Nutrition and Behavior

A Multidisciplinary Approach

Dedication

To Harriet, whose love for me makes all things possible (JW).
To Mark, for his patience, encouragement and loving support (BJT).
To John, Daniel and Jacob for their continuous support and love (RBK).

NUTRITION AND BEHAVIOR

A Multidisciplinary Approach

John Worobey

Department of Nutritional Sciences
Rutgers University, New Brunswick, New Jersey
USA

Beverly J. Tepper

Department of Food Science
Rutgers University, New Brunswick, New Jersey
USA

and

Robin B. Kanarek

Department of Psychology
Tufts University, Medford, Massachusetts
USA

with a contribution by

Kristen E. D'Anci

Tufts University
USA

CABI Publishing

CABI Publishing is a division of CAB International

CABI Publishing
CAB International
Wallingford
Oxfordshire OX10 8DE
UK
Tel: +44 (0)1491 832111
Fax: +44 (0)1491 833508
E-mail: cabi@cabi.org

CABI Publishing
875 Massachusetts Avenue
7th Floor
Cambridge, MA 02139
USA
Tel: +1 617 395 4056
Fax: +1 617 354 6875
E-mail: cabi-nao@cabi.org

Website: www.cabi-publishing.org

A catalogue record for this book is available from the British Library, London,
UK.

Library of Congress Cataloging-in-Publication Data
Worobey, John.
  Nutrition and behavior: a multidisciplinary approach / John Worobey,
Beverly J. Tepper, Robin B. Kanarek; with a contribution by Kristen E. D'Anci.
    p.cm.
Includes bibliographical references and Index.
ISBN-13: 978-0-85199-674-5 (alk. paper)
ISBN-10: 0-85199-674-4 (alk. paper)
1. Human behavior--Nutritional aspects.   I. Tepper, Beverly J.   II. Kanarek,
  Robin B.   III. Title.

QP141.N7763 2005
612.3-dc22
                            2005014126

ISBN-10: 0-85199-674-4
ISBN-13: 978-0-85199-674-5

Typeset by SPI Publisher Services, Pondicherry, India.
Printed and bound in the UK by Biddles Ltd., King's Lynn.

Contents

Acknowledgements

The authors wish to collectively thank Kirsten Cooke and Crystal Levanon for their help with the typing and proofing of references, Jeanette Lopez for her artistic contribution to the graphics in the text, Karen Hamberger for preparing the subject index and Suzy Kiefer for facilitating the electronic delivery of the manuscript to the publisher. John Worobey would like to express his appreciation for the sabbatical awarded by Rutgers University that provided the time, and Dr. Michael Lewis of the University of Medicine and Dentistry of New Jersey who provided the place, which enabled him to work full-time on this project.

1 Introduction

J. Worobey

Why a book on nutrition and behavior? You might have heard some friends say on more than one occasion that they 'live to eat'. Every one of us, however, must eat in order to live. Besides ensuring that life will be sustained, the type of diet we follow does much to affect our quality of life. Hunger, of course, causes discomfort, while a full stomach brings contentment. Both are affective states, suggesting that what we eat may impact upon our emotions, with an influence on what we feel and in all likelihood, how we think. From the beginning of recorded history right up through the present, humans have believed that the food they eat can have a powerful effect on their behavior. Ancient Egyptians, for example, believed that salt could stimulate passion, onions induce sleep, cabbage prevent a hangover, and lemons protect against 'the evil eye'. Aside from the latter, perhaps, each of these goals are still desired by thousands of individuals, and the possibility that a type of diet or a particular nutrient can help to achieve sexual, emotional or cognitive equilibrium is viewed as a natural way to cope in a frantic world.

To be sure, the subject of this book is in some ways a scientific examination of the popular adage, 'You are what you eat' – a question that has interested people for centuries. Based on hunches, anecdotal reports, or conventional wisdom, statements such as 'Fish is brain food', 'Oysters are an aphrodisiac', or 'Sugar causes hyperactivity' have appeared in the popular press, or have likely been uttered by friends or relatives in the spirit of well-meaning advice. More directly, advertisers have flat out told consumers to 'Be a coffee achiever' and even that 'Milk drinkers make better lovers', in order to sell a product. Recent endorsements are just as zealous in their claims, as various herbs are now being hawked as a natural means for reducing depression or boosting energy, while the fatty acids in fish oil are touted as improving intelligence. The last 25 years have witnessed a phenomenal increase in the number of magazine articles, self-help books, cable shows and websites devoted to nutrition and the idea of eating well, with an information explosion regarding the relationships between diet and behavior. Unlike previous centuries, however, we now have research data from scores of investigations that bear on the diet and behavior connection. That is to say, after little attention historically being paid by scientists to the relationship between our dietary practices and our everyday behavior, we have slowly but surely accumulated a body of scientific evidence that allows us to better distinguish fact from folly as pertains to the relationship between nutrition and behavior.

The statements cited above about the relationships between nutrition and behavior may or may not be true. Some of them may turn out to be partially supported by objective data and taken as fact, at least by the objective data that we have to date. Others are, at best, unverified. But even verified facts can some-times change as data continue to accrue. Besides guiding you through the current research evidence that exists to support or dis-prove various diet and behavior connections, we will also describe for you the means by which scientists examine these relationships and base their conclusions. To do this, we will be drawing from the literature in the nutri-tional and behavioral sciences, meaning nutri-tion, biochemistry and psychology, of course, but also anthropology, medicine, public health and sociology whenever appropriate. The area of nutrition and behavior is an inter-disciplinary one, with research in all these fields having something to offer as we exam-ine their dynamic relationship.

You will thus become acquainted with what we know at present regarding the nutri-tion and behavior connections that hold up to scientific scrutiny. But perhaps more important, you will also learn why certain questions are asked in the first place, how they are posed so as to be studied scientifically, how the appro-priate research ought to be conducted, and just how far the findings may extend. Even if you are not contemplating a career in research, you will nevertheless learn to make sense of the 'latest study' that you will inevitably hear about in the news, and should be able to evaluate the validity of the claims made by its authors.

As the topic may warrant, from time to time the results of animal studies may be drawn on throughout this book. To be sure, a phenomenal amount of research on feeding behavior and the effects of nutritional depriva-tion has been conducted using animal models, as there are certain manipulations that cannot be done with humans. But the focus of this book is decidedly human. For one thing, enough studies of nutrition–behavior issues are now available on humans to justify such a vol-ume. For another, the variables that have been investigated, whether cognitive (e.g. attention), emotional (e.g. mood), or social (e.g. peer interaction), if not uniquely human, are the most interesting when applied to humans.

This book gives us an appreciation of just how much food and the act of eating touches our everyday lives – indeed, nearly every aspect of our behavior and development. Infants are fed almost immediately after they are born, children learn of the world through tasting new foods, families bond through shar-ing countless mealtimes, parents must work in order to put food on the table, young adults often choose a restaurant for a first date, and so forth. Not only does the act of eating provide a script for our lives, the satisfaction that we expect to get from eating may also serve as an end in itself. Which person who has ever flown on a commercial airplane has not complained about the food, and which socialite would dare to arrange a wedding, a bar mitzvah or a funeral for that matter without catering a meal to legitimize the event?

Such major life events are colored by cul-ture, which is an underlying premise of this book. While many of the topics that we cover will address how nutrition influences or modi-fies behavior, we will also endeavor to explore how behavior influences nutrition. How or what a person eats obviously determines nutritional status, but our approach to behavior will consist of far more than the behavior of eating. That is, what factors determine the behavior that leads to the diet that the individual ultimately selects? At a global level, cultural and familial factors may influence food preferences, with economics helping to determine food choice. As will be seen, however, the individual's respect for his or her traditions, concerns about health or fixation on appearance can all interact to determine how that person behaves around food.

Historical Perspective

Reference has already been made to the ancient Egyptians and their beliefs about food and behavior. The ancient Greeks also thought that diet was an integral part of psy-chological functioning, but added a personal-ity component to the process. They conceived of four temperaments, that is, choleric, melan-cholic, phlegmatic and sanguine, that were responsive to heat, cold, moisture and dryness. Because these characteristics were consid-ered to be inherent properties of food, it was believed that consuming particular dietary items could correct humoral imbalances (Farb and Armelagos, 1980).

During the Middle Ages, the view that food and health were connected was extended to beliefs about sexuality, as medieval men and women used food in an attempt to both encourage and restrain their erotic impulses. Figs, truffles, turnips, leeks, mustard and savory were all endowed with the ability to excite the sexual passions, as were rare beef in saffron pastry, roast venison with garlic, suckling pig, boiled crab and quail with pomegranate sauce (Cosman, 1983). To dampen sexual impulses, foods such as lettuce, cooked capers, rue and diluted hemlock-wine concoctions were sometimes employed, though seldom as often as the stimulants (Cosman, 1983).

The French philosopher and gourmand Jean Anthelme Brillat-Savarin wrote 'Tell me what you eat, and I will tell you what you are' in his treatise, *The Physiology of Taste*, first published in 1825 (Drayton, 1970). He postulated a number of direct relationships between diet and behavioral outcomes, being among the first to document the stimulating effects of caffeine. He also believed that certain foods, such as milk, lettuce or rennet apples, could gently induce sleep, while a dinner of hare, pigeon, duck, asparagus, celery, truffles or vanilla could facilitate dreaming.

In the early years of the last century a health reform movement erupted in the USA, with many of the claims made by its leaders concerning food and behavior. Diet was believed to affect mental health, intelligence, spirituality and sexual prowess. One of the most prominent leaders of this movement was John Harvey Kellogg – known best for introducing breakfast cereals, but brutally satirized in the book and movie of the same name, *The Road to Wellville* (Boyle, 1994). Kellogg lectured widely throughout the USA, promoting the use of natural foods and decrying the eating of meat, which he believed would lead to the deterioration of mental functioning while arousing animal passions. He further claimed that the toxins formed by the digestion of meat produced a variety of symptoms including depression, fatigue, headache, aggression and mental illness, while spicy or rich foods could lead to moral deterioration and acts of violence (Kellogg, 1888, 1919).

While amusing by 21st-century standards, such early convictions about the interaction between nutrition and behavior are not merely of historical significance, but have survived and are indeed flourishing. For example, in your authors' lifetimes, we have heard dire warnings that food additives cause hyperactivity in children (Feingold, 1975), that monosodium glutamate (MSG) causes headaches and heart palpitations (Schaumberg and Byck, 1968), and that refined carbohydrates cause criminal behavior in adults (Duffy, 1975). As you shall see later, however, research done in well-controlled studies shows little support for such claims. In recent years, bee pollen has been advocated as a means to enhance athletic prowess, garlic as a cure for sleep disorders, ginger root as a remedy for motion sickness, ginseng as an aid to promote mental stamina, and multivitamin cocktails as a tonic for boosting intelligence (Jarvis, 1983; Dubick, 1986; Herbert and Barrett, 1986; Yetiv, 1986; White and Mondeika, 1988). Again, in some instances there may be some valid basis for these claims. However, in many cases these 'facts' may be based on anecdotal evidence, insufficient observations, misinterpretation of findings or just poor science.

Whether concerned with ensuring our mental health, reducing our levels of stress or simply losing weight, most of us share a belief that diet and behavior are intimately related. You may have relied on an energy bar yourself on occasion, in the belief that it would help you concentrate, while you observe your parents attempting to slow the aging process by trying the herbal supplement they see advertised on a nightly infomercial. While we may not think we are exactly what we eat, we nevertheless seem predisposed to accept claims about nutrition and behavior that promise us whatever we think is desirable, no matter how improbable. Our task throughout this book will be to help you recognize the associations that current scientific evidence suggests are most likely true, given our current understanding of work that bridges nutrition and behavior.

References

Boyle, T.C. (1994) *The Road to Wellville*. Penguin Books, London.

Cosman, M.P. (1983) A feast for Aesculapius: historical diets for asthma and sexual pleasure. *Annual Review of Nutrition* 3, 1–33.

Drayton, A. (1970) *The Philosopher in the Kitchen* (translation of J.A. Brillat-Savarin, *La physiologie du goût,* first published 1825). Plenum, New York.

Dubick, M.A. (1986) Historical perspective on the use of herbal preparations to promote health. *Journal of Nutrition* 116, 1348–1354.

Duffy, W. (1975) *Sugar Blues.* Warner Books, New York.

Farb, P. and Armelagos, G. (1980) *Consuming Passions: The Anthropology of Eating.* Houghton-Mifflin, Boston, Massachusetts.

Feingold, B.F. (1975) Hyperkinesis and learning disabilities linked to artificial food flavors and colors. *American Journal of Nursing* 75, 797–803.

Herbert, V. and Barrett, S. (1986) Twenty-one ways to spot a quack. *Nutrition Forum Newsletter,* September, 65–68.

Jarvis, W.T. (1983) Food faddism, cultism and quackery. *Annual Review of Nutrition* 3, 35–52.

Kellogg, J.H. (1888) *Plain Facts for Old and Young.* Segner, Burlington, Iowa.

Kellogg, J.H. (1919) *The Itinerary of a Breakfast.* Funk & Wagnalls, New York.

Schaumberg, H.H. and Byck, R. (1968) Sin cib-syn.: accent on glutamate (letter). *New England Journal of Medicine* 279, 105.

White, P.L. and Mondeika, T.D. (1988) Food fads and faddism. In: Shils, M.E. and Young, V.R. (eds) *Modern Nutrition in Health and Disease.* Lea & Febiger, Philadelphia, Pennsylvania, pp. 666–671.

Yetiv, J.Z. (1986) *Popular Nutritional Practices: A Scientific Appraisal.* Popular Medicine Press, Toledo, Ohio.

2 Concepts and Models in Nutrition and Behavior

J. Worobey

The constructs of nutrition and behavior relate in a rather circuitous manner. What does such a statement mean? Stated simply, that nutrition affects or influences behavior, but that behavior *can be just as powerful* in determining nutritional status (see Fig. 2.1). To give an example, if malnourished, a person is likely to be lethargic, that is, low in activity or display of energy, disinterested in the environment and flat in affect. An adequate diet is necessary for the individual to exhibit a reasonable amount of activity. In this case, *under*nutrition is having an effect on *active* behavior. But what of the opposite scenario? A woman who initiates an exercise regimen combined with running and weightlifting, in order to reduce her waistline and regain muscle tone, finds herself being hungry more often. Moreover, her best friend suggests that she make efforts to improve her diet, eating regularly and even adding a protein milkshake so as to maintain and boost her energy level. She complies, and in this case *active* behavior has now had a direct effect on her nutritional status, namely increasing her energy intake.

In later chapters we will explore in detail the research that supports specific nutrition–behavior relationships, as well as behavior–nutrition sequences. In Fig. 2.1, we can see that certain behavioral phenomena may be conceptualized as directly affecting nutrition, while others may more logically be construed as nutritional variables that affect behavior. In reality, very few associations will be as straightforward (i.e. direct) as these examples suggest. Other mediating variables will influence most associations. However, as a first step these examples should serve to illustrate the vast amount of interesting nutrition–behavior associations that have been explored by scientists.

Starting with the behavioral side, the temperament trait of sensation seeking, a reliable individual difference, has been shown to be associated with a person's enjoyment of hot, spicy foods like chilli peppers. Hence, knowing this personality trait in a male may be useful in predicting what items he might choose from a menu. A teenage girl who wants to make her high school cheerleading squad may deliberately starve herself before the upcoming tryouts. In this case her effort to conform to the model that her peers provide can place her at risk of an eating disorder. A woman who grew up with a relatively happy childhood, may find herself preparing, serving and eating meatloaf every weekend, using the recipe her mother swore by as she now raises her own family. In each of these cases, certain behavioral antecedents have influenced nutritional status or diet quality.

Conversely, nutritional factors may exert a powerful role in affecting performance or modifying behavior. As we shall see in later chapters, severe malnutrition can greatly depress physical and cognitive functioning. But even temporary lapses in adequate nutrient intake, as shown with skipping a meal like

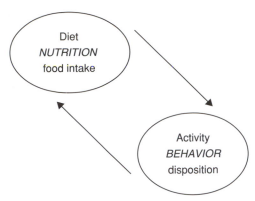

Fig. 2.1. Nutrition and behavior – the circle of life.

breakfast, can reduce a child's attention span on a learning task. Substances such as caffeine, a natural ingredient of coffee but an additive to certain soft drinks, will boost attention and arousal. In contrast, a high-starch meal may serve to calm a stressed adult just as much through its perception as a comfort food as by its facilitating the release of neurotransmitters.

Finally, to illustrate the bi-directionality that is inherent in the nutrition–behavior relationship, consider this example. It is extremely likely that an overweight child will display less activity in school or at play relative to an average-sized child. If teased by his or her peers, such a child will tend to spend a lot of his or her after-school hours watching television and, not incidentally, will eat more snacks while watching TV. In all likelihood he or she will choose to spend even less time playing outdoors, and will thereby get even less exercise. Additional weight gain would be predicted, with obesity as a possible outcome. In this case we have a vicious cycle of behavior (i.e. low activity) leading to poorer nutrition (i.e. excessive snacking) that further impacts on behavior (i.e. even less activity).

Nutrition versus Behavior: Which is Key?

Many of you who are reading this book may already have a background in the nutritional sciences, but have sometimes wondered why you like foods that your best friend just cannot stand, whether or not certain foods can really improve your mood, or why you seem to crave popcorn while at the movies but never eat it at home. Others may be more familiar with the psychological sciences, and are reading this book to decide whether particular nutrients may be worth adding to the list of independent variables like age, sex or socio-economic status that you have come to accept as being important in understanding human behavior. We will attempt to answer these questions in the chapters that follow, as well as pose and address additional queries that you may not have considered. In other words, there should be of much interest here to the budding life scientist, and intriguing though no less instructive insights to be gained by the future behavioral scientist. None the less, you may still be partial to the 'world view' that your training up to now represents. After all, what could a psychological perspective possibly add to your understanding of the importance of nutrition, or vice versa?

Perhaps a way of illustrating just how essential both perspectives are to ensuring optimal human development is to consider two situations where development has been compromised in much the same way, yet via markedly different paths. Phenylketonuria (PKU) is an inborn error of metabolism that results in mental retardation in childhood if unidentified and left untreated. In infants with the disorder, the absence of a single enzyme – phenylalanine hydroxylase – prevents the conversion of the amino acid phenylalanine into tyrosine (Nyhan, 1981). The ingestion of a *normal* diet, containing typical amounts of protein, results in the accumulation of phenylalanine, which in turn exerts a toxic effect on the central nervous system. The effects are manifested in the form of severe mental retardation, decreased attention span and unresponsiveness. Fortunately, the early detection of PKU, through a newborn screening test, can allow for immediate treatment through a low protein diet, which avoids the certain likelihood of any brain damage. Nevertheless, this example shows the powerful effects that diet can impose on a developing infant. But by what other means might mental development be impaired?

Deprivational dwarfism is a condition of retarded growth and mental development directly attributable to a caregiving environment that is characterized as emotionally detached and lacking in normal affection (Gardner, 1972). Infants reared by hostile parents, or by caregivers that are emotionally unavailable and who do not respond to the infant's signals for attention, often fail to thrive and show stunted growth with little interest in their environment (Spitz and Wolf, 1946). Despite regular feedings, adequate nutrient intake, and no metabolic irregularities, a lack of environmental stimulation in infancy will here have as powerful an effect on the developing infant as did undetected PKU in the previous example. It is almost certain that a normal diet for a PKU baby will have devastating consequences, no matter how good the caregiver–infant relationship. But an infant deprived of appropriate behavioral interaction with a caregiver will also be delayed, no matter how good the nutrition.

It should be clear then that nutrition and behavior, both inherently interesting phenomena in their own right, are on an equal footing in terms of their treatment in this book. As stated at the outset in so many words, nutrition obviously sustains life. But besides helping to regulate nutrient intake, behavior and its expression serve to define who we are, what we attain, and how much of life we enjoy.

The Scientific Method

A researcher who studies nutrition may have as her long-term goal the promotion of physical well-being. Over the short run, she may conduct studies on the role of iron in ensuring proper muscle functioning and physical stamina. In contrast, a researcher who studies behavior may wish to serve society by eventually optimizing mental health. His day-to-day research program may consist of examining the myriad of factors that lead to depression. Despite somewhat different goals for the application of their work, these two scientists are nevertheless alike in a fundamental way – they both assume an underlying order, regularity and predictability in the laws of nature. In conducting their research, they seek to identify the patterns of relationships that serve to link what may appear to the untrained eye as unrelated

phenomena. To do this, both the nutritional and behavioral scientist will follow the scientific method. And in doing so, they are more alike than different in terms of how they attempt to discover truth.

The scientific method is the approach used by all scientists in their efforts to identify the truth about relationships between natural events. As can be seen in Table 2.1, the method comprises the following series of steps:

1. *State the research question.* The scientists may build upon a theory that they encounter, on personal observation, or on previous research, and will pose a research question that has relevance to the phenomena of interest.
2. *Develop a hypothesis.* The scientists will next reformulate the research question into a specific hypothesis that can be tested.
3. *Test the hypothesis.* In this major step the scientists design a systematic plan that will be useful in testing the hypothesis, implement the plan by conducting the study, collect the appropriate data and then analyze the results.
4. *Interpret the results.* Based on the results, the scientists either accept or reject the hypothesis, and formulate conclusions that derive solely from the data.
5. *Disseminate the findings.* The scientists share the findings with the scientific community by publishing the results, describing the study procedures and data in sufficient detail so that others may evaluate or replicate the results.

For the sake of illustration, suppose you are at a party and overhear a conversation wherein a woman confides to a male friend that she is a 'closet chocaholic'. Listening in more intently, you hear him ask her if she feels guilty about this. She replies that she really does not feel guilty; rather, she just seems to crave chocolate whenever she feels stressed, as

Table 2.1. The scientific method.

1. State the research question.
2. Develop a hypothesis.
3. Test the hypothesis.
4. Interpret the results.
5. Disseminate the findings.

it never fails to pick her up. You find this exchange somewhat amusing but nevertheless interesting, and as you drive home you wonder how you could determine whether eating chocolate might in fact alleviate stress. How would the scientific method be used by you to study this possibility?

The *research question* was posed when you asked yourself whether or not there was some validity to the woman's claim that, for her at least, eating chocolate helped to reduce stress. Might there really be a relationship between eating chocolate and improving one's mood? You realize that someone may already have asked this question, so you do a little homework before you begin. Reviewing the literature on a topic is a critical phase of the research process, so that you can see if someone else has already answered the question that interests you, or has studied a problem close to the one you are thinking about. Thanks to modern computers and library search engines, you can now rapidly search the literature by using a few keywords. *PsychInfo* and *Medline,* which list published papers that appear in psychological and medical journals, respectively, are extremely useful search engines that are available through most academic libraries. Entering 'chocolate+mood' you find that some studies have indeed been published on chocolate cravings, some on food and mood, and even some on chocolate and mood (e.g. Macdiarmid and Hetherington, 1995; Schuman *et al.*, 1987). You discover, however, that the studies all seemed to focus on women who define themselves as 'chocolate addicts'. You wonder if chocolate eating might make a difference in the moods of everyday people, and particularly men. To employ the scientific method, you need to formulate an actual hypothesis in order to operationalize your question. You therefore propose that eating chocolate will help to improve mood, or more specifically, that eating greater quantities of chocolate will reduce depression in women *and* men.

As you may have already guessed, testing even this relatively straightforward proposition involves more than simply handing out *Nestlé*™ chocolate bars and asking individuals how they feel. In Chapter 3 we will describe the methods used by researchers in designing

their investigations, and we will differentiate between experimental and observational approaches. For the moment, however, you decide that as an initial *test of your hypothesis*, conducting a survey might be a useful strategy. Reviewing the articles that you located earlier, you find references to a number of dietary recall instruments, as well as some questionnaires that measure depression. So you develop a questionnaire that includes a section on depression and dietary patterns, and add some questions that specifically ask about consumption of chocolate. You also include some questions that will provide you with demographic information (e.g. age, sex), though you are careful not to ask any questions that would allow you to identify who an individual respondent might be. Mostly any study you would do will require approval by the university's Institutional Review Board, though an anonymous survey, where you cannot identify your respondents and their participation is voluntary, may be exempt. We will discuss issues of confidentiality later in this chapter.

In order to access a reasonable number of subjects in an expedient fashion, you ask your biology professor from last semester if you can hand out your questionnaires in one of her large lecture classes. She agrees, and after administering the survey you find that you have close to 200 completed questionnaires. Although you can derive a depression score from the original instrument's instructions, you would need to use a packaged computer program to reduce the dietary information into a usable format. So rather than analyze their overall dietary quality at present, you decide to simply create a chocolate score by counting up the number of times per week that each respondent reported that they ate a serving of chocolate. Analyzing the data statistically, you find no relationship for the men, but a small, negative correlation between the depression and chocolate scores for the women (more will be said about the meaning of a statistical correlation in Chapter 3). This would seem to indicate partial support for your hypothesis.

Before concluding that eating chocolate may be the ideal cure for depression, however, you must first endeavor to accurately *interpret your results*. While the correlation coefficient was in the right direction for the women, its magnitude was too small as to be statistically significant. This might mean that the relationship is not really there, or perhaps it would have reached significance if you had a larger sample. But even if the associations were higher, it would still only indicate that chocolate intake and depression were associated in a way that might not yet be understood. It might be the case, for example, that women who are happier eat chocolate more often because they view it as a suitable way of rewarding themselves. Alternatively, the amounts of chocolate eaten by men may not have been very much, so a comparison by sex was misleading. In contrast, a number of the respondents may be bothered by their weight, and now avoid chocolate because of dieting to reduce their calorie intake. For that matter, some other aspect of their diet may be at work, as a literature exists on the effect of carbohydrates on mood. It may be that chocolate eaters eat a whole lot of things, the sum of which could play a role in preventing depression.

The results of your survey would seem to support what was already known about chocolate and mood in women, but they did not seem to break any new ground. To *disseminate your findings*, you could present your results to your classmates, or by analyzing the dietary data that you already collected, add to your findings and get a better understanding of how diet, chocolate intake and depression might interact. Thinking over some alternate explanations for your findings, or better yet, designing an experiment where you could evaluate mood states after eating chocolate might be your next step. By developing a new hypothesis, you are back at the start of the scientific method, and now on your way to contributing to the process of scientific inquiry.

Ethical Issues in the Conducting of Research

While not a line-item of the scientific method, implicit within the design and implementation of a research investigation, as well as in the application of the findings, are a number of issues that relate to the conduct of any research that involves human subjects. The formal codification of ethical guidelines for the conduct of research involving humans, at least in the USA, began well over 50 years ago in the aftermath of the Second World War. In 1946, a number of Nazi physicians went on trial at Nuremberg because of research atrocities they had performed on prisoners as well as on the general citizenry. For example, dried plant juice was added to flour fed to the general population in an experiment aimed at developing a means for sterilizing women, while men were exposed to X-rays without their knowledge to achieve the same effect. In another experiment, hundreds of prisoners in the Buchenwald concentration camp were injected with the typhus fever virus in an effort to develop a vaccine. After the trial and through the efforts of the Nazi War Crimes Tribunal, fundamental ethical principles for the conduct of research involving humans were generated and made part of the Nuremberg Code, which sets forth 10 conditions that must be met before research involving humans is ethically permissible. Primary among its tenets is that the voluntary consent of the human subject is absolutely essential, with additional elements concerning safety considerations in designing, conducting and terminating the experiment.

Despite the issuance of this code in 1947, many researchers in the USA were either unaware of its principles or did not apply these guidelines to their research activities. The infamous Tuskegee Syphilis Study, where black men with syphilis were left untreated to track its effects, is a sobering example. When the study was started in the 1930s the men had not given their informed consent. However, when penicillin became available in the 1940s the men were neither informed of this nor treated with the antibiotic. In fact, the study continued until 1972, when accounts of it finally appeared in the American press. Yet other atrocities have also occurred. From 1946 to 1956, mentally retarded boys at the Fernald State School in Massachusetts who thought they were joining a science club were fed radioactive milk with their breakfast cereal. The researchers were interested in how radioactive forms of iron and calcium were absorbed by the digestive system. In 1963, studies were undertaken at New York City's Chronic Disease Hospital to gather information on the nature of the human transplant rejection process.

Patients who were hospitalized with various debilitating diseases were injected with live cancer cells, with the rationale that the patients' bodies were expected to reject the cancer cells. Finally, from 1963 to 1966 'mentally defective' children at the Willowbrook State School in New York were deliberately infected with the hepatitis virus, drawn from the infected stools of others or in a more purified form. The investigators argued that since their contracting hepatitis was likely to occur anyway, much could be learned by studying the disease under controlled conditions.

The above examples were not intended to frighten or disgust the reader, but to illustrate that such shameful instances of abuse of children and adults have occurred in the name of research, and not all that long ago. As federal funding for biomedical research increased dramatically during the 1960s, and news of these research horror stories surfaced, the US Government, in conjunction with the research community, gradually designed one of the most comprehensive systems in the world for the conduct of research involving humans. In 1974, the National Research Act (PL 93-348) was signed into law and established the National Commission for the Protection of Human Subjects of Biomedical and Behavioral Research to identify the ethical principles that should guide the conduct of all research involving humans. The Commission's efforts resulted in a document called *The Belmont Report – Ethical Principles and Guidelines for the Protection of Human Subjects*, which was published in 1979. This report outlines three basic ethical principles:

1. *Respect for persons*. This principle requires that researchers acknowledge the autonomy of every individual, and that informed consent is obtained from all potential research subjects (or their legally authorized representative if they are immature or incapacitated).
2. *Beneficence*. This principle requires that researchers treat their subjects in an ethical manner not only by respecting their decisions and protecting them from harm, but also by making efforts to secure their well-being. Risks must be reasonable in light of expected benefits.

3. *Justice*. This principle requires that selection and recruitment of human subjects is done fairly and equitably, to ensure that a benefit to which a person is entitled is not denied without good reason or a burden is not imposed unduly.

It is clear then that all researchers have a fundamental responsibility to safeguard the rights and welfare of the individuals who participate in their research activities. In addition, government regulations require that any institution that conducts federally-funded research must adhere to the principles of *The Belmont Report*; must set forth in writing ethical principles, policies, and procedures for protecting the rights of human research subjects; and must maintain an Institutional Review Board (IRB) that reviews and approves prospective and continuing research.

At most colleges and universities, an IRB approval is mandatory even if the research is not federally funded, or even funded at all. IRBs have one paramount role – to protect the rights and welfare of human subjects. Members of such committees bring diverse skills, perspectives and insights to the responsibility of reviewing research activities involving humans. They take into account ethical standards of research on an individual protocol-by-protocol basis. Rather than disapproving proposed research activities, the IRB strives to work interactively with research investigators to assure that their research design is appropriate, that risks to participants are minimized (with benefits maximized), and that consent procedures are adequate.

Nutrition Quackery and Psychological Misconduct

Aside from these issues regarding the conduct of research with human subjects, ethics are of relevance to the subject of nutrition and behavior because of the therapeutic claims that have been made on behalf of various dietary and psychological interventions. Clinical psychologists, whose very profession is built upon the application of their training to assist individuals in achieving mental health, are obviously bound to a code of conduct that mandates trust between the therapist and client. Different psychological therapies exist, of course, but to become a psychologist one has to master graduate work in psychology, complete an extensive internship wherein their training as a therapist is supervised, and finally pass an examination for licensure. One psychologist's mode of therapy with a particular client may be less effective than that of a colleague's, but no blame is attributable given the psychologist's disclosure of alternative approaches and the client's free choice. But a psychologist must terminate a consulting or clinical relationship when it is reasonably clear that the client is not benefiting from it. Adherence to the *Ethical Principles of Psychologists* (2002) is demanded, and a psychologist can have his or her license suspended if he or she is found to have violated any of these principles. For example, disclosing personal information about a client to someone other than another professional concerned with the case, or for whom the client has given permission would be grounds for suspension. For that matter, any information obtained about a research participant during the course of an investigation is also considered confidential, with the researcher responsible for assuring anonymity in any report of the investigation.

In contrast, under current laws in the USA and abroad, individuals do not have to possess a particular credential to call themselves a nutritionist. They may have had some nutrition coursework, or may have had none at all. They may have an advanced degree, or may not have a diploma from an accredited college. Even if they have an advanced degree, however, it need not be in nutrition, medicine, or even science! For example, an individual could claim to be a nutritionist, nutrition expert, nutrition consultant or nutrition counselor armed only with the confidence of having taken some nutrition courses. To draw a relevant analogy, would you have confidence in someone who claimed to be a psychotherapist if the person disclosed that the only basis for the claim was that in college the individual was a psych major?

In point of fact, a nutrition credential does exist, in the form of the Registered Dietitian (RD). The designation of RD indicates that the individual has completed at least a bachelor's degree from an accredited college or university, has mastered a body of nutrition-related courses

specified by the American Dietetics Association, has successfully completed a supervised work experience, and has passed a national qualifying examination. So a Registered Dietitian is clearly the nutrition professional as regards the health aspects of nutritional sciences. If looking for sound nutrition advice for your own health, then, you would be wise to seek the counsel of a Registered Dietitian. In lieu of that, your primary physician, who would have had human physiology and biochemistry in medical school, is likely the next best person to consult.

But the reality is, anyone can call herself a nutritionist and not be breaking any laws. There are far more individuals who call themselves nutritionists than there are Registered Dietitians. Check the listings under 'Nutritionists' of any suburban telephone directory, for example, and you are likely to find the letters RD after fewer than one in three 'experts'. Why is this bad you may ask? Granted, a good number of individuals who call themselves nutritionists may in fact be trained in the science of nutrition, and may be sincere in their desire to help people. Others, however, while meaning well, may be misinformed and can inadvertently cause health problems by their overzealous advice. Consider the findings that parents who raise their children under a strict vegetarian regimen can induce nutritional deficiencies (Sanders and Reddy, 1994; Dwyer, 2000). Still others may have enough of a science background to sound convincing, but are unscrupulous in their attempts to promote particular nutrients or weight-loss strategies. As will be seen in Chapter 7, megadoses of vitamin A can cause headache, fatigue and vertigo (Hathcock *et al.*, 1990), with high doses of vitamin C being shown as possibly damaging DNA (Lee *et al.*, 2001).

Unfortunately, the field of nutrition is broad enough that quackery presents a real danger, financially if not physically. The word 'quack' derives from *quacksalver*, which is an archaic term used to identify a salesman who quacked loudly about a medical cure such as a salve, lotion, or in today's world, the wonders of a particular nutritional product or regimen. How might one protect oneself from such a charlatan? Dr Victor Herbert, a respected physician, lawyer and authority on nutrition, devoted much of his career to warning consumers about 'doctors of nutramedicine', 'vitamiticians' and other nutrition quacks. Some of the telltale signs of questionable practitioners appear in Table 2.2.

Nutrition quacks may attempt to market their alternative treatments to just about anyone, but there are certain populations who may be the most likely targets. Certainly, those who naïvely believe the testimonials they hear regarding health claims of supplemental products are at risk. However, those who may be suffering from an as yet incurable disease and are desperate for a cure, or those who may simply mistrust the medical/scientific establishment are also suitable targets for fraudulent pill pushers (Anderson *et al.*, 1998). For example, individuals suffering from arthritis, stricken with cancer or battling AIDS may be particularly susceptible to health claims for a miracle cure. But even athletes, teenagers and the elderly may look to supplements in order to boost performance, help them gain or lose weight, or delay the aging process.

Conclusion

As we have tried to illustrate, the linkages between nutrition and behavior are intuitively interesting, but inherently complex. For example, the effect of overall malnutrition (of the insufficient nourishment variety) would likely be fatigue and apathy in addition to poor

Table 2.2. Ten ways to spot 'nutrition quacks'.

1. They display credentials not recognized by responsible scientists or educators.
2. They promise quick, dramatic, miraculous cures.
3. They use disclaimers couched in pseudo-medical jargon.
4. They claim that most Americans are poorly nourished.
5. They tell you that supplements will offset a poor diet.
6. They allege that modern processing removes all nutrients from food.
7. They claim you are in danger of being poisoned by our food supply.
8. They recommend that everyone take vitamins or other food supplements.
9. They tell you it is easy to lose weight.
10. They warn you not to trust your doctor.

Source: Herbert, 1993.

health. In contrast, the impairments due to a particular vitamin or mineral deficiency may be subtler, depending on the levels of other nutrients as well as the individual's overall health status. Alternately, the individual's background, including education, assets and even desire for good health, does much to determine the food choices he or she will make. As will be seen in the chapters that follow, hundreds of studies have been conducted to assess the behavioral consequences of numerous dietary components. Vitamins, minerals, food additives, herbal supplements and sweeteners have all been studied in an effort to shed light on the real, but often misunderstood, relationships between what we eat and how we behave. At the same time, a growing number of studies have looked at the myriad number of variables that determine our patterns of dietary intake. In other words, how culture, family, peers, personality and other individual characteristics influence our behavior, to predict our eating style and determine our nutritional status.

The proper study of nutrition and behavior relies on the Scientific Method – the modus operandi of both the nutritional and behavioral sciences. The facts about nutrition–behavior relationships that we report will be based on the results of studies that employed research designs that are best suited for testing a particular hypothesis. When such studies consistently show the same results, these results will be generally accepted as representing the truth, at least as the current body of evidence suggests it to be. Regardless of the research question, however, there are ethical considerations that must be addressed in the recruitment of subjects, design of the research and the application of the findings. In Chapter 3, we will describe the research designs that have proven to be the most useful in testing hypotheses about nutrition and behavior.

References

American Psychological Association (2002) *Ethical Principles of Psychologists and Code of Conduct*. Washington, DC. Available at: http://www.apa.org/ethics/code2002

Anderson, J., Patterson, L. and Daly, B. (1998) Nutrition quackery. *Annual Editions: Nutrition* 13, 166–169.

Dwyer, J. (2000) Should dietary fat recommendations for children be changed? *Journal of the American Dietetics Association* 100, 36.

Gardner, L. (1972) Deprivation dwarfism. *Scientific American* 227, 76–82.

Hathcock, J.N., Hatton, D.G., Jenkins, M.Y., McDonald, J.T., Sundaresan, P.R. and Wilkening, W.L. (1990) Evaluation of vitamin A toxicity. *American Journal for Clinical Nutrition* 52, 183–202.

Herbert, V. (1993) Vitamin pushers and food quacks. *Annual Editions: Nutrition* 6, 192–198.

Lee, S.H., Oe, T. and Blair, I.A. (2001) Vitamin C-induced decomposition of lipid hydroperoxides to endogenous genotoxins. *Science* 292(5524), 2083–2086.

Macdiarmid, J.I. and Hetherington, M.M. (1995) Mood modulation by food: an exploration of affect and cravings in 'chocolate addicts'. *British Journal of Clinical Psychology* 34, 129–138.

Nyhan, W.L. (1981) Nutritional treatment of children with inborn errors of metabolism. In: Suskind, R.M. (ed.) *Textbook of Pediatric Nutrition*. Raven Press, New York, pp. 563–576.

Sanders, T.A. and Reddy, S. (1994) Vegetarian diets and children. *American Journal of Clinical Nutrition* 59, 1176S.

Schuman, M., Gitlin, M.J. and Fairbanks, L. (1987) Sweets, chocolate and atypical depressive traits. *Journal of Nervous and Mental Disorders* 175, 491–495.

Spitz, R.A. and Wolf, K. (1946) Anaclitic depression. *Psychoanalytical Study of Children* 2, 313–342.

The Belmont Report (1979) National Institutes of Health, Bethesda, Maryland. Available at: http://ohsr.od.nih.gov/mpa/belmont/php3

3 Research Methods and Analytic Strategies

J. Worobey

As we outlined in Chapter 2, the proper way to establish the validity of claims about nutrition and behavior is to employ established scientific research methods. Our knowledge of relationships between nutritional and behavioral variables comes from a wide array of research designs. A team of nutrition researchers might be inclined to employ a certain type of design, such as the epidemiological approach, while a group of psychologists may be more likely to choose a cross-sectional design in order to study changes with development. For example, suppose a research team surveyed all the children of elementary school age in a certain school district in order to test their knowledge of the Food Guide Pyramid, and then related the children's most recent spelling test scores to their pyramid scores. In such a scenario, they would be conducting an epidemiological study. In contrast, if the researchers compared the classes of 1st, 3rd and 5th graders in just one school, to see if their understanding of and compliance to the pyramid (and not incidentally, their spelling test results) improved with increasing age, they would be conducting a cross-sectional study. Both of these approaches would tell the investigators something about the relationship between dietary knowledge and academic achievement. But one approach would be chosen over another depending on what specific question the researchers were most interested in answering.

Experimental and Correlational Strategies

Regardless of the slightly different tactics illustrated in the above examples, in actual practice both nutrition researchers and behavioral scientists share a good number of research approaches, which should not be surprising since they both endeavor to follow the Scientific Method. Despite the wide variety of research designs, most of them can be subsumed under one of two general strategies, the experimental versus the correlational approach (see Table 3.1). Although the true experiment is the sine qua non of scientific research, we will address the correlational approach first, because such studies often serve as precursors to experiments.

Correlational approaches

Correlational studies are used to identify associations between variables, and in nutrition-behavior research, to generate hypotheses about the manner in which certain nutrition and behavior variables are related. In the general case, specific linkages are sought between nutrition variables (e.g. dietary intake) and behavioral variables (e.g. mental states). Linkages between two or more variables are determined by the use of statistical procedures that produce an index of association, known as

Table 3.1. Correlational vs. experimental approaches.

Correlational designs	Experimental designs
Exploratory	Dietary challenge
Epidemiological	Crossover design
Retrospective	Dose response
Cross-sectional	Dietary replacement
Longitudinal	Quasi-experiment

a correlation coefficient, which reflects the strength as well as direction of the relationship. (Some rudimentary statistical procedures are addressed in the Appendix.) Recall the example from Chapter 2 where we described a simple study of chocolate intake and depression. In that made-up example, we found that a slight inverse relationship existed between chocolate intake and depression in women. The inverse relationship, indicated by a negative correlation, suggested that as more chocolate was reported eaten (intake was higher), depression scores decreased (were lower).

When the correlational approach is used, the investigator observes or measures a number of variables that are of particular interest. Behavior or other phenomena are observed as they occur naturally, and observation is the primary means for obtaining data. Existing records may be analyzed, tests may be administered, questions may be asked, or behavior may be observed, but nothing is manipulated. As will be seen, this method is rather different from the approach taken by an experiment. In a correlational study of the relationship between variables, the researcher would operationally define the variables of interest and then observe or obtain measures of the relevant variables.

Suppose an investigator was interested in studying the relationship between sugar and hyperactivity. The researcher might ask a group of children to complete a diet record of everything that they ate over a weekend, and also ask their parents to report on how active their children were at bedtime, using a standardized activity rating scale. The researcher would then determine the total sugar content of the children's diets using a packaged computer program. Currently available programs can accurately and rapidly calculate energy intake,

as well as grams ingested, for sugar and assorted micro- and macronutrients. Similarly, the children's scores on the activity scale could be easily tabulated, with higher scores indicating higher activity levels. Finally, the researcher would run a correlational analysis to learn if there is a relationship between sugar intake and activity level – is it really the case that children who ingested more sugar also displayed higher activity?

Let us assume that such a study was conducted and it was indeed found that there was a significant, positive relationship between sugar intake and activity level. It might be tempting to conclude at this point that eating sugary foods does in fact cause hyperactivity. However, such a conclusion would be premature for a number of reasons, some specific to this little investigation, but others that are problematic to all correlational studies. In any study of this nature that attempts to demonstrate a nutrition–behavior connection there are several conditions that must be met before we can accept the validity of the results.

First, reliable and valid measures of nutrient intake must be obtained (see Table 3.2). One of the standard approaches for measuring dietary intake is the 24 h recall, in which subjects are asked to record everything they have eaten over the previous day. There are wide day-to-day variations in any individual's food intake, so one 24 h record is not likely to provide an accurate determination of average dietary patterns. While our fictional study used a 2 day record, weekend patterns of foods eaten are likely to be different than that of a

Table 3.2. Methods of recording dietary intake.

Diet history – Through an interview, information is obtained about client's current and previous eating patterns.

Food record – Using a diary, the client self-reports all food and beverages consumed over a defined period, usually 3–7 days.

Food frequency questionnaire – Client completes a fixed-choice instrument that asks about daily, weekly, and monthly consumption of various foods.

24 h diet recall – Interviewer takes client through 24 h period to itemize what was consumed during previous day.

weekday. Partly for this reason, some experts suggest that a minimum of 7 days of records be kept when running correlational studies (Anderson and Hrboticky, 1986). Moreover, the accuracy of children's records of their own meals, snacks, and portion sizes leaves much to be desired (Baxter *et al.*, 1998).

Second, appropriate sampling techniques must be used to minimize extraneous variables that might affect the behavioral outcome. By sampling, we are referring both to the subjects that comprise the group of individuals who are studied, as well as to the segments of behavior that are used to represent the variables of interest. In general, a larger number of subjects is preferred relative to a smaller number. If the N-size (number of subjects) is too small, the probability of observing relationships between a nutrient variable and a particular behavior is reduced, and it may be falsely concluded that no relationship exists. On the other hand, correlational studies that use a great number of subjects risk the possibility of finding 'false positives', that is, associations that appear to be present but may only be an artifact of the large N-size. For example, when correlations are run between several nutrition variables and a behavioral measure, the chances of achieving statistically significant results increase with the number of subjects as well as with the number of correlation coefficients that are calculated. When N-sizes are relatively large, as in epidemiological research, even small correlations can reach statistical significance, making it necessary for the researcher to be careful in determining whether or not the association is conceptually meaningful (Anderson and Hrboticky, 1986).

Aside from the number of subjects, the sampling of behavior is also a concern. In our sugar and activity study, for example, the measurement of sugar intake was derived from a 2 day dietary record, which may or may not be adequate. But the parental ratings of activity may have been colored in some cases by the parents' perceptions of their child's general activity level. That is, they may be overestimating the child's activity at bedtime based on their general perceptions from years of living with the child, and not on their bedroom display. Ratings of activity may be particularly subjective, but ratings of sociability, aggres-

siveness, shyness, helpfulness – in fact, anything that may be personality-based – will all depend on how much time the subject has been observed. Human behavior can vary from day to day, hour to hour, so while an assessment at bedtime may have seemed like a reasonable index of the child's activity level, it may not be enough time to condemn or acquit sugar if its effects are short-lived. Whenever behavior is being observed and rated, one has to address whether *enough* behavior has been sampled to make a valid estimate of what is typical of that person's behavior.

Third, and most important, it must be stressed that correlational studies *cannot establish causality*. Because the question in our example asked if sugar was related to hyperactivity, the finding that they were associated implied that sugar intake caused an increase in activity level. But one might just as rationally conclude that increased activity level demands an increase in sugar intake. That is, children who are more active may happen to crave more sweets so as to sustain their activity level via increased energy intake. Since sugar intake and bedtime activity were measured at more or less the same time, we do not know which preceded the other, a necessary condition if we are to attribute causality. Related to this problem is the possibility that a third, unidentified variable is actually responsible for the measured levels of sugar and activity. For example, if the children watched a great deal of television over the weekend, they would likely have been exposed to endless attractive commercials for candy, cookies and other sugary snacks. Under the guise of entertainment, they would also have witnessed countless examples of jumping, dancing, kickboxing, etc., whether through cartoons or live action shows. A 2 day diet of children's programming could have led to both an increased desire for sweets and the imitation of active role models.

Even if television watching were to correlate with sugar intake and increased activity, however, it would still be incorrect to attribute causality to the children's viewing habits, as all the problems with correlational approaches would still apply. Again, measuring television watching at approximately the same time as diet and activity were observed would only imply that these variables varied together.

Another factor, perhaps undisciplined parenting, might directly affect the child's display of activity, with the other variables merely serving as covariates. In spite of such ambiguity, the apparent weaknesses of the correlational approach are still offset by the value it holds in terms of exploring possible associations between variables. If a correlation between two variables is found to exist, a formal hypothesis about the nature of their relationship may be generated that can be subsequently tested using an experimental design.

In addition to the exploratory function of the above example, a number of variants of the correlational approach exist. In contrast to the *epidemiological* studies that include large sample sizes as well as large numbers of variables, the correlational approach also encompasses designs that may be much more modest, but share the observational method of data acquisition. The *retrospective* approach consists of obtaining data on a pool of subjects, but instead of linking nutritional status to certain behaviors by drawing on an array of concurrent measures, efforts are made to identify relevant variables from the past that may help to inform the present circumstances. For example, a psychologist who counsels young women with anorexia nervosa may be trying to identify factors in her family history that are relevant to her current condition. He would thus be starting with an individual who was diagnosed with an eating disorder, and then examine elements of her past that seemed to characterize her family of origin. If enough of his clients disclosed similar memories of growing up, the psychologist might infer a relationship between parental hostility, for example, and the daughters' disorder. Despite the appeal of such a correlation, he would have to recognize that other factors might be the actual cause of his clients' eating difficulties.

Two additional designs, quite prevalent in developmental psychology, can answer questions about changes in behavior that accompany age. The cross-sectional approach may be familiar to you from reports where a cross-section of the population, for example, rich, poor and middle-class, is surveyed on some issue in order to draw conclusions about peoples' lifestyles as a function of socio-economic status. There are actually numerous studies of this nature, where the eating habits of social groups by income, ethnicity, or geographic region are of interest. In the behavioral sciences, however, the *cross-sectional* design refers to a study in which subjects of different ages are observed in order to determine how behavior may change as a function of age. For example, if a nutrition professor were interested in the use of vitamin supplements in adulthood, and had a hunch that older people are likelier to use them, the professor might survey first-year students enrolled in an English composition class, the graduate students in the English department, and the faculty in English as well. If a higher percentage of faculty members used supplements than graduate students, who were higher in turn than the undergraduates, the professor's hypothesis would be supported, though only at a descriptive level, that is, there would be no explanation why the older subjects used more supplements, but only that they did so.

This last point may seem relatively unimportant, but this flaw is serious insofar as the professor cannot predict based on the data whether the younger subjects will elect to use more vitamin supplements when they get older. Because age does not explain behavior, the age differences between the subjects is only a marker variable. For all the professor knows, the majority of first-year students may never reach the level of vitamin use seen even in the graduate students, perhaps because of a nutrition course they take in the spring. The cross-sectional design thus has its limitations, despite the relative ease with which an investigator can learn about age differences across wide ranges.

Fortunately, an alternate approach for studying changes with age exists. Instead of studying separate groups of different-aged subjects, in a *longitudinal* design the investigator would identify a group of subjects and study them on separate occasions. Depending on the age range in which she was interested, she would start with subjects at the lower end, observe them on some variable, and contact them at one or more later points in time to observe them again with the same measure. In the example just described, the professor might survey the first-year composition students, put the data away for a few years, locate them in their senior year, and try to follow them up some years later after graduation. But there are some problems that beset this approach, as well. For one thing, just locating the students as seniors will be more challenging than it had been when they were all in one class. Some may have dropped out of college, some may have graduated early. Some may have married and changed their names. Moreover, those who are still there will be scattered throughout the university, so just getting them to respond to the survey will require mailing them the questionnaires, at a minimum. It will thus cost more to get the data collected. Imagine how hard it would be to track them down when they are five or ten years out of school. But a bigger issue should also be apparent. This longitudinal study will have taken some 8–13 years to complete – a lot of time and trouble in this case to learn the answer to a relatively simple question. Obviously, having to wait years for subjects to age is not a preferred use of an investigator's time or money.

It is primarily for this reason that longitudinal studies of adults are conducted by research groups at institutes or universities, where several investigators (with a large budget) can arrange for their successors to continue to gather the data. For example, the Fels Research Institute began the Fels Longitudinal Study in 1929 in Yellow Springs, Ohio, in order to study the effects of the Great Depression on child development. Psychological data were collected for well over 40 years, with a switch to physical growth measures in the mid-1970s. Dozens of individuals are enrolled every year, with data now available on the children, grandchildren and great-grandchildren of the original volunteers. To this day, serial data are still collected, sometimes with changes in areas of interest, but data on body composition continues to be gathered. Similarly, the Framingham Heart Study was started in Framingham, Massachusetts, by the National Heart Institute in order to identify the general causes of heart disease and stroke. A cohort of 5209 adult men and women were enrolled in 1948, with the subjects returning every 2 years for extensive physical examinations. A second generation of enrollees began participating in 1971. Since its inception, over 1000 research articles have been published using this database, with much of our present knowledge of cardiovascular risk factors deriving from the study.

Experimental approaches

In contrast to the correlational approaches, experimental designs have the potential to identify causal links between diet and behavior. Where a correlational study may include a number of variables, equivalent in value until associations are determined, an experimental study includes two specific types of variables. The *independent variable*, manipulated by the experimenter, constitutes the treatment that the subjects receive. It may be the addition of a particular nutrient to the subjects' diets, or the application of a nutrition lesson to a class of students, but in either case the experimenter is controlling what the subjects are exposed to or how their experience within the investigation differs. The *dependent variable* refers to the observation, measure, or outcome that results from the manipulation of the independent variable. If the manipulation of a specific dietary component (the independent variable) significantly alters the form or magnitude of a behavioral measure (the dependent variable), a causal relationship can then be postulated.

While different nutrition–behavior studies can vary widely in terms of their complexity, certain common elements will characterize any sound experiment. First, an experiment will include a minimum of two groups of subjects. The group of greatest interest, indeed, the real test of the experiment, is referred to as the experimental or *treatment group*. As you might expect, this group of subjects is the one that receives the treatment, that is, the independent variable. The second but just as essential group is referred to as the *control group*. In the simplest case, the control group receives nothing, but serves as a standard for comparison purposes. Using a control group makes it possible to eliminate alternative explanations for changes in the dependent variable, such as maturation, history or other experiences aside from the treatment. Any difference that is seen between the treatment and control groups at the end of the experiment can therefore be attributed to the independent variable.

To be more certain that such differences are due to the independent variable alone, it is important to ensure that the groups are similar in all respects prior to the application of the treatment. Similarity between the treatment and control groups is accomplished by *random assignment*, where subjects are randomly assigned to one group or the other. This procedure increases the likelihood that the two groups will be equivalent, as individual differences between subjects in each group are likely to be evenly distributed. As an added check, and if the situation allows, measures may also be made prior to the implementation of the treatment. For example, a pretest on the subjects from both groups should reveal comparable scores. If post-test scores then differ in the predicted direction, the researcher has further evidence that the treatment was effective.

In studies where the participating subjects have reason to expect that their receiving a treatment might change their behavior or feelings of well-being, a placebo control group may also be included. The *placebo effect* refers to the phenomenon that when human beings take any treatment that they believe will be beneficial, their chances of improving are increased (Hrobjartsson and Gotzsche, 2001). Because food is a part of so many aspects of everyday life, it holds significance far beyond its nutritional value. Research on nutrition and behavior is particularly susceptible to a subject's belief that specific nutritional supplements may improve their disposition or performance. To control against this false effect, an experimenter interested in the effectiveness of St. John's Wort in relieving depression could give to the experimental group the actual treatment (pills containing the herb), to a placebo group a mock treatment (sugar pills), and to the control group nothing. If the herbal treatment is effective, following the experiment depression scores should be lowest for the treatment group.

Since even experimenters may harbor biases about the expected outcome of a treatment (they are human, too), their experiments should be conducted under *double-blind* conditions. In this condition neither the individuals who are collecting data nor the subjects know whether the subjects are receiving treatment or placebo (the research director obviously keeps track of who is receiving what, or the outcome would be meaningless).

Recall for a moment the correlational study that we outlined earlier in this chapter on sugar and hyperactivity. At the time, we concluded that there appeared to be a link between sugar intake and bedtime activity, but we also cautioned that the results may not be definitive due to the limitations of such a design. We also mentioned, however, that correlational studies are often useful in generating hypotheses that can be tested using an experimental design. How might we design an experiment to answer a question about sugar and activity that could address the issue of causality?

First, we might decide on an age range on which to focus our attention – not too broad, because we want to reduce excessive sources of variance across our subject pool. We obtain the cooperation of a 1st grade teacher who is willing to volunteer his or her class for this experiment, and completes the activity rating forms. With the permission of the Board of Education, the children's parents, and the children themselves, the following procedure is implemented. On a given Wednesday (pizza day in the cafeteria) we arrive at school just before lunch. The researcher announces to the class that as a special treat that day, in addition to their fat-free milk each child will be given a 12-ounce bottle of root beer. After the children are seated in the cafeteria, they are handed a bottle each. The bottles have had their manufacturer's labels covered with special labels of yellow or green that include the school's name and picture of their mascot. The children alternately receive a yellow bottle and a green bottle. Neither the teacher nor the students are informed that the yellow bottles contain diet root beer (with no sugar), and the green bottles regular root beer (with 40 g of sugar). We note the children's names and the color of bottle they received. We also observe that all the children ate a slice of pizza and drank all their root beer, though some did not finish their salad or milk. Following lunch the children go outside to the playground for recess, and we ask their teacher to spend a little time observing each of her students during the next 20 min. After recess is over, the teacher completes the activity rating scales for each child while the children are read a story by the researcher.

Let us now suppose that after comparing the activity scores between the children who had the regular root beer (treatment) and the diet root beer (control), we find that activity scores for the treatment group are slightly higher than for the control group. Can we conclude that sugar invariably increases activity level? Even an experiment has its limitations, so a wholesale acceptance of the hypothesis may not yet be warranted. Despite our expected finding, why must we still be careful in our conclusions?

Our having randomly distributed the two kinds of sodas gives us confidence that the groups of children who received either beverage should have been equivalent before they drank their root beer. Some children may have been better nourished than others, some may have skipped breakfast, some may have had more sleep, some may have come from single-parent families, etc., but these differences should have been randomly dispersed across groups. While a correlational study benefits from a larger sample size, equivalent sub-samples are a greater concern in an experiment. Our target class may have been too small to ensure that individual differences in children were evenly distributed across the two halves.

In our correlational study we also insisted that our measures be valid and reliable. While the activity scale we used was the same, our treatment variable and its administration bears some scrutiny. Perhaps 40 g of sugar was not enough to be effective. Maybe 60 g of sugar is the amount necessary to demonstrate a behavioral effect. This problem and a viable strategy will be addressed shortly. Aside from the amount of the treatment, the *duration of the treatment* should also be considered. Although an acute study (one-shot treatment) permits the evaluation of the immediate effects of a nutrition variable, it cannot provide information about long-term or chronic exposure. Perhaps a steady diet of highly sugared food does increase activity, but this one drink intervention did not. As behavioral effects may only appear with prolonged exposure, both acute and long-term studies should be used to assess nutrition–behavior relationships.

The *time of day* that a nutrient is tested may possibly influence its behavioral effects. Diurnal rhythms of alertness may be different between morning and afternoon, and a greater effect may have been seen if the sodas were distributed at snack time as opposed to lunch. Timing is also relevant to the behavioral outcome, as immediately after lunch may have been too short an interval in which to see an effect on activity level.

Finally, the greater *nutritional context* of any dietary manipulation must be considered when designing an experiment. What the children had for breakfast may have varied from child to child, which is why some studies require that the subjects fast before eating a test meal. Our random assignment should have controlled for this. But altering one dietary variable can often alter the intake of others, as with low fat foods that contain more sodium. Although the use of root beer as opposed to a cola beverage eliminated caffeine as a confound (root beer has no caffeine, regular cola does), serving the soda with lunch as opposed to on an empty stomach may also have made a difference, rather, reduced the differences between groups that could have been found.

Despite these possible weaknesses, the experimental approach is still our best bet for demonstrating causality. As with correlational studies, a number of variants also exist. The example just covered is commonly referred to a *dietary challenge* study. In such an experiment, behavior is usually evaluated for several hours after the subjects have consumed either the substance being studied or a placebo. This approach is also referred to as a *between subjects* design. An advantage of this approach is that double-blind procedures are usually easy to implement, as the food component can be packaged so that neither the subjects nor the experimenter can detect what is being presented. Furthermore, to control for potential order effects a *crossover design* can be used. Half of the subjects are given the food component on the first day of testing and the placebo on the second, while the other half are given the placebo on the first day and the treatment on the second. In this manner each subject experiences both the treatment and serves as his or her own control, and the N-size has in effect been doubled. This approach is also referred to as a *within subjects* design.

In certain studies of nutrition and behavior, *dose response* procedures are sometimes used. Because a low dose or amount of a dietary variable (e.g. 40 g of sugar) may have different behavioral consequences than a higher one, several doses of the dietary variable should be tested whenever feasible. In practice, this is simply a matter of administering a number of treatments, with experimental groups differing only by the amount of the independent variable. For example, multiple doses of caffeine (32, 64, 128 and 256 mg) have been tested to determine if there is a systematic relationship between that dietary variable and alertness (Lieberman *et al.*, 1987). The lack of a systematic relationship may be a warning that the apparent effect is spurious or that the variability is greater than expected.

In *dietary replacement* studies the behavioral effects of two diets – one containing the food component of interest and the other as similar as possible to the experimental diet except for that component – are compared over a period of time. For example, regular tub margarine could be replaced with a fat substitute in order to determine if subjects will compensate for the reduction in calories by eating more food (Rolls *et al.*, 1992). Such a manipulation would be relatively mild if done over a day or two, but differences in energy intake could be attributed to a change in perceived hunger due to the experiment. An obvious advantage of dietary replacement studies is that chronic dietary effects can be examined. However, it is often difficult to make two diets equivalent except for the food component that is being studied, making double-blind techniques relatively hard to employ. Furthermore, it is usually not feasible to test more than one dose of the dietary variable, and replacement studies are usually expensive and time consuming.

Finally, quasi- or *naturalistic-experiments* are sometimes conducted when a characteristic or trait that cannot be manipulated is the variable of interest. For example, one would not intentionally deprive children of iron to observe the behavioral effects of anemia. However, one could identify children who were alike on a number of variables (age, SES) except for the presence or absence of iron deficiency, and compare their performance on a battery of psychomotor tests (Lozoff *et al.*, 1991). In such a study, iron deficiency would

be viewed as the independent variable. Alternately, researchers who study the effects of breastfeeding on infant behavior recognize that mothers cannot be randomly assigned to breast- or bottle-feed their infants. Therefore, great pains must be taken when sampling to ensure that mothers who breast- or formula-feed are alike on as many demographic measures as possible (Worobey, 1999).

Independent and Dependent Variables in Nutrition and Behavior Research

The aforementioned examples of correlational and experimental studies have included a wide array of variables, and should give you a sense of just how much territory the research that links nutrition to behavior covers. Is there a logic to which variables may be looked at, however? That is, are there certain 'usual suspects' that most scientists would find intriguing? As a matter of fact, there are a good number of variables that investigators of food-and-behavior connections find appealing. Table 3.3 provides a listing of variables that are typically tested in studies of

Table 3.3. Variables in diet and behavior research.

Independent variables
Organismic or individual characteristics.
Social and cultural factors.
Setting and context.
External cues.
Cognitions about food.
Palatability of food.
Energy density of food.
Texture and volume.
Liquid or solid form.

Dependent variables
Amount of food consumed.
Rate of eating.
Manner of eating.
Frequency of eating.
Motivation for food.
Physiological responses.
Judgement of food quality.
Hedonic ratings of food.
Feelings of satiety.

Source: adapted from Rodin, 1991.

peoples' eating behavior, when using an experimental approach (Rodin, 1990).

Under the heading of independent variables, weight, gender, personality and diet history may be considered *organismic* or individual factors, but greater attention has been paid to setting variables and characteristics of the food itself. *Social* and *cultural factors* refer to regionalism in dietary habits, such as deep-fried foods in the American southwest, or pasta in families of Italian heritage. The *setting* or *context* factor may be illustrated by the phenomenon of people eating and drinking more when they are in a social situation like a party. Eating at noon on a Saturday, even after having had a late breakfast because of sleeping in, would suggest that you are regulated more by *external cues* like the clock than by any feelings of hunger. *Variety* in foods offered, as currently popular in the buffet-style restaurants across the USA, encourages sampling, and more eating. *Cognitions* refer to our ideas about food, such as what is food in the first place? In certain cultures insects, eyeballs, or dog meat, might be considered palatable or even a delicacy, while to most western citizens they conjure up feelings of disgust. *Palatability*, of course, refers to ease in acceptance. For most children, a mild cheddar is likelier to be preferred over a mottled blue cheese. Food cravings that are based on a deficiency, or a perceived need for some quick calories, may be considered *nutrient-related* or *energy density* variables, respectively. Finally, some diet and behavior researchers have investigated how other food characteristics like *volume*, *texture*, and whether it is presented in a *solid* or *liquid* form may influence consumptive behavior.

Also appearing in Table 3.3 are the typical outcome variables, the dependent variables that diet and behavior researchers find the most interesting. Some may be measured through observational methods. For example, the *amount consumed* or the *rate of eating* that the subject exhibits can be video-recorded for later coding. The manner in which the subject approaches the meal, eating the greens first, or slicing the meat throughout before taking one bite refer to the microstructure of food intake. How the individual spaces the meals or snacks denotes the *frequency of ingestion*, while

choosing a salad instead of his usual steak after hearing a Public Service Announcement on cholesterol would indicate a departure from the usual *motivation for food*. More sophisticated observation can be made of a subject's *physiological responses*, such as an increase in heart rate after ingesting caffeine, or perspiring after some very hot Szechuan food. While such objective measures may be preferred, asking the subjects themselves about their perceptions can also advance our knowledge of food and behavior connections. For example, how much did taste or texture affect their enjoyment speaks to their judgement of *food quality*. How good they perceived the food to be can be assessed via *hedonic ratings*. And finally, do their ratings of *hunger* or *satiety* suggest that the test meal was adequate to promote contentment?

The reader may be thinking that these are two fairly long lists. In fact, Rodin (1990) drew them from descriptions of published experiments that represent a great deal of the research done by herself and many others who are interested in the study of diet and behavior. So these are well thought out and widely accepted listings. But do they do it all? What is missing, or rather, what is *limiting* about using just these variables in experiments on nutrition and behavior?

From our perspective on the area of nutrition and behavior, there are at least two deficiencies that are apparent. First, while conducting experiments with such variables allows us to be confident that the difference in taste between sucrose and aspartame may be inconsequential to most people if they are chewing on a gumball in a laboratory, it may not help us to predict whether the same people will purchase gum at all when they shop at their local supermarket. The ill-fated introduction of *New Coke*, and necessary re-marketing of *Coca-Cola*™ in a 'Classic' form is testimony to the gap that exists between the laboratory and everyday behavior of the man on the street. While *New Coke* tasted better to those who tried it under laboratory conditions, the general citizenry wanted no part of it when the company trumpeted its superiority, and expressed their displeasure by refusing to buy. While the laboratory provides control over specific variables, then, the external validity or generalizability of the results may be limited.

The model in Fig. 3.1 illustrates the myriad factors that go into an individual's making a food choice (Krondl and Lau, 1979; Furst *et al.*, 1996). The 'who' category contains the characteristics that pertain to the individual, whether descriptive (e.g. age, sex), biological (e.g. health, heredity) or personality-based (e.g. depression, activity level). The 'where' category relates to the physical environment (e.g. time and place of food choice) and social and cultural norms that influence the individual's decision making. The 'why' category refers to food perceptions that relate to the individual's food choices as belief- or sensory-based, as opposed to hunger cues (Krondl, 1990). As you can see from this model, there is a lot more that goes into planning a meal at home, or making selections in a restaurant, than simply knowing what the characteristics are of the food that is available.

The second limitation of the preceding list of independent and dependent variables, given the perspective on nutrition and behaviour relationships that we have taken for this book, is that while they all have something to do with eating, they seem to go no further. In fairness, the Krondl (1990) and Rodin (1990) models were developed to assist in our understanding

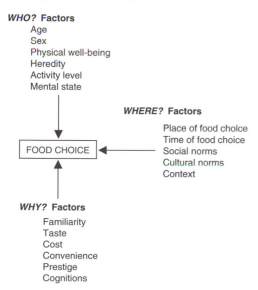

Fig. 3.1. Model of food selection behaviour. (Source: adapted from Krondl, 1990.)

of a large body of work in diet and behaviour that focuses on food choice and dietary intake. Indeed, *eating behaviour* is the stuff of which many diet and behaviour studies are based, and what a person eats has at the very least, indirect effects on other behaviours. As we shall readily discuss, however, dietary components may influence mood states, activity levels, social interactions, cognitive performance as well as a host of other behavioural variables. While the 'who, where, why' formulation may be useful in predicting the diet on which an individual may subsist, in the chapters that follow we will describe far more behavioural outcomes than simply what foods are chosen, or how much is eaten.

Conclusion

In this chapter we have outlined the most common approaches to conducting research in the area of nutrition and behaviour. While you may not be conducting studies yourself, your ability to understand the research that you will be reading about can only be enhanced by your familiarity with how research is designed. For exploratory questions, correlational approaches are extremely useful in identifying associations between different variables. If a certain variable is believed to impact on the status of another, the researcher may set up an experiment in order to test a particular hypothesis about the nature of their relationship. Correlational approaches can document relationships between variables, but only experiments can determine causality. The list of variables that may be of interest in studying diet–behaviour relationships is nearly endless, as both the disciplines of nutrition and psychology are fair game. While not addressed in this chapter, statistics are used to help in our understanding of the relationships between variables we seek to uncover. The Appendix provides a primer on basic statistics that may be useful for interpreting any empirical articles on nutrition that you may come across. While statistically significant correlations or differences are the resultant goal of any scientific investigation, the substantive significance of a study's findings must also be considered when evaluating the contribution it makes.

References

Anderson, G.H. and Hrboticky, N. (1986) Approaches to assessing the dietary component of the diet-behavior connection. *Nutrition Reviews: Diet and Behavior – A Multidisciplinary Evaluation,* 44, 42–51.

Baxter, S.D., Thompson, W.O. and Davis, H.C. (1998) Accuracy of children's school lunch recalls according to how they remembered what they ate. *Current Clinical Nutrition Issues* 14(1), 58–66.

Furst, T., Connors, M., Bisogni, C.A., Sobal, J. and Falk, L.W. (1996) Food choice: a conceptual model of the process. *Appetite* 26, 247–265.

Hrobjartsson, A. and Gotzche, P.C. (2001) Is the placebo powerless? An analysis of clinical trials comparing placebo with no treatment. *The New England Journal of Medicine* 344(21), 1594–1602.

Krondl, M. (1990) Conceptual models. In: Anderson, G.H. (ed.) *Diet and Behavior: Multidisciplinary Approaches.* Springer-Verlag, London, pp. 5–15.

Krondl, M. and Lau, D. (1979) Social determinants in human food selection. In: Barker, L.M. (ed.) *The Psychobiology of Human Food Selection.* AVI, Westport Connecticut, pp. 139–152.

Lieberman, H.R., Wurtman, R.J., Emde, C.G., Roberts, C. and Coviella, H.G. (1987) The effects of low doses of caffeine on human performance and mood. *Psychopharmacology* 92, 308–312.

Lozoff, B., Jimenez, E. and Wolf, A.W. (1991) Long-term developmental outcome of infants with iron deficiency. *The New England Journal of Medicine* 325(10), 687–694.

Rodin, J. (1990) Behavior: its definition and measurement in relation to dietary intake. In: Anderson, G.H. (ed.) *Diet and Behavior: Multidisciplinary Approaches* Springer-Verlag, London, pp. 57–72.

Rolls, B.J., Pirraglia, P.A., Jones, M.B. and Peters, J.C. (1992) Effects of olestra, a non-caloric fat substitute, on daily energy and fat intakes in lean men. *American Journal of Clinical Nutrition* 56, 84–92.

Worobey, J. (1999) Feeding method and motor activity in 3-month old human infants. *Perceptual and Motor Skills* 86, 883–895.

4 Direct Effects of Nutrition on Behavior: Brain-Behavior Connections

J. Worobey

Whether human or animal, alterations in behavior are ultimately the result of changes in the functioning of the central nervous system. To put it simply, whatever affects the brain affects behavior. Over the last 30–40 years, a growing body of research has shown that the chemistry and function of the brain are influenced by diet. Although large gaps exist at the biochemical, physiological and behavioral levels in terms of our knowledge of the precise effects of nutrition on brain functioning, we do know that diet exerts an effect on both the developing and mature brain. Indeed, many constituents of the diet, such as vitamins, minerals and macronutrients, have long been shown to influence brain function. In recent decades research has further determined that essential fatty acids, as well as certain amino acids, also play a role in brain development and function. In the case of the fatty acids, functional effects are evident but the underlying mechanisms are poorly understood, while the process of influence for amino acids is well documented but their consequences are not yet fully fathomed (Fernstrom, 2000). Since the central nervous system is, in a word, central to our understanding of brain and behavior connections, we will begin with a review of its structure and development.

Structure of the Central Nervous System

The brain is one of the two major components that comprise the central nervous system (CNS), the other being the spinal cord. The adult human brain weighs from 1.3 to 1.4 kg (about 3 lb), while the spinal cord is approximately 44 cm in length (about 17 in). *Neurons*, or nerve cells, comprise about half of the volume of the brain, and form the structural foundation for the organ. Neurons serve as the information processing and transmitting elements of the CNS. Their capacity to process and transmit information depends on their ability to generate and conduct electrical signals as well as to manufacture and secrete chemical messengers. These chemical messengers are known as *neurotransmitters*, and much will be said about their form and function later in this and the following chapters.

It is estimated that the adult human brain contains about 100 billion neurons (Changeux and Ricoeur, 2000). That's 10^{11} or 100,000,000,000! Neurons are similar to other cells in the body in terms of their general make up. For example, they have a nucleus that contains genes, they contain cytoplasm, mitochondria, endoplasmic reticulum and other organelles, and a membrane surrounds them.

However, they differ from other cells in terms of their special properties that allow them to function as the components of a rapid communication network. Their ability to communicate is facilitated because they have specialized projections called dendrites and axons, special connections called synapses and special chemicals called neurotransmitters. Like snowflakes, no two neurons are identical, but most share certain structural features that make it possible to recognize their component parts – the soma, the dendrites, and the axon (see Fig. 4.1).

The *soma* (or cell body) contains the nucleus of the neuron, much of the biochemical material for synthesizing enzymes and other molecules necessary for ensuring the life of the cell. The *dendrites* are fine extensions that branch out to form a treelike structure around the soma (the word dendrite derives from the Greek word for tree, i.e. 'dendron'). Dendrites serve as the main physical surface through which the neuron receives incoming information from other neurons, meaning that dendrites bring information to the cell body. The surface of the dendrites is somewhat rough or corrugated, with outgrowths known as *spines* that receive the chemical messages.

Each dendrite receives messages from hundreds of other nerve cells that will affect the activity of the neuron. As a result of these competing messages, the information that the neuron receives may or may not be transmitted down its axon to another nerve cell. The *axon* extends from the cell body and provides the pathway over which signals travel from the soma to other neurons. In other words, the axon takes information away from the cell body. Axons are usually thinner and longer than dendrites and exhibit a different type of branching pattern. While the branches of the dendrites tend to surround the cell body, the branches of the axon occur near the far end, away from the soma where the axon will communicate with other neurons.

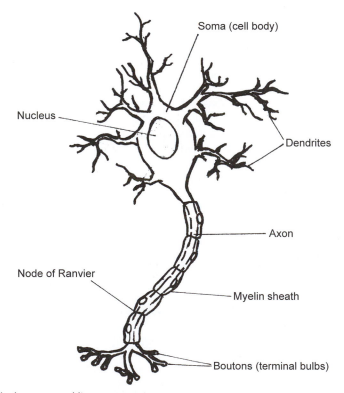

Fig. 4.1. A typical neuron and its components.

The point at which information flows from one neuron to another is referred to as a *synapse* (from the Greek *syn-haptein* or 'together to clasp'). The synapse is a small gap that separates two neurons, and consists of a pre-synaptic ending (that contains neurotransmitters, mitochondria and other cell organelles), a post-synaptic ending (that contains receptor sites for neurotransmitters), and the synaptic cleft (a space between the pre-synaptic and post-synaptic endings) (see Fig. 4.2). Each of the branched ends of the axon is enlarged and forms a terminal bulb known as a bouton. The bouton contains numerous small spherical structures called synaptic *vesicles* that hold the chemical messenger, that is, the neurotransmitter.

For neurotransmission between nerve cells to occur, an electrical impulse first travels down the axon to the synaptic terminal. At the pre-synaptic ending, the electrical impulse triggers the migration of vesicles (containing the neurotransmitters) toward the pre-synaptic membrane. The vesicle membrane then fuses with the pre-synaptic membrane and its neurotransmitters are released into the synaptic cleft. The neurotransmitter molecules then diffuse across the synaptic cleft where they bind with the receptor sites of the post-synaptic ending. When a neurotransmitter binds to a receptor at the dendritic spine of another nerve cell, the electrical response of the receiving neuron is affected. The neurotransmitter can either excite or inhibit the post-synaptic cell, which will determine its action potential. If the excitatory post-synaptic events are numerous enough, they will combine to cause an action potential in the receiving cell that will result in a continuation of the message.

It is estimated that there are one *quadrillion* synapses in the human brain (Changeux and Ricoeur, 2000). That translates into 10^{15} or 1,000,000,000,000,000 synapses. At a relatively more modest level, a typical neuron has 1000–10,000 synapses and might receive information from 1000 nerve cells.

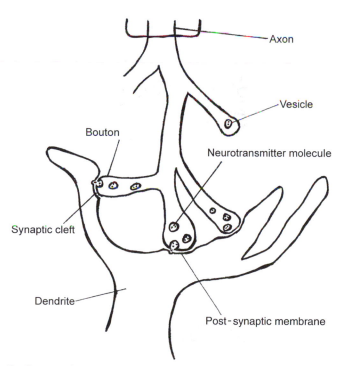

Axon

Vesicle

Bouton

Neurotransmitter molecule

Synaptic cleft

Dendrite

Post-synaptic membrane

Fig. 4.2. Schematic diagram of a synapse.

Despite the phenomenal size of these numbers, recall that all of the nerve cells together only account for about half of the brain's volume. The remainder of the brain comprises a variety of support cells, the most important of which are the *glial* cells (from the Latin word for glue). It is estimated that there are about one trillion glial cells within the CNS, or 10^{12}. The glia occupy essentially all of the space in the CNS that is not filled by neurons, and there are several different types of these cells in the brain, with each having a special role.

The largest of the glial cells are the *astrocytes*, or astroglia, named for their star like shape. Some astrocytes are wrapped around the dendritic and somatic portions of the neuron, while others form a layer around blood vessels. It has been hypothesized that astrocytes supply neurons with nutrients from the blood, but astrocytes may also be important in transporting ions from the brain to the blood. As some astrocytes surround synapses, they limit the dispersion of neurotransmitters that are released into the synaptic cleft and prevent cross-talk among neurons that may be performing different functions. Finally, certain types of astrocytes act like the PacMan™ video game character, that is, they serve as eating cells or *phagocytes* that clean up the debris of neurons killed by head injury, infection or stroke. A significant as well as interesting property of neurons is that they do not undergo cell division, so that if a neuron is fatally damaged, it is lost forever.

A second type of glial cells are the *oligodendrocytes*, or oligodendroglia, that provide support for axons and coat axons in the brain and spinal cord with myelin. *Myelin* serves to insulate axons from one another, and is made up of lipid and protein. It is produced by the oligodendrocytes in the form of a tubular sheath that surrounds the axon (see Fig. 4.1). The sheath is not continuous, but consists of a series of segments, with a small portion of each axon left uncoated between segments. This uncoated, segmental end is called the node of Ranvier. Myelin isolates axons from each other and helps to conserve the neuron's metabolic energy. A third type of glial cells, the *microglia*, are extremely small cells that remain dormant until damage occurs in the CNS. They are then transformed into phagocytes, which like certain of the astrocytes, move throughout the brain to clean up the debris left by dead neurons.

Development of the Central Nervous System

As described in elementary biology, a single fertilized egg gives rise to all of the cells in the human body. In the second week after conception and following implantation in the uterine wall, the blastocyst differentiates into three distinct cell layers. These layers, the endoderm, the mesoderm, and the ectoderm, serve as the beginnings of all the body's tissues. As the outer layer, the *ectoderm* is the origin of both the skin and the nervous system. By the third week after conception, the first perceptible sign of body formation appears, specifically a pear-shaped neural plate that arises from the dorsal ectoderm. All of the cells that will become neurons develop from this neural plate. Shortly after formation, a fold appears in the neural plate that joins together in forming the *neural tube*. The neural tube contains approximately 125,000 cells, and is the precursor to the CNS. Once the neural tube is fully formed, the mass of cells is officially called the embryo (Moore, 1988).

If the neural tube does not close properly, a number of possible anomalies can result. One is anencephaly, where the forebrain fails to develop correctly because the anterior portion of the neural tube does not close. A second is spina bifida, which results from the failure to close of the posterior portion of the neural tube. As you will see in Chapter 7, the likelihood of these neural tube defects occurring may be reduced through increased intake of folic acid in the diet.

Once the neural tube is closed, during the fourth week after conception, the nerve cells begin to proliferate rapidly. Based on an average gestation period of 270 days, neurons are produced at the rate of about 250,000/min during prenatal development. With few exceptions, neurons in the human nervous system stop forming around the time of birth, which means that the 100 billion neurons that comprise the adult's brain are actually present in the brain of the newborn. However, the period of proliferation does vary for different populations of cells. But in general, the proliferation of larger neurons (which tend to serve long distance functions within the CNS) precedes the proliferation of smaller cells (which are destined primarily for 'local circuits' within the brain).

Before they differentiate into their final form, nerve cells are referred to as neuroblasts. When they have finished dividing, neuroblasts migrate to their ultimate location within the brain. The radial glia (a type of glial cell) play a prominent role in directing neural migration. Present only during prenatal development and disappearing shortly before birth, they extend from the inner to outer surfaces of the emerging nervous system. The radial glia appear to act as guide wires on which the migrating neuroblasts move slowly to their destinations. Some later-forming neuroblasts migrate in a different manner, being attracted to the surfaces of nerve cells and migrating along the axons of earlier formed neurons (Rakic, 1981).

After migrating to its final location, a neuroblast must orient itself properly and associate with other cells of a similar kind. This process, called aggregation, is important for the development of functional units within the CNS, for example, layers of the cortex. Neural cell adhesion molecules, on the neuronal surface, promote the aggregation of nerve cells destined to have similar functions (Hoffman and Edelman, 1983). Initially neuroblasts bear no more resemblance to mature nerve cells than to other cells in the body. Once at its destination, however, the neuroblast begins to acquire the distinctive appearance of neurons characteristic of its particular location in the CNS. During this process of differentiation, each neuron will develop its own specific dendritic pattern, axonal structure and distinctive neurotransmitter.

Once nerve cells have begun to differentiate, they must also make appropriate connections with other nerve cells. As indicated earlier, connections between neurons occur at the synapse level. *Synaptogenesis*, or the formation of synapses, begins during prenatal development, but is not confined to this period. Indeed, the formation of most synapses in the human neocortex occurs after birth. This process actually accounts for the largest change in brain cells between birth and adulthood. A variety of environmental factors, notably nutrition, can alter post-natal synaptogenesis.

Despite the 100 billion or so neurons that are present at birth, far more nerve cells are produced than are actually found in the newborn's brain. Somewhat surprisingly, extensive cell death is a crucial phase of brain development. Depending on the location in the brain, some 15% and up to 85% of neurons die during fetal development. One possible explanation for the death of some neurons versus the survival of others is competition for the life-maintaining linkages they must make with their proper synaptic targets. That is, neurons that do not make appropriate synaptic connections would be most likely to die. As with synaptogenesis, the death of nerve cells continues after birth. In fact, it has been suggested that behavioral maturity results not from synaptic formations that occur after birth, but instead from the elimination of excess connections and the increasing efficiency of those connections that remain (Bloom and Lazerson, 1988; Kimble, 1988).

At birth, the human newborn's brain weighs from 300 to 350 g (less than 0.75 lb). Although all of its neurons are already in place, there is still a great deal of post-natal growth ahead. In fact, the infant's brain grows quite rapidly during early post-natal development, more than doubling in weight by 1 year, and reaching approximately 80% of its adult weight by the time the child is 4 years of age. But if not nerve cells, what growth takes place? There are actually three to four areas of growth that appear to continue and are critical in brain development.

The first area of growth is in the proliferation of glial cells. Glial cells begin to rapidly proliferate at about 30 weeks gestation, and continue to develop throughout life. In humans as well as many other mammalian species, the most intense phase of glial production occurs shortly after birth. The second area is the development of the myelin sheath around the nerve cells' axons. Myelination greatly hastens the rate at which axons conduct messages, as well as keeps them from interfering with proximal neurons that may be programmed for different functions. In humans, rapid myelination begins shortly after birth and continues until the child reaches age 4. The first nerve tracts in the CNS to become myelinated are in the spinal cord, followed by the hindbrain, midbrain, and forebrain. Within the cerebral cortex, sensory neurons are myelinated before motor neurons, and as a result, sensory function precedes motor function. The third area of growth is in the aforementioned synaptogenesis, which as already indicated, represents the largest increase in brain cells between birth and maturity.

Finally, some research suggests that certain nerve cells may in fact develop postnatally. For example, there are a few areas around the brain ventricles in which the proliferation of neurons remain evident after birth. Small neurons that are derived from these areas may be added to portions of the brain such as the hippocampus throughout the first few years of post-natal life (Spreen et al., 1984; Rosenzweig and Leiman, 1989).

The Role of Nutrients in Brain Development

Lipids and fatty acids

The perinatal period is critical for brain growth, as the number of neurons and the myelination process are being established. The first post-natal year is also important, as the infant brain continues to grow by approximately 120%. In fact, some 60% of the infant's total energy intake during the first year after birth is used by the brain, in constructing neuronal membranes and depositing myelin (Tacconi et al., 1997). Most of this energy intake comes from dietary fat, with lipids accounting for over half the dry weight of the brain. A vast number of compounds fall under the definition of lipids, which are variably distributed in the grey and white matter of the brain, as well as in neurons and glia. The lipids found most in the brain are cholesterol, phospholipids, cerebrosides, gangliosides, sulfatides and an array of fatty acids.

Cholesterol is a key component of the neuronal plasma membrane, indeed of all plasma membranes, and regulates and maintains the internal milieu of the nerve cell. The basic structural unit of the membrane is the plasma membrane lipid bilayer, which provides a complex chemical environment for the protein molecules that mediate cell function (Mason et al., 1997). During intrauterine growth the fetus receives no cholesterol of dietary origin but synthesizes its own using glucose and fatty acids. At birth, most of the plasma cholesterol comes from high-density lipoprotein. In the first weeks after birth, the concentration of plasma total and lipoprotein cholesterol rise steeply until they reach levels that are maintained until adulthood (Kwiterovich, 1986). Alterations in neuronal plasma membrane cholesterol content seem to be important in modulating the activity of neurotransmitter receptors, so cholesterol also appears to be involved in the regulation of brain function (Hu et al., 1987), a phenomenon to be addressed later.

Phospholipids, which are also important for building the bilayers of the various brain cell membranes, play an important role as secondary messengers and signal mediators (Shukla and Halenda, 1991). Apart from the necessity of gangliosides to the development of ganglion, the specific roles of lipids such as cerebrosides and sulfatides have been less clearly established, although their abundance in nerve axons suggests their importance in nerve impulse conduction (Hannum and Bell, 1989).

Fatty acids are normally present as esters in phospholipids, and their composition has an impact on the fluidity of membranes (Spector and Yorer, 1985). When released after stimulation, some of them act as secondary messengers or may be precursors of eicosanoids, hormone-like chemical regulators that influence blood vessel dilation and constriction (Insel et al., 2004). As will be discussed later, the fatty acid profile of the brain is unique in that it contains large amounts of essential fatty acids. These fatty acids become polyunsaturated acids, and whose availability is a limiting factor in brain development (Tacconi et al., 1997).

Macro- and micronutrients

The role of macro- and micronutrients as they affect behavior will be addressed in Chapters 6 through 8. For the moment, how their deficiency may impact on brain lipids are of interest, and for obvious reasons, much of our knowledge derives from animal models. In general, undernutrition during development adversely affects the growth of the brain, especially the production of myelin, in experimental animals. For example, suckling rats with restricted food intake have lower brain weight and content of protein and lipids, with phospholipids and cholesterol reduced by about 80% relative to their normally fed littermates (Perry *et al.*, 1986). In one study of normally fed rats who were undernourished during the suckling period by restricting their feeding time, the ganglioside was reduced in areas of the brain such as the cerebellum (Bhargava *et al.*, 1984), while individual phospholipids and cholesterol in brain myelin was decreased in another investigation (Yeh, 1988). Such results suggest that a general reduction of food intake, particularly of protein, impairs brain growth and lipid deposition, altering the composition of myelin glycolipids in particular.

Vitamins are of obvious importance given the rapid development of the infant's brain in the first year. Experiments with animals may again be instructive. In studies using rat pups, thiamine deficiency has been shown to impair deposition of cerebrosides, phospholipids and cholesterol (Trostler *et al.*, 1977), niacin deficiency impairs cerebroside content and myelination (Nakashima and Suzue, 1982), and pyroxidine deficiency reduces levels of myelin lipids and polyunsaturated fatty acids in the cerebellum (Thomas and Kirksey, 1976). As stated previously, folate deficient human mothers appear to have a greater likelihood of delivering infants who display malformations of the CNS, including microcephaly (Growden, 1979).

Trace elements seem to exert a greater role in brain functioning than on brain development, although zinc and copper deficiencies are particularly damaging to the maturation of the brain (Odutaga, 1982; Cunnane *et al.*, 1986). Scientists have determined that sodium and potassium are necessary for electrical activity, fluid balance, and synaptic communication, that selenium facilitates antioxidant activity, and that calcium, cobalt, copper, iron, magnesium, manganese, molybdenum and zinc are all essential for brain function (Smith, 1990; Levander and Burk, 1992).

Polyunsaturated Fatty Acids and Early Behavior

As mentioned earlier, the long-chain polyunsaturated fatty acids, or *PUFAs*, that are located on the cell membrane phospholipids serve as important structural components of the brain. Studies on PUFAs represent one of the most rapidly growing areas of research in the study of early human development and functioning. The major brain PUFAs are docosohexaenoic acid (22:6n-3), arachidonic acid (20:4n-6), and adrenic acid (22:4n-6). The abbreviations in parentheses reflect the standard nomenclature for fatty acids, with the first number representing the length of the carbon chain, the number before the letter *n* representing the number of double bonds, and the number after the dash referring to the number of carbons from the methyl end of the molecule to the first double bond. Because they are prevalent in green plants, algae, and phytoplankton on which fish feed, fish oils are a rich source of docosohexaenoic acid (or DHA), while egg lipids can provide both DHA and arachidonic acid (or AA). Two fatty acids, namely linoleic acid (18:2n-6 also known as omega-6) and alphalinolenic acid (18:3n-3 also known as omega-3) are precursors of these PUFAs and must be obtained from the diet because they cannot be synthesized (see Table 4.1). They are termed *essential fatty acids* (EFAs) and if provided by the diet, the CNS and liver have enzymes that can convert them into the longer chain PUFAs (Sprecher, 1992). Vegetable oils are a rich source of both linoleic and alphalinolenic acids.

The long-chain DHA and AA fatty acids are believed to be critical components of membrane phospholipids and major constituents of the nervous system (Innis, 1991; Lucas, 1997). DHA is present in high concentrations in the retina – in some ways an extension of the brain – and comprises 30–40% of fatty acids in certain phopholipids of the rod outer segment membranes (Pleisler and Anderson, 1983). This suggests that visual acuity would be quite dependent on adequate DHA. However, it is also true that the non-myelin membranes of the CNS contain proportionally high amounts of DHA and AA (Innis, 1997), so a number of organ systems are likely affected by their

Table 4.1. Nomenclature of lipids.

Main fatty acids	Fatty acid carbon #
Palmitic acid	16:0
Palmitoleic acid	16:1
Stearic acid	18:0
Oleic acid	18:1n-9
Omega-3s (ω-3)	
α-Linolenic acid	18:3n-3
Eicosapentaenoic acid (marine)	20:5n-3
Docosapentaenoic acid	22:5n-3
Docosahexaenoic acid (DHA)	22:6n-3
Omega-6s (ω-6)	
Linoleic acid	18:2n-6
γ-linolenic	18:3n-6
Dihomo-γ-linolenic (DHLA)	20:3n-6
Arachidonic acid	20:4n-6
Eicosapentaenoic acid (mammal)	20:5n-6
Adrenic acid	22:4n-6
Glycolipids	
Cerebrosides	
Gangliosides	
Phospholipids	
Phosphatidylcholine	
Phosphatidylethanolamine	
Phosphatidylserine	
Phosphatidylinositol	
Phosphatidylglycerol	
Diphosphatidylglycerol	
Sulfolipids	
Cholesterol	
Cholesteryl esters	
Triglycerides	

uptake. In the brain, DHA is most abundant in membranes that are associated with synaptic function, and is accumulated in the CNS late in gestation and early in post-natal life. Studies that have manipulated DHA in the diet (e.g. animals given animal diets that are deficient in DHA or human infants given formulas containing DHA) have shown results that support its role in brain functioning (Dobbing, 1997).

In studies with Rhesus monkeys, Reisbick and his colleagues found that a diet deficient in omega-3 fatty acids led to changes in both photoreception and cortical functions related to the visual system (Connor et al., 1992). This may explain the longer time that the monkeys spend in looking at test stimuli, a behavior that actually suggests lower cognitive competence (Reisbick et al., 1997). Experiments with rats

have shown that diets deficient in omega-3s produce abnormal retinal functioning (Bazan, 1990) and heightened motor activity, as indicated by increased exploration of novel environments (Enslen et al., 1991). However, a rat that spends more time exploring may not spend as much time in trying to learn a task, and the confound between visual acuity and learning may also be problematic (Benton, 1997). For example, Lamptey and Walker (1976) trained rats with a Y-maze, where the rodents must learn to run to either a white or black arm to receive their food reward. The researchers found that rats who consumed a diet that was deficient in omega-3s performed worse, but was it due to the experimental rats' inability to learn and remember or to their reduced visual acuity?

Regardless of the learning task, rats given diets containing omega-3 or omega-6 fatty acids versus diets deficient in these EFAs, have been more successful in performing on traditional mazes, water mazes and shock avoidance tasks. Although the impact on their learning cannot always be distinguished from other mental abilities, the consistency of these findings strongly suggest that the fatty acid content of the diet influences learning and memory (Benton, 1997). But rats, or even rat pups, are not the same as human infants. And depriving human infants of *essential* fatty acids for the sake of an experiment would certainly not be ethical. Nevertheless, there may be circumstances in which infants are already being deprived of EFAs.

Essential fatty acids and infant development

The fact is, most infants do not obtain certain PUFAs in their diet if they are being fed with a factory manufactured infant formula. Breastmilk contains DHA, but standard formulas in the USA do not. Great Britain and Canada began to make omega-3 formulas available to consumers for infant use in the mid-1990s, and in late 2001 the USA gave approval for the same. This recent change in the composition of commercial formulas illustrates how policy makers weigh scientific evidence before making their decisions, yet may still be influenced by lobbyists. The European Society for Pediatric Gastroenterology and Nutrition in 1991 and the British Nutrition Foundation in 1992 recommended not only that omega-3s be present, but that DHA and AA be added to infant formulas. In 1995, the Food and Drug Administration of the USA commissioned the American Society for Nutritional Sciences to appoint an interdisciplinary team of nutrition experts to study the issue of supplementing infant formulas and make recommendations regarding their implementation. Their findings, published in 1998 as a special issue of the *Journal of Nutrition*, led them to suggest minimum and maximum levels for omega-3s, but they refrained from giving manufacturers the go-ahead to add DHA to infant formula at that time. Given the relevance of this issue to the role of nutrition in brain and behavior connections, let us look at the kind of evidence the panel considered.

The Expert Panel was convened to review the published work from the 1980s through late 1990s that addressed the role of any nutrients (i.e. macro- and micro-) that were considered as suitable for inclusion in infant formulas. They used six types of supportive evidence for determining what the minimum levels should be for each conceivable nutrient, namely: direct experimental evidence, metabolic balance studies, clinical observations of deficiency, extrapolation from experimental evidence to older age groups, theoretically-based calculations and its analogy to breast-fed infants (Raiten *et al.*, 1998). This last criterion is particularly meaningful, because the utility of formula has always been evaluated by comparing its effects on infant growth and development to how babies fare if they are fed with breast milk. Indeed, breast milk is considered 'The Gold Standard' to which all formulas should be compared.

Breast- versus formula feeding

One area in which such a comparison has been made surrounds the frequent claim that breast-fed infants seem to be smarter as children than are formula-fed infants. About 75 years ago, Hoefer and Hardy (1929) reported that children of 7–13 years who had been breastfed for 10 months or more had higher IQ scores than those who were formula fed or weaned by 3 months of age. In the last decades of the 20th century, investigators again began to look for differences in intelligence between breast- and formula-fed babies, and often found them usually favoring the breast-fed infants (e.g. Rodgers, 1978; Taylor and Wadsworth, 1984; Johnson and Swank, 1996). From a scientific standpoint, however, breastfeeding was not the only factor that would seem to be favoring infants who are nursed, as numerous studies have also shown that breast-feeding is associated with higher socio-economic status, or SES (e.g. Worobey, 1992; Horwood and Fergusson, 1998). Higher SES is a marker for more involved parenting, which usually translates into more attention being paid to the infant – whether through reading, playing or all around caregiving – which in turn has been shown to facilitate cognitive development in childhood. To address this important confound, efforts have been made to try and control for SES when evaluating the impact of breastfeeding on childhood intelligence. A recent meta-analysis concluded that children who were breastfed have IQ scores from 2–3 points higher than children who were formula fed (Anderson *et al.*, 1999), with another study reporting that the duration of breastfeeding may even display a dose–response effect on adult intelligence (Mortensen *et al.*, 2002). However, ongoing work still suggests that other family factors, like maternal IQ and parental education, may better account for higher childhood IQ scores than does breastfeeding (Malloy and Berendes, 1998; Jacobson *et al.*, 1999).

If we accept for the moment the premise that breastfeeding makes a positive difference in terms of childhood IQ, the question still remains as to why this may be the case. It should not be surprising that as scientists began to look for an explanation as to why something like early intelligence would be improved with breastfeeding, they would eventually target the substances that make up breast milk versus formula. In fact, much of the impetus for analyzing the role of PUFAs in particular was due to recognizing that a major difference between breast milk and commercial formula is the absence of certain fatty acids in the latter, notably DHA. It stands to reason that a substance so essential to nerve functioning would just have to make a difference in the evolution of intelligence. While those who investigate feeding differences in IQ or behavior have been quick to endorse this explanation (e.g. Lucas *et al.*, 1992; Anderson *et al.*, 1999; Mortensen *et al.*, 2002), their data are surely wanting, as the composition of breast milk was not ascertained in such studies. For that matter, studies of breast- versus formula-fed infants are not very useful in answering this question anyway, since DHA is but one of a very large number of substances that differ between these fluids. Instead, groups of infants who are fed formulas that differ in composition by only a single variable, say DHA, should be used to best address this type of question (Shaw and McEachem, 1997). Fortunately, the results of studies that have looked at one fatty acid at a time and effects on infant developmental outcomes are now available.

PUFA supplementation and infant behavior

The Expert Panel reviewed some 30 studies that focused specifically on PUFAs, the bulk of which tested standard infant formulas against formulas with added DHA or DHA+AA, and in some cases, against human milk. Although measures of growth, metabolism and plasma were of also interest, let us examine the behavioral outcomes. Recognize that because infants are pre-verbal, the tasks used to determine their abilities are of rather a different form than you would use if you were testing intelligence in, say, a 10-year-old child.

Since the retina is laden with DHA, a number of investigators have used what amounts to a preferential looking technique in order to test the infant's visual acuity. In a relatively simple procedure, the examiner holds up a card that has two stimuli printed on one side, visible to the infant but unseen by the examiner. The examiner looks through a peephole in the center of the back of the card at the infant, and by watching the infant's gaze attempts to determine whether the infant is looking at the image on the left or the right. One of the two stimuli is a circular grating of dark lines of variable thickness; the other is of a gray circle. The infant's score is determined

by the number of cards for which he or she shows a preference for the grated image (Teller, 1979; Mayer and Dobson, 1997). Although some of the investigators using this approach found the PUFA formula to result in better visual acuity than a standard formula (e.g. Birch *et al.*, 1992), particularly in *preterm* infants (e.g. Carlson *et al.*, 1992), a number of other sound investigations did not (e.g. Auestad *et al.*, 1997).

While the testing of infant intelligence may appear to be more sophisticated, the certainty that one is really measuring IQ in a pre-verbal child is much more tenuous. One approach to inferring intelligence is based on an assessment device called the Infantest (Fagan and Shepherd, 1987). Also relying on the infant's ability to look, the infant is first given the opportunity to habituate to one stimulus. When a new stimulus is paired with the first, the baby is expected to spend more time looking at the novel stimulus. A retrospective study with infants whose formula contained either omega-6 or omega-3 fatty acids revealed no differences in novelty preference with this test (Innis *et al.*, 1996).

The most popular assessment tool for testing infant mental performance is the Bayley (1993) Scales of Infant Development. It comprises items that measure sensory orientation, fine and gross motor skills, imitative ability and early receptive and expressive language. Although suitable for testing infants, its sensitivity to a particular aspect of brain function has not been hypothesized; nevertheless, it comes closest to measuring what psychometricians would call infant intelligence. The Expert Panel evaluated one study using the Bayley Scales that tested standard formula against DHA, DHA+AA, and human milk. Its authors found no significant differences on Bayley scores (Scott *et al.*, 1998), although they used the older version of the infant assessment. Using the current version of the Bayley Scales, it was recently shown that supplementation of formula with DHA or DHA+AA did improve mental scores (Birch *et al.*, 2000). In fact, scores were highest for the DHA+AA group, followed by the DHA group, which was followed by the control group.

As a consultant to the panel's review concluded, inconsistency would best describe the general pattern of findings regarding the literature on dietary PUFA supplementation and infant cognition. In situations where positive findings did occur, they were 'not particularly impressive in size, stability, or clinical significance' (Raiten *et al.*, 1998: p. 2276S). Moreover, in one study it was determined that improvements in visual acuity were offset by reduced growth and head circumference in DHA-fed infants relative to a group receiving regular formula (Carlson *et al.*, 1996). As a result, the Expert Panel did not recommend the addition of DHA or AA to infant formulas at that time, although minimum levels for omega-3 and omega-6 fatty acids were approved.

In making this decision not to mandate DHA, the Expert Panel recognized that weaknesses of the previous studies, including small sample sizes, variable demographics, numerous confounds, and short-term follow-ups, could all have factored into the inconsistencies in findings across investigations. Aware that this is a rather recent area of research, the panel endorsed the continuation of basic science and clinical studies to further examine the role of PUFAs in infant development, and recommended a reappraisal of newer data by the year 2003. In 1997, a second Expert Panel began examining the scientific evidence that pertained to nutrient requirements for *preterm* infant formulas. In their 2002 report, also published as a special issue of the *Journal of Nutrition*, the panel did make recommendations for minimum and maximum AA:DHA ratios, but reiterated their non-endorsement of AA:DHA levels in formula for full-term infants (Klein, 2002).

That the Food and Drug Administration nevertheless gave approval in 2001 for companies to market such formulas for full-term infants instead of waiting until a subsequent Expert Panel assessed the more recent data may be a better indicator of corporate pressure and public demand than of consistent scientific results. None the less, some research suggests that even better measures of cognitive development may reveal more robust effects (Willatts *et al.*, 1998; Helland *et al.*, 2003). However, recent studies with full-term infants have been convergent in showing no differences between DHA-supplemented versus control groups on mental measures (Lucas

et al., 1999; Makrides *et al.*, 2000; Auestad *et al.*, 2001). And given the complexity of brain-behavior relationships, it is likely that in the near future we will see reports of PUFA studies which look at aspects of infant behavior that go beyond visual acuity and cognition, such as language development, attention deficit, sleep patterns, and temperament (Wachs, 2000; Auestad *et al.*, 2001; Richardson and Puri, 2002).

Cholesterol and Adult Behavior

Besides the recent explosion of interest in the role of essential fatty acids in altering infant behavior, lipid research in the past decade has also targeted dietary cholesterol. To be sure, scientists have long established the link between serum cholesterol and cardiovascular disease, and the medical community has sounded a warning for quite some time about the need to restrict our intake of foods high in saturated fats (Grundy, 1990). Related to our previous discussion, it has been proposed that newborns exposed to higher levels of cholesterol via breast milk may be better able to cope with dietary cholesterol when adults (Reiser and Sidelman, 1972). But most efforts to improve cardiovascular health have been aimed at lowering levels of serum cholesterol in adulthood, by improving diet, increasing exercise or using antilipidemic drugs (Smith *et al.*, 1993).

If the stated goal in reducing levels of cholesterol is to reduce the number of deaths due to cardiovascular disease or to slow its progression, then the effectiveness of preventive and therapeutic interventions has been amply demonstrated (Oliver, 1991; Goldman, 1992). However, recent research indicates that although fatal and non-fatal cardiovascular events have declined in cholesterol-treated samples, overall mortality has not been significantly reduced in such patients (Lindberg *et al.*, 1992; Smith *et al.*, 1993). That is, while deaths due to cardiovascular disease did show a decline among treated patients, the number of deaths due to non-cardiovascular causes actually seemed to increase (Schwartz and Ketterer, 1997).

This most surprising and unpredicted finding prompted a team of researchers to conduct a meta-analysis of six prevention studies aimed at reducing cholesterol through dietary or pharmacological lipid lowering (Muldoon et al., 1990). All the studies used random assignment when assigning patients to treatment, mortality served as the outcome measure, and data were available for nearly 25,000 male patients. In evaluating the results of the studies, the investigators found that mortality was in fact not reduced, despite the reduction in the number of deaths due to cardiovascular disease. While cancer claimed some of the victims, the investigators were surprised to discover that an increase in non-illness-related deaths was what kept the mortality rate at the level that would have been expected if no treatment was provided. These unpredicted deaths were due to suicides, homicides, and accidents – all behavioral phenomena! A subsequent review of 19 cohort studies reiterated this finding across different cultures and geographic locations, namely, the USA, Europe, and Japan (Jacobs et al., 1992).

Cholesterol and antisocial behavior

The relationship between cholesterol and non-illness-related deaths remains controversial, as contrary data do exist (e.g. Gould et al., 1995; Iribarren et al., 1995). However, since the possibility has been raised that attempts at lowering cholesterol may be linked to emotional distress, a number of recent investigations have focused on outcome variables other than non-cardiovascular mortality. There now exists a small but compelling literature that links low serum cholesterol levels (i.e. below 160–180 mg/dl) to psychiatric and behavioral manifestations of affective disorders and violence (Kaplan et al., 1997). For example, depression has been found to be higher in men taking lipid-lowering medication (Ketterer et al., 1994), as well as correlating negatively with cholesterol levels in older males (Morgan et al., 1993). Individuals with antisocial personality disorder, whether of a psychopathic or sociopathic nature, have also been shown to have significantly lower levels of cholesterol (Virkkunen, 1979; Freedman et al., 1995). As summarized by Kaplan et al. (1997), low cholesterol concentrations have also been

observed in prisoners, homicidal offenders, those who attempt suicide, and patients hospitalized for violence.

Kaplan and his colleagues have tested the association between plasma cholesterol and aggressive behavior under laboratory conditions using Asian monkeys. The cynomolgus macaque is closely related to the rhesus monkey, but about half the size. In a series of carefully controlled studies, the monkeys were raised in social groupings, were fed diets that were either high or low in saturated fat and cholesterol, and were subjected to routine plasma lipid sampling as well as behavioral observations (Kaplan et al., 1997). Depending on the specific study, monkeys in the low-fat condition exhibited more aggression involving physical contact, spent more time alone if they consumed the low cholesterol diet, and sought less body contact with their peers (Kaplan et al., 1994). Clearly then, a low fat or cholesterol diet for these monkeys resulted in a variety of antisocial behaviors.

Cholesterol and cognitive functioning

On the basis of animal studies, it has been proposed that dietary manipulations may modify behavior by changing brain cholesterol levels and the fluidity of neuronal membranes. At the same time, learning in and of itself has been shown to alter cholesterol levels in the hippocampus and cortex of rats, with accompanying increases in membrane fluidity (Kessler and Yehuda, 1985). In humans, almost no research has been conducted to date on the role of fat in the diet and learning ability, although some other aspects of cognitive functioning have been explored. For example, reaction time has been linked to diet in a few reports. Reaction time, or the speed of mental processing, may not only underlie cognitive ability but can also serve as a convenient index of human intelligence (Eysenck, 1987).

Relative to this topic, the data from a British study of diet and reaction time are quite provocative. As part of the Health and Lifestyle Survey (1987), health researchers obtained information from a representative, random sample of over 7000 adults from various social classes. The respondents completed a Food

Frequency Questionnaire on which they indicated how often they ate 31 types of food, on a scale of '(a) Never or on very rare occasions' through '(f) More than once a day'. To measure reaction times, individuals were instructed to press one of four buttons on a keypad marked 'one' to 'four' when the digits 1, 2, 3 or 4 appeared on a screen.

The responses to the food questionnaire were submitted to a factor analysis, with factors such as vegetables, fruit/salad and fatty foods emerging. For our present discussion, the fatty foods factor is of particular interest. The food items clustering onto this factor were potato chips (crisps), French fries (chips), fried foods and sausage/meat products. Based on their consumption of fatty foods, the sample was subdivided into categories of low, medium or high, with roughly a third in each grouping. To state the results simply, the fatty foods factor was uniquely and strongly associated with reaction time. Specifically, the more fatty food in the diet, the faster the reaction time, regardless of age, gender, or socio-economic class. These results are correlational, however, so causality cannot be assumed. However, the linear direction of the results (high = fastest, > medium > low = slowest), the specificity of association (no other diet factors showed a correlation), and the plausibility of the relationship (that dietary fat could influence neural functioning) does make for a testable hypothesis (Benton, 1997).

In a naturalistic experiment, Benton (1995) measured the cholesterol levels of 274 undergraduates who consumed freely chosen diets. For the reaction time task, the subjects were presented with an 8-lamp testing apparatus. The lamps were arranged in a semicircle, each with a push button below, and surrounded a central push button. The subjects depressed the center button with their dominant index finger, and when one or more of the lights lit up, they would lift their finger to push the appropriate button/s. Reaction time were scored in two ways – decision time (the time taken to raise the finger from the center button) and movement time (the time taken from leaving the center button to pushing the appropriate button/s). The 'treatment' variable was one of eight levels of cholesterol, scaled along one-tenth increments (e.g. <1.3 g/l, 1.31–1.4 g/l, 1.41–1.5 g/l, etc.). For the female subjects, a linear relationship was shown between plasma cholesterol and both movement and decision times. That is, lower cholesterol values were associated with slower reaction times and vice versa. For males, the results were not as direct, as movement times for the males did not follow a pattern, while decision times were curvilinear. By curvilinear, we mean that decision times were slower for both the low and high levels of cholesterol, with mid-levels of cholesterol being the fastest. Based on these results, it cannot be concluded that lower levels of cholesterol directly affect cognitive functioning, although future research on this question would appear to be justified.

The cholesterol-serotonin hypothesis

Throughout our discussion of cholesterol and its possible influence on brain functioning, we have provided little in the way of an explanation as to how it may exert its influence. As part of the cell membrane, its role in the structure of the CNS is well established. But by what mechanism does dietary cholesterol affect brain function, or in plainer terms, human behavior?

Taken together, the studies just reviewed build an intriguing, though tentative, case for what has been termed the *cholesterol-serotonin hypothesis*. Recall the work of Kaplan and his colleagues who manipulated levels of dietary cholesterol and produced behavioral changes in their cynomolgus monkeys. The most compelling changes observed in the monkeys took the form of antisocial behaviors, especially acts of aggression (Kaplan *et al.*, 1997). Based on their results with these primates, Kaplan and colleagues have posited a neurological basis for aggression. Their hypothesis is that lowered cholesterol will result in a decrease in the neurotransmitter serotonin, which in turn results in an increase in aggression and impulsivity. The manner in which serotonin is manufactured and operates will be discussed in detail in Chapter 5, along with some other important neurotransmitters. For the moment let us say that serotonin and serotonergic activity have been shown to play an important role in mood disorders.

Kaplan *et al.* (1997) acknowledge that their hypothesis presumes three associations:

(i) an inverse relationship between plasma cholesterol and aggressive or violent behavior; (ii) a positive association between cholesterol and central serotonergic activity; and (iii) a link between reduced central serotonergic activity and increased aggression or violent behavior. Kaplan and his colleagues have been studying these associations in earnest, and have amassed experimental evidence, albeit with monkeys, for all three conditions. They suggest that their hypothesis may be useful in making sense of the epidemiological associations found between low cholesterol and the increased incidence of violent deaths that we discussed earlier. They even speculate that early in history, a cholesterol-serotonin-behavior linkage may have served as a mechanism to increase competitive behavior for high-fat foods (Bunn and Ezzo, 1993).

Observational studies with humans have shown a trend of lower serotonin in those with lower cholesterol (Ringo et al., 1994). And some work with humans has demonstrated that naturally low and experimentally lowered serotonin can attenuate violent behavior. A recent meta-analysis of cohort, case-control and cross-sectional studies showed increased numbers of violent deaths and violent behaviors by persons with low cholesterol levels (Golomb, 1998). Golomb et al. (2000) have also shown that low cholesterol is associated with subsequent criminal behavior, but their data were limited to 100 individuals who were only screened for cholesterol on one occasion.

In point of fact, however, the relevant studies with humans have just not been done. Nevertheless, the cholesterol-serotonin hypothesis is an intriguing starting point for helping us try to understand the paradox of lowering cholesterol being shown as ineffective in reducing mortality. Researchers over the next decade will likely continue to investigate this hypothesis to further delineate the role of cholesterol and other lipids in facilitating brain development and function.

Conclusion

Over the last 20 years, the field of behavioral neuroscience has contributed much to our understanding of brain–behavior relationships.

In this chapter we have attempted to provide a rudimentary overview of the developing central nervous system and how nutrition affects its ontogeny. The growth and proliferation of neurons, myelinization, and the process of synaptogenesis occur quite rapidly during the prenatal period. None the less, many of these aspects of brain development still continue in the period surrounding birth and throughout the first years of extrauterine life. As we have seen, the role of nutrition, particularly of certain lipids such as cholesterol and essential fatty acids, is critical to CNS development. Dietary fat is also becoming appreciated for a number of effects it may have on behavior. From this perspective, the quality of diet over a sustained period may exert its influence through a change in brain functioning, which may lead to increases or decreases in cognitive ability or even aggressive tendencies. Yet short-term changes in diet may also be of some consequence. While we have refrained from saying much about the importance of neuro-transmitters and their impact on brain functioning in the present chapter, it will become increasingly evident that nutrition plays a prominent role in their synthesis and release. We are now ready to begin our discussion of neurotransmitters, serotonin being chief among them, to consider their direct role in linking nutrition to behavior.

References

Anderson, J.W., Johnstone, B.M. and Remley, D.T. (1999) Breastfeeding and cognitive development: a meta-analysis. American Journal for Clinical Nutrition 70, 525–535.

Auestad, N., Montalto, M., Hall, R., Fitzgerald, K., Wheeler, R., Connor, W., Neuringer, M., Connor, S., Taylor, J. and Hartmann, E. (1997) Visual acuity, erythrocyte fatty acid composition, and growth in term infants fed formulas with long-chain polyunsaturated fatty acids for one year. Pediatric Research 41, 1–10.

Auestad, N., Halter, R., Hall, R.T., Blatter, M., Bogle, M.L., Burks, W., Erickson, J.R., Fitzgerald, K.M., Dobson, V., Innis, S.M., Singer, L.T., Montalto, M.B., Jacobs, J.R., Qiu, W. and Bornstein, M.H. (2001) Growth and development in term infants fed long-chain polyunsaturated fatty acids: a double-masked, randomized, parallel, prospective, multivariate study. *Pediatrics* 108, 372–381.

Bayley, N. (1993) *Bayley Scales of Infant Development,* 2nd edn. Psychological Corporation, San Antonio, Texas.

Bazan, N.G. (1990) Supply of n-3 polyunsaturated fatty acids and their significance in the central nervous system. In: Wurtman, R.J. and Wurtman, J.J. (eds) *Nutrition and the Brain*, Vol. 8. Raven Press, New York, pp. 1–24.

Benton, D. (1995) Do low cholesterol levels slow mental processing? *Psychosomatic Medicine* 57, 50–53.

Benton, D. (1997) Dietary fat and cognitive functioning. In: Hillbrand, M. and Spitz, T. (eds) *Lipids, Health, and Behavior*. American Psychological Association, Washington, DC.

Bhargava, P., Rao, P.S., Vajreshwari, A. and Shankar, R. (1984) Total gangliosides, ganglioside species and the activity of neuraminidase in different brain regions and spinal cord of normal and undernourished rats. *Lipids* 19, 179–186.

Birch, E., Birch, D., Hoffman, D. and Uauy, R. (1992) Dietary essential fatty acid supply and visual development. *Investigative Ophthalmology and Visual Science* 33, 3242–3253.

Birch, E.E., Garfield, S., Hoffman, D.R., Uauy, R. and Birch, D.G. (2000) A randomized controlled trial of early dietary supply of long-chain polyunsaturated fatty acids and mental development in term infants. *Developmental Medicine & Child Neurology* 42, 174–181.

Bloom, R.E. and Lazerson, A. (1998) *Brain, Mind, and Behavior*. W.H. Freeman, New York.

Bunn, H.T. and Ezzo, J.A. (1993) Hunting and scavenging by Plio-Pleistocene hominids: nutritional constraints, archaeological patterns, and behavioural implications. *Journal of Archaeological Science* 20, 365–398.

Carlson, S.E., Cooke, R.J., Werkman, S.H. and Tolley, E.A. (1992) First year growth of pre-term infants fed standard compared to marine oil n-3 supplemental formula. *Lipids* 27(11), 901–907.

Carlson, S.E., Werkman, S.H. and Tolley, E.A. (1996) Effect of a long-chain n-3 fatty acid supplementation on visual acuity and growth of preterm infants with and without bronchopulmonary dysplasia. *American Journal of Clinical Nutrition* 63, 687–697.

Changeux, J.P. and Ricoeur, P. (2000) *What Makes Us Think?* Princeton University Press, Princeton, New Jersey, p. 78.

Connor, W.E., Neuringer, M. and Reisbick, S. (1992) Essential fatty acids: the importance of n-3 fatty acids in the retina and brain. *Nutrition Review* 50, 21–29.

Cunnane, S.C., McAdoo, K.R. and Prohaska, J.R. (1986) Lipid and fatty acid composition of organs from copper-deficient mice. *Journal of Nutrition* 116, 1248–1256.

Dobbing, J. (1997) *Developing Brain and Behavior: The Role of Lipids in Infant Formula*. Academic Press, California.

Enslen, M., Milon, H. and Malone, A. (1991) Effect of low intake of n-3 fatty acids during development on brain phospholipids fatty acid composition and exploratory behaviour in rats. *Lipids* 26, 203–208.

Eysenck, H.J. (1987) Speed of information processing reaction time and the theory of intelligence. In: Vernon, P.A. (ed.) *Speed of Information Processing and Intelligence*. Ablex, Norwood, New Jersey, pp. 21–67.

Fagan, J.F. and Shepherd, P.A. (1987) *The Fagan Test of Infant Intelligence*. Infantest Corporation, Cleveland, Ohio.

Fernstrom, J.D. (2000) Can nutrient supplements modify brain function? *American Journal for Clinical Nutrition* 71, 1669S–1673S.

Freedman, D.S., Byers, T., Barrett, D.H., Stroop, N., Eaker, E. and Monroe-Blum, H. (1995) Plasma lipid levels and psychologic characteristics in men. *American Journal of Epidemiology* 141, 507–517.

Goldman, L. (1992) Cost-effectiveness strategies in cardiology. In: Braunwald, E. (ed.) *Heart Disease: A Textbook of Cardiovascular Medicine*. Philadelphia: W.B. Saunders, Philadelphia, Pennsylvania, pp. 1694–1707.

Golomb, B.A. (1998) Cholesterol and violence: is there a connection? *Annals of Internal Medicine* 128(6), 478–487.

Golomb, B.A., Stattin, H. and Mednick, S. (2000) Low cholesterol and violent crime. *Journal of Psychiatric Research* 34, 301–309.

Gould, J.A., Roussow, J.E., Santanello, N.C., Heyse, J.F. and Furber, C.D. (1995) Cholesterol reduction yields clinical benefit: a new look at old data. *Circulation* 91, 2274–2282.

Growdon, J.H. (1979) Neurotransmitter precursors in the diet: their use in the treatment of brain diseases. In: Wurtman, R.J. and Wurtman, J.J. (eds) *Nutrition and the Brain*, Vol. 3. Raven Press, New York, pp. 117–181.

Grundy, S.M. (1990) Cholesterol and coronary heart disease: future directions. *Journal of the American Medical Association* 264, 3053–3059.

Hannun, Y.A. and Bell, R.M. (1989) Functions of sphingolipids and sphingolipid breakdown products in cellular regulation. *Science* 243, 500–507.

Health and Lifestyle Survey (1987) Health Promotion Research Trust, London.

Helland, I.B., Smith, L. Saarem, K., Saugstad, O.D. and Drevon, C.A. (2003) Maternal supplementation with very-long-chain n-3 fatty acids during pregnancy and lactation augments children's IQ at 4 years of age. *Pediatrics*, 111(1). Available at: http://www.pediatrics.org/cgi/content/full/111/1/e39

Hoefer, C. and Hardy, M.C. (1929) Later development of breast fed and artificially fed infants: comparison of physical and mental growth. *Lancet* 92(8), 615–619.

Hoffman, S. and Edelman, G.M. (1983) Kinetics of homophilic binding by embryonic and adult forms of the neural cell. *Proceedings of the National Academy of Sciences USA* 80, 5762–5766.

Horwood, I.J. and Fergusson, D.M. (1998) Breastfeeding and later cognitive and academic outcomes. *Pediatrics* 101(1). Available at: http://www.pediatrics.org/cgi/content/full/101/1/e9

Hu, Z.Y., Borreau, E., Jung-Testas, I., Robel, P. and Baulieu, E.E. (1987) Neurosteroids: oligodendrocyte mitochondria convert cholesterol to pregnenolone. *Proceedings of the National Academy of Sciences USA* 84, 8215–8219.

Innis, S.M. (1991) Essential fatty acids in growth and development. *Progress in Lipid Research,* 30, 39–103.

Innis, S.M. (1997) Polyunsaturated fatty acid nutrition in infants born at term. In: Dobbing, J., (ed.) *Developing Brain and Behavior: The Role of Lipids in Infant Formula.* Academic Press, California.

Innis, S.M., Nelson, C.M., Lwanga, D., Rioux, F.M. and Waslen, P. (1996) Feeding formula without arachidonic acid and docosahexaenoic acid has no affect on preferential looking acuity or recognition memory in healthy full term infants at 9 months of age. *American Journal of Clinical Nutrition* 64, 40–46.

Insel, P., Turner, R.E. and Ross, D. (2004) *Nutrition,* 2nd edn). Jones and Bartlett Publishers, Sudbury, Massachusetts.

Iribarren, C., Reed, D.M., Wergowske, G., Burchfiel, C.M. and Dwyer, J.H. (1995) Serum cholesterol level and mortality due to suicide and trauma in the Honolulu Heart Program. *Archives of Internal Medicine* 155, 695–700.

Jacobs, D., Blackburn, H., Higgins, M., Reed, D., Iso, H., McMillan, G., Neaton, J., Nelson, J., Potter, J., Rifkind, B., Rossouw, J., Shekelle, R. and Yusuf, S. (1992) Report of the conference on low blood cholesterol: mortality associations. *Circulation* 86, 1046–1060.

Jacobson, S.W., Chiodo, L.M. and Jacobson, J.L. (1999) Breastfeeding effects on intelligence quotient in 4- and 11-year-old children. *Pediatrics* 103(5), 1–6.

Johnson, D.L. and Swank, P.R. (1996) Breastfeeding and children's intelligence. *Psychological Reports* 79, 1179–1185.

Kaplan, J.R., Shively, C.A., Botchin, M.B., Morgan, T.M., Howell, S.M., Manuck, S.B., Muldoon, M.F. and Mann, J.J. (1994) Demonstration of an association among dietary cholesterol, central serotonergic activity, and social behavior in monkeys. *Psychosomatic Medicine* 56, 479–484.

Kaplan, J.R., Manuck, S.B., Fontenot, M.B., Muldoon, M.F., Shively, C.A. and Mann, J.J. (1997) The cholesterol-serotonin hypothesis: interrelationships among dietary lipids, central serotonergic activity, and social behavior in monkeys. In: Hillbrand, M. and Spitz, R.T. (eds) *Lipids, Health, and Behavior.* American Psychological Association, Washington, DC.

Kessler, R.A. and Yehuda, S. (1985) Learning-induced changes in brain cholesterol and fluidity: implication for brain aging. *International Journal of Neuroscience* 28, 73–82.

Ketterer, M.W., Brymer, J., Rhoads, K., Kraft, P., Goldberg, D. and Lovallo, W.A. (1994) Lipid lowering therapy and violent death: is depression a culprit? *Stress Medicine* 10, 233–237.

Kimble, D.P. (1988) *Biological Psychology.* Holt, Rinehart & Winston, New York.

Klein, C.J. (ed.) (2002) Nutrient requirements for preterm infant formulas. *The Journal of Nutrition* 132(6S1).

Kwiterovich, P.O. (1986) Biochemical, clinical, epidemiologic, genetic, and pathologic data in the pediatric age group relevant to the cholesterol hypothesis. *Pediatrics* 78, 349–362.

Lamptey, M.S. and Walker, B.L. (1976) A possible essential role for dietary linolenic acid in the development of the young rat. *Journal of Nutrition* 106, 89–93.

Levander, O.A. and Burk, R.F. (1992) Selenium. In: Brown, M.L. (ed.) *Present Knowledge in Nutrition* 6th edn.. International Life Science Institute – Nutrition Foundation.

Lindberg, G., Rastam, L., Gulberg, B. and Eklund, G.A. (1992) Low serum cholesterol concentration and short term mortality from injuries in men and women. *British Medical Journal* 305, 277–279.

Lucas, A. (1997) Long-chain polyunsaturated fatty acids, infant feeding and cognitive development. In: Dobbing, J. (ed.) *Developing Brain and Behavior: The Role of Lipids in Infant Formula.* Academic Press, California.

Lucas, A., Morley, R., Cole, T.J., Lister, G. and Lesson-Payne, C. (1992) Breast milk and subsequent intelligence quotient in children born preterm. *Lancet* 339, 261– 264.

Lucas, A., Stafford, M., Morley, R., Abbott, R., Stephenson, T., MacFayden, U., Elias- Jones, A. and Clements, H. (1999) Efficacy and safety of long-chain polyunsaturated fatty acid supplementation of infant-formula milk: a randomised trial. *Lancet* 354, 1948–1954.

Makrides, M., Neumann, M.A., Simmer, K. and Gibson, R.A. (2000) A critical appraisal of the role of dietary long-chain polyunsaturated fatty acids on neural indices of term infants: a randomized, controlled trial. *Pediatrics* 105, 32–38.

Malloy, M.H. and Berendes, H. (1998) Does breast-feeding influence intelligence quotients at 9 and 10 years of age? *Early Human Development* 50, 209–217.

Mason, R.P., Rubin, R.T., Mason, P.E. and Tulenko, T.N. (1997) Molecular mechanisms underlying the effects of cholesterol on neuronal cell membrane function and drug-membrane interactions. In: Hillbrand, M. and Spitz R.T. (eds) *Lipids, Health, and Behavior.* American Psychological Association, Washington, DC.

Mayer, D.L. and Dobson, V. (1997) Grating acuity cards: validity and reliability in studies of human visual development. In: Dobbing, J. (ed.) *Developing Brain and Behavior: The Role of Lipids in Infant Formula.* Academic Press, California.

Moore, K.L. (1988) *The Developing Human: Clinically Oriented Embryology,* 4th edn. W.B. Saunders, Philadelphia, Pennsylvania.

Morgan, R.E., Palinkas, L.A., Barett-Connor, E.L. and Wingard, D.L. (1993) Plasma cholesterol and depressive symptoms on older men. *The Lancet* 341, 75–79.

Mortensen, E.L., Michaelsen, K.F., Sanders, S.A. and Reinisch, J.M. (2002) The association between duration of breastfeeding and adult intelligence. *Journal of the American Medical Association* 287(18), 2365–2371.

Muldoon, M.F., Manuck, S.B. and Matthews, K.A. (1990) Lowering cholesterol concentrations and mortality: a quantitative review of primary prevention trials. *British Medical Journal* 301, 309–314.

Nakashima, Y. and Suzue, R. (1982) Effect of nicotinic acid on myelin lipids in brain of the developing rat. *Journal of Nutritional Science and Vitaminology Tokyo* 28, 491–500.

Odutaga, A.A. (1982) Effects of low-zinc status and essential fatty acid deficiency on growth and lipid composition of rat brain. *Clinical Experimental of Pharmacology and Physiology* 9, 213–221.

Oliver, M.F. (1991) Might treatment of hypercholesterolemia increase non-cardiac mortality. *Lancet* 337, 1529–1531.

Perry, M.L., Gamallo, J.L. and Bernard, E.A. (1986) Effect of protein malnutrition on glycoprotein synthesis in rat cerebral cortex slices during the period of brain growth spurt. *Journal of Nutrition* 116, 2486–2489.

Pleisler, S.J. and Anderson, R.E. (1983) Chemistry and metabolism of lipids in vertebrate retina. *Progress in Lipid Research* 22, 79–131.

Rakic, P. (1981) Developmental events leading to laminar and areal organization of the neocortex. In: Schmidt, F.O. (ed.) *The Organization of the Cerebral Cortex.* MIT Press, Cambridge, Massachusetts, pp. 7–28.

Raiten, D.J., Talbot, J.M. and Waters, J.H. (1998) Executive summary for the report: assessment of nutrient requirements for infant formulas. *The Journal of Nutrition* 128(11S), 2059S–2294S.

Reisbick, S., Neuringer, M., Gohl, E., Wald, R. and Anderson, G.J. (1997) Visual attention in infant monkeys: effects of dietary fatty acids and age. *Developmental Psychology* 33, 387–395.

Reiser, R. and Sidelman, Z. (1972) Control of serum cholesterol homeostasis by cholesterol in the milk of the suckling rat. *Journal of Nutrition* 102, 1009–1016

Richardson, A.J. and Puri B.K. (2002) A randomized double-blind, placebo-controlled study of the effects of supplementation with highly unsaturated fatty acids on ADHD-related symptoms in children with specific learning disabilities. *Progress in Neuro-Psychopharmacology & Biological Psychiatry* 26(2), 233–239.

Ringo, D., Lindley, S., Faull, K. and Faustman, W. (1994) Cholesterol and serotonin: seeking a possible link between blood cholesterol and CSF 5-HIAA. *Biological Psychiatry* 35, 957–959.

Rodgers, B. (1978) Feeding in infancy and later ability and attainment: a longitudinal study. *Developmental Medicine and Child Neurology* 20, 421–426.

Rosenzweig, M.R. and Leiman, A.L. (1989) *Physiological Psychology.* Random House, New York.

Schwartz, S.M. and Ketterer, M.W. (1997) Cholesterol lowering and emotional distress: current status and future directions. In: Hillbrand, M. and Spitz, R.T. (eds) *Lipids, Health, and Behavior.* American Psychological Association, Washington, DC.

Scott, D.T., Janowsky, J.S., Carroll, R.E., Taylor, J.A., Auestad, N. and Montalto, M.B. (1998) Formula supplementation with long-chain polyunsaturated fatty acids: are there developmental benefits? *Pediatrics* 102, 59.

Shaw, C.A. and McEachem, J.C. (1997) The effects of early diet on synaptic function and behavior: pitfalls and potentials. In: Dobbing, J. (ed.) *Developing Brain and Behavior: The Role of Lipids in Infant Formula*. Academic Press, California.

Shukla, S.D. and Halenda, S.P. (1991) Phospholipase D in cell signaling and its relationship to phospholipase C. *Life Sciences* 48, 851–866.

Smith, D.G., Song, F. and Sheldon, T.A. (1993) Cholesterol lowering and mortality. The importance of considering initial level of risk. *British Medical Journal* 306, 1367–1373.

Smith, Q.R. (1990) Regulation of metal uptake and distribution within brain. In: Wurtman, R.J. and Wurtman, J.J. (eds) *Nutrition and the Brain*, Vol. 8. Raven Press, New York, pp. 25–74.

Spector, A.A. and Yorek, M.A. (1985) Membrane lipid composition and cellular function. *Journal of Lipid Research* 26, 1015–1035.

Sprecher, H. (1992) Long chain fatty acid metabolism. In: Bracco, U. and Deckelbaum, R.J. (eds) *Polyunsaturated Fatty Acids in Human Nutrition*. Nestlé Nutrition Workshop Series, Vol. 28. Raven Press, New York, pp. 13–24.

Spreen, O., Tupper, D., Risser, A., Tuokko, H. and Edgell, D. (1984) *Human developmental neuropsychology*. Oxford University Press, New York.

Tacconi, M.T., Calzi, F. and Salmona, M. (1997) Brain, lipids, and diet. In: Hillbrand, M. and Spitz, R.T. (eds) *Lipids, Health, and Behavior*. American Psychological Association, Washington, DC.

Taylor, B. and Wadsworth, J. (1984) Breast feeding and child development at five years. *Developmental Medicine and Child Neurology* 26, 73–80.

Teller, D.Y. (1979) The forced-choice preferential looking procedure: a psychophysical technique for use with human infants. *Infant Behavior & Development* 2, 135–153.

Thomas, M.R. and Kirksey, A. (1976) Post-natal patterns of fatty acids in brain of progeny from vitamin B-6 deficient rats before and after pyridoxine supplementation. *Journal of Nutrition* 106, 1415–1420.

Trostler, N., Guggenheim, K., Havivi, E. and Sklan, D. (1977) Effect of thiamine deficiency in pregnant and lactating rats on the brain of their offspring. *Nutrition and Metabolism* 21, 294–304.

Virkkunen, M. (1979) Serum cholesterol in antisocial personality. *Neuropsychology* 5, 27–30.

Wachs, T.D. (2000) Linking nutrition and temperament. In: Molfese, D. and Molfese, T. (eds) *Temperament and Personality Development Across the Life Span*. Erlbaum, Hillsdale, New Jersey.

Willatts, P., Forsyth, J.S., DiModugno, M.K., Varma, S. and Colvin, M. (1998) Effect of long-chain polyunsaturated fatty acids in infant formula on problem solving at 10 months of age. *Lancet* 352, 688–691.

Worobey, J. (1992) Development milestones related to feeding status: evidence from the Child Health Supplement to the 1981 National Health Interview Survey. *Journal of Human Nutrition and Dietetics* 5, 545–552.

Yeh, Y.Y. (1988) Long chain fatty acid deficits in brain myelin sphingolipids of undernourished rat pups. *Lipids* 23, 1114–1118.

5 Short-term Effects of Nutrition on Behavior: Neurotransmitters

J. Worobey and R.B. Kanarek

In Chapter 4 we outlined how nutritional variables such as essential fatty acids play an important role in the functioning of the central nervous system (CNS) and the expression of certain behaviors. In subsequent chapters we will examine how deficiencies in essential nutrients like vitamins or minerals can also impair the CNS and result in profound behavioral disturbances. Brain functioning may additionally be impaired by the contamination of our food supply with pesticides or heavy metals such as lead or mercury. In such cases, however, relatively long-term nutritional deficiencies or sustained exposure to environmental toxins would be necessary before alterations in brain functioning and behavior are observed.

The results of research conducted over the last 25 years suggest that changes in short-term nutritional variables may also affect brain functioning, and thereby influence behavior. As we have already indicated, abundant research has been conducted to demonstrate that the consumption of certain types of food can affect the chemical composition of the brain. Altering the chemistry of the brain has in turn been linked to changes in specific behaviors. For example, as shown in Chapter 4 a diet high in fatty foods may influence the activity of neurons containing serotonin, which may be linked to behaviors such as aggression or violence. As we shall see a bit later, serotonin uptake has also been linked to mood disorders,

sleep and appetite. More generally, it has been proposed that moment-to-moment changes in nutrient availability can modify neurotransmitter synthesis and activity in the CNS.

If valid, such modifications have important consequences for behavior, as it suggests that in altering the production of neurotransmitters in the brain, certain foods themselves may be operating like psychoactive drugs. Such alterations would have implications for the treatment of psychological or neurological disorders, as specific diets or nutrients could act as therapeutic agents for such conditions. On the other hand, there may be certain nutrients that in exerting their effect could offset the expected benefits of a prescription drug, and thereby be countertherapeutic. But perhaps we are getting a bit ahead of ourselves. Before we address the utility of dietary interventions that can stimulate the production of neurotransmitters, let us first describe the ways in which nutrients may alter neurotransmitter synthesis and activity, and then examine how these alterations may modify behavior.

Neurotransmitters and Precursor Control

There are approximately three dozen substances that are believed to act as neurotransmitters in the CNS of mammals. These chemical substances can be categorized under one of three major headings:

1. *Monoamines*, which include substances such as serotonin, acetylcholine and the catecholamines (dopamine and norepinephrine).
2. *Peptides,* which include substances such as endorphins, cholecystkinin, somatostatin and thyrotropin-releasing hormone.
3. *Non-essential Amino Acids*, such as aspartate, glutamine and glycine.

(Christensen, 1996)

Of these three groups, the synthesis and activity of the monoamines have been the most thoroughly investigated. With all due respect to the peptides and non-essential amino acids, the monoamines will be addressed exclusively because they have probably been the most frequently investigated from a dietary perspective, and they also seem to have the most pronounced behavioral effects. The monoamine neurotransmitters are all low molecular weight, water-soluble amines that carry an ionic charge. They are synthesized in the neurons from *precursor* molecules that ordinarily must be obtained in whole or in part from the diet. Precursor control means that the availability of the neurotransmitter is controlled by the presence of its precursor or the substance from which it is synthesized. For example, tryptophan is the precursor to the neurotransmitter serotonin. The cells of the body cannot produce tryptophan, so individuals must consume it in sufficient amounts through the protein in their diet. In contrast, choline is the precursor to the neurotransmitter acetylcholine, but it can be formed in the liver and brain. However, the major portion of choline is obtained through dietary lecithin.

Under appropriate conditions increasing the dietary intake of a precursor should stimulate neurotransmitter formation. However, a number of conditions must be met before it can be assumed that the rate at which neurons will synthesize a given neurotransmitter is dependent on the intake of a dietary precursor:

1. *It must be demonstrated that the precursor is obtained from the general circulation and cannot be synthesized in the brain.*
2. *Plasma levels of the precursor must fluctuate with dietary intake and not be kept within a narrow range by a physiological mechanism.*
3. *The enzyme transforming the precursor into the neurotransmitter must be unsaturated, so that the synthesis of the neurotransmitter will accelerate when additional precursor material is made available.*
4. *The enzyme that catalyzes the synthesis of the neurotransmitter is not modified by feedback inhibition that could decrease its activity after the neurotransmitter levels have increased.*
5. *The rate at which the precursor enters the brain must vary directly with its concentration in plasma – there must not be an absolute blood–brain-barrier for the precursor.*

(Growden, 1979; Wurtman *et al.*, 1981a)

As its name suggests, the blood–brain-barrier is the structural means by which most substances in the blood are prevented from entering the brain. The barrier is semi-permeable, allowing some materials to cross into the brain, but stopping others from doing so. A number of special characteristics contribute to this ability. First, a discontinuous sheath of astrocyte cells that are interspersed between blood vessels and neurons envelops the cerebral capillaries, or small blood vessels of the brain. As in most parts of the body the capillaries are lined with endothelial cells. In muscles, for example, the endothelial tissue has small spaces in between each individual cell so that substances can move readily between the inside and outside of the capillaries. However, the endothelial cells of the capillaries in the brain differ ultrastructurally from those in muscle. That is, they fit together with extremely tight junctions, which serves to prevent substances from passing out of the bloodstream. Finally, the plasma membranes of the cerebral endothelial cells provide a continuous lipid barrier between blood and brain, and are the anatomical basis of the barrier (Pardridge *et al.*, 1975).

The blood–brain-barrier has several important functions. Most notably, it helps in maintaining a constant environment for the brain. It serves to protect the brain from foreign substances in the blood that may injure the brain.

It also protects the brain from hormones in the rest of the body. Large molecules do not pass easily through the barrier, and those that have a high electrical charge are slowed. However, lipid soluble molecules, such as alcohol or barbiturate drugs, can pass rapidly into the brain. And relevant for our present discussion, the precursors to the monoamine neurotransmitters are also able to cross through the blood–brain-barrier. For that matter, serotonin, acetylcholine and the catecholamines appear to meet all five of the conditions for precursor control that were outlined above. These neurotransmitters, their dietary sources and their behavioral implications will be described next.

Serotonin

The synthesis of the neurotransmitter serotonin, also called 5-hydroxytryptamine (5-HT), is accomplished within the serotonergic neurons located in the brain. The first step in its synthesis is the uptake of the amino acid tryptophan from the blood into the brain. Tryptophan is an amino acid, one of the building blocks of protein, which should suggest to the reader that serotonin levels are related to nutrient intake. As shown in Fig. 5.1, tryptophan enters the neurons of the brain where it is converted to 5-hydroxytryptophan in a reaction catalyzed by the enzyme tryptophan hydroxylase. In the next step 5-hydroxytryptophan is converted to serotonin (5-HT) through an action controlled by the enzyme 5-hydroxy-

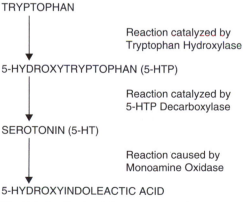

Fig. 5.1. Synthesis of the neurotransmitter serotonin.

tryptophan decarboxylase. With the help of monoamine oxidase, the metabolite 5-hydroxy-indoleacetic acid is ultimately produced.

It is generally accepted that the primary factor limiting the synthesis of serotonin is the hydroxylation of tryptophan to 5-hydroxytryptophan, the reaction catalyzed by tryptophan hydroxylase. For additional tryptophan to increase the rate of serotonin synthesis, tryptophan hydroxylase must not be saturated with tryptophan. If it were, no more tryptophan could be converted to 5-hydroxytryptophan, no matter how much additional tryptophan was available. The availability of tryptophan hydroxylase thus serves as the rate-limiting step in the synthesis of serotonin (Christensen, 1996).

Studies of tryptophan hydroxylase on animals have shown that this enzyme is only half saturated at the concentrations of tryptophan normally found in the rat brain (Sved, 1983). This would suggest that increasing the availability of tryptophan could as much as double the rate of tryptophan synthesis. In their groundbreaking research in the early 1970s, Fernstrom and Wurtman (1971, 1972, 1974) attempted to do just this. Rats given varying amounts of tryptophan showed a clear dose response. As brain tryptophan levels increased, serotonin synthesis demonstrated a corresponding rise. Serotonin levels are therefore sensitive to tryptophan levels, with even small changes in brain levels of tryptophan producing significant effects on 5-HT (Young, 1986).

Since increasing plasma tryptophan elevates brain tryptophan levels and accelerates the synthesis of serotonin, Fernstrom and Wurtman predicted that similar results would occur following the consumption by rats of a high protein meal that naturally contained tryptophan. But much to their surprise, brain tryptophan and serotonin levels were depressed, although plasma tryptophan levels were elevated. This paradox was found to occur because tryptophan is relatively scarce in protein, when compared to the other large neutral amino acids (LNAA). The LNAAs (namely tryptophan, valine, tyrosine, leucine, isoleucine, phenylalanine and methionine) share a common transport mechanism in crossing the blood–brain-barrier (Pardridge, 1977). The system transporting the LNAAs is relatively unsaturated at normal plasma LNAA concentrations. So if plasma levels of the LNAAS rise, as happens following the consumption of a protein-rich meal, the saturation of the transport system increases and the transport of LNAAs into the brain also increases (Christensen, 1996).

But because the LNAAs share this common transport system, all of them compete with each other to enter the brain. The amount of a given LNAA that is transported into the brain therefore depends on the level of that amino acid in the blood relative to the other LNAAs (see Fig. 5.2). And since tryptophan only comprises some 1–1.5% of most dietary proteins, it is not a very good competitor (Sved, 1983). Following a high protein meal, plasma levels of the other LNAAs increase to a greater degree than plasma tryptophan levels. Thus, a high protein meal will give the other LNAAs a competitive advantage in crossing the blood–brain-barrier.

But another paradox was soon to emerge, as scientists soon discovered that in contrast to a high protein meal, a high carbohydrate meal increased brain levels of tryptophan and serotonin. As the high carbohydrate test meals contained no protein or tryptophan, this finding again begged for an explanation. It was soon recognized that brain tryptophan and serotonin levels rose in fasted animals because carbohydrate intake stimulated secretion of the hormone insulin. Indeed, Fernstrom and Wurtman (1971, 1972) tested rats with carbohydrate diets versus insulin injections, and found that the same results occurred for both experimental groups – that plasma tryptophan, brain tryptophan and serotonin levels increased.

As it turns out, plasma tryptophan has the unusual ability to bind itself loosely to circulating albumin. When insulin is administered or secreted, non-esterified fatty acid molecules,

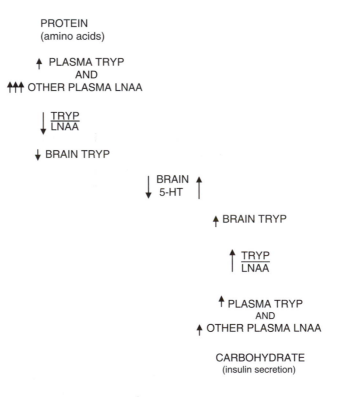

Fig. 5.2. Modulation of brain serotonin by dietary protein vs. carbohydrate.

which are usually bound to albumin, dissociate themselves and enter adipocytes. As a result, the tryptophan that binds to the albumin is protected from being taken up by peripheral cells. The result of this action is that little change occurs in plasma tryptophan levels following insulin secretion, but the plasma levels of many other LNAAs decrease. Because the bound tryptophan is nearly as able to cross into the brain as is the unbound tryptophan that is still in circulation, insulin spares tryptophan levels rather than interfering with its transport (Yuwiler *et al.*, 1977). Furthermore, insulin decreases plasma levels of other LNAAs by stimulating their uptake into muscle. The increase in the total tryptophan/LNAA ratio that results causes an increase in the amount of tryptophan that crosses the blood–brain-barrier.

It should be noted that only a small amount of high quality protein – as little as 4% – is necessary to block the effects of carbohydrate on brain tryptophan levels (Teff *et al.*, 1989). A diet consisting of both carbohydrate and protein will increase the plasma levels of tryptophan, but the brain levels of tryptophan and subsequent uptake of 5-HT will decrease (Fernstrom and Faller, 1978; Yokogoshi and Wurtman, 1986). In addition, the extent to which a high carbohydrate meal can raise tryptophan levels depends on whether other foods are present in the person's stomach. For instance, if sufficient protein remains in your stomach from your last meal, the effects of carbohydrate on brain tryptophan and serotonin will be blunted. So it is highly unlikely that a typical meal consumed under normal circumstances, even if high in carbohydrate, will significantly boost serotonin levels (Christensen, 1997).

To further complicate matters, the time of day when foods are consumed may also affect serotonin levels. Diets high in carbohydrate or low in protein do not alter the tryptophan/LNAA ratio when ingested in the evening unless tryptophan is added directly. However, a high carbohydrate meal can alter the tryptophan/LNAA ratio if ingested in the morning (Levine, 1990).

These findings show none the less that brain tryptophan and 5-HT are dependent on the ratio of plasma concentration of tryptophan to the total plasma concentration of the other LNAAs, rather than on absolute plasma tryptophan levels. If blood tryptophan levels rise but the levels of the other LNAAs do not, brain tryptophan and 5-HT will increase. But if blood tryptophan remains constant and blood levels of the other LNAAs increase, brain tryptophan and 5-HT will decrease. Finally, if blood levels of both tryptophan and the other LNAAs rise concomitantly, no change in levels of brain tryptophan or serotonin should occur (Fernstrom and Wurtman, 1971; 1974; Fernstrom, 1986; Wurtman, 1987).

Diet, Serotonin and Behavior

As mentioned in Chapter 4, serotonin is believed to play a significant role in the mediation of mood and antisocial behaviors such as aggression. Serotonin also appears to be important in sleep and arousal, as well as in food intake and nutrient selection. Given the impact of carbohydrate intake on the serotonergic system, diet-induced alterations in serotonin could well serve to modulate these behaviors (Sayegh *et al.*, 1995; Innis *et al.*, 1998). There is evidence that both supports and refutes this proposition, to which we will now turn.

Food intake, serotonin and sleep

Research with experimental animals has established that serotonin plays an important role in sleep. Manipulations that lower brain serotonin levels have been shown to produce insomnia, while those that increase 5-HT levels serve to increase sleepiness. For example, giving enough tryptophan to increase brain 5-HT by 10–20% decreases the latency to sleep in rats (Leathwood, 1986). In an interesting demonstration with cats, sleep was significantly reduced when the neurons of the raphe nuclei were destroyed (Jouvet, 1968). The raphe nuclei are an area of the hypothalamus, rich in 5-HT, and their destruction depressed cerebral levels of serotonin.

Tryptophan can also increase sleep in normal human beings and has been recommended for the treatment of insomnia. Small doses have been shown to shorten sleep latency, increase sleep duration and decrease the frequency of waking up during sleep in both men and women (Hartman *et al.*, 1983a; Leathwood, 1986). Others have found that subjects report greater feelings of fatigue and lower levels of self-rated vigor after ingesting a tryptophan-laced meal (Lieberman *et al.*, 1986). In addition, it has been demonstrated that increasing the tryptophan content of infant formula can prolong sleep time in human infants (Yogman and Zeisel, 1983).

In an elegant double-blind experiment with infants, Steinberg *et al.* (1992) randomly assigned newborns to one of four experimental formulas, differing only in amounts of added tryptophan. Each formula contained 13.2 g of protein/l, with either 0, 294, 588 or 882 μmoles/l of added tryptophan, respectively (all within the range of concentrations of commercially available formulas). An additional number of breast-fed infants served as a comparison group. Babies were fed their assigned formula from birth through the duration of the study, which lasted eight weeks. Infant states of arousal following a feeding were observed on multiple occasions over eight weeks. While plasma tryptophan levels showed a definite dose response (highest in the high tryptophan-added group), it was differences in the plasma tryptophan/LNAA ratios that were predictive of the amount of time infants took to fall asleep following a feeding. Given the better metabolizing of nutrients from breast milk, the breast-fed infants were on a par with the high-tryptophan group in terms of this ratio, though they were at the mean in terms of sleep latency. But this study clearly showed that higher levels of dietary tryptophan resulted in a shorter time for the infants to fall asleep.

Given the findings that carbohydrate-rich meals can elevate brain serotonin, it would be expected that carbohydrate intake should increase feelings of sleepiness. In support of such a prediction, it has been reported that subjects who eat high-carbohydrate meals feel less alert than those who eat high-protein meals (Spring *et al.*, 1986; 1989). Males characterized themselves as calmer after consuming carbohydrate meals than after protein meals, while females described themselves as sleepier. These effects were shown whether the meal was breakfast or lunch, and were unaffected by the age of the subjects. These results suggest that a high carbohydrate meal may in fact increase the level of brain serotonin, given the reduction in mental alertness.

As mentioned earlier, tryptophan has been prescribed by some for the treatment of insomnia, as an alternative to medication. Despite the findings that it may promote sleep, however, a few studies have failed to find sleep-enhancing effects (Nicholson and Stone, 1979; Hartman *et al.*, 1983b). To reconcile the results of studies that show an effect versus those that do not, it should be considered that dosages of tryptophan have varied across studies, and that the length of time between ingestion and observed outcomes may make a difference (Hartman and Greenwald, 1984). Since tryptophan is not absorbed as rapidly as standard prescriptive drugs, waiting an hour before seeing an effect may be necessary. Since individuals without insomnia will likely fall asleep in less than 15 min, any experiments that employ normal volunteers and look for an immediate effect may not show results.

Food intake, serotonin and nutrient selection

As opposed to the findings on serotonin and sleep, there is a substantial body of evidence for the neurons that produce serotonin being important in the regulation of food intake. Treatments that increase the activity of serotonergic neurons have consistently led to reduced food intake. Conversely, decreasing serotonergic activity has been associated with increasing food consumption (Blundell, 1984; Sanamin and Garattini, 1990). Serotonergic neurons appear to play a role in overall energy consumption, as well as macronutrient intake. The evidence for this comes from studies that examined the changes in nutrient choice following experimental alterations in serotonergic systems. Most of these experiments have assessed the effect of chemicals like tryptophan, fenfluramine or fluoxetine on nutrient intake in animals. For example, rats are given a choice of diets that contain varying proportions of the macronutrients protein, carbohydrate and fat.

Initial experiments that used this paradigm found that increases in serotonergic activity were accompanied by selective reduction in carbohydrate intake. Subsequent research, however, has indicated that a number of independent variables, such as the age of the animals, diet composition, and feeding schedule, must be considered when assessing the effects of serotonin on nutrient choice. When these variables are taken into account, an elevation in serotonin may lead to certain reductions in carbohydrate intake, though it is not a very robust phenomenon (Blundell, 1984; Kanarek, 1987).

Although it has been assumed that the effects of serotonin on food intake and diet selection are mediated via the CNS, adjustments in food intake may also result from changes in peripheral serotonergic systems. In point of fact, the largest stores of serotonin are not in the brain, but in the gastrointestinal tract. So modifying peripheral 5-HT, without changing its levels in the brain, can still affect feeding behavior. For example, peripheral administration of serotonin that does not cross the blood–brain-barrier nevertheless inhibits total energy intake and selectively reduces fat intake (Pollack and Rowland, 1981; Amer et al., 2004). These results indicate that both the CNS and peripheral serotonergic system must be considered when evaluating the relationship of serotonin and feeding behavior.

In humans, it has also been proposed that manipulations that would increase serotonergic activity should result in reductions in energy intake. Some evidence in support of this proposition comes from experiments demonstrating that drugs like fenfluramine, which increase serotonergic activity, suppress energy intake in obese individuals (see Chapter 15). Investigators who have analyzed meal patterns in painstaking detail have shown that such drugs influence energy consumption by reducing meal size and slowing the rate of food intake (Silverstone, 1981; Nathan and Rolland, 1987).

From what we have said so far, an obvious way of increasing cerebral serotonin levels is simply to administer tryptophan to willing subjects. Studies that have employed this method have found that large doses of tryptophan reduce energy intake in individuals of normal weight. In general, adding tryptophan to the diet leads to equivalent reductions in protein and carbohydrate intake (Silverstone and Goodall, 1984; Hrboticky et al., 1985). However, there does exist data to indicate that tryptophan combined with a high protein meal can selectively decrease the amount of carbohydrate that is subsequently consumed (Blundell and Hill, 1987). In a study that used a clever reversal of this approach, Young and his colleagues provided their male volunteers with meals that were deficient in tryptophan. After an overnight fast, the subjects received either a nutritionally-balanced mixture for breakfast, or one that was tryptophan deficient. Five hours later, the men were given the opportunity to eat all they wished for lunch from an experimenter-furnished buffet. The results indicated that relative to the men who ate the balanced breakfast, those who ate the tryptophan-deficient breakfast ingested significantly *less* protein at lunch (Young, 1991). Carbohydrate intake did not appear to be affected.

Taken together, these studies suggest that increases in serotonergic activity are associated with reductions in energy intake in animals and humans. While it is too soon to determine if increases in 5-HT lead to selective reduction in carbohydrate intake, some research does suggest that the brain may signal less of a need for certain macronutrients if tryptophan levels are manipulated.

Diet, serotonin and mood

Over the last 20 years, some persuasive evidence has accumulated that implicates serotonin in mood disorders (Spring, 1986; Lucki, 1998; Van der Does, 2001). Individuals who suffer from mood disorders or depression report pervasive and sustained alteration in their emotions that, when extreme, will markedly decrease their quality of life. Indeed, feeling severely depressed may be the most common reason that an individual seeks psychiatric help or is referred for psychological counseling. The *Diagnostic and Statistical Manual of Mental Disorders* (DSM-IV, 1994) of the American Psychiatric Association has a diagnostic category titled Major Depressive Disorder, which distinguishes between single or recurrent major depressive episodes. As can be seen in Table 5.1, the primary characteristics of a depressive episode include depressed mood, a diminished interest in daily activities, fatigue, inability to concentrate, sleep disturbances, changes in appetite and so forth. As you can see, a number of these symptoms of depression look somewhat like the phenomena that we have been touching on throughout this book.

In truth, the etiology of depressive illness cannot be explained by a single biological, social or developmental theory. A variety of

Table 5.1. Criteria for a major depressive disorder.

1. Five or more of the following symptoms have been present during the same 2-week period and represent a change from previous functioning. At least one of the symptoms is depressed mood or a loss of interest/pleasure.
   - Depressed mood most of the day, nearly every day, as indicated by either subjective report or observation made by others.
   - Markedly diminished interest or pleasure in all, or almost all, activities most of the day, nearly every day.
   - Significant weight loss when not dieting or weight gain or decrease or increase in appetite nearly every day.
   - Insomnia or hypersomnia nearly every day.
   - Psychomotor agitation or retardation nearly every day.
   - Fatigue or loss of energy nearly every day.
   - Feelings of worthlessness or excessive or inappropriate guilt nearly every day.
   - Diminished ability to think or concentrate, or indecisiveness, nearly every day.
   - Recurrent thoughts of death, recurrent suicidal ideation with or without a specific plan, or a suicide attempt.
2. The symptoms cause clinically significant distress or impairment in social, occupational, or other important areas of functioning.
3. The symptoms are not due to the direct physiological effects of a drug or a general medical condition.
4. Bereavement well after the loss of a loved one, where symptoms are associated with marked functional impairment, preoccupation with worthlessness, suicidal ideation, psychomotor retardation or psychotic symptoms.

Source: adapted from the *DSM-IV – Diagnostic and Statistical Manual of Mental Disorders*, 4th edn., 1994.

factors must interact in order to precipitate the disorder. However, it does appear that alterations in brain serotonin likely contribute to the symptoms of depression, at least in some patients. As pharmacological research has shown, drugs that increase serotonergic activity are useful in treating depression, while drugs that decrease serotonergic activity may actually produce depressive symptoms. But it would also be an oversimplification to regard any treatment as acting just on a single neurotransmitter (Spring et al., 1992). Nevertheless, the available evidence clearly indicates that serotonin is involved in some capacity.

The results of studies with healthy adults appear to be mixed. For example, tryptophan-depleted beverages have been shown to increase feelings of depression in men (Young et al., 1985) and women (Ellenbogen et al., 1996). While some studies have shown that a carbohydrate-rich meal can induce calmness in healthy adults (Spring et al., 1983; Spring et al. 1989), others have reported no effects of such a meal (Smith et al., 1988; Christensen and Redig, 1993).

As an alternate strategy, studies have also been conducted with depressed subjects to examine the effect of diet on serotonin as it may relate to their depression. In the first type, researchers examine the plasma tryptophan levels of depressed and non-depressed individuals and look for differences in tryptophan level by group, predicting lower levels in depressed subjects. Recent studies have shown that depressed individuals have a lower tryptophan/LNAA ratio than the non-depressed (Maes et al., 1990; Lucca et al., 1992), which you will recall reduces the ability of tryptophan to cross the blood–brain-barrier. In the second type of study, researchers provide depressed individuals with tryptophan-depleted foods to determine the effect on their subsequent mood. Patients whose depression has gone into remission after antidepressant treatment are suitable subjects for these trials. For example, patients are given a tryptophan-depleted beverage versus one that includes a mixture of other LNAAs, and the maintenance of remission is observed. Some researchers have found that twice as many subjects who receive the tryptophan-depleted beverage relapse, relative to the LNAA subjects (Delgado et al., 1991), but others indicate that this is more likely the case for individuals who have a family history of depression (Benkelfat et al., 1994; Leyton et al., 2000a).

In a related vein, some recent work has shown that tryptophan-depletion may lead to increased aggression (Bond et al., 2001). However, others have found no significant changes in hostility during acute tryptophan-depletion, at least among psychiatric inpatients with intermittent explosive disorder (Salomon et al., 1994). To complicate matters further, some recent studies have shown that treatment with tryptophan decreased aggressive behavior in adults, but increased dominant behavior (Moskowitz et al., 2001; Young and Leyton, 2002).

Carbohydrate cravings and mood

Over the last 20 years, interest has grown in the possible relationship between certain forms of mental functioning and carbohydrate intake. For example, Markus et al. (1998, 2000) have shown that stress and coping may be affected by diet, irrespective of the individual's ability to control the stressor.

In terms of depression, one of its forms has been linked to appetite, namely, the condition known as Seasonal Affective Disorder (SAD). Depressive symptoms of SAD typically appear in the late fall or early winter and decline in the spring as the days get noticeably longer. Besides the characteristic of seasonality, individuals with SAD differ from the classically depressed in that they experience increases in sleep and marked carbohydrate cravings during the fall and winter months (Garvey et al., 1988; Oren and Rosenthal, 1992). Some of these individuals anecdotally report that they consume carbohydrates in order to combat their feelings of depression (Leibenluft et al., 1993).

An association between depressive symptoms and carbohydrate cravings has also been identified in women who report suffering from Pre-Menstrual Syndrome (PMS). While the definitions of PMS may vary across investigations, most emphasize the presence of symptoms and an impairment in functioning during the late luteal phase of the menstrual cycle (Halbreich et al., 1993). Women with PMS increase their carbohydrate consumption premenstrually, but after menstruation both their cravings and consumption decrease. Moreover, acute tryptophan-depletion has been shown to aggravate symptoms of PMS, particularly irritability (Menkus et al., 1994).

In addition, there appears to be a subgroup of obese individuals, mostly women, who describe frequent and powerful cravings for carbohydrate-rich foods (Wurtman et al., 1981b; Wurtman et al., 1987). Moreover, many overweight carbohydrate cravers report negative mood states such as being tense or restless prior to a snack, but relaxed and calm after snacking. For these women, high carbohydrate/high fat snacks are preferred, and the addition of upwards of 800 cal/day may very well contribute to the maintenance of their excessive weight.

It has been hypothesized that the strong desire for carbohydrates exhibited by individuals with SAD, PMS and carbohydrate craving obesity may reflect the body's need to increase serotonin levels. The intake of pure carbohydrates by experimental animals elevates cerebral 5-HT levels, and we have already suggested that a similar process may be operating in humans. A consistent finding for all three of these groups of individuals is that carbohydrate cravings seem to be stimulated following the experience of depressive symptoms (Christensen, 1996). It is therefore possible that individuals who suffer from SAD, PMS or carbohydrate craving obesity may consume excessive carbohydrates because doing so will elevate their cerebral 5-HT levels, which in turn will lead to a positive change in mood. Under these circumstances, it seems that carbohydrate ingestion may be a form of self-medication, where individuals crave carbohydrates because they work to alleviate their depressive symptoms (Christensen, 1997).

While the idea of individuals consuming particular foods to modulate their mood is intriguing, it also presents numerous problems. For one thing, an objective definition of what constitutes excessive carbohydrate intake is not available. Most of the studies that have addressed the role of carbohydrate consumption on mood have used subjects that defined themselves as cravers. Thus, the designation of individuals as carbohydrate cravers has been based on their own perceptions of their behavior, rather than on objective criteria. Second, the definition of a high carbohydrate food is often problematic. It is often the case that the foods that the subjects define as high in carbohydrates are also high in fat, for example, cake, chocolate and ice cream. Given the high palatability of such foods, cravings for them may indicate a desire for a pleasant gustatory experience rather than for a particular nutrient.

Some physiological data indicate that dietary-induced alterations in the plasma ratio of tryptophan to the other LNAAs may have less effect on brain serotonin and function than was previously thought. For example, receptors for serotonin are located in the dendrites and cell body of the serotonergic neurons. Feedback from these receptors serves to limit the dietary-induced effects of alterations in neurotransmitter activity (Carlsson, 1987; Garattini, 1989). The injection of tryptophan thus leads to a reduction in the firing of the serotonergic neurons, which serves to counteract the increased release of serotonin that might have otherwise occurred. In addition, recall that even minimal amounts of protein in a high carbohydrate food can suppress that food's ability to raise brain tryptophan and serotonin levels. Taken together, these problems must lead us to question the idea that individuals who suffer from SAD, PMS or carbohydrate craving obesity seek to consume high carbohydrate foods in order to modulate their mood (Fernstrom, 1988).

Acetylcholine

The neurotransmitter acetylcholine is synthesized from the acetyl coenzyme-A and choline. Similar to tryptophan, choline enters the brain via a transport system that allows it to cross the blood–brain-barrier. Once it enters the brain, choline is taken up by the neuron, where in the presence of the enzyme choline acetyltransferase the acetate ion is transferred from acetyl coenzyme-A to the choline molecule. This process yields one molecule of acetylcholine and one of coenzyme-A.

As you might expect, the synthesis of acetylcholine is influenced by the availability of choline within the cholinergic neuron. Choline can be synthesized in the liver, but neuronal choline concentrations can also be altered by dietary choline intake, in the form of either free choline or as a constituent of the phospholipid lecithin (Hirsch and Wurtman, 1978). Lecithin, or phosphatidylcholine, is present in a variety of foods including eggs, fish, liver, peanuts and wheat germ, and is also an ingredient of many processed foods where it serves as an antioxidant and emulsifying agent. In addition, lecithin is available as a dietary supplement and is sold as such in health and vitamin stores. The lecithin found in foods or in nutritional supplements is absorbed into the intestinal mucosa where it is rapidly hydrolyzed by free choline. Any lecithin that is not hydrolyzed enters the bloodstream and is transported to the lymphatic circulation where it is broken down more slowly to choline.

The intake of foods that contain substantial amounts of choline or lecithin will lead to elevations in plasma choline levels. Since choline can readily cross the blood–brain-barrier, elevations in choline levels translate into increased brain choline levels. Furthermore, because the enzyme choline acetyltransferase is unsaturated when choline is within normal limits, increased neuronal levels of the precursor will stimulate the synthesis of acetylcholine. Diet induced increases in neuronal acetylcholine levels are therefore associated with enhanced release of choline when cholinergic neurons are stimulated (Wurtman, 1987; Wecker, 1990).

A number of neurological diseases such as Huntington's chorea, tardive dyskinesia and Alzheimer's disease, are thought to involve deficiencies in the activity of cholinergic neurons (Fernstrom, 2000). Drugs that serve to increase cholinergic transmission are typically used in the treatment of these diseases, however, their effectiveness has been inconsistent. In addition, the majority of these drugs have a short duration of action and produce unpleasant side effects such as nausea, vomiting and mental dullness, which further limit their application. It has therefore been proposed that increasing acetylcholine through dietary manipulations may be a more effective and benign approach for the treatment of diseases associated with deficiencies in cholinergic neurotransmission. To assess the utility of acetylcholine therapy, a number of clinical experiments have been conducted, the results of which are now summarized.

Huntington's chorea

Huntington's disease is an inherited progressive neurological disorder whose symptoms usually begin when an individual reaches middle age. The characteristic symptoms include involuntary muscular contractions known as chorea that involves all of the skeletal muscles. Chronic chorea results in poor balance, difficulty in walking, and restlessness. As the disease progresses, signs of mental disturbance develop such as confusion, forgetfulness, inability to concentrate, personality changes, paranoia and dementia. Autopsies performed on deceased patients who suffered from Huntington's disease reveal that their brain weights were reduced, particularly in regions of the cortex and basal ganglia.

By examining neurotransmitter functioning in patients with Huntington's disease, some evidence has been provided for a role for acetylcholine. For example, patients with Huntington's disease show reduced levels of acetylcholine as well as choline acetyltransferase, and decreased numbers of post-synaptic acetylcholine receptors. When drugs are used to increase acetylcholine activity the choreic movements characteristic of the disorder appear to be reduced, while drugs that decrease activity of the neurotransmitter tend to aggravate them.

It has thus been suggested that administering choline or lecithin would increase acetylcholine levels and thereby reduce some of the symptoms of Huntington's disease. In fact, a few investigators have reported that treatment with choline significantly improved balance, gait and choreic movements in some patients (Aquilonius and Eckernas, 1977). However, their use has not generally been successful, as improvements when found did not persist for more than a week or two, even when choline was administered for a contin-

ued period (Growden, 1979; Rosenberg and Davis, 1982).

Tardive dyskinesia

Tardive dyskinesia is the unfortunate side effect of certain antipsychotic mediations. It is a neurological disorder that can develop after prolonged treatment of three months or more with drugs such as haloperidol or chlorpromazine. Tardive dyskinesia is characterized by hyperkinetic activity of the mouth and jaw region, protrusion of the tongue, lip smacking and puckering, and difficulty in swallowing. In addition, involuntary spastic movements of the hands, arms, feet and legs may be present. The disease is not an inevitable consequence of using antipsychotic medication, but does develop in 10–20% of patients who use the drugs for more than a year. Individuals who have experienced sustained exposure to antipsychotic medications, electroconvulsive therapy or organic brain syndrome, as well as those with histories of drug or alcohol abuse, are at particular risk (Tarsy, 1983; Batey, 1989).

Why tardive dyskinesia develops in certain individuals is unknown, though some suspect that an imbalance between the cholinergic and dopaminergic neurons in the basal ganglia may be involved. This imbalance would seem to favor the transmission of the neurotransmitter dopamine at the expense of acetylcholine being transmitted. Research with drugs shows that enhancing the activity of acetylcholine relieves the symptoms of tardive dyskinesia, while drugs that reduce its activity will exacerbate the individual's symptoms. Thus, some support exists for the role of decreased cholinergic activity in tardive dyskinesia.

In a number of investigations, the use of choline or lecithin has been associated with reducing the frequency of abnormal movements of some patients with tardive dyskinesia. In a double-blind crossover study, Growdon and his colleagues found that choline administration increased plasma choline levels and suppressed involuntary facial movements in nearly half of their patients with the disease. A problem with their study, however, was the telltale odor that characterized the patients who ingested the choline (Growdon *et al.*, 1977). The treatment group developed the aroma of rotten fish in their urine and perspiration, as well as in their breath, which made the likelihood of the study being truly blind somewhat questionable. The odor was produced by the action of intestinal bacteria on choline, and does not occur after lecithin administration.

Subsequent studies that used lecithin instead of choline indicate that lecithin is as effective as choline in suppressing tardive dyskinesia (Growden *et al.*, 1978; Jackson *et al.*, 1979). However, many patients report feeling nauseated, or experience abdominal cramps and diarrhea when taking high doses of lecithin. Because of these side effects, and more recent work that has shown choline to be less effective than first believed, current recommendation are that the dietary treatment of tardive dyskinesia is of limited clinical utility (Gelenberg *et al.*, 1989).

Alzheimer's disease

In recent years, a great deal of attention has been focused on the abnormal deterioration of the brain known as Alzheimer's disease, which may affect one in 20 adults by age 65, and one in five of those over age 80 (Whitney and Rolfes, 2002). It is characterized by the slow, progressive deterioration of cognitive functions, with dementia usually occurring within five to ten years. The onset of Alzheimer's disease is usually inconspicuous and very often is difficult to distinguish from other psychological problems. Initially, the individual suffers from periods of short-term memory loss and may find it hard to concentrate. As the disease progresses, however, memory loss becomes more severe while disorientation, anxiety, depression and difficulty in completing simple tasks becomes more and more common.

The cognitive declines that accompany Alzheimer's disease occur as neurons in the brain die and communication between the cells breaks down, but may also be due in part to alterations in cholinergic activity in the CNS. Acetylcholine neurons in the hippocampus play an important role in memory, and post-mortem examinations of Alzheimer's patients reveal significant reduction in levels of choline acetyltranferase in the hippocampus and neocortex. Moreover, dementia and low choline acetyltranferase levels appear to be positively correlated. Recent work suggests that there may be selective degeneration of cholinergic nicotinic receptors in certain regions of the brain, such as the nucleus basalis (Ereshefsky *et al.*, 1989).

Researchers who study memory have determined that anticholinergic agents will disrupt performance on tests that rely on the recall of words and digits (Safer and Alen, 1971; Mohs *et al.*, 1981). Since problems with memory are a major symptom of Alzheimer's disease, much attention has been paid to the question of whether the consumption of choline or lecithin can bring about improvements in memory or alleviate deficits. In rats, the administration of choline has been shown to elevate brain acetylcholine levels (Hirsch *et al.*, 1977), and in mice, to reduce age-related declines in retention of learned behavior (Bartus *et al.*, 1980). In humans, lecithin consumption does raise choline levels in plasma (Wurtman *et al.*, 1977), and in at least one study with normal young adults choline produced improvements in memory performance (Sitaram *et al.*, 1978).

However, in elderly samples for which the memory problems that accompany Alzheimer's disease may represent a significant clinical problem, acetylcholine precursors have produced disappointing results, as neither choline nor lecithin seem to offer much improvement in memory (Spring, 1986). Work with normal, healthy subjects has not shown an effect of acetylcholine on improving memory either (Nathan *et al.*, 2001). Furthermore, it has also been noted that depressed mood is a side effect of choline and lecithin treatments employed to reverse memory deficits in Alzheimer's patients (Davidson *et al.*, 1991).

There are a number of possible explanations for the limited benefits of acetylcholine precursors, but first among them would be the choice of patient groups for study. The subjects used primarily were, after all, Alzheimer's patients with a chronic, degenerative disease of the CNS, so the extent of losses due to changes beyond those involving cholinergic neurons may be too much to realize any beneficial action of acetylcholine precursors (Fernstrom, 2000). In the aged brain, deficiencies in choline uptake, presynaptic cholinergic receptors, choline acetyltranferase activity, or the loss of cholinergic neurons of the cortex could prevent the synthesis of choline into acetylcholine (Bartus *et al.*, 1982).

Despite these mixed results with Alzheimer's patients, some researchers are still convinced that the exploration of cholinergic mechanisms in affective disorders such as mania may offer important clues concerning the physiology behind psychopathology (Janowsky and Overstreet, 1998). For example, the brains of patients with major depression do show higher levels of choline than the brains of control subjects (Charles *et al.*, 1994). Advances in neuroimaging and molecular genetics may one day help in identifying cholinergic linkages to mood.

In sum, however, it must be concluded that based on the studies to date, the administration of choline and lecithin appear to have limited benefits in the treatment of neurological disorders such as Huntington's disease, tardive dyskinesia or Alzheimer's disease. It may be the case that the dosages of choline or lecithin studied are not in the right amounts to produce dramatic changes in the synthesis of brain acetylcholine (Bartus *et al.*, 1982). But if choline acetyltranferase levels are decreased, as in the case of Huntington's disease and Alzheimer's disease, the transformation of brain choline to acetylcholine would be reduced and thereby prevent the effectiveness of precursor loading. Finally, the functioning of other neurotransmitters, such as dopamine, are also altered in Huntington's disease, tardive

dyskinesia and Alzheimer's disease. Thus it is possible that even if acetylcholine synthesis and release were corrected, other CNS systems would still be defective, and neurological functioning would continue to be abnormal (Growdon, 1979; Ereshefsky *et al.*, 1989).

Dopamine and Norepinephrine

In the brains of mammals, including humans, the catecholamine neurotransmitters dopamine and norepinephrine are synthesized from the amino acid tyrosine. The synthesis of dopamine occurs within the dopaminergic neurons, while the synthesis of norepinephrine occurs within the noradrenergic neurons. As shown in Fig. 5.3, the rate-limiting initial step in this synthetic pathway is the conversion of tyrosine into dihydroxyphenylalanine by the enzyme tyrosine hydroxylase. This intermediate product, called DOPA, is then synthesized into dopamine by the action of the enzyme DOPA decarboxylase. In noradrenergic neurons that also contain the enzyme dopamine-B-hydroxylase, dopamine is then converted into norepinephrine.

Tyrosine, like the neurotransmitter tryptophan that we discussed earlier in this chapter, is obtained from the diet, but facilitated by protein sources. As serotonin increases when the relative level of plasma tryptophan increases, so does catecholamine synthesis increase as the relative level of tyrosine increases. Tyrosine meets most of the precursor conditions that we listed earlier, as its plasma levels increase following protein intake, its rate-limiting enzyme is unsaturated, and a transport system exists for

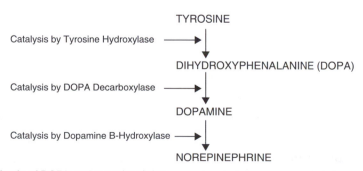

Fig. 5.3. Synthesis of DOPA and norepinephrine.

ferrying it across the blood–brain-barrier (Christensen, 1996). While most of the conditions that are necessary for tyrosine to increase the synthesis of its neurotransmitter products are met, most studies have revealed that tyrosine administration has no effect on the synthesis of catecholamines. Indeed, not only have most studies indicated that tyrosine administration is ineffective in increasing DOPA, but brain levels of the metabolites of the catecholamines have not been shown to increase (Sved, 1983). However, there are situations under which administering tyrosine has been shown to enhance catecholamine synthesis.

Relative to the carbohydrate-tryptophan-serotonin link we discussed earlier in this chapter, the dietary control of the catecholamines is a more straightforward process that is connected directly to the consumption of protein or the administration of tyrosine. When protein is consumed, levels of plasma tyrosine increase, providing greater amounts of available tyrosine for transporting across the blood–brain-barrier. As we have previously seen, the carrier system is a competitive one, transporting tyrosine and the other LNAAs, so the relative level of a given amino acid is the most important factor. The most efficient way to increase the tyrosine/LNAA ratio is to administer tyrosine, allowing more tyrosine to cross into the brain. The increase in brain tyrosine levels then stimulates an increase in catecholamine synthesis, *but only if the catecholaminergic neurons are firing*. When they are quiescent, tyrosine appears to have little influence on catecholamine synthesis, which indicates that the enzyme tyrosine hydroxylase may be subject to end-product inhibition (Christiansen, 1996).

Tyrosine and stress

Exposing laboratory animals to acute, unavoidable stress will result in behavioral deficits, including reductions in spontaneous motor activity and aggression. These behavioral changes are described as learned helplessness, and have been attributed by some to hypothalmic and brainstem depletions in norepinephrine (Weiss *et al.*, 1981). Scientists have

asked if tyrosine would be able to reverse both the behavioral deficits and the norepinephrine depletion that follows an uncontrolled stressor. Some work with mice suggests that this does happen, as a cold-swim stress test decreased brain norepinephrine and dopamine levels, but tyrosine prevented the reduction in aggression and activity that ordinarily would have been seen. However, while the dietary tyrosine supplements increased brain tyrosine and dopamine levels, tyrosine did not produce significant changes in brain norepinephrine in this study (Brady *et al.*, 1980). In a different study, with rats exposed to a tail-shock stressor, investigators found that tyrosine supplementation prevented both the behavioral changes and the depletion of norepinephrine, but had no effect on the control animals that were not stressed (Lehnert *et al.*, 1984). Given their results, Lehnert and his colleagues hypothesized that under stressful conditions noradrenergic neurons must show an increase in activity, and may become deficient in brain tyrosine and norepinephrine. But can the same be said for humans?

Research has shown that in the absence of stress, administering tyrosine does nothing to affect performance levels in humans, a finding that supports the animal work (Lieberman *et al.*, 1983; Owasoyo *et al.*, 1992). But when male subjects were subjected to environmental stressors like severe cold or high altitudes, tyrosine supplements served to counteract the detrimental effects and improved their cognition and performance on coding, mathematical and pattern recognition problems (Banderet and Lieberman, 1989; Ahlers *et al.*, 1994). The same was true for a platoon of cadets who were given cognitive tests during a demanding military training course (Deijen *et al.*, 1999). The cadets who received a tyrosine-rich drink performed better on memory and tracking tasks.

Tyrosine and mood

Deficiencies in both dopamine and norepinephrine have been implicated in depression, so it is not surprising that a number of studies have investigated the relationship of tyrosine to mood. The ingestion of tyrosine has been shown, after all, to modify the neurotransmission of these catecholamines (Wurtman et al., 1981). Plasma levels of tyrosine are significantly decreased in depressed patients as compared to controls, and plasma levels rise as depressed patients recover. Less tyrosine may be transported into the brains of depressed individuals, and a reduced ratio of plasma tyrosine to the other LNAAs seems to correlate with responsiveness to imipramine, a prescription antidepressant (Gelenberg et al., 1983; Spring, 1986).

In a study that enrolled non-depressed subjects, Leathwood and Pollett (1983) administered 500 mg of tyrosine along with a low protein, high carbohydrate meal. No significant effects were shown for mood, but the high carbohydrate content of the meal likely enhanced tryptophan levels, and thereby counteracted any effects of the tyrosine supplement. To improve upon this experimental flaw, Lieberman and his colleagues administered 100 mg/kg of tyrosine to 20 healthy males in a double-blind crossover study, but on an empty stomach following an overnight fast. However, they also found no mood-altering effect of tyrosine (Lieberman et al., 1983). Since no apparent stress was involved in either of these investigations, the catecholaminergic neurons may have been quiescent. In other words, the enzyme tyrosine hydroxylase may have displayed end-product inhibition, with catecholamine synthesis left unstimulated. Interestingly enough, in the environmental stress paradigm mentioned earlier, non-depressed subjects not only showed better cognitive performance with tyrosine, but reported fewer psychological problems such as fatigue and dizziness (Banderet and Lieberman, 1989).

Since many of the drugs that are used to treat depression appear to enhance neurotransmission of norepinephrine, the hypothesis that depression results from a deficiency in norepinephrine has been posited (Schildkraut, 1965; van Praag, 1985). Some early work with a handful of depressed patients showed improvement in symptoms with tyrosine treatment, and a relapse when placebo was substituted (Gelenberg et al., 1980; Goldberg, 1980). However, in none of these case studies was tyrosine administered in a blind manner.

Using the catecholamine-depletion approach, some investigators have reported that inhibiting tyrosine can lead to depressed mood. In a recent study, albeit with nine subjects (8 females), the tyrosine-depleted group had higher depression ratings after three days of taking AMPT, a tyrosine inhibitor (Lam et al., 2001). In another study of 41 women, subjects received either a tyrosine-depleted mixture, a tryptophan-depleted mixture, or a nutritionally balanced amino acid mixture. In response to a psychological challenge, mood was lowered for both the tyrosine- and tryptophan-depleted groups (Leyton et al., 2000b). So in this case, vulnerability to stress was increased by virtue of depleting the neurotransmitters.

Employing a double-blind experimental design, Gelenberg and his colleagues assigned outpatients suffering from severe depression to either a tyrosine treatment group (100 mg/kg/day) or to a placebo control condition for a four week period. Although 67% of the treatment group improved as compared to 38% of the placebo group, these results are less dramatic when one considers that the tyrosine and placebo groups comprised just six and eight patients, respectively (Gelenberg et al., 1983). Hence, tyrosine was effective in four out of six patients, while the placebo produced similar effects in three out of eight. More recently, the Gelenberg group conducted a larger trial, randomly assigning 65 depressed outpatients to tyrosine (100 mg/kg/day), imipramine (2.5 mg/kg/day), or placebo for a minimum of 4 weeks. Although catecholamine production was enhanced, the tyrosine group was no different than the placebo group at the end of treatment (Gelenberg et al., 1990). In fact, all three groups did improve, but the imipramine group showed a trend toward the greatest improvement.

These results seem to provide modest support for the efficacy of tyrosine in elevating mood or treating depression. However, research in this area may still continue, as it could still be possible that a subgroup of individuals who suffer from depression may be responsive to tyrosine (Gelenberg et al., 1990). Indeed, brain-imaging techniques now available have shown that dopamine neurotransmission may influence cognitive performance, independent of variables like age or Huntington's disease (Baeckman and Farde, 2001).

Conclusion

Research with animal models has demonstrated that dietary variables can influence neurotransmitter synthesis. For example, the production and release of the neurotransmitters serotonin, acetylcholine and the catecholamines can be stimulated by increasing the intake of tryptophan, choline and dopamine, respectively. Depending on the particular neurotransmitter, dietary intake of carbohydrate, protein or lecithin serve to house neurotransmitter precursors, and can thereby augment neurotransmitter synthesis. These findings with experimental animals have lead to the hypothesis that the intake of specific nutrients can lead to short-term, but relatively rapid alterations in human behavior. Although this hypothesis is intriguing, research that has examined the role of dietary precursors in regulating mood, sleep or appetite has produced equivocal results. None the less, work is currently underway that suggests both tryptophan (Luciana et al., 2001; McAllister-Williams et al., 2002) and tyrosine (Thomas et al., 1999) influence memory, with dopamine hypothesized as being linked to excessive eating and obesity (Wang et al., 2001). Further research is therefore needed to identify beneficial effects of neurotransmitters and their potential for therapeutic use. As too little is known about dose-response relationships and possible side effects, more definitive results must be obtained before the use of neurotransmitter synthesis as a form of diet therapy for disorders such as depression or weight control can be recommended.

References

Ahlers, S.T., Thomas, J.R., Schrot, J. and Shurtrleff, D. (1994) Tyrosine and glucose modulation of cognitive deficits resulting from cold stress. In Marriott B.M. (ed) Food Components to Enhance Performance. National Academy Press, Washington, DC, pp. 301–320.

Amer, A., Breu, J., McDermott, J., Wurtman, R.J. and Maher, T.J. (2004) 5-hydroxy-L-tryptophan suppresses food intake in food-deprived and stressed rats. Pharmacology, Biochemistry & Behavior 77(1), 137–143.

Aquilonius, S. and Eckernas, S. (1977) Choline therapy in Huntington's chorea. Neurology 27, 887–889.

Baeckman, L. and Farde, L. (2001) Dopamine and cognitive functioning: brain imaging findings in Huntington's disease and normal aging. Scandinavian Journal of Psychology 42(3), 287–296.

Banderet, L.E. and Lieberman, H.R. (1989) Treatment with tyrosine, a neurotransmitter precursor; reduces environmental stress in humans. Brain Research Bulletin 22, 759–762.

Bartus, D., Dean, R.L., Goas, J.A. and Lippa, A.S. (1980) Age-related changes in passive avoidance retention: modulation with dietary choline. Science 209, 301–303.

Bartus, R.T., Dean, R.L., Beer, B. and Lippa, A.S. (1982) The cholinergic hypothesis of geriatric memory dysfunction. Science 216, 408–417.

Batey, S.R. (1989) Schizophrenic disorders. In DiPiro, J.T. Talbert, R.L. Hayes, P.E. Yee, G.C. and Posey L.M. (eds) Pharmacotherapy: A Pathophysiological Approach. Elsevier, New York, pp. 714–728.

Benkelfat, C., Ellenbogen, M.A., Dean, P., Palmour, R.M. and Young, S.N. (1994) Mood-lowering effect of tryptophan depletion: enhanced susceptibility in young men at genetic risk for major affective disorders. Archives of General Psychiatry 51, 687.

Blundell, J.E. (1984) Serotonin and appetite. Neuropharmacology 23, 1537–1551.

Blundell, J.E. and Hill, A.J. (1987) Influence of tryptophan on appetite and food selection in man. In Kaufman S. (ed.) Amino acids in health and disease: New perspectives. Alan R. Liss, New York, pp. 403–409.

Bond, A.J., Wingrove, J. and Critchlow, D.G. (2001) Tryptophan depletion increases aggression in women during premenstrual phase. Psychopharmacology 156(4), 477–480.

Brady, K., Brown, J.W. and Thurmond, J.B. (1980) Behavioral and neurochemical effects of dietary tyrosine and neurochemical effects in young and aged mice following cold-swim stress. Pharmacological and Biochemical Behavior 12, 667–674.

Carlsson, A. (1987) Commentary. Integrative Psychiatry 5, 238.

Charles, H.C., Lazeyras, F., Krishnan, K.R.R., Boyko, O.B., Payne, M. and Moore, D. (1994) Brain choline in depression: in vivo detection of potential pharmacodynamic effects of antidepressant therapy using hydrogen localized spectroscopy. Progress in Neuropsychopharmacology & Biological Psychiatry 118, 1121–1127.

Christensen, L. (1996) *Diet-behavior Relationships: Focus on Depression.* American Psychological Association, Washington, DC.

Christensen, L. (1997) The effect of carbohydrates on affect. *Nutrition* 13(6), 503–514.

Christensen, L. and Redig, C. (1993) Effect of metal composition on mood. *Behavioral Neuroscience* 107, 346–353.

Davidson, M., Stern, R.G., Bierer, L.M., Horvath, T.B., Zemishlani, Z., Markofsky, R. and Mohs, R.C. (1991) Cholinergic strategies in the treatment of Alzheimer's Disease. *Acta Psychiatrica Scandinavica* 366, 47–51.

Deijen, J.B., Wientjes, C.J.E., Vullinghs, H.F.M., Cloin, P.A. and Langefeld, J.J. (1999) Tyrosine improves cognitive performance and reduces blood pressure in cadets after one week of a combat training course. *Brain Research Bulletin* 48(2), 203–209.

Delgado, P.L., Price, L.H., Miller, H.L., Salomon, R.M., Licinio, J., Krystal, J.H., Heninger, G.R. and Charney, D.S. (1991) Rapid serotonin depletion as a provocative challenge test for patients with major depression: relevance to antidepressant action and the neurobiology of depression. *Psychopharmacology Bulletin* 27, 321–329.

Diagnostic and Statistical Manual of Mental Disorders (DSM-IV) (1994) American Psychiatric Association, Washington, DC.

Ellenbogen, M.A., Young, S.N., Dean, P., Palmour, R.M. and Benkelfat, C. (1996) Mood response to acute tryptophan depletion in healthy volunteers: sex differences and temporal stability. *Neuropsychopharmacology* 15(5), 465–474.

Ereshefsky, L., Rospond, R. and Jann, M. (1989) Organic brain syndromes, Alzheimer type. In DiPiro, J.T., Talbert, R.L., Hayes, P.E., Yee, G.C. and Posey, L.M. (eds) *Pharmacotherapy: A Pathophysiological Approach.* Elsevier, New York, pp. 678–696.

Fernstrom, F.D. (1986) Acute and chronic affects of protein and carbohydrate ingestion on brain tryptophan levels and serotonin synthesis. *Nutrition Reviews* 44, 25–36.

Fernstrom, J.D. (1988) Tryptophan, serotonin, and carbohydrate appetite: will the real carbohydrate craver please stand up! *Journal of Nutrition* 118, 1417–1419.

Fernstrom, J.D. (2000) Can nutrient supplements modify brain function? *American Journal of Nutrition* 7, 1669S–73S.

Fernstrom, F.D. and Faller, D.V. (1978) Neutral amino acids in the brain: changes in response to food ingestion. *Journal of Neurochemistry* 30, 1531–1538.

Fernstrom, J.D. and Wurtman, R.J. (1971) Brain serotonin content: increase following ingestion of carbohydrate diet. *Science* 174, 1023–1025.

Fernstrom, J.D. and Wurtman, R.J. (1972) Elevation of plasma tryptophan by insulin in rat. *Metabolism* 21, 337–341.

Fernstrom, J.D. and Wurtman, R.J. (1974) Nutrition and the brain. *Scientific American* 230, 84–91.

Garattini, S. (1989) Further comments. *Integrative Psychiatry* 6, 235–238.

Garvey, M.J., Wesner, R. and Godes, M. (1988) Comparison of seasonal and non-seasonal affective disorders. *American Journal of Psychiatry* 145, 100–102.

Gelenberg, A.J., Wojcik, J.D., Growdon, J.H., Sved, A.F. and Wurtman, R.J. (1980) Tyrosine for the treatment of depression. *American Journal of Psychiatry* 137, 622–623.

Gelenberg, A.J., Wojcik, J.D., Gibson, C.J. and Wurtman, R.J. (1983) Tyrosine for depression. *Journal of Psychiatric Research* 17, 175–180.

Gelenberg, A.J., Wojcik, J., Falk, W.E., Bellinghausen, B. and Joseph, A.B. (1989) CDP-choline for the treatment of tardive dyskinesia: a small negative series. *Comprehensive Psychiatry* 30, 1–4.

Gelenberg, A.J., Wojcik, J.D., Falk, W.E., Baldessarini, R.J., Zeisel, S.H., Schoenfeld, D. and Mok, G.S. (1990) Tyrosine for depression: a double-blind trial. *Journal of Affective Disorders* 19, 125–132.

Goldberg, I.K. (1980) L-tyrosine in depression. *Lancet* 2, 364.

Growden, J.H. (1979) Neurotransmitter precursors in the diet: their use in the treatment of brain disease. In Wurtman R.J. and Wurtman J.J. (eds) *Nutrition and the Brain*, Vol. 3. Raven Press, New York, pp. 117–181.

Growden, J.H., Hirsch, M.J., Wurtman, R.J. and Wiener, W. (1977) Oral choline administration to patients with tardive dyskinesia. *New England Journal of Medicine* 297, 524–527.

Growden, J.H., Gelenberg, A.J., Doller, J., Hirsch, M.J. and Wurtman, R.J. (1978) Lecithin can suppress tardive dyskinesia. *New England Journal of Medicine* 298, 1029–1030.

Halbreich, U., Bancroft, J., Dennerstein, L., Endicott, J., Faccinetti, F., Genazzani, A., Morse, C., Parry, B., Rubinow, D. and Reid, R. (1993) Menstrually related disorders: points of consensus, debate, and disagreement. *Neuropsychopharmacology* 9, 13.

Hartman, E. and Greenwald, D. (1984) Tryptophan and human sleep: an analysis of 43 studies. In Schlossberger, H.G. Kochen, W. Linzen, B. and Steinhart H. (eds) *Progress in Tryptophan and Serotonin Research*. Walter de Gruyter, New York, pp. 297–304.

Hartman, E., Lindsley, J.G. and Spinweber, C. (1983a) Chronic insomnia: effect of tryptophan, flurazepam, secobarbital, and placebo. *Psychopharmacology (Berlin)* 80, 138–142.

Hartman, E., Spinweber, C. and Ware, J.C. (1983b) Effect of amino acids on quantified sleepiness. *Nutrition and Behavior* 1, 179–183.

Hirsch, M.J. and Wurtman, R.J. (1978) Lecithin consumption elevates acetylcholine concentration in rat brain and adrenal gland. *Science* 202, 223–225.

Hirsch, M.J., Growden, J.H. and Wurtman, R.J. (1977) Increase in hippocampal acetylcholine after choline administration. *Brain Research* 125, 383–385.

Hrboticky, N., Leiter, L.A. and Anderson, G.H. (1985) Effects of L-tryptophan on short term food intake in lean men. *Nutrition Research* 5, 595–607.

Innis, R.B., Nestler, E.J. and Charney, D.S. (1998) The spectrum of behaviors influenced by serotonin. *Biological Psychiatry* 44(3), 151–162.

Jackson, I., Nuttall, A. and Perez-Cruet, J. (1979) Treatment of tardive dyskinesia with lecithin. *American Journal of Psychiatry* 136, 1458–1459.

Janowsky, D.S. and Overstreet, D.H. (1998) Acetylcholine. In Goodnick, P.J. (ed.) *Mania: Clinical and Research Perspectives*. American Psychiatric Press, Washington, DC, pp. 135–155.

Jouvet, M. (1968) Insomnia and decrease of cerebral 5-hydroxytryptamine after destruction of the raphe system in the cat. *Advances in Pharmacology* 6, 265–279.

Kanarek, R.B. (1987) Neuropharmacological approaches to studying diet selection. In S. Kaufman (ed.) *Amino acids in health and disease: New perspectives*. Alan R. Liss, New York, pp. 383–401.

Lam, R.W., Tam, E.M., Grewal, A. and Yatham, L.N. (2001) Effects of alpha-methyl-para-tyrosine-induced catecholamine depletion in patients with seasonal affective disorder in summer remission. *Neuropsychopharmacology* 25(5), S97–S101.

Leathwood, P.D. (1986) Neurotransmitter precursors: from animal experiments to human applications. *Nutrition Reviews* 44, 193–204.

Leathwood, P.D. and Pollett, P. (1983) Diet-induced mood changes in normal populations. *Journal of Psychiatric Research* 17(2), 147–154.

Lehnert, H., Reinstein, D.K., Strowbridge, B.W. and Wurtman, R.J. (1984) Neurochemical and behavioral consequences of acute, uncontrollable stress: effects of dietary tyrosine. *Brain Research* 303, 215–223.

Leibenluft, E., Fiero, P., Bartko, J.J., Moul, D.E. and Rosenthal, N.E. (1993) Depressive symptoms and the self-reported use of alcohol, caffeine, and carbohydrates in normal volunteers and four groups of psychiatric outpatients. *American Journal of Psychiatry* 150, 294–301.

Levine, A.S. (1990) Nutrition and behavior. In Morley, J.E., Glick, Z. and Rubenstein, L.Z. (eds) *Geriatric Nutrition*. Raven Press, New York.

Leyton, M., Ghadirian, A.M., Young, S.N., Palmour, R.M., Blier, P., Helmers, K.F. and Benkelfat, C. (2000a) Depressive relapse following acute tryptophan depletion in patients with major depressive disorder. *Journal of Psychopharmacology* 14(3), 284–287.

Leyton, M., Young, S.N., Pihl, R.O., Etezadi, S., Lauze, C., Blier, P., Baker, G.B. and Benkelfat, C. (2000b) Effects on mood of acute phenylalanine/tyrosine depletion in healthy women. *Neuropsychopharmacology* 22(1), 52–63.

Lieberman, H.R., Corkin, S., Spring, B.J., Growden, J.H. and Wurtman, R.J. (1983). Mood, performance, and pain sensitivity: changes induced by food constituents. *Journal of Psychiatric Research* , 135–145.

Lieberman, H.R., Spring, B.J. and Garfield, G.S. (1986) The behavioral effect of food constituents: strategies used in studies of amino acids, protein, carbohydrate, and caffeine. *Nutrition Reviews* 44, 51–60.

Lucca, A., Lucini, V., Piatti, E., Ronchi, P. and Smeraldi, E. (1992) Plasma tryptophan levels and plasma tryptophan/neutral amino acids ratio in patients with mood disorder, patients with obsessive-compulsive disorder, and normal subjects. *Psychiatric Research* 44, 85–91.

Luciana, M., Burgund, E.D., Berman, M. and Hanson, K.L. (2001) Effects of tryptophan loading on verbal, spatial, and affective working memory functions in healthy adults. *Journal of Psychopharmacology* 15(4), 219–230.

Lucki, I. (1998) The spectrum of behaviors influenced by serotonin. *Biological Psychiatry* 44(3), 151–162.

Maes, M., Vandewoude, M., Schotte, C., Martin, M., D'Hondt, P., Scharpe, S. and Block, P. (1990) The decrease available of L-tryptophan in depressed females: clinical and biological correlates. *Progress in Neuropsychopharmacology & Biological Psychiatry* 14, 903–919.

Markus, R., Panhuysen, G., Tuiten, A., Koppeschaar, H., Fekkes, D. and Peters, M.L. (1998) Does carbohydrate-rich, protein-poor food prevent a deterioration of mood and cognitive performance of stress-prone subjects when subjected to a stressful task? *Appetite* 31, 49–65.

Markus, R., Panhuysen, G., Tuiten, A. and Koppeschaar, H. (2000) Effects of food on cortisol and mood in vulnerable subjects under controllable and uncontrollable stress. *Physiology and Behavior* 70(3–4), 333–342.

McAllister-Williams, R.H., Massey, A.E. and Rugg, M.D. (2002) Effects of tryptophan depletion on brain potential correlates of episodic memory retrieval. *Psychopharmacology* 160(4), 434–442.

Menkes, D.B., Coates, D.C. and Fawcett, J.P. (1994) Acute tryptophan depletion aggravates premenstrual syndrome. *Journal of Affective Disorders* 32(1), 37–44.

Mohs, R.C., Davis, K.L. and Levy, M.L. (1981) Partial reversal of anticholinergic amnesia by choline chloride. *Life Sciences* 29, 1317–1323.

Moskowitz, D.S., Pinard, G., Zuroff, D.C., Annable, L. and Young, S.N. (2001) The effect of tryptophan on social interaction in everyday life: a placebo-controlled study. *Neuropharmacology* 25(2), 277–289.

Nathan, C. and Rolland, Y. (1987) Pharmacological treatments that affect CNS activity: serotonin. *Annals of the New York Academy of Sciences* 499, 277–296.

Nathan, P.J., Baker, A., Carr, E., Earle, J., Jones, M., Nieciecki, M., Hutchison, C. and Stough, C. (2001) Cholinergic modulation of cognitive function in healthy subjects: acute effects of donepezil, a cholinesterase inhibitor. *Human Psychopharmacology* 16(6), 481–483.

Nicholson, A.N. and Stone, B.M. (1979) L-tryptophan and sleep in healthy man. *Electroencephalography and Clinical Neurophysiology* 47, 539–545.

Oren, D.A. and Rosenthal, N.E. (1992) Seasonal affective disorders. In Paykel E.S. (ed.) *Handbook of affective disorders*. The Guilford Press, New York.

Owasoyo, J.O., Neri, D.F. and Lamberth, J.G. (1992) Tyrosine and its potential use as a countermeasure to performance decrement in military sustained operations. *Aerospace Medical Association* 63, 364–369.

Pardridge, W.M. (1977) Regulation of amino acid availability to the brain. In Wurtman R.J. and Wurtman J.J. (eds) *Nutrition and the brain*, Vol. 1. Raven Press, New York, pp. 141–204.

Pardridge, W.M., Connor, J.D. and Crawford, I.L. (1975) Permeability changes in the blood-brain barrier: causes and consequences. *CRC Critical Reviews of Toxicology* 3, 159–199.

Pollack, J.D. and Rowland, N. (1981) Peripherally administered serotonin decreases food intake in rats. *Pharmacology, Biochemistry and Behavior* 15, 179–183.

Rosenberg, G.S. and Davis, K.L. (1982) The use of cholinergic precursors in neuropsychiatric diseases. *American Journal of Clinical Nutrition* 36, 709–20.

Safer, D.J. and Allen, R.P. (1971) The central effects of scopolamine in man. *Biological Psychiatry* 3, 347–355.

Salomon, R.M., Mazure, C.M., Delgado, P.L., Mendia, P. and Charney, D.S. (1994) Serotonin function in aggression: the effect of acute plasma tryptophan depletion in aggressive patients. *Biological Psychiatry* 35(8), 570–572.

Saminin, R. and Garattini, S. (1990) The pharmacology of serotoninergic drugs affecting appetite. In Wurtman R.J. and Wurtman J.J. (eds) *Nutrition and the brain*, Vol. 8. Raven Press, New York, pp. 163–192.

Sayegh, R., Schiff, I. and Wurtman, J. (1995) The Effect of a carbohydrate-rich beverage on mood, appetite, and cognitive function in women with premenstrual syndrome. *Obstetrics and Gynecology* 86, 520–528.

Schildkraut, J.J. (1965) The catecholamine hypothesis of affective disorder: a review of supporting evidence. *American Journal of Psychiatry* 122, 509–522.

Silverstone, T. (1981) Clinical pharmacology of anorectic drugs. In Garattini S. and Saminin R. (eds) *Anorectic agents: Mechanisms of action.* Raven Press, New York, pp. 211–222.

Silverstone, T. and Goodall, E. (1984) Serotonergic mechanism in human feeding: the pharmacological evidence. *Appetite* 7, 85–87.

Sitaram, N., Weingartner, H., Caine, E.D. and Gillin, J.C. (1978) Choline: selective enhancement of serial learning and encoding of low imagery words in man. *Life Sciences* 22, 1555–1560.

Smith, A., Leekam, S., Ralph, A. and McNeil, G. (1988) The influence of meal composition on post-lunch changes in performance efficiency and mood. *Appetite* 10, 195–203.

Spring, B. (1986) Effects of foods and nutrients on the behavior of normal individuals. In Wurtman R.J. and Wurtman J.J. (eds) *Nutrition and the brain* Raven Press, New York, pp. 1–48.

Spring, B., Maller, O., Wurtman, J., Digman, L. and Cozolino, L. (1983) Effects of protein and carbohydrate meals on mood and performance: interactions with sex and age. *Journal of Psychiatric Research* 17, 155–157.

Spring, B., Lieberman, H.R., Swope, G. and Garfield, G.S. (1986) Effects of carbohydrates on mood and behavior. *Nutrition Reviews* 44, 51–70.

Spring, B., Chiodo, J., Harden, M., Bourgeois, M.J., Mason, J.D. and Lutherer, L. (1989) Psychobiological effects of carbohydrates. *Journal of Clinical Psychiatry* 50(5), 27–33.

Spring, B., Gelenberg, A.J., Garvin, R. and Thompson, S. (1992) Amitriptyline, clovoxamine and cognitive function: a placebo-controlled comparison in depressed patients. *Psychopharmacology* 108(3), 327–332.

Steinberg, L.A., O'Connell, N.C., Hatch, T.F., Picciano, M.F. and Birch, L.L. (1992) Tryptophan intake influences infants' sleep latency. *Journal of Nutrition* 122, 1781–1791.

Sved, A.F. (1983) Precursor control of the function of monoaminergic neurons. In Wurtman R.J. and Wurtman J.J. (eds) *Nutrition and the brain*, Vol. 6. Raven Press, New York, pp. 223–275.

Tarsy, D. (1983) History and definition of tardive dyskinesia. *Clinical Neuropharmacology* 6, 91–99.

Teff, K.L., Young, S.N. and Blundell, J.E. (1989) The effect of protein or carbohydrate breakfasts on subsequent plasma amino acid levels, satiety, and nutrient selection in normal males. *Pharmacology, Biochemistry, and Behavior* 34, 829–837.

Thomas, J.R., Lockwood, P.A., Singh, A. and Deuster, P.A. (1999) Tyrosine improves working memory in a multitasking environment. *Pharmacology, Biochemistry, & Behavior* 64(3), 495–500.

Wang, G.J., Volkow, N.D., Logan, J., Pappas, N.R., Wong, C.T., Zhu, W., Netusil, N. and Fowler, J.S. (2001) Brain dopamine and obesity. *Lancet* 357(9271), 354–357.

Wecker, L. (1990) Choline utilization by central cholinergic neurons. In Wurtman R.J. and Wurtman J.J. (eds) *Nutrition and the Brain*, Vol. 8. Raven Press, New York, pp. 147–162.

Weiss, J.M., Goodman, P.A., Losito, B.G., Corrigan, S., Carry, J.M. and Bailey, W.H. (1981) Behavioral depression produced by an uncontrollable stressor: relationship to norepinephrine, dopamine and serotonin levels in various regions of rat brain. *Brain Research Review* 3, 167–205.

Whitney, E.N. and Rolfes, S.R. (2002) *Understanding Nutrition*. 9th edn. Wadsworth Publishing Company, California.

Wurtman, R.J. (1987) Nutrients affecting brain composition and behavior. *Integrative Psychiatry* 5, 226–257.

Wurtman, R.J., Hirsch, M.J. and Growdon, J.H. (1977) Lecithin consumption raises serum free choline levels. *Lancet* 2, 68–69.

Wurtman, R.J., Hefti, F. and Melamed, E. (1981a) Precursor control of neurotransmitter synthesis. *Pharmacological Reviews* 32, 315–335.

Wurtman, R.J., Wurtman, J.J., Growden, J.H., Henry, P., Lipscomb, A. and Zeisel, S.H. (1981b) Carbohydrate craving in obese people: suppression by treatments affecting serotoninergic neurotransmission. *International Journal of Eating Disorders* 1, 2–15.

Wurtman, J., Wurtman, R., Reynolds, S., Tsay, R. and Chew, B. (1987) Fenfluramine suppresses snack intake among carbohydrate cravers but not among noncarbohydrate cravers. *International Journal of Eating Disorders* 6, 687–699.

van der Does, A.J.W. (2001) The effects of tryptophan depletion on mood and psychiatric symptoms. *Journal of Affective Disorders* 64(2–3), 107–119.

van Praag, H.M. (1985) Monoamines and depression: the present state of the art. In Plutchik, R. and Kellerman, H. (eds) *Biological Foundations of Emotion*. Academic Press, New York, pp. 335–356.

Yogman, M.W. and Zeisel, S.H. (1983) Diet and sleep patterns in newborn infants. *New England Journal of Medicine* 309(19), 1147–1149.

Yokogoshi, H. and Wurtman, R.J. (1986) Meal composition and plasma amino acid ratios: effects of various proteins on carbohydrates, and of various protein concentrations. *Metabolism* 35, 837–842.

Young, S.N. (1986) The clinical psychopharmacology of tryptophan. In Wurtman R.J. and Wurtman J.J. (eds) *Nutrition and the Brain*, Vol. 7. Raven Press, New York, pp. 49–88.

Young, S.N. (1991) Some effects of dietary components (amino acids, carbohydrate, folic acid) on brain serotonin synthesis, mood, and behavior. *Canadian Journal of Pharmacology* 69, 893–903.

Young, S.N and Leyton, M. (2002) The role of serotonin in human mood and social interaction: insight from altered tryptophan levels. *Pharmacology, Biochemistry & Behavior* 71(4), 857–865.

Young, S.N., Smith, S.E., Pihl, R.O. and Ervin, F.R. (1985) Tryptophan depletion causes a rapid lowering of mood in normal males. *Psychopharmacology* 87, 173–177.

Yuwiler, A., Oldendorf, W. H., Geller, E. and Braun, L. (1977) Effect of albumin binding and amino acid competition on tryptophan uptake into brain. *Journal of Neurochemistry* 28, 1015–1023.

6 Effects of Chronic and Acute Forms of Undernutrition

J. Worobey

When you hear the term 'malnutrition' what image comes to mind? A scrawny child with a bloated stomach in a far-off Third World country that you saw in an infomercial for Save the Children? Or a youngster with bad teeth dressed in torn clothes in a rural area of your own country? How about an urban child in a 10th floor tenement apartment, who lives with his loving grandmother but goes to bed hungry every night? Perhaps you thought of an old man failing to thrive in a nursing home, moved there because his broken hip never quite healed even after his hospitalization. But what of an 11-year-old girl who has been dieting like mad ever since she menstruated for the first time and a classmate snickered at her budding breasts?

All of these examples comprise malnutrition, if we take it to mean a condition caused by deficient nutrient intake. But even an obese individual may be considered *malnourished*, if we take it to mean his caloric consumption is far in excess of what he needs to maintain a healthier weight. In this chapter, however, we are interested in malnutrition in the traditional sense of the word, the condition caused by acute or prolonged undernutrition. While those of us fortunate enough to live in developed countries may only be acquainted with severe undernutrition from watching television, protein–energy malnutrition (PEM) continues to be a major problem in the world. Also referred to as protein–calorie malnutrition, PEM has long been recognized as a consequence of poverty, but it has become increasingly clear that it is also a *cause* of poverty (UNICEF, 1997). Having been robbed of their mental and physical potential, children who manage to survive PEM and live into adulthood have lessened intellectual ability, lower levels of productivity and higher incidences of chronic illness and disability.

Although we usually associate malnutrition with conditions of poverty in the Third World, recent reports have clearly demonstrated that modern societies, including the USA and UK, are not immune to this problem. In the USA, it is estimated that more than one in every four children under age 12 do not get all the food they need, while researchers in the UK have documented the health risks linked to diet in poor families. Among low-income populations in these developed societies, low-birth-weight, anemia, growth failure, weakened resistance to infection, increased susceptibility to lead poisoning, dental disease and so forth are all associated with undernutrition, and unfortunately are not all that infrequent (James *et al.*, 1997).

In this and the following chapter, the behavioral consequences of PEM and deficiencies of essential vitamins and minerals are discussed. In the preceding chapters we have described the development and functioning of the central nervous system. That background should now be helpful as we explore the role of malnutrition as it impacts on behavior. Before we begin our examination of the pertinent studies, however, we will first define the forms that PEM usually takes.

Features of Protein–Energy Malnutrition

To be sure, there is not just one kind of malnutrition. Besides PEM, deficiencies in iron, iodine and vitamin A may appear in combination and contribute to the debilitating effects of each other. These deficiencies will be covered in Chapters 7 and 8. But PEM is the most common form of malnutrition in the world, affecting an estimated 200 million children (UNICEF, 1997). Of the nearly 12 million children under age 5 who die each year in developing countries from preventable causes, the deaths of over 6 million, or 55%, are either directly or indirectly attributable to malnutrition – due to its association with diarrhea, malaria, measles, respiratory infections and perinatal problems (Murray and Lopez, 1996). Adults also suffer from hunger and starvation; however, PEM occurs most frequently and also has its most devastating consequences in infancy and early childhood.

Severe PEM in infants and children has traditionally been classified as either marasmus or kwashiorkor. *Marasmus* results from insufficient energy intake, that is, an extremely low intake of both protein and calories. The word derives from the Greek *marasmos* which means 'to waste away.' It is most often observed in infants under 1 year of age at the time of weaning (see Fig. 6.1). However, in developed countries a form of it can strike young women who have dieted excessively, as in anorexia (see Chapter 14), as well as the elderly poor who have difficulty in obtaining or ingesting sufficient calories. In contrast, *kwashiorkor* results from the insufficient intake of protein, with caloric needs usually satisfied. The word itself literally means 'the disease of the deposed baby when the next one is born,' and derives from the language of the Ga tribe of Ghana. As this meaning suggests, kwashiorkor is most likely to occur in the second or third year of

life, when a baby is weaned to make way for the next one born (see Fig. 6.2). The majority of severely malnourished children in underdeveloped nations often exhibit symptoms of both conditions or alternately display one and then the other, and this is referred to as *marasmic kwashiorkor*. An adult form of malnutrition, known as *iatrogenic PEM*, characterizes the individual whose nutritional status deteriorates after prolonged hospitalization, when hospitalization is not due to a dietary or gastrointestinal problem.

As shown in Table 6.1, marasmus is the form of PEM most commonly affecting infants aged 6–18 months, when they are weaned from breast milk to formula. In attempting to stretch their limited resources, the impoverished mother will dilute the commercial formula, further contaminating it with dirty water, which leads to bacterial infection. The

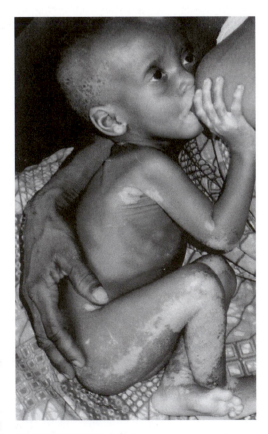

Fig. 6.1. Marasmic infant.

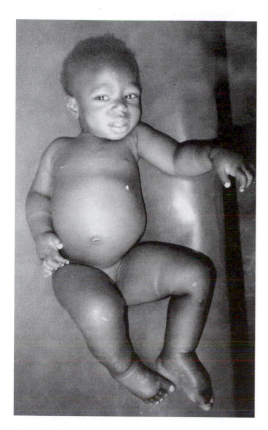

Fig. 6.2. Kwashiorkor infant.

infant then suffers from repeated episodes of gastroenteritis, resulting in diarrhea, dehydration and anemia. In an attempt to cure the baby, the mother may even withhold food. Recurrent infections, coupled with little or no food, subsequently lead to marasmus. In terms of resultant behavior, the marasmic infant is typically irritable, but may also appear to be weak and apathetic. The infant is also understandably hungry, but can seldom tolerate large amounts of food and will vomit easily (Torun and Viteri, 1988).

Kwashiorkor, which typically develops when the toddler is from 18 to 24 months of age, comes about when a newborn sibling arrives, and the toddler is weaned from the breast and fed the high carbohydrate-low protein diet that the rest of the family subsists on. While this diet may be adequate for the adult, it is insufficient for the rapidly growing toddler. Since the child of this age is beginning to explore the environment, the opportunity for exposure to bacteria and viruses can further exacerbate the consequences of the poor diet. However, one of the behavioral characteristics of kwashiorkor is a lessened interest in the environment, along with irritability, apathy and frequently anorexia. But most notably, the toddler with kwashiorkor cries easily and often displays an expression of sadness and misery (Torun and Viteri, 1988).

Iatrogenic PEM most commonly occurs in patients, often seniors, who are hospitalized

Table 6.1. Comparison of different forms of protein-energy malnutrition.

Feature	Marasmus	Kwashiorkor	Iatrogenic
Type of victim	Infants, elderly poor	Toddlers	Hospitalized adults
Growth failure	Severe	Somewhat severe	Not applicable
Muscle changes	Wasting	Wasting	Weakness
Subcutaneous fat	Absent	Present	Decreased
Edema	Absent	Always	Absent
Skin changes	Rare	Frequent	Capillary fragility
Hair changes	Frequent	Very frequent	Frequent
Liver enlargement	Rare	Frequent	Rare
Diarrhea	Frequent	Frequent	Frequent
Blood changes	Frequently anemic	Anemia	Low lymphocyte count
Serum albumin	Normal	Low	Low
Appetite	Ravenous	Anorectic	Anorectic
Irritability	Always	Always	Frequent
Apathy	Always	Always	Apathy toward eating
Other psychological	Failure to thrive	Whimpering cry	Altered taste sensation

longer than 2 weeks, and can result from acts and omissions by health care providers or from institutional policies and practices that undermine optimal nutritional care. Patients may report a lack of interest in, an aversion toward, or a perceived inability to eat, along with altered taste sensations. Less eating combined with extended time in bed leads to poor muscle tone (including those muscles required for chewing and swallowing) and mental irritability or confusion (Wendland et al., 2003).

PEM, Brain Development and Behavior in Rats

As we discussed in Chapters 4 and 5, nutrition plays an important role in normal brain development, affecting the growth and number of neurons, the development of synapses, the myelination of axons, the production of neurotransmitters and so on. The detrimental effects of early PEM on brain development have been demonstrated in neuroanatomical and neurochemical studies in experimental animals. In rats, for example, low maternal energy or protein intake have been associated with decreases in brain weight, reductions in numbers of both neurons and glial cells and impairments in dendritic development. In terms of their implications for functional deficits, three types of enduring brain changes due to PEM have been observed. Namely, changes in hippocampal structure and electrophysiology, changes in the number and sensitivity of adrenergic receptors and changes in the cerebellum (Strupp and Levitsky, 1995).

Regarding the hippocampus, observed effects in rats include a significant reduction in the size of cells taken from the dentate gyrus and in the degree of dendritic branching (Cintra et al., 1990). The number of granule cells (the tiniest neurons) is also reduced by early malnutrition and cannot be reversed with nutritional rehabilitation. However, there is some evidence that the number of synapses per neuron may increase relative to controls in animals that are malnourished and are then rehabilitated (Ahmed et al., 1987).

Alterations in various neurotransmitter systems are evident during and immediately after early malnutrition, however, the nature of these changes is not clear. Most investigators have shown that either pre- or post-natal malnutrition causes an increase in brain concentrations of the monoamines, but others have reported a decrease (Levitsky and Strupp, 1995). The activity of the neurotransmitter systems may be permanently altered, however, as the number of norepinephrine receptors has been shown to be reduced, while adrenaline-activated receptors are less able to exhibit down regulation. Down regulation refers to the compensatory reduction in receptor numbers that occurs as a result of repeated stimulation of the receptor by the relevant neurotransmitter.

Finally, it is generally agreed that early post-natal malnutrition produces enduring changes in the cerebellum of the rat. When compared to well-fed controls, the cerebella of malnourished rats are smaller and contain less DNA. Early malnutrition causes abnormal electrophysiological activity of Purkinje cells and a suppression of the synapse/neuron ratio. Nutritional rehabilitation has been shown to normalize the low density of these cerebellar neurons, though it does not seem to reverse the reduced ratio of granule/Purkinje cells (Levitsky and Strupp, 1995).

The impact of these compromises to brain development on the behavior of animals has been shown in a number of broad areas, namely, motivation, emotional reactivity and cognitive inflexibility. Rats that have been malnourished show higher levels of appetitive motivation than control rats in situations that manipulate aversive learning conditions (Tonkiss et al., 1993). Heightened emotionality or anxiety is inferred by their increased spilling, altered behavior in unfamiliar environments and their heightened sensitivity to shocks (Levitsky and Barnes, 1970). Both motivation and emotional reactivity can likely affect the animals' ability to solve problems in experimental situations. But spatial abilities may be further reduced in their own right, as malnourished rats are less capable of certain type of maze-learning (Tonkiss and Galler, 1990). Because such cognitive inflexibility is associated with damage to the frontal lobes, it may be the case that prefrontal dysfunction is an effect of early malnutrition (Strupp and Levitsky, 1995).

PEM and Early Human Development

Although most of us associate PEM with extreme poverty and relatively large families, severe malnutrition and food deprivation can actually reduce fertility (Whitney and Rolfes, 2002). From a behavioral perspective, both men and women have little interest in sex during times of starvation. Biologically speaking, women may develop amenorrhea, while men may lose their ability to produce viable sperm. As will be seen in Chapter 14, women who diet excessively to the point of anorexia suffer from malnutrition, and are neither interested nor capable of becoming pregnant.

But if a malnourished woman does become pregnant, she must face the challenge of supporting both the growth of her fetus and her own physical health with less than sufficient nutrient stores. Years ago it was believed that through a protective relationship with the mother, the fetus would be spared any adverse consequences of maternal malnutrition. There are, in fact, two mechanisms that buffer the fetus from inadequate nutrition. First of all, the mother's intake of food provides a direct nutritional source. But in addition, the placenta transfers nutrients that are stored by the mother to the developing fetus. However, malnutrition before or around the time of conception can prevent the placenta from developing fully.

Severe PEM early in development will typically result in a failure to maintain embryonic implantation, resulting in a spontaneous abortion. Moderate malnutrition throughout gestation will generally permit the continued development of the fetus, but will also lead to changes in the growth of both the placenta and the fetus. If the placenta is poorly developed it cannot deliver proper nourishment to the fetus, and the infant may subsequently be born prematurely, small for gestational age, and with reduced head circumference (Hay et al., 1997). In human infants, a reduced head circumference may be the first indication that malnutrition, particularly during gestation and infancy, has resulted in permanent brain

damage. Since marasmus typically develops at a younger age than kwashiorkor, the marasmic child is likelier to have a reduced head circumference than one with kwashiorkor.

In recent years, a veritable explosion of interest in the effects of malnutrition on the developing fetus has occurred. A current topic of widespread interest, widely referred to as the *Barker Hypothesis*, proposes that a significant number of adulthood diseases may trace their origins to undernutrition during fetal development (Barker, 1998). Barker and his colleagues have shown that during prenatal development the fetus responds to severe malnutrition by favoring the metabolic demands of the growing brain and central nervous system, as well as heart, *at the expense of other tissues*. In other words, in an intrauterine environment that is lacking in the nutrients the infant needs for proper organ growth, the fetus may react by slowing its metabolism to conserve all the energy-rich fat that it can. This in turn may lead to obesity (see Chapter 15), heart disease, hypertension and diabetes in later life (Barker, 2003). Alternately, the fetus may favor the brain over an organ like the liver, for example, when it must subsist on inadequate sources of energy. Despite some convincing epidemiological evidence for the hypothesis, the scientific and medical communities have not universally embraced the concept (Susser and Levin, 1999). However, scores of studies to test this 'fetal programming' hypothesis are now underway and the coming years should see further evidence that bears on this important question (Langley-Evans, 2004).

As may be understandable, studies that have examined the consequences of early malnutrition on the cellular growth of the infant brain are limited. Over 30 years ago, Winick and Russo (1969) observed significant reductions in the brain weight, total protein and total DNA content in infants who died of marasmus before they were a year old. Those infants with extremely low birth weights, indicative of prenatal malnutrition, had lower brain DNA content than did the malnourished infants with higher birth weights. The reduced DNA content is particularly meaningful, as it indicates a decrease in both neurons and glial cells.

Future efforts to determine the effects of malnutrition on brain development will likely rely on the availability of magnetic resonance imaging, or MRI, which can even be done on the fetus before birth. For example, research using the MRI procedure has confirmed the early reports that brain myelination is impaired in malnourished infants. Current reports have also shown that fetal growth retardation appears to reduce grey brain matter volume more than white brain matter, although brain sparing may occur despite growth retardation (Gong et al., 1998).

Evidence concerning the role of malnutrition on the development of the post-natal brain has generally supported the hypothesis that development is most impaired in those cell types and regions that are showing maximum growth at the time that the nutritional deficiency is present. Therefore, post-natal malnutrition is usually not associated with a reduction in the number of neurons, but in the number of glial cells. However, the primary effect of post-natal malnutrition is a reduction in the size of both neurons and glial cells, with synaptogenesis and myelination possibly being inhibited.

Because kwashiorkor occurs later in post-natal life, it has a less permanent effect on brain development than marasmus. For example, kwashiorkor does not lead to a marked reduction in the number of neurons. An early investigation of infants who died during their second year of life showed only minor deficits in brain DNA levels, though their decreased brain weight/DNA ratios indicated a reduction in brain cell size (Winick, 1976). Despite these effects, some degree of recovery from malnutrition does occur if an adequate diet is provided later in the infant's life (Spreen et al., 1984). Using MRI to monitor changes in cerebral atrophy, a relatively recent study demonstrated that brain shrinkage accompanying kwashiorkor could be rapidly reversed with nutritional rehabilitation (Gunston et al., 1992).

Behavioral Effects of Severe Malnutrition

Over the last 40 years, the relationship of PEM to behavioral development, particularly the development of intellectual competence, has been the subject of much inquiry. A major question posed by scientists has been whether malnutrition of various degrees of severity, which typically leads to impaired brain development, will also cause impaired cognitive development (Pollitt, 1988; Ricciuti, 1993). Throughout the decade of the 1960s, the findings of reduced brain size and cell numbers in malnourished animals were supplemented with studies that reported lower IQ scores and school performance by impoverished children who experienced early clinical malnutrition.

Based on such findings, policymakers, and well meaning scientists as well, concluded that malnutrition in children was a direct cause of impaired mental development due to its effect on brain growth. In essence, a straightforward explanatory model was endorsed, namely, malnutrition → brain damage → impaired behavior. A corollary to this model was that improving the dietary intake of children at risk for chronic malnutrition would produce a significant enhancement of their intellectual development (Ricciuti, 1993). It is now generally acknowledged that this model, despite its simplistic elegance, falls rather short in explaining how malnutrition compromises mental development (Gorman, 1995; Brown and Pollitt, 1996). Rather, a myriad of adverse health and socioenvironmental conditions are now seen as interacting with nutritional status to influence mental development, as well as other behavioral outcomes.

The ecology of malnutrition

The primary cause of PEM is a lack of sufficient protein and calories, but the problem of PEM cannot be viewed in isolation from other socioenvironmental conditions (Wachs, 1995). Indeed, the environment of the malnourished child is different in countless ways beyond the mere deficiencies of food intake. As one researcher describes the many disadvantages that the families of malnourished children typically endure:

> These include poor physical and economic resources, such as overcrowded homes with poor sanitation and water supply, few household possessions and low income. They also tend to have unstable family units, with

large numbers of closely spaced children. Parental characteristics associated with infant malnutrition include poor health and nutritional status, poor obstetric history, extreme youth or age, low intelligence and educational levels, little media contact, few social contacts, traditional life styles, and low skilled occupations. The stimulation in the home is poor with few toys or books and little participation by the parents in play activities.

(Grantham-McGregor, 1995, p. 2234S)

Instead of attributing cognitive deficiencies solely to brain damage from malnutrition, the model in Fig. 6.3 displays the numerous forces that are likely to interact in reducing intellectual development. To be sure, the brain may be directly affected as a consequence of PEM, but this model allows for a reversal if adequate nutrition is made available. Health may also be compromised, but illness itself can further reduce the child's level of nutrient intake. From an ecological perspective, however, it is the reduction in the child's energy level, slowed motor development, minimal exploration of the environment and lowered expectations by parents that may place the impoverished child at greater risk for impaired cognitive development (Brown and Pollitt, 1996).

The impact of poverty cannot be underestimated when discussing the effects of PEM,

because a child's state of malnourishment is invariably confounded with socio-economic status. The term *confound* means that poor socio-economic status co-varies with poor nutrition, and since both of these factors may be independently associated with reduced cognitive performance in children, it is difficult to determine if one, the other or their interaction is most responsible for the mental deficits. From what we have said so far, the hypothesized link from malnutrition to impaired mental development should now be obvious. But the link from lower socio-economic status to child development merits further explanation.

Less money available for food means less food on the table, of course. But less food also means less variety of foods served and conceivably less interest in eating. Children learn much from their experiences with food, in terms of tastes that stimulate their gustatory and olfactory senses. Early food experiences also teach children labels, amounts and physical processes inherent in preparing and cooking different food items (Endres *et al.*, 2004). Less money available also means fewer resources in general, for clothing and shelter. When one is trying to survive, play is a luxury that poor families can ill afford. Not only is the opportunity for play restricted, but less money also means few if any toys that would serve to stimulate

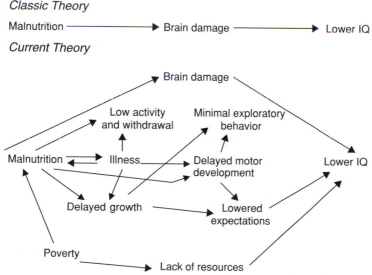

Fig. 6.3. Effect of malnutrition on cognitive development. (Source: adapted from Brown and Pollitt, 1996.)

cognitive development. Parents in poor villages or neighborhoods may not view the area as safe, so they further prevent their children from freely exploring the local environs.

However, parents do more than supply food or toys. Stated simply, family economic background and parental education are known to be positively associated with children's cognitive development (Garcia-Coll, 1990). Lower socio-economic status connotes less education, and less educated parents may have less time to spend with their children because of their jobs, are not aware of the importance of reading to their toddler (and may be illiterate themselves), or are less capable of effective parenting when they are available. It has been well demonstrated that responsive and sensitive caregiving plays an essential role in facilitating the infant's secure attachment to the parent (Lewis, 2002). But parents of malnourished children are likely to be malnourished themselves, further reducing their interest in making time to stimulate their offspring. It is worth noting that in the only published prospective study of children that included observations of mother–child dyads before the children were malnourished, mothers were found to be less responsive and affectionate to their children, and spoke less to them as well (Cravioto, 1977). Reviewing a number of recent correlational studies, Wachs (1995) concludes that the strongest predictions of developmental outcomes can be made when based on the interaction of nutrient status with such contextual factors as low socio-economic status, low parental education, family illiteracy and specific types of caregiver–child transactions.

Effects in infants

A number of investigators have researched the effects of malnutrition concurrent with infant cognitive development. While tests of normative abilities are better at gauging performance relative to peers of the same age than in estimating actual intelligence, a number of tools such as the Bayley Scales of Infant Development or the Griffiths Mental Development Scales have been used in studies of malnourished infants. Regardless of the type of malnutrition, the development of infants and toddlers

on such tests is significantly delayed (Grantham-MacGregor, 1995). In general, language and verbal development appear to be the most negatively affected by PEM.

Malnutrition in infants has also been associated with abnormalities in cerebral functioning as measured by psychophysiological tests of arousal. For example, heart rate deceleration is expected to occur when an infant is presented with a novel stimulus, with habituation occurring when the infant becomes accustomed to the stimulus. As it turns out, this effect may only be seen with well-nourished infants. When malnourished infants viewed a novel stimulus, they displayed no alterations in heart rate (Lester et al., 1975). The infants' ability to integrate intersensory information, that is, to tell that a particular sound and image go together, is also delayed in malnourished infants (Cravioto and Arrieta, 1986). These data suggest that severe malnutrition leads to a diminished responsiveness to environmental signals and therefore to a reduction in the infant's capacity for information processing. It is likely that these deficits in information processing will persist even after nutritional rehabilitation has occurred.

As discussed earlier, both marasmus and kwashiorkor are associated with distinctive alterations in the infant's behavior. Recall that the behavioral symptoms of marasmus include irritability and apathy, with kwashiorkor additionally including anorexia and withdrawal, often accompanied by a whimpering, monotonous cry. Of all the behavioral symptoms associated with these two malnourished states, lethargy and reduced activity are the most commonly observed. In fact, it has been hypothesized that this reduction in motor activity may serve to isolate malnourished infants from their environment, resulting in limited opportunities for learning and thereby depressing mental development (Schurch and Scrimshaw, 1990).

Specifically, the *functional isolation* hypothesis posits that the decreased activity, affect, and attention that characterize malnourished infants make them less likely to seek stimulation from their environment (Strupp and Levitsky, 1995; Brown and Pollitt, 1996). In turn, the caregivers are less responsive to their infants and offer them less stimulation.

Over time, this repeating circle of less seeking/less receiving of stimulation interferes with the infant's normal acquisition of information from the social and physical environment. Left unchecked, the child's development is adversely affected (Pollitt *et al.*, 1993; Wachs, 1993). The functional isolation hypothesis will be revisited in Chapter 8 as a potential explanation for decreased responsiveness of iron-anemic infants to their environments. Thus, functional isolationism may be a common thread linking various types of nutritional insult to reduced cognitive development in children.

Evidence that motor development is compromised by PEM is also provided by studies that have used supplementary feeding in malnourished infants. Regardless of the assessment of motor performance employed, undernourished infants who received nutritional interventions in the form of high calorie feeding supplements show improved motor scores through 2 years of age (Husaini *et al.*, 1991; Pollitt *et al.*, 1993).

Besides the reduction in motor activity that characterizes PEM, however, other non-cognitive aspects of the malnourished infant's behavior may bear on the interaction between mother and baby, and further exacerbate the risk of lowered stimulation. Brazelton and his colleagues have shown that malnourished newborns are low in social responsiveness and display poor orienting to visual stimuli such as human faces (Brazelton *et al.*, 1977). An infant who shows little social responsiveness to his mother, and who persists in fussing and crying when awake, cannot be much fun to be around. Add to this scenario the fact that the mother is likely to be malnourished herself. With less energy to stimulate, rouse up or play with her baby, her caregiving efforts are likely to be minimal, and the infant's cognitive development is bound to suffer.

Such a cycle of depressed mother–infant interaction is sometimes seen in cases of *non-organic failure to thrive*. Even in developed societies like the USA, some 1–5% of infants who by all accounts should be well nourished nevertheless can show deterioration in their rate of growth. Although some cases of failure to thrive are classified as organic in origin, the more common, non-organic type consists of abnormal behavior and distorted caregiver–infant interactions, in association with the retarded weight gain (Krugman and Dubowitz, 2003). Although apathy and reduced activity are characteristic of malnourished infants, many of the behaviors of infants failing to thrive cannot be attributed to malnutrition alone. Instead, the infants' irritability may discourage social interaction, which the mother may interpret as a personal rejection. In other cases, the mother may not be very good at recognizing hunger signals. Alternately, the mother may recognize the signals, but because she is under stress or frustrated with her unresponsive baby she may be less likely to respond herself (Ricciuti, 1993).

Effects on children

Investigators in many countries have attempted to assess the effects of severe PEM on concurrent and subsequent behaviors. In recent years, however, investigations have also examined the effects of mild-to-moderate malnutrition in children. As might be expected, certain metabolic consequences of severe malnutrition may rapidly recover, whereas other outcomes such as physical growth and behavior may only improve rather slowly over an extended period, or may never reach normal levels. Even moderate undernutrition, if chronic, may prevent children from behaving at a level that is appropriate for their age. The majority of these studies have focused on measuring intellectual performance, partly because testing procedures are readily available but also because the demonstration of permanent cognitive deficits would have obvious implications for social policy and preventive or remedial interventions (Brown and Sherman, 1995).

Cognitive Deficits. Cravioto and his colleagues found that in comparison to their non-malnourished siblings, twice as many of their Mexican children who experienced severe malnourishment before 3 years of age had IQs below 70, even after two or more years of recovery. Since much of the content of intelligence tests for children consists of language and verbal items, the impact of malnutrition on these areas can directly reduce IQ scores. Unfortunately, malnutrition may have been confounded with poor parenting, as the mothers were generally less sensitive, verbally communicative, emotionally involved or interested in their child's performance relative to their behavior with the unaffected child (Cravioto and Arrieta, 1986). These investigators also reported that early episodes of malnutrition were associated with deficits in intersensory integration, which in childhood has been associated with reading and writing disabilities.

Galler and her colleagues conducted a meticulous study of the cognitive consequences of malnutrition in Barbados. Using a quasi-experimental design known as a *case control* approach, the investigators carefully matched malnourished children, who had suffered from marasmus as infants, with children of similar social and economic backgrounds but with no history of malnutrition. As is often true of case control studies, however, even when socio-economic status is equated by matching, there can be distinct differences between the home environments of malnourished and well-nourished children. This study was no exception, as a retrospective analysis revealed that fathers of the malnourished children held less skilled jobs, and the mothers of those children had less education, were less sociable and were more depressed than the parents of the matched controls (Galler and Ramsey, 1985).

Taking the effects of the home environment into account using multivariate statistical procedures, Galler and her colleagues found that a history of malnutrition still had a strong association with IQ scores. For example, IQ scores measured between the ages of 5 and 11 years were consistently lower for the previously malnourished children than for the controls. Nearly 50% of the previously malnourished children had IQ scores of 90 or lower (100 is considered average), but only 17% of the control children had scores in that range. Follow-up studies of the same children when they reached the ages of 9 and 15 years revealed sustained impairment in the intellectual development of the previously malnourished children. In the later assessments, approximately 50% of the previously malnourished children had IQ scores of 70 or less in contrast to fewer than 15% of the control children with scores at 70 or below (Galler et al., 1986).

An extremely ambitious study of malnutrition and its effects on cognitive abilities was conducted in Guatemala, consisting of an early supplementary feeding intervention in four rural villages carefully selected for their high prevalence of PEM (Townsend et al., 1982). Using a placebo-controlled design, two of the villages were randomly assigned to receive a high protein/high calorie supplement (known as *atole*), with the other two villages receiving a low calorie supplement (*fresco*). The *atole* supplement was developed by the investigators to serve as a high protein substitute for the traditional corn gruel that Guatemalan mothers often feed their children, and contained 11.5 g of protein and 163 kcal of energy per cup. The *fresco* drink, common to the villagers, served as the control supplement, and contained 59 kcal per cup, with no protein. Both drinks were fortified with vitamins and minerals. Supplements were administered twice daily *ad libitum* to all pregnant women, infants and children 7 years of age and younger, with data collected on over 2300 subjects.

The primary hypothesis of the experiment concerned the effects of the high protein/energy supplement (*atole*) on cognitive development. The cognitive measures used included individual tests of embedded figures, incomplete figures, odd figures, block design, memory for designs, verbal analogies, memory for objects and vocabulary recognition. Given the large number of tests that were employed at the pre-school level, the investigators ran a factor analysis over all the tests. The analysis revealed a general perceptual–organizational–verbal factor that served as a composite score. A main effect of treatment was obtained at 4 and 5 years on this factor score, with *atole* subjects performing significantly better than *fresco* subjects (Pollitt et al., 1993).

The children were seen again for follow up testing when they were from 13 to 19 years old. Again, a battery of tests was administered, including intelligence, general knowledge, literacy, numeracy, reading comprehension, vocabulary, information processing, reaction time, memory and paired associates. Significant differences between groups were shown on four of the ten tests, and in all cases favored the *atole* subjects. Specifically, numeracy, general knowledge, vocabulary and reading comprehension were higher for the *atole* than *fresco* conditions. In addition, intelligence scores for the *fresco* group were higher as socio-economic status increased, though this effect was not seen for the *atole* groups (Pollit *et al.*, 1993).

Results from other intervention studies also support the utility of nutrition supplements in rectifying the effects of PEM. To date, reports of significant effects of supplementation have been shown for malnourished children in Columbia (Waber *et al.*, 1981) and Jamaica (Grantham-McGregor *et al.*, 1994). The Jamaica group has also tested an educational intervention with their malnourished cohort, and has reported improvements in verbal intelligence. Finally, a relatively recent correlational study in Kenya showed positive associations between food intake and cognitive scores in 8-year-old children (Sigman *et al.*, 1989). What is remarkable about this work is that the children were only mildly to moderately malnourished, yet cognitive scores were lower if protein and kilocalorie intake was found to be lower.

Motor Delays. Some of the studies just described also measured motor abilities, and the investigators have generally found that motor skills are delayed in children with PEM (Cravioto and Arrieta, 1986), although this is not always the case (Bartel *et al.*, 1978). In an early study, teachers described malnourished children as clumsy (Richardson *et al.*, 1972). In Chapter 8, we will review research that identifies iron deficiency as exerting a negative influence on motor development. Though PEM may be less a threat to motor abilities, it can nevertheless be of some consequence in terms of its impact on activity level.

We have already described the process by which lessened motor activity in infants may reduce their exploration of the environment and contact with stimulation. Evidence exists that school age children who are only mildly undernourished can have their activity level reduced as well. In the Kenyan study referred to above, the researchers had the opportunity to observe 7-year-old children who were receiving about 95% of their recommended intake relative to their rather small size. Using a valid coding system, the researchers looked at play-

ground behavior over the course of 6–8 months, and separately coded low and high demonstrations of activity. They found that high activity was positively correlated with protein–calorie intake, and that low activity was negatively correlated with intake (Espinosa *et al.*, 1992). The latter association means that lower protein–energy intake corresponded to more instances of low activity. It would seem to make sense that children who are more active require higher levels of food intake, but the data from this correlational study are consistent with the results of the studies that examined severely malnourished children.

Behavior Problems. The observation of playground behaviors in the Kenyan study was not limited to just the coding of activity. Espinosa and his colleagues found that energy intake was positively associated with observed happiness and leadership, and was negatively associated with observed anxiety. Given our stated emphasis on the environmental context, it should also be mentioned that these aspects of behavior were similarly associated with socio-economic status, which additionally correlated negatively with aggression in boys (Espinosa *et al.*, 1992).

Children in the Mexican study were shown to be less responsive when given a task (Cravioto and Arrieta, 1986), and the Jamaican children gave less attention to playing with toys (Grantham-McGregor *et al.*, 1989). Reports from teachers suggest that formerly malnourished children show less emotional control, are more distractible, have lower attention spans and develop poorer relationships with their peers as well as with the teachers themselves. Families who report food insecurity – the uncertain availability of adequate and safe foods – have children who are rated as higher in hyperactivity and other problematic behavior (Murphy *et al.*, 1998b).

Despite cultural differences in expectations for behavior, malnourished children generally seem to have more behavioral problems than do the children to whom they are compared, even when no longer hungry. For example, in a recently published longitudinal study of children in Mauritius (an island of the coast of Africa), children categorized as malnourished at age 3 were found to be higher in externalizing behavior at later ages. That is, compared to adequately nourished controls (n = 1206), the malnourished children (N = 353) were higher in aggression and hyperactivity at ages 8 and 11 years, and higher in conduct disorders and excessive motor activity at age 17 (Liu *et al.*, 2004).

School Performance. Given the effects that malnutrition appears to have on cognitive abilities, it might be expected that school performance would also suffer. Indeed, a number of studies have shown that children who were severely malnourished in infancy were found to earn poorer grades in school than matched controls (Galler *et al.*, 1990; Grantham-McGregor *et al.*, 1994). This effect is apparent even when children are matched by their class year in school. However, in several studies differences have not been found between the formerly malnourished children and their siblings (Graham and Adrianzen, 1979; Moodie *et al.*, 1980). It may be the case that families whose circumstances allowed a child to suffer from severe malnutrition in the first place may have attitudes toward education, school enrollment or regular school attendance that override any additional effects that the malnourished child's experience would entail (Grantham-McGregor, 1995).

Relatively speaking, there has not been much research conducted on school-age children with respect to the long-term effects of malnutrition on their school performance. Some exemplary studies have been published, but they are not directly comparable in ages examined, interventions attempted, tests used or results that were found (Pollitt *et al.*, 1993; Grantham-McGregor *et al.*, 1994; Wachs *et al.*, 1995). Studies of PEM and its effects have typically included observations of infants and pre-school age children, with children of school age not targeted for nutritional interventions. A related exception would appear to be the recent efforts to promote school breakfast programs, although the children who participate are not suffering from chronic starvation in the PEM sense. The effect of these programs in promoting school performance will be addressed later in this chapter.

Effects in adults

Compared to our knowledge of the behavioral consequences of PEM in children, our knowledge of the effects of malnutrition on adults is scant. Alaimo and her colleagues (Alaimo *et al.*, 2002) have recently found that adolescents from low-income households that experience food insufficiency report higher levels of dysthymia, or mild depression, suggesting that persistent food deprivation may affect mental health. Given the changes in behavior that characterizes the work we have reviewed with infants and children, one might expect lethargy and lessened activity to be natural outcomes of persistent malnutrition in adults. From what we know of individuals who have experienced periods of severe famine or survived the deprivations of a concentration camp, for example, lethargy and reduced activity are indeed likely to be observed, with apathy, social isolation and impairments in memory not at all unusual. Binge eating has also been seen among malnourished prisoners of war after their rescue (Polivy *et al.*, 1994), and Holocaust survivors maintain disturbed attitudes toward food (Sindler *et al.*, 2004). Given the special circumstances of these conditions of malnutrition, however, it is impossible to determine if such behavioral changes were directly related to PEM or to the other devastating aspects of those environments (Widdowson, 1985).

Interestingly enough, the most extensive information we have on the behavioral effects of malnutrition in adults comes from work conducted half a century ago on individuals who were not starving at all, at least not until they agreed to participate in the research project we will now discuss. During the Second World War, Ancel Keys and his colleagues at the University of Minnesota undertook a study on the effects of moderate malnutrition to provide a basis for nutritional rehabilitation programs in Europe for after the war (Keys *et al.*, 1950, also described in Garner, 1997). Thirty-six conscientious objectors volunteered as subjects, agreeing to participate in the experiment after being told the purposes of the study. The men were housed at the university and were permitted to attend classes and participate in other activities. Following a baseline period during which time their daily caloric intake averaged 3500 kcal, the investigators reduced their daily energy intake by 55% – 1570 kcal, for 6 months. While the physiological effects were of major interest to the investigators, the behavioral findings due to the marked reduction in caloric intake are what made this a landmark study.

The behavioral consequences of undernutrition were assessed quantitatively through the use of questionnaires and psychological inventories and qualitatively by personal interviews and observations. At the outset of the study, the subjects displayed a keen interest in all aspects of the program. With the passage of time and the loss of body weight, however, their interest declined. One of the first changes observed in the subjects was a reduction in their social initiative. That is, the men became reluctant to make decisions or plan and participate in group activities. They preferred spending more and more time alone, reporting that it was just 'too much trouble' or 'too tiring' to have to contend with other people. Those subjects who had started classes at the university dropped out. The psychological inventories revealed decreases in activity, motivation, self-discipline, sex drive and mental alertness, with increases in apathy, irritability and moodiness.

Although motivation and interest in the social environment declined, the subjects' cognitive abilities, as measured by an extensive battery of intelligence tests, were not impaired. Their constriction of cognitive pursuits, however, did show an interesting change. As the subjects' interest in intellectual, political and cultural issues lost their appeal, their interest in food increased. In fact, it became the principal topic of conversations, daydreams and reading for nearly all of the men, with cookbooks, menus and information bulletins on food production becoming the primary interest of many. The men also extended their mealtimes by consuming their allotted food more slowly, and adding spices and condiments to their limited rations.

At the completion of the study, nutritional rehabilitation led to a reversal of the majority of behavioral changes that had been observed. Anecdotal reports, however, suggested that the heightened interest in food that was expressed by many of the subjects had continued even after their complete rehabilitation (Keys *et al.*, 1950). For ethical reasons, a study like this is unlikely to ever be undertaken again. However, its results are a powerful demonstration of the effects of undernutrition on the behavior of heretofore-healthy adult subjects, particularly in the areas of activity and social interaction.

More recently, anecdotal evidence from an experimental living arrangement known as Biosphere 2 supports these classic results by Keys. Biosphere 2 was a 3-acre living space on the Arizona desert that contained an ecosystem that was materially closed but energetically open to sunlight and electric power. Air, water and organic material were recycled in an effort to simulate what life on a space colony would be like. The four men and four women scientist/subjects who were sealed inside the station initially subsisted on 2500 calories per day. When the Biosphere environment was unable to produce enough food to maintain this level of nutrition, the project director placed all of the inhabitants, including himself, on a 1780 calories per day regimen. After 6 months of caloric restriction, the men lost 25 lb and women 15 lb on the average, with both groups significantly reducing their cholesterol, blood pressure and blood sugar (Walford *et al.*, 1992). However, much like the Keys' subjects, thoughts of food were paramount. The individuals reportedly stared at one another's plates at mealtimes to make sure no one was getting more than their fair share, while any food shown in the movies they watched at night served to mesmerize them (Schardt, 2003).

Consequences of Short-term Nutritional Deficits

As we have discussed, the vast majority of studies on the consequences of PEM have focused on the effects of severe episodes of marasmus or kwashiorkor on concurrent or subsequent cognitive capacities, motor behavior, or other behavioral problems in infants and young children. Over the last 20 years, however, an increasing number of studies have examined the effects of short-term nutritional deprivation, as exemplified by skipping breakfast, on academic and test performance in school-age children. Ernesto Pollitt and his colleagues have done substantial work in this area, and have repeatedly shown that skipping breakfast can have detrimental effects on behavior. With both undernourished children in Peru and middle-class children in the USA, his research team has demonstrated that going without breakfast can have deleterious effects on problem-solving performance, which could derive from metabolic changes associated with the lack of glucose available to the brain.

In a typical study by this group, elementary-grade children who are given breakfast after an overnight fast are tested against a comparable group of children who are fed nothing, or are given a non-caloric soft drink. In their investigations, children who did not receive breakfast did worse on tests of figure-matching, scanning and discrimination (Pollitt and Matthews, 1995; Jacoby et al., 1996). Other investigators have used similar designs, and have found that eating breakfast is associated with improved scores on tests of matching, arithmetic and verbal fluency (Chandler et al., 1995).

Indirect support for the importance of breakfast also comes from studies that have examined the efficacy of School Breakfast Programs (SBP). In the USA, a government-sponsored SBP must provide 25% of the day's Recommended Dietary Allowance. An SBP breakfast should at a minimum contain: one serving of milk; one serving of fruit or vegetable or full-strength juice; and two servings from the bread, meat or bread or meat alternate groups (Burghardt et al., 1995). Although some investigators do not indicate what or how much the children who participate in SBPs actually eat, they have demonstrated that school attendance increases, and rates of tardiness decrease, when breakfast is provided at school (Murphy et al., 1998a). In a recent study that examined school performance at the end versus the beginning of the month, it was reported that 3rd grade children in an urban school performed better at the time of first testing. The investigators, who also obtained information on what the children ate for breakfast on test days, hypothesized that the quality of their breakfasts deteriorated over the month due to their families' food stamps or wages running out (Worobey et al., 2001).

Despite the apparent convergence of these results, there are some limitations to these studies on breakfast and its effects on cognition. For one thing, most of the studies have been conducted on children who are at nutritional risk due to conditions of poverty (Chandler et al., 1995; Jacoby et al., 1996). If one recalls our discussion on the ecology of malnutrition, it should be obvious that these children have many stresses in their lives, and that missing breakfast is just another insult relative to poor hygiene, sleeping conditions or even depression. At one level, providing breakfast to children who are constantly undernourished may exaggerate its effectiveness. At the same time, it is difficult to justify not feeding the control children in such experiments for the sake of an experiment.

A second issue concerns the age of the target children, who for indeterminate reasons are usually age 8–11 (Chandler et al., 1995; Jacoby et al., 1996; Worobey et al., 2001). This age range does warrant study, but it is somewhat striking that the focus has been narrowly applied to 3rd through 5th graders. Actually, a few studies have looked at teenagers as well as college students, but differences between breakfast and fasting groups have been inconsistent or non-existent (Cromer et al., 1990; Benton and Sargent, 1992; Smith et al., 1994).

A recent study attempted to address some of these limitations by using a sample of children who were at little or no risk of undernutrition, who regularly ate breakfast, and who were younger than those described in previous reports. Middle-class 4-year-olds attending a university-run preschool served as their own controls in a study that tested the impact of a school-provided breakfast against their usual fare at home (Worobey and Worobey, 1999). Baseline pretesting was done prior to the inception of the breakfast program, with mothers of the children keeping records of what their children ate for breakfast all that week. A custom battery of tasks was employed, including mazes, the figure-matching test that has been shown to be sensitive to breakfast skipping and some computer tasks that required the matching of shapes and discrimination of stimuli. Six weeks after the SBP was initiated, the researchers retested the children on parallel forms of the tasks, while food intake during breakfast was recorded at preschool. Not all children participated in the SBP, so testers were kept blind as to whether the children ate breakfast at school or at home at the time of the second assessment. The results showed that while total protein and calorie intake was not affected by home versus school breakfast status, the children's diets were qualitatively better at preschool than at home. That is, fewer calories were ingested from fat or simple sugars. Relative to themselves and to their peers, who ate breakfast at home, the preschoolers who participated in the SBP did better on the figure-matching test and the computer discrimination task (Worobey and Worobey, 1999).

The results of these studies on breakfast indicate that even short-term nutritional deficits can have significant consequences for children's school attendance and academic performance, and are not confined to children who suffer from severe malnutrition. However, poor children in underdeveloped countries and low-income children in developed countries are likely to be at greatest risk for skipping breakfast. Since children who miss breakfast are unlikely to achieve their recommended daily allowances for calories and other nutrients, efforts to improve the nutritional status of children should include the continued support of School Breakfast Programs (Sampson et al., 1995).

Conclusion

It is abundantly clear that malnutrition does not occur in a vacuum, but is just one component of an ecological framework that includes poverty, illiteracy, disease, inadequate parenting and the lack of other support systems. With this complex system in mind, it is safe to conclude that malnutrition has adverse behavioral consequences. In the human infant, severe PEM can affect brain growth. Infants who suffer from marasmus or kwashiorkor may be permanently saddled with reduced brain weight, impairments in myelination and decreased synaptogenesis. Early irritability and inactivity can depress mother–infant interactions, and lead to a vicious circle of less attention paid to the developing child, with less interest and attention in the environment displayed by the child as well. Lowered intellectual abilities are the likely result, with reduced attention span, poor memory and emotional instability also possible. In adults, malnutrition can lead to

alterations in mood, and decreases in motivation, alertness and social interaction.

Although we did not address it in this chapter, PEM also increases a child's vulnerability to environmental toxins such as lead, further illustrating the complexity of the system to which malnutrition contributes. While fasting increases the absorption of ingested lead, lead also competes with trace minerals such as calcium and zinc. In Chapters 7 and 8 we will examine how vitamins and trace minerals, when deficient, may also be linked to the cognitive, motor and affective outcomes we have just covered.

References

Ahmed, M.G., Bedi, K.S., Warren, M.A. and Kamel, M.M. (1987) Effects of a lengthy period of undernutrition from birth and subsequent nutritional rehabilitation on the synapse: granule cell neuron ratio in the rat dentate gyrus. *Journal of Comparative Neurology* 263, 146–158.

Alaimo, K., Olson, C. and Frongillo, E.A. (2002) Food insufficiency, but not low family income, is positively associated with dysthymia and suicide symptoms in adolescents. *Journal of Nutrition* 132(4), 719–725.

Barker, D.J.P. (1998) *Mothers, Babies and Health in later Life*. Churchill Livingstone, Edinburgh, UK.

Barker, D.J.P. (2003) The fetal origins of obesity. In Bray, G.A. and Bouchard, C. (eds) *Handbook of Obesity: Etiology and Pathophysiology*, 2nd edn. Marcel Dekker, New York, pp. 823–851.

Bartel, P.R., Griesel, R.D., Burnett, L.S., Freiman, I., Rosen, E.U. and Geefhuysen, J. (1978) Long-term effects of kwashiorkor on psychomotor development. *South African Medical Journal* 53, 360–362.

Benton, D. and Sargent, J. (1992) Breakfast, blood glucose and memory. *Biology and Psychology* 33, 207–210.

Brazelton, T.B., Tronick, E., Lechtig, A., Lasky, R.E. and Klein, R.E. (1977) The behavior of nutritionally deprived Guatemalan infants. *Developmental Medicine & Child Neurology* 19, 364–372.

Brown, J.L. and Pollitt, E. (1996) Malnutrition, poverty, and intellectual development. *Scientific American* 274(2), 38–43.

Brown, J.L. and Sherman, L.P. (1995) Policy implications of new scientific knowledge. *Journal of Nutrition* 125(8), 2281S–2284S.

Burghardt, J.A., Gordon, A.R. and Fraker, T.M. (1995) Meals offered in the National School Lunch Program and the School Breakfast Program. *American Journal of Clinical Nutrition* 61, 187S–198S.

Chandler, A.M.K., Walder, S.P., Connolly, K. and Grantham-McGregor, S. (1995) School breakfast improves verbal fluency in undernourished Jamaican children. *Journal of Nutrition* 125, 894–900.

Cintra, L., Diaz-Cintra, S., Galvan, A., Kemper, T. and Morgane, P.J. (1990) Effects of protein undernutrition on the dentate gyrus in rats of three age groups. *Brain Research* 532, 271–277.

Cravioto, J. (1977) Not by bread alone: effect of early malnutrition and stimuli deprivation on mental development. In Ghai, O.P. (ed) *Perspectives in Pediatrics,* Interprint, New Delhi, pp. 87–104.

Cravioto, J. and Arrieta, R. (1986) Nutrition, mental development, and learning. In Faulkner, F. and Tanner, J.M. (eds) *Human Growth*, Vol. 3. Plenum Publishing, New York and London, pp. 501–536.

Cromer, B.A., Tarnowski, K.J., Stein, A.M. and Harton, P. (1990) The school breakfast program and cognition in adolescents. *Journal of Developmental & Behavioral Pediatrics* 11, 295–300.

Endres, J.B., Rockwell, R.E. and Mense, C.G. (2004) *Food, Nutrition, and the Young Child.* Macmillan, New York.

Espinosa, M.P., Sigman, M.D., Neumann, C.G., Bwibo, N.O. and McDonald, M.A. (1992) Playground behaviors of school-age children in relation to nutrition, schooling, and family characteristics. *Developmental Psychology* 28, 1188–1195.

Galler, J.R. and Ramsey, F. (1985) The influence of early malnutrition on subsequent behavioral development: the role of the microenvironment of the household. *Nutrition & Behavior* 2, 161–173.

Galler, J.R., Ramsey, F. and Forde, V. (1986) A follow-up study of the influence of early malnutrition on subsequent development. 4. Intellectual performance during adolescence. *Nutrition & Behavior* 3, 211–222.

Galler, J.R., Ramsey, F., Morley, D.S., Archer, E. and Salt, P. (1990) The long-term effects of early kwashiorkor compared with maramus. IV. Performance on the national high school entrance examination. *Pediatric Research* 28, 235–239. *Journal of the American Academy of Child Psychiatry* 22, 16–22.

Garcia-Coll, C.T. (1990) Developmental outcome of minority infants: a process- oriented look into our beginnings. *Child Development* 61(2), 270–289.

Garner, D.M. (1997) The effects of starvation on behavior: implications for eating disorders. In Garner, D.M. and Garfinkel, P.E. (eds) *Handbook for Treatment of Eating Disorders*. Guilford Press, New York, pp. 145–177.

Gong, Q.Y., Roberts, N., Garden, A.S. and Whitehouse, G.H. (1998) Fetal and fetal brain volume estimation in the third trimester of human pregnancy using gradient echo MR imaging. *Magnetic Resonance Imaging* 16(3), 235–240.

Gorman, K.S. (1995) Malnutrition and cognitive development: evidence from experimental/quasi-experimental studies among the mild-to-moderately malnourished. *Journal of Nutrition* 125, 2239S–2244S.

Graham, G.G. and Adrianzen, B. (1979) Status in school of Peruvian children severely malnourished in infancy. In Brozek, J. (ed) *Behavioral Effects of Energy and Protein Deficits*. NIH Pub. 9–1906. Department of Health, Education, and Welfare, Washington, DC, pp. 185–194.

Grantham-McGregor, S. (1995) A Review of Studies of the Effect of Severe Malnutrition on Mental Development. *The Journal of Nutrition* 125(8S), The American Institute of Nutrition, p. 2235S.

Grantham-McGregor, S.M., Schofield, W. and Haggard, D. (1989) Maternal child interaction in survivors of severe malnutrition who received psychosocial stimulation. *European Journal of Clinical Nutrition* 43, 45–52.

Grantham-McGregor, S.M., Powell, C., Walker, S., Chang, S. and Fletcher, P. (1994) The long-term follow up of severely malnourished children who participated in an intervention program. *Child Development* 65, 428–439.

Gunston, G.D., Burkimsher, D., Malan, H. and Sive, A.A. (1992) Reversible cerebral shrinkage in kwashiorkor: an MRI study. *Archives of Disabilities in Children* 67(8), 1030–1032.

Hay, W.W., Catz, C.S., Grave, G.D. and Yaffe, S.J. (1997) Workshop Summary: Fetal growth: its regulation and disorders. *Pediatrics* 99, 585–591.

Husaini, M., Karyadi, L., Husaini, Y.K., Sandjaja, Karyadi, D. and Pollitt, E. (1991) Developmental effects of short-term supplementary feeding in nutritionally-at-risk Indonesian infants. *American Journal of Clinical Nutrition* 54(4), 799–804.

Jacoby, E., Cueto, S. and Pollitt, E. (1996) Benefits of a School Breakfast Program among Andean children in Peru. *Food & Nutrition Bulletin* 17(1), 54–64.

James, W.P.T., Nelson, M., Ralph, A. and Leather, S. (1997) Socioeconomic determinants of health: the contribution of nutrition to inequalities of health. *British Medical Journal* 314, 1545.

Keys, A.J., Brozek, J., Henschel, A., Mickelson, O. and Taylor, H.L. (1950) *The Biology of Human Starvation*. University of Minnesota Press, Minneapolis, Minnesota.

Krugman, S.D. and Dubowitz, H. (2003) Failure to thrive. *American Family Physician* 68, 879–886.

Langley-Evans, S.C. (ed.) (2004) *Fetal Nutrition and Adult Disease: Programming of Chronic Disease Through Fetal Exposure to Undernutrition*. CAB International, Wallingford, UK.

Lester, B.M., Klein, R.E. and Martinez, S.J. (1975) The use of habituation in the study of the effects of infantile malnutrition. *Developmental Psychobiology* 8, 541–546.

Levitsky, D. and Barnes, R.H. (1970) The effects of early malnutrition on the reaction of adult rats to aversive stimuli. *Nature* 225, 468–469.

Levitsky, D.A. and Strupp, B.J. (1995) Malnutrition and the brain: changing concepts, changing concerns. *The Journal of Nutrition* 125(8S), 2212S–2220S.

Lewis, M. (2002) Social development. In Slater, A. and Lewis, M. (eds) *Introduction to Infant Development*. Oxford University Press, New York, pp. 210–228.

Liu, J., Raine, A., Venables, P.H., and Mednick, S.A. (2004) Malnutrition at age 3 years and externalizing behavior problems at ages 8, 11, and 17 years. *American Journal of Psychiatry* 161(11), 2005–2013.

Moodie, A.D., Bowie, M.D., Mann, M.D. and Hansen, J.D.L. (1980) A prospective 15-year follow up study of kwashiorkor patients. Part II. Social circumstances, educational attainment and social adjustment. *South African Medical Journal* 58, 677–680.

Murphy, J.M., Pagano, M.E., Nachmani, J., Sperling, P., Kane, S. and Kleinman, R.E. (1998a) The relationship of school breakfast to psychosocial and academic functioning. *Archives of Pediatric Adolescent Medicine* 152, 899–906.

Murphy, J.M., Wehler, C.A., Pagano, M.E., Little, M., Kleinman, R.E. and Jellinek, M.S. (1998b) Relationship between hunger and psychosocial functioning in low-income American children. *Journal of the American Academy of Child & Adolescent Psychiatry* 37(2), 163–170.

Murray, C.J.L. and Lopez, A.D. (1996) *The Global Burden of Disease*. Harvard School of Public Health, Cambridge, Massachusetts, pp. 360–367.

Pollitt, E. (1988) A critical review of three decades of research on the effects of chronic energy malnutrition on behavioral development. In Schurch, B. and Scrimshaw, N. (eds) *Chronic Energy Deficiency: Consequences and Related Issues*. Proceedings of the International Dietary Energy Consultative Group meeting held in Guatemala City, Guatemala. Nestlé Foundation, Switzerland.

Pollitt, E. and Matthews, R. (1995) Breakfast and cognition: an integrative summary. *American Journal of Clinical Nutrition* 67(4), 804S–813S.

Pollitt, E., Gorman, K.S., Engle, P.L., Martorell, R. and Rivera, J. (1993) Early supplemental feeding and cognition: effects over two decades. *Monographs of the Society for Research in Child Development* 58(7, Serial No. 235).

Polivy, J., Zeitlin, S., Herman, C. and Beal, A. (1994) Food restriction and binge eating: a study of former prisoners of war. *Journal of Abnormal Psychology* 103, 409–411.

Ricciuti, H. (1993) Nutrition and mental development. *Current Directions in Psychological Science* 2, 43–46.

Richardson, S.A., Birch, H.G., Grabie, E., and Yoder, K. (1972) The behavior of children in school who were severely malnourished in the first two years of life. *Journal of Health and Social Behavior* 13, 276–284.

Sampson, A.E., Dixit, S., Meyers, A.F. and Houser, R. (1995) The nutritional impact of breakfast consumption on the diets of inner-city African-American elementary school children. *Journal of the National Medical Association* 87(3), 195–202.

Schardt, D. (2003) Eat less live longer? Does calorie restriction work? *Nutrition Action Health Letter* 30(7), 1, 3–6.

Schurch, B. and Scrimshaw, N.S., (eds) (1990) *Activity, Energy Expenditure and Energy Requirements of Infants and Children*. Nestlé Foundation Lausanne, Switzerland.

Sigman, M. Neumann, C., Jansen, A. and Bwibo, N. (1989) Cognitive abilities of Kenyan children in relation to nutrition, family characteristics, and education. *Child Development* 60, 1463–1474.

Sindler, A.J., Wellman, N.S. and Stier, O.B. (2004) Holocaust survivors report long-term effects on attitudes toward food. *Journal of Nutrition Education and Behavior* 36(4), 189–196.

Smith, A., Kendrick, A., Maben, A. and Salmon, J. (1994) Effects of breakfast and caffeine on cognitive performance, mood, and cardiovascular functioning. *Appetite* 22, 39–55.

Spreen, O., Tupper, D., Risser, A., Tuokko, H. and Edgell, D. (1984) *Human Developmental Neuropsychology*. Oxford University Press, New York.

Strupp, B.J. and Levitsky, D.A. (1995) Enduring cognitive effects of early malnutrition: a theoretical reappraisal. *The Journal of Nutrition* 125(8S), 2221S–2232S.

Susser, M. and Levin, B. (1999) Ordeals for the fetal programming hypothesis. *British Medical Journal* 318, 885–886.

Tonkiss, J. and Galler, J.R. (1990) Prenatal protein malnutrition and working memory performance in adult rats. *Behavioral Brain Research* 40, 95–107.

Tonkiss, J., Galler, J.R., Morgane, P.J., Bronzino, J.D. and Austin-LaFrance, R.J. (1993) Prenatal protein malnutrition and postnatal brain function. In *Annals of the New York Academy of Science: Maternal Nutrition and Pregnancy Outcome* 678, 215–227.

Torun, B. and Viteri, F.E. (1988) Protein-energy malnutrition. In Shils, M.E. and Young, V.R. (eds) *Modern Nutrition in Health and Disease*. Lea & Febiger, Philadelphia, pp. 746–773.

Townsend, J.W., Klein, R.E., Irwin, M.H., Owens, W., Yarbrough, C. and Engle, P.L. (1982) Nutrition and preschool mental development. In Wagner, D.A. and Stevenson, H.W. (eds), *Cross-cultural Perspectives on Child Development*. W.H. Freeman, San Francisco.

UNICEF (United Nations Children's Emergency Fund), (1997) *The State of the World's Children 1998*. Oxford University Press, Oxford, UK.

Waber, D.P., Vuori-Christiansen, L., Ortiz, N., Clement, J.R., Christiansen, N.E., Mora, J.O., Reed, R.B. and Herrera, M.G. (1981) Nutritional supplementation, maternal education, and cognitive development of infants at risk of malnutrition. *American Journal of Clinical Nutrition* 34, 807–913.

Wachs, T.D. (1993) Environment and the development of disadvantaged children. In Karp, R.J. (ed.), *Malnourished Children in the United States Caught in the Cycle of Poverty*. Springer, New York, pp. 13–30.

Wachs, T.D. (1995) Relation of mild-to-moderate malnutrition to human development: correlational studies. *Journal of Nutrition* 125, 2245S–2254S.

Wachs, T.D., Bishry, Z., Moussa, W., Yunis, F., McCabe, G., Harrison, G., Sweifi, E., Kirksey, A., Galal, O., Jerome, H. and Shaheen, F. (1995) Nutritional intake and context as predictors of cognition and adaptive behavior of Egyptian age school children. *International Journal of Behavioral Development* 18(3), 425–450.

Walford, R.L., Harris, S.B., and Gunion, M.W. (1992) The calorically restricted low-fat nutrient dense diet in Biosphere 2 significantly lowers blood glucose, total leukocyte count, cholesterol, and blood pressure in humans. *Proceedings of the National Academy of Sciences* 89, 11533–11537.

Wendland, B.E., Greenwood, C.E., Weinberg, I. and Young, K.W.H. (2003) Malnutrition in institutionalized seniors: the iatrogenic component. *Journal of the American Geriatric Society* 51, 85–90.

Whitney, E.N. and Rolfes, S.R. (2002) *Understanding Nutrition*, 9th edn. Wadsworth Publishing Company, California.

Widdowson, E.M. (1985) Responses to deficits of dietary energy. In Blaxter, K. and Waterlow, J.C. (eds) *Nutritional Adaptation in Man*. John Libby, London, pp. 97–104.

Winick, M. (1976) *Malnutrition and brain development*. Oxford University Press, New York.

Winick, M. and Rosso, P. (1969) Head circumference and cellular growth of the brain in normal and marasmic children. *Journal of Pediatrics* 74, 774–778.

Worobey, J. and Worobey, H. (1999) The impact of a two-year school breakfast program for preschool-aged children on their nutrient intake and pre-academic performance. *Child Study Journal* 29(2), 113–129.

Worobey, J., Worobey, H., Johnson, E. and Hamm, M. (2001) Effects of nutrient intake in a sample of inner city elementary school children. *Resources in Education*. ERIC (ED 453 963), Champaign, Illinois.

7   B Vitamins, the Central Nervous System and Behavior

B.J. Tepper and R.B. Kanarek

Vitamins are organic compounds that are essential for the metabolism of other nutrients and the maintenance of a variety of physiological functions. As a virtue of being organic compounds, all vitamins contain the element carbon. However, the 13 vitamins vary greatly in chemical composition and in the roles they play in the body. Vitamins, in contrast to the macronutrients, protein, fat and carbohydrate, are required in relatively small amounts in the diet and are not a source of energy. The primary function of many vitamins is catalytic; they often serve as coenzymes which facilitate the actions of enzymes involved in essential metabolic reactions.

The significance of vitamins for human health was first recognized as a result of the deficiency diseases which are associated with the lack of these nutrients in the diet. Research conducted primarily at the turn of the 20th century led to the hypothesis that certain diseases such as scurvy, rickets, pellagra and beriberi were caused by the lack of an essential substance in the diet and cured by adding this substance back. In 1912, Casimir Funk coined the term 'vitamine', 'vita' for life and 'amine' because the substance contained nitrogen. Later work demonstrated that there was not one, but many, of these vital substances and that only a few were amines, and so the final 'e' was dropped, leading to the term vitamin.

There are a variety of causes for vitamin deficiencies. Some individuals, due to genetic abnormalities or disease conditions, have a decreased ability to absorb vitamins provided in food. For example, chronic alcoholism can impair the absorption of thiamin from the gastrointestinal tract. A second cause of vitamin deficiency is the increased need for a vitamin, leading to deficiency symptoms on an intake that would normally be adequate. Increased need for vitamins can occur during pregnancy or lactation, or as a result of intake of medications or therapeutic agents. For example, individuals treated with anticonvulsant drugs to control seizures demonstrate an increased need for vitamin B_6. The most common cause of vitamin deficiencies, however, is inadequate intake. In many parts of the world, inadequate amounts or varieties of food continue to be the rule, and incidence of classic deficiency diseases such as beriberi and pellagra remain common. Deficiency diseases are rare among healthy individuals in developed countries except in pockets of the population with special requirements or with poor dietary intakes.

Several of the B vitamins – thiamin (B_1), niacin, pyridoxine (B_6), folate and cobalamin (B_{12}), – play important roles in the functioning of the central nervous system, and in human behavior and development. These functions will be described in subsequent sections following a brief discussion of dietary reference values for the intake of nutrients.

Dietary Reference Intakes

The Dietary Reference Intakes (DRIs) are a comprehensive set of reference values for nutrient intakes for healthy populations in the USA and Canada. The DRIs are derived from scientifically-based estimates of nutrient intakes and are used for planning and assessing the diets of healthy individuals, and for establishing guidelines for the military and federal food assistance such as the School Lunch Program and Women, Infants and Children (WIC) Program. The DRIs consist of three categories of reference intakes; Estimated Average Requirements (EAR); the Recommended Dietary Allowances (RDA); and, Adequate Intakes (AI). The fourth component of the DRIs is the Tolerable Upper Intake level (UL), an indicator of excess intake (see Table 7.1 for definitions). The UL is not intended to be a recommended level of intake. There is no established benefit for healthy individuals if they consume nutrient intakes above the RDA or AI (Food and Nutrition Board, 1998a).

The RDAs have traditionally served as the authoritative guideline for nutrient assessment. The RDAs have been in existence since 1941 and are updated periodically as new information becomes available, typically every 10 years. Since the RDAs are based on nutrient requirements, EAR is used in setting the RDA for a nutrient. The EAR is the daily intake value of a nutrient that is estimated to meet the nutrient requirement of half of the healthy individuals in a life stage and gender group. The RDA for most nutrients is set at 2 standard deviations above the EAR to provide a margin of safety. If there is insufficient data to set the RDA for a nutrient, AI is used as the guideline instead. The current DRI tables include RDAs for nutrients about which there is a high degree of certainty about their requirements (e.g. B vitamins); AIs are used for nutrients for which requirements are less certain (Food and Nutrition Board, 1998a). The current DRIs for selected B vitamins and folate described in this chapter appear in Table 7.2.

Table 7.1. Reference values comprising the dietary reference intakes.

Dietary Reference Intakes
Recommended dietary allowances (RDAs): the average daily, dietary intake level that is sufficient to meet the nutrient requirements of nearly all (97–98%) healthy individuals in a particular life stage and gender group.
Estimated average requirement (EAR): a daily nutrient intake value that is estimated to meet the requirement of half the healthy individuals in a group.
Adequate intake (AI): a recommended daily intake value based on observed or experimentally determined approximations of nutrient intake by a group (or groups) of healthy people that are assumed to be adequate – used when an RDA cannot be determined.
Tolerable upper intake level (UL): the highest level of daily nutrient intake that is likely to pose no risks of adverse health effects to almost all individuals in the general population. As UL increases, the risk of adverse effects increases.

Source: Food and Nutrition Board, 1998h.

Thiamin (Vitamin B$_1$)

The symptoms of inadequate thiamin intake that constitute the disease known as beriberi were described by the Chinese as early as the 7th century. The disease was relatively uncommon until the Industrial Revolution when the consumption of refined cereal grains increased dramatically. During commercial milling of grains, the thiamin-rich bran or outer covering is removed. As a result, white flour and polished white rice have little if any thiamin. The consumption of white bread, considered a sign of affluence in late-18th-century Europe resulted in a significant increase in the prevalence of thiamin deficiency among the wealthy. Studies by Eijkman in the late 1800s showed that rice bran extract was effective in curing beriberi in experimental animals. In 1926, an anti-beriberi factor was isolated from rice bran, and in 1936, this factor named thiamin was identified and synthesized (Haas, 1988; Tanphaichitr, 1998; Bates, 2001).

Table 7.2. Dietary reference intakes for selected B vitamins and folate.

Life stage group		Thiamin (mg/d)	Niacin (mg/d)	Vitamin B_6 (mg/d)	Vitamin B_{12} (µg/d)	Folate (µg/d)
Infants	0–6 mo	0.2	2	0.1	0.4	65
	7–12 mo	0.3	4	0.3	0.5	80
Children	1–3 y	0.5	6	0.5	0.9	150
	4–8 y	0.6	4	0.6	1.2	200
Males	9–13 y	0.9	12	1.0	1.8	300
	14–18 y	1.2	16	1.3	2.4	400
	19–30 y	1.2	16	1.3	2.4	400
	31–50 y	1.2	16	1.3	2.4	400
	51–70 y	1.2	16	1.7	2.4	400
	>70 y	1.2	16	1.7	2.4	400
Females	9–13 y	0.9	12	1.0	1.8	300
	14–18 y	1.0	14	1.2	2.4	400
	19–30 y	1.1	14	1.3	2.4	400
	31–50 y	1.1	14	1.3	2.4	400
	51–70 y	1.1	14	1.3	2.4	400
	>70 y	1.1	14	1.3	2.4	400
Pregnancy		–	1.4	18	1.9	2.6	600
Lactation		–	1.4	17	2.0	2.8	500

Source: Food and Nutrition Board, 1998h.

Functions, requirements and dietary sources

Thiamin is a component of the coenzyme thiamin pyrophosphate (TPP) which is necessary for the metabolism of carbohydrate and branched-chain amino acids. In addition to its coenzyme functions, thiamin is important for membrane functionality and normal conduction of electrical impulses in the nervous system. The mechanisms by which thiamin affects neural activity remains poorly understood, but several roles for the vitamin have been identified. Thiamin may play a role in the control of sodium conductance at axonal membranes. Thiamin may also be involved in the utilization and turnover of major neurotransmitters including acetylcholine, norepinephrine and serotonin. Decreased brain levels of glutamate, aspartate and GABA have also been described in thiamin-deficient rats. Since thiamin plays a role in energy metabolism at the cellular level, lack of the vitamin may result in impaired central glucose metabolism leading to energy depletion and neuronal cell death (Haas, 1988; Butterworth, 1993; Jeffrey, 1998; Tanphaichitr, 1998). More will be said shortly about the biochemical functions of thiamin in brain and peripheral nervous tissues in deficiency states.

Cereal grains contain substantial amounts of thiamin, but the commercial milling processes used in most Western countries remove the outer portions of the grain which are the richest sources of the vitamin. In the USA, Canada and most countries, grain products including flour, bread, pasta and ready-to-eat cereals are fortified with B vitamins. Major food sources of thiamin in the US population are grain products, processed meats and pork, followed by fish, soy-based meat substitutes and seeds (see Table 7.3). The current DRI for men and women, 19–50 years of age is 1.2 mg and 1.1 mg of thiamin per day. There are no reports of adverse effects from consumption of excess thiamin from food or supplements (Food and Nutrition Board, 1998b).

Despite awareness of the dietary sources of thiamin and the availability of synthetic thiamin, beriberi continues to be a serious health problem in parts of the world where high-carbohydrate diets are common and rice and wheat are not enriched as a common practice. In Southeast Asia, where the diet of

Table 7.3. Thiamin, niacin and vitamin B₆ content of selected foods (per serving).

Food	Serving	Thiamin (mg)	Niacin (mg)	Vitamin B₆ (mg)
Branflakes cereal	3/4 cup	1.57	20.01	2.03
Cornflakes	1 cup	0.36	5.10	0.50
Sliced ham	2 slices	0.36	1.65	0.19
Whole-wheat bread, enriched	1 slice	0.10	1.07	0.05
Ground beef patty, broiled	3 oz	0.04	4.10	0.33
Lamb chop, broiled	3 oz	0.09	5.82	0.14
Kidney beans, canned	1 cup	0.28	1.17	0.06
Peanuts, dry roasted	1 oz	0.12	3.83	0.07
Tuna fish, canned	3 oz	0.03	11.29	0.88
Chicken breast, roasted	3 oz	0.06	11.79	0.53
Raisins	1 cup	0.15	1.10	0.25
Milk, whole	1 cup	0.11	0.26	0.09
Spinach, frozen	1 cup	0.15	0.83	0.26
Green peas, frozen	1 cup	0.45	2.37	0.18
Baked potato w/skin	1 medium	0.16	2.85	0.63

Source: US Department of Agriculture, 2003.

the poorer segment of the population consists primarily of polished rice, beriberi is prevalent. Additionally, the predominance of carbohydrate in the diet raises the metabolic requirement for the vitamin and may precipitate the disease. Infantile beriberi frequently occurs when pregnancy and lactation raise the mother's requirement for thiamin. Breast-fed infants develop the disease when the milk of malnourished mothers is deficient in the vitamin (Jeffrey, 1998; Suter, 2001). As recently as the late 1980s, studies from Thailand reported that beriberi was a leading cause of infant mortality, accounting for 250 deaths per 1000 live births. Infant mortality fell to 78 deaths per 1000 live births in the mid-1990s following initiation of a thiamin supplementation program (McGready et al., 2001). Finally, a number of foods including fermented fish, tea leaves and betel nuts contain compounds that act as thiamin antagonists, decreasing the availability of thiamin. Individuals living on marginal diets and consuming large amounts of these foods have an increased risk of developing thiamin deficiency (Wang and Kies, 1991; Bates, 2001).

In industrialized countries, thiamin deficiency occurs almost exclusively in alcoholics, primarily due to poor diet with inadequate vitamin intake. Alcohol consumption also contributes to thiamin deficiency because it leads to degeneration of the intestinal wall and thus impairs absorption of the vitamin (Jeffrey, 1998; Suter, 2001).

Clinical effects of inadequate intake

Because thiamin deficiency in humans usually occurs in conjunction with decreased intake of other B vitamins, it is often difficult to attribute symptoms specifically to a lack of thiamin. However, early stages of thiamin deficiency include anorexia, weight loss, short-term memory loss, confusion, irritability, muscle weakness and enlarged heart. The deficiency of thiamin known as beriberi can present as two separate clinical entities; both wet and dry forms have been described. Wet beriberi is primarily characterized by edema and abnormalities of the cardiovascular system. Malnutrition and low levels of activity favor the development of dry beriberi, which is characterized by muscle wasting and principally affects the nervous system. The signs of beriberi are described in Table 7.4 (Food and Nutrition Board, 1998b).

The exact role of thiamin in nerve conduction in the peripheral nervous system is not known. The vitamin is found in nerve cell membranes and mitochondria, and in the form of the coenzyme TPP, may play a fundamental role in the control of sodium conductance at axonal membranes. Additionally, thiamin deficiency leads to axonal degeneration and demyelination of peripheral neurons. These changes contribute to the painful distal neuropathy experienced by patients with dry beriberi (Jeffrey, 1998; Bates, 2001).

Wernicke-Korsakoff syndrome is characterized by a wide range of neurological and psychological deficits, as well as a specific constellation of neuropathological damage. Most frequently Wernicke-Korsakoff syndrome is seen in chronic alcoholics who also present with clinical symptoms of malnutrition. In these patients, Wernicke-Korsakoff syndrome is a direct result of thiamin deficiency.

The early stage of the disease termed Wernicke's encephalopathy includes cognitive and psychomotor deficits (see Table 7.4). Following administration of thiamin, the mental symptoms of Wernicke's encephalopathy rapidly improve; however, the psychomotor aspects of the disease including nystagmus (involuntary rapid eye movements), ophthalmoplegia and ataxia may become more apparent. If the deficiency remains untreated,

Korsakoff's psychosis may develop, which is characterized by an inability to learn and to form new memories (anterograde amnesia), unpredictable loss of past memories, hallucinations and confabulation. Korsakoff's psychosis is only minimally or slowly responsive to thiamin administration. The rapidity of the response to thiamin depends upon the conversion of the vitamin to its active form in the liver. Thus, alcoholics with advanced liver disease, such as cirrhosis, have a delayed response to vitamin therapy (Jeffrey, 1998; Tanphaichitr, 1998; Bates, 2001).

CNS alterations associated with thiamin deficiency

Thiamin deficiency in both experimental animals and humans is associated with bilaterally symmetrical lesions throughout the brain, particularly in the thalamus, the hypothalamus, mammillary bodies, the midbrain, the brain stem and the cerebellum. Damage to the cere-

Table 7.4. Clinical manifestations of thiamin deficiency.

Beriberi	Wernicke-Korshakoff Syndrome
Wet: Enlargement of the heart, heartbeat irregularities, hypertension, edema, congestive heart failure.	Wernicke's encephalopathy: Anorexia, nystagmus (involuntary rapid eye movements), ophthalmoplegia (paralysis of the eye muscles) and ataxia (difficulty maintaining balance while walking). Apathy, inattentiveness, confusion, drowsiness and decreased spontaneity of speech.
Dry: Early signs: decreased initiative, increased irritability, inability to concentrate, fatigue and depression. Progressing to: peripheral neuropathy including bilateral symmetrical impairment of sensory, motor and reflex functions particularly the distal parts of the lower extremities. Paresthesias ('pins and needles') of the toes, followed by a burning sensation in the feet. Without treatment: decreased perception of light touch, loss of vibratory sense and normal reflexes, motor weakness and secondary muscle atrophy.	Korsakoff psychosis: Inability to learn and to form new memories (anterograde amnesia), unpredictable loss of past memories, hallucinations and confabulation.

Sources: Jeffrey, 1998; Tanphaichitr, 1998; Bates, 2001.

bellum and brain stem, both involved in the control of movement, are the probable basis for the ataxia and ophthalmoplegia characteristic of Wernicke's encephalopathy. Atrophy of the mammillary bodies and damage to thalamic nuclei are commonly observed and are hypothesized to be the primary cause of the memory deficits seen in the disorder. Atrophy of the cerebral cortex, abnormalities of cerebellar structure, enlargement of the cerebral ventricles and alterations in the myelin sheath surrounding neurons are also typical of Wernicke-Korsakoff syndrome. Purkinje cells, which are densely branching neurons found in the cerebral cortex are selectively vulnerable to thiamin deficiency. Loss of Purkinje cell density may contribute to the clinical signs of Wernicke's encephalopathy (Witt and Goldman-Rakic, 1983a,b; Victor et al., 1989; Baker et al., 1999).

Research on the effects of intermittent thiamin deficiency in rhesus monkeys has demonstrated that the number of damaged central nervous system structures increases with successive periods of thiamin deficiency (Witt and Goldman-Rakic, 1983a). Additionally, these researchers have observed significant correlations between the severity of neurological symptoms and the extent of neuroanatomical damage. These results indicate that the effects of thiamin deficiency are cumulative in the sense that clinical symptoms appear sooner with repetitions of the deficiency, and that the number of damaged central nervous system structures tends to increase with increasing periods of deficiency. These results emphasize the importance of early detection and treatment of thiamin deficiency.

Animal models of Wernicke-Korsakoff syndrome suggest that brain pathways utilizing particular neurotransmitters may be specifically damaged by thiamin deficiency. For example, thiamin deficiency reduces serotonin metabolism within the central nervous system. The development of neurological symptoms, particularly ataxia, thermoregulatory abnormalities and memory loss, have been attributed to changes in the functioning of serotonergic neurons in the cerebellum, brain stem and diencephalic structures. Following intermittent thiamin deficiency in monkeys, pathological changes are found predominantly in areas containing serotonergic neurons. Because these animals display a pattern of memory loss similar to that seen in patients with Wernicke-Korsakoff syndrome, it has been proposed that amnesia in these individuals results from a loss of serotonergic neurons (Witt and Goldman-Rakic, 1983b). Indeed, examination of the brains of deceased patients with Wernicke-Korsakoff syndrome revealed a profound loss of serotonin-containing neurons within functional zones of the cerebellum (Halliday et al., 1994).

Thiamin deficiency also leads to a reduction in the turnover of acetylcholine and thus alters the function of cholinergic neurons. Damage to central cholinergic systems may be responsible for motor deficits observed in thiamin-deficient animals. Cholinergic cell loss has also been described in alcoholics with Wernicke-Korsakoff syndrome and is associated with memory dysfunction in those individuals. However, cholinergic cell loss is also characteristic of other types of dementia such as Alzheimer's disease, and is not unique to patients with Wernicke-Korsakoff syndrome. Finally, whole brain and regional concentrations of three amino acid neurotransmitters, gamma-aminobutyric acid (GABA), glutamate and aspartate, are also decreased in the thiamin-deficient rat (Butterworth, 1993; Halliday et al., 1994; Jeffrey, 1998).

In conclusion, thiamin deficiency alters the activity of several neurotransmitter systems in the mammalian central nervous system. However, the association between these alterations in neurotransmitters and the damage found in the brains of thiamin-deficient individuals, remains poorly understood. The activity of four of these neurotransmitters, acetylcholine, GABA, glutamate and aspartate, is related to glucose metabolism in the brain. Thus, one theory suggests that thiamin deficiency reduces the activity of TPP-dependent enzymes, which leads to impaired cellular energy metabolism and neuronal cell death. Alternatively, dendritic and synaptic changes associated with thiamin deficiency may lead to alterations in neurotransmitter function within the central nervous system (Witt and Goldman-Rakic, 1983a,b; Haas, 1988; Butterworth, 1993; Halliday et al., 1994; Jeffrey, 1998).

Niacin (Vitamin B₃)

During the early part of the 20th century, large numbers of people in the southern USA suffered from a disease characterized by skin lesions, severe gastrointestinal disturbances and mental disabilities. The disease occurred predominantly among the poor and those in institutions where extremely limited diets were common. In severe cases, the prognosis was always unfavorable: death within 2 to 3 weeks. Although new to North America, this disease had long been known in Europe. Don Gaspar Casal, a physician in the Spanish court, first described the disease in 1735 as 'mal de la rosa' (sickness of the rose) because of a characteristic redness of the skin that worsened when patients were exposed to the sun. In 1770, the disease was noted in Italy and given the name 'pellagra', meaning rough skin. As in the USA, the disease in Europe was particularly common among the poor, whose dietary staple was corn. Corn is limiting in the amino acid tryptophan which the body converts to nicotinamide, contributing to the requirement for niacin (Cervantes-Laurean et al., 1998; Jacob, 2001).

Pellagra was identified as a major public health problem in the southern USA, where it affected more than 200,000 people per year. The endemic nature of the disease resulted in its becoming the focus of extensive investigations by the Public Health Service (PHS). Initial work concentrated on the possibility that an infectious agent or toxic substance in spoiled corn caused the disease. However, pioneering work by Joseph Goldberger of the PHS demonstrated that the disease was consistently associated with rural poverty and was the result of the lack of a critical dietary component. Due to the absence of an appropriate animal model for the disease, however, the dietary factor responsible for preventing or curing pellagra was not identified for 20 years. In 1937, Elvehjem, working at the University of Wisconsin, found that nicotinic acid was effective in curing black tongue, a condition in dogs similar to pellagra. Treatment of pellagra with nicotinic acid quickly led to dramatic improvements, with the number of pellagra victims in southern hospitals and mental institutions rapidly decreasing toward zero (Etheridge, 1972). Elmore and Feinstein (1994) give a fascinating account of the political context and social implications of Goldberger's work for improving public health nutrition.

Today, pellagra has virtually disappeared from industrialized countries, occurring primarily in alcoholics or individuals suffering from pancreatic disease. However, it continues to be a problem in many parts of the world, and is still encountered in India and parts of China and Africa. Pellagra is not found in South America or Mexico, although corn forms a major portion of the diet. In this part of the world, the traditional preparation of corn with alkalis (e.g. soda lime) liberates the niacin bound to protein, making it more available for absorption (Malfait et al., 1993; Jacob, 2001).

Functions, requirements and dietary sources

Nicotinic acid and nicotinamide are organic compounds with relatively simple chemical structures and equivalent biological activity. Niacin is the generic term that includes both forms of the vitamin. Niacin is required by all living cells. The vitamin is a component of two coenzymes; nicotinamide adenine dinucleotide (NAD), which is crucial for intracellular respiration and oxidation of fuel molecules such as lactate, pyruvate and α-ketoglutarate; and nicotinamide adenine dinucleotide phosphate (NADP), which plays an important role in the biosynthesis of fats and steroids (Cervantes-Laurean et al., 1998; Food and Nutrition Board, 1998c; Jacob, 2001).

Niacin is widely distributed in food with flesh foods being a rich source of the vitamin. Major dietary sources in the USA adult population come from poultry, mixed dishes high in meat, poultry or fish, enriched and whole-grain breads and bread products and ready-to-eat cereals (see Table 7.3). Additionally, the essential amino acid tryptophan serves as a major biosynthetic precursor for niacin. Most dietary proteins contain about 1% tryptophan, with approximately 60 mg of tryptophan yielding 1 mg of niacin or one niacin equivalent (NE). Thus, 6 g of protein would provide 60 mg of tryptophan or 1 NE.

Dietary requirements for niacin are expressed as niacin equivalents representing niacin itself plus that obtained from tryptophan. The dietary reference intake for niacin for men and women throughout adult life (19–70+ years of age) is 16 mg NE/day and 14 mg NE/day, respectively (Food and Nutrition Board, 1998c).

Clinical effects of inadequate intake

Pellagra is the clinical manifestation of severe niacin deficiency. The disease is characterized by a pigmented symmetrical rash that develops on areas of the body exposed to sunlight, changes in the digestive system and a bright red tongue. Chronic, severe niacin deficiency leads to neurological symptoms including irritability, sleeplessness, dizziness, loss of memory, confusion and signs of emotional instability. In advanced cases, hallucinations, delusions of persecution, severe depression and catatonia are observed. These latter symptoms are similar to those of schizophrenia. Indeed, many individuals diagnosed as schizophrenic and placed in mental institutions in the USA at the turn of the 20th century were probably suffering from pellagra. Niacin therapy leads to a rapid reversal of clinical symptoms (Cervantes-Laurean et al., 1998; Jeffrey, 1998; Jacob, 2001).

Physiological and biochemical correlates

Examination of the brains of chronic pellagra victims has revealed degeneration, especially in the large neurons of the motor cortex, brain stem and anterior horn of the spinal cord. Similar alterations have been found in the brains of dogs suffering from black tongue, which is also caused by niacin deficiency. These findings suggest that chronic niacin deficiency leads to permanent structural changes within the central nervous system (McIlwain and Bachelard, 1985).

Experimental pellagra has been induced in a variety of animals by feeding them diets low in niacin and tryptophan, or by the administra-

tion of the niacin antimetabolite 6-aminonicotinamide (6-AN). Several hours after the administration of 6-AN, mice exhibit paralysis and loss of motor control. Chronic treatment with 6-AN leads to degeneration of neurons and glial cells in adult animals. Studies with experimental animals have also revealed that niacin deficiency is associated with a reduction in brain levels of NAD and NADP. The reductions in these coenzymes that are critical for normal nutrient metabolism may contribute to the alterations in nervous system function associated with niacin deficiency (Lipton et al., 1979; McIlwain and Bachelard, 1985).

The exact mechanism by which niacin influences neuronal cells remains elusive. However, some studies have identified a role for poly (ADP-ribose) polymerase (PARP), a nuclear enzyme that participates in DNA repair, in neuronal functioning. PARP cleaves NAD into nicotinamide and ADP-ribose, permitting ADP-ribose to be transferred onto nuclear proteins at DNA strand breaks. However, excessive activation of PARP rapidly depletes stores of NAD, leading to cellular energy exhaustion and neuronal cell death. Increased activation of PARP typically follows traumatic brain injury such as stroke and neuro-degenerative insults such as Alzheimer's disease. Recent findings suggest that administration of nicotinamide preserves cellular energy reserves and protects against this catastrophic cell loss. Whether this mechanism explains the neural damage in niacin deficiency and pellagra is unclear. It is intriguing, however, that PARP knockout mice (genetically altered mice that lack the PARP gene) display a skin disease similar to the dermatitis of pellagra. This observation has led to the speculation that pellagra could result from niacin deficiency limiting PARP activity in neuronal cells (Cervantes-Laurean et al., 1998; Jacob, 2001).

Adverse effects and toxicity

There are no adverse effects of the consumption of naturally occurring niacin in food. Side effects of large therapeutic doses of nicotinic acid (i.e. 3 g/day) include flushing (burning, tingling, itching and a reddened flush on the face, arms and chest), pruritus, nausea, vomiting and headache. The niacin UL is set at 35 mg/day (Food and Nutrition Board, 1998c).

Pyridoxine (Vitamin B$_6$)

Functions, requirements and dietary sources

The terms pyridoxine or vitamin B$_6$ are used to denote a group of three related compounds, pyridoxine, pyridoxal and pyridoxamine. The active form of this vitamin is the coenzyme pyridoxal phosphate (PLP) which can be formed from any of the three compounds. PLP is the coenzyme for a large number of enzyme systems, most of which are involved in amino acid metabolism. For example, PLP is essential for the process of transamination in which the amino group (NH$_2$) from one amino acid is transferred to another substance, and for deamination, in which an amino group is removed so that protein, which is not necessary for growth can be used as energy. PLP is also required for decarboxylation, or the removal of carboxyl groups (COOH) from amino acids, which is a necessary step in the synthesis of several neurotransmitters including GABA, serotonin, norepinephrine and histamine. Further, pyridoxine is involved in several biochemical steps in the conversion of the amino acid tryptophan to niacin (Leklem, 1998; McCormick, 2001).

Pyridoxine is widely distributed in both plant and animal foods. Major sources of the nutrient in the US diet are fortified cereals, meats, poultry and fish as well as starchy vegetables and non-citrus fruits (see Table 7.3). Freezing can lead to a 15% to 70% decrease in the pyridoxine content of vegetables, and as much as 50% to 90% of the vitamin is lost in the milling of grains. The DRI for B$_6$ for adult men and women (19–50 years of age) is 1.3 mg/d. After 50 years of age, the requirement increases slightly to 1.7 mg/d and 1.5 mg/d for men and women, respectively (Food and Nutrition Board, 1998d).

Clinical effects of inadequate intake

The classic signs of B$_6$ deficiency include seborrheic dermatitis, microcytic anemia, elipti-form convulsions, depression and confusion. Microcytic anemia is the result of decreased hemoglobin synthesis. The first enzyme and committed step in heme biosynthesis uses PLP as a coenzyme. PLP also functions as a coenzyme for decarboxylases which are involved in the synthesis of several neuotransmitters including dopamine, serotonin and GABA. The levels of these neurotransmitters are reduced in B$_6$ depleted experimental animals (Dakshinamurti, 1982). Convincing evidence of the necessity of the vitamin for humans was shown in 1952 when infants were inadvertently fed an autoclaved commercial formula in which the B$_6$ content was not properly preserved. These infants were normal at birth and in good health until 8 to 16 weeks of age when they suddenly displayed nervous irritability and convulsive seizures. These symptoms, which were noted in more than 300 infants, were eliminated by pyridoxine treatment (Coursin, 1954). EEG abnormalities have also been noted in some young women fed low amounts of B$_6$ in a depletion–repletion study. These abnormalities promptly reversed themselves following adequate intake (Food and Nutrition Board, 1998d; Leklem, 1998).

Uncomplicated primary B$_6$ deficiency is rarely encountered in adults, since ingestion of diets with insufficient amounts of the vitamin would likely also lack adequate amounts of other B vitamins. Interactions between PLP and certain therapeutic agents could increase the need for B$_6$ as has been reported with the drug isoniazid which is used in the treatment of tuberculosis, and L-DOPA which is used in the treatment of Parkinson's disease. PLP also interacts with steroid hormones. Studies in the 1970s reported that the use of high-dose oral contraceptives was associated with decreased B$_6$ status indicators in women. This is not a problem today since the amount of estrogen used in oral contraceptives has been reduced 3–5 times (Food and Nutrition Board, 1998d; Leklem, 1998).

Adverse effects and toxicity

There are no adverse effects associated with high intakes of B$_6$ from foods. However, large oral doses of B$_6$ as dietary supplements have been used in the treatment of many conditions including carpal tunnel syndrome, and premenstrual syndrome. Daily intake of pyridoxine (>1g) can lead to peripheral sensory neuropathy and painful dermatological lesions. Schaumburg *et al.*, (1983) reported on seven adult patients consuming 2–6 g/day of pyridoxine for periods ranging from 2 to 40 months. All seven individuals initially experienced an unstable gait and numb feet. Numbness and clumsiness of the hands followed within several months. All patients had a 'stocking glove' distribution of sensory loss affecting all modalities (i.e. light touch, temperature, pinprick). Studies of nerve conduction indicated dysfunction of the distal portions of the sensory nerves, and nerve biopsies in two patients revealed widespread non-specific axonal degeneration. Neurological disabilities gradually improved once the supplements were discontinued. The UL for B_6 is 100 mg/day (Food and Nutrition Board, 1998d).

Cobalamin (Vitamin B_{12})

Until the 1920s pernicious anemia was a fatal disease of unknown origin with no known cure. In 1926, however, Minot and Murphy (cited in Weir and Scott, 1998) reported that feeding patients large amounts of liver (approximately a pound a day) could cure the anemia and prevent the neurological symptoms that accompanied the disease. In the same year, Castle (cited in Weir and Scott, 1998) set forth the hypothesis that an antipernicious anemia substance was formed by the combination of an extrinsic factor in food and an intrinsic factor in normal gastric secretion. It was subsequently shown that the extrinsic and intrinsic factors do not combine to form an antipernicious anemia substance, but rather that the intrinsic factor is necessary for intestinal absorption of the extrinsic factor. The search for the active substance in liver culminated in 1948 when scientists in the USA and England isolated a few micrograms of a red crystalline substance that was dramatically effective in the treatment of pernicious anemia. This substance, which was designated vitamin B_{12}, was found to be a complex molecule containing the mineral cobalt in its center. The presence of cobalt in the vitamin led to the term 'cobalamin'.

It is now known that B_{12} binds to intrinsic factor, a glycoprotein produced by the parietal cells of the stomach after stimulation with food, and forms a complex. The B_{12}-intrinsic factor complex attaches to specific receptors on the intestinal surface and becomes internalized. Lack of intrinsic factor leads to malabsorption of B_{12} and if this condition is left untreated, it leads to severe neurological deficit and life-threatening anemia (Weir and Scott, 1998; Stabler, 2001).

Functions, requirements and dietary sources

B_{12} functions as a coenzyme for a critical methyl transfer reaction that converts homocysteine to methionine. B_{12} also participates as a coenzyme in a second reaction that converts L-methymalonyl-coenzyme A (CoA) to succinyl-CoA, which is involved in the metabolism of fatty acids. The need for B_{12} is small as compared with the other B vitamins; the current DRI for adult men and women, 19 to 70+ years of age is 2.4 ug/day (Food and Nutrition Board, 1998e).

All vitamin B_{12} found in food is made by microorganisms. The vitamin is absent in plants except where they are contaminated by microorganisms (e.g. nodules on roots of legumes). Thus, B_{12} is obtained almost exclusively from foods of animal origin. As shown in Table 7.5, major sources of the vitamin include beef, mixed dishes with meat, fish or poultry as major ingredients, milk and milk products and fortified ready-to-eat cereals. No adverse effects of excess intake of B_{12} from foods or supplements have been identified (Food and Nutrition Board, 1998e).

B_{12} is continuously secreted in bile and in healthy individuals, is mostly reabsorbed and available for metabolic functions. Because the body can store B_{12}, deficiencies develop slowly even on a diet completely lacking the vitamin. It takes a number of years for B_{12} deficiency to develop in adults who are strict vegetarians (vegans) consuming no dairy products or eggs, as well as no meat. It is recommended that strict vegetarians take vitamin B_{12} supplements. Low B_{12} concentrations in human milk commonly occur in two situations; when the mother is a strict vegetarian or in developing

Table 7.5. Folate and vitamin B$_{12}$ content of selected foods (per serving).

Food	Serving	Folate (mcg)	Food	Serving	Vitamin B$_{12}$ (µg)
White rice, cooked	1 cup	222	Chicken liver	3 oz	14.85
Branflakes cereal	3/4 cup	170	Salmon, baked	3 oz	9.00
Spaghetti, cooked	1 cup	172	Tuna fish, canned	3 oz	2.54
Orange juice, fresh	1 cup	74	Roast beef	3 oz	2.47
Chickpeas, canned	1 cup	160	Cornflakes	1 cup	1.51
Green peas, frozen	1 cup	90	Milk, whole	1 cup	1.07
Spinach, raw	1 cup	58	Yogurt, low-fat w/fruit	8 oz	1.09
Melon	1 cup	34	Egg, fried	1 large	0.64
Banana	1 cup	30	Chicken breast, roasted	3 oz	0.30
Summer squash, raw	1 cup	33	Cheddar cheese	1 oz	0.24
Spaghetti sauce	1 cup	28	Chocolate ice cream	1/2 cup	0.19

Source: US Department of Agriculture, 2003.

countries where the usual consumption of animal products is low. Infants born to vegan mothers should be supplemented from birth because their initial stores are low and their mother's milk is unlikely to supply adequate amounts of the vitamin (Food and Nutrition Board, 1998e; Stabler, 2001).

Clinical effects of inadequate intake

B$_{12}$ deficiency in human beings is almost exclusively the result of limited intake and/or inadequate absorption. Pernicious anemia, which is the classic example of B$_{12}$ deficiency, usually develops because of decreased absorption of the vitamin due to a lack of the intrinsic factor, complete or partial removal of the stomach, atrophic gastritis, infection or pancreatic insufficiency. The underlying cause of the anemia is the interference with normal DNA synthesis in red blood cells, resulting in larger-than-normal erythrocytes (macrocytosis). These large, abnormally-shaped erythrocytes interfere with the ability of hemoglobin to carry oxygen to cells in the body. Clinically, the disease is characterized by pallor, fatigue, decreased exercise tolerance, shortness of breath and palpitations. These clinical symptoms are indistinguishable from those of folate deficiency (see following section). Gastrointestinal problems are also common including sore tongue, loss of appetite and constipation. The hematological symptoms of

B$_{12}$ deficiency are completely reversed with B$_{12}$ treatment (Weir and Scott, 1998; Stabler, 2001).

B$_{12}$ deficiency also has profound effects on the nervous system. Neurological complications are present in 75–90% of individuals with clinically observable B$_{12}$ deficiency. The neurological signs of deficiency include numbness and tingling in the hands and feet, diminution of vibratory and position senses, and poor motor coordination including ataxia. These changes result from demyelination of peripheral nerves. With continued B$_{12}$ deficiency, demyelination progresses gradually to include damage to the spinal cord and eventually the brain. Cognitive changes can include moodiness, loss of concentration, memory loss, confusion, depression, visual disturbances, insomnia and dementia. It was originally thought that the occurrence of neurological symptoms in the absence of anemia was rare. However, in about 25% of cases, patients suffering from B$_{12}$ deficiency display neuropsychiatric abnormalities without anemia. Furthermore, the occurrence of neurological symptoms is inversely correlated with the degree of anemia; individuals who are less anemic show more prominent neurological complications and vice versa (Jeffrey, 1998; Weir and Scott, 1998; Stabler, 2001).

The pathogenesis of neuropathy in B$_{12}$ deficiency is complex and poorly understood. However, some evidence points to a disruption in the activity of methionine synthase, the enzyme which regulates the conversion of homocysteine to methionine. B_{12} serves as a cofactor for this enzyme. In B_{12} deficiency, this pathway is inhibited, leading to a fall in the production of methionine (an essential amino acid for protein synthesis) and a net reduction in the availability of methyl groups for the synthesis of phospholipids and neurotransmitters. The demyelination of peripheral nerves observed in B_{12} deficiency might be associated with decreased synthesis of myelin basic proteins. More will be said shortly about the homocysteine-to-methionine conversion pathway as it relates to folate metabolism (Jeffrey, 1998; Weir and Scott, 1998; Stabler, 2001).

Aging. Aging is associated with a decrease in the absorption and digestion of food-bound B_{12} which may lead to a decline in B_{12} status among elderly individuals. One factor contributing to this decline may be atrophic gastritis, a condition that affects 10–30% of the elderly population and is responsible for low stomach acid secretion and the inability to digest food-bound B_{12}. However, laboratory studies of B_{12} absorption in the elderly are contradictory with some studies showing no difference in absorption of the vitamin between young and elderly subjects and other studies showing a reduction in B_{12} absorption with age. These discrepancies may be due in part, to the fact that absorption of cyanocobalamin, the form of the vitamin used in fortified foods and supplements, is not compromised in the elderly. A recent study in Southern California reported a prevalence of undiagnosed, untreated, pernicious anemia of 2% among free-living elderly individuals aged 60 years or more (Carmel, 1996). Based on these findings and the high prevalence of atrophic gastritis among older individuals, it is recommended that adults over the age of 50 consume foods fortified with B_{12}, or B_{12} supplements (Food and Nutrition Board, 1998e).

Folate

Folate was originally discovered in the 1930s during the search for the factor in liver responsible for its effectiveness in curing pernicious anemia. It was subsequently discovered that although folate cures megaloblastic anemia by stimulating the regeneration of red blood cells and hemoglobin, it is ineffective in relieving the neurological symptoms of pernicious anemia. Thus, it was concluded that folate was not the true antipernicious anemia factor. Subsequent work, however, has established that folate is necessary for the synthesis of essential nulceic acids, which in turn are required for normal cell division and replication (Herbert, 1998; Bailey *et al.*, 2001).

Functions, requirements and dietary sources

Folate is a generic term for a family of related compounds that function as coenzymes in numerous reactions in the body. These functions include DNA and purine synthesis, which is required for normal cell growth and division, and single-carbon transfers, which are involved in amino acid interconversions. Folate is required for the conversion of homocysteine to methionine. In this pathway (depicted in Fig. 7.1), the enzyme 5-10-methylene tetrahydrofolate reductase (MTHFR) converts 5-10-methylene tetrahydrofolate to 5-methyl tetrahydrofolate, liberating a methyl group that is used by homocysteine in the synthesis of methionine. As mentioned previously, B_{12} is a cofactor in this reaction. The homocysteine-to-methionine conversion is also responsible for maintaining of this pathway via the regeneration of the parent compound (tetrahydrofolate) and subsequent conversion to 5-10-methylene tetrahydrofolate. Because of the close interrelationship between folate and B_{12} in this pathway, deficiency of either vitamin leads to the accumulation of homocysteine in the blood and the same hematologic abnormalities that lead to megaloblastic anemia (Food and Nutrition Board, 1998f; Herbert, 1998; Bailey *et al.*, 2001).

There is strong evidence implicating inadequate folate intake in the development of neural tube defects (NTDs) in pregnancy and cardiovascular disease. Poor folate status has also been associated with a greater risk of cancer and psychiatric disorders. The role of folate in NTDs and psychiatric illness will be considered later in this chapter; cancer and cardio-

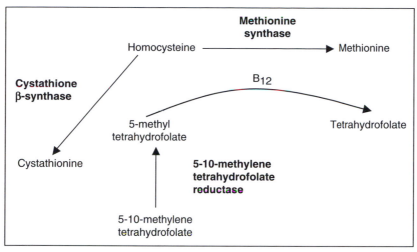

Fig. 7.1. Involvement of vitamin B_{12} and folate in the homocysteine-to-methionine conversion pathway. (Source: Food and Nutrition Board, 1998h.)

vascular disease are beyond the scope of this book.

Folate from food sources is assumed to be approximately 50% bioavailable. Folic acid is the form of the vitamin used in fortification and dietary supplements. It is estimated that 85% of folic acid is absorbed from supplements consumed with food and 100% from supplements consumed without food. The intake of other nutrients does not influence the requirement for folate although lower intake of the vitamin has been reported in alcoholics and smokers. Interactions between folate and certain medications have been reported including non-steroidal anti-inflammatory drugs (NSAIDS) at high doses, and methotrexate which is used in the treatment of rheumatoid arthritis. The DRI for folate for adults (19 to 70 yrs) has been set at 400 µg/day dietary folate equivalents. Dietary folate equivalents are a way to express the mixed bioavailablity of naturally-occurring folate from food and folic acid from fortified foods and supplements (Food and Nutrition Board, 1998f).

Although folate is found in a wide variety of foods, cooking and storage can lead to significant losses of the vitamin. In addition, food composition tables underestimate the folate content in food because the traditional method of folate analysis (on which the food database was derived) failed to extract all the folate from the food matrix. New methods of analysis, which can precisely measure total folate content of foods, will eventually be used to update the foods database. These factors make it difficult to determine the actual amount of the vitamin consumed in the diet. However, data collected during the 1990s indicate that the intake of folate in the US population is low. Among women of child-bearing age in particular, dietary intake of folate was approximately half of the current DRI. In 1998, the USA began a program of mandatory fortification of all cereal grains with folate. This strategy was adopted, in part, to help women of child-bearing age to increase their intake of folate and reduce the risk of NTDs. Recent data estimate that folate intake has increased twofold since fortification began (Choumenkovitch *et al.*, 2002). Fortified, ready-to-eat cereals and vegetables (excluding dark green types) are the major sources of food folate in the population (see Table 7.5) (Food and Nutrition Board, 1998f).

Adverse effects and toxicity

Although folic acid corrects the hematological changes associated with B_{12} deficiency, it not only fails to alleviate the degeneration of nervous tissue, but it may accentuate the changes.

Thus, the use of folic acid supplements by B_{12} deficient individuals may be dangerous, allowing severe and irreversible nervous system symptoms to progress undetected. In addition, high doses of the vitamin consumed as dietary supplements may have toxic consequences including irritability, excitability, sleep disturbances and gastrointestinal upsets. No adverse effects have been associated with amounts of folic acids present in fortified foods. The folate UL for adults from fortified foods and supplements (combined) is 1000 µg/day (Food and Nutrition Board, 1998f).

Neural tube defects

Neural tube defects (NTDs) are the most common congenital malformations of the central nervous system with an incidence rate, worldwide of <1 to 9 per 1000 births. NTDs arise from a failure of the embryonic process of neurulation – closure of the neural tube. Closure of the neural tube begins separately and consecutively in at least three sites: the cervical hindbrain boundary, the forebrain–midbrain boundary and the rostral extremity of the forebrain. In the human embryo, neurulation begins at approximately 21 days post-fertilization and is complete by 28 days. Thus, the critical period for neurulation is short, occurring before a woman may be aware that she is pregnant. The abnormalities associated with NTDs vary in severity; some are fatal whereas others can be corrected with surgery or managed with medical care. Different forms of NTDs could arise at different times during neurulation by specific mechanisms that are poorly understood (Food and Nutrition Board, 1998f; Jeffrey, 1998).

Convincing evidence that folic acid was protective against the development of NTDs came from a double-blind study conducted in the early 1980s among pregnant women who had previously given birth to a child with a NTD. Women were randomly assigned to groups; one group received 4 mg/day folic acid and the other group received a mixture of other vitamins. Women receiving folic acid had a 72% reduction in risk of giving birth to a child with NTDs (MRC Vitamin Study Research Group, 1991).

The etiology of NTDs is complex with both heredity and nutritional status playing contributing roles. The heritability of NTDs is thought to be 60% with a 3–5% risk of recurrence in a sibling birth (Food and Nutrition Board, 1998f). Recent studies have shown a mutation in the gene which codes for the enzyme MTHFR in mothers of children with NTDs. The reader will recall that MTHFR is a critical enzyme in the metabolism of homocysteine to methionine (see Fig. 7.1). The variant of this gene (T^{677}) produces MTHFR with reduced enzymatic activity that is associated with elevated plasma homocysteine concentrations. However, the effect of this gene variant on homocysteine levels is dependent on folate. Individuals with low folate status who homozygously express the T^{677} mutation display lower MTHFR activity and higher plasma homocysteine concentrations. Conversely, individuals with good folate status can overcome the destabilizing effects of the mutation on the enzyme; these individuals do not show elevated homocysteine levels (Food and Nutrition Board, 1998f,g; Bailey et al., 2001).

A recent study on NTDs underscores the importance of examining gene–nutrient interactions when assessing the risk of disease in the population. The risk of NTDs was 5-fold higher in women who were homozygous for the T^{677} mutation if they did not use vitamin supplements; the risk was not increased if they did use supplements (Botto and Mulinare, 1999).

The emerging field of nutrigenomics should be mentioned as a side note to this discussion. Nutrigenomics is the study of the effects of nutrients on gene expression. Although our understanding of gene–nutrient relationships is limited at present, the field is rapidly advancing. New discoveries in nutrigenomics will provide a better understanding of disease prevalence in genetically-diverse population groups and could ultimately lead to the development of individualized and more effective treatments (Muller and Kersten, 2003).

Associations with other psychiatric disorders

A variety of observations suggest that folic acid deficiency may also have significant effects on behavior. For example, studies have shown that anticonvulsant-induced folate deficiency is associated with a higher than usual incidence of psychiatric symptoms including depression and psychotic behavior. It is impossible, however, to establish a cause-and-effect relationship from this association since higher intakes of anticonvulsant medications, which cause greater inhibition of folate absorption, may be the cause of some symptoms. Other studies have found that in medical patients with folic acid deficiency, psychiatric symptoms including irritability, hostility and paranoia occur more frequently. In psychiatric patients, these same symptoms are more severe in those with low serum folate than in those with normal levels of the vitamin (Food and Nutrition Board, 1998f).

Finally, some studies have suggested that folic acid may lead to improvements in neuropsychological functioning and in symptoms of affective disorder. A double-blind, placebo-controlled study found that treatment with methylfolate significantly improved the clinical and social recovery of both depressed and schizophrenic patients (Godfrey et al., 1990). The benefits of the vitamin over the placebo increased gradually over time, in keeping with the view that the response of the nervous system to folate occurs slowly. Improvements in psychological functioning have not been universally documented, however, particularly when high doses of the vitamin have been used (Food and Nutrition Board, 1998f).

Conclusion

It is clear that vitamins play a significant role in the functioning of the nervous system and behavior. Vitamins are important in the synthesis of neurotransmitters, maintenance of neuronal integrity, myelination of neurons and conduction of electrical potentials. Vitamin deficiencies can result in neurological and psychological problems ranging from impairments of sensory and motor functioning to overt psychotic behavior. Observations that vitamin deficiencies are associated with alterations in the central nervous system and behavior that can be reversed by vitamin administration have led to the idea that increased intake may be useful in the treatment of a variety of psychological disorders. However,

as was already seen in Chapter 5 on dietary supplements for the treatment of behavioral illnesses, the evidence for this idea is controversial.

References

Bailey, L., Moyers, S. and Gregory, J. III (2001) Folate. In: Bowman, B. and Russell, R. (eds), *Present Knowledge in Nutrition*, 8th edn., International Life Sciences Institute Press, Washington, DC, pp. 214–229.

Baker, K., Harding, A., Halliday, G., Kril, J. and Harper, C. (1999) Neuronal loss in functional zones of the cerebellum of chronic alcoholics with and without Wernicke's encephalopathy. *Neuroscience* 91, 429–438.

Bates, C. (2001) Thiamin. In: Bowman, B. and Russell, R. (eds), *Present Knowledge in Nutrition*, 8th edn., International Life Sciences Institute Press.

Botto, L. and Mulinare, J. (1999) Maternal vitamin use, genetic variation in methylenetetrahydrofolate reductase and risk for spina bifida. *American Journal of Epidemiology* 150, 323–324.

Butterworth, R. (1993) Pathophysiology of cerebellar dysfunction in the Wernicke-Korsakoff syndrome. *Canadian Journal of Neurological Sciences* 20(Suppl. 3), S123–126.

Carmel, R. (1996) Prevalence of undiagnosed pernicious anemia in the elderly. *Archives of Internal Medicine* 156, 1097–1100.

Cervantes-Laurean, D., McElvaney, N. and Moss, J. (1998) Niacin. In: Shils, M., Olson, J., Shike, M. and Ross A. (eds), *Modern Nutrition in Health and Disease*, 9th edn. Lippincott Williams & Wilkins, Philadelphia, pp. 401–411.

Choumenkovitch, S., Selhub, J., Wilson, P., Rader, J., Rosenberg, I. and Jacques, P. (2002) Folic acid intake from fortification in United States exceeds predictions. *Journal of Nutrition* 32, 2792–2798.

Coursin, D. (1954) Convulsive seizures in infants with pyridoxine-deficient diets. *Journal of the American Medical Association* 154, 406–408.

Dakshinamurti, K. (1982) Neurobiology of Pyridoxine. *Advances in Nutrition Research* 4, 143–179.

Elmore, J. and Feinstein, A. (1994) Joseph Goldberger: an unsung hero of American clinical epidemiology. *Annals of Internal Medicine* 121, 372–375.

Etheridge, E.W. (1972) The butterfly caste: a social history of Pellagra in the South. Greenwood, Westport, Connecticut.

Food and Nutrition Board, Institute of Medicine, National Academy of Sciences (1998a) Introduction to Dietary Reference Intakes.

Dietary Reference Intakes for Thiamin, Riboflavin, Niacin, Vitamin B6, Folate, Vitamin B12, Pantothenic Acid, Biotin and Choline. National Academy Press, Washington, DC, pp. 17–26.

Food and Nutrition Board, Institute of Medicine, National Academy of Sciences (1998b) Thiamin. Dietary Reference Intakes for Thiamin, Riboflavin, Niacin, Vitamin B6, Folate, Vitamin B12, Pantothenic Acid, Biotin and Choline. National Academy Press, Washington, DC, pp. 58–86

Food and Nutrition Board, Institute of Medicine, National Academy of Sciences (1998c) Niacin. Dietary Reference Intakes for Thiamin, Riboflavin, Niacin, Vitamin B6, Folate, Vitamin B12, Pantothenic Acid, Biotin and Choline. National Academy Press, Washington, DC, pp. 123–149.

Food and Nutrition Board, Institute of Medicine, National Academy of Sciences (1998d) Vitamin B6. Dietary Reference Intakes for Thiamin, Riboflavin, Niacin, Vitamin B6, Folate, Vitamin B12, Pantothenic Acid, Biotin and Choline. National Academy Press, Washington, DC, pp. 150–195.

Food and Nutrition Board, Institute of Medicine, National Academy of Sciences (1998e) Vitamin B12. Dietary Reference Intakes for Thiamin, Riboflavin, Niacin, Vitamin B6, Folate, Vitamin B12, Pantothenic Acid, Biotin and Choline. National Academy Press, Washington, DC, pp. 306–356.

Food and Nutrition Board, Institute of Medicine, National Academy of Sciences (1998f) Folate. Dietary Reference Intakes for Thiamin, Riboflavin, Niacin, Vitamin B6, Folate, Vitamin B12, Pantothenic Acid, Biotin and Choline. National Academy Press, Washington, DC, pp. 196–305.

Food and Nutrition Board, Institute of Medicine, National Academy of Sciences (1998g) Methylenetetrahydrofolate Reductase (Appendix L). Dietary Reference Intakes for Thiamin, Riboflavin, Niacin, Vitamin B6, Folate, Vitamin B12, Pantothenic Acid, Biotin and Choline. National Academy Press, Washington, DC, pp. 520–522.

Food and Nutrition Board, Institute of Medicine, National Academy of Sciences (1998h) Dietary Reference Intakes for Thiamin, Riboflavin, Niacin, Vitamin B6, Folate, Vitamin B12, Pantothenic Acid, Biotin and Choline. National Academy Press, Washington, DC, p. 244.

Godfrey, P., Toone, B., Carney, M., Flynn, T., Bottiglieri, T., Laundy, M., Chanarin, I. and Reynolds, E. (1990) Enhancement of recovery from psychiatric illness by methylfolate. Lancet 336, 392–395.

Haas, R. (1988) Thiamin and the brain. Annual Review of Nutrition 8, 483–515.

Halliday, G., Cullen, K. and Harding, A. (1994) Neuropathological correlates of memory dysfunction in the Wernicke-Korsakoff syndrome. Alcohol Alcohol Supplement 2, 245–251.

Herbert, V. (1998) Folic Acid. In: Shils, M., Olson, J., Shike, M. and Ross A. (eds), Modern Nutrition in Health and Disease, 9th edn. Lippincott Williams & Wilkins, Philadelphia, pp. 433–446.

Jacob, R. (2001) Niacin. In: Bowman, B. and Russell, R. (eds), Present Knowledge in Nutrition, 8th edn. International Life Sciences Institute Press, pp. 199–206.

Jeffrey, D. (1998) Nutrition and diseases of the nervous system. In: Shils, M., Olson, J., Shike, M. and Ross, A. (eds), Modern Nutrition in Health and Disease, 9th edn. Lippincott Williams & Wilkins, Philadelphia, pp. 1543–1554.

Leklem, J. (1998) Vitamin B6. In: Shils, M., Olson, J., Shike, M. and Ross, A. (eds), Modern Nutrition in Health and Disease, 9th edn. Lippincott Williams & Wilkins, Philadelphia, pp. 413–421.

Lipton, M.A., Mailman, R. and Nemeroff, C. (1979) Vitamins, megavitamin therapy, and the nervous system. In: Wurtman, R. and Wurtman, J. (eds), Nutrition and the Brain, Vol. 3. Raven Press, New York, pp. 183–264.

Malfait, P., Moren, A., Dillon, J., Brodel, A., Begkoyian, G., Etchegorry, M., Malenga, G. and Hakewell, P. (1993) An outbreak of pellagra related to changes in dietary niacin among Mozambican refugees in Malawi. International Journal of Epidemiology 22, 504–511.

McCormick, D. (2001) Vitamin B-6. In: Bowman, B. and Russell, R. (eds), Present Knowledge in Nutrition, 8th edn. International Life Sciences Institute Press, pp. 207–213.

McGready, R., Simpson, J., Cho, T., Dubowitz, L., Changbumrung, S., Bohm, V., Munger, R., Sauberlich, H., White, N. and Nosten, F. (2001) Postpartum thiamine deficiency in a Karen displaced population. American Journal of Clinical Nutrition 74, 808–813.

McIlwain, H. and Bachelard, H. (1985) Biochemistry and the Central Nervous System. Churchill Livingstone, New York.

MRC Vitamin Study Research Group (1991) Prevention of neural tube defects: results of the Medical Research Council Vitamin Study. Lancet 338, 131–137.

Muller, M. and Kersten, S. (2003) Nutrigenomics: goals and strategies. Nature Reviews Genetics 4, 315–322.

Schaumburg, H., Kaplan, J., Windbank, A., Vick, N., Rasmus, S., Pleasure, D. and Brown, M. (1983) Sensory neuropathy from pyridoxine abuse. *New England Journal of Medicine* 309, 445–448.

Stabler, S. (2001) Vitamin B-12. In: Bowman, B. and Russell, R. (eds), *Present Knowledge in Nutrition*, 8th edn International Life Sciences Institute Press, Washington, DC, pp. 230–240.

Suter, P. (2001) Alcohol. In: Bowman, B. and Russell, R. (eds), *Present Knowledge in Nutrition*, 8th edn International Life Sciences Institute Press, Washington, DC, pp. 497–507.

Tanphaichitr, V. (1998) Thiamin. In: Shils, M., Olson, J., Shike, M., and Ross, A. (eds), *Modern Nutrition in Health and Disease*, 9th edn. Lippincott Williams & Wilkins, Philadelphia, pp. 381–389.

USDA (2003) *National Nutrient Database for Standard Reference, Release 16. Nutrient Data Laboratory Home Page*. USA Department of Agriculture, Agricultural Research Service. Available at: http://www.nal.usda.gov/fnic/foodcomp

Victor, M., Adams, R. and Collins, G. (1989) The Wernicke-Korsakoff Syndrome and related neurological disorders due to alcoholism and malnutrition, 2nd edn. FA Davis, Philadelphia.

Wang, R. and Kies, C. (1991) Niacin, thiamin, iron and protein status of humans as affected by the consumption of tea (Camellia sinensis) infusions. *Plant Foods in Human Nutrition* 41, 337–353.

Weir, D. and Scott, J. (1998) Vitamin B12 Cobalamin. In: Shils, M., Olson, J., Shike, M., and Ross, A. (eds), *Modern Nutrition in Health and Disease*, 9th edn. Lippincott Williams & Wilkins, Philadelphia, pp. 447–458.

Witt, E. and Goldman-Rakic, P. (1983a) Intermittent thiamine deficiency in the rhesus monkey: Part I. Progression of neurological signs and neuroanatomical lesions. *Annals of Neurology* 13, 376–395.

Witt, E. and Goldman-Rakic, P. (1983b) Intermittent thiamine deficiency in the rhesus monkey: Part II. Evidence for memory loss. *Annals of Neurology* 13, 396–401.

8 Minerals, the Central Nervous System and Behavior

B.J. Tepper

Awareness that small amounts of inorganic compounds are imperative for normal growth began over a century ago when it was recognized that iron, copper and zinc were essential for the maturation of plants and microorganisms. Further evidence of the importance of minerals for animal nutrition was subsequently derived from two major sources: basic studies on the effects of specially formulated diets, low or high in a specific mineral, on growth and reproduction in animals; and the realization that a number of endemic diseases of man and animals resulted from mineral deficiencies.

A large number of mineral elements are found in living cells; however, not all minerals are considered essential. Essential minerals participate in functions that are vital for life, growth or reproduction. When an essential mineral is removed from the diet, a deficiency syndrome develops. Improvement in growth or health occurs when these minerals are included in the diet.

Essential minerals are divided into *macronutrient* elements, which are present in relatively high amounts in animal tissues (>0.005% body weight), and *micronutrients* or trace elements, which are present in extremely small amounts (<0.005% body weight). For humans, the essential macronutrient elements, in order of the amounts found in the body, are calcium, phosphorous, potassium, sulfur, sodium, chlorine and magnesium. Trace elements presently recognized as necessary and

nutritionally important to humans include iron, iodine, copper, zinc, selenium, chromium, manganese, molybdenum and cobalt. Other trace elements are known to be biologically important but are not considered essential because their precise biochemical function is not known. Elements such as boron, nickel and silicon fall into this latter class.

Biological Functions of Minerals

Minerals serve a variety of critical functions. They are necessary constituents of a number of enzymes, such as iron in the catalases and cytochromes; of hormones, such as iodine in thyroxine; of vitamins, such as cobalt in vitamin B_{12}; and of body tissues, such as calcium and phosphorous in bone and teeth. Minerals also act as catalysts or cofactors for biological reactions; they are necessary for the absorption of nutrients from the gastrointestinal tract and the uptake of nutrients by cells. Lastly, minerals help to maintain the acid-base balance in the body as well as regulate the physiology of cell membranes (Yip, 2001).

Major minerals and the central nervous system

Minerals such as sodium, potassium and calcium are vital for the normal functioning of

©J. Worobey, B.J. Tepper and R.B. Kanarek 2006. *Nutrition and Behavior: A Multidisciplinary Approach* (J. Worobey, B.J. Tepper and R.B. Kanarek)

the nervous system. Like all living cells, nerve cells maintain an electric gradient across the membrane. At rest, the inside of the cell is slightly negatively charged relative to the outside of the cell, which is slightly positively charged. This electrical gradient is regulated by the action of the sodium–potassium pump, which controls the movement of positively charged ions of sodium (Na+) and potassium (K+) through specific channels in the membrane. The Na+–K+ pump pushes Na+ into the extracellular fluid at a slightly higher rate than it permits K+ to cross into the cell. The net effect of this movement (as well as the contribution of other ion fluxes) is the accumulation of more positive charge on the outside of the membrane (Erlij, 1998; Purves et al., 2001).

When a nerve impulse is generated, the permeability of the membrane is momentarily altered. Ion channels, which are selectively permeable to Na+ and K+ open, allowing the rapid flux of Na+ into the cell and K+ out of the cell. This leads to a temporary change in the electrical charge on the membrane (i.e. depolarization), generating an action potential. This charge then alters the permeability of the next portion of the membrane, which in turn changes the electrical charge in that portion of the membrane, and so on. Thus, the nerve impulse is passed down the fiber (Erlij, 1998; Purves et al., 2001). See Chapter 4 for a general description of the anatomy and physiology of the nerve cell. An animation of these events can also be viewed on the internet at http://www.blackwellpublishing.com/matthews/channel.html.

When a nerve impulse reaches the synapse or end terminal of a nerve fiber, it triggers the release of a neurotransmitter, which then crosses the synaptic space to activate a second nerve fiber. We can illustrate this process using the neurotransmitter glutamate as an example. The action of glutamate is dependent on the presence of calcium ions (Ca^{2+}) in the extracellular fluid. As we have already seen for Na+ and K+, specialized pumps actively remove Ca^{2+} from cells so that the concentration of Ca^{2+} is much higher on the outside of cells than on the inside of cells. Glutamate binds directly to these channels causing them to open. The momentary influx of Ca^{2+} shifts the permeability of the membrane generating an action potential in the second neuron (Hille, 1992; Purves et al., 2001).

It should be clear from this discussion that the neural circuitry is regulated by processes that are critically sensitive to the presence of minute concentrations of minerals in the fluids surrounding nerve cells. Factors that modify the concentrations of these ions can disrupt the integrity of neuronal membranes and interfere with the transmission of nerve impulses.

Neither sodium nor potassium deficiency is a common nutritional problem. Nevertheless, sodium deficiency or hyponatremia can occur in a variety of medical conditions. These include chronic wasting diseases, such as cancer, liver disease, semi-starvation and ulcerative colitis; major surgical treatment or extensive trauma; as a result of abnormal external loss of sodium without adequate replacement including gastrointestinal losses due to diarrhea or vomiting; excessive sweating; and as the result of severe dietary restriction (McLaren, 1998; Oh and Uribarri, 1998).

Potassium deficiency or hypokalemia is often associated with abnormal food intake such as occurs in severe malnutrition, anorexia nervosa, chronic alcoholism and low carbohydrate diets for weight reduction. Additionally, surgical trauma or any condition that reduces the availability of nutrients for absorption, such as prolonged vomiting and diarrhea, can lead to potassium depletion. Hypokalemia can have profound effects on neural functioning and can alter neuronal connections to both smooth and cardiac muscles (McLaren, 1998; Oh and Uribarri, 1998).

Calcium deficiency in otherwise healthy individuals is insufficient to produce nervous system abnormalities. However, calcium deficiency or hypocalcemia has been associated with hypoparathyroidisim, chronic renal failure and the intake of certain drugs such as tetracycline antibiotics, which bind calcium and make it unavailable for use. Symptoms of hypocalcemia include depression and psychosis progressing to dementia or encephalopathy; neuromuscular irritability; and tetany consisting of parasthesias of the lips and spasm of the facial muscles and extremities (McLaren, 1998; Oh and Uribarri, 1998).

Trace minerals and the central nervous system

It has been well established that trace elements including iron, zinc, selenium and iodine are important for normal functioning of the nervous system. These micronutrients are crucial for normal growth and maintenance of the nervous system and deficiencies of these elements can lead to a variety of cognitive and behavioral deficits. As detailed in the following sections, iron deficiency can lead to apathy, fatigue and diminished cognitive performance, whereas zinc deficiency is accompanied by anorexia and mood changes. Finally, iodine deficiency during neonatal development results in permanent damage to the central nervous system (CNS) and severe mental retardation.

Iron (Fe)

Iron is found in all cells and is crucial for many biochemical reactions in the body. Its primary role is to facilitate the transfer of oxygen and carbon dioxide across tissues. Most of the body's iron is found in hemoglobin, the principal component of red blood cells. Hemoglobin combines with oxygen in the lungs and releases oxygen in the tissues whenever a need exists. Hemoglobin also aids in the return of carbon dioxide from tissues to the lungs. In muscle tissue, oxygen is taken up by another iron-protein complex, myoglobin, which serves as a temporary oxygen acceptor and reservoir. Cytochromes are heme-containing compounds that are critical for cellular respiration and energy metabolism. In addition to its role in oxygen transport, iron is a structural component or a cofactor for a number of enzymes which neutralize oxidative damage to cells (such as the peroxidases) or participate in DNA synthesis, neurotransmitter synthesis and degradation (Fairbanks, 1998; Yip, 2001). Unless otherwise stated, information on iron requirements and metabolism in the following section is drawn from Fairbanks (1998) and Yip (2001).

Requirements and dietary sources of iron

The total amount of iron in the body varies as a function of age, gender, weight, hemoglobin mass and size of the organs that store iron. The average body content of iron in adult males is typically 4.0 g; and in adult females, 2.5 g. Over two-thirds of the iron in the body is contained in the functional pool in the form of hemoglobin, myoglobin and tissue enzymes; or in blood (bound to the protein transferrin). The remaining one-third is stored in the liver, spleen and bone marrow as ferritin, a soluble iron complex, or hemosiderin, an insoluble iron-protein complex.

The normal adult male must assimilate about 1 mg of iron a day to balance the natural losses that occur via the gastrointestinal tract, urinary system and skin. As a result of the blood lost in menstruation, women must absorb 1.5 mg of iron a day. Estimating the iron adequacy of the diet by tabulating the iron content of foods can be misleading since only a portion of the iron present in food can be assimilated. The bioavailability of iron, that is, the amount that is absorbed and utilized is influenced by a number of factors including the composition of the diet and the iron status of the individual.

Absorption of heme and non-heme iron

Iron is present in food as part of heme, found in muscle fibers such as meats, poultry and fish and as non-heme iron, found in dairy products and plant foods. The iron from meat is well-absorbed and is little affected by dietary factors. In contrast, the iron from plant foods is poorly assimilated and is strongly influenced by gastrointestinal and dietary factors. This is because ingested, non-heme iron is insoluble. In order to absorb non-heme iron, it must combine with acid gastric juice, which both liberates and stabilizes the iron. Thus, changes in the acidity of the stomach can play an important role in the absorption of iron. The consumption of ascorbic acid (vitamin C) in a plant-based meal can increase iron absorption twofold. Conversely, decreased stomach acidity due to overuse of antacids can reduce iron absorption.

Phytates associated with the fiber in legumes, rice, grains and nuts inhibit the absorption of non-heme iron because they combine with iron to form insoluble compounds that pass through the intestinal tract without being absorbed. Drinking coffee or tea with a meal also decreases iron absorption by

40% and 60% respectively, due to the presence of iron-binding substances called polyphenols in these beverages. Interestingly, the absorption of iron from plant foods is more efficient when these foods are consumed with meats than when eaten alone. Cooking methods also influence iron availability. Iron is lost from foods if they are cooked in large amounts of water, which is subsequently discarded. In contrast, the use of cast-iron cookware can add to daily iron intake. Finally, an individual's iron status alters iron absorption. Iron-deficient individuals are twice as efficient in absorbing iron than non-deficient individuals.

Although heme iron is approximately 2–3 times better absorbed than non-heme iron, the majority of iron consumed in typical mixed diets in the USA and Canada is predominantly in the non-heme form. Therefore, for the purposes of setting the dietary requirement for iron, the bioavailability of ingested iron from mixed diets is estimated to be 18%. The bioavailability of iron from a vegetarian diet is approximately half that of a mixed diet (~10%). Thus, vegetarians may have difficulty consuming adequate iron (Food and Nutrition Board, 2000a).

Dietary sources

Liver is an excellent dietary source for iron, however, it is not a popular food for many individuals and has recently fallen into disfavor because of its high cholesterol content. Other good sources of iron include lean meats, shellfish and poultry. Eggs, green leafy vegetables, whole-grain cereals and fruits provide progressively less absorbable iron (see Table 8.1) (Food and Nutrition Board, 2000a).

Current dietary patterns may be having a negative impact on iron status. Approximately half the iron in the average American diet is from bread or grain products from which iron is poorly absorbed. The consumption of pizza, snack foods and soft drinks is increasing, but these foods provide negligible iron to the diet. Efforts have been made to improve the iron adequacy of Westernized diets through iron enrichment of bread and flour. However, elemental iron, the type of iron used for fortification is poorly absorbed and provides little benefit. This practice has been discontinued in several European countries (Fairbanks, 1998).

Table 8.1. Iron content of selected foods (per serving).

Food	Serving	Iron (mg)
Cornflakes enriched	1 cup	8.4
Beef liver	3 oz	5.2
Green peas	1 cup	3.2
Raisins	1 cup	2.7
Ground beef	3 oz	2.2
White rice	1 cup	1.9
Tuna fish	3 oz	1.3
Green beans	1 cup	1.2
Chicken	3 oz	1.0
Whole-wheat bread	1 slice	0.9
Fried egg	1 large	0.9
Baked potato	1 medium	0.6
Tomatoes	1 cup	0.5
Cheddar cheese	1 oz	0.2

Source: USDA, 2003.

Outcomes have been different in certain South American countries where iron-deficiency anemia is widespread. In Venezuela, for example, a program of iron fortification of flour reduced iron-deficiency anemia by half in less than 2 years (Layrisse *et al.*, 1996).

Requirements across the lifecycle

During periods of rapid growth and development, the need for iron increases. The iron 'cost' of pregnancy is particularly high. Pregnant women require supplemental iron to make up for normal losses, the increased demand due to the enlargement in red cell mass that accompanies pregnancy, and the requirements of the fetus and placenta. These increased needs develop primarily during the last half of pregnancy, when the fetus is growing most rapidly and iron requirements can reach 5–6 mg/day. As this amount cannot be supplied by diet alone, iron stores in the body are utilized to prevent the development of maternal iron deficiency. Iron supplementation is necessary during pregnancy to offset the risk of iron-deficiency anemia, which is high during the third trimester of pregnancy.

Infants of mothers who consume adequate iron during pregnancy are born with iron stores sufficient to meet their needs for approximately the first 6 months of life. Thereafter, iron needs of infants increase to keep pace with the demands of rapid development. When one considers normal losses and the demands of rapid growth, the iron requirement for an infant at 6 months of age approaches that estimated for an adult male. This increased demand for iron persists in older infants and toddlers between the ages of 9 and 18 months who are highly vulnerable to iron deficiency.

The growth spurt of puberty represents another critical period of iron need for both male and female adolescents. Throughout the childbearing years, women maintain a greater demand for iron due to loss from the menses. If women of childbearing age do not maintain adequate stores of iron they are at increased risk of developing iron deficiency during pregnancy. RDAs for iron according to life stage and gender are shown in Table 8.2. Iron requirements from early childhood through adolescence are in the general range of 7–15 mg/day. The RDA for adults is 8 mg/day, increasing to 18 mg/day for women of childbearing age (Food and Nutrition Board, 2000a).

Although the risk of adverse effects of iron from dietary sources is low, high intake of iron supplements by adults is associated with gastrointestinal effects including constipation, nausea, vomiting and diarrhea. Children, on the other hand, are highly susceptible to acute iron toxicity from the inadvertent ingestion of iron tablets intended for adults. Accidental iron overdose is the most common cause of poisoning deaths in children under 6 years of age. Symptoms include damage to the gastrointestinal tract, kidneys, liver, CNS and hematological defects. The upper limit (UL) for adults and children is 45 mg/day and 40 mg/day, respectively (Food and Nutrition Board, 2000a).

Iron deficiency

Iron deficiency can be categorized in three stages ranging from mild to severe. The first stage involves depletion of iron stores and is evidenced by a decrease in the concentration of serum ferritin. During the second stage,

Table 8.2. Dietary reference intakes for iron, zinc and iodine.

Life stage category		Iron (mg/d)	Zinc (mg/d)	Iodine (µg/d)
Infants	0–6 months	0.27	2	110
	7–12 months	11	3	130
Children	1–3 years	7	3	90
	4–8 years	10	5	90
Males	9–13 years	8	8	120
	14–18 years	11	11	150
	19–30 years	8	11	150
	31–50 years	8	11	150
	51–70 years	8	11	150
	>70 years	8	11	150
Females	9–13 years	8	8	120
	14–18 years	15	9	150
	19–30 years	18	8	150
	31–50 years	18	8	150
	51–70 years	8	8	150
	>70 years	8	8	150
Pregnancy	14–18 years	27	13	220
	19–50 years	27	11	220
Lactation	14–18 years	10	14	290
	19–50 years	9	12	290

Source: Food and Nutrition Board, 2000.

termed iron deficiency there is a reduction in body transport of iron and an increase in iron absorption. Although the production of hemoglobin is compromised in iron deficiency, no functional impairments are observed. In the final stage, anemia develops leading to weakness, fatigue, difficulty breathing during exercise, headache and palpitations. Severe iron-deficiency anemia is characterized by low hemoglobin concentrations resulting in reduced oxygen-carrying capacity of the blood and decreased capacity to perform physical work. Clinical signs of iron deficiency are shown in Table 8.3. These include changes to the skin and mucous membranes, which appear pale in proportion to the reduction in circulating hemoglobin. Nails may become pale, thin, brittle, longitudinally ridged and then concave or spoon-shaped. Coldness and paresthesia of the hands and feet are also common (Food and Nutrition Board, 2000a).

Iron deficiency is the most common nutritional problem in the world second only to starvation and famine. Worldwide, it is estimated to affect more than 2 billion people. In tropical areas of Asia, Africa and Central and South America where intestinal diseases such as parasites and dysentery are common, iron deficiency and iron-deficiency anemia is widespread (Fairbanks, 1998).

Iron deficiency is also a common nutritional problem in the USA although it rarely captures public attention. According to national health statistics, iron deficiency occurs in ~9% of toddlers and ~9–11% of adolescent females. Among women of childbearing age, iron deficiency occurs in 16% of black women and 20% Mexican–American women (Looker et al., 1997). Low socio-economic status is the primary determinant of poor iron status in the USA, but the problem cuts across all socio-economic groups. A survey conducted in a middle-class community in Minnesota found that the prevalence of iron-deficiency anemia peaked at 21% in women 25–29 years of age (Ania et al., 1994). As described earlier in this chapter, pregnancy and early childhood are critical periods for neural development. Thus, poor iron status at these stages can have far-reaching consequences for cognitive behavior and intellectual performance. These effects will be described in greater detail in the following section.

Finally, the elderly are also at high risk for iron deficiency (Ania et al., 1994). However, iron deficiency in elderly individuals is usually the result of gastrointestinal illness such as malabsorption, or the presence of tumors or ulcers (Food and Nutrition Board, 2000a).

Iron deficiency and behavior

In children, iron-deficiency anemia is strongly associated with impaired cognitive development and intellectual performance (see Table 8.3). The behavioral disturbances of iron-deficiency anemia in both adults and children frequently include irritability, mental fatigue, shortened attention span, impaired memory, anxiety and depression (Food and Nutrition Board, 2000a; Beard and Connor, 2003).

During the 1980s and 1990s, a wealth of information about the behavioral effects of iron deficiency has come from research on infants and young children conducted in Central America, Africa and elsewhere around the globe. Studies in infants have used the Bayley Scales of Infant Development, which measures mental and motor abilities during the first 24 months of life as well as temperament. Iron-deficient infants generally score

Table 8.3. Symptoms of iron deficiency.

Anemia.
Fatigue and lack of energy.
Decreased capacity for physical work.
Impaired thermal regulation.
Impaired immune function.
Decreased mental acuity.
Impaired mental performance.
Glossitis.
Koilonychia (spooned nails).
Blue sclera.
Pregnancy complications.
Restless Leg Syndrome – involuntary muscle contractions associated with alterations in CNS motor control centers.
Pica – consumption of non-food items.
Developmental delays in children affecting language ability, fine motor skills, problem solving.

Source: adapted from Beard, 2001.

lower on the Bayley Scales than non-deficient infants. For example, Lozoff et al., (1998) working in Costa Rica reported that developmental test scores of anemic infants aged 6 to 24 months were significantly lower than those of non-anemic control infants. Moreover, anemic infants were more wary and fearful, more hesitant, less likely to show pleasure, and less active than non-anemic infants. During play, anemic infants were less likely to explore their environment and were more likely to stay close to their caregiver. These behaviors characterize a paradigm of 'functional isolation' which can limit an infant's stimulation and learning from his or her environment. It is still unclear if functional isolation is directly related to a lack of iron in specific brain areas or is a more generalized response to the quality of the care-giving environment. That is, an anemic infant may be less likely to receive attention from caregivers which might further compromise the infant's cognitive development. Moreover, iron deficiency often occurs in the context of poverty, and among families coping with a variety of stressors that can hinder the healthy development of their infant. These factors include large family size, food insecurity, poor housing, low maternal education and poor maternal health. Thus, a variety of socio-economic factors can confound the association between iron deficiency and delayed infant development. Some studies have attempted to control for these confounders, but this poses a substantial challenge in supplementation trials (Beard and Connor, 2003; Black, 2003). Functional isolationism has also been associated with protein-calorie malnourishment, which is discussed in Chapter 6.

A critical question is whether iron deficiency early in life produces long-standing cognitive and behavioral deficits in children. Hurtado et al. (1999) conducted a population-based study to investigate the association between early childhood anemia and mental retardation. The health records of >5400 children, who had been enrolled in the Special Supplemental Program for Women, Infants and Children (WIC) at 1–5 years of age were linked with the school records of these same children at 10 years of age. Results showed an association between early iron-deficiency anemia and increased likelihood of mild or moderate mental retardation after controlling for confounding factors. Another study reported by Halterman et al. (2001) investigated the relationship between iron deficiency and cognitive test scores in a nationally, representative sample of ~5000 children and adolescents. Average math scores were lower for children with iron deficiency (either with or without anemia) than for children with normal iron status. Moreover, iron deficient children were more than twice as likely to score below average in math than children with adequate iron status. Finally, Lozoff et al. (2000) conducted a follow-up study in the group of Costa Rican children who had been tested and treated for iron deficiency in infancy. At 12 years of age, children who were iron deficient as infants lagged behind their peers with good iron status in math, writing, reading and overall school progress. Children who had been iron deficient in infancy also experienced more anxiety, depression and social problems and they performed less well in cognitive and motor tasks. Taken together, these studies provide strong evidence that early iron deficiency places children at risk for reduced intellectual performance later in development.

Numerous studies have investigated the effectiveness of iron therapy for reversing the behavioral deficits of iron deficiency. Among iron-deficient pre-school children studied by Pollitt et al. (1986), iron therapy for 3–4 months improved performance on tests of discrimination learning and attention. In agreement with Pollitt's work, another study observed a reversal of attention deficits following 2 months of iron therapy (Soewondo et al., 1989). However a third study found that iron therapy lead to no improvement in cognition or Stanford-Binet test intelligence scores, but did improve language acquisition and motor development (Deinard et al., 1986). Studies in older children and adolescents have reported improved math and verbal scores in iron-treated groups as well as better problem solving skills (Seshadri and Golpaldas, 1989; Soewondo et al., 1989).

Although results across studies were not identical, the general conclusion is that iron supplements from 2–4 months' duration were sufficient to improve performance on learning and memory as well as attention tasks in children. However, complete reversal of cognitive deficits by iron therapy was rare even when the clinical deficiency was corrected.

Iron and the Central Nervous System

Animal studies

Studies in rats and other species have been extremely valuable for understanding the functions of iron in the brain. Several regions in the adult brain are rich in iron including the nucleus accumbens, basal ganglia, substantia nigra, deep cerebellar nuclei, the red nuclei and portions of the hippocampus. However, the distribution of iron in the developing brain is quite different than in the adult brain and reflects the stage of brain development at the time of the investigation. For example, in the rat, the substantia nigra does not become rich in iron until after 60 days of life, when the majority of neural development has been completed. A similar observation has been made in humans who do not reach peak iron in this region until adolescence (Beard and Connor, 2003).

Studies of dietary iron deficiency illustrate how withholding iron at different stages of development influences the pattern of brain iron. To induce iron deficiency in rat pups, lactating animals are reared by dams fed iron-deficient diets. Iron deprivation in lactating rats (post-natal day 10–21) resulted in a large 25% drop in iron content of the cortex, striatum and cerebellum, but only a 5% decrease in the iron content of the thalamus. Iron deprivation after weaning produced similar declines in the cortex, striatum and cerebellum, but the decrease in iron content of the thalamus was much greater, 25% (Pinero et al., 2000; Beard, 2003).

It is important to consider the functional significance of these changes in brain iron on neural development and functioning. We now turn our attention to this question. The primary iron-containing cell type in the CNS is the oligodendrocyte. Oligodendrocytes are responsible for the synthesis of fatty acids and cholesterol for myelin synthesis, and are therefore critical for the proper myelination of nerve fibers of the spinal cord and gray matter (Beard and Connor, 2003).

Lack of iron during critical periods of brain development results in the presence of immature oligodentrocytes and hypomylenization of nerve fibers. Myelinization in the rat occurs between post-natal day 8 and day 14. Feeding iron deficient diets to rats before myelinization leads to irreversible brain damage in these animals. Partial recovery of function is observed if iron deficiency occurs during late lactation and is corrected by feeding adequate iron. Nevertheless, it remains uncertain whether complete reversal of brain abnormalities can be achieved despite complete normalization of iron status. The situation is quite different in adult animals in which iron therapy promptly normalizes brain functioning (Beard, 2003; Beard and Connor, 2003).

Together, these observations suggest that the timing of the nutritional insult can alter the distribution of brain iron producing markedly different effects on cognition and behavior. These findings are consistent with the idea of 'critical periods' of development for which adequate iron is essential for normal development to occur (Beard, 2003; Beard and Connor, 2003).

Brain iron is also involved in neurotransmitter metabolism and therefore has a role in nerve conduction. Iron is a cofactor for the enzymes tyrosine hydroxylase and tryptophan hydroxylase, which are essential for the synthesis of the neurotransmitters dopamine, norepinephrine and serotonin. Iron is also involved in several steps in the packaging and degradation of these transmitters (Beard, 2003; Beard and Connor, 2003).

In addition to its influence on the synthesis and breakdown of neurotransmitters, iron's most important effects may be on the binding of these molecules to post-synaptic receptor sites. The dopaminergic system may be particularly sensitive to regional brain, iron deficiency. For example, decreased brain iron in the striatum and the nucleus accumbens, has been associated with a decrease in dopamine receptor binding sites in these regions. Since dopamine is involved in perception, memory, motivation and motor control, alterations in dopaminergic function could partially explain the behavioral abnormalities associated with iron deficiency.

Although the majority of studies have focused on dopamine, other neurotransmitter systems such as serotonin, norepinephrine and GABA may be involved as well (Beard, 2003; Beard and Connor, 2003).

Human studies

Since it is not possible to directly observe changes in brain iron metabolism in living humans, much of what is known about brain iron biochemistry has come from deprivation studies in animals. However, directly linking the biochemical changes observed in animals with alterations in human cognition and behavior is a challenging task. In a unique study, Rocangliolo *et al.* (1998) demonstrated slower nerve conduction velocity in the auditory nerve of 6-month-old, iron-deficient infants. In humans, peak myelinization of neurons occurs at 8–12 months of age. Thus, the most likely explanation for this finding was altered mylenization of auditory nerve fibers resulting in delayed maturation of auditory brainstem responses. These findings could have important implications for language acquisition, which emerges near the end of the first year of life.

In conclusion, it seems clear that iron deficiency is associated with a range of deficits in brain functioning and cognitive behavior. This represents a major public health concern, not only in underdeveloped countries but also in the USA, where the prevalence of iron-deficiency anemia has remained steady at ~5% for young children across more than two decades (Fairbanks, 1998).

Zinc (Zn)

Zinc is a cofactor for nearly 100 enzymes that catalyze vital biological functions. Zinc facilitates the synthesis of DNA and RNA and thus participates in protein metabolism. The mineral is particularly important in protein metabolism in tissues that undergo rapid turnover such as the gonads, gastrointestinal tract, taste buds and skin. Zinc also plays a critical role in immune function, physical growth and the actions of a number of hormone systems. Because zinc plays an essen-

tial role in so many diverse biologic processes, deficiencies of the nutrient lead to a broad range of non-specific deficits. Thus, it can be difficult to link a specific clinical abnormality directly to zinc nutrition (Food and Nutrition Board, 2000b).

Requirements and dietary sources of zinc

The total amount of zinc in the human body is 1.5 to 2.5 g, with three-fourths of this amount concentrated in the skeleton. High concentrations of zinc are also found in the eyes, skin and male reproductive system (King and Keen, 1998).

Zinc is widely distributed in foods. However, like non-heme iron, the bioavailability of zinc depends on several gastrointestinal factors including intestinal pH and the presence or absence of other food components such as phytates, which interfere with zinc absorption. Zinc also competes with other elements such as calcium and iron and for absorption. High intakes of iron as dietary supplements can inhibit zinc absorption (Food and Nutrition Board, 2000b).

Good sources of zinc include seafood, muscle meats and nuts (see Table 8.4). Legumes and whole-grain products contain significant amounts of phytates that decrease the amount of available zinc in these foods. Fruits and vegetables are low in zinc. The relatively minimal amounts of absorbable zinc in plant foods make zinc deficiency a serious concern for individuals eating a strictly vegetarian diet (Food and Nutrition Board, 2000b).

The recommended dietary allowance for zinc increases from 3 mg/day for infants to 9–11 mg/day through adolescence and adulthood. The RDA for zinc increases to 11–14 mg/day for pregnant and lactating women (Table 8.2). Zinc requirements may be as much as 50% higher for strict vegetarians because of the relatively poor absorption of zinc from plant foods (Food and Nutrition Board, 2000b).

There are no adverse effects of intake of zinc from food. However, high zinc intake from supplements can cause gastrointestinal distress and can interfere with copper status. Thus, the UL for adults is set at 40 mg/day of

Table 8.4. Zinc content of selected foods (per serving).

Food	Serving	Zinc (mg)
Oysters	4 oz	74.1
Ground beef–patty	3 oz	5.3
Ham, cooked	3 oz	2.2
Kidney beans, canned	1 cup	1.4
Green peas, frozen	1 cup	1.1
Corn, canned	1 cup	1.0
Chicken breast, roasted	3 oz	0.9
Peanut butter	2 tbl	0.9
Cheddar cheese	1 oz	0.9
Broccoli, cooked	1 cup	0.7
Bread, wholewheat	1 slice	0.5
Salmon, baked	3 oz	0.4
Tuna fish, canned	3 oz	0.4
Apple	1 medium	0.1

Source: USDA, 2003.

zinc from food, water and as supplements (Food and Nutrition Board, 2000b).

Animal studies

The need for zinc for growth and development in animals has been recognized for over 60 years. In adult animals, zinc deficiency is characterized by depressed gonadal function, skin lesions, impaired wound healing and suppressed immune responses. In rats, a zinc-deficient diet rapidly leads to anorexia characterized by large fluctuations in daily food intake and weight loss. Alterations in the concentrations and receptor function of norepinephrine in the hypothalamus has been associated with anorexia in zinc-deficient animals (King and Keen, 1998). Changes in neuropeptides involved in the regulation of feeding including galanin and neuropeptide Y (NPY) have also been observed in zinc-deficient rats (Selvais et al., 1997).

Severe zinc deficiency during gestation or lactation adversely affects growth, physical development and the subsequent behavior of the offspring. Pups of rats made zinc deficient for even short periods of time during pregnancy frequently develop major congenital malformations involving the skeleton, heart, eyes, gastrointestinal tract and lungs. Brain development

is particularly impaired in zinc deficiency and is associated with neural tube defects, hydroencephaly and spina bifida (King and Keen, 1998). Significant reductions in brain weight and brain levels of DNA, RNA and protein have been observed in zinc-deficient fetal rats. These changes are associated with impaired cell growth and maturation of CNS structures including the hippocampus and cerebellum. For example, one study showed that granule cell number was decreased in the cerebellum of 21-day old rat pups and dendritic arboring and branching of Purkinje cells was severely reduced, consistent with immature development (Dvergsten et al., 1983; 1984).

Zinc concentrations are highest in the hippocampus followed by the gray matter. In the hippocampus, approximately 8% of the zinc is located in synaptic vesicles. Zinc is released from axon terminals during electrophysiological activity. This release may modulate postsynaptic receptors for glutamate. Thus zinc may play a role in the neuromodulation of glutaminergic neurons. Zinc may also be involved in biogenic-amine synthesis and monoamine oxidase metabolism (Sandstead et al., 2000).

Zinc deficiency during fetal or early postnatal development also alters later behavior. A series of studies by Halas et al. (1977, 1986; reviewed in Sandstead et al., 2000) showed that rats that had been zinc deprived during gestation and/or lactation then rehabilitated made more errors in a running maze, showed impaired shock avoidance behavior, and were more aggressive than their normal counterparts. Moderate or mild zinc deficiency in monkeys was associated with lethargy, apathy and hypoactivity (Golub et al., 1995). Zinc-deprived, pre-pubertal and adolescent monkeys also showed lower spontaneous motor activity as well as impaired performance of a visual-attention task and short-term-memory task (Golub et al., 1994, 1995).

Human studies

Zinc deficiency in humans is relatively prevalent throughout the developing world. Symptoms of severe zinc deficiency were first documented in the early 1960s in Iran and Egypt. Subsequently, zinc deficiency has been reported as a significant health problem in Turkey, Portugal, Morocco and Yugoslavia. In the USA, severe zinc deficiency is rare, but mild zinc deficiency has been associated with strict vegetarian diets, inflammatory bowel disease such as ulcerative colitis or Crohn's disease, parenteral nutrition feeding, pregnancy or the genetic disorder, acerodermatitis enteropathica (AE) (King and Keen, 1998). Individuals with eating disorders might also be at greater risk for zinc deficiency (as well as other nutrients). One study reported mild zinc deficiency among women with anorexia nervosa. Although zinc status improved after weight recovery in these women, zinc concentrations did not reach normal levels (Castro et al., 2004).

Acerodermatitis enteropathica

Much of what is known about the clinical features of human zinc deficiency has come from observations of patients with AE (King and Keen, 1998). AE is a rare genetic disorder that is inherited as an autosomal recessive characteristic. Individuals with AE have an inability to absorb zinc from the gastrointestinal tract leading to functional zinc deficiency. The underlying biochemical defect responsible for AE is unknown. The onset of the disease occurs in infants at weaning and is characterized by acute growth retardation, severe gastrointestinal problems including diarrhea and malabsorption, hyperpigmented skin lesions and increased susceptibility to infection. Alterations in mood and behavior are also a common feature of AE. Children with the disease are generally lethargic and irritable, and rarely smile or display an interest in their environment. They may also suffer from emotional disorders including depression. If undiagnosed and untreated, AE is often fatal, with death resulting from infection and/or malnutrition. Zinc supplementation rapidly reverses the symptoms of the disease (King and Keen, 1998).

Nutritional zinc deficiency

Severe nutritional zinc deficiency was first described by Prasad and colleagues in young Egyptian and Iranian men suffering from growth retardation and hypogonadism (Prasad, 1988). Many of these men looked like young adolescent boys although they were actually in their early twenties. In addition to growth retardation and delayed sexual maturation, they displayed anemia, dermatitis, impaired liver function, anorexia and neurosensory and behavioral abnormalities. The majority came from the lowest socioeconomic strata of their villages and lived on cereal-based diets consisting mainly of unleavened wheat bread and vegetables. Meat and dairy products were rarely available. Parasitic infections, which can interfere with zinc absorption and are common among these populations might have contributed to the deficiency. The effects of zinc supplementation on these young men's symptoms, was striking. After several months of therapy, many of the men had grown several inches, gained substantial weight, displayed accelerated sexual maturation and demonstrated improvements in liver function, and dermatological symptoms (Prasad, 1985, 1988).

Abnormalities in sensory function are also common in zinc-deficient individuals including a decreased sense of taste (hypogeusia), night blindness and photophobia. One study showed that prescription of zinc to zinc-deficient patients relieved the symptoms of hypogeusia after 6 months of treatment (Tanaka, 2002). The mechanisms by which zinc affects taste function remain poorly understood but may be related to pathological changes in taste bud anatomy (Henkin et al., 1999).

Pregnancy

Poor zinc status is also associated with negative pregnancy outcomes including birth defects, premature delivery and maternal complications. Although a direct relationship has not been established between zinc deprivation and abnormal CNS development in humans, current evidence suggests that the human fetus is no less vulnerable to zinc depletion than the offspring of other species. Support for this hypothesis comes from observations that in regions of the world where zinc deficiency is prevalent, there is a high incidence of anencephaly and other developmental CNS defects

(Sandstead *et al.*, 2000). Additional evidence of the damaging effects of zinc deficiency comes from studies that examined pregnancy outcomes of women with AE, prior to the recognition of the therapeutic value of zinc. In three women with AE, seven pregnancies resulted in one spontaneous abortion, and two infants born with major congenital defects similar to the CNS and skeletal anomalies seen in the offspring of zinc-deficient rats. This percentage of abnormal births (43%) greatly exceeded that found in normal populations (<4%). Finally, it has been suggested that poor maternal zinc status may be a cause of intrauterine growth retardation. A recent epidemiological study in Sweden revealed that women with the lowest zinc intakes were twice as likely to deliver a preterm infant after controlling for confounding variables (Scholl *et al.*, 1993). However, not all studies agree that zinc supplements increase birth weight (Tamura *et al.*, 2000).

Brain development and behavior

Several studies have investigated the effects of zinc deficiency on behavior and brain function in children. Working in a semi-rural Egyptian population, Kirksey *et al.* (1991) reported a positive association between maternal intakes of foods high in zinc and infant performance on attention tasks soon after birth. At 6 months of age, motor development was also associated with maternal intakes of zinc during gestation (Kirksey *et al.*, 1994). In an earlier study, Thatcher *et al.* (1984) reported a positive association between hair zinc concentrations and reading ability in school children in Baltimore, Maryland.

The effects of zinc supplementation on brain development and behavior are somewhat controversial. Supplementation trials have generally produced mixed results with some studies showing improvements in cognitive development and learning skills, and others showing no benefit (Penland, 2000; Black, 2003).

Since zinc deficiency can coincide with other trace elements deficiencies, it is often difficult to isolate the specific effects of zinc on behavioral outcomes. Sanstead *et al.* (1998) investigated the effects of zinc therapy on cognitive performance and psychomotor function in a large population of Chinese children, 6–9 years of age. Half of the subjects were from an urban area and the other half were from a rural one (to assess the influence of socio-economic factors on the study's results). Subjects participated in a 10-week supplementation trial and received either zinc alone, a mineral supplement (without zinc) or a zinc-mineral supplement. Results showed that zinc supplementation either with or without other minerals resulted in improved performance in a complex reasoning task. Other neurophysiological functions were also improved including recognition memory, attention and psychomotor function. This study was able to demonstrate a relationship between zinc therapy and improvements in cognitive and psychomotor function in older children. These results highlight the importance of considering zinc deficiency in the context of other micronutrient deficiencies which could have similar effects on cognition and behavior.

Mild zinc deficiency

As mentioned earlier in this chapter, severe zinc deficiency is uncommon in North America except in medical conditions. However, mild zinc deficiency may be more widespread and is typified by diminished physical growth in children. Increased growth velocity is observed in growth-retarded children supplemented with zinc (King and Keen, 1998).

Iodine (I)

Iodine is an indispensable component of the thyroid hormones. The thyroid hormones regulate the rate of cellular oxidation thereby influencing physiological and mental development, the functioning of nervous and muscle tissue, and energy metabolism. Iodine is particularly important during fetal development and is critical for normal maturation of the CNS. Goiter or enlargement of the thyroid gland is the hallmark of iodine deficiency (Hetzel and Clugston, 1998; Stanbury and Dunn, 2001).

Requirements and dietary sources of iodine

Approximately three-quarters of the 15 – 25 mg of iodine in the body is concentrated in the thyroid gland with the remainder found in the salivary and mammary glands, gastric mucosa and kidneys. Iodine is found in both plant and animal foods. However, the iodine content of foods depends primarily on the iodine content of the soil on which they were raised and therefore is highly variable. Soils from areas near ocean waters, which have a high concentration of iodine, typically contain large amounts of iodine. In contrast, mountainous parts of the world, including the Andes, Alps, Pyrenees and Himalayas, have soils from which most of the iodine has been removed by the natural forces of glaciation, weathering and erosion. Iodine-deficient soils are also found in flooded river valleys such as the Ganges in India. In North America, iodine-deficient soils are found in areas surrounding the Great Lakes. This region was considered a 'goiter belt' prior to the iodination of salt (Hetzel and Clugston, 1998; Stanbury and Dunn, 2001).

With the exception of saltwater fish, shellfish and seaweed, which are high in iodine, most foods are considered poor sources of iodine. For most people in the USA and many other countries, iodized salt is the major source of dietary iodine. In the USA, iodized salt contains 0.01% potassium iodine or 76 µg of iodine/g (Food and Nutrition Board, 2000c).

RDAs for iodine range from 90–150 µg/day in infancy through adulthood. Values are increased for pregnant women to 220 µg/day (see Table 8.2). Median intakes typically exceed requirements and are estimated to be ~1100 µg/day. The general population is highly tolerant of excess iodine intake from foods, and toxic effects are rarely encountered except in sensitive subpopulations. Thus, the UL for iodine corresponds to usual intakes in the population (Food and Nutrition Board, 2000c).

Metabolism and physiology

Iodine is rapidly absorbed from the gut into the circulation. The majority of the absorbed iodine is taken up by the thyroid gland and used in the production of thyroid hormones. The remainder is taken up by the kidney and excreted in the urine. The thyroid gland is remarkably efficient at removing iodine from the blood and concentrating it, a process called 'iodine trapping'. This is evidenced by the high concentration gradient for iodine between the thyroid gland and the blood, which is 100:1, increasing to 400:1 during iodine deficiency. Thyroglobulin is the primary storage form of the thyroid hormones and contains 90% of the iodine in the thyroid gland. Thyroglobulin is a glycoprotein that attaches iodine molecules to residues of the amino acid tyrosine. Two precursors are formed; monoiodotyrosine (MIT) and diiodotyrosine (DIT). As shown in Fig. 8.1, these molecules couple to produce the prohormone T_4 (thyroxine), the major circulating form, and T_3 (triiodothyronine) the active form of thyroid hormone (Hetzel and Clugston, 1998; Stanbury and Dunn, 2001).

The thyroid gland is regulated by a complex mechanism involving the thyroid hormones, the pituitary, the brain and peripheral tissues. When blood levels of thyroid hormones fall, the pituitary gland is stimulated to release thyroid-stimulating hormone (TSH). TSH then travels to the thyroid gland to increase the rate of iodine uptake and hormone synthesis. When iodine status is adequate, hormone synthesis increases and TSH levels fall, restoring normal hormone balance. In iodine deficiency, TSH levels remain elevated. The thyroid gland responds by increasing iodine turnover, but it cannot keep pace with the demands for increased hormone synthesis. Cellular hyperplasia follows leading to an enlargement of the thyroid gland known as goiter. The thyroid gland in a normal individual weighs ~15 g. Goiter can be detected by physical examination as a mass or swelling in the neck and in severe cases may be visible to the casual observer even at a distance (Hetzel and Clugston, 1998; Stanbury and Dunn, 2001).

Iodine deficiency

Thyroid hormone has multiple functions as a regulator of cellular metabolism and growth. Reduced metabolic rate is the principal

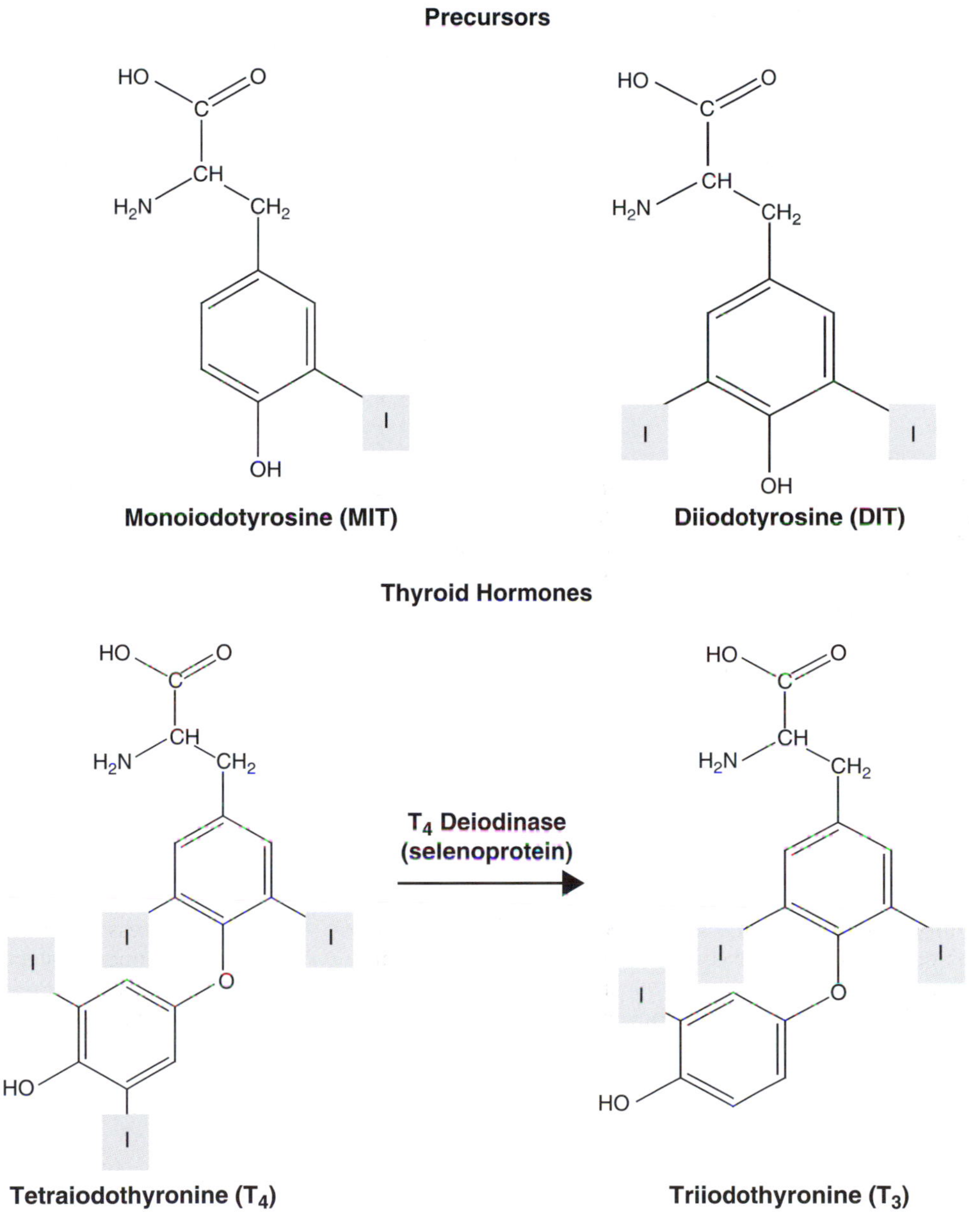

Precursors

Monoiodotyrosine (MIT)   Diiodotyrosine (DIT)

Thyroid Hormones

T$_4$ Deiodinase
(selenoprotein)

Tetraiodothyronine (T$_4$)   Triiodothyronine (T$_3$)

Fig. 8.1. Thyroid hormones and their precursors. Precursors MIT (1 iodine molecule) and DIT (2 iodine molecules) couple to produce T$_4$ or T$_3$. T$_4$ can also be converted to T$_3$ by the selenium-containing enzyme T$_4$ deiodinase. The latter pathway is compromised in selenium deficiency.

biological consequence of iodine deficiency. Other manifestations include impaired physical growth and maturation, slowness of movement, impaired reflexes, hoarseness of the voice, skin changes and cardiac insufficiency (Hetzel and Clugston, 1998).

Iodine deficiency can be defined as mild, moderate or severe. Moderate iodine deficiency is associated with reduced visual and motor performance, perceptual abnormalities and reduced and intellectual capabilities in both children and adults (Delange, 2000).

Severe iodine deficiency causes goiter in adults and children. Cretinism is the result of severe iodine deficiency during fetal development and is associated with permanent physical and mental abnormalities. Two subtypes of cretinism have been identified: neurological and myxedematous. Individuals with neurological cretinism, which is more common, typically are deaf–mute and display spastic movement and gait, as well as profound mental retardation. In comparison, myxedematous cretins are short in stature and display symptoms of severe hypothyroidism, but they are not deaf or mute. The two subtypes of cretinism tend to predominate in different geographical areas, but they are not mutually exclusive. Mixed forms of cretinism with both neurological and myxedematous features do occur (Hetzel and Clugston, 1998; Stanbury and Dunn, 2001).

Inadequate intake of iodine is the primary cause of iodine deficiency. But, certain foods contain substances called goitrogens that interfere with the production of thyroid hormones. Many of these foods (e.g. cassava, maize, bamboo shoots, millet and sweet potatoes) are dietary staples in areas of the world where iodine deficiency is prevalent. It has been postulated that when dietary-iodine intake is low, goitrogen overload may exacerbate existing iodine deficiency. Cassava, for example, contains the goitrogen, linamarin. When cassava is improperly prepared, linamarin is hydrolyzed in the gut to thiocyanate. Thiocyanate competes with iodine for uptake by the thyroid gland, thereby reducing thyroid hormone synthesis (Delange, 2000; Stanbury and Dunn, 2001).

A third factor to consider is selenium deficiency. The selenium-containing enzyme T_4 deiodinase is responsible for the conversion of T_4 to T_3, the active form (see Fig. 8.1). Also, the detoxifying enzyme glutathione peroxidase requires selenium. In selenium deficiency, the production of T_3 is reduced, and peroxides accumulate damaging the thyroid gland (Delange, 2000).

It is only recently that the complex etiology of endemic goiter and cretinism has been unraveled. It is now understood that the development of goiter and cretinism reflects iodine deficiency (as the primary cause), and the probable involvement of selenium deficiency and goitrogen overload (Delange, 2000;

Stanbury and Dunn, 2001). These secondary mechanisms may explain discrepancies in the clinical picture of cretinism in different population groups around the world. For example, in regions with isolated, severe iodine deficiency such as New Guinea, China, Indonesia and Thailand, the neurological type of cretinism predominates. However, the myxedemous form is more common in the Democratic Republic of Congo (formerly Zaire) where iodine deficiency is complicated by selenium deficiency and a goitrogenic diet. Thus, the combined effects of selenium deficiency and goitrogenic overload tend to accentuate the hypothyroidism of iodine deficiency and mitigate the brain damage (Contempre et al., 1994; Delange, 2000). The mechanisms responsible for these different clinical outcomes are discussed below.

Iodine deficiency in most Western countries has virtually been eliminated by the use of iodized salt and the availability of food from a variety of geographical areas. However, iodine deficiency continues to be a major public health problem in parts of the world characterized by iodine-poor soil and primitive food transportation systems. In 1993, The World Health Organization (WHO) estimated that 1.6 billion people live in iodine-deficient environments and are at risk for iodine deficiency (World Health Organization, 1993).

Endemic cretinism occurs when iodine intake is below 25 μg/day. In severely affected areas of India, Indonesia, China and elsewhere, endemic cretinism can affect up to 10% of the population (Hetzel and Clugston, 1998). Moreover, in severely affected communities, a substantial proportion of the population may also have lesser degrees of retardation as a result of brief or intermittent iodine deficiency during early development. These individuals are not so readily identifiable because they lack the physical characteristics and developmental impairments of cretinism. For example, observations by Green (1977, 1994) in rural Ecuador revealed that in addition to the 5.7% of the adult population who were deaf–mute cretins, another 17.4% of the population displayed more moderate neurological deficits and behavioral limitations. Thus, the presence of large subgroups of people exhibiting a spectrum of physical and/or intellectual limitations can adversely affect the social and economic well-being of a community (Dunn, 1994).

Iodine deficiency can be completely avoided by iodine supplementation. Iodized salt is the preferred method of correcting iodine deficiency, although iodized oil injections have been used successfully in some high-risk populations. Due to the combined efforts of numerous governments and international agencies, substantial progress has been made in implementing a universal salt iodination policy to eliminate iodine deficiency as a public health problem worldwide. However, significant challenges still exist in ensuring adequate supply and distribution of iodized salt to populations in need. The presence of political and social unrest in some countries further impedes supplementation efforts (Hetzel and Clugston, 1998).

Fetal development

It was originally believed that thyroid hormone was not important for early brain development. It is now known that the fetal brain needs thyroid hormone throughout gestation to develop normally (Morreale de Escobar et al., 1994; Delange, 2000). During early gestation, the fetus obtains T_4 exclusively from the maternal circulation. By 9–10 weeks gestational age, T_3 is already present in the fetal brain and is likely to have been converted locally from T_4 of maternal origin. Since fetal production of T_3 is regulated by the presence of maternal T_4, a constant supply of T_4 from the mother is critical during early brain development when neuronal cell proliferation and migration is maximal. Thus, maternal T_4 is thought to exert a protective effect on fetal brain development even before fetal thyroid function begins at midpregnancy. Moreover, at term, up to half of the T_4 present in cord blood is still of maternal origin. Together, these findings suggest that maternal T_4 protects the fetal brain throughout pregnancy, but seems to be most critical during early neurodevelopment. This mechanism might explain why severe maternal iodine deficiency during early fetal growth results in neurological cretinism,

whereas maternal iodine deficiency later in gestation leads to myxedematous form in which profound brain damage to the fetus is avoided (Morreale de Escobar et al., 1994; Delange, 2000). Stated another way, neurological cretinism is caused by a failure of the mother to provide adequate T_4 to her fetus early in neural development, whereas myxedematous cretinism is caused by fetal thyroid failure that occurs later in gestation. As noted previously in this chapter, the fetal thyroid is particularly vulnerable to damage when iodine deficiency is accompanied by selenium deficiency and goitrogen overload. Thus, severe fetal hypothyroidism would be the most likely outcome of iodine deficiency and its complications late in pregnancy (Morreale de Escobar et al., 1994).

The maternal protection hypothesis is supported by early studies conducted in Papua New Guinea showing that iodine supplementation of deficient women either before pregnancy or early in gestation protected against neurological damage of the fetus (Pharoah and Connolly, 1994). In another study in China, maternal iodine supplementation early in gestation led to a 2% prevalence of neurologic abnormalities in infants as compared with a 9% prevalence in infants whose mothers had received iodine during the last trimester of pregnancy. Also, treatment during the 3rd trimester or after delivery improved brain growth but not neurological status of the infants (Cao et al., 1994).

Numerous studies have investigated the relationship between early iodine deficiency and intellectual development in children. In pre-term or small-for-gestational-age infants the thyroid gland is underdeveloped and T_4 levels at birth are low. Den Ouden et al. (1996) followed the intellectual development of such children up to pre-adolescence. At 9 years of age, 27% of these children had been held back a grade in school and 18% required special education. Tiwari et al. (1996) found that pre-adolescent and adolescent boys with severe iodine deficiency were slow learners and showed low motivation to achieve. These results are reinforced by the findings of Bleichrodt and Born (1994) who conducted a meta-analysis[1] of nineteen studies on iodine deficiency and cognitive function. They showed that

---

[1] A meta-analysis is a statistical procedure that allows direct comparison of data across studies, even if the methods vary.

iodine deficiency resulted in a striking loss of 13.5 points in IQ score. Quite clearly, iodine deficiency can lead to a devastating loss of intellectual potential in children.

Experimental animals

Brain development proceeds according to a sequence of precisely-timed and coordinated-steps of cell differentiation and migration. Studies in rodents have demonstrated that thyroid hormones are involved in the regulation of migration and differentiation of a variety of brain cell types including neurons, oligodendrocytes, astrocytes and glial cells. In iodine deficiency, Purkinje cells of the cerebellum are characteristically affected by a lack of dendritic branching. Oligodendrocytes are also decreased in number and myelinization drops (Bernal et al., 2003).

Studies on the molecular mechanisms of hormone action have shown that T_3 binds to receptors in the nucleus of cells to initiate a sequence of changes in gene transcription. In the developing brain, for example, T_3 regulates a variety of genes involved in the myelinization of neurons in the brain stem, cerebellum, midbrain, hippocampus and neocortex. In the absence of T_3, myelinization proceeds at a slower rate, leading to delayed development as compared to normal animals. These studies demonstrate that the thyroid hormones are critical for synchronizing a number of cellular events that control brain maturation (Bernal et al., 2003).

Studies have also investigated the influence of thyroid gene expression on behavioral abnormalities in mice (Guadano-Ferraz et al., 2003). Mice lacking the T_3 receptor subtype, TRα1, performed less well than normal mice in an open-field test, and they were hyperresponsive in a fear-conditioning test. In the open-field test, TRα1-deficient mice exhibited more freezing (behavioral immobility) and less exploratory behavior than their normal counterparts. In the fear-conditioning task, freezing levels were higher in TRα1-deficient mice 1 week after training. Since both behaviors depend on the integrity of the hippocampus, these findings suggested that alternations in the circuitry of the hippocampus might underlie these behavioral deficits. Further investigation revealed that the behavioral abnormalities of TRα1-deficient mice correlated with fewer GABAergic terminals on pyramidal neurons in the dorsal hippocampus in these animals (Guadano-Ferraz et al., 2003). Studies such as this one can provide powerful clues about the involvement of specific genes and neural pathways in behavioral changes in animals that could have important parallels in human biology.

Conclusion

The intake of essential minerals is as crucial for normal brain development and functioning as the intake of sufficient protein, energy and vitamins. In adults, mineral deficiencies can lead to a variety of alterations in behavior. These consequences can be rapidly reversed by providing sufficient quantities of the mineral in the diet. Unfortunately, the deleterious effects of mineral deficiencies are not reversible if the deficiency occurs during a critical stage of brain development. As we have seen, maternal deficiencies of both zinc and iodine during fetal development can lead to permanent impairments in brain function and behavior.

Because mineral deficiencies are among the most common nutritional problems in children, serious consideration must be given to ways to combat these deficiencies. Improved methods of food distribution, better monitoring of nutrient intakes at the population level and progress in maternal and nutrition education may help alleviate these problems.

References

Ania, B., Suman, V., Fairbanks, V. and Melton, L.R. (1994) Prevalence of anemia in medical practice: community versus referral patients. Mayo Clinic Proceedings 69, 730–735.

Beard, J. (2003) Iron deficiency alters brain development and functioning. Journal of Nutrition 133, 1468S–1472S.

Beard, J. and Connor, J. (2003) Iron status and neural functioning. Annual Review of Nutrition 23, 41–58.

Bernal, J., Guadaño-Ferraz, A. and Morte, B. (2003) Perspectives in the study of thyroid hormone action on brain development and function. Thyroid 13, 1005–1012.

Black, M. (2003) Micronutrient deficiencies and cognitive functioning. *Journal of Nutrition* 133, 3927S–3931S.

Bleichrodt, N. and Born, M. (1994) A metaanalysis of research on iodine and its relationship to cognitive development. In: Stanbury, J. (ed.) *The Damaged Brain of Iodine Deficiency* Cognizant Communication, New York.

Cao, X., Jiang, X., Dou, Z., Rakeman, M., Zhang, M., O'Donnell, K., Ma, T., Amette, K., DeLong, N. and DeLong, G. (1994) Timing of vulnerability of the brain to iodine deficiency in endemic cretinism. *New England Journal of Medicine* 331, 1739–1744.

Castro, J., Deulofeu, R., Gila, A., Puig, J. and Toro, J. (2004) Persistence of nutritional deficiencies after short-term weight recovery in adolescents with anorexia nervosa. *International Journal of Eating Disorders* 35, 169–178.

Contempre, B., Many, M., Vanderpas, J. and Dumont, J. (1994) Interaction between two trace elements: selenium and iodine. Implications for both deficiencies. In: Stanbury, J., (ed.) *The Damaged Brain of Iodine Deficiency* Cognizant Communication, New York.

Deinard, A., List, A., Lindgren, B., Hunt, J. and Chang, P. (1986) Cognitive deficits in iron-deficient and iron-deficient anemic children. *Journal of Pediatrics* 108, 681–689.

Delange, F. (2000) The role of iodine in brain development. *Proceedings of the Nutrition Society* 59, 75–79.

Den Ouden, A., Kok, J., Verkerk, P., Brand, R. and Verloove-Vanhorick, S. (1996) The relation between neonatal thyroxine levels and neurodevelopmental outcome at age 5 and 9 years in a national cohort of very preterm and/or very low birth weight infants. *Pediatric Research* 39, 142–145.

Dunn, J. (1994) Societal implications of iodine deficiency and the value of its prevention. In: J. Stanbury, (ed.) *The Damaged Brain of Iodine Deficiency* Cognizant Communication, New York.

Dvergsten, C., Fosmire, G., Ollerich, D. and Sandstead, H. (1983) Alterations in the postnatal development of the cerebellar cortex due to zinc deficiency. I. Impaired acquisition of granule cells. *Brain Research* 271, 217–226.

Dvergsten, C., Fosmire, G., Ollerich, D. and Sandstead, H. (1984) Alterations in the postnatal development of the cerebellar cortex due to zinc deficiency. II. Impaired maturation of Purkinje cells. *Brain Research* 318, 11–20.

Erlij, D. (1998) Membrane channels and transporters: paths of discovery. In: Shils, M., Olson, J., Shike, M. and Ross, A. (eds) *Modern Nutrition in Health and Disease*, 9th edn. Lippincott Williams & Wilkins, Philadelphia.

Fairbanks, V. (1998) Iron in medicine and nutrition. In: Shils, M., Olson, J., Shike, M. and Ross, A. (eds) *Modern Nutrition in Health and Disease*, 9th edn. Lippincott Williams & Wilkins, Philadelphia.

Food and Nutrition Board, Institute of Medicine, National Academy of Sciences. (2000a) *Iron. Dietary Reference Intakes for Thiamin A, Vitamin K, Arsenic, Boron, Chromium, Copper, Iodine, Iron, Manganese, Molybdenum, Nickel, Silicon, Vanadium and Zinc*. National Academy Press, Washington, DC, 9.1–9.78.

Food and Nutrition Board, Institute of Medicine, National Academy of Sciences. (2000b) *Zinc. Dietary Reference Intakes for Thiamin A, Vitamin K, Arsenic, Boron, Chromium, Copper, Iodine, Iron, Manganese, Molybdenum, Nickel, Silicon, Vanadium and Zinc*. National Academy Press, Washington, DC, 12.1–12.47.

Food and Nutrition Board, Institute of Medicine, National Academy of Sciences. (2000c) *Iodine. Dietary Reference Intakes for Thiamin A, Vitamin K, Arsenic, Boron, Chromium, Copper, Iodine, Iron, Manganese, Molybdenum, Nickel, Silicon, Vanadium and Zinc*. National Academy Press, Washington, DC, 8.1–8.27.

Golub, M., Takeuchi, P., Keen, C., Gershwin, M., Hendrickx, A. and Lonnerdal, B. (1994) Modulation of behavioral performance of prepubertal monkeys by moderate dietary zinc deprivation. *American Journal of Clinical Nutrition* 60, 238–243.

Golub, M., Keen, C., Gershwin, M. and Hendrickx, A. (1995) Developmental zinc deficiency and behavior. *Journal of Nutrition* 125(Suppl. 8), 2263S–2271S.

Greene, L. (1977) Hyperendemic goiter, cretinism, and social organization in highland Ecuador. In: Greene, L. (ed.) In *Malnutrition, Behavior and Social Organization*. Academic Press, New York.

Greene, L. (1994) A retrospective view of iodine deficiency, brain development and behavior from studies in Ecuador. In: Stanbury, J. (ed.) *The Damaged Brain of Iodine Deficiency* Cognizant Communication, New York.

Guadano-Ferraz, A., Benavides-Piccione, R., Venero, C., Lancha, C., Vennstrom, B., Sandi, C., DeFelipe, J. and Bernal, J. (2003) Lack of thyroid hormone receptor alpha1 is associated with selective alterations in behavior and hippocampal circuits. *Molecular Psychiatry* 8, 30–38.

Halas, E., Reynolds, G. and Sandstead, H. (1977) Intra-uterine nutrition and its effects on aggression. *Physiology and Behavior* 19, 653–661.

Halas, E., Hunt, C. and Eberhardt, M. (1986) Learning and memory disabilities in young adult rats from mildly zinc deficient dams. *Physiology and Behavior* 37, 451–458.

Halterman, J., Kaczorowski, J., Aligne, C., Auinger, P. and Szilagyi, P. (2001) Iron deficiency and cognitive achievement among school-aged children and adolescents in the United States. *Pediatrics* 107, 1381–1386.

Henkin, R., Martin, B. and Agarwal, R. (1999) Decreased parotid saliva gustin/carbonic anhydrase VI secretion: an enzyme disorder manifested by gustatory and olfactory dysfunction. *American Journal of Medical Sciences* 318, 380–391.

Hetzel, B., and Clugston, G. (1998) Iodine. In: Shils, M., Olson, J., Shike, M. and Ross, A. (eds) *Modern Nutrition in Health and Disease*, 9th edn. Lippincott Williams & Wilkins, Philadelphia.

Hille, B. (1992) *Ionic channels of excitable membranes*. Sinauer, Sunderland, Massachussetts.

Hurtado, E., Claussen, A. and Scott, K. (1999) Early childhood anemia and mild or moderate mental retardation. *American Journal of Clinical Nutrition* 69, 115–119.

King, K., and Keen, C. (1998) Zinc. In: Shils, M., Olson, J., Shike, M. and Ross, A. (eds) *Modern Nutrition in Health and Disease*, 9th edn. Lippincott Williams & Wilkins, Philadelphia.

Kirksey, A., Rahmanifar, A., Wachs, T., McCabe, G., Bassily, N., Bishry, Z., Galal, O., Harrison, G. and Jerome, N. (1991) Determinants of pregnancy outcome and newborn behavior of a semirural Egyptian population. *American Journal of Clinical Nutrition* 54, 657–667.

Kirksey, A., Wachs, T., Yunis, F., Srinath, U., Rahmanifar, A., McCabe, G., Galal, O., Harrison, G. and Jerome, N. (1994) Relation of maternal zinc nutriture to pregnancy outcome and infant development in an Egyptian village. *American Journal of Clinical Nutrition* 60, 782–792.

Layrisse, M., Chavez, J., Mendez-Castellano, S., Bosch, V., Tropper, E., Bastardo, B. and Gonzalez, E. (1996) Early response to the effect of iron fortification in the Venezuelan population. *American Journal of Clinical Nutrition* 64, 903–907.

Looker, A., Dallman, P., Carroll, M., Gunter, E. and Johnson, C. (1997) Prevalance of iron deficiency in the United States. *Journal of the American Medical Association* 277, 973–976.

Lozoff, B., Klein, N., Nelson, E., McClish, D., Manuel, M. and Chacon, M. (1998) Behavior of infants with iron-deficiency anemia. *Child Development* 69, 24–36

Lozoff, B., Jiminez, E., Hagen, J., Mollen, E. and Wolf, A. (2000) Poorer behavioral and developmental outcome more than 10 years after treatment for iron deficiency in infancy. *Pediatrics* 105, E51 http://pediatrics.aappublications.org/cgi/content/full/105/4/e51.

McLaren, D. (1998) Clinical manifestations of human vitamin and mineral disorders: a resumé. In: Shils, M., Olson, J., Shike, M. and Ross, A. (eds) *Modern Nutrition in Health and Disease*, 9th edn. Lippincott Williams & Wilkins, Philadelphia.

Morreale de Escobar, G., Obregón, M., Calvo, R. and Escobar del Ray, F. (1994) Hormone nurturing of the developing brain: the rat model. In: Stanbury, J. (ed.) *The Damaged Brain of Iodine Deficiency*. Cognizant Communication, New York.

Oh, M. and Uribarri, J. (1998) Electrolytes, water and acid-base balance. In: Shils, M., Olson, J., Shike, M. and Ross, A. (eds) *Modern Nutrition in Health and Disease*, 9th edn. Lippincott Williams & Wilkins, Philadelphia.

Penland, J. (2000) Behavioral data and methodology issues in studies of zinc nutrition in humans. *Journal of Nutrition* 130, 361S–364S.

Pharoah, P. and Connolly, K. (1994) Iodine deficiency in Papua New Guinea. In: Stanbury, J. (ed.) *The Damaged Brain of Iodine Deficiency*. Cognizant Communication, New York.

Pinero, D., Li, N., Connor, J. and Beard, J. (2000) Variations in dietary iron alter brain iron metabolism in developing rats. *Journal of Nutrition* 130, 254–263.

Pollitt, E., Saco-Pollitt, C., Leibel, R.L. and Viteri, F. (1986) Iron deficiency and behavioral development in infants and preschool children. *American Journal of Clinical Nutrition* 43, 555–565.

Prasad, A. (1985) Clinical manifestations of zinc deficiency. *Annual Review of Nutrition* 5, 341–363.

Prasad, A. (1988) Clinical spectrum and diagnostic aspects of human zinc deficiency. *Essential and Toxic Trace Elements in Human Health and Disease* Alan R. Liss, New York.

Purves, D., Augustine, G., Fitzpatrick, D., Katz, L., LaMantia, A.-S., McNamara, J. and Williams, S. (2001) *Neuroscience*. Sinauer Associates, Sunderland, Massachussetts.

Roncagliolo, M., Garrido, M., Walter, T., Peirano, P. and Lozoff, B. (1998) Evidence of altered central nervous system development in infants with iron deficiency anemia at 6 months: delayed maturation of auditory brainstem responses. *American Journal of Clinical Nutrition* 68, 683–690.

Sandstead, H., Penland, J., Alcock, N., Dayal, H., Chen, X., Li, J., Zhao, F. and Yang, J. (1998) Effects of repletion with zinc and other micronutrients on neuropsychologic performance and growth of Chinese children. *American Journal of Clinical Nutrition* 68, 470S–475S.

Sandstead, H., Fredrickson, C. and Penland, J. (2000) History of zinc as related to brain function. *Journal of Nutrition* 130, 496S–502S.

Scholl, T., Hediger, M., Schall, J., Fischer, R. and Khoo, C. (1993) Low zinc intake during pregnancy: its association with preterm and very preterm delivery. *American Journal of Epidemiology* 137, 1115–1124.

Selvais, P., Labuche, C., Nguyen, X., Ketelslegers, J., Denef, J. and Maiter, D. (1997) Cyclic feeding behaviour and changes in hypothalamic galanin and neuropeptide Y gene expression induced by zinc deficiency in the rat. *Journal of Neuroendocrinology* 9, 55–62.

Seshadri, S. and Golpaldas, T. (1989) Impact of iron supplementation on cognitive function in preschool and school aged children: the Indian experience. *American Journal of Clinical Nutrition* 50, 675–686.

Soewondo, S., Husaini, M. and Pollitt, E. (1989) Effects of iron deficiency on attention and learning processes in preschool children: Bandung, Indonesia. *American Journal of Clinical Nutrition* 50, 667–674.

Stanbury, J. and Dunn, J. (2001) Iodine and iodine deficiency disorders. In B. Bowman, and R. Russell, (eds) *Present Knowledge in Nutrition*, 8th edn. International Life Sciences Institute Press, Washington, DC.

Tamura, T., Goldenberg, R., Johnston, K. and DuBard, M. (2000) Maternal plasma zinc concentrations and pregnancy outcome. *American Journal of Clinical Nutrition* 71, 109–113.

Tanaka, M. (2002) Sensory function of the salivary gland in patients with taste disorders or xerostomia: correlation with zinc deficiency. *Acta Otolaryngology* Supplement 546, 134–141.

Thatcher, R., McAlaster, R., Lester, M. and Cantor, D. (1984) Comparisons among EEG, hair minerals and diet predictions of reading performance in children. *Annals of the New York Academy of Sciences* 433, 87–96.

Tiwari, B.D., Godbole, M.M., Chattopadhyay, N., Mandal, A. and Mithal, A. (1996) Learning disabilities and poor motivation to achieve due to prolonged iodine deficiency. *American Journal of Clinical Nutrition* 63, 782–786.

USDA (2003) *National Nutrient Database for Standard Reference, Release 16*. Nutrient Data Laboratory Homepage, US Department of Agriculture, Agricultural Research Service. http://www.nal.usda.gov/fnic/foodcomp

World Health Organization (1993) Micronutrient deficiency information system (MDIS) working paper no 1. *Global prevalence of iodine deficiency disorders*. WHO/UNICEF/ICCIDD, Geneva.

Yip, R. (2001) Iron. In: Bowman, B. and Russell, R. (eds) *Present Knowledge in Nutrition*, 8th edn. International Life Sciences Institute Press, Washington, DC.

9 Dietary Supplements, Mental Performance and Behavior

B.J. Tepper

The popularity of complementary, self-help and alternative medicines is growing rapidly. At the forefront of this trend is strong consumer interest in dietary supplements. Sales of dietary supplements including vitamins, minerals, medicinal herbs and other botanicals have sky-rocketed in the past decade, exceeding $15 billion per year. In 1998, the five top selling herbs in the USA were Ginkgo biloba, St. John's Wort, ginseng, garlic and Echinacea, totaling more than $540 million in sales (Blumenthal, 1998).

Dietary supplements make numerous claims – from enhancing mood and memory, to decreasing anxiety and stress and improving sleep. Are these claims fact or fantasy? Do the benefits outweigh the risks or are consumers too eager to embrace 'unproven' therapies? Some of the primary reasons for using dietary supplements are to preserve overall health and well-being and to reduce the effects of aging. Some supplements show promise in slowing cognitive decline in the elderly and reducing the severity of neurodegenerative diseases such as Alzheimer's and Parkinson's disease. On the other hand, the extent to which dietary supplements can improve cognitive function in otherwise healthy people is open to debate. Consumers may also use supplements as an alternative to mainstream medicine, or because they have exhausted conventional treatment options. For example, St. John's Wort

has been promoted as beneficial in the treatment of mild depression with fewer side effects than pharmaceutical therapy.

The public perceives these products as 'natural' and 'healthy' and therefore without health risks. However, some botanicals can have side effects or can interfere with the actions of other medications. Effects of long-term use of these products are largely unknown. Moreover, dietary supplements are sold as foods not as drugs. According to current legal statutes, dietary supplements do not have to meet the same rigorous safety standards applied to the manufacture and sale of pharmaceuticals. Serious health consequences or death have resulted from the use of some supplements.

Traditional vitamins and minerals (e.g. vitamin E, vitamin C, β-carotene and selenium) are also consumed as dietary supplements. However, as opposed to herbs and botanicals, the functions of these nutrients in the human body are better understood, and safety levels have been clearly established. Whether ingesting these constituents in large quantities is effective or not is an ongoing research question. This is particularly important in light of some evidence that vitamins consumed as supplements may not provide the same health benefits as consuming these same vitamins from foods.

Hundreds of compounds are sold as dietary supplements in the USA and Western Europe. This chapter will focus only on dietary supplements that affect cognitive function and mood states and for which there is general agreement among experts of a potential health benefit. Thus, the popular herb valerian (Echinacea) will not be discussed as numerous studies have failed to show a consistent effect of this herb on cognitive function. The chapter begins by defining a dietary supplement and continues with a discussion of the functions and uses of two general classes of dietary supplements: antioxidant vitamins and minerals; and herbs and botanicals.

What is a Dietary Supplement?

Dietary supplements are marketed as foods in the USA and Britain. In the USA, the Food and Drug Administration regulates the sale of dietary supplements under rules established by the Dietary Supplement Health and Education Act (DSHEA) of 1994. The legal definition of a dietary supplement is shown in Table 9.1.

Various types of statements can be used on the label of dietary supplements, but claims cannot be made about the use of a

Table 9.1. Definition of a dietary supplement.

According to the US Dietary Supplement Health and Education Act (DSHEA) of 1994, the term dietary supplement means:
- A product (other than tobacco) that is intended to supplement the diet that bears or contains one or more of the following ingredients:
  - a vitamin
  - a mineral
  - an herb or other botanical
  - an amino acid
  - a dietary substance for use by man to supplement the diet by increasing total dietary intake (e.g. enzymes, or tissues from organs or glands), or
  - a concentrate, metabolite, constituent or extract.
- Is intended for ingestion in pill, capsule, softgel, gelcap, tablet, liquid or powder form.
- Is not represented for use as a conventional food or as the sole item of a meal or diet.
- Is labeled as a dietary supplement.

Source: US Food and Drug Administration, Dietary Supplement and Health Education Act, 1994. (http://www.cfsan.fda.gov/~dms/dietsupp.html)

dietary supplement to diagnose, prevent, mitigate, treat or cure a disease. For example, a product cannot carry the claim 'treats cardiovascular disease' or 'reduces cholesterol levels'. The FDA has authorized a list of claims that is identical to that used for claims on food products. The manufacturer is permitted to describe the supplement's effects on structure or function of the body or the well-being achieved by consuming the supplement. Examples of appropriate claims include the claim of linking folic acid with neural tube defects or that calcium reduces the risk of osteoporosis (US FDA, 1994).

Popular, but are they safe?

Although the FDA has the authority to regulate the sale of dietary supplements, the law does not require that a dietary supplement be approved by the FDA prior to marketing. According to current statutes, if a dietary supplement contains an ingredient that is suspected to be unsafe, the burden of proof is on the FDA. In other words, the FDA cannot remove a product from the market unless there is compelling evidence that the supplement can cause harm to public health. This is in stark contrast to pharmaceuticals, which are highly regulated by the FDA and must satisfy strict safety and efficacy standards before they are placed on the market. Under DSHEA, it is the manufacturer who is responsible for determining that its supplements are safe and that claims made about them are supported by scientific evidence that is not false or misleading. Currently, there are no regulations that establish a minimum standard of practice for manufacturing dietary supplements to ensure their identity, purity, quality strength and composition. In the USA, the non-profit group, US Pharmacopeia (USP) has developed a voluntary national certification program for dietary supplements (http://www.uspverified.org/standards/). This program will verify that a supplement contains the declared ingredients on the product label at the amounts specified, meets requirements for limits on contaminants, and complies with good manufacturing practices.

There have been several highly publicized cases in which dietary supplements have led to serious illness or even death. In 1989–90, 1536 cases, including 27 deaths, from eosinophilia-myalgia syndrome (EMS) were reported to the FDA. EMS is a blood disorder characterized by high fever, acute joint and muscle pain, swelling of the arms and legs, weakness and paralysis, which can lead to respiratory arrest. EMS was associated with the ingestion of the amino acid L-tryptophan as a dietary supplement and was traced to a contaminant in the manufacture of L-tryptophan by a single company (Varga et al., 1993). It is believed that lack of attention to good manufacturing standards contributed to this tragedy.

Ephedra is the dried stem of a plant that is indigenous to China, Pakistan and India and is a popular dietary supplement for enhancing athletic performance. Ephedra has potent biological effects on the central and peripheral nervous system, the cardiovascular system, kidney and lung (Lieberman, 2001). This controversial herb was withdrawn from the US market the year following the death of a professional baseball player who collapsed while taking ephedra during training (Noguchi, 2003). In 2002, FDA issued a warning for Kava which has been associated with toxic liver damage (US FDA, 2002). Two British cases of severe neuropathy have also been reported with the use of Chinese herbal teas for the treatment of eczema (Lord et al., 1999).

Since herbs and botanicals are extracts of natural products rather than pure compounds, the active ingredient(s) may be unknown and appropriate doses cannot be determined. For example, it was originally believed that hypericin, one of three components of St. John's Wort, was responsible for the herb's antidepressant effects. Consequently, this compound was adopted as the basis for standardization. Currently, all St. John's Wort sold in the USA contains 0.3% hypericin. However, it was subsequently learned that another compound, hyperforin, was the active principle and that only hyperforin, or whole plant extract containing hyperforin, had a therapeutic effect (Muller et al., 1998).

As mentioned earlier, interactions between medicinal herbs and common medications can also pose serious health problems. For instance, consuming Gingko biloba with anticoagulants, vitamin E or even aspirin can cause internal bleeding. It is likely that many other interactions occur between herbs and common medications, but are largely unknown at present. Because of the numerous complaints and potential risks associated with these products, critics such as the Public Citizen Health Research Group have argued that controls on the dietary supplements industry are far too lax and new and tougher regulations are needed.

Separating science from hype

The public is bombarded with information about dietary supplements by the industry, media, government and consumer groups. Evaluating this information and making informed decisions can be a difficult task. Internet sources of reliable and up-to-date information on dietary supplements are listed at the end of this chapter and include the NIH Office of Dietary Supplements, the FDA and the International Food Information Council.

Hundreds of clinical studies have been conducted on dietary supplements. Unfortunately, the bulk of this research is flawed by the use of inappropriate study designs. Many trials are too short to show reliable effects and others do not include a 'placebo' control group that receives an inert substance. The reader should be aware that the randomized, placebo-controlled, double-blind trial is considered the gold-standard for clinical studies (Spilker, 1991). In this type of trial, subjects are randomly assigned to treatment or placebo. The reason for random assignment of subjects is to minimize the influence of extraneous factors on study outcomes. Consider the outcome of a clinical trial on Ginkgo biloba for the treatment of Alzheimer's disease without randomization. If patients with more severe symptoms were assigned to the treatment group, the results of the study would be biased against the treatment. Conversely, if subjects with more severe symptoms were assigned to the placebo group, the results would be biased in favor of the treatment. In either scenario, the true effects of the treatment cannot be ascertained. It is also known that merely receiving a treatment has a powerful influence on mitigating symptoms. Double-blinding ensures that neither the subjects nor the experimenters are biased by the knowledge of who is receiving active versus inactive ingredients. The blinding codes are broken at the end of the study. For a treatment to be successful, the effect of the treatment must exceed the effect of placebo. These methods are identical to those used to test the efficacy of pharmaceuticals.

Oxidative Stress and Dietary Antioxidants

Aerobic metabolism produces energy, waste products such as carbon dioxide, and a steady stream of reactive by-products. All cells of the body are exposed to oxidants generated by normal metabolic processes and from a variety of environmental toxins such as plant alkaloids, pesticides, air pollutants and heavy metals. The principal reactive species include reactive oxygen species (ROS) and reactive nitrogen species (RNS) (see Table 9.2). Approximately 1–3% of the total oxygen utilized by the body is involved in the production of ROS. ROS includes oxygen radicals such as superoxide (O_2^-), hydroxyl (OH), peroxyl (RO_2), and non-radicals such as hydrogen peroxide (H_2O_2) and singlet oxygen ($^1O_2$). RNS includes nitric oxide (NO) and several related compounds. Also called 'free radicals', ROS and RNS have a free or unpaired electron that

makes them highly unstable and reactive with biologic molecules such as proteins, lipids, carbohydrates and nucleic acids. As described below, this reactivity can damage cells and may contribute to the aging process and the development of chronic diseases (Food and Nutrition Board, 2000a).

The body has two antioxidant defense mechanisms, which counteract the damaging effects of reactive species. The first mechanism involves free-radical scavenging to remove ROS, RNS and their precursors before they damage cells and cellular components. The antioxidant vitamins vitamin C (ascorbic acid), vitamin E (α-tocopherol) and β-carotene function as free-radical scavengers in the human body. The second mechanism involves enzymatic processes which neutralize ROS and RNS to harmless compounds. The major protective enzyme systems include superoxide dismutases, glutathione peroxidases and catalases. Selenium is a weak antioxidant on its own but is an essential component of the detoxifying enzyme, glutathione peroxidase (Food and Nutrition Board, 2000b).

Oxidative stress is a disturbance in the equilibrium between the presence of free radicals (pro-oxidants) and antioxidants. An imbalance favoring pro-oxidants leads to oxidative damage to a variety of biologic molecules including, lipid peroxidation of cell membranes, DNA strand breakage and inactivation of cellular proteins. It has been hypothesized that over time, oxidative stress may play a role in the aging process because this imbalance produces damage at a faster rate than the body's repair processes can cope with. Oxidative stress has also been implicated in the development of degenerative diseases such as cardiovascular disease, stroke and senile dementia. Although there is little doubt that oxidative stress directly damages biologic molecules, it has not been firmly established that degenerative diseases result from the imbalance between formation and removal of reactive species. It is also not known if ingestion of dietary antioxidants is directly related to development or prevention of degenerative diseases or how much is needed to afford protection (Food and Nutrition Board, 2000b). As we will see below, numerous studies have been conducted to answer these important questions.

Table 9.2. Examples of reactive oxygen and nitrogen species.

Name	Formula	Description
Superoxide	O_2^-	An oxygen-centered radical with limited activity
Hydroxyl	OH	A highly-reactive oxygen-centered radical
Peroxyl,alkoxyl	RO_2; RO	Oxygen-centered radicals
Oxides of nitrogen	NO; NO_2	Nitric oxide (NO) is formed in the body from the amino acid L-arginine

Source: Food and Nutrition Board, 2000a.

Antioxidant vitamins and minerals

In addition to their conventional role in preventing deficiency diseases, a number of nutrients are known to have antioxidant properties. At present, only vitamin C, vitamin E, β-carotene and the trace mineral, selenium are recognized as dietary antioxidants by the US Food and Nutrition Board. According to the current definition, a dietary antioxidant is a substance found in human diets that significantly decreases the adverse effects of RNS and ROS on normal physiologic functions in humans (Food and Nutrition Board, 2000b).

The following descriptions are taken from the Dietary Reference Intakes (DRIs) for antioxidants and related compounds (Food and Nutrition Board, 2000b), except as otherwise noted.

Vitamin E

Vitamin E is a fat-soluble vitamin that primarily functions as chain-breaking antioxidant in lipids. Vitamin E prevents the propagation of free-radical reactions that would otherwise cause lipid peroxidation of membranes and cellular lipoproteins. Specifically, the vitamin protects polyunsaturated fatty acids (PUFAs, see Chapter 4) from attack by peroxyl radicals. This protection derives from the fact that peroxyl radicals react 1000 times more rapidly with vitamin E than with PUFAs.

Vitamin E deficiency is extremely rare in humans and is only associated with malabsorption of the vitamin (as in cystic fibrosis) or inborn errors in vitamin E metabolism. Experimental vitamin E deficiency is characterized by peripheral neuropathy and degeneration of axons of sensory neurons. Vitamin E is the common name for the active form of the vitamin known as α-tocopherol. α-tocopherol exists in one natural and three synthetic forms. Vitamin E supplements are sold as esters (to protect the shelf life) of the natural form or as the synthetic mixture. When α-tocopherol is derived from vegetable oils it is labeled as a natural source of vitamin E. There are other naturally occurring forms of vitamin E (β-, γ-, and δ-tocopherols), but these compounds are not metabolically active in humans.

Dietary sources of vitamin E include fats and oils as the primary source followed by vegetables; meat, poultry and fish; desserts; and breakfast cereals. The RDA for vitamin E ranges from 12–15 mg/day for adult men and women. The upper limit (UL) is set at 1000 mg/day. There are few adverse effects of consuming large doses of α-tocopherol as dietary supplements. High doses of the vitamin lead to hemorrhage in experimental animals, but large studies in humans showed no evidence of hemorrhagic stroke.

Vitamin C (Ascorbic Acid)

Vitamin C is a broad-based, water-soluble antioxidant that quenches a variety of reactive oxygen and nitrogen species. In addition to its own antioxidant activity, vitamin C can also regenerate or spare α-tocopherol. When α-tocopherol intercepts a radical, a tocopheroxyl radical is formed. This radical can be reduced by vitamin C (or other reducing agents), thereby oxidizing vitamin C and returning vitamin E to its reduced state. Thus, vitamin C has the capacity to recycle vitamin E.

Vitamin C is also a cofactor for enzymes involved in a variety of biological functions including the synthesis of collagen and other connective tissues, the biosynthesis of carnitine for cellular energy production and the interconversion of several major neurotransmitters including dopamine and norepinephrine. Specifically, ascorbic acid is a cofactor for dopamine β-hydroxylase which converts dopamine to norepinephrine and is also involved in the hydroxylation of tryptophan in brain to form serotonin (5-HT). Ascorbic acid has other functions in nervous tissues, as well. It modulates the activity of glutamatergic and dopaminergic neurons and is involved in the synthesis of glial cells and myelin (Martin et al., 2002). Vitamin C is highly concentrated in the central nervous system (CNS) and local brain concentrations change rapidly with neuronal activity. Moreover, brain pools are relatively resistant to vitamin C depletion. Together, these observations suggest a major role for vitamin C in CNS functioning.

The protective effects of vitamin C in the brain may arise from its free-radical scavenging ability or may be related to its actions on central vascular tissue. Which mechanism predominates is uncertain. In the periphery, vitamin C has vasodilatory and anti-clotting effects, and is thought to play a role in the reduction of cardiovascular disease by inhibiting plasma low-density lipoproteins (LDL) cholesterol oxidation. Oxidized LDL tends to aggregate on vascular cell walls resulting in the accumulation of plaques that narrow blood vessels. Since senile dementia and other neurodegenerative diseases may involve narrowing of cerebral blood vessels, vitamin C may serve similar functions in the brain.

Scurvy is the classic deficiency disease associated with low vitamin C intakes. Symptoms of the disease include bleeding gums, swollen and inflamed joints, dark blotches on the skin and muscle weakness. Scurvy is rare in Western countries although it is occasionally seen in individuals consuming restricted diets such as alcoholics. However, low plasma concentrations of vitamin C have been observed in some segments of the population including the elderly and those of low socio-economic status.

Approximately 90% of vitamin C in Western diets comes from fruits and vegetables. Major dietary contributors include citrus fruits and juices, green vegetables, tomatoes and tomato products and potatoes. The RDA for vitamin C for adult men and women is 90 mg/day and 75 mg/day, respectively. Dietary supplements containing vitamin C are popular, but estimated intakes from both food and supplements rarely exceed 200 mg/day. Although serious risk of adverse effects from excess vitamin C intake from food and supplements is low, some individuals experience gastrointestinal disturbances such as nausea, cramps and diarrhea from large oral doses. The UL for vitamin C for adults is 2000 mg/day.

β-Carotene

The carotenoids are a family of water-soluble, plant sterols which include α-carotene, β-carotene, lycopene, lutein, zeaxanthin and β-crytoxanthin. β-carotene is the most studied carotenoid in the human diet and has been shown to have antioxidant activity *in vitro*. Although consumption of β-carotene and other carotenoids has been linked to reduced risk of

chronic diseases such as cancer and cardiovascular disease, these effects have not been firmly established. At present, there is no dietary reference intake for carotenoids, per se since the biological functions of these compounds are diverse and are poorly understood. However, several carotenoids including α-carotene, β-carotene and β-crytoxanthin have well-known pro-vitamin A activity. In other words, these compounds can be converted to vitamin A in the body and contribute to vitamin A requirements. Vitamin A is an essential nutrient for vision, growth, reproduction and the integrity of the immune system. The pro-vitamin A activity of carotenoids is distinct from their role as antioxidants.

Good dietary sources of β-carotene include bright orange and yellow fruits, vegetables and green leafy vegetables. Carrots are the major source of β-carotene in the US diet, followed by cantaloupe, broccoli, broth-based soups, spinach and collard greens. The bioavailability of β-carotene from raw foods is low since it is bound to proteins in the plant matrix. But, several factors can alter its bioavailability. On the one hand, mild cooking, especially steaming, improves bioavailability. However, prolonged heating, especially boiling, destroys the compound. Also, consuming a small amount of fat with a meal containing β-carotene increases its solubility and its utilization in the body. β-carotene from supplements has a much higher bioavailability than from foods. This is because the β-carotene from supplements is not bound to proteins and has been solubilized with emulsifiers. There are no health risks from consuming large amounts of carotenoids from foods or supplements except for carotenoiderma, a yellow discoloration of the skin that is not harmful. No upper limit has been set for β-carotene or other carotenoids.

Selenium

Selenium is a trace metal that is required for human health. Selenium principally functions as selenoproteins. Two classes of selenoproteins are known. The first class consists of a family of selenium-dependent, glutathione-peroxidase enzymes which serve as the body's primary defense mechanism against oxidative stress. Glutathione peroxidase is widely distributed in the body but is highly concentrated in the brain where it is localized in glial cells in central gray matter, hippocampus and temporal cortex (Chen and Berry, 2003). Decreased activity of this enzyme has been documented in patients with Alzheimer's and Parkinson's disease which could imply a general increased level of oxidative stress in these individuals.

Another class of selenium-dependent enzymes, the iodothyronine deiodinases regulate thyroid-hormone metabolism. These enzymes were described in Chapter 8 in conjunction with their role in iodine deficiency disease and cretinism. Given the importance of the thyroid hormones in CNS function, it is plausible that even subclinical deficiencies of selenium may play a role in psychological functioning (Benton, 2002). This possibility will be discussed later in the chapter.

Selenium is ubiquitous in the food supply being present in meats, shellfish, dairy products and plant foods. Selenium is found in the soil, and the concentration of selenium in soil varies widely by region. Thus, the amount of selenium present in foods depends on the selenium content of the soil on which it was grown. Industrialized countries utilize extensive food distribution systems which minimize variations in selenium content of the food supply. Thus, selenium deficiency is rare in humans except in isolated populations living in selenium-poor environments. Typical intakes in the USA and Canada from foods are well above the recommended 55 μg/day for adult men and women.

Many dietary supplements also contain selenium. However, the risk to the general population of adverse effects from high doses appears to be low. The UL for selenium is 400 μg/day.

Herbs and botanicals

Ernst (2002) and Fugh-Berman and Cott (1999) comprehensively reviewed the risks and benefits of commonly used herbal therapies. The following descriptions are taken from these reviews except as noted. When the neuroprotective mechanism(s) of an herb or botanical are known (or at least strongly suspected), they are described as well.

Ginkgo biloba

Ginkgo biloba is an herb derived from the leaves and nuts of the ginkgo or maidenhair tree. It has been used to treat asthma and chilblains (sores of the hands and feet from exposure to the cold) in Chinese medicine for thousands of years. Pharmacological studies suggest that this herb has anti-edemic, antihypoxic, free radical scavenging, antioxidant and anticoagulant activity. Together, these actions could protect vascular tissues from ischemic damage (hypoxia). Ginkgo has been used experimentally to protect against myocardial reperfusion injury, depression, brain trauma, memory impairment, dementia and intermittent claudation. Extracts contain the active ingredients, flavonoid glycosides and terpene lactones. The former may act as free-radical scavengers which could explain their actions on brain trauma, cardiac injury, memory loss and dementia. The latter may be responsible for antagonizing platelet clotting factors and increasing blood fluidity. Standardized extracts of ginkgo (designated as EGb 761) contain 22–27% flavonoid glycosides and 5–7% terpene lactones (consisting of gingkoglides A, B and C and bilobalide).

Ginkgo may provide neuroprotection by several mechanisms of action. EGb 761 has effects on the cholinergic, dopaminergic and serotonergic systems. For example, in one study, EGb 761 was shown to block the age-related decline in the density of acetylcholine and 5-HT_{1A} receptors in the brains of aged rats. The 5-HT_{1A} receptor subtype is thought to play an important role in learning and memory. This action has been attributed to the ability of EGb 761 to inhibit lipid oxidation of membranes as well as modulate receptor synthesis. EGb 761 also has antioxidant activity *in vitro*. In a variety of experiments, EGb 761 reduced the production of hydroxyl and peroxyl radicals, increased the activity of antioxidant-enzyme systems and inhibited oxidative damage to mitochondria. The latter activity is of major importance in aging since oxidative damage to mitochondrial DNA is a major target of free-radical attack (Ahlemeyer and Krieglstein, 2003).

Ginseng

The roots of Asian ginseng (*Panax ginseng*) are believed to have sedative, hypnotic and anti-depressant properties. Ginseng extract also acts as a CNS stimulant and potentiates the stimulatory effects of caffeine from coffee, tea and cola. The herb is used in traditional Chinese medicine to improve cognitive performance, vigilance, stamina and concentration. Ginseng has been investigated as a therapeutic agent for improving cognitive performance, memory and mood. *P. ginseng* is often confused with other plant species such as Russian, American or Japanese ginseng. 'Ginseng' as discussed in this chapter pertains to *P. ginseng*.

Ginseng can have a number of side effects including insomnia, nausea, diarrhea and headache. It also lowers blood glucose. Thus, the use of this herb might be counterindicated in individuals taking anti-diabetic medications. Ginseng is also reported to interact with monoamine oxidase (MAO) inhibitors, used in the treatment of depression, and anticoagulants such as warfarin.

St. John's Wort

St. John's Wort (*Hypericum perforatum*) is a wild-growing herb with yellow flowers. It has been used since ancient times to treat mental disorders and nerve pain. When applied topically as a balm, it was used to treat insect bites, wounds and burns. Today, St. John's Wort (SJW) is used primarily to treat mild to moderate depression. However, it is not effective in treating major depression.

The main active constituents of SJW are hypericin and hyperforin, although other components may be active as well. The mechanism(s) of action of SJW in depression are uncertain, but at least two pathways have been proposed. First, brain serotonin levels are low in depression. The herb may act by selectively inhibiting reuptake of serotonin (and perhaps the other monoamines) to prolong neurotransmitter action at post-synaptic membranes. Additional evidence that SJW enhances monoamine metabolism comes from studies showing that SJW administered in the prefrontal cortex of awake rats, increased 5-HT and especially dopamine turnover in these animals (Yoshitake et al., 2004). These data imply that SJW may act via the same mechanisms as conventional antidepressant medications such as the tricyclic antidepressants (e.g. imipramine) and the newer generation of selective serotonin reuptake inhibitors (SSRIs) such as sertraline (Zoloft™) (Gupta and Moller, 2003).

Second, high levels of interleukin-6 (IL-6) have also been associated with increased concentrations of adrenal regulatory hormones, a hallmark of depression. There is some evidence that SJW reduces IL-6 concentrations helping to moderate adrenal regulatory responses (Thiele et al., 1994). More research needs to be done to determine precisely how SJW counteracts depression.

St. John's Wort has fewer side effects than conventional antidepressants which make it an attractive treatment alternative. Although the use of SJW has been associated with dry mouth, dizziness, gastrointestinal effects, increased sensitivity to light and fatigue, the frequency of such complaints is quite low. However, other, more serious side effects have been associated with the use of this herb. SJW rapidly deactivates several classes of drugs by inducing liver detoxifying enzymes. Serious interactions are known to occur with protease inhibitors used to treat HIV infection, immunosuppressant drugs, birth control pills, cholesterol lowering drugs, cancer and anti-seizure medications and blood anticoagulants (Izzo, 2005). Thus, SJW is considered safe when taken alone, but can lead to significant health problems when combined with other medications.

Kava

Kava is made from the dried rhizome of the plant *Piper methysticum* and was traditionally used as a recreational drink in the South Pacific. Kava has anxiolytic properties and also acts as a muscle relaxant, mood enhancer, analgesic and sedative. Today, it is generally used to treat seizures and psychotic illnesses. The active compounds are a family of kavapyrones, the anxiolytic actions of which are complex. The kavapyrones enhance GABA binding in the amygdala, and inhibit norepinephrine uptake. Their muscle-relaxing effects are due to inhibition of sodium and calcium channels as well as effects on the glutamate system.

Kava potentiates the effects of other anxiolytics and alcohol, and should be avoided in individuals taking psychotrophic medications. Long-term use has been associated with yellow discoloration of the skin, hair and nails, visual disturbances, dizziness, ataxia, hair loss, hearing loss, appetite loss and weight loss. Most disturbing are reports that kava may induce toxic liver damage. These reports have led FDA to issue a consumer warning on kava (US FDA, 2002).

Oxidative Damage and CNS Disorders

The brain has high, energy needs, and a high rate of oxygen utilization which renders it highly susceptible to oxidative damage. The brain also has a high content of fatty acids incorporated into neural membranes and much of these are polyunsaturated fatty acids (PUFAs) that are especially vulnerable to lipid peroxidation. In addition, the brain has high levels of transition metals such as copper and zinc that readily form reactive hydroxyl species (Martin *et al.*, 2002; Fariss and Zhang, 2003).

Alzheimer's disease

Alzheimer's disease (AD) is the major cause of dementia in older persons, accounting for one-half to two-thirds of all cases of dementia in North America and Europe. The prevalence of AD is ~3% in persons 65 years of age and rises to 50% in persons 85 years of age and older (Martin *et al.*, 2002). Since the proportion of elderly persons in the population is rising rapidly, AD is of growing public-health concern both from a medical and societal perspective. The disease is characterized by a long latency period followed by a progressive decline in long-term episodic memory and impairments in other cognitive functions. The person crosses a threshold of cognitive loss after which the full syndrome is evident and therapy should be initiated. These changes include the presence of dementia, loss of ability to perform activities of daily living, institutionalization and death (Emilien, 2004).

As shown in Table 9.3, the deficits associated with AD fall into three domains which encompass declines in cognition, functioning (the ability to perform tasks of everyday living), and behavior. Cognitive losses in individuals with AD include forgetfulness, memory loss, lack of concentration and declines in language ability. Since AD affects executive functions, the ability to perform basic life tasks can be compromised. Thus, in the functioning domain motor skills are compromised which can affect the ability to walk and talk. Incontinence can also develop during the later stages of the disease. Finally, behavioral changes such as mood swings, depression and irritability also accompany AD. Agitation and the incidence of aggressive behaviors (screaming, hitting, biting) increase with disease progression and

Table 9.3. Deficits associated with Alzheimer's disease.

Cognitive	Functional	Behavioral
Forgetfulness, loss of memory, memory distortions. Deficits in concentration, attention, learning, problem solving. Language deficits. Ability to draw figures.	Loss of motor skills including the ability to walk and talk. Incontinence. In later stages – emergence of primitive reflexes such as grasping and sucking.	Mood swings, apathy, depression, irritability, restlessness. Delusions and hallucinations.

Source: Emilien (2004).

place a particularly heavy burden on care-givers (Emilien, 2004).

Pathophysiology

The primary neurodegenerative changes in AD include the accumulation of β-amyloid protein which forms neuritic plaques, and the presence of neurofibrillary tangles. These lesions are the hallmarks of AD and are associated with the loss of neurons and synapses in many brain areas including the basal forebrain, amygdala, hippocampus and cerebral cortex. These changes are observed at post-mortem examinations (Emilien, 2004).

There is a hierarchy of damage in AD. Structures involved in executive functions such as the medial and temporal lobes of the cerebral cortex are initially affected. As the disease progresses the damage spreads to other areas, finally encompassing primary sensory and motor regions. The clinical course of AD reflects these pathological changes. During the early stages of the disease, isolated neural degeneration and minimal pathology is observed. By the later stages, severe and widespread neuronal damage is apparent which coincides with the appearance of severe psychiatric symptoms and motor deficits (Emilien, 2004).

AD is a complex disease that is poorly understood. A host of mechanisms are thought to play a role in the pathogenesis of AD, but the predominance of any particular mechanism is uncertain. Oxidative damage to CNS tissues is considered a critical factor in the development of the disease. Oxidative stress may result from aging, cellular energy deficit, overproduction of ß-amyloid protein or inflammation. Because ß-amyloid can initiate protein oxidation and lipid peroxidation, and eventually lead to neuronal death, it is considered a key factor in the neurotoxicity of AD. Interestingly, oxidative stress can also lead to the overproduction of β-amyloid precursor and β-amyloid protein fragments. This process can lead to a vicious cycle wherein oxidative stress leads to more β-amyloid, and β-amyloid, in turn, leads to more oxidative stress (Grundman and Delaney, 2002).

Following trauma or stress, tissues mount an inflammatory response including the release of cytokines such as interleukin-1 (IL-1) or tumor necrosis factor-α (TNF-α), and adhesion factors. Cytokines are proteins that function as mediators of intercellular communication. Abnormalities in the production of these substances might also contribute to AD and other brain diseases (Martin et al., 2002; Emilien, 2004).

Activation of glial cells (gliosis) represents another acute response to trauma and other forms of injury that lead to CNS damage. Glial cell activation generates free radicals, the release of inflammatory cytokines and the production of β-amyloid protein. Vascular disease is also common in the elderly and may also lead to cognitive impairment in AD (Martin et al., 2002; Emilien, 2004).

Neurotransmitter mechanisms

Multiple neurotransmitter systems are involved in cognition and memory and may be affected in AD (Emilien, 2004). For example, acetylcholine neurons are widely distributed in the CNS. Acetylcholine is thought to play a role in cognitive function, and cognitive impairments in AD are strongly associated with the loss of forebrain cholinergic neurons. In experimental animals deafferentation of cholinergic neurons leads to cortical deposition of β-amyloid protein, a characteristic sign of AD (Beach et al., 2000).

Serotonin is involved in memory, and a variety of observations suggest that the integrity of the 5-HT system may also be compromised in AD. For example, histopathological studies have shown the presence of neuritic plaques and neurofibrillary tangles in serotonergic neurons in the hippocampus in patients with AD (Emilien, 2004). In addition, the concentration of free, active neurotransmitter in the synaptic cleft is known to modulate neuronal activity. In the serotonergic system, the serotonin transporter (5-HTT) clears the synaptic cleft of serotonin, terminating the signal. An autoradiographic study showed that the number of 5-HTT sites was decreased in specific brain area of AD patients including the hippocampus (Tejani-Butt et al., 1995).

Experimental manipulation of the serotonergic system has also been shown to affect cognition and memory, and may have implications for AD. For example, in one study, acute serotonin depletion impaired cognitive function in AD patients (Newhouse et al., 2002). The role of the 5-HT$_{1A}$ receptor subtype in memory functions was described earlier in this chapter. Administration of a 5-HT$_{1A}$ agonist to healthy volunteers impaired verbal memory in a dose-dependent manner (Yasuno *et al.*, 2003).

There might also be a link between dopaminergic dysfunction and the development of psychotic symptoms in AD. Studies have shown an increase in monoamine oxidase B activity in the brains of patients with AD. This enzyme is responsible for deactivating dopamine at the synaptic cleft, thereby terminating neurotransmission. There is some evidence that giving MAO inhibitors can lead to cognitive and behavioral improvements in such patients (Sunderland *et al.*, 1987).

Parkinson's disease

Parkinson's disease (PD) is a chronic, late onset, neurodegenerative disease that affects ~1% of US and European populations over the age of 60 years. The disease is characterized by the intraneuronal deposition of alpha-synuclein proteins (Lewy bodies) and the destruction of dopaminergic neurons in the substantia nigra. The most common symptoms of PD involve the motor system and include tremors of the hand or foot on one side of the body, rigidity, and bradykinesia or slowing of voluntary movement. Secondary symptoms include speech and posture problems; changes in facial expression and difficulty swallowing; memory loss; anxiety; depression; mental confusion and dementia. The etiology of this disease is not well understood but is thought to arise from environmental exposure to toxins, breakdown products of dopamine metabolism and genetic factors to a lesser extent. Epidemiological studies indicate that environmental factors play a prominent role in the vast majority (90%) of PD cases that are not due to familial causes (Fariss and Zhang, 2003).

Pathophysiology and neurotransmitter mechanisms

The critical event(s) that lead to the accumulation of alpha-synuclein proteins and neurotoxicity in PD remain to be elucidated. However, there is convincing evidence that oxidative stress and mitochondrial dysfunction in dopaminergic neurons may be involved. Normal dopamine metabolism generates reactive oxygen species and is associated with increased concentrations of trace metals such as iron. Iron is abundant in mitochondria of dopaminergic neurons and for reasons that are not well understood, levels of iron are elevated in the substantia nigra of patients with PD. The release of free iron from mitochondria promotes the production of ROS, which can damage neuronal lipids and proteins. Moreover, exposure to endogenous iron and other toxic metabolites inhibits mitochondrial electron transport leading to energy depletion and neuronal cell death. As noted earlier, environmental exposure to pesticides, herbicides and toxic metals such as iron, copper and manganese are thought to play a key role in the pathophysiology of PD. For example, manganese miners are known to develop PD-like symptoms and manganese has been shown to induce oxidative stress and mitochondrial dysfunction in laboratory animals. Thus, it is generally believed that the majority of cases of PD are the result of exposure to environmental toxins that target dopaminergic neurons (Fariss and Zhang, 2003).

Animal models

The experimental neurotoxin, MPTP (1-methyl-4-phenyl-1,2,3,6-tetrahydropyridine) induces PD-like symptoms in rodents and monkeys and has been a useful tool for investigating the pathogenesis of this disease. Studies by Duan *et al.* (2002) examined the possibility that dietary factors, specifically dietary folate, might protect dopaminergic neurons from damage by MPTP. First, separate groups of mice were fed either a folate-deficient or folate-replete diet. All mice were then given a subtoxic dose of MPTP that was not sufficient to induce complete dopaminergic neurodegeneration. Folate-deficient mice exhibited poor motor performance on a rotorod test which assesses the ability of an animal to hang on to a rotating rod. These researchers also observed a 50–60% loss of tyrosine hydroxylase-positive neurons in the substantia nigra of folate-deficient mice as compared to control mice. Tyrosine hydroxylase is required for dopamine synthesis and is considered a marker of dopaminergic neurons

(Duan *et al.*, 2002). The specific role of folate in cognitive decline and dementia is discussed in more detail later in this chapter.

Studies have also examined the protective effects of acute doses of vitamin E against MPTP destruction of striatal dopaminergic neurons. Unfortunately, much of these data are conflicting with some studies showing a protective effect of vitamin E and others showing a lack of protection. Differences in the dose of vitamin E used, the timing of vitamin E administration relative to the dose of MPTP and route of administration could, in part, explain these discrepancies (Fariss and Zhang, 2003).

Other studies (which did not use MPTP pretreatment) investigated the effects of dietary vitamin E supplementation on vitamin E concentrations and neurological functions in different brain regions in rats. One study showed a positive effect of 2 months of dietary vitamin E supplements on brain levels and brain function as assessed by dopamine release from striatum (Martin *et al.*, 1999). Interestingly, brain levels were maximally enriched by a moderate dose of vitamin E. Higher doses did not lead to further enhancement, suggesting that the brain has limited capacity to incorporate vitamin E. This limitation could explain why discrepant findings have been observed for supplementary vitamin E in the MPTP model of neural toxicity.

Animal studies have also shown a potent protective effect of selenium on the induction of PD. In one experimental model, multiple doses of methamphetamine were administered to mice to induce neurotoxicity of the nigrostriatal dopaminergic system. This damage was avoided by pretreating mice with selenium. In another experimental model, administration 6-hydroxydopamine to rats lead to neurotoxicity of catecholaminergic neurons and the induction of PD. Selenium prevented the neurodegeneration in a dose-dependent manner (Chen and Berry, 2003).

Dietary Supplements, Dementia and Cognitive Decline in Humans

Antioxidant vitamins

A number of human studies have shown a beneficial effect of vitamins E and C on neuro-

degenerative processes in older individuals (Martin *et al.*, 2002). For example, one study showed that in patients with moderate AD, high doses of vitamins E and C slowed the progression to severe dementia and delayed the time to institutionalization for these patients by approximately 7 months (Sano *et al.*, 1997). However, no differences were observed between treatment and controls in tests of cognitive functioning, possibly because of the advanced stage of the disease in these patients.

Epidemiological studies have been useful for examining associations between antioxidants and the risk of neurodegenerative diseases in the general population. This research has suggested that vitamin C and especially vitamin E may be associated with lower risk of AD (Martin *et al.*, 2002). However, there is controversy about whether antioxidants from foods or supplements provide the benefits. In a large population study conducted in Rotterdam, the Netherlands, more than 5300 adults who were over the age of 55 years and free of dementia at baseline were prospectively studied over a 6-year period (Engelhart *et al.*, 2002). High dietary intakes of vitamins C and E were strongly associated with lower risk of AD among current smokers, but the effect was less pronounced among non-smokers. One explanation for these findings could be that smoking is associated with lower plasma concentrations of the major antioxidants and consequently, smokers may be less protected against the formation of free radicals and oxidative stress than non-smokers. The relatively short time frame of this study might have also contributed to the weaker association between the dietary parameters and AD among those who never smoked.

Surprisingly, intake of vitamin E from supplements (as opposed to diet) was not associated with reduction in risk for AD in the Rotterdam study (Engelhart *et al.*, 2002). These data seem to conflict with the studies of Sano *et al.* (1997) mentioned earlier, which showed a benefit of vitamin E supplements in AD patients. The reasons for this discrepancy are puzzling. It seems that large oral doses of supplements can slow the progression of established disease, but are not effective in reducing the long-term risk of developing AD. One explanation could be that whole foods contain mixtures of antioxidants that complement each other in unique ways, and these unique ratios cannot be duplicated by dietary supplements. Moreover, the presence of fiber in foods or perhaps other biologic molecules whose functions are not currently known may provide some of the long-term protection. Thus, the benefits of antioxidants from foods and supplements may not be synonymous. More studies need to be done to address this potentially important distinction (Grundman and Delaney, 2002; Martin et al., 2002).

A number of epidemiological studies have also investigated the associations between dietary antioxidants and cognitive functioning in healthy, community-dwelling elderly populations. The objective of these studies was to determine if antioxidants played a role in the development of mild cognitive impairments that could predispose older individuals to AD or other forms of dementia. However, the results of these studies are not in agreement. No associations were observed between dietary vitamins A, C, E and cognitive decline in a cohort of men participating in the Zutphen elder study (Kalmijn et al., 1997). Cognitive decline was evaluated in this study using the Mini-Mental State Examination (MMSE), a global assessment of memory, orientation, attention and language. In contrast, another study in older individuals in the USA showed that high vitamin E intake from either food or supplements was associated with less cognitive decline over a 3-year period as measured by a battery of cognitive tests (Morris et al., 2002). Yet another study conducted in Australia showed that vitamin C intake from supplements was associated with a lower prevalence of decline in MMSE scores over a 4-year period, but not other tests of cognitive function (Paleologos et al., 1998).

Data on the effects of antioxidant vitamins on the progression to PD are also conflicting (Fariss and Zhang, 2003). Fahn (1991) reported that high doses of vitamins E and C delayed the need for medication in patients with PD by 2.5 years. However, the Fahn study (1991) was not blinded or controlled, and patients were permitted to take other medications concurrently with vitamin supplements. Another double-blind, placebo-controlled trial of vitamin E supplementation led to no benefits to PD patients (Vatassery et al., 1999).

The possibility that antioxidants could protect against the future development of PD has also been studied. However, combined data from the Nurses Health Study and the Health Professionals Follow-up Study which monitored >147,000 individuals over 12–14 years showed no benefit of vitamins E, C or A from supplements on PD risk but did find that dietary vitamin E was protective (Zhang et al., 2002).

There are a number of problems inherent in observational studies that depend on recall of dietary behaviors as a means of linking nutrient intakes with the risk of disease. One concern that has been raised in previous chapters is over-reporting or underreporting of dietary intakes that could skew study results. In addition, the ability of participants to recall the frequency, amount or specific type of supplements they consume may not be reliable. This is particularly relevant for interpreting studies in older individuals who are vulnerable to memory problems. These factors are likely to reduce the strength of the associations between diet and supplement use, and cognitive outcomes (Martin, 2003).

Another approach for assessing relationships between antioxidants and cognitive impairments is to measure serum concentrations of nutrients as markers of dietary behavior. Several studies have shown that serum concentrations of vitamins E, C and A are lower in patients with AD than age-matched controls without the disease (Grundman and Delaney, 2002). Since serum indices reflect dietary intakes over time, these data imply that low habitual intakes of these vitamins might have contributed to the development of the disease. A population-based study of elderly individuals living in Basel, Switzerland investigated the protective effects of antioxidants on memory performance over a 12-year period. Results showed that higher concentrations of plasma C and A, but not E, predicted better semantic memory in a vocabulary test but not other memory tasks such as free-recall, recognition and working-memory (Perrig et al., 1997).

Selenium

As mentioned earlier, selenium is a major component of the detoxifying enzyme glutathione peroxidase. Decreased activity of this enzyme has been demonstrated in patients with AD and PD and may be indicative of higher oxidative stress in these individuals. However, as is the case for many age-related cognitive diseases, it is unclear whether this decrease in enzyme activity is a root cause or a consequence of the neurodegenerative changes. Although animal models point to a protective role for selenium in both AD and PD, convincing data are lacking on the usefulness of selenium in preventing age-related cognitive impairments in humans (Grundman and Delaney, 2002).

It is notable that a few studies have shown an association between selenium and other psychiatric conditions. For example, Benton and Cook (1991) showed in a double-blind, placebo-controlled trial that selenium supplementation improved the mood states of individuals with low or marginal intakes of selenium. However, other well-controlled, clinical trials of selenium on mood enhancement are scarce. One area where selenium may be potentially useful is in the support of patients with HIV/AID who exhibit a high level of psychological burden. In one double-blind, placebo-controlled trial, daily selenium therapy for 12 months reduced anxiety several-fold in the treatment group relative to the placebo group (Shor-Posner et al., 2003).

Efficacy of antioxidant vitamins and minerals

These conflicting reports are difficult to interpret, but a few general conclusions can be drawn from these data. Antioxidants, especially vitamins C and E may have the potential to protect against age-related declines in cognitive performance and reduce the incidence or severity of neurodegenerative diseases. Whether antioxidants from food or supplements are superior for these purposes is presently unclear. Additional studies will be needed to make this determination.

Folate, B_{12} and homocysteine

There is also convincing evidence that elevated homocysteine may be involved in the development of cognitive decline and dementia in the elderly. As discussed in Chapter 7,

folate and B_{12} are required for the conversion of homocysteine to the essential amino acid, methionine. Lack of either vitamin reduces the activation of this pathway and leads to the accumulation of homocysteine in the blood. Homocysteine is thought to have direct toxic effects on CNS neurons by exacerbating oxidative stress or eliciting DNA damage. Elevated plasma homocysteine has also been implicated as a strong risk factor for AD (LeBoeuf, 2003).

A histological study examining the brains of deceased individuals showed that elderly persons with increased plasma homocysteine were 4.5 times more likely to have had AD than age-matched, healthy controls (Clarke et al., 1998). High plasma homocysteine has also been observed in patients with PD (Kuhn et al., 1998). Moreover, results from the Framingham study have shown that high plasma homocysteine at baseline, was a strong predictor of AD over an 8-year period (Seshadri et al., 2002). After controlling for age, sex and other vascular and dietary factors, high homocysteine nearly doubled the risk of AD. Whether homocysteine is a causative factor in the development of neurodegenerative disorders or is merely a marker for coexisting cerebrovascular disease remains uncertain.

Elevated plasma homocysteine is typically associated with low and marginal intakes of folate and vitamin B_{12}. The elderly are at greater risk for deficiencies of these nutrients due to reduced absorption of folate and vitamin B_{12} that naturally occurs with aging (Food and Nutrition Board, 2000b). Thus, it has been hypothesized that elderly individuals with lower concentrations of folate or B_{12}, and higher concentrations of homocysteine may have poorer cognitive functioning than elders with normal indices of these constituents. Several studies have investigated these associations in free-living populations. Morris et al. (2002) reported that elderly respondents in the NHANES II study with low folate status and hyperhomocysteinemia had poorer story recall than those with low homocysteine concentrations. Two additional studies were conducted in elderly Hispanic populations in the USA. The first study (Lindeman et al., 2000) reported a modest association between low serum folate and low MMSE scores as well as performance on other memory tasks. The second study (Miller *et al.*, 2003) showed that elevated homocysteine was only a modest predictor of MMSE scores. In the latter study, demographic variables including education, age and acculturation were more strongly associated with cognitive functioning than homocysteine.

Oral supplements of folate and B_{12} restore normal plasma indices of these nutrients and reduce homocysteine levels. Thus, one strategy would be to supplement the diets of older individuals with folate and B_{12} to correct the disturbance in homocysteine. Thus far, trials on the effects of folate supplementation (either with or without B_{12}) on preventing or slowing neurological impairments in elderly people have been disappointing. Although folic acid plus B_{12} reduced serum homocysteine concentrations, they did not protect against declines in cognitive performance (Malouf *et al.*, 2003).

Ginkgo biloba and ginseng

A number of double-blind, placebo-controlled trials have tested the efficacy of standardized ginkgo extracts (EGb 761) for the treatment of AD or multi-infarct dementia. LeBars *et al.*, (1997) showed that after 1 year of treatment with EGb 761, 29% of patients showed at least a 4-point improvement on the Alzheimer's Disease Assessment Scale–cognitive subscale (ADAS-Cog) compared with 14% of patients receiving placebo. This effect was clinically meaningful and comparable with results achieved with high doses of the psychoactive medication, tacrine (Fugh-Berman and Cott, 1999). Likewise, another double-blind, placebo-controlled trial showed improvements in memory, attention, psychopathology and behavior in patients with AD after 6 months of treatment with standardized ginkgo extracts (Kanowski *et al.*, 1996).

Oken *et al.* (1998) conducted a meta-analysis to summarize the results of more than 50 double-blind, placebo-controlled trials of standard ginkgo extracts as treatment for AD or dementia. The majority of studies did not meet inclusion criteria primarily due to a lack of clear diagnosis of AD or dementia. Other exclusions included lack of objective assessment of cognitive function or insufficient sta-

tistical information. In all, only four studies were of sufficient methodological quality to be included in the analysis. These studies showed a small but significant improvement in objective measures of cognitive performance after 3–6 months of treatment with standardized gingko extracts. A more recent review of published studies also revealed that standard ginkgo extracts led to clinical global improvements in patients with AD as assessed by the physician, cognitive performance tasks and activities of daily living (Birks *et al.*, 2002).

Solomon *et al.* (2002) investigated whether ginkgo could improve memory performance in healthy, elderly individuals. However, no differences were observed between treatment and placebo on a battery of neuropsychological tests including verbal and non-verbal learning and memory, attention, concentration and language or subjective ratings. On the basis of these results and others (Moulton *et al.*, 2001; Cieza *et al.*, 2003), it can be concluded that ginkgo extracts provide positive therapeutic benefits to patients with cerebral disorders but little or no improvement in mental functioning for healthy individuals.

In contrast to ginkgo, the therapeutic usefulness of ginseng for cognitive impairments remains questionable. A systematic review of clinical trials showed no evidence of a benefit from ginseng for the treatment of psychiatric disorders or improvement of quality of life in geriatric populations (Ernst, 2002).

Memory and Mood

Ginseng is popularly used to enhance memory and for the relief of stress and fatigue. Several studies have explored the usefulness of ginseng either alone or in combination with gingko on memory and mood in healthy, non-geriatric populations. The results of two recent studies from the same laboratory typify the effects of these herbs on cognitive performance and memory.

In the first study, Wesnes *et al.* (2000) examined healthy, middle-aged volunteers who received either a gingko/ginseng combination or placebo for 14 weeks. Subjects performed a battery of cognitive tasks using a standardized assessment (CDR computerized assessment) at repeated intervals during the trial. The gingko/ginseng combination improved working memory (spatial and numeric), but had no effects on other aspects of cognitive performance including word or picture recognition, reaction time, or attention. In the second study, Kennedy *et al.* (2002) examined the effects of a single dose of ginkgo extracts, ginseng extracts or a ginkgo/ginseng combination on short-term attention and memory tasks in college students using the same assessment battery as Wesnes *et al.* (2000). Kennedy *et al.* (2002) reported some improvements in overall quality of memory (all tasks), secondary memory (word and picture recall and recognition) and working memory for selected treatments at some time-points but not others. Gingko alone and the gingko/ginseng combination improved mood in the study by Kennedy *et al.* (2002) but the gingko/ginseng combination did not improve mood in the earlier study by Wesnes *et al.* (2000). These inconsistencies raise questions about the reliability of the effects of these herbs. Together, these studies provide suggestive evidence but not conclusive support for memory improvements with combinations of these herbs.

Depression and Anxiety

St. John's Wort

One of the more successful herbal therapies is the use of St. John's Wort (SJW) for the treatment of mild to moderate depression. Depression is a common psychiatric illness that affects approximately 19 million Americans each year, with a lifetime prevalence of 17% (Kessler *et al.*, 1994). Antidepressant medications are widely used for the treatment of depression, however they can lead to unpleasant side effects such as impaired sleep or sexual function, headache, dry mouth, nausea and diarrhea. Because SJW may act on the same mechanisms as antidepressants and has fewer of these side effects, it has gained a great deal of attention as an alternate therapy for depression.

More than 40 randomized clinical trials have been conducted on SJW for depression.

The general conclusion from these earlier studies was that SJW was more effective than placebo and comparable to tricyclic antidepressants for improving depressive symptoms. However, many of the earlier trials were criticized for lack of objective diagnostic or outcome measures (Gupta and Moller, 2003). More recently, systematic reviews of well-designed studies confirmed the earlier findings and showed that SJW was almost twice as effective as placebo and not statistically different than tricyclics in treating depression (Whiskey *et al.*, 2001).

It is notable that two, large, multicenter trials performed in the USA failed to show a therapeutic benefit of SJW on major depressive symptoms (Shelton *et al.*, 2001; Hypericum Depression Trial Study Group, 2002). Both studies used strict diagnostic criteria and standardized outcome measures such as change in severity of the Hamilton Depression Rating Scale, among others. However, both studies admitted patients who suffered from major, recurrent depressive illness. The inclusion of patients who may have been chronically ill and resistant to treatment may have contributed to the negative results in these trials. These findings support the conclusion that SJW is beneficial for treating mild to moderate depressive symptoms, but is not effective in major depression.

Kava

Kava has been shown to be beneficial in the treatment of anxiety disorders. In several double-blind, placebo-controlled trails, kava was more effective in reducing anxiety than placebo and comparable to standard anxiolytic drugs (Fugh-Berman and Cott, 1999). A meta-analysis which used total score on the Hamilton Anxiety scale as the common outcome measure, showed a 5-point reduction in score with Kava as compared to placebo (Pittler and Ernst, 2003). In a recent study on sleep disturbances associated with anxiety disorders, kava was more effective than placebo in improving the quality of sleep. Kava also reduced anxiety and improved self-rating of well-being (Lehrl, 2004). Despite the beneficial effects of kava, questions regarding its safety profile remain (Clouatre, 2004).

Conclusion

Research on dietary supplements is still in its infancy but continues to evolve and mature. Whereas earlier studies were more likely to have serious methodological flaws, more recent trials have used more rigorous designs and have yielded more reliable results. Controversies surrounding the benefits of dietary supplements are likely to diminish as gaps in knowledge about the safety and efficacy of these products are filled.

References

Ahlemeyer, B. and Krieglstein, J. (2003) Pharmacological studies supporting the therapeutic use of Ginkgo biloba extract for Alzheimer's disease. *Pharmacopsychiatry* 36(Suppl. 1), S8–14.

Beach, T.G., Potter, P.E., Kuo, Y.M., Emmerling, M.R., Durham, R.A., Webster, S.D., Walker, D.G., Sue, L.I., Scott, S., Layne, K.J. and Roher, A.E. (2000) Cholinergic deafferentation of the rabbit cortex: a new animal model of Abeta deposition. *Neuroscience Letters* 283, 9–12.

Benton, D. (2002) Selenium intake, mood and other aspects of psychological functioning. *Nutritional Neuroscience* 5, 363–374.

Benton, D. and Cook, R. (1991) The impact of selenium supplementation on mood. *Biological Psychiatry* 29, 1092–1098.

Birks, J., Grimley, E.V. and Van Dongen, M. (2002) Ginkgo biloba for cognitive impairment and dementia. *Cochrane Database System Reviews* (4), CD003120.

Blumenthal, M. (1998) Herbal market levels after five years of boom. *HerbalGram* 47, 64–65.

Chen, J. and Berry, M.J. (2003). Selenium and selenoproteins in the brain and brain diseases. *Journal of Neurochemistry* 86, 1–12.

Cieza, A., Maier, P. and Poppel, E. (2003) Effects of Ginkgo biloba on mental functioning in healthy volunteers. *Archives of Medical Research* 34, 373–381.

Clarke, R., Smith, A.D., Jobst, K.A., Refsum, H., Sutton, L. and Ueland, P.M. (1998) Folate, vitamin B12, and serum total homocysteine levels in confirmed Alzheimer disease. *Archives of Neurology* 55, 1449–1455.

Clouatre, D.L. (2004) Kava kava: examining new reports of toxicity. *Toxicology Letters* 150, 85–96.

Duan, W., Ladenheim, B., Cutler, R.G., Kruman, II, Cadet, J.L. and Mattson, M.P. (2002) Dietary folate deficiency and elevated homocysteine levels endanger dopaminergic neurons in models of Parkinson's disease. *Journal of Neurochemistry* 80, 101–110.

Emilien, G. (2004) Alzheimer disease: neuropsychology and pharmacology. Basel, Birkhauser.

Engelhart, M.J., Geerlings, M.I., Ruitenberg, A., van Swieten, J.C., Hofman, A., Witteman, J.C. and Breteler, M.M. (2002) Dietary intake of antioxidants and risk of Alzheimer disease. *Journal of the American Medical Association* 287, 3223–3229.

Ernst, E. (2002) The risk-benefit profile of commonly used herbal therapies: ginkgo, St. John's wort, ginseng, echinacea, saw palmetto and kava. *Annals of Internal Medicine* 136, 42–53.

Fahn, S. (1991) An open trial of high-dosage antioxidants in early Parkinson's disease. *American Journal of Clinical Nutrition* 53(Suppl.1), 380S–382S.

Fariss, M.W. and Zhang, J.G. (2003) Vitamin E therapy in Parkinson's disease. *Toxicology* 189, 129–146.

Food and Nutrition Board, Institute of Medicine, National Academy of Sciences (2000a) *Dietary Reference Intakes: Proposed Definition and Plan for Review of Dietary Antioxidants and Related Compounds.* National Academy Press, Washington, DC, pp. 1–13.

Food and Nutrition Board, & National Academy of Sciences (2000b). *Dietary Reference Intakes for Vitamin C, Vitamin E, Selenium, and Carotinoids.* National Acadamy Press, Washington, DC.

Fugh-Berman, A. and Cott, J.M. (1999) Dietary supplements and natural products as psychotherapeutic agents. *Psychosomatic Medicine* 61, 712–728.

Grundman, M. and Delaney, P. (2002) Antioxidant strategies for Alzheimer's disease. *Proceedings of the Nutrition Society* 61, 191–202.

Gupta, R.K. and Moller, H.J. (2003) St. John's Wort: an option for the primary care treatment of depressive patients? *European Archives of Psychiatry and Clinical Neuroscience* 253, 140–148.

Hypericum Depression Trial Study Group. (2002) Effect of Hypericum perforatum (St John's Wort) in major depressive disorder: a randomized controlled trial. *Journal of the American Medical Association* 287, 1807–1814.

Izzo, A. (2005) Herb-drug interactions: an overview of the clinical evidence. *Fundamentals of Clinical Pharmacology* 19, 1–16.

Kalmijn, S., Feskens, E.J., Launer, L.J. and Kromhout, D. (1997) Polyunsaturated fatty acids, antioxidants, and cognitive function in very old men. *American Journal of Epidemiology* 145, 33–41.

Kanowski, S., Herrmann, W.M., Stephan, K., Wierich, W. and Horr, R. (1996) Proof of efficacy of the ginkgo biloba special extract EGb 761 in outpatients suffering from mild to moderate primary degenerative dementia of the Alzheimer type or multi-infarct dementia. *Pharmacopsychiatry* 29, 47–56.

Kennedy, D.O., Scholey, A.B. and Wesnes, K.A. (2002) Modulation of cognition and mood following administration of single doses of Ginkgo biloba, ginseng, and a ginkgo/ginseng combination to healthy young adults. *Physiology and Behavior* 75, 739–751.

Kessler, R.C., McGonagle, K.A., Zhao, S., Nelson, C.B., Hughes, M., Eshleman, S., Wittchen, H.U. and Kendler, K.S. (1994) Lifetime and 12-month prevalence of DSM-III-R psychiatric disorders in the United States. Results from the National Comorbidity Survey. *Archives of General Psychiatry* 51, 8–19.

Kuhn, W., Roebroek, R., Blom, H., van Oppenraaij, D., Przuntek, H., Kretschmer, A., Buttner, T., Woitalla, D. and Muller, T. (1998) Elevated plasma levels of homocysteine in Parkinson's disease. *European Neurology* 40, 225–227.

Le Bars, P.L., Katz, M.M., Berman, N., Itil, T.M., Freedman, A.M. and Schatzberg, A.F. (1997) A placebo-controlled, double-blind, randomized trial of an extract of Ginkgo biloba for dementia. North American EGb Study Group. *Journal of the American Medical Association* 278, 1327–1332.

LeBoeuf, R. (2003) Homocysteine and Alzheimer's disease. *Journal of the American Dietetic Association* 103, 304–307.

Lehrl, S. (2004) Clinical efficacy of kava extract WS 1490 in sleep disturbances associated with anxiety disorders: results of a multicenter, randomized, placebo-controlled, double-blind clinical trial. *Journal of Affective Disorders* 78, 101–110.

Lieberman, H.R. (2001) The effects of ginseng, ephedrine, and caffeine on cognitive performance, mood and energy. *Nutrition Reviews* 59, 91–102.

Lindeman, R.D., Romero, L.J., Koehler, K.M., Liang, H.C., LaRue, A., Baumgartner, R.N. and Garry, P.J. (2000) Serum vitamin B12, C and folate concentrations in the New Mexico elder health survey: correlations with cognitive and affective functions. *Journal of the American College of Nutrition* 19, 68–76.

Lord, G.M., Tagore, R., Cook, T., Gower, P. and Pusey, C.D. (1999) Nephropathy caused by Chinese herbs in the UK. *Lancet* 354, 481–482.

Malouf, M., Grimley, E.J. and Areosa, S.A. (2003) Folic acid with or without vitamin B12 for cognition and dementia. *The Cochrane Database of Systematic Reviews* (4), CD004514.

Martin, A. (2003) Antioxidant vitamins E and C and risk of Alzheimer's disease. *Nutrition Reviews* 61, 69–79.

Martin, A., Janigian, D., Shukitt-Hale, B., Prior, R.L. and Joseph, J.A. (1999) Effect of vitamin E intake on levels of vitamins E and C in the central nervous system and peripheral tissues: implications for health recommendations. *Brain Research* 845, 50–59.

Martin, A., Youdim, K., Szprengiel, A., Shukitt-Hale, B. and Joseph, J. (2002) Roles of vitamins E and C on neurodegenerative diseases and cognitive performance. *Nutrition Reviews* 60, 308–326.

Miller, J.W., Green, R., Ramos, M.I., Allen, L.H., Mungas, D.M., Jagust, W.J. and Haan, M.N. (2003) Homocysteine and cognitive function in the Sacramento Area Latino Study on Aging. *American Journal of Clinical Nutrition* 78, 441–447.

Morris, M.C., Evans, D.A., Bienias, J.L., Tangney, C.C. and Wilson, R.S. (2002) Vitamin E and cognitive decline in older persons. *Archives of Neurology* 59, 1125–1132.

Moulton, P.L., Boyko, L.N., Fitzpatrick, J.L. and Petros, T.V. (2001) The effect of Ginkgo biloba on memory in healthy male volunteers. *Physiology and Behavior* 73, 659–665.

Muller, W.E., Singer, A., Wonnemann, M., Hafner, U., Rolli, M. and Schafer, C. (1998) Hyperforin represents the neurotransmitter reuptake inhibiting constituent of hypericum extract. *Pharmacopsychiatry* 31(Suppl. 1), 16–21.

Newhouse, P., Tatro, A., Naylor, M., Quealey, K. and Delgado, P. (2002) Alzheimer disease, serotonin systems, and tryptophan depletion. *American Journal of Geriatric Psychiatry* 10, 483–484.

Noguchi, I. (2003) *Is Ephedra Dangerous?* Online NewsHour. Available at: http://www.pbs.org/newshour/extra/features/jan-june03/ephedra.html [posted 3.05.03].

Oken, B.S., Storzbach, D.M. and Kaye, J.A. (1998) The efficacy of Ginkgo biloba on cognitive function in Alzheimer disease. *Archives of Neurology* 55, 1409–1415.

Paleologos, M., Cumming, R.G. and Lazarus, R. (1998) Cohort study of vitamin C intake and cognitive impairment. *American Journal of Epidemiology* 148, 45–50.

Perrig, W.J., Perrig, P. and Stahelin, H.B. (1997) The relation between antioxidants and memory performance in the old and very old. *Journal of the American Geriatric Society* 45, 718–724.

Pittler, M.H. and Ernst, E. (2003) Kava extract for treating anxiety. *The Cochrane Database of Systematic Reviews* (1), CD003383.

Sano, M., Ernesto, C., Thomas, R.G., Klauber, M.R., Schafer, K., Grundman, M., Woodbury, P., Growdon, J., Cotman, C.W., Pfeiffer, E., Schneider, L.S. and Thal, L.J. (1997) A controlled trial of selegiline, alpha-tocopherol, or both as treatment for Alzheimer's disease. The Alzheimer's Disease Cooperative Study. *New England Journal of Medicine* 336, 1216–1222.

Seshadri, S., Beiser, A., Selhub, J., Jacques, P.F., Rosenberg, I.H., D'Agostino, R.B., Wilson, P.W. and Wolf, P.A. (2002) Plasma homocysteine as a risk factor for dementia and Alzheimer's disease. *New England Journal of Medicine* 346, 476–483.

Shelton, R.C., Keller, M.B., Gelenberg, A., Dunner, D.L., Hirschfeld, R., Thase, M.E., Russell, J., Lydiard, R.B., Crits-Cristoph, P., Gallop, R., Todd, L., Hellerstein, D., Goodnick, P., Keitner, G., Stahl, S.M. and Halbreich, U. (2001) Effectiveness of St John's Wort in major depression: a randomized controlled trial. *Journal of the American Medical Association* 285, 1978–1986.

Shor-Posner, G., Lecusay, R., Miguez, M.J., Moreno-Black, G., Zhang, G., Rodriguez, N., Burbano, X., Baum, M. and Wilkie, F. (2003) Psychological burden in the era of HAART: impact of selenium therapy. *International Journal of Psychiatry and Medicine* 33, 55–69.

Solomon, P.R., Adams, F., Silver, A., Zimmer, J. and DeVeaux, R. (2002) Ginkgo for memory enhancement: a randomized controlled trial. *Journal of the American Dietetic Association* 288, 835–840.

Spilker, B. (1991) *Guide to clinical trials*. Raven Press, New York.

Sunderland, T., Tariot, P.N., Cohen, R.M., Newhouse, P.A., Mellow, A.M., Mueller, E.A. and Murphy, D.L. (1987) Dose-dependent effects of deprenyl on CSF monoamine metabolites in patients with Alzheimer's disease. *Psychopharmacology* 91, 293–296.

Tejani-Butt, S.M., Yang, J. and Pawlyk, A.C. (1995) Altered serotonin transporter sites in Alzheimer's disease raphe and hippocampus. *Neuroreport* 6, 1207–1210.

Thiele, B., Brink, I. and Ploch, M. (1994) Modulation of cytokine expression by hypericum extract. *Journal of Geriatric Psychiatry and Neurology* 7(Suppl. 1), S60–62.

US Food and Drug Administration, Center for Food Safety and Applied Nutrition. (1994) *Dietary Supplement and Health Education Act*. Available at: http://www.cfsan.fda.gov/~dms/dietsupp.html.

US Food and Drug Administration, Center for Food Safety and Applied Nutrition (2002) *Consumer Advisory: Kava-containing Dietary Supplements may be Associated with Severe Liver Damage*. Available at: http://www.cfsan.fda.gov/~dms/addskava.html [February, 2005].

Varga, J., Jimenez, S.A. and Uitto, J. (1993) L-tryptophan and the eosinophilia-myalgia syndrome: current understanding of the etiology and pathogenesis. *Journal of Investigative Dermatology* 100, 97S–105S.

Vatassery, G.T., Bauer, T. and Dysken, M. (1999) High doses of vitamin E in the treatment of disorders of the central nervous system in the aged. *American Journal of Clinical Nutrition* 70, 793–801.

Wesnes, K.A., Ward, T., McGinty, A. and Petrini, O. (2000) The memory enhancing effects of a Ginkgo biloba/Panax ginseng combination in healthy middle-aged volunteers. *Psychopharmacology* 152, 353–361.

Whiskey, E., Werneke, U. and Taylor, D. (2001) A systematic review and meta-analysis of Hypericum perforatum in depression: a comprehensive clinical. review. *International Clinical Psychopharmacology* 16, 239–252.

Yasuno, F., Suhara, T., Nakayama, T., Ichimiya, T., Okubo, Y., Takano, A., Ando, T., Inoue, M., Maeda, J. and Suzuki, K. (2003) Inhibitory effect of hippocampal 5-HT1A receptors on human explicit memory. *American Journal of Psychiatry* 160, 334–340.

Yoshitake, T., Iizuka, R., Yoshitake, S., Weikop, P., Muller, W.E., Ogren, S.O. and Kehr, J. (2004) Hypericum perforatum L (St John's Wort) preferentially increases extracellular dopamine levels in the rat prefrontal cortex. *British Journal of Pharmacology* 142, 414–418.

Zhang, S.M., Hernan, M.A., Chen, H., Spiegelman, D., Willett, W.C. and Ascherio, A. (2002) Intakes of vitamins E and C, carotenoids, vitamin supplements, and PD risk. *Neurology* 59, 1161–1169.

Internet sources of information on dietary supplements:

National Institutes of Health, Office of Dietary Supplements (http://dietary-supplements.info.nih.gov)
US Food and Drug Administration, Center for Food Safety and Nutrition (http://vm.cfsan.fda.gov~dms/supplmnt.html)
International Food Information Council (http://www.ific.org/index.cfm).

10 Bio-behavioral and Psychosocial Influences on Nutrition

B.J. Tepper

Introduction

As pointed out in Chapter 2, the effect of nutrition on behavior is bidirectional. On the one hand, nutritional state can have a profound effect on our mental state, sense of well-being and our responses to physical and emotional stress. On the other hand, certain aspects of our social or physical environment such as cultural and family background, where we live and our educational and income level affect our attitudes toward foods. This combination of social and environmental variables can have far-reaching consequences for eating behavior, mediating both the types and amounts of foods we choose to consume, ultimately influencing nutritional state.

This chapter will explore how major biological variables such as sex, age, genetic background and disease influence the nutrition–behavior paradigm. Fig. 10.1 illustrates this theoretical model. The reader will recognize this as the same basic model introduced in Chapter 2 with some additional complexities. Certain variables such as the presence of a disease (e.g. diabetes) can directly alter nutritional state and thereby influence eating behavior. Other variables (e.g. genetic variation in taste) do not affect nutritional state directly, but exert a strong influence on eating behavior which subsequently influences nutrition and health. Moreover, social and environ-

mental variables (we will henceforth call these psychosocial variables) can operate in a similar fashion. As we have seen in Chapter 7, low folic acid intake during pregnancy is a leading cause of neural tube defects in newborns. Low socio-economic status can limit the availability of fresh fruits and vegetables, which are a rich source of folic acid. In this example, low socio-economic status is seen to have a direct influence on the nutritional state of the mother, which has a subsequent impact on the physical and cognitive development of her child.

Alternately, psychosocial variables can mediate or modify behaviors which have a subsequent effect on nutritional state. An excessive drive for thinness is a risk factor for eating disorders such as anorexia nervosa. If left unchecked, this attitude and the behaviors it entails (self-imposed food restriction) can lead to severe weight loss and poor nutritional status, conditions which have multiple physiological effects on the body including sleep disturbances, anemia, decreased heart rate, low blood pressure and kidney dysfunction, among others (see Chapter 13 for a complete description).

It should be obvious from this discussion that the nutrition–behavior paradigm consists of a complex mosaic of direct, indirect and interactive influences. This complexity presents a significant challenge to nutrition researchers attempting to disentangle these complex rela-

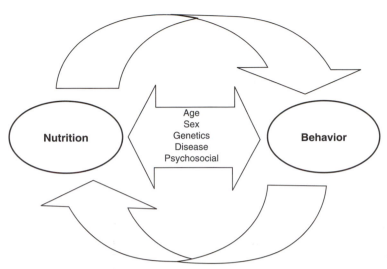

Fig. 10.1. Flow diagram of the nutrition–behavior paradigm.

tionships. In free-living humans, it is extremely difficult if not impossible to isolate the effects of a single variable on behavior. For example, suppose a researcher is interested in studying the effects of aging on appetite changes in the elderly. Since aging is known to diminish the ability to perceive the flavor of food, the researcher hypothesizes that reduced satisfaction with eating is the underlying cause of the loss of appetite. However, the elderly are also more likely to suffer from a range of medical conditions including systemic diseases such as diabetes, thyroid disorders and cancer or psychiatric conditions such as Alzheimer's disease or Parkinson's disease. These disorders, or their treatments can also influence taste and smell ability or could alter metabolism which ultimately affects appetite. Moreover, psychosocial factors such as living alone, depression or loss of independence can influence appetite. How can the researcher be sure that the loss of taste and smell is the underlying cause of the appetite loss when so many other variables contribute to this outcome? Basically, he or she cannot draw a firm conclusion about causality when other contributing factors are present. Hence, we call these contributing factors *confounding variables* because they reduce the confidence with which we can conclude that a specific outcome (here appetite loss) is directly related to a cause (reduced flavor perception).

Generally speaking, confounding variables cannot be eliminated. But, there are various ways to control for confounding variables in nutritional studies. Briefly, this involves the use of appropriate study design and execution. In an epidemiological study, there are statistical methods that permit the researcher to examine the influence of a single variable (e.g. age) on an outcome (e.g. amount consumed in a meal), while holding other variables constant (gender, medication use, etc.). In order to assess the effects of living in a nursing home on appetite in the elderly, the researcher can employ a case-control study in which each nursing home subject (case) is matched to a free-living subject (control) in relevant characteristics such as gender, income and overall health. If differences in appetite are confirmed between the cases and controls, then the researcher can begin looking at specific aspects of the nursing home environment that might explain these differences. Animal studies may be useful in some cases as they more readily permit control of confounding variables. The reader is referred to Willett (1998) for a more in-depth discussion of experimental design issues.

The relevant point to be made here is that caution must always be used in drawing conclusions from nutritional studies. Careful consideration of the experimental design is a critical step in determining whether the conclusions drawn from a study are appropriate and valid. A researcher's claim that reduced flavor perception causes appetite loss in the elderly (or that sugar causes food cravings or ginko biloba improves mental performance, for that matter) may be unwarranted if other variables that are known to influence this relationship were not considered as part of the experiment.

We begin the next section by describing some of the major genetic and biological determinants of the nutrition–behavior paradigm, followed by the psychosocial variables. Given the integrative and often intimate relationships among these variables, it may be necessary to skip ahead, so to speak, and incorporate some of the psychosocial variables into our earlier discussion.

Taste Perception and Preference

How foods are perceived

According to consumers, taste is the most important determinant of food choice (Glanz *et al.*, 1998). The word 'taste' as it is commonly used encompasses a number of dimensions of a food including its aroma, flavor and texture. Aromas and flavors are complex mixtures of volatile odor compounds (Lawless and Heymann, 1998). These volatile compounds can be inhaled directly through the nose or released in the mouth during chewing and swallowing a food. In both cases, the odor molecules become dissolved in the mucus layer that lines the nasal passages and are conducted upward to the olfactory epithelium where they bind to odor receptor cells (See Fig. 10.2).

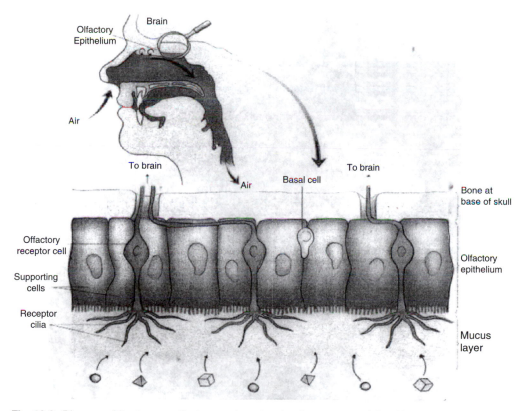

Fig. 10.2. Diagram of the human olfactory system showing the anatomy of the olfactory epithelium and the routes by which volatile odor molecules reach the olfactory epithelium. Reproduced with permission from Matthews, G. Neurobiology: molecules, cells and systems. London: Blackwell Science (http://www.blackwellpublishing.com/matthews/about.html)

Although the specific mechanisms of odor perception largely remain a mystery, recent discoveries have revealed much about the structure and functional properties of odor receptors and the neural pathways and brain centers with which they communicate. Approximately 500–750 odor receptor genes have been identified in humans (Mombaerts, 1999). However, humans are capable of perceiving thousands of individual odor molecules. Since the number of individual compounds that can be perceived greatly exceeds the number of receptors, it is believed that different combinations (or families) of receptors fire in concert to encode a complex aroma. For instance, coffee is composed of >800 individual aroma compounds (Illy, 2002). Separately, these compounds have little resemblance to coffee, but when present together they stimulate a unique pattern of neural firing that the brain interprets as the familiar aroma of coffee.

The basic tastes also contribute to flavor perception. The basic tastes are perceived within the oral cavity by the taste buds that are distributed primarily on the tip and edges of the tongue (see Fig. 10.3). Each taste bud is composed of a series of elongated taste receptor cells that are arranged around a central core, like sections of an orange. The top of the taste bud or taste 'pore' is open to the flow of saliva. This configuration permits taste molecules that are dissolved in the saliva to gain access to the taste cells (Lawless and Heymann, 1998).

The taste buds are arranged on the surface of specialized structures called papillae. Taste papillae vary in size and shape. Humans have three types of functional taste papillae: fungiform (mushroom shaped), foliate (appearing as parallel rows of ridges and valleys) and circumvallate (button-shaped). Each taste papilla contains from two to several hundred taste buds depending on its, size, type and location. Although the taste buds are too small to be seen without magnification, taste papillae are easily viewed by the naked eye as small mounds on the tip and margins of the tongue. The circumvallate papillae are the largest papillae on the human tongue. They are arranged in an inverted 'V' on the back of the tongue. Additional taste buds are also found on the soft palate and epiglottis, at the back of the throat (Lawless and Heymann, 1998).

Taste buds respond to the four classic basic tastes including sweet, salt, bitter and sour. Specific receptors for sweet and bitter taste have been identified and are localized to the surface of the taste cells. However, salt and sour taste are detected through another mechanism; namely by activation of ion channels that reside within the taste cell membrane (Lindemann, 2001). Umami is another distinct oral taste sensation. Umami is loosely translated as 'delicious taste' and refers to the sensation associated with the amino acid L-glutamate and 5' ribonucleotides such as inosine 5'-monophosphate (IMP) and guanine 5'-monophosphate (GMP) (Yamaguchi and Ninomiya, 2000). Monosodium glutamate (MSG) has long been used as a meat tenderizer. However, MSG and 5'-ribonucleotides also function as flavor enhancers, lending a savory richness to vegetables and meats. Accumulating evidence, including the identification of a specific oral receptor mechanism for glutamate, suggests that umami is a 5th basic taste (Brand, 2000).

Oral irritation, touch, temperature and pain represent a broadly-defined class of sensations that are associated with free nerve endings of the Trigeminal (5th cranial) nerve and specialized receptors of somatosensory fibers. Chemesthesis is a term used to describe the close anatomical and functional relationship between these two systems (Bryant and Silver, 2000). Trigeminal sensations include the hotness of chili peppers and horseradish, the coolness of mint, the tingle of carbonation and the astringency of tea. Trigeminal nerve fibers innervate the surfaces of the mouth, nasal cavities and the soft tissues around the eye. This explains why strong horseradish simultaneously produces mild burning in the mouth and nose, and tearing of the eyes.

Texture relates to the feel of the food in the mouth (e.g. grainy, lumpy, oily) and its mechanical properties – how it responds to forces in the mouth during chewing (Lawless and Heymann, 1998). For example, hardness is defined as the amount of force required to compress a sample of food between the molars; springiness is defined as the degree to which the sample returns to its original shape after compression. Premium quality chocolate

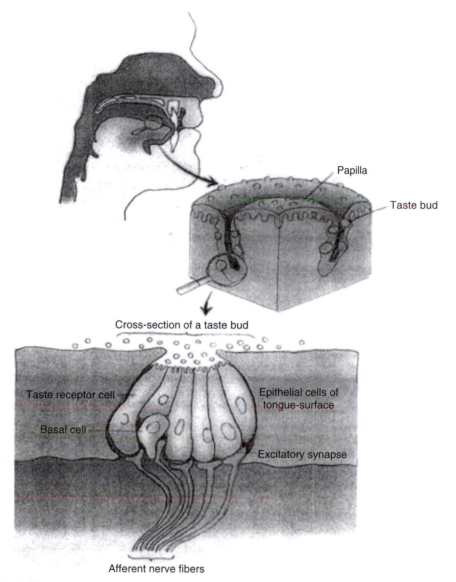

Fig. 10.3. Diagram of the anatomy of the human taste system showing a taste papilla and a cross-section of a taste bud. Reproduced with permission from Matthews, G. Neurobiology: molecules, cells and system. London: Blackwell Science (http://www.blackwellpublishing.com/matthews/about.html)

might be described by its silky-smooth, mouth-feel whereas a freshly-baked cake might be defined by its soft, springy crumb.

All of the sensations just described, at the appropriate levels, along with color and other appearance characteristics ultimately determine whether a food is accepted or rejected. Hedonic reactions to foods are considered in the following section.

Genetic taste predispositions

Many species, including humans have a strong, genetic predisposition to prefer or reject certain tastes. In a now classic study, Steiner (1977) photographed the facial expressions of newborn infants who were exposed to basic taste solutions, prior to their first feeding. The infants displayed a positive facial expression (smiling) to sweet taste, pursing of the lips to sour taste and mouth-gaping to bitter taste. The reader is cautioned, however, that observational studies such as this one can be subjective because the interpretation of the findings depends on the researchers' unbiased recording of the infants' responses. Although facial expressions can be misinterpreted, similar responses have also been recorded from numerous primate species and other animals (Steiner et al., 2001). The decerebrate rat also displays facial reactions to oral taste stimuli suggesting that this response is an unconscious reflex (Grill and Norgren, 1978).

Another method for assessing the hedonic taste reactions of infants is to measure their fluid consumption. In one study, infants were fed either sugar water or plain water by bottle. The infants consumed more sugar water than plain water and their consumption of sugar water increased with increasing sugar concentration (Desor et al., 1973). Together these findings support several conclusions about the taste reactions of infants. First, infants are capable of detecting basic taste stimuli at birth. Second, they can distinguish different concentrations of these stimuli and third, these stimuli elicit hedonic reactions in infants similar to those seen in children and adults.

Throughout evolutionary history, humans have been faced with the task of selecting nutritionally-adequate foodstuffs from plant and animal materials in their natural environment. The availability of digestible items was limited and often unpredictable. The innate preference for sweet taste and rejection of bitter taste may have provided survival advantages for ancestral human societies. The attraction to sweet foods such as fruits and berries provided a concentrated source of calories. On the other hand, many plants contain bitter-tasting alkaloids and other compounds that are toxic to humans and should be avoided (Fenwick et al., 1990; Glendinning, 1994). Technological advances in agriculture and animal husbandry have stabilized the food supply for contemporary societies. The advent of the modern supermarket with its seemingly endless selection of items is a very recent phenomenon in the long course of human food ways. The implications of overabundance of food to the development of obesity will be discussed in Chapter 14. Suffice it to say here, that current food patterns seem to reflect our innate predispositions quite

well, favoring the selection of calorically-dense sweets and fats at the expense of fruits and vegetables, some of which are bitter-tasting.

The preference for salt deserves particular attention. There is a biological need for salt and a strong preference for salt is ubiquitous in most species. Blood and kidney concentrations of sodium are tightly regulated to maintain proper fluid balance and cellular function. Individuals must seek out salt from the environment to meet dietary needs. Both animals and humans exhibit cravings for salt when they are salt depleted either by dietary restriction, drug intervention (diuretics) or as a result of disease affecting the adrenal glands or kidneys (Denton et al., 1996). In contrast to the other basic tastes, the ability to detect salt appears to be absent in the neonate suggesting that the taste apparatus for salt is not fully developed at birth. But, this situation rapidly changes. Infants who are initially indifferent to salt solution at birth develop a strong preference for salt water by 4 months of age (Beauchamp et al., 1986). Today, we worry about consuming too much salt. Prior to industrialization, however, salt supplies were limited in many geographic locations and salt was considered a precious commodity. Salt was carried as part of the spice trade and wars have been fought over it. Indeed, public opposition to the salt tax was a precipitating factor in the French Revolution (see Tannahill, 1989).

Fat

There is little doubt that fat is highly palatable to humans, but how the preference for this nutrient develops is not well understood. It is widely believed that the preference for fat is a learned rather than an innate phenomenon. This conclusion is supported, in part, by data showing that newborn infants are indifferent to the taste of corn oil placed on the tongue (Graillon et al., 1997). Moreover, young children rapidly learn to prefer high-fat calorie-dense foods and readily associate flavors paired with the delivery of calories from fat. In one feeding experiment, children consumed either a high-fat yogurt drink with a distinctive flavor or a low-fat yogurt drink with a different distinctive flavor on different days. When both drinks were offered simultaneously, the children preferred the high-fat paired flavor to the low-fat paired flavor (Johnson *et al.*, 1991). These experiments and similar experiments in rats have led to the general conclusion that strong hedonic appeal coupled with positive caloric consequences contributes to the reinforcing properties of fat.

Unlike the basic tastes for which a specific taste and receptor type can be linked (e.g. sweet taste), no oral receptor for fat has ever been identified. The search for a putative oral fat receptor is hindered by the fact that the perception of fat does not depend on a single sensory quality. Fats impart a wide range of sensory attributes to foods including flavor, texture and mouthfeel. It has been suggested that the perception of these fat-associated flavors and textures rather than the sensory properties of the fats themselves drive acceptance. This is because triglycerides (oils stripped of volatile flavors) are generally unpalatable to humans (Mela, 1990). Thus, the absence of any strong evidence for a neonatal response to fats coupled with more compelling evidence for learning, has led most researchers to support the learning hypothesis.

Nevertheless, recent evidence challenges this traditional view. Biophysical studies in rats suggest the existence of a receptor that depolarizes in response to the topical application of cis-polyunsaturated fatty acids to the tongue (Gilbertson *et al.*, 1997). Moreover, rats rendered anosmic (odor blind) by intranasal application of zinc sulfate could distinguish oleate (long-chain fatty acid) from triolein (triglyceride of oleate) in a two-bottle preference test presumably based on taste (Fukuwatari *et al.*, 2003). Human studies also suggest that the mere taste of fat on the tongue (without the subject being able to see, smell or swallow it) was sufficient to elicit a physiological response (rise in blood triglycerides) (Mattes, 2001). These findings seem to suggest that human beings posses some type of oral fat detector but the exact nature of this mechanism has yet to be elucidated.

Developmental Factors and Early Taste Experiences

Early taste experiences and developmental factors each play a critical role in shaping the food preferences of infants and young children. To address this issue, we return to studies in infants. We have already discussed the strong innate preference for sweet taste in the neonate. At 6 months of age, infants who had previously been fed sugar water by bottle preferred the sweetened water more than infants with no prior exposure to sugar water suggesting that innate preferences can be modified by early taste experiences (Beauchamp and Moran, 1982). Interestingly, the strong preference for highly concentrated, sweet fluids seems to be specific to young children and diminishes with age. When subjects from different age groups rated sugar solutions, younger subjects preferred the sweeter solutions, whereas older subjects preferred the less sweet solutions (Desor *et al.*, 1975; De Graaf and Zandstra, 1999). These results are supported by longitudinal studies in which the same group of subjects gave higher preference ratings to sugar solutions when they were 11–15 years of age than they did when they were retested at 19–24 years of age (Desor and Beauchamp, 1987). An age decline in the preferred level of saltiness in soups has also been reported (Desor *et al.*, 1975). Thus, older children show a maturational shift in the preferred concentration of sweetness in beverages and saltiness in soups, more like those of adults. These findings suggest that as children gain experience with the foods and cuisines of their culture, they begin to adopt more adult-like preferences. More will be said shortly about family and cultural influences on food selection.

Milk is the primary source of nourishment for infants and is often the first oral sensory stimulus they encounter. Milk is a fat-in-water emulsion consisting of milkfat, proteins, sugars and salts. Cow's milk can vary in flavor depending on the type of feed the animals consume. Menella and Beauchamp (1993) have shown that certain flavors present in a mother's diet can be transmitted into her breast milk. Evaluation by trained human judges revealed that garlic aroma was detectable in the breast milk of women who consumed garlic approximately 2 hours before. Infants of these mothers nursed for longer periods of time and consumed more milk when the milk smelled like garlic than before garlic ingestion or after garlic aroma declined.

Additional evidence suggests that early flavor associations might occur prenatally, by exposure of the fetus to flavors in amniotic fluid. For example, newborns of mothers who consumed anise during late pregnancy showed a preference for anise aroma 4 hours after birth (Schaal *et al.*, 2000). Flavor learning *in utero* has also been shown to influence post-natal food ingestion, as well. In one study, three groups of mothers were studied: group 1 consumed carrot juice during pregnancy and water during lactation, group 2 consumed water during pregnancy and carrot juice during lactation, and group 3 consumed water during both periods. Infants of mothers who consumed carrot juice during pregnancy consumed more carrot-flavored cereal during feeding tests at 6 months of age than did the other groups of infants (Mennella and Beauchamp, 1999). These findings suggest that early flavor experiences, both in the womb and during lactation, increase a child's familiarity with flavors and facilitates the learning of cuisine. Some researchers have hypothesized that these early experiences may have long-term consequences for food selection later in development (Stein *et al.*, 1996).

Neophobia and familial interactions

Food selection by young children is strongly determined by familiarity with and exposure to specific foods. Fear of trying new foods or 'neophobia' is a trait commonly observed in young children as they make the transition to adult-like foods. Neophobia may have adaptive significance by protecting the young organism against the inadvertent consumption of foods that might be harmful (Rozin, 1996). The fact that rats and other omnivores show a similar behavior (called 'bait shyness') underscores the strong biological origins of this behavior. However, studies have shown that children can overcome neophobia with repeated exposure to the taste of a novel food (Birch and Fisher, 1998). Since the consumption of a varied diet is consistent with good health (Anonymous, 2000), repeated exposure to new foods during childhood could promote diversity in children's food choices and ultimately lead to the selection of healthier diets. Pliner and Hobden (1992) developed a simple paper and pencil instrument to measure food neophobia in older children and adults.

Since young children have little control over the types and amounts of foods served to them,

parental-feeding practices play a critical role in shaping a child's eating environment. Parents frequently use food in contingencies (e.g. 'Eat your broccoli and you can go play outside') or as rewards for good behavior (e.g. 'Put your toys away and you can have ice cream'). However, research has shown that these coercive strategies can have the unintended consequences of reducing preferences for nutritionally desirable foods (broccoli) and increasing preferences for palatable sweet foods (ice cream) (Birch *et al.*, 1996). In another example, Fisher and Birch (1999) found that daughters of mothers who withheld snacks showed a higher preference for snacks and consumed more snacks in a free-choice paradigm than daughters of mothers who were less controlling of snack food intake.

Aside from direct attempts by parents to control their children's eating, parents particularly mothers also communicate their own attitudes about food and eating to their children. One study showed that mothers who were chronic dieters and who were overweight themselves had daughters who overate and were heavier (Birch and Fisher, 2000). Other research has shown, however, that when children are encouraged to follow their own internal hunger/satiety cues they are capable of self-regulating their energy intake (Johnson, 2000).

A final point to be made is that parents and children share not only a common eating environment but a common genetic background as well, and the nature of this interaction remains poorly understood. Studies in identical twins may be promising for teasing apart the contributions of genes and environment to the development of eating behaviors in children (Faith *et al.*, 2002).

Preference shifts in adults

An important consideration is whether taste and eating experiences acquired in childhood, are fixed and resistant to change. This is a relevant question since the primary focus of dietary intervention is on modifying the consumption of highly preferred sensory qualities such as fat, salt or sugar. Common, everyday experience tells us that dietary change is difficult to sustain, supporting the argument that food preferences are fixed. Other evidence indicates that food preferences may be more malleable. One example is the observed population shift in the acceptance of low-fat milk (White, 1993). Diet manipulation studies have also shown that consumption of a reduced-salt diet for 8–12 weeks resulted in a downward shift in the preferred level of salt in foods (Bertino et al., 1982). Similar results were reported for reduced-fat diets, but only when the fat reduction was achieved by substituting foods that were naturally lower in fat for higher fat versions (not with fat-replaced items) (Mattes, 1993). Whether this hedonic shift promotes long-term adherence to sodium- or fat-reduced diets in real life remains an open question.

The acquisition of liking for chili pepper is another example of the malleability of food preferences. Chili peppers are one of the most widely consumed spices in the world with 2.3 M tonnes (dry weight) produced each year (DeWitt, 1999). Most humans find chili peppers aversive the first time they taste them. But, with repeated exposure, some individuals eventually show a strong preference for them. The explanation for this phenomenon is unclear. Some researchers have suggested that preference for chili develops as a benign form of sensation or thrill seeking (Rozin, 1990). Other evidence suggests that repeated exposure to capsaicin (the active ingredient in chili pepper) reduces overall sensitivity (Green and Rentmeister-Bryant, 1998), perhaps promoting its acceptance and long-term use. This shift in sensitivity could partially explain why habitual chili pepper eaters rate the hotness of capsaicin less intense than do non-eaters (Lawless et al., 1985). It is also possible that individuals vary in their perception of hotness that could mediate their acceptance of hot foods. We now consider the influence of individuality in taste responses on food selection.

Genetic Variation in Taste and Food Selection

In the previous section, the genetic predispositions and environmental influences that shape taste preferences and food selection were described. However, humans show large individual variation in preferences for specific foods that cannot be explained on the basis of innate preferences alone. The emerging field of 'taste genetics' has provided additional clues about the role of human variation in taste perception in food preferences and eating behavior (Tepper, 1998; Tepper and Ullrich, 2002).

It has been known for some time that many plant species contain a class of bitter-tasting compounds called thioureas. All compounds in this family contain the chemical moiety N-C=S which is responsible for their bitter taste. Thioureas are commonly found in vegetables of the Brassica family including cabbage, broccoli, Brussels sprouts and kale (Fahey et al., 2001). An accidental discovery by A.L. Fox in 1931 revealed that taste sensitivity to these compounds was a genetically determined trait (Fox, 1932). The two most studied compounds are phenylthiocarbamide (PTC) and its chemical derivative 6-n-propylthiouracil (PROP). PTC and PROP are moderately to extremely bitter to some individuals (they are called 'tasters') and tasteless to others (they are called 'non-tasters'). Approximately 70% of Caucasians living in North America and Western Europe are tasters; the remaining 30% are non-tasters. These percentages vary dramatically among different ethnic groups across the globe. For example, comparatively fewer Blacks, and ethnic Chinese and Koreans are non-tasters (~3–11%); whereas, non-tasters comprise ~40% of individuals among certain indigenous groups in India (Guo and Reed, 2001). The implications of these ethnic differences on food preferences are not well understood.

It was originally believed that the ability to taste PTC/PROP was inherited as a classic Mendelian trait; tasters were assumed to posses at least one dominant allele (TT or Tt), whereas non-tasters posses two recessive alleles (tt). However, taste studies seem to indicate that the large group of tasters consists of two distinct subgroups, medium tasters (Tt) who are moderately sensitive to PTC/PROP and supertasters (TT) who show the most extreme sensitivity to these compounds (Bartoshuk et al., 1994). A major gene responsible for this phenotype has recently been mapped to human chromosome 7 although additional loci may reside on other chromosomes (Drayna et al., 2003).

Early interest in the inheritance of this trait arose from field studies in which observers

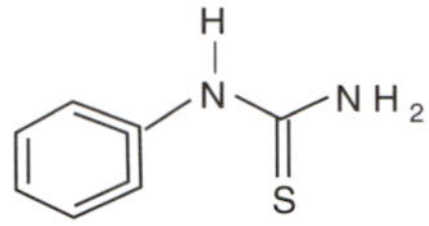

Phenylthiocarbamide (PTC)

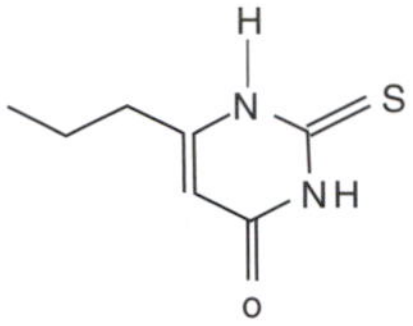

6-n-Propylthiouracil (PROP)

Fig.10.4. Chemical structure of PTC and PROP.

noted an association between the incidence of PTC taste blindness and the iodine deficiency disease known as goiter (see Chapter 8 for a description of this disease). Although low dietary iodine is the primary cause of this disease, goitrogens in the food supply may play a contributing role by interfering with the ability of the thyroid gland to utilize iodine. It had been known for some time that the thioureas possess anti-thyroid properties (Gaitan, 1989). While studying isolated populations in the Andes Mountains of Ecuador, Greene (1974) observed that most athyroitic cretins (individuals suffering from an extreme form of iodine deficiency disease characterized by severe mental retardation) were non-tasters. He hypothesized that taster status might be protective against the overconsumption of goitrogens in the food supply and might have provided a selective advantage in populations consuming diets that were marginal in iodine.

The relevance of this phenotype to well-nourished populations with adequate iodine intakes appears less certain. Some contemporary studies support the relationship between greater taste sensitivity to PTC/PROP and rejection of thiourea-containing vegetables and fruits (Drewnowski et al., 2000), but other studies have failed to do so (Mattes and Labov, 1989; Jerzsa-Latta et al., 1990). Nevertheless, liking of fruits and vegetables is influenced by a variety of factors including attitudes, social norms and health considerations making it difficult to isolate the effects of taste factors on acceptability. Interestingly, current dietary recommendations encourage the consumption of

fruits and vegetables, which are a rich source of cancer preventive phytochemicals and antioxidants. However, many of these compounds are bitter tasting. With respect to cancer risk, PROP tasters may be at a disadvantage since bitter taste might serve as a barrier for the acceptance of these foods (Drewnowski and Gomez-Carneros, 2000).

Studies suggest that PROP tasters are more sensitive to a variety of oral stimuli including bitter tastes (not related to thioureas), sweet taste, the texture of fats and oral irritation. A partial list of these relationships is shown in Table 10.1. A striking feature of the data presented in Table 10.1 is that PROP taster status appears to play a role in the perception of so many diverse sensory qualities. How these differences arise and why they exist, are only beginning to be understood. However, emerging evidence suggests that tasters and non-tasters are anatomically different. PROP tasters have more taste buds on the tip of the tongue which could explain their greater sensitivity to basic taste sensations. Tasters are also hypothesized to have more trigeminal fibers, which play a role in the perception of fats and irritation. Thus, anatomical variation in the oral taste apparatus might explain why tasters are physiologically more responsive to these stimuli (Bartoshuk et al., 1994; Tepper and Nurse, 1997).

A broader question is whether these differences in perception influence food preferences and dietary selection. A number of studies have shown that as compared to non-tasters, PROP tasters show lower acceptance of many foods that have the key sensory qualities listed in

Table 10.1. A partial list of sensory properties that vary with genetic taste sensitivity to 6-n-propylthiouracil.

Taste

Bitter
  Caffeine
  Quinine
  Naringin (grapefruit)
  Isohumulones (beer)
  Green tea
  Dark beer
  L-Amino acids
  Epicatechins [1]
Bitter (aftertaste)
  Potassium chloride
  Sodium benzoate
  Saccharin
Sweet
  Sucrose
  Saccharin
  Aspartame
Irritation
  Chili
  Cinnamaldehyde
  Ethanol
Texture (fat)
  Salad dressing
  Dairy products

[1] Phytochemicals commonly found in black tea, grape juice and red wine. Compiled from: Delwiche *et al.*, 2001; Tepper and Ullirch, 2002; Tepper *et al.*, 2003; Kirkmeyer and Tepper 2004.

Table 10.1, including high-fat salad dressings and dairy products, bitter vegetables and fruits, and soy products (Akella *et al.*, 1997; Tepper and Nurse 1998; Drewnowski *et al.*, 2000; Duffy and Bartoshuk, 2000; Tepper *et al.*, 2003).

Hot and pungent foods represent another interesting group of foods that are perceived differently by tasters and non-tasters (Prescott and Swain-Campbell, 2000). In one study, subjects rolled a series of cotton-tipped applicators across the center of their tongues which contained increasing concentrations of capsaicin (see Fig. 10.5). As expected, burn intensity increased with increasing capsaicin concentration for all subjects. However, tasters (medium and supertasters combined) perceived greater burn intensity from the capsaicin starting with the third sample. Although the differences between groups were statistically significant, the magnitude of the effect was modest (Tepper and

Nurse, 1997). Nevertheless, a subsequent study showed that these differences in perception had a meaningful impact on acceptance and use of hot/pungent foods. The responses of 232 adult subjects to a food preference survey revealed that fewer tasters reported that they liked chili peppers, hot sauce and salsa and they used these items less frequently than did non-tasters (Tepper and Ullirch, 2002). Our previous discussion on the acquisition of liking of chili pepper seems relevant here. It is possible that genetic taste differences might predispose an individual to either like or dislike chili peppers. The contribution of genetic taste factors, cultural and social variables on acceptance of chili would make an interesting research study.

The significance of the PROP phenotype to nutrition and health is an area of intense scientific scrutiny. There is some evidence, at least in children, that non-tasters consume more discretionary fats in their diets than tasters (Keller *et al.*, 2002). This finding is consistent with some studies in adults that have reported higher preferences for high-fat foods by non-tasters as compared to tasters (Tepper and Nurse, 1998; Duffy and Bartoshuk, 2000). It is conceivable that PROP status serves as a genetic marker for underlying differences in fat preference and dietary fat intake. Over time, increased dietary fat intake could lead to higher body weights among non-tasters. In support of this hypothesis studies are showing that non-tasters are heavier than other groups (Tepper, 2004). Thus, the PROP phenotype might constitute a critical link between an individual's personal taste world and his or her food consumption behavior. Further study of this relationship could provide considerable insight into individual differences in susceptibility to diet-induced obesity. This area is not without controversy, however, as other studies have shown no relation between PROP status and either food preferences or body weight (Drewnowski, 2004).

Disease, Aging and Other Physiological Differences

Disease

A variety of systemic diseases can influence food and fluid appetite. Some of these include:

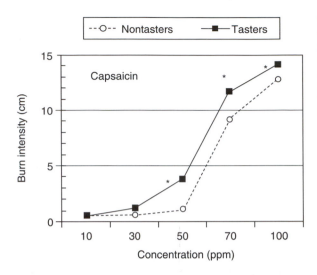

Fig. 10.5. Burn intensity ratings for capsaicin applied to the center of the tongue with a cotton swab. *Super-tasters gave higher ratings to capsaicin at 50–100 ppm than non-tasters ($p < 0.05$). Adapted from Tepper and Nurse, 1997, with kind permission from Elsevier Ltd.

thyroid disorders, which affect overall energy metabolism and food intake; chronic renal disease, which affects the ability of the kidney to regulate sodium excretion and influences salt appetite; and diabetes mellitus, which affects the body's ability to secrete or utilize insulin. Changes in taste and appetite in diabetes mellitus have been relatively well-studied and will be briefly discussed here.

Diabetes mellitus occurs in two forms: Type 1 or juvenile onset diabetes affects the ability of the islet cells of the pancreas to secrete insulin; Type 2 also known as adult-onset, or non-insulin dependent diabetes occurs when the cells of the body become resistant to the action of insulin. Both diseases are characterized by an inability to utilize glucose leading to an accumulation of glucose in the blood if left untreated. Historical descriptions of diabetes have suggested that the disease is associated with cravings for sweet foods. In both forms of the disease, patients experience a disruption in taste function, with sweet taste being most vulnerable (Settle, 1991). Individuals with Type 2 diabetes show higher preferences for sucrose solutions and consume more sweet foods in their diets (Tepper *et al.*, 1996). Women with gestational diabetes (a form of the disease that occurs in pregnancy associated with Type 2 symptoms) liked sweet-fat dairy drinks more than pregnant women without the disease. In this same study, plasma glucose was positively corre-

lated with both liking of glucose solutions and intake of sweet carbohydrates (as fruit and fruit juice) in women with GDM, but not in women without the disease. Thus, women who had the more severe diabetic symptoms liked the glucose solutions more and also had higher dietary intakes of sweet carbohydrates (Tepper and Seldner, 1999). Together, these findings support the notion of a 'sweet-tooth' in diabetes, which could have important implications for the management of this disease.

The cachexia-anorexia syndrome is a term used to describe the severe appetite loss, anorexia and body wasting associated with advanced cancers and other chronic inflammatory states such as HIV infection, inflammatory bowel disease, liver disease and rheumatoid arthritis. The origins of this condition are not well understood, but involve malabsorption of nutrients, changes in metabolic and immune function and modulation of brain neurotransmitter or neuropeptide activity. Cachexic patients can experience disruptions in taste or smell function, food aversions, nausea and vomiting. Chemotherapeutic and immunosuppressive agents seem to exacerbate these effects (Plata-Salaman, 2000).

Aging

As mentioned in the introduction to this chapter, taste and smell problems are prevalent in the elderly (Hoffman *et al.*, 1998; Murphy *et al.*, 2002) and may reduce the quality of life for elderly persons. Although subtle declines in chemosensory function could begin as early as mid-adulthood, noticeable losses first appear during the 6th decade of life and function continues to diminish thereafter (Ship and Weiffenbach, 1993; Doty, 2001). It has been reported that aromas are 2–15 times harder for the elderly to detect, and when they are detected, they are weaker to the elderly than to young subjects (Schiffman, 1993; Stevens and Cain, 1993). The age decline in taste perception is much more modest than for aroma perception, but, interestingly, all taste qualities are not equally affected. Elderly subjects are more likely to experience a decline in bitter taste than in sweet taste; decreased sour and salty taste has been reported in some studies on aging but not others (Murphy and Gilmore, 1989; Cowart *et al.*, 1994). Nevertheless, even subtle taste and smell losses can influence the perception of foods and beverages. In one study, only 45% of middle-aged and elderly subjects reliably discriminated differences in salt concentration in tomato soup or the pres-

ence of the spice marjoram in carrot soup. In contrast, 88–95% of young subjects reliably discriminated these differences (Stevens and Cain, 1993).

Diminished appetite may be a risk factor for weight loss, poor nutritional status and other health consequences in geriatric populations. As the population ages, these problems are likely to intensify (Drewnowski and Shultz, 2001). The sources of appetite changes in the elderly are many but can be grouped into three major categories; functional changes to the taste/smell system, physiological changes associated with the diseases of aging or their treatments; and demographic/psychosocial factors. These factors are outlined in Table 10.2.

Functional causes of taste/smell loss include reduction in the number or activity of taste buds or olfactory receptors, changes in conduction along nerve pathways, or reduced activity at higher brain centers. Other changes associated with the aging process include dry mouth and changes in dentition which directly affect the ability to chew and swallow food, as well as functional changes in the digestive tract that affect the absorption and utilization of

Table 10.2. Sources of chemosensory and appetite changes in the elderly.

Chemosensory losses	Diseases of aging and their treatments	Psychosocial
Decreased turnover and renewal of taste buds; thickening of taste epithelium, atrophy of salivary glands. Decreased axonal transport across gustatory nerves. Decreased number of mitral cells and glomeruli in olfactory bulb.	Allergic rhinitis, upper respiratory infection; oral pathology including glossitis, burning mouth syndrome, periodontal disease, dry mouth, changes in dentition or difficulty swallowing; radiation, chemotherapy, surgical trauma; tobacco smoking and lung disease. Alzheimer's disease: neurofibrillary tangles and senile plaques in multiple olfactory structures. Parkinson's disease: decreased neurotransmission through dopaminergic pathways in olfactory bulb. Nutritional: cancer, chronic renal failure, liver disease, zinc deficiency. Endocrine: hypothyroidism, diabetes. Medications (including): anticholesteremics, anticoagulants, immunosuppressives, antihypertensives, hypoglycemics.	Education, income, bereavement, depression, living alone, immobility, food monotony.

Sources: Schiffman, 1993; Doty, 2001; Drewnowski and Shultz, 2001.

nutrients (Drewnowski and Shultz, 2001). Both Alzheimer's disease and Parkinson's disease affect the myelin sheathing of central nerve fibers and patients with these diseases have reduced ability to identify odors (Doty, 2001). Systemic diseases were discussed earlier in this chapter. Both over-the-counter and prescription medications can interfere with taste and smell function (Schiffman and Zervakis, 2002). Although these effects can occur in any age group, the elderly may be more vulnerable to the effects of pharmaceuticals since they often suffer from multiple diseases and may be taking several medications simultaneously.

Demographic and psychosocial factors are another source of appetite changes in the elderly. Low socio-economic status can directly affect the ability of the elderly to obtain or prepare palatable meals. Psychological factors such as bereavement, living alone or depression can exacerbate loss of interest in food. Monotonous diets lacking in variety have been linked to lower food intake in the elderly which can be overcome with more imaginative diet planning (Duffy et al., 1995). Flavor enhancement of foods is another strategy that could improve the acceptability of foods to the elderly (Francoise et al., 2001).

Pregnancy

Appetite changes are common in pregnancy and are generally of two types; those involving food aversions which typically occur during the early stages of pregnancy, and food cravings which appear later in gestation (Worthington-Roberts et al., 1989; Pope et al., 1992). Neither the natural history of pregnancy cravings and aversions – their timing, duration and intensity – nor their underlying causes are well understood. Food aversions are closely associated with nausea and vomiting during pregnancy (Crystal et al., 1999). This suite of symptoms is commonly referred to as 'morning sickness'. The term morning sickness is probably a misnomer since the vast majority of women who report nausea during pregnancy experience their symptoms throughout the day. Although 50% of women reported that their symptoms subsided by the end of the first trimester, 90% had nausea that lasted well into mid-pregnancy (Lacroix et al., 2000). Salty and spicy foods, including meats and shellfish are common targets of aversion during pregnancy as are alcohol and coffee. Alcohol and caffeine are of particular concern since these compounds are well-known teratogens that increase the risk of miscarriage and stillbirth (Flaxman and Sherman, 2002). It has been hypothesized that avoidance of these foods helps to protect the fetus from exposure to the toxic effects of these compounds. Other theories suggest that the steep rise in gestational hormones during early pregnancy triggers nausea and vomiting. Neither of these theories have been extensively supported.

Approximately 85% of women report food cravings at some point in their pregnancies. Cravings appear to be most frequent and intense during mid-pregnancy and to decline thereafter. Generally, sweet-fat foods are preferred during mid-pregnancy, whereas salty and spicy foods are preferred late in pregnancy (Bowen, 1992; Pope et al., 1992). As noted for nausea and vomiting in pregnancy, researchers have questioned whether changes in food cravings can be linked with fluctuations in the gestational hormones. Gestational hormones begin to rise in early pregnancy and reach a peak at mid-pregnancy before falling toward baseline at delivery. These hormonal changes are associated with metabolic adaptations that ensure a constant flow of energy to the developing fetus, primarily in the form of glucose (Boden, 1996). It is possible that the timing of peak cravings for sweets in mid-pregnancy coincides with this spike in gestational hormones. Studies documenting this relationship have yet to be done.

Ethnicity/Culture/Social Interactions

Social norms, attitudes and beliefs are critical determinants of food selection within a culture. Every culture has food traditions, which are passed down from generation to generation. These traditions determine which foods are to be eaten or avoided, what foods are to be eaten together or within certain social contexts. A complex code of rituals surrounds the preparation, presentation and consumption of foods (Long, 2000). Prohibitions against the consumption of pork, meats of any type, seafood or alcohol can be found selectively among the tenets of major religious and ethnic groups across the globe (Tannahill, 1989). Some foods are avoided only during religious observances such as the avoidance of meat during Lent or Ramadan. As discussed earlier in this chapter, through experience, children learn what foods are appropriate to consume and when.

Cuisine

All peoples cook their food, an activity that distinguishes humans from animal species. To a large extent cooking and transforming food has practical significance for releasing nutrients from the food. Cooking legumes disables protease inhibitors and lectins that lower their digestibility. For centuries, Native American cultures treated maize with lime (alkali), which enhances its amino acid profile and releases niacin (McGee, 1984). Cuisine refers to methods of food preparation and presentation that express the aesthetic, gustatory, social and nutritional ideals of a people or culture. Cuisines vary markedly around the world. Yet, there are three universal components of cuisine. These include dietary staples, cooking techniques and flavor principles – recurring combination of flavorings/ingredients that define main dishes (Rozin 1982; Rozin 2000). Examples are shown in Table 10.3.

The interested reader is referred to a collection of works describing the traditional meal patterns of Japan, China, Northern Europe and Britain (Marshall, 2000; Newman 2000; Otsuka 2000; Prattala, 2000).

Aside from burgers and fries, one can argue if the USA has a national cuisine. Our

Table 10.3. Components of 'Cuisine'.

- Dietary staples (maize – Mexico; rice – Asia).
- Cooking techniques (stir-fry – Asia; stewing – Mexico).
- 'Flavor Principles' – recurring combination of flavorings/ingredients that define main dishes:
  ○ Greece – lemon, oregano, olive oil
  ○ Indonesia – soy sauce, coconut, chili, ground nuts
  ○ China – soy sauce, ginger, garlic, sesame oil
  ○ Italy – tomato, oregano, garlic, olive oil.

Sources: Rozin, 1982, 2000.

basic food traditions derive from Northern Europe and Britain but strong regional and ethnic traditions flourish. Hush puppies and grits are more likely to be eaten in the American South, whereas, New England-style clam chowder is more commonly consumed in the Northeast. The presence of a large food manufacturing industry in the USA and an extensive national food distribution chain gives US consumers a large variety of food choices. Consumers from coast to coast can purchase a box of Rice Krispies cereal or a can of Campbell's soup in almost any grocery store. However, the nationalization of brands is a two-edged sword in some respects; it increases consumer access to a wide range of products, but it also tends to homogenize the food supply so that a supermarket shelf in Galveston, Texas might be undistinguishable from one in Freeport, Maine.

Food plays an indelible role in life, as a source of pleasure, health and personal identity. This philosophy is clearly revealed in the writings of the 19th-century gastronome and food writer Brillat-Savarin, who once wrote, 'tell me what you eat, and I will tell you what you are' (Brillat-Savarin 2000). However, attitudes toward foods do vary cross-culturally. In a study comparing the food attitudes of French, Belgian, Japanese and US consumers, the French were most likely to view food in terms of cuisine and pleasure; Americans were most influenced by nutritional value and health risks (Rozin et al., 1999). The latter orientation is not surprising given the strong Puritan food ethic that persists in the USA, which tends to equate food with morality. In the Puritan tradition, dietary excess of all kinds and consumption of meat in particular was blamed for a variety of societal ills including aggressiveness, poor digestion, degenerative diseases and gout, as well as mental and moral insufficiency. These ideals were brought to an extreme in the writings of Sylvester Graham and William Kellogg during the Health Reform Movement that flourished during the 19th century (see Introduction to this volume). Kellogg opened a sanitarium in Battle Creek Michigan (today this would be called a spa) where wealthy clients came to take 'the cure', a regimen of self-denial, vegetarianism and (closely following the teachings of Graham) copious consumption of bran to cleanse the colon. Kellogg and C.W. Post (a former patient of Kellogg) are recognizable names today as the founders of what was to become the modern breakfast food industry (Stacey, 1994; Brenner, 1999).

Also, a series of scientific and technological advancement that began during the mid-19th century and extending well into the 20th century fundamentally shifted the way we thought about food. An understanding of microbes and 'germ theory' emerged that eventually led to better preservation and distribution of food by canning, freezing and aseptic packaging. The vitamins were being discovered and the processes of digestive physiology were being revealed. The Domestic Science movement (also known as Home Economics in the USA) redefined home cookery as a precise, efficient and systematic endeavor. Foods were defined less in terms of their sustenance and more in terms of their fuel economy – how much fat, protein and carbohydrate they contained. Perhaps in response to powerful public scandals about widespread food adulteration practices several years before, advocates of Domestic Science emphasized purity, wholesomeness and hygiene over taste and satisfaction (Stacey, 1994; Brenner, 1999).

As medical theories advanced about the role of food in health, specific nutrients began to emerge as dietary culprits including salt, sugar, carbohydrates, fat and cholesterol. The vilification of fat in the popular press is a particularly compelling example of the public's fixation on an individual nutrient. Counting fat calories seemed to be a national obsession during the 1980s–1990s as revealed by the thousands of popular books and articles written on fat-reduction diets and the proliferation of reduced-fat and fat-free products introduced onto supermarket shelves (Ornish, 1990; Anonymous, 1991; Stacey, 1994). More recently, the pendulum has swung away from concern about too much fat to concern about too many carbohydrates (Atkins, 2002). Although the media tends to sensationalize each new scientific discovery, it is important to recognize that this expanding body of scientific evidence is the corner stone of national food policy and has made a vital impact on improving the health and well-being of the population (Anonymous, 2000). Undoubtedly,

these policies will continue to evolve and change as new knowledge becomes available.

The public's perceptions about food seem to constantly fluctuate from indulgence to sin, from celebrating the triumph of technology to a source of anxiety about pesticides or genetically modified organisms (GMOs). Each new technological advance seemed to spawn a backlash of sorts, a desire to look back to a simpler, more uncomplicated, time. Hence, the emergence of California cuisine (a style of cooking emphasizing the use of the most fresh, in-season, local ingredients), renewed interest in farmer's markets, the preservation of heirloom varieties of fruits and vegetables and finally, the Slow Food Movement, a global organization that seeks to preserve local cuisine and cooking techniques across cultures (http://www.slowfood.org). Although it is difficult to quantify the effects of these fluctuations on our food patterns, they occur with such regularity and capture our national food consciousness so completely that they are likely to remain a powerful force in shaping our eating habits (Stacey, 1994; Brenner, 1999).

Eating Attitudes Defined

As mentioned earlier, we are becoming an increasingly nutrition and weight-conscious society. After taste, nutrition and health attitudes are strong predictors of dietary behavior (Glanz et al., 1998). However, attitudes about health and nutrition often overlap with concerns about weight and obesity making it difficult to disentangle the two. At present there is no unified theory to address all the motivations that influence eating decisions. Traditionally, these issues have been examined in separate literatures to which we now turn.

Nutrition attitudes and beliefs

The Fishbein-Ajzen (1980) theory of reasoned action has been especially useful in capturing the effects of attitudes and beliefs on food selection. This model is based on the theory that an individual's behavioral intention is mainly determined by two components: the individual's own attitude (i.e. whether the individual perceives the behavior to be good or beneficial) and the subjective norm (i.e. the perceived social pressure to behave in a certain way). This model has been useful for predicting the selection (avoidance) of high-fat foods (Tuorila, 1987; Towler and Shepherd, 1992) including milk and meat. Extensions of this model have been used to understand other types of consumer behavior such as consumption of organic products, attitudes toward pesticides and genetically engineered foods (Shepherd and Raats, 1996).

Food avoidance and rejection

Rozin and Fallon (1987) describe three major elements of food rejection – distaste, danger and disgust. Disgust relates to the contamination of a food through contact with offensive substances such as insects, or hair. More recent work has broadened the concept of disgust to include sociocultural reasons for rejecting a food such as ethical implications related to the environment and animal rights. Mooney and Walbourn (2001) measured the relative contribution of concerns about weight, health, ethics and unnatural ingredients to food avoidance in college students. Men and women avoided different foods and had different reasons for doing so. Meat avoidance was stronger among women than men and ethical concerns about animals distinguished meat-avoiders from those who avoided other foods. Weight concern was a predominant factor for avoiding other foods in women, whereas taste was more critical for men. Studies in adolescents also revealed more weight dissatisfaction, the use of extreme weight control behaviors, and more symptoms of disordered eating among vegetarians as compared to non-vegetarians (Lindeman et al., 2000; Perry et al., 2001). Thus, for some individuals the practice of vegetarianism might mask an increased susceptibility to eating problems. The reader is referred to Chapter 13 for a discussion of the major concepts and theories of eating disorders.

Dietary Restraint and Disinhibition

Dietary restraint is defined as the conscious control of food intake to lose weight or main-tain current weight. The concept of dietary restraint arose from the work of early theorists who were attempting to understand distinctions between the eating patterns of obese and normal weight individuals (see Lowe, 1993). Prevailing theories at the time suggested that overeating in the obese was due to overresponsiveness to external cues such as food palatability, and underresponsiveness to internal physiologic hunger-satiety signals. Furthermore, it was thought that obese individuals were biologically programmed to maintain a higher body weight 'set-point' than normal weight individuals. Thus, it was posited that by dieting, many obese individuals were artificially suppressing their bodyweight under their biologically-defended set point. This behavior would inevitably lead to overeating, precipitating a vicious cycle of weight loss and regain. Herman and Polivy (1975) developed the 'boundary' model to describe the effects of dieting on eating. This model was eventually applied to normal weight dieters as well.

The boundary model of eating

According to the boundary model, food intake is regulated along a continuum ranging from hunger to fullness (see Fig. 10.6) (Herman and Polivy, 1984). At the extremes of this continuum, biological processes drive food consumption. At one extreme, energy depletion gives rise to aversive sensations of hunger and at the other extreme, energy excess gives rise to aversive sensations of discomfort. The hunger and satiety boundaries represent the points at which eating is either initiated or terminated. Inbetween these two extremes is the 'zone of biological indifference'. The zone of biological indifference reflects an interim state of neither extreme hunger nor extreme fullness where cognitive and social factors control food intake. The eating continua of restrained eaters (dieters in the Herman and Polivy model) and unrestrained eaters (non-dieters in the model) vary in two fundamental ways. First, dieting expands the zone of biological indifference disrupting normal physiologic regulation of eating. Restrained eaters have a lower hunger boundary (they are less sensitive to hunger sensations) and they also have a higher satiety boundary (they are less sensitive to satiety signals). Second, restrained eaters maintain a self-imposed diet boundary or calorie quota that they strongly defend against diet excursions. Unrestrained eaters have no need of a diet boundary because their food intake is governed by normal physiologic control.

Laboratory eating studies

The diet-boundary model also helps to explain why restrained and unrestrained eaters respond differently to standard laboratory preload manipulations (Herman and Polivy, 1984). In these experiments, subjects consume a fixed amount of a palatable food (ice cream or milkshake) as a preload then have free access to another palatable food (which we will call the target food). Unrestrained eaters show normal regulation of intake; they eat less of the target food following a preload than they do when no preload is given. Restrained eaters show the opposite responses; when no preload is given restrained eaters defend their diet boundary and eat very little. However, after the forced consumption of a preload, the restrained eater feels that all is lost (I 'blew' it) and overeats. This loss of control over eating is called 'counterregulation' or 'disinhibition'. Numerous experiments

have used variations in the basic preloading paradigm to investigate counterregulatory eating in the laboratory including the use of low-calorie preloads to assess the influence of palatability, or the use of deception to make the subject believe that the preload is high in calories (Lowe, 1993). Disinhibition was eventually used to describe susceptibility to overeating in response to a variety of external cues including palatable foods, social situations and emotional eating associated with anxiety or loneliness. Although restraint and disinhibition do not completely explain variations in eating behavior in the laboratory (i.e. some restrained eaters fail to disinhibit in response to palatable foods), these constructs have provided the conceptual framework which has guided research on eating behavior for the last 30 years. Dietary restraint and disinhibition can be assessed using validated questionnaires (Stunkard and Messick, 1985; van Strien et al., 1986). Representative questions from the 3-Factor Eating Questionnaire, which measures restraint, disinhibition and perceived hunger are shown in Table 10.4. Since dietary restraint and disinhibition are so closely associated with weight concern and the drive for thinness in women, they are indispensable for understanding variations in food intake and body weight in females. Consequently, most of the research on restraint and disinhibition has focused on female subjects.

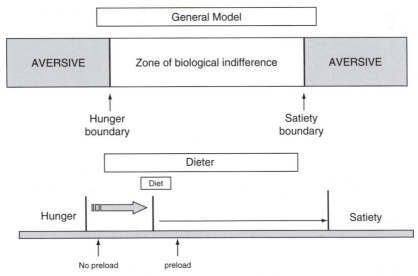

Fig. 10.6. The Boundary Model for the Regulation of Eating. Reproduced with permission from Herman and Polivy, 1984. pp. 149.

Table 10.4. Representative items from the 3-Factor Eating Questionnaire[1].

Restraint
I have a pretty good idea of the number of calories in common foods.
I deliberately take small helpings as a means of controlling my weight.
When I have eaten my quota of calories, I am usually good about not eating any more.

Disinhibition
When I feel anxious, I find myself eating.
I usually eat too much at social occasions like parties and picnics.
Sometimes things just taste so good that I keep on eating even when I'm no longer hungry.

Hunger
I often feel so hungry I just have to eat something.
Dieting is hard for me because I just get too hungry.

[1] Respondents indicate whether each statement is True or False about them. Source: Stunkard and Messick, 1985.

Everyday eating behavior and body weight

Studies have shown that restraint and disinhibition are correlated with eating behaviors in everyday life. Dietary restraint has been associated with lower fat and energy intakes and more frequent use of low-fat foods in community-dwelling women and female college students (Tuschl et al., 1990; Alexander and Tepper, 1995). However, some studies have shown either no differences or higher body weights in diet-restrained women as compared to unrestrained women suggesting that restrained women may be struggling to control their weight with varying degrees of success. These findings are consistent with the notion that dietary restraint represents the intention to control one's weight, not necessarily the act of doing so (Lowe, 1993). Another factor is an individual's approach to weight control and dieting. In one study, restrained eaters who adopted more flexible and realistic weight control strategies (flexible control) achieved better long-term weight maintenance than restrained eaters who resorted to chronic food restriction (rigid control), the latter group priming themselves to fail (Westenhoefer et al., 1999).

On the other hand, disinhibition is consistently related to emotional eating, binging and weight cycling (Lawson et al., 1995).

Consequently, in most situations where it has been studied, individuals with high disinhibition are heavier than those with low disinhibition (Westenhoeffer et al., 1994; Lawson et al., 1995; Williamson et al., 1995). According to the boundary model, restrained eating was thought to give rise to disinhibition. More recent findings suggest that restraint and disinhibition might be independent constructs such that an individual might exhibit one characteristic but not the other. Evidence for this independence comes from studies showing that some restrained eaters do not disinhibit in the laboratory (Lowe 1993) and conversely, that some individuals who score high on disinhibition are not restrained eaters (Westenhoefer et al., 1990). If these two factors are present in the same individual, they tend to oppose each other with restraint promoting weight loss and disinhibition promoting weight gain (Williamson et al., 1995; Hays et al., 2002). Because early studies did not investigate the interactive effects of restraint and disinhibition on body weight, they might have missed the importance of this relationship. Figure 10.7 shows the body mass indices (BMI; kg/m^2) of a group of community-dwelling, middle-aged women characterized by both dietary restraint and disinhibition. Women with high disinhibition, unopposed by restraint had the highest BMIs in the study (27.6 kg/m^2), whereas women with both high disinhibition and high restraint had somewhat lower BMIs (26.3 kg/m^2). Women with high restraint and low disinhibition had still lower BMIs (24.9 kg/m^2) that were within the healthy range. Women who were neither restrained nor disinhibited had the lowest BMIs in the study (22.2 kg/m^2). In addition to showing that restraint and disinhibition interact in predictable ways to influence body weight, these findings imply that a modest amount of restraint can have a moderating effect on body weight. It is important to note that severe restraint and disinhibition are risk factors for eating disturbances such as anorexia, bulimia and binge eating disorder. These issues will be covered in Chapters 13 and 14.

Gender Differences

It is unclear whether gender differences in eating behavior reflect true biological variability or sociocultural differences in eating attitudes.

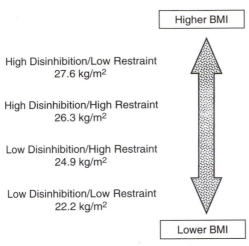

Higher BMI

High Disinhibition/Low Restraint
27.6 kg/m²

High Disinhibition/High Restraint
26.3 kg/m²

Low Disinhibition/High Restraint
24.9 kg/m²

Low Disinhibition/Low Restraint
22.2 kg/m²

Lower BMI

Fig. 10.7. Interaction between dietary restraint and disinhibition on body mass index (BMI; kg/m²) in women.

Food preferences of men and women differ with women preferring vegetables and sweets and men preferring meats (Logue and Smith, 1986; Rappoport *et al.*, 1993). Among young adults, particularly college students, concern about physical appearance is a dominant theme. These ideals are pursued differently by women and men; women want to lose weight and men want to gain weight (Streigel-Moore *et al.*, 1986; Alexander and Tepper, 1995). Overall, women's food choices appear to be more strongly motivated by health/nutrition beliefs than those of men (Towler and Shepherd, 1992; Rappoport *et al.*, 1993).

Cost/Convenience/Availability

Expenditures on food eaten away from the home have risen dramatically in Westernized countries (Byrne *et al.*, 1998). In 1998, per capita expenditures on meals eaten away-from-home exceeded £296/annum ($400) in the UK and exceeded $1000/annum in the USA (Edwards, 2000). Foods eaten away from home are generally higher in energy content and portion sizes have increased substantially. As discussed in Chapter 14, of this book , these factors may contribute to the growing problem of obesity in the population. Consumer

demand for convenience continues to escalate and convenience foods represent a major area of growth and innovation for the food industry. Today, convenience foods represent a range of meal options from single-portion, microwavable soups to complete meals or meal solutions (a package containing semi-prepared ingredients). The impact of these rapidly-developing changes on eating patterns have yet to be determined.

Finally, cost is an important consideration for food purchases across all socio-economic groups. However, low-income groups are at greater risk for inadequate nutrition than their more affluent counterparts with infants and children, pregnant women and the elderly being the most vulnerable (Dixon *et al.*, 2001). Consumption of fruits and vegetables and dairy products is lower in low-income households and has been linked to lower intakes of several nutrients including vitamins A, C, B-6, folate, zinc, iron and calcium. Persons living in poverty may not have the financial resources to afford a healthy diet, a condition known as food insufficiency. This recognized as a worldwide problem even in affluent countries (Nelson, 2000; Dixon *et al.*, 2001; Giskes *et al.*, 2002). Low intakes of B-6, folate, zinc and iron have direct effects on behavior as discussed in Chapters 7 and 8.

Conclusion

Throughout this chapter we have tried to emphasize the multidisciplinary nature of the nutrition–behavior paradigm. It would appear that no single theory or factor can completely explain what is eaten, how it is eaten or why – food selection and eating remain a complex and highly personal human behavior. This assertion is not meant to discourage the reader from pursuing this understanding further. Rather, we stress that multidimensional approaches to eating that incorporate biological, genetic and sociocultural factors into the model are much more likely to reveal important insights into eating behavior than the dependence on a single factor or group of factors.

References

Ajzen, I. and Fishbein, M. (1980) *Understanding Attitudes and Predicting Social Behavior*. Prentice-Hall, Englewood Cliffs, New Jersey.

Akella, G., Henderson, S. and Drewnowski, A. (1997) Sensory acceptance of Japanese green tea and soy products is linked to genetic sensitivity to 6-n-propylthiouracil. *Nutrition and Cancer* 29, 146–151.

Alexander, J. and Tepper, B. (1995) Use of reduced-calorie/reduced-fat foods by young adults: influence of gender and restraint. *Appetite* 25, 217–30.

Anonymous (1991) *Trends: Consumer Attitudes and the Supermarket 1991*. Food Marketing Institute, Washington, DC.

Anonymous (2000) *Nutrition and your Health: Dietary Guidelines for Americans*. Department of Health and Human Services and United States Department of Agriculture, Washington, DC.

Atkins, R. (2002) *Dr. Atkins' New Diet Revolution*. HarperCollins, New York.

Bartoshuk, L., Duffy, V. and Miller, I. (1994) PTC/PROP tasting: anatomy, psychophysics, and sex effects. *Physiology and Behavior* 56, 1165–1171.

Beauchamp, G. and Moran, M. (1982) Dietary experience and sweet taste preference in human infants. *Appetite* 3, 139–152.

Beauchamp, G., Cowart, B. and Moran, M. (1986) Developmental changes in salt acceptability in human infants. *Developmental Psychobiology* 19, 17–25.

Bertino, M., Beauchamp, G. and Engelman, K. (1982) Long-term reduction in dietary sodium alters the taste of salt. *American Journal of Clinical Nutrition* 36, 1134–44.

Birch, L. and Fisher, J. (1998) Development of eating behaviors among children and adolescents. *Pediatrics* 101, 539–549.

Birch, L. and Fisher, J. (2000) Mothers' child-feeding practices influence daughters' eating and weight. *American Journal of Clinical Nutrition* 71, 1054–1061.

Birch, L., Fisher, J. and Grimm-Thomas, K. (1996) The development of children's eating habits. In: Meiselman, H. and MacFie, H. (eds) *FoodChoice, Acceptance and Consumption*. Chapman & Hall, London, pp. 161–206.

Boden, G. (1996) Fuel metabolism in pregnancy and in gestational diabetes mellitus. *Obstetrics and Gynocology Clinics of North America* 23, 1–10.

Bowen, D. (1992) Taste and food preference changes across the course of pregnancy. *Appetite* 19, 233–242.

Brand, J. (2000) Receptor and transduction processes for umami taste. *Journal of Nutrition* 130, 942S–945S.

Brenner, L. (1999) *American Appetite: the Coming of Age of Cuisine*. Avon Books, New York.

Brillat-Savarin, J. (2000) The physiology of taste or meditations on transcendental gastronomy. Counterpoint Press, New York.

Bryant, B. and Silver, W. (2000) Chemesthesis: the common chemical sense. Finger, T., Silver, W. and Restrepo, D. *The Neurobiology of Taste and Smell*. Wiley-Liss, New York.

Byrne, P., Capps Jr., O. and Saha, O. (1998) Analysis of quick-serve, mid-scale, and up-scale food away from home expenditures. *International Journal of Food and Agribusiness Management Review* 1, 51–72.

Cowart, B.J., Yokomukai, Y. and Beauchamp, G. (1994) Bitter taste in aging: compound-specific decline in sensitivity. *Physiology and Behavior* 56, 1237–41.

Crystal, S., Bowen, D. and Bernstein, I. (1999) Morning sickness and salt intake, food cravings, and food aversions. *Physiology and Behavior* 67, 181–187.

De Graaf, C. and Zandstra, E. (1999) Sweetness intensity and pleasantness in children, adolescents, and adults. *Physiology and Behavior.* 67, 513–520.

Delwiche, J., Buletic, Z. and Breslin, P. (2001) Covariation in individuals' sensitivities to bitter compounds: evidence supporting multiple receptor/transduction mechanisms. *Perception Psychophysics* 63, 761–776.

Denton, D., McKinley, M. and Weisinger, R. (1996) Hypothalamic integration of body fluid regulation. *Proceedings of the National Academy of Sciences USA.* 93, 7397–7404.

Desor, J. and Beauchamp, G. (1987) Longitudinal changes in sweet preferences in humans. *Physiology and Behavior* 39, 639–641.

Desor, J., Maller, O. and Turner, R. (1973) Taste in acceptance of sugars by human infants. *Journal of Comparative and Physiological Psychology.* 84, 496–501.

Desor, J., Greene, L. and Maller, O. (1975) Preferences for sweet and salt in 9-to 15-year-old and adult humans. *Science* 190, 686–687.

DeWitt, D. (1999) *The Chile Pepper Encylopedia*. William Morrow, New York.

Dixon, L., Winkleby, M. and Radimer, K. (2001) Dietary intakes and serum nutrients differ between adults from food-insufficient and food-sufficient families: Third National Health and Nutrition Examination Survey, 1988–1994. *Journal of Nutrition* 131, 1232–1246.

Doty, R. (2001) Olfaction. *Annual Review of Psychology* 52, 423–452.

Drayna, D., Coon, H., Kim, U., Elsner, T., Cromer, K., Otterud, B., Baird, L., Peiffer, A. and Leppert, M. (2003) Genetic analysis of a complex trait in the Utah Genetic Reference Project: a major locus for PTC taste ability on chromosome 7q and a secondary locus on chromosome 16p. *Human Genetics* 112, 567–572.

Drewnowski, A. (2004) PROP-sensitivity, food choices, and food consumption. In: Prescott J. and Tepper, B.J. (eds) *Sensitivity to PROP (6-n-Propylthiouracil): Its Measurement, Significance and Implications.* Marcel Dekker, New York, pp. 179–194.

Drewnowski, A. and Gomez-Carneros, C. (2000) Bitter taste, phytonutrients, and the consumer: a review. *American Journal of Clinical Nutrition* 72, 1424–1435.

Drewnowski, A. and Shultz, J. (2001) Impact of aging on eating behaviors, food choices, nutrition, and health status. *Journal of Nutrition Health and Aging* 5, 75–79.

Drewnowski, A., Henderson, S., Hann, C., Berg, W. and Ruffin, M. (2000) Genetic taste markers and preferences for vegetables and fruit of female breast care patients. *Journal of the American Dietetic Association* 100, 191–197.

Duffy, V. and Bartoshuk, L. (2000) Food acceptance and genetic variation in taste. *Journal of the American Dietetic Association* 100, 647–655.

Duffy, V., Backstrand, V. and Ferris, A. (1995) Olfactory dysfunction and related nutritional risk in free-living, elderly women. *Journal of the American Dietetic Association* 95, 879–884.

Edwards, J. (2000) Food service/catering restaurant and institutional perspectives of the meal. In: Meiselman, H. (ed.) *Dimensions of the Meal: The Science, Culture, Business and Art of Eating.* Aspen, New York, 223–244.

Fahey, J., Zalcmann, A. and Talalay, P. (2001) The chemical diversity and distribution of glucosinolates and isothiocyanates among plants. *Phytochemistry* 56, 5–51.

Faith, M., Tepper, B., Hoffman, D. and Pietrobelli, A. (2002) Genetic and environmental influences on childhood obesity. *Clinics in Family Practice* 4, 277–294.

Fenwick, G., Curl, C., Griffiths, N., Heaney, R. and Price, K. (1990) Bitter principles in food plants. In: Rouseff, R.L. (ed.) *Bitterness in Foods and Beverages; Developments in Food Science.* Elsevier, Amsterdam, 205–250.

Fisher, J. and Birch, L. (1999) Restricting access to foods and children's eating. *Appetite* 32, 405–419.

Flaxman, S. and Sherman, P. (2002) Morning sickness: a mechanism for protecting mother and embryo. *Quarterly Review of Biology* 75, 113–148.

Fox, A. (1932) The relationship between chemical constitution and taste. *Proceedings of the National Academy of Sciences of USA* 18, 115–120.

Francoise, M., Mathey, A., Siebelink, E., Graaf, C. and Van Staveren, W. (2001) Flavor enhancement of food improves dietary intake and nutritional status of elderly nursing home residents. *Journal of Gerontology* 56A, 200–205.

Fukuwatari, T., Shibata, K., Iguchi, K., Saeki, T., Iwata, A., Tani, K., Sugimoto, E. and Fushiki, T. (2003) Role of gustation in the recognition of oleate and triolein in anosmic rats. *Physiology and Behavior* 78, 579–583.

Gaitan, E. (1989) *Environmental Goitrogenesis.* CRC Press, Boca Raton, Florida.

Gilbertson, T., Fontenot, D., Liu, L., Zhang, H. and Monroe, W. (1997) Fatty acid modulation of K+ channels in taste receptor cells: gustatory cues for dietary fat. *American Journal of Physiology* 272(4 Pt 1), C1203–10.

Giskes, K., Turrell, G., Patterson, C. and B., N. (2002) Socioeconomic differences among Australian adults in consumption of fruits and vegetables and intakes of vitamins A, C, and folate. *Journal of Human Nutrition and Dietetics* 15, 375–385.

Glanz, K., Basil, M., Maibach, E., Goldberg, J. and Snyder, D. (1998) Why Americans eat what they do: taste, nutrition, cost, convenience, and weight control concerns as influences on food consumption. *Journal of the American Dietetic Association* 98, 1118–1126.

Glendinning, J. (1994) Is the bitter rejection response always adaptive? *Physiology and Behavior* 56, 1217–1227.

Graillon, A., Barr, R., Young, S., Wright, J. and Hendricks, L. (1997) Differential response to intraoral sucrose, quinine and corn oil in crying human newborns. *Physiology and Behavior* 62, 317–325.

Green, B. and Rentmeister-Bryant, H. (1998) Temporal characteristics of capsaicin desensitization and stimulus-induced recovery in the oral cavity. *Physiology and Behavior* 65, 141–149.

Greene, L. (1974) Physical growth and development, neurological maturation, and behavioral functioning in two Ecuadorian Andean communities in which goiter is endemic. *American Journal of Physical Anthropology* 41, 139–152.

Grill, H.J. and Norgren, R. (1978) The taste reactivity test. II. Mimetic responses to gustatory stimuli in chronic thalamic and chronic decerebrate rats. *Brain Research* 143, 281–97.

Guo, S. and Reed, D. (2001) The genetics of phenylthiocarbamide perception. *Annals of Human Biology* 28, 111–142.

Hays, N., Bathalon, G., McCrory, M., Roubenoff, R., Lipman, R. and Roberts, S. (2002) Eating behavior correlates of adult weight gain and obesity in healthy women aged 55–65 y. *American Journal of Clinical Nutrition* 75, 476–483.

Herman, C. and Polivy, J. (1975) Anxiety, restraint and eating behavior. *Journal of Abnormal Psychology* 43, 647–660.

Herman, P. and Polivy, J. (1984) The boundary model for the regulation of eating. In: Stunkard, A. and Stellar, E. (eds) *Eating Disorders*. Raven Press, New York,141–156.

Hoffman, H., Ishii, E. and MacTurk, R. (1998) Age-related changes in the prevalence of smell/taste problems among the United States adult population. Results of the 1994 disability supplement to the National Health Interview Survey (NHIS). *Annals of the New York Academy of Science* 855, 716–722.

Illy, E. (2002) The complexity of coffee. *Scientific American,* 86–91.

Jerzsa-Latta, M., Krondl, M. and Coleman, P. (1990) Use and perceived attributes of cruciferous vegetables in terms of genetically-mediated taste sensitivity. *Appetite* 15, 127–134.

Johnson, S. (2000) Improvong preschoolers' self–regulation of energy intake. *Pediatrics* 106, 1429–1435.

Johnson, S., McPhee, L. and Birch, L. (1991) Conditioned preferences: young children prefer flavors associated with high dietary fat. *Physiology and Behavior* 50, 1245–1251.

Keller, K., Steinmann, L., Nurse, R. and Tepper, B. (2002) Genetic taste sensitivity to 6-n-propylthiouracil influences food preference and reported intake in preschool children. *Appetite* 38, 3–12.

Kirkmeyer, S. and Tepper, B. (2004) A current perspective on creaminess perception and PROP taster status. In: Prescott, J. and Tepper, B. (eds) *Sensitivity to PROP (6-n-Propylthiouracil): Its Measurement, Significance and Implications.* Marcel Dekker, New York, pp. 117–136

Lacroix, R., Eason, E. and Melzack, R. (2000) Nausea and vomiting during pregnancy: a prospective study of its frequency, intensity, and patterns of change. *American Journal of Obstetrics and Gynecology* 182, 931–937.

Lawless, H. and Heymann, H. (1998) Physiological and psychological foundations of sensory function. In: *Sensory Evaluation of Food: Principles and Practices.*Chapman & Hall, New York.

Lawless, H., Rozin, P. and Shenker, J. (1985) Effects of oral capsiacin on gustatory, olfactory, and irritant sensations and flavor identification in humans who regularly or rarely consume chili pepper. *Chemical Senses* 10, 579–589.

Lawson, O., Williamson, D., Champagne, C., DeLany, J., Brooks, E., Howat, P., Wozniak, P., Bray, G. and Ryan, D. (1995) The association of body weight, dietary intake, and energy expenditure with dietary restraint and disinhibition. *Obesity Research* 3, 153–161.

Lindeman, M., Stark, K. and Latvala, K. (2000) Vegetarianism and eating-disordered thinking. *Eating Disorders* 8, 157–165.

Lindemann, B. (2001) Receptors and transduction in taste. *Nature* 413, 219–225.

Logue, A. and Smith, M. (1986) Predictors of food preferences in adult humans. *Appetite* 7, 109–125.

Long, L. (2000) Holiday meals: rituals of family traditions. In: Meiselman, H. (ed.) *Dimensions of the Meal: The Science, Culture, Business and Art of Eating.* H. Meiselman. Aspen Publishers, Gaithersburg, Maryland, 143–159.

Lowe, M. (1993) The effects of dieting on eating behavior: a three factor model. *Psychological Bulletin* 114, 100–121.

Marshall, D. (2000) British meals and food choice. In: Meiselman, H. (ed.) *Dimensions of the Meal: The Science, Culture, Business and Art of Eating.* Aspen Publishers, Gaithersburg, Maryland, 202–220.

Mattes, R. (1993) Fat preference and adherence to a reduced-fat diet. *American Journal of Clinical Nutrition* 57, 373–81.

Mattes, R. (2001) The taste of fat elevates postprandial triacylglycerol. *Physiology and Behavior* 74, 343–8.

Mattes, R.D. and Labov, J. (1989) Bitter taste responses to phenylthiocarbamide are not related to dietary goitrogen intake in human beings. *Journal of the American Dietetic Association* 89, 692–694.

McGee, H. (1984) Grains, legumes and nuts. In: *On Food and Cooking.* Simon & Schuster, New York, 226–263.

Mela, D. (1990) Sensory preferences for fats: what, who, why? *Food Quality & Preference* 2, 95–101.

Mennella, J. and Beauchamp, G. (1993) The effects of repeated exposure to garlic-flavored milk on the nursling's behavior. *Pediatric Research* 34, 805–8.

Mennella, J. and Beauchamp, G. (1999) Experience with a flavor in mother's milk modifies the infant's acceptance of flavored cereal. *Developmental Psychobiology* 35, 197–203.

Mombaerts, P. (1999) Seven-transmembrane proteins as odorant and chemosensory receptors. *Science* 286, 707–711.

Mooney, K. and Walbourn. L. (2001) When college students reject food: not just a matter of taste. *Appetite* 36, 41–50.

Murphy, C. and Gilmore, M. (1989) Quality-specific effects of aging on the human taste system. *Perception Psychophysics* 45, 121–128.

Murphy, C., Schubert, C., Cruickshanks, K., Klein, B.E., Klein, R. and Nondahl, D.M. (2002) Prevalence of olfactory impairment in older adults. *Journal of the American Medical Association* 288, 2307–2312.

Nelson, M. (2000) Childhood nutrition and poverty. *Proceedings of the Nutrition Society* 59, 307–315.

Newman, J. (2000) Chinese meals. In: Meiselman, H. (ed.) *Dimensions of the Meal: The Science, Culture, Business and Art of Eating.* Aspen Publishers, Gaithersburg, Maryland, 163–177.

Ornish, D. (1990) *Dr. Dean Ornish's Program for Reversing Heart Disease without Drugs or Surgery.* Random House, New York.

Otsuka, S. (2000) Japanese meals. In: Meiselman, H. (ed.) *Dimensions of the Meal: The Science, Culture, Business and Art of Eating.* Aspen Publishers, Gaithersburg, Maryland, 178–190.

Perry, C., McGuire, M., Neumark-Sztainer, D. and Story, M. (2001) Characteristics of vegetarian adolescents in a multiethnic population. *Journal of Adolescent Health* 29, 406–416.

Plata-Salaman, C. R. (2000) Central nervous system mechanisms contributing to the cachexia-anorexia syndrome. *Nutrition* 16, 1009–1012.

Pliner, P. and Hobden, K. (1992) Development of a scale to measure the trait of food neophobia in humans. *Appetite* 19, 105–120.

Pope, J., Skinner, J. and Carruth, B. (1992) Cravings and aversions of pregnant adolescents. *Journal of the American Dietetic Association* 92, 1479–1482.

Prattala, J. (2000) North European Meals: Observations from Denmark, Finland, Norway and Sweden. In: Meiselman, H. (ed.) Dimensions of the Meal: The Science, Culture, Business and Art of Eating. Aspen Publishers, Gaithersburg, Maryland, 191–201.

Prescott, J. and Swain-Campbell, N. (2000) Responses to repeated oral irritation by capsaicin, cinnamaldehyde and ethanol in PROP tasters and non-tasters. *Chemical Senses* 25, 239–246.

Rappoport, L., Peters, G., Downey, R., McCann, T. and Huff-Corzine, L. (1993) Gender and age differences in food consumption. *Appetite* 20, 33–52.

Rozin, E. (2000) The role of flavor in the meal and the culture. In: Meiselman, H. (ed.) *Dimensions of the Meal: The Science, Culture, Business and Art of Eating.* Aspen Publishers, Gaithersburg, Maryland, 134–142.

Rozin, P. (1982) Human food selection: the interaction of biology, culture and individual experience. In: Barker, L. (ed.) *The Psychobiology of Human Food Selection.* AVI Publishing, Westport, Connecticut.

Rozin, P. (1990) Getting to like the burn of chili pepper: biological, psychological and cultural perspectives. In: Green, B., Mason, J. and Kare, M. (eds) *Chemical Senses: Irritation.* Marcel Dekker, New York, 2, 231–273.

Rozin, P. (1996) The Socio-cultural context of eating and food choice. In: Meiselman, H. and MacFie, H. (eds) *Food Choice, Acceptance and Consumption.* Chapman & Hall, London, 83–104.

Rozin, P. and Fallon, A. (1987) A perspective on disgust. *Psychological Review* 94, 23–41.

Rozin, P., Fischler, C., Imada, S., Sarubin, A. and Wrzesniewski, A. (1999) Attitudes to food and the role of food in life in the U.S.A., Japan, Flemish Belgium and France: possible implications for the diet-health debate. *Appetite* 33, 163–180.

Schaal, B., Marlier, L. and Soussignan, R. (2000) Human foetuses learn odours from their pregnant mother's diet. *Chemical Senses* 25, 729–37.

Schiffman, S. (1993) Perception of taste and smell in elderly persons. *Critical Reviews in Food Science and Nutrition* 33, 17–26.

Schiffman, S.S. and Zervakis, J. (2002) Taste and smell perception in the elderly: effect of medications and disease. *Advances in Food and Nutriton Research* 44, 247–346.

Settle, R. (1991) The chemical senses in diabetes mellitus. In: Getchell, T.V., Doty, R.L. Bartoshuk, L.M., and Snow, J.B. (eds) *Smell and Taste in Health and Disease.* Raven Press, New York, 829–845.

Shepherd, R. and Raats, M. (1996) Attitudes and beliefs in food habits. In: Meiselman, H. and MacFie, H. (eds) *Food Choice, Acceptance and Consumption.* pp. 346–364. Chapman & Hall, London.

Ship, J. and Weiffenbach, J. (1993) Age, gender, medical treatment and medication effects on smell identification. *Journal of Gerontology* 48, M26–M32.

Stacey, M. (1994) *Consumed: Why Americans Love, Hate and Fear Food.* Simon & Schuster, New York.

Stein, L., Cowart, B., Epstein, A., Pilot, L., Laskin, C. and Beauchamp, G. (1996) Increased liking for salty foods in adolescents exposed during infancy to a chloride-deficient feeding formula. *Appetite* 27, 65–77.

Steiner, J. (1977) Facial expressions of the neonate infant indicating the hedonics of food-related stimuli. In: Weiffenbach, J. (ed.) *Taste and Development*. US Department of Health, Education and Welfare, Bethesda, Maryland.

Steiner, J., Glaser, D., Hawilo, M. and Berridge, K. (2001) Comparative expression of hedonic impact: affective reactions to taste by human infants and other primates. *Neuroscience and Biobehavioral Reviews* 25, 53–74.

Stevens, J. and Cain, W. (1993) Changes in taste and flavor in aging. *Critical Reviews in Food Science and Nutrition*. 33, 27–37.

Streigel-Moore, R., Silberstein, L. and Rodin, J. (1986) Toward and understanding of risk factors for bulimia. *American Psychologist* 41, 246–263.

Stunkard, A. and Messick, S. (1985) The three-factor eating questionnaire to measure dietary restraint, disinhibition and hunger. *Journal of Psychosomatic Research* 29, 41–83.

Tannahill, R. (1989) *Food in History*. Crown Publishers, New York.

Tepper, B. (1998) 6-n-Propylthiouracil: a genetic marker for taste, with implications for food preference and dietary habits. *American Journal of Human Genetics* 63, 1271–1276.

Tepper, B. and Nurse, R. (1997) Fat perception is related to PROP taster status. *Physiology and Behavior* 61, 949–954.

Tepper, B. and Nurse, R. (1998) PROP taster status is related to fat perception and preference. *Annals of the New York Academy of Sciences* 855, 802–804.

Tepper, B. and Seldner, A. (1999) Sweet taste and intake of sweet foods in normal pregnancy and pregnancy complicated by gestational diabetes mellitus. *American Journal of Clinical Nutrition* 70, 277–84.

Tepper, B. and Ullirch, N. (2002) Taste, smell and the genetics of food preference. *Topics in Clinical Nutrition* 17, 1–14.

Tepper, B., Hartfiel, L. and Schneider, S. (1996) Sweet taste and diet in type II diabetes. *Physiology and Behavior* 60, 13–8.

Tepper, B., Keller, K. and Ullrich, N. (2003) Genetic variation in taste and preferences for bitter and pungent foods: implications for chronic disease risk. In: Hofmann, T., Ho, C.-T. and Pickenhagen, W. (eds) *Challenges in Taste Chemistry and Biology*, Vol. 867. American Chemical Society, Washington, DC, pp. 60–74

Tepper, B.J. (2004) Genetic sensitivity to 6-n-propylthiouracil as a marker for fat intake, obesity and chronic disease risk: current evidence and future promise. In: Prescott, J. and Tepper, B.J. (eds) *Sensitivity to PROP (6-n-Propylthiouracil): Its Measurement, Significance and Implications*. Marcel Dekker, New York, pp. 155–178.

Towler, G. and Shepherd, R. (1992) Application of Fishbein and Ajzen's expectancy-value model to understanding fat intake. *Appetite* 18, 15–27.

Tuorila, H. (1987) Selection of milks with varying fat contents and related overall liking, attitudes, norms and intentions. *Appetite* 8, 1–14.

Tuschl, R., Laessle, R., Platte, P. and Pirke, K. (1990) Differences in food choice frequencies between restrained and unrestrained women. *Appetite* 14, 9–13.

van Strien, T., Frijters, J., Van Staveren, W., Defares, P. and Deurenberg, P. (1986) The predictive validity of the Dutch restrained eating scale. *International Journal of Eating Disorders* 5, 747–755.

Westenhoefer, J., Pudel, V. and Maus, N. (1990) Some restrictions on dietary restraint. *Appetite* 14.

Westenhoeffer, J., Broekmann, P., Munch, A. and Pudel, V. (1994) Cognitive control of eating and the disinhibition effect. *Appetite* 23, 27–41.

Westenhoefer, J., Stunkard, A. and Pudel, V. (1999) Validation of the flexible and rigid control dimensions of dietary restraint. *International Journal of Eating Disorders* 26, 53–68.

White, C. (1993) Low-fat dairy products. In: Altschul, A. (ed.) *Low-calorie Foods Handbook*. Marcel Dekker, New York, 253–271.

Willett, W. (1998) *Nutritional Epidemiology*, 2nd edn. Oxford Press, New York.

Williamson, D., Lawson, O., Brooks, E., Wozniak, P., Ryan, D., Bray, G. and Duchmann, E. (1995) Association of body mass with restraint and disinhibition. *Appetite* 25, 31–41.

Worthington-Roberts, B., Lambert, M. and Wu, R. (1989) Dietary cravings and aversions in the postpartum period. *Journal of the American Dietetic Association* 89, 647–651.

Yamaguchi, S. and Ninomiya, K. (2000) Umami and food palatability. *Journal of Nutrition* 130 (Suppl. 4S), 921S–926S.

11   Dietary Sugar and Behavior

K.E. D'Anci and R.B. Kanarek

Introduction

Most of us have a love–hate relationship with sugar. On the one hand, as children, we learn 'a spoonful of sugar helps the medicine go down' and that 'little girls are made of sugar and spice, and everything nice'. As adults, we call those we care most about 'sweetheart', 'honey bun' and 'sweetie pie'. On holidays such as Valentine's Day, Easter and Halloween, and events such as birthdays and anniversaries, we celebrate with gifts of candy and other sweets. Sweet foods taste good, and they can make us feel good. On the other hand, it is commonly believed that sugar intake is associated with a myriad of ills including obesity, diabetes, hyperactivity in children, depression and other psychological disorders. People describe themselves as 'sugar addicts' and we're all familiar with the infamous 'Twinkie defense[1]'. Moreover, 'common wisdom' states that sugars from natural sources such as honey are nutritionally superior to the empty calories obtained from refined white sugar. Given these conflicting views, it is important to sort through the evidence to determine the actual consequences of sugar intake.

In this chapter, we will define what nutritionists mean when they use the term sugar, provide information on how much sugar is found in foods, discover how much sugar Americans are consuming, and explore whether sugar intake does lead to physiological and psychological woes. Finally, we will present the results of recent studies that suggest that sugar intake may have beneficial effects on cognition and mood, pain and substance abuse.

What is sugar?

Before beginning to assess the effects of sugars on behavior, it is necessary to understand what sugars are. Sugars belong to the group of foods known as carbohydrates that are composed of the elements carbon, hydrogen and oxygen.

---

[1] Twinkie defense: **n.** A claim by a criminal defendant that at the time of the crime he or she was of diminished mental capacity due to intake of too much sugar, as from eating 'Twinkies,' sugar-rich snacks. The defense was argued successfully by a defense psychiatrist in the notorious case of former San Francisco County Supervisor Dan White, who shot and killed San Francisco Mayor George Moscone and County Supervisor Harvey Milk, resulting in White's conviction for only manslaughter instead of murder. (Online Law Dictionary: http://www.law.com/)

There are hundreds of different carbohydrates, however, our interests lie only in the carbohydrates that are important for human nutrition. These carbohydrates are classified as sugars, starches and fibers.

When we talk about sugar in the diet, we are referring to more than the granulated white powder in bowls on kitchen counters across the nation. Dietary sugars can be divided into three groups. The simple sugars or monosaccharides, are the building blocks for all carbohydrates. The general chemical formula for monosaccharides is $(CH_2O)n$ where n is three or greater. Monosaccharides can have as few as three or as many as nine carbon atoms. However, the ones most commonly encountered in the human diet contain six carbons (Berdanier, 1995; Brody, 1999; Sapllholz et al., 1999). Glucose is the most important of these six carbon sugars. Although glucose, itself, is not a major component of foods, it is the primary breakdown product of more complex dietary carbohydrates. Fructose, the sweetest of the monosaccharides is found in fruits, honey and is now commonly used as a sweetener in soft drinks and other foods. Galactose, the third of the nutritionally relevant monosaccharides, is seldom found free in foods, but is a component of the disaccharide, lactose.

Most of our sugar intake comes in the form of disaccharides, which are made up of two monosaccharides. Until recently, Americans consumed most of their sugar in the form of sucrose, a disaccharide comprised of one molecule of glucose and one molecule of fructose. Sucrose, a very sweet carbohydrate, is what we find on our tables and what most people mean when they use the term sugar. Sucrose is produced commercially from sugar beets and sugar cane and is also found in molasses, maple syrup and in small quantities in fruits and vegetables. Another important disaccharide is lactose, which contains one molecule of glucose and one molecule of galactose and is found in milk products. Finally, maltose is a disaccharide containing two molecules of glucose. Maltose does not occur naturally to any great degree.

The less familiar trisaccharides are made up of three monosaccharide units, such as raffinose, found in sugar beets (Wildman and Medeiros, 2000). These are not common compounds in the diet.

Metabolism of Sugar

It is important to begin by recognizing that (i) all carbohydrates are ultimately broken down into the monosaccharide glucose and (ii) the body treats sugars added to foods in exactly the same way as it treats the sugars naturally occurring in fruits and other foods. Thus, natural sugars are not any better or worse for the body than added sugars (see Wolke, 2002 for a discussion of so-called 'raw' sugars). An enzyme, sucrase, breaks down sucrose in the small intestine into its monosaccharide components, fructose and glucose. Because fructose is rapidly metabolized to glucose in the intestinal mucosa, any description of sugar metabolism is basically a description of glucose metabolism. After absorption from the gastrointestinal tract, glucose is carried in the blood stream to the liver, brain and other tissues. Glucose is removed from the bloodstream by insulin, and stored in the liver in the form of glycogen. The liver can store glycogen, sufficient to see us through a 10 h fast; any excess that the liver cannot accommodate is converted into fat and stored in adipose tissue in fat cells. Other enzymatic processes in the liver convert fats and amino acids into glucose as well, thus we can maintain blood glucose when eating a variety of macronutrients.

When needed, glycogen is removed from storage and broken back down into glucose by glucagon. Glucose is the primary fuel for the brain, and is not stored in the brain (Wenk, 1989; Sieber and Trastman, 1992; Morris and Saril, 2001). Furthermore, the brain lacks the enzymes that are present in the liver for converting amino acids and fats into glucose. Thus, the brain is dependent upon circulating blood glucose levels for fuel, and experiences consequences related to fluctuations in blood glucose levels (McCall, 2002). We will discuss later how varying levels of blood glucose can directly impact cognitive functioning.

Sweet taste

The primary reason for our consumption of sweet foods is their pleasant taste. Most animals, including humans, have strong preferences for sweet-tasting substances. Ancient cave paintings by prehistoric artists provide evidence of the high esteem in which sweet-tasting foods such as honey, figs and dates were held. Moreover, paintings from tombs dating as early as 2600 BCE depict the beekeeping practices of ancient Egyptians (Darby, Ghalioungui and Grivetti, 1977).

There are chemoreceptors for four basic flavors: salt, sour, bitter and sweet as well as a 'savory' taste known as umami (Lindemann, 1996; Lindemann, 2001). When you eat something sweet, taste receptor cells on your tongue are activated and communicate via neurotransmission to the brain. The complete cascade of events that occurs between initial stimulation of your taste buds and the final perception of sweet taste has yet to be completely determined. It is thought, however, that sweet taste is communicated to the brain via at least two means of transmission: via a G-protein second-messenger system and via calcium and potassium ion gated channels (Lindemann, 2001). Recent research investigating transduction of sweet taste has uncovered the sweet-receptor gene: T1R3 (Matsunami et al., 2000; Max et al., 2001; Bachmanov et al., 2004). This gene, when expressed, stimulates the generation of the receptor that binds sugars and sweet-tasting molecules (Matsunami et al., 2000; Lindemann, 2001; Max et al., 2001).

We know that sweet foods taste good, but what mediates the pleasurable, or hedonic, response to sweet food? Although the nature of the hedonic response is not completely understood, there is considerable evidence supporting the actions of certain neurotransmitter systems in this response. Moreover, the preponderance of the literature indicates that the hedonic response is mediated in the brain rather than in the periphery (e.g. Dum et al., 1983; Marks-Kaufman et al., 1989; Berridge and Robinson, 1998).

Research in humans and animals investigating hedonics suggests that the endogenous opioid system (the same system in which drugs like morphine and heroin act to alleviate pain) (Yeomans and Gray, 2002; Bodnar, 2004; Levine and Billington, 2004) as well as the dopamine system (Berridge and Robinson, 1998; Yamamoto, 2003) may be involved. Merely eating or anticipating eating sweet foods can cause the release of beta-endorphin in the brain (Dum et al, 1983; Yamamoto et al., 2000). This release of beta-endorphin may then produce a rewarding feeling resulting from direct actions at endogenous opioid receptors and via indirect or direct actions in the dopamine system. Finally, the two neurotransmitter systems can be separated into distinct categories such that dopamine seems to be involved in 'wanting' (Berridge and Robinson, 1998; Berridge, 2000) palatable foods and the endogenous opioid system is more involved in 'liking' (Berridge, 2000; Pecina and Berridge, 2000).

Drewnowski et al. (1995) showed that when a drug is given that blocks the opioid receptor (naloxone), intake of and preference for highly palatable sweet foods (and high fat foods) is reduced in women with binge-eating disorder – but not controls. In other studies, Hsiao and Smith (1995) showed that administration of the dopamine antagonist raclopride decreased sucrose intake in rats. By blocking the effects of endogenous opioids and dopamine, therefore, the hedonic response to tasty foods is decreased. We will discuss more in a later section how sweet taste preferences in people with substance-abuse problems may differ from that of the rest of the population.

Sugar consumption

How much sugar do you think you consume each day – 5 teaspoons, 15 teaspoons or 30 teaspoons? Do you think that since you don't add sugar to your food or you drink diet beverages that you eat very little sugar? Don't bet on it. The USDA (2000) reports that US consumption of nutritive sweeteners is at an all time high (Fig. 11.1). You can see in the figure that even though consumption of non-nutritive sweeteners has increased over the past few decades, there is no compensating decrease in consumption of nutritive sweeteners. Although a number of variables such as one's age, gender and snacking patterns will influence one's answer, it is estimated that Americans consume an average of 53 teaspoons of added sugars a day (USDA, 2000). The recommended limit for sugar intake for people consuming a

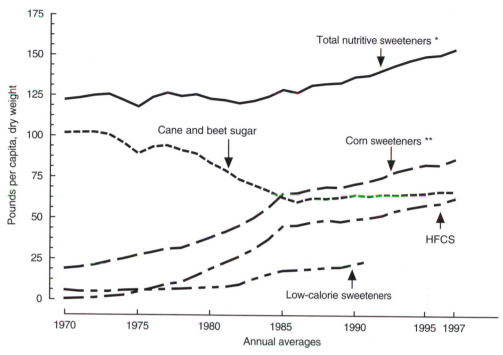

Fig. 11.1. American consumption of nutritive sweeteners through 1997. Source: USDA/Economic Research Service, 1999.

* Cane and beet sugar and corn sweeteners are subsets of total nutritive sweetener consumption.
** High fructose corn syrup (HFCS) is a subset of corn sweeteners. Low-calorie sweetener data consist of saccharin and aspartame. Data are not available for low-calorie sweeteners after 1991.

2000/cal/day diet is no more than 40 g of added sugars (which is a mere 10 teaspoons, or one 12 oz can of soda, and totals 8% of total caloric intake)[2]. In fact, most of the sugar we eat is not added at the table, or during cooking, but at the factory[3]. It is important to realize that food manufacturers add a variety of sugar-containing products to our foods – often referred to as 'hidden sugars'. Most of these products are added to enhance the sweetness of the food, however, these products also can extend the shelf life of a product, promote browning in foods, help to retain moisture in bakery items, and improve food consistency.

However, because most sugar-containing products are used for their sweetening capacity, as a group they are called nutritive sweeteners.

For many years, sucrose was the most commonly added nutritive sweetener, however, in the mid-1980s corn sweeteners became the product of choice for many food manufacturers (USDA, 2000). Corn sweeteners are produced by the enzymatic breakdown of maize starch. They are similar in taste to sucrose, but are significantly less expensive to produce. Corn sweeteners are now the predominant sweeteners in a number of foods

---

[2] The WHO (2003) recommends a diet that contains no more than 10% dietary sugars for the prevention of obesity, diabetes and dental caries. This recommendation has come under considerable fire from sugar lobbying groups.

[3] Don't just take our word for it. Take a few days and keep a 'sugar diary'. For everything that you eat, look at the nutritional label, or a nutritional table, and write down how many grams of 'sugars' are in the portion you eat. Be sure to measure your portions. Every 4 g of sugar equals 1 teaspoon of sugar – and 16 cal.

including carbonated soft drinks, jellies, jams, canned fruits and salad dressings. While most of us know that nutritive sweeteners are important ingredients in foods such as candies, soft drinks, ice cream, gelatin desserts, cereals and cookies and other baked goods, we may not be as aware that sweeteners are added to foods as varied as pizza, hot dogs, lunch meats, soups, spaghetti sauce, ketchup, salad dressings, boxed rice mixes and canned vegetables (USDA, 2000). As shown in Table 11.1, nutritive sweeteners come in a variety of forms. Many foods contain more than one sweetener, which makes it difficult for the consumer to calculate the total amount of nutritive sweeteners in a food product.

Several methods have been used for calculating the amount of sugar Americans consume; the most common being disappearance rates. This method subtracts the amount of sugars used from the total amount of sugar available in the food supply. Note that disappearance rates don't take into account wastage, or use of products for non-human consumption and therefore over estimate consumption patterns. However, from year to year, disappearance rates can be considered relatively consistent with respect to the level of over estimation. Therefore, looking at disappearance data over many years is still illustrative of gross measures of food consumption.

The National Health and Nutrition Examination Survey (NHANES) carried out by the Centers for Disease Control and National Center for Health Statistics is also used to calculate per capita sugar intake. The NHANES has advantages over merely looking at disappearance data in that people are surveyed in their homes regarding foods they eat and their health. Data are collected every 2 years, and the data are reasonably current. However, it is important to note that individuals frequently

underestimate their food intake, particularly of foods consumed between meals and foods that might have negative connotations – such as candy, desserts and soft drinks.

Although there are problems in estimating actual sugar intake, it is evident from the data that sugar intake has increased dramatically over the past 100 years. At the turn of the 20th century, Americans were consuming, on average, approximately 60 lb of nutritive sweeteners per year (Lecos, 1985). In comparison, as we enter the 21st century, yearly sweetener intake has risen to over 155 lb per person (USDA, 2000). The past few decades have seen an explosion of sugar-containing foods including soda, high-fructose corn syrup flavored fruit beverages and low-fat snack foods (Briefel and Johnson, 2004; Kranz et al., 2005). Low-fat foods are often a surprising source of sugar for consumers. Fat carries flavor in foods, and when fat is removed, more of other ingredients need to be added to boost flavor. Since sugar is a relatively inexpensive and flavor-enhancing ingredient, these foods have more added sugar than their higher-fat counterparts.

Sugar and Behavior

Sugar and cognition

With today's growing focus on relationships between nutrition, health and behavior, a growing body of research supports a link between sugar consumption and cognitive ability (Bellisle, 2004). In contrast to what is sometimes presented in the popular press, researchers have found that, in some circumstances, intake of sugars can boost performance on cognitive tasks. The positive effects of sugar consumption on cognition have been demonstrated in all age groups, from infants to the elderly (Kaplan et al., 2000; Blass and Camp, 2001; Sünram-Lea et al., 2001; Busch et al., 2002; Bellisle 2004; Messier, 2004) as well as in people with Down's syndrome (Manning et al., 1998) and Alzheimer's disease (Craft et al., 1992; Manning et al., 1993).

Beginning with the youngest age group, research by Blass and colleagues (Zeifman et al., 1996; Blass, 1997; Blass and Camp, 2001) has suggested that intake of sugar can

Table 11.1. Nutritive sweeteners used in foods.

Sucrose	Honey
Corn syrup	Dextrose
Fructose	High fructose corn syrup
Maltose	Crystalline fructose
Sorbitol	Glucose syrup
Mannitol	Tagatose
Molasses	Maple syrup

promote eye contact and face recognition in infants. For example, in an experiment investigating the effects of sucrose and experimenter eye contact to calm infants, Blass (1997) found age-related differences in the ability of sucrose to facilitate calming. Crying babies of varying ages were given sucrose by an experimenter while the experimenter maintained eye contact with the infant. In young infants (2–4 weeks old), eye contact and sucrose were more effective at reducing crying than eye contact alone. This effect persisted, but was less pronounced in older infants (6–9 weeks old) and was no longer present at 12 weeks of age. In a subsequent study, Blass and Camp (2001) showed that a preference for a face previously paired with sucrose and eye contact is greater than preference for a face pair with either eye contact or sucrose alone. Furthermore, they found that infants given sucrose and no eye contact gazed more at a stranger's face than at the face that had been seen when sucrose was given. These results indicate that sucrose in the absence of social interaction may be aversive to infants. It is argued that the preference for sweet foods and for faces develops early in humans to help the infant form a bond with the mother, thus increasing survival. These studies suggest an important role in palatable foods and social engagement on the development of face recognition and face preference.

As in infants, intake of sugar can have positive effects on cognitive behavior in young children. For example, 9–12-year-old boys performed significantly better on a vigilance task when they had consumed a sugar-containing confectionery product than when given a sweet-tasting, but non-nutritive placebo (Busch et al., 2002). While sugar intake did improve performance on the vigilance task, intake did not alter the children's ability to complete tasks measuring memory or visual perception. Reasons why one cognitive task, but not others may be influenced by sugar intake are mentioned in an upcoming section.

Moving on into adult populations, we continue to see improvements in cognition following ingestion of sugar (Messier et al., 1999; Kennedy and Scholey, 2004; Messier, 2004; Benton, 2005; Mahoney et al., 2005). Morris and Saril (2001) found that working memory, as measured by the listening span test, was significantly improved in college-aged students given a glucose drink relative to those given a non-caloric saccharin drink. In older subjects, Kaplan et al. (2000) showed a relationship between glucose regulation and cognitive performance. More specifically, poor blood glucose regulation was associated with poorer performance on a battery of cognitive tests. These same people, however, were more sensitive to the effects of subsequent glucose or carbohydrate ingestion on cognitive performance than those with better blood glucose regulation. Thus glucose intake produced greater improvements in cognitive test scores in people who performed more poorly on the cognitive test under control conditions, and who had poor glycemic control.

Given what we know about the relationship between fasting and blood glucose (namely if you go a long period of time without eating, your blood glucose is used by your body and thus there is less in your blood), fast duration is an important experimental consideration. Sünram-Lea et al. (2001) examined the difference between a short (2 h) and a long (9–12 h) fast on a variety of cognitive tests. Blood glucose for individuals fasting overnight was lower than for those who had fasted for only 2 h. Blood glucose was elevated following glucose ingestion, but was still lower in those who fasted overnight relative to those who fasted for 2 h. However, although individuals had different levels of blood glucose, all of them performed better on the battery of cognitive tests when they had consumed glucose than when they were given a placebo containing the non-nutritive sweetener, aspartame. The findings in this experiment are important in that they studied the effects of glucose in a more naturalistic manner. People typically eat every few hours that they are awake, and positive effects of sugars on cognition can be produced under these conditions.

One possible confound in experiments looking at the effects of something consumed on a certain behavior is the placebo, or expectancy effect. It is possible that subjects' performances can be influenced by what they think they should do based on their expectations about what they are eating. In experiments assessing the effects of sugar intake on cognitive behavior, researchers try to control for expectation by using a non-nutritive sweet-tasting placebo (such as aspartame), and sometimes employ a third condition where no sweet substance is given at all. Green *et al.* (2001) set out to characterize the effects of expectancy on the interaction between sucrose intake and cognition. They did this by comparing performance on cognitive tasks when participants were told correctly that they were drinking a beverage containing either glucose or aspartame, or when they were told that the glucose beverage contained aspartame, and the aspartame beverage contained glucose. Glucose intake was associated with improved performance on a word recognition memory task, and a task measuring attention. However, for the attention task, glucose only improved performance when people were told that they were receiving glucose. The authors suggest that, although glucose produced some improvements in cognitive performance, their findings show contributions of expectancy to glucose effects on performance. In this study, subjects showed the strongest effects for glucose intake on cognition in the more challenging tasks: word recognition and the Bakan task. Immediate recall (short-term memory) and motor speed were not affected.

The previous findings lead us to the final piece of the puzzle: task difficulty. Typically, intake of sugar improves cognitive performance more on difficult than easy cognitive tasks (Sünram-Lea *et al.*, 2001; Sünram-Lea *et al.*, 2002; Kennedy and Scholey, 2004; Benton, 2005). For example, Kennedy and Scholey (2004) reported that glucose enhanced performance more on tasks that participants rated as difficult relative to those they rated as easy. Additionally, these researchers (Scholey *et al.*, 2001) found that blood glucose levels fell more sharply following more demanding tasks than for easier ones. On the basis of these and similar findings, it is hypothesized that difficult cognitive tasks require the brain to work harder than easier tasks. This mental work leads to a depletion of glucose, and is reflected in falling blood sugar levels. By consuming a food or beverage containing sugar, the resulting elevation in blood glucose levels enhances cognitive performance.

Indirectly supporting this hypothesis, glucose is typically not effective in increasing performance in lower-demand cognitive tasks. The absence of a facilitating effect on easier cognitive tasks may represent a floor effect. Namely, the tasks may not be demanding enough to result in substantial use of glucose by the brain, and thus not responsive to further manipulation by diet.

Other evidence of the importance of glucose for brain functioning comes from studies investigating cognitive behavior in individuals suffering from diabetes. Decrements in cognitive functioning have been reported in people with diabetes (Weigner *et al.*, 1999; McCall, 2002; Awad *et al.*, 2004), and improvements in glycemic control in diabetic individuals associated with the ameliorations of these deficits in cognitive performance (Gradman *et al.*, 1993; Greenwood *et al.*, 2003). New research on insulin resistance suggests that people with impaired glucose tolerance, but who are not yet diabetic may also have problems with short-term memory (Convit *et al.*, 2003).

In conclusion, intake of glucose and other sugars has been related to improvements in cognitive behavior in children, young adults and the elderly (Scholey *et al.*, 2001; Busch *et al.*, 2002; Sünram-Lea *et al.*, 2002; Kennedy and Scholey, 2004; Benton, 2005). However, there is much we need to know about the effects of sugar on cognitive behavior. For example, additional information is needed about the quantity of sugar that should be consumed to enhance cognitive performance. While intake of a moderate amount of sugar may improve an individual's ability to attend to a mental task, intake of a larger amount may have less beneficial effects (Benton, 2005). Additionally, few studies have followed the time course of the effects of sugar on behavior, and it is important to know the duration of sugar's actions on behavior. Another issue to be resolved is whether one type of sugar is more beneficial than another at improving the performance on mental tasks. Most research in this area has assessed the effects of either glucose or sucrose on behavior. However, as noted earlier, in the USA, intake of these sugars is decreasing, while consumption of fructose is increasing. Thus, future research should investigate the effects of fructose, as well as glucose and sucrose, on cognitive behavior.

Sugar and mood

It may come as no surprise that intake of sweet foods influences mood. After all, high-carbohydrate drinks and meal replacement bars promise increased energy if you consume them. Indeed, part of the cultural attitude toward sugar is the belief that sugar intake enhances mood and decreases fatigue. People with depression and anxiety often report 'self-medicating' with palatable high sugar/high fat foods. One argument linking carbohydrate intake and mood is that carbohydrate intake increases blood glucose levels which, in turn, elevate mood (Benton, 2003). To some extent, research supports this argument. However, one critical aspect of the mood literature is that people may be victims of expectation effects rather than true post-ingestive effects. Another is that it is difficult to separate out the effects of carbohydrate intake from those of fat intake or the palatability of the food items. Foods consumed to enhance mood are typically highly palatable and not only contain sugars, but also fat (e.g. ice cream, cookies or cake) (Drewnowski and Schwartz, 1990). Other carbohydrate foods such as bread, pasta and potatoes are usually eaten with a sauce or topping that adds fat and/or protein. Indeed, many of these foods require the addition of fat or protein to make them palatable. Consider plain boiled pasta versus macaroni and cheese, plain potatoes versus mashed potatoes, or plain popcorn versus popcorn topped with salt and butter. It is rare to encounter a person who eats pure sugar foods such as hard candy to combat cravings or elevate mood. Therefore, some of the effects of sweet foods on mood may be attributable either to other nutrients in the food itself or to sensory characteristics including taste, mouth feel and smell. However, in many cases, the salient feature reported by people about the foods eaten is that they are sweet.

Although the literature on intake of pure sugar and mood is quite small, there is a large body of research examining carbohydrate intake and mood. Although much of this research is in special populations such as restrained-eaters, people with eating disorders, or people with clinical mood disorders, there is some research in non-clinical populations that support the hypothesis that sugar intake influences mood. Christensen and Pettijohn (2001) found that people who report greater levels of anxiety, depression and fatigue also report greater cravings for high carbohydrate/high fat foods than people who crave protein-rich foods. Participants in this study were given questionnaires asking what types of foods they typically craved, and scales assessing mood prior to and following eating the foods they reported craving the most. The majority of the participants classified themselves as 'carbohydrate cravers'. These people reported that they felt anxious, depressed and fatigued prior to craving carbohydrates and that eating the foods which they craved alleviated these negative moods. In other research, Willner et al. (1998) showed that humans in an experimental model of depression increase 'craving' for highly palatable sweet foods. Participants were asked to listen to music intended to produce either elated or depressed moods, and to concentrate on the mood that the music attempted to evoke, and try to experience that mood. They then were told that chocolate candy could be earned in an operant progressive ratio task[4]. Participants were also asked to complete mood questionnaires throughout the study. Music significantly influenced participants' reported mood. Furthermore, breakpoints for participants listening to depressing music were significantly higher, and they earned significantly more chocolate reinforcers than those that listened to uplifting music. Finally,

---

[4] A progressive ratio is an operant procedure where the requirements for reinforcement (usually pressing a button or lever) increase in a predetermined manner thereby increasing the interval of reinforcement (here, chocolate candy). In the present model, the further a participant continues in the progressive ratio (the higher the breakpoint), the more that individual is said to demonstrate 'craving'.

self-reports of craving for chocolate increased and remained elevated throughout the experiment in the group listening to the depressing music relative to those listening to uplifting music. In both of these studies, it is important to note that the effects of mood and palatable sweet foods were indirectly determined. In the first study, mood and food cravings were assessed using a battery of questionnaires (Christensen and Pettijohn, 2001). In the second study, participants achieved an experimentally-induced depressed mood, and then subsequent operant responding for chocolate was measured (Willner et al., 1998). These studies do show differences in affect and craving in relationship to mood, but they do not assess the immediate post-ingestive effects of carbohydrate on mood.

Reid and Hammersley (1995, 1999) more specifically investigated the ability of sucrose intake to alter mood in humans. In the first study (Reid and Hammersley, 1995), after a 9 h fast, participants were asked to complete the Profile of Mood States (POMS) at the start of the study and at subsequent time points. To avoid any influence of taste on mood, all subjects were given a benzocaine anesthetic lozenge prior to drinking one of the beverages: a sugar sweetened drink, a saccharin sweetened drink, or water. There were no differences as a function of drink condition on any mood measures with the exception of an elevation of energy in the sucrose condition in women who ordinarily ate breakfast – there were no differences for other women or for any of the men. It seems likely that in this experiment, the effects of mood related to sugar are attributable to the consumption of calories in people experiencing an abnormal caloric deprivation. It is possible that the benzocaine lozenge itself contributed to the results of this study since the lozenge is unpalatable and produces numbness of the mouth, tongue and upper throat.

In a subsequent study, Reid and Hammersley (1999) examined the effects of diet on mood in non-fasted participants. In this study, participants were asked to eat yogurt containing added corn oil, sugar, both corn oil and sugar, or saccharin, and then completed a variety of scales to determine mood, hedonic response, fullness and thirst. The results from this study differ from the first in two areas. First, intake of sucrose did not increase subjective feelings of energy. This may be due, in part, to the fact that participants were not food deprived in this study. In the first study, however, increased energy was reported by those participants who were accustomed to having breakfast. The second finding indicated that intake of sugar and corn oil or sugar alone significantly increased self-ratings of calmness on a scale ranging from 'calmer' to 'more angry'.

Interestingly, research investigating the effect of glucose intake on psychosocial stress responses showed that glucose intake increased the stress response (Gonzalez-Bono et al., 2002). In this experiment, fasted participants were given a glucose solution, protein, fat, or water prior to experiencing experimentally-induced social stress. Blood glucose and cortisol (a 'stress hormone') were measured throughout the study. Cortisol levels were significantly higher in participants who consumed glucose relative to the other dietary conditions. However, measures of calmness decreased in all subjects, and there were no differences in these parameters for those given glucose relative to the other groups. It is well known that activation of stress hormones such as cortisol and adrenaline produce elevations in blood glucose. Since after fasting, the stress response is blunted, increasing blood glucose levels by consumption of the sugar may reverses the decrements in glucose levels which occur during fasting to a greater extent than intake of fats or proteins which must be converted to glucose by more metabolically expensive methods. These data suggest that sugar has a subtle, yet demonstrable post-ingestive effect on mood. Moreover, these effects can be profoundly different depending upon the fasting state of the individual and the nature of the psychological test.

Sugar and hyperactivity

One of the more enduring myths surrounding sucrose intake is its role in hyperactivity in children. Many parents and teachers believe that intake of sugary foods leads to an increase in activity in children in general and, specifically, an aggravation of ADHD symptoms in children with ADHD (Liem *et al.*, 2004; Sinha and Efron, 2005). This myth has endured for decades despite an overwhelming lack of scientific evidence to support it (Kanarek, 1994; Wolraich *et al.*, 1995).

Over the years, hyperactivity and ADHD in children have drawn considerable attention from the medical and lay communities. More and more children are diagnosed with ADHD each year (Root and Resnick, 2003). ADHD presents with a constellation of symptoms ranging from impulsivity to aggression. Children diagnosed with the syndrome have difficulty coping with overstimulation, changes in daily routine, and periods of concentrated focus. These problems become more pronounced with increasing external stimulation, such as from group gatherings, parties and classroom situations.

A meta-analysis[5] conducted by Wolraich *et al.* (1995) examined findings of 16 studies on sugar intake and behavior in children. They only included experiments in which sugar consumption was compared to a placebo condition where subjects were given aspartame or saccharin, and the experimenters were blind to the diet manipulation. Subjects were children with or with ADHD and the experiments analyzed examined the effects of sugar intake on motor skills, aggression and mood. The ultimate conclusion of the meta-analysis was that there was that sugar consumption had no little or no effects on behavior.

One possible reason for the persistence of the sugar-hyperactivity myth could be that situations in which children typically show signs of overstimulation and hyperactivity are also situations in which sugary foods are prevalent (i.e. birthday parties, Halloween). Moreover, it is important to note that at such events, other foods are also available such as sodas (many of which contain caffeine in addition to sugar), chips and even nutritious food choices. However, since parents *expect* that the children will be affected by high sugar intake, sugar becomes the culprit at the end of the party. Hoover and Milich (1994) examined this

possibility by rating mother's perceptions of their child's hyperactivity in a deception experiment. All children were given an aspartame drink. The mothers were either told that the child had consumed aspartame (the truth), or that the child had consumed a sugar-sweetened drink (the deception). The key manipulation in this experiment was the mothers' expectancies. Mothers who believed their childhad consumed sugar (high expectancy) gave higher ratings for hyperactive behavior than mothers who believed their child consumed aspartame (low expectancy). These findings are supported by the observation that the children in the high expectancy group were not more active than the children in the low expectancy group. It was noted in this experiment that the high expectancy mothers engaged in a greater amount of mothering behavior toward their children, including maintaining physical closeness, verbal criticism and talking to them. The researchers argued that negative expectations can lead to a self-fulfilling prophecy, where mothers 'see' behavioral disruptions that may not be present and, furthermore, the children may react in some manner to the behavior elicited in their mothers through these expectations (Hoover and Milich, 1994).

Sugar and drug/alcohol interactions

Interactions between sucrose and drugs of abuse have been well established in both humans and animals (Kanarek *et al.*, 2005). Since more rigorous and controlled experiments are possible in animals than in humans for obvious ethical reasons, and animal studies can provide insights for understanding the human condition, a brief review of animal studies follows.

Intake of sucrose-containing foods can predict subsequent drug intake (Gosnell and Krahn, 1998; DeSousa *et al.*, 2000; Gosnell, 2000), alter the rewarding properties of drugs (Kanarek *et al.*, 1996; Vitale *et al.*, 2003),

---

[5] A meta-analysis is a type of statistical literature review that standardizes and analyzes the statistical findings from a number of different published papers. Meta-analysis requires that the analyst define and adhere to stringent criteria for the papers to be included in analysis.

and increase the pain relieving properties of drugs such as morphine (D'Anci *et al.*, 1997; Kanarek *et al.*, 2001) and nicotine (Mandillo and Kanarek, 2001). Although each drug sub-class acts on different areas of the brain and involves different neurotransmitter mecha-nisms, the findings with respect to sugar and drugs of abuse suggests a universal relation-ship between seemingly disparate substances.

It is a challenge to study interactions bet-ween diet and psychoactive substances in humans. First and foremost, it is extremely dif-ficult to design a study that can control for all of the possible variables that can influence eat-ing behavior and drug-related behavior. For example, it is unethical to give human partici-pants in a research study a potentially addict-ing drug, especially if they have never used the drug before. Moreover, many studies are per-formed in populations of 'at risk' people or recovering addicts. This presents additional concerns, since so little is known about what really produces addiction or how to treat addic-tion with a high-success rate. Additionally, there are many physiological changes brought about not only by long-term abuse of the drug itself, but also from other side effects of drug abuse – such as poor nutritional status, codependence on other substances and disease.

One observation about people with sub-stance dependence is that they typically eat abnormally high levels of sugar. This is seen in both stimulant abuse (Shaner, 2002; Janowsky *et al.*, 2003) and opiate abuse (Perl *et al.*, 1997; Morabia *et al.*, 1989; Bogucka-Bonikowska *et al.*, 2002). Additionally, drug dependence is associated with a greater preference for sweet foods in comparison with non-drug dependent individuals (Maone *et al.*, 1992; Perl *et al.*, 1997; Kampov-Polevoy *et al.*, 2003). This effect is seen in both infants born drug-dependent (Maone *et al.*, 1992) and drug-dependent adults (Perl *et al.*, 1997; Kampov-Polevoy *et al.*, 2003). For example, Maone *et al.* (1992) found that newborns exposed to cocaine in utero pre-ferred a pacifier dipped in sucrose over a non-sweetened pacifier to a greater degree than did control newborns. Similarly, Morabia *et al.* (1989) found that opioid-dependent men ate more high-sugar foods than non-dependent men, and that these low-nutrient foods tend to crowd out other foods in the diet, such as

foods rich in protein and fat. These observa-tions suggest that there is an interaction between the hedonic response to drugs of abuse and palatable sweet foods.

To explore the relationship between nutri-ent intake and drug abuse further, Kampov-Polevoy *et al.* (1997) compared sweet taste perception and preference in recently detoxi-fied alcoholics and controls. All participants were asked to taste solutions containing vary-ing concentrations of sucrose. They were asked to rate each fluid on how sweet they thought the solution was, and how pleasant they found it. Kampov-Polevoy and colleagues showed that alcoholic men preferred the higher con-centrations of sucrose more than non-alco-holic controls, but that their perception of sweet taste was not different from controls. Therefore, although drug-dependent people prefer sweet solutions, and prefer sweeter solu-tions than non-drug-dependent people, the dif-ference is not due to an underlying difference in sweet–taste perception (Kampov-Polevoy *et al.*, 1997). In a similar study, Bogucka-Bonikowska *et al.* (2002) measured sweet taste preference and perception in opioid-depend-ent individuals. However, in contrast to Kampov-Polevoy and colleagues, Bogucka-Bonikowska and colleagues found no differ-ences in preferences for sweet tastes in opioid dependent and non-opioid-dependent people. Finally, since drug and alcohol abuse is often accompanied by cigarette smoking, the effects of smoking on taste reactivity cannot be ruled out. Neither study mentioned whether smokers were excluded from participating, however the Kampov-Polevoy study mentions that partici-pants were medication-free for several days prior to the experiment.

As mentioned above, high initial prefer-ence for sweetened foods is predictive of future drug intake in animals. However, this relationship has yet to be established in humans. One study attempted to determine whether one known risk factor for developing alcoholism – paternal alcoholism – paralleled high-sugar preference – a predictor of drug intake in animals (Kranzler *et al.*, 2001). Kranzler and colleagues looked at two groups of non-alcoholic adults: participants in one group had fathers who were alcoholic; and those in the other group had non-alcoholic fathers. Sweet taste preference and perception were measured as described above (Kampov-Polevov et al., 1997). There were no group differences for either sweet perception or sweet preference. While the results of this study suggest that there is sweet preference is not correlated with the predilection for alcohol use, they are limited because we cannot know who among the participants ultimately will be alcohol-dependent. Finally, it is also possible that, in humans, one physiological consequence of long-term alcohol or drug abuse may be alterations in preference for sweets that would not be seen prior to substance abuse. In anecdotal support of this idea, the handbook used in Alcoholics Anonymous (Anonymous, 1975) lists eating something, 'usually sweet' as one of the primary ways to offset the desire to drink. Furthermore, the handbook mentions that even those members who previously were not partial to sweet foods found that eating something sweet was beneficial in staying sober.

In alcoholic populations, the preference for highly sweet solutions may be due, in part to interactions with the GABA-ergic system. Alcohol exerts its actions via many mechanisms, including the GABA system (Kiianmaa et al., 2003). Recent research in animals (Reynolds and Berridge, 2002) suggests that GABA is also implicated in appetitive behavior – and that GABA may be related to 'liking' of palatable foods (Berridge, 2000). More specifically, activation of GABA systems with ethanol may lead directly to an enhanced hedonic response to sweet foods. Moreover, chronic stimulation of the GABA system may result in conformational alterations at the neuronal level that may persist even after ethanol abuse ceases – leading to a longer-term preference for intensely sweet foods.

We mentioned earlier that some of the postingestive effects of sweet-tasting foods include interactions with dopamine and beta-endorphin in the brain. These neurotransmitter systems are associated with the rewarding and reinforcing properties of drugs. Thus, it is possible that highly palatable foods act in a reinforcing and/or rewarding manner. The reward obtained from food intake may, therefore, act to offset or reduce some of the negative consequences of abstaining from drugs or alcohol.

Furthermore, the interaction may work both ways, such that administration of drugs can enhance the rewarding properties of palatable foods, and thus increase preference for and intake of highly preferred foods.

Sugar and Pain

Since biblical times, sweet-tasting foods and fluids have been advocated for pain relief. To lessen the pain of ritual circumcision, in Jewish tradition, a drop of sweet wine is placed in the mouth of newborn babies, while in the Muslim religion, pieces of dates are rubbed inside the infant's mouth (Katme, 1995). More recent validation of these ancient prescriptions comes from research assessing the effects of short-term intake of palatable fluids and fluids on pain sensitivity in both humans and experimental animals. The first scientific investigation of sugar's pain relieving properties was completed by Blass et al. (1987) who found that infusions of sucrose into the oral cavity of infant rats reduced pain sensitivity, and led to a diminution of distress vocalizations when these animals were isolated from their dam and siblings. Within 3 years, this research was extended to humans in whom it was found that small quantities of sucrose placed on the tongue of 1- to 3-day old infants reduced crying in response to a painful stimulus (e.g. circumcision, heel prick, or venepuncture) (Smith et al, 1990). In the intervening years, these findings have repeatedly confirmed and extended (e.g. Blass and Watt, 1999; Masters-Harte and Abdel-Rahman, 2001; Yamada and Ohlsson, 2004). These studies indicate that in human infants, pain relief begins approximately 30 s after exposure to a sweet solution, and lasts at least 4 min after exposure (Blass and Shah, 1995; Yamada and Ohlsson, 2004).

One question raised by these initial experiments was whether the pain-relieving properties of sugars are restricted to sucrose or extend to other simple carbohydrates. Studies aimed at answering this question found that in both rat pups and human infants, sucrose and fructose were most effective in producing analgesia followed by glucose. In contrast, lactose, the sugar found in milk, failed to relieve pain in either rats or humans (Blass and Hoffmeyer, 1991; Blass and Smith, 1992). These findings are interesting when compared with results of earlier studies demonstrating that human infants can discriminate among different sugars, and prefer sucrose, fructose and glucose to lactose (Desor *et al.*, 1973). Taken together, these studies imply that when examining the acute effects of a food or fluid, the palatability of the substance, rather than its nutritive consequences, may be critical in determining analgesic responses.

Additional evidence of the importance of palatability in mediating the pain-relieving actions of foods and fluids comes from work demonstrating that intake of non-nutritive (e.g. aspartame), as well as nutritive sweet-tasting solutions, have analgesic properties (Ramenghi *et al.*, 1996). Moreover, in human infants, administration of a sweet solution directly into the stomach through a feeding tube fails to produce analgesia, indicating that the sweet-tasting solution must come in contact with taste receptors in the mouth and/or tongue to relieve pain (Ramenghi *et al.*, 1999, 2002).

Most studies investigating the effects of intake of palatable solutions on pain sensitivity in young organisms have used relatively brief pain stimuli, such as a heel prick or venepuncture in humans, and exposure to radiant heat in rats. However, there are suggestions from studies using laboratory rodents that intake of palatable foods and fluids may allow individuals to better cope with a variety of painful or stress-producing stimuli (Ren *et al.*, 1997; Anseloni *et al.*, 2002).

Although the analgesic actions of palatable foods and fluids tend to wane with age, the consumption of palatable foods and fluids can reduce pain sensitivity in adults as well as younger organisms (Mercer and Holder, 1997; Zmarzty *et al.*, 1997; Fontella *et al.*, 2004; Kanarek and Carrington, 2004). As an example, Mercer and Holder (1997) measured adults' sensitivity to pressure-induced pain and found that women who consumed a palatable sweet food displayed increased pain tolerance relative to women consuming either an unpalatable or neutral-tasting food. However, in men, no differences in pain sensitivity were observed as a function of nutrient palatability (Mercer and Holder, 1997).

It is hypothesized that the endogenous opioid system plays a role in mediating the effects of acute intake of palatable foods and fluids on pain sensitivity. In support of this hypothesis, pretreatment with the opioid antagonist naltrexone, blocks the pain-relieving effects of sucrose solutions in infant rats (Blass *et al.*, 1987). Additionally, intake of palatable foods and fluids elevates plasma and brain levels of endogenous opioid peptides (Dum *et al.*, 1983; Yamamoto *et al.*, 2000; Yamamoto, 2003), and increases neural activity in a number of brain areas containing opioid receptors.

Conclusion

In summary, dietary intake of sugars influences behavior through a variety of means. Ingestion of sugars alters blood glucose levels, endogenous opioid and dopamine functioning as well as insulin levels. These alterations, in turn, affect behaviors such as pain perception, mood and cognition. Furthermore, there is a relationship between drug abuse and sugar preferences, such that preferences for sweet foods are higher in individuals who abuse drugs such as alcohol and opioids. These effects may be altered by expectations of those consuming sweet substances, or by other people interacting with them. Finally, initial food preferences, current mood or stress levels, motivation or blood glucose status can modify these effects. Taken together, the available data are suggestive of a powerful relationship between ingestion of sugary foods and a wide range of brain functioning.

References

Alcoholics Anonymous (1975) *Living Sober.* Alcoholics Anonymous World Services, New York, p.87.

Anseloini, V.C.Z, Weng, H.R., Terayama, R., Letizia, D., Davis, B.J., Ren, K., Dubner, R. and Ennis, M. (2002) Age-dependency of analgesia elicited by intraoral sucrose in acute and persistent pain models. *Pain* 97, 93–103.

Awad, N., Gagnon, M. and Messier, C. (2004) The relationship between impaired glucose tolerance, type 2 diabetes and cognitive function.

Journal of Clinical and Experimental Neuropsychology 26, 1044–1080.

Bachmanov, A.A., Reed, D.R., Li, X. and Beauchamp, G.K. (2004) Genetic dissection of sweet taste in mice. *ACS Symposium Series* 867, 75–90.

Bellisle, F. (2004) Effects of diet on behaviour and cognition in children. *Britrish Journal of Nutrition* 92, S227–S232.

Benton, D. (2003) Carbohydrate, memory and mood. *Nutrition Reviews* 61, S61–S67.

Benton, D. (2005) Diet, cerebral energy metabolism, and psychological functioning. In: Lieberman, H.R., Kanarek, R.B., and Prasad, C. (eds) *Nutritional Neuroscience.*, CRC Press, Boca Raton, Florida, pp. 57–72.

Berdanier, C.D. (1995) *Advanced Nutrition: Macronutrients,* 2nd edn. CRC Press, Boca Raton, Florida.

Berridge, K.C. (2000) Measuring hedonic impact in animals and infants: microstructure of affective taste reactivity patterns. *Neuroscience and Biobehavioural Reviews* 24, 173–198.

Berridge, K.C. and Robinson, T.E. (1998) What is the role of dopamine in reward: hedonic impact, reward learning, or incentive salience? *Brain Research Review* 28, 309–369.

Blass, E.M. (1997) Changing influences of sucrose and visual engagement in 2- to 12-week-old human infants: implications for maternal face recognition. *Infant Behavior and Development* 20, 423–434.

Blass, E.M. and Camp, C.A. (2001) The ontogeny of face recognition: eye contact and sweet taste induce face preference in 9- and 12-week-old human infants. *Developmental Psychology* 37, 762–774.

Blass, E.M. and Hoffmeyer, L.B. (1991) Sucrose as an analgesic for newborn infants. *Pediatrics* 87, 215–218.

Blass, E.M. and Shah, A. (1995) Pain-reducing properties of sucrose in human newborns. *Chemical Senses* 20, 29–35.

Blass, E.M. and Smith, B.A. (1992) Differential effects of sucrose, fructose, glucose, and lactose on crying in 1–3-day-old human infants: qualitative and quantitative considerations. *Developmental Psychology* 28, 804–810.

Blass, E.M. and Watt, L.B. (1999) Suckling- and sucrose-induced analgesia in human newborns. *Pain* 83, 611–623.

Blass, E.M., Fitzgerald, E. and Kehoe, P. (1987) Interactions between sucrose, pain and isolation distress. *Pharmacology, Biochemistry & Behavior* 26, 483–489.

Bodnar, R. (2004) Endogenous opioids and feeding behavior: a 30-year historical perspective. *Peptides* 25, 697–725.

Bogucka-Bonikowska, A., Baran-Furga, H., Chmielewska, K., Habrat, B., Scinska, A., Kukwa, A., Koros, E., Kostowski, W., Polanowska, E. and Bienkowski, P. (2002) Taste function in methadone-maintained opioid-dependent men. *Drug and Alcohol Dependence* 68, 113–117.

Briefel, R.R. and Johnson, C.L. (2004) Secular trends in dietary intake in the United States. *Annual Review of Nutrition* 24, 401–431.

Brody, T. (1999) *Nutritional Biochemistry,* 2nd edn. Academic Press, New York.

Busch, C.R., Taylor, H.A., Kanarek, R.B. and Holcomb, P.J. (2002) The effects of a confectionary snack on attention in young boys. *Physiology and Behavior* 77, 333–340.

Carbajal, R., Lenclen, R., Gajdos, V., Jugie, M. and Paupe, A. (2002) Crossover trial of analgesic efficacy of glucose and pacifier in very preterm neonates during subcutaneous injections. *Pediatrics* 110, 389–393.

Christensen, L. and Pettijohn L. (2001) Mood and carbohydrate cravings. Appetite 36: 137–145.

Convit, A., Wolf, O.T., Tarshish, C. and de Leon, M.J. (2003) Reduced glucose tolerance is associated with poor memory performance and hippocampal atrophy among normal elderly. *Proceedings of the National Acadamy of Sciences USA* 10.1073/pnas.0336073100.

Craft, S., Zallen, G. and Baker, L.D. (1992) Glucose and memory in mild senile dementia of the Alzheimer type. *Journal of Clinical and Experimental Neuropsychology* 14, 253–267.

D'Anci K.E., Kanarek, R.B. and Marks-Kaufman, R. (1997) Beyond sweet taste: saccharin, sucrose, and polycose differ in their effects upon morphine-induced analgesia. *Pharmacology, Biochemistry & Behavior* 56, 341–345.

Darby, W.J.P., Ghalioungui, P. and Grivetti, L. (1977) *Food: The Gift of Osiris,* Academic Press, New York.

Desor, J.A., Maller, O. and Turner, R.E. (1973) Taste in acceptance of sugars by human infants. *Journal of Comparative and Physiogical Psychology* 84, 496–501.

DeSousa, N.J., Bush, D.E. and Vaccarino F.J. (2000) Self-administration of intravenous amphetamine is predicted by individual differences in sucrose feeding in rats. *Psychopharmacolology (Berl)* 148, 52–58.

Drewnowski, A. and Schwartz, M. (1990) Invisible fats: sensory assessment of sugar/fat mixtures. *Appetite* 14, 203–217.

Drewnowski, A., Krahn, D.D., Demitrack, M.A., Nairn, K. and Gosnell, B.A. (1995) Naloxone, an opiate blocker, reduces the consumption of sweet high-fat foods in obese and lean female binge eaters. *American Journal of Clinical Nutrition* 61, 1206–1212.

Dum, J., Gramsch, C.H. and Herz, A. (1983) Activation of hypothalamic beta-endorphin pools by reward induced by highly palatable foods. *Pharmacology, Biochemistry & Behavior* 18, 443–448.

Fontella, F.U., Nunes, M.L, Crema, L.M., Balk, R.S., Dalmaz, C. and Netto, C.A. (2004) Taste modulation of nociception differently affects chronically stressed rats. *Physiology and Behavior* 80, 557–561.

Gonzalez-Bono, E., Rohleder, N., Hellhammer, D.H., Salvador, A. and Kirschbaum, C. (2002) Glucose but not protein or fat load amplifies the cortisol response to psychosocial stress. *Hormones and Behavior* 41, 328–333.

Gosnell, B.A. (2000) Sucrose intake predicts rate of acquisition of cocaine self-administration. *Psychopharmacology (Berl)* 149, 286–292.

Gosnell, B.A. and Krahn, D.D. (1998) Taste and diet preferences as predictors of drug self-administration. *NIDA Research Monograph* 169, 154–175.

Gradman, T.J., Laws, A., Thompson, L.W. and Reaven, G.M. (1993) Verbal learning and/or memory improves with glycaemic control in older subjects with non-insulin-dependent diabetes mellitus. *Journal of American Geriatric Society* 41, 1305–1312.

Green, M.W., Taylor, M.A., Elliman, N.A. and Rhodes, O. (2001) Placebo expectancy effects in the relationship between glucose and cognition. *British Journal of Nutrition* 86, 173–179.

Greenwood, C.E., Kaplan, R.J., Hebblethwaite, S. and Jenkins, D.J.A. (2003) Carbohydrate-induced memory impairment in adults with type 2 diabetes *Diabetes Care* 26, 1961–1966.

Hoover, D.W. and Milich, R. (1994) Effects of sugar ingestion expectancies on mother-child interactions. *Journal of Abnormal Child Psychology* 22, 501–515.

Hsiao, S. and Smith, G.P. (1995) Raclopride reduces sucrose preference in rats. *Pharmacology Biochemistry and Behavior* 50, 121–125.

Janowsky, D., Pucilowski, O. and Buyinza, M. (2003) Preference for higher sucrose concentrations in cocaine abusing-dependent patients. *Journal of Psychiatric Research*. 37, 35–41.

Kampov-Polevoy, A., Garbutt, J.C. and Janowsky, D. (1997) Evidence of preference for a high-concentration sucrose solution in alcoholic men. *American Journal of Psychiatry* 154, 269–270.

Kampov-Polevoy, A., Garbutt, J.C. and Khalitov, E. (2003) Family history of alcoholism and response to sweets. *Alcoholism, Clinical and Experimental Research* 27, 1743–1749.

Kanarek, R.B. (1994) Does sucrose or aspartame cause hyperactivity in children? *Nutrition Reviews* 52, 173–175.

Kanarek, R.B. and Carrington, C. (2004) Sucrose consumption enhances nicotine-induced analgesia in male and female smokers. *Psychopharmacology (Berl)* 173, 56–63, 2004.

Kanarek, R.B., Mathes, W.F. and Przypek, J. (1996) Intake of dietary sucrose or fat reduces amphetamine drinking in rats. *Pharmacology, Biochemistry & Behavior* 54, 719–723.

Kanarek, R.B., Mandillo, S. and Wiatr, C. (2001) Chronic sucrose intake augments antinociception induced by injections of mu but not kappa opioid receptor agonists into the periaqueductal gray matter in male and female rats. *Brain Research* 920, 97–105.

Kanarek, R.B., D'Anci, K.E., Foulds Mathes, W., Yamamoto, R., Coy, R.T. and Leibovici, M. (2005) Dietary modulation of the behavioral consequences of psychoactive drugs. In: Lieberman, H.R., Kanarek, R.B. and Prasad, C. (eds) *Nutritional Neuroscience*, CRC Press, Boca Raton, Florida, pp. 187–206.

Kaplan, R.J., Greenwood, C.E., Winocur, G. and Wolever, T.M.S. (2000) Cognitive performance is associated with glucose regulation in healthy elderly persons and can be enhanced with glucose and dietary carbohydrates. *American Journal of Clinical Nutrion* (72), 825–836.

Katme, A.M. (1995) Analgesic effects of sucrose were known to the prophet. *British Medical Journal* (311), 1169.

Kennedy, D.O. and Scholey, A.B. (2004) A glucose-caffeine 'energy drink' ameliorates subjective and performance deficits during prolonged cognitive demand. *Appetite* 42, 331–333.

Kiianmaa, K., Hyytia, P., Samson, H.H., Engel, J.A., Svensson, L., Soderpalm, B., Larsson, A., Colombo, G., Vacca, G., Finn, D.A., Bachtell And, R.K. and Ryabinin, AE. (2003) New neuronal networks involved in ethanol reinforcement. *Alcoholism, Clinical and Experimental Research* 27, 209–219.

Kranz, S., Smicklas-Wright, H., Siega-Riz, A.M. and Mitchell, D. (2005) Adverse effect of high added sugar consumption on dietary intake in American preschoolers. *Journal of Pediatrics* 146, 105–111.

Kranzler, H.R., Sandstrom, K.A., and Van Kirk, J. (2001) Sweet taste preference as a risk factor for alcohol dependence. *American Journal of Psychiatry* 158, 813–815.

Lecos, C.W. (1985) Sugar, how sweet it is – and isn't. *FDA Consumer*, February, 21–23.

Levine, A.S. and Billington, C.J. (2004) Opioids as agents of reward-related feeding: a consideration of the evidence. *Physiology and Behavior* 82, 57–61.

Liebman, B. (1999) The changing American diet. *Nutrition Action Newsletter*, April, 8–9.

Liem, D.G., Mars, M. and De Graff, C. (2004) Sweet preferences and sugar consumption of 4- and 5-year-old children: role of parents. *Appetite* 43, 235–245.

Lindemann, B. (1996) Taste reception. *Physiological Reviews* 76, 718–766.

Lindemann, B. (2001) Receptors and transduction in taste. *Nature* 413, 219–225.

Mahoney, C.R., Taylor, H.A. and Kanarek, R.B. (2005) The acute effects of meals on cognitive performance. In: Lieberman, H. R., Kanarek, R. B. and Prasad, C. (eds) *Nutritional Neuroscience*, CRC Press, Boca Raton, Florida, pp. 73–91

Mandillo, S. and Kanarek, R.B. (2001) Chronic sucrose intake enhances nicotine-induced antinociception in female but not male Long-Evans rats. *Pharmacology, Biochemistry & Behavior* 68, 211–219.

Manning, C.A., Ragozzino, M.E. and Gold, P.E. (1993) Glucose enhancement of memory in patients with probable senile dementia of the Alzheimer's type. *Neurobiology of Aging* 14, 523–528.

Manning, C.A., Honn, V.J., Stone, W.S., Jane, J.S. and Gold, P.E. (1998) Glucose effects on cognition in adults with Down's syndrome. *Neuropsychology* 12, 479–484.

Maone, T.R., Mattes, R.D. and Beauchamp, G.K. (1992) Cocaine-exposed newborns show an exaggerated sucking response to sucrose. *Physiology & Behavior* 51, 487–491.

Marks-Kaufman, R., Hamm, M.W. and Barbato, G.F. (1989) The effects of dietary sucrose on opiate receptor binding in genetically obese (ob/ob) and lean mice. *Journal of the American College of Nutrition* 8, 9–14.

Masters-Harte, L.D. and Abdel-Rahman, S.M. (2001) Sucrose analgesia for minor procedures in newborn infants. *The Annals of Pharmacotherapy* 35, 947–952.

Matsunami, H., Montmayeur, J.P. and Buck, L.B. (2000) A family of candidate taste receptors in human and mouse. *Nature* 404, 601–604.

Max, M., Shanker, Y.G., Huang, L.Q., Rong, M., Liu, Z., Campagne, F., Weinstein, H., Damak, S. and Margolskee, R.F. (2001) Tas1r3, encoding a new candidate taste receptor, is allelic to the sweet responsiveness locus Sac. *Nature Genetics* 28, 58–63.

McCall, A.L. (2002) Diabetes mellitus and the central nervous system. *International Review of Neurobiology* 51, 415–453.

Mercer, M.E. and Holder, M.D. (1997) Antinociceptive effects of palatable sweet ingesta on human responsivity to pressure pain. *Physiology & Behavior* 61, 311–318.

Messier, C. (2004) Glucose improvement of memory: a review. *European Journal of Pharmacology* 490, 33–57.

Messier, C., Desrochers, A. and Gagnon, M. (1999) Effect of glucose, glucose regulation, and word imagery value on human memory. *Behavioral Neuroscience* 113, 431–438.

Miller, A., Barr, R.G. and Young, S.N. (1994) The cold pressor test in children: methodological aspects and the analgesic effect of intraoral sucrose. *Pain* 56, 175–183.

Morabia, A., Fabre, J., Chee, E., Zeger, S., Orsat, E. and Robert, A. (1989) Diet and opiate addiction: a quantitative assessment of the diet of non-institutionalized opiate addicts. *British Journal of Addiction* 84, 173–180.

Morris, N and Saril, P. (2001) Drinking glucose improves listening span in students who miss breakfast. *Educational Research* 43, 201–207.

Pecina, S. and Berridge, K.C. (2000) Opioid site in nucleus accumbens shell mediates eating and hedonic 'liking' for food: map based on microinjection Fos plumes. *Brain Research* 863, 71–86.

Perl, E., Schufman, E., Vas, A., Luger, S. and Steiner, J.E. (1997) Taste- and odor-reactivity in heroin addicts. *The Israel Journal of Psychiatry and Related Sciences* 34, 290–299.

Ramenghi, L.A., Wood, C.M., Griffiths, G.C. et al., (1996) Reduction of pain respones in premature infants using intraoral sucrose. *Archives of Diseases in Childhood* 74, F126–F127.

Ramenghi, L.A., Evans, D.J. and Levene, M.I. (1999) "Sucrose analgesia": absorptive mechanism or taste perception. *Archives of Diseases in Childhood* 80, F146–F147.

Ramenghi, L.A., Webb, A.V., Shevlin, P.M., Green, M., Evans, D.J. and Levine, M.I. (2002) Intra-oral administration of sweet-tasting substances and infants' crying response to immunization: a randomized, placebo-controlled trial. *Biology of the Neonate* 81, 163–169.

Reid, M. and Hammersley, R. (1995) Effects of carbohydrate intake on subsequent food intake and mood state. *Physiology & Behavior* 58, 421–427.

Reid, M. and Hammersley, R. (1999) The effects of sucrose and maize-oil on subsequent food intake and mood. *British Journal of Nutrition* 82, 447–455.

Ren, K., Blass, E.M., Zhou, Q-o. and Dubner, R. (1997) Suckling and sucrose ingestion suppress persistent hyperalgesia and spinal Fos expression after forepaw inflammation in infant rats. *Proceedings of the National Academy of Sci USA* 94, 1472–1475.

Reynolds, S.M. and Berridge, K.C. (2002) Positive and negative motivation in nucleus accumbens shell: bivalent rostrocaudal gradients for GABA-elicited eating, taste 'liking'/'disliking' reactions, place preference/avoidance, and fear. *The Journal of Neuroscience* 22, 7308–7320.

Root, W. and Resnick, R.J. (2003) An update on the diagnosis and treatment of attention-deficit/hyperactivity disorder in children. *Professional Psychology – Research and Practice* 34, 34–41.

Scholey, A.B., Harper, S. and Kennedy, D.O. (2001) Cognitive demand and blood glucose. *Physiology & Behavior* 73, 585–592.

Shaner, J.W. (2002) Caries associated with methamphetamine abuse. *Journal of Michigan Dental Association* 84, 42–47.

Sieber, F.E. and Trastman, R.J. (1992) Special issues: glucose and the brain. *Critical Care Medicine* 20, 104–114.

Sinha, D. and Efron, D. (2005) Complementary and alternative medicine use in children with attention deficit hyperactivity disorder. *Journal of Paediatrics and Child Health* 41, 23–26.

Smith, B.A., Fillion, T.J. and Blass, E.M. (1990) Orally mediated sources of calming in 1- to 3-day-old human infants. *Developmental Psychology* 26, 731–737.

Spallholz, J.E., Boylan, L.M. and Driskell, J.A. (1999) *Nutrition, Chemistry and Biology*, 2nd edn. CRC Press, Boca Raton, Florida.

Sünram-Lea, S.I., Foster, J.K., Durlach, P. and Perez, C. (2001) Glucose facilitation of cognitive performance in healthy young adults: examination of the influence of fast-duration, time of day and pre-consumption plasma glucose levels. *Psychopharmacology (Berl)* 157, 46–54.

Sünram-Lea, S.I., Foster, J.K., Durlach, P. and Perez, C. (2002) Investigation into the significance of task difficulty and divided allocation of resources on the glucose memory facilitation effect. *Psychopharmacology (Berl)* 160, 387–397.

USDA (2000) Agriculture fact book 2000. Washington, DC. p.314.

Vitale, M.A., Chen, D. and Kanarek, R.B. (2003) Chronic access to a sucrose solution enhances the development of conditioned place preferences for fentanyl and amphetamine in male

Long-Evans rats. *Pharmacology, Biochemistry & Behavior* 74, 529–539.

Weinger, K., Kinsley, B.T., Levy, C.J., Bajaj, M., Simonson, D.C., Cox, D.J., Ryan, C.M. and Jacobson, A.M. (1999) The perception of safe driving ability during hypoglycemia in patients with type 1 diabetes mellitus. *The American Journal of Medicine* 107, 246–253.

Wenk, G.L. (1989) An hypothesis on the role of glucose in the mechanism of action of cognitive enhancers. *Psychopharmacology (Berl)* 99, 431–438.

Wildman, R.E.C. and Medeiros, D.M. (2000) *Advanced Human Nutrition*. CRS Press, New York, p. 585p

Willner, P., Benton, D., Brown, E., Cheeta, S., Davies, G., Morgan, J. and Morgan, M. (1998) 'Depression' increases 'craving' for sweet rewards in animal and human models of depression and craving. *Psychopharmacololy (Berl)* 136, 272–283.

Wolke, R.L. (2002) *What Einstein Told His Cook*. Norton, New York.

Wolraich, M.L., Wilson, D.B. and White, J.W. (1995) The effect of sugar on behavior or cognition in children. *JAMA* 274, 1617–1621.

World Health Organization (2003) WHO technical report series 916: diet, nutrition, and the prevention of chronic diseases. Geneva, Switzerland, 160 p.

Yamada, S.B. and Ohlsson, A. (2004) Sucrose for analgesia in newborn infants undergoing painful procedures. *Cochrane Database of Systematic Reviews* CD001069. pub2.

Yamamoto, T. (2003) Brain mechanisms of sweetness and palatability of sugars. *Nutrition Reviews* 61, S5–S9.

Yamamoto, T., Sako, N. and Maeda, S. (2000) Effects of taste stimulation on beta-endorphin levels in rat cerebrospinal fluid and plasma. *Physiology & Behavior* 69, 345–350.

Yeomans, M.R. and Gray R.W. (2002) Opioid peptides and the control of human ingestive behaviour. *Neuroscience and Biobehavioral Reviews* 26, 713–728.

Zeifman, D., Delany, S. and Blass, E.M. (1996) Sweet taste, looking, and calm in 2- and 4- week old infants: the eyes have it. *Developmental Psychology* 32, 1090–1099.

Zmarzty, S.A., Wells, A.S. and Read, N.W. (1997) The influence of food on pain perception in healthy human volunteers. *Physiology & Behavior* 62, 185–191.

12 Caffeine, the Methylxanthines and Behavior

K.E. D'Anci and R.B. Kanarek

Each morning, millions of individuals around the world wake up and begin their day with a cup of coffee. Indeed, you may be one of them. Americans consume approximately 20% of the world's coffee. Over half of the adults in the USA drink coffee every day, while another 25% drink the beverage on a more occasional basis (Dictum and Luttinger, 1999).

While millions consume coffee, tea remains the most popular beverage in the world. As might be expected, the highest per capita intake of tea is in the UK where individuals consume an average of three to four cups of tea each day. Although tea consumption in the USA has increased over the last 10 years, Americans continue to consume only one-third as much tea as individuals in Great Britain.

Young people often find the taste of coffee and tea unpalatable. However, children and adolescents drink substantial quantities of soft drinks both at home and away. For example, soda dispensing machines are becoming increasingly common in schools throughout the USA (Pollak and Bright, 2003).

While coffee, tea and soft drinks differ widely in taste and nutrient composition, they share an important characteristic – they all contain chemicals called methylxanthines. There are a large number of methylxanthines, but only three are commonly found in foods: caffeine, theophylline and theobromine. Caffeine is naturally found in coffee, kola nuts,

tea and chocolate, and is an added ingredient in over 70% of the soft drinks manufactured in the USA (Bernstein et al., 2002). As well as caffeine, theophylline is found in tea, and theobromine in chocolate. As noted below, all three of these compounds have significant physiological actions. However, it is the action of these drugs on the central nervous system, which contributes most significantly to their use. As a group, the methylxanthines are the most commonly consumed psychoactive substances in the world (James, 1997).

A Very Brief History of Coffee, Tea and Chocolate

Coffee

The actual beginning of coffee use and cultivation remains lost to history. But, according to legend, the power of the coffee plant was first discovered over 1500 years ago by a young Ethiopian goat herder named Kaldi. One evening, after spending the day walking the hills, Kaldi, much to his surprise, found his animals behaving in a most unusual manner – running about, butting one another, dancing on their hind legs, and darting off at the sight of the young goat herder. These antics lasted through the night, and were repeated the following day. Careful observation revealed that this frenetic behavior resulted from the intake of the glossy green leaves and red berries of a tree never seen before by the goat herder. A curious youth, Kaldi tasted the plant, and was rewarded with a burst of energy and feeling of euphoria. In his quest to sustain these positive effects, Kaldi became the first habitué of coffee. As word of these magical plants spread, coffee became an integral part of Ethiopian culture (Rall, 1985; Dictum and Luttinger, 1999; Pendergast, 1999).

In Ethiopia and other parts of the Arab world, the berries of the plant, *Coffea arabica*, were originally chewed. Later, the berries were crushed and mixed with balls of animal fat to produce the first 'energy bars', which provided concentrated nourishment for long travels and bloody battles. Over time, the populace developed more palatable recipes for the plant, and by 1000 BCE, the leaves and berries of the plant were being mixed with boiled water to make a beverage called kavah, the Arabic word for coffee. As experience with the plant grew, its value as a medication with the potential to alleviate a myriad of maladies including gastrointestinal distress, fatigue and pain, became well recognized (Dicum and Luttinger, 1999; Pendergast, 1999; Lieberman, 2001).

By the 1500s, throughout the Levant, coffeehouses, where men congregated to discuss politics, play games and listen to music, were an integral part of the culture. Although foreigners visiting the Middle East could experience the pleasures of drinking coffee, until the 1600s, coffee remained a monopoly of the Arab world. Foreigners were prohibited from visiting coffee farms, and extreme care was taken to prevent coffee beans from being exported. In the middle of the 1600s, however, Dutch spies managed to smuggle coffee plants from the Middle East. From these plants, the world's love of coffee grew. In the ensuing 100 years, coffee drinking became common-place throughout Europe, with coffeehouses becoming important political and culture venues in Holland, Italy, France, Austria and England (Dicum and Luttinger, 1999).

The first coffeehouse in the USA opened in Boston in 1689. By the beginning of the 1700s, coffeehouses were found in all of the major cities in the country. As in Europe, these coffeehouses became centers for political, social and commercial activities. Coffee intake grew with the nation, and coffee became a staple of life in both the cities and country. By the mid-1800s, enterprising entrepreneurs began roasting green coffee beans and packaging the beans into one-pound bags, further increasing the availability and popularity of the beverage. At the beginning of the last century, manufacturers developed a process for refining coffee crystals from brewed coffee. These crystals could be dissolved in hot water leading to the first instant coffee. Although the beverage did not possess the taste, smell or body of coffee brewed from fresh beans, it did resemble the real thing. During the First World War, instant coffee provided soldiers with a reasonable source of warmth and caffeine. By the middle of the century, freeze-drying allowed instant coffee to more closely mimic coffee made directly from beans. In 1978, instant coffee represented 34% of all coffee in this country. However the intervening years, with a rise in gourmet and specialty coffees, have witnessed a decline in the popularity of instant coffee, which now accounts for only 10% of coffee intake (Dicum and Luttinger, 1999; Pendergast, 1999).

Tea

As with coffee, the origins of tea are swathed in myth. One of the most popular suggestion is that the founder of Zen Buddhism, Daruma, fell asleep while meditating. Upon awakening, he was so distraught that he cut off his eyelids and cast them to the ground. The first tea plant grew from this spot – and the leaves were used to brew a beverage that produced alertness (Ray and Ksir, 2002). Whatever its origins, tea has been consumed for thousands of years. For much of its history, drinking hot tea was safer than drinking water – due in part to the fact that the water for tea needed to be boiled. Indeed, when drinking tea in times before modern plumbing, the first 'cup' of tea was poured to rinse out the cup and clean it for subsequent use.

Chocolate

Chocolate is made from the cacao bean. The cacao tree is native to the new world, and was used by the Aztecs to make 'xocolatl' – a frothy drink made from cacao bean paste, water, maize and chilies. Cacao was considered a gift from Quetzalcoatl, the god of air. Recalling the legends, the official name of the cacao tree is *Theobroma cacao* – 'food of the gods'. To the Aztecs, the seeds of the cacao tree were as valuable as gold and silver, and often used to pay tribute to their rulers.

Christopher Columbus, the first European who had the pleasure of consuming 'xocolatl', brought the fruits of the cacao tree back to Spain. In Europe, as in the new world, chocolate was reserved for the aristocracy, and associated with indulgence and luxury. Although initially consumed as a beverage, by the mid-1700s, cacao beans had been transformed into bars, which were used as a food. Later innovations, such as the addition of milk to the confection, added to the allure of chocolate. Like coffee, chocolate won praises for its medicinal qualities – and was recommended as a cure for mental stress, tuberculosis and fever. By the 1800s, the connection between chocolate and romance was established with physicians recommending that patients scorned by suitors should consume chocolate to alleviate their travails (Ray and Ksir, 2002).

Sources of Caffeine

In the USA, more than 75% of all caffeine consumed comes from coffee. In Table 12.1, you can see that the caffeine levels in a cup of coffee vary depending on the way the beverage has been brewed. An additional influence on caffeine content in coffee is the duration of roast in that lighter roasts, which are roasted for shorter periods of time contain significantly more caffeine than the darker roasts, which result from longer roasting. A common misconception is to equate caffeine content with the strength of the coffee's flavor. In fact – the opposite is true.

When calculating daily caffeine intake from coffee, it is important to note that the data displayed in Table 12.1 represent the amount of caffeine found in a 12 oz cup or standard mug of coffee. However, as for many other foods in our diet, the size of a typical cup of coffee has increased substantially over the past

decade. An 8 oz cup of coffee, where available, is now considered 'small', a 12 oz cup 'medium', and a 16 oz cup 'large'. As 'large' is the most common size sold in retail coffee establishments, a 'cup' of coffee, now contains anywhere from 160 to 350 mg of caffeine (Harland, 2000; McCusker *et al.*, 2003).

Tea is the second largest source of caffeine in the American diet. Approximately 15% of the caffeine consumed in the USA comes from tea. By weight, tea leaves contain more caffeine than an equal amount of coffee beans. However, since a smaller quantity of tea leaves is required to brew a cup of tea than the quantity of coffee beans required to make a cup of coffee, a cup of tea generally contains less caffeine (45 to 75 mg) than a cup of coffee. A cup of tea also contains 1–2 mg of the methylxanthine known as theophylline.

Caffeine is also found in chocolate with a cup of cocoa or glass of chocolate milk containing between 5–10 mg of caffeine and 250 mg of theobromine (Barone and Roberts, 1996; Harland, 2000). Caffeine from chocolate makes up only a small part of total caffeine intake in adults. However, chocolate provides a major source of methylxanthines for many children.

A growing source of caffeine for children and adolescents comes from soda, sports drinks and waters with added amounts of the drug. Over 70% of soft drinks including not only cola beverages, but also drinks that on first glance may appear to be caffeine-free (fruit drinks), contain the drug. Caffeine content in these products ranges from approximately 20 mg per 16 oz serving in bottled ice tea to over 90 mg per 12 oz serving in soft drinks and waters marketed directly for their high caffeine content (e.g. Joltand Java Water).

In addition to being components of coffee, tea, chocolate and soft drinks, caffeine, theophylline and theobromine are found in a wide variety of foods (e.g. yogurt, ice cream and energy bars) and pharmaceutical products (e.g. analgesics, allergy and asthma medications, and weight control products) (Barone and Roberts 1996; Harland, 2000).

As evident from Table 12.1, even if you don't regularly drink caffeine-containing beverages, you may still be consuming significant

Table 12.1. Caffeine content of common foods and over-the-counter (OTC) medications.

Product	Serving size (oz) (unless otherwise stated)	Milligrams of caffeine (approximate values)
Coffee		
Brewed	12	200
Roasted and ground, percolated	12	180
Roasted and ground, filter drip	12	268
Roasted and ground, decaffeinated	12	5
Espresso	2	35
Double espresso	2	70
Instant	12	110–150
Instant decaffeinated	12	7.5
Tea		
Average blend	12	65
Green	12	45
Instant	12	22
Leaf or bag	12	75
Decaffeinated tea	12	0
Cola beverages		
Cola beverage, regular	12	36–46
Cola beverage, diet	12	39–50
Non-cola beverages		
Sunkist orange soda	12	35
Mountain Dew	12	56
Barq's root beer	12	22
Glaceau vitamin water		
Energy Tropical Citrus	12	32
Cocoa products		
Chocolate milk	12	12
1 envelope hot-cocoa mix	12	8
Candy, milk chocolate	1	7
Candy, sweet chocolate	1	19
Baking chocolate, unsweetened	1	25–58
Chocolate cake	2.8	6
Chocolate brownies	1.5	10
Chocolate mousse	3.2	15
Chocolate pudding	5.1	9
Other foods		
Dannon natural flavors low fat coffee-flavored yogurt	6	36
Häagen-Dazs coffee ice cream	4	24
Starbucks coffee java chip ice cream	4	28
OTC medications		
Excedrin tension headache	2 tablets	130
Excedrin extra strength	2 tablets	130
Midol menstrual complete	2 tablets	130

Sources: Schardt and Schmidt (1996); Shils *et al.* (1999); Harland (2000); Consumer Reports (2003); Product labels.

amounts of the drug in other foods and medicines. While this may not be a major cause of concern for most adults, it may be an important issue for children who are smaller, and thereby are consuming a proportionally larger amount of caffeine. It may also be a consideration for pregnant women and others who wish to avoid caffeine.

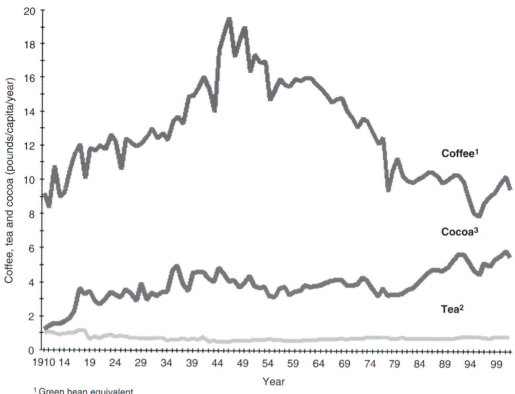

[1] Green bean equivalent
[2] Dry leaf equivalent
[3] Bean equivalent

Fig. 12.1. Intake of caffeine-containing beverages since 1910. Source: USDA/Economic Research Service.

Trends in coffee, tea and chocolate consumption

Although the size of a cup of coffee has increased over the years, coffee intake in the USA has actually declined since peaking in the late 1940s (Fig. 12.1) (Dicum and Luttinger, 1999). It is important to note that per capita data cannot distinguish between people who do and do not consume coffee. Thus, there are people who consume no coffee and people who consume 20 lb of coffee annually. However, the general trend for Americans is to drink less coffee than they did in the middle of the 20th century. The one exception to this trend is the specialty coffee market (e.g. cappuccino, latte and espresso), which has experienced significant growth in the last decade, especially among younger consumers (Dicum and Luttinger, 1999; Pendergast, 1999).

Across the globe, tea and tea intake has remained stable for the last 100 years. However, over the last decade, Americans seem to be enjoying more tea, both green and black, than ever before with per capita tea intake now estimated to be 1 lb per year. This increase in tea consumption may be due, in part, to reports in the popular press about the potential health benefits of drinking tea. These reports are based on the fact that polyphenols and other compounds found in tea can serve as potent antioxidants. These antioxidants may reduce the risk factors for cardiovascular disease and certain types of cancers by neutralizing the damage to our cells produced over time by the oxidative by-products of normal metabolism. However, it is important to note that while some studies have supported a role for tea in the prevention of cancer and heart disease, this had not universally been the case. As in many studies on the health benefits of nutrients, confounding variables such as other lifestyle factors (e.g. smoking and exercise habits) and intake of other nutrients (e.g. alcohol and dietary fat) must be taken into account when evaluating the health benefits of tea (McKay and Blumberg, 2002; Lambert and Yang, 2003; Rietveld and Wiseman, 2003).

Intake of cocoa and other chocolate-containing foods has increased slightly since the 1950s, with per capita cocoa intake now equaling approximately 6 lb per year. Intake of chocolate confections is also on the rise. It is estimated that in 2001, on average, each American consumed 11.7 lb of chocolate, which means that overall in the USA, approximately 3 billion lb of chocolate are consumed each year. Americans, however, are not the largest consumers of chocolate. That honor goes to the Swiss, who consume almost twice as much chocolate as Americans, or approximately 22.4 lb per person each year (Table 12.2).

Studies of the nutritional habits of children and adolescents clearly show that intakes of soft drinks and related beverages have grown over the last two decades. Over 95% of Americans between the ages of 5 and 18, consume caffeine-containing soft drinks at least once a week. Moreover, soft drink intake of children between the ages of 6 to 17 years has more than doubled from an average of 5 oz of soft drinks per day in 1978 to over 12 oz of soft drinks per day in 2000. As the numbers above represent average intakes, it means that many children are consuming substantially more than 12 oz of soft drinks a day. Adolescent boys consume the largest amounts of these beverages, with an average intake of 25 oz/day (Castellanos and Rapoport, 2002; Forshee and Storey, 2003; French et al., 2003; Pollak and Bright, 2003).

Recent evaluations of actual caffeine intake indicate that on average, Americans consume 193 mg of caffeine per day. Men between the ages of 35 to 54 have the greatest caffeine intake, with a daily average of 336 mg, followed by men between the ages of 55 and 64 who take in 318 mg/day. Women in these age groups consume a daily average of 250 mg of caffeine (35 to 54 years) and 228 mg (55 to 64 years). Young children between the ages of 2 and 11, consume approximately 21 mg of caffeine per day, which increases to approximately 70 mg/day in the teenage years (Frary et al., 2005).

Table 12.2. Yearly per capita intake of chocolate.

Country	Intake of chocolate (lb)
Switzerland	22.4
Austria	20.1
Ireland	19.5
United Kingdom	18.5
Norway	18.0
Denmark	18.0
Germany	18.0
Sweden	18.0
Belgium	15.4
United States	11.7
Finland	11.0
France	10.6
Netherlands	9.9
Australia	9.7
Italy	6.8
Greece	4.6
Japan	4.0
Portugal	3.5
Spain	3.5
Brazil	2.0

Metabolism of the Methylxanthines

The three methylxanthines – caffeine, theophylline and theobromine – are chemically similar and metabolized in a similar manner Fig. 12.2). Therefore, discussion of metabolism of these drugs will focus on caffeine, as it is the most frequently consumed member of the group. In adults, when caffeine is consumed in beverages, over 99% is rapidly absorbed from the digestive tract. Within 5 min, caffeine is distributed to all of the tissues in the body including the brain. Additionally, caffeine easily crosses the placental barrier to enter fetal tissue, and passes from mother to infant in the breast milk (Rall, 1985). Once consumed, peak effects are seen within 15 min to 2 h. The wide variation in peak effects is related to speed of gastric emptying and presence of other dietary compo-

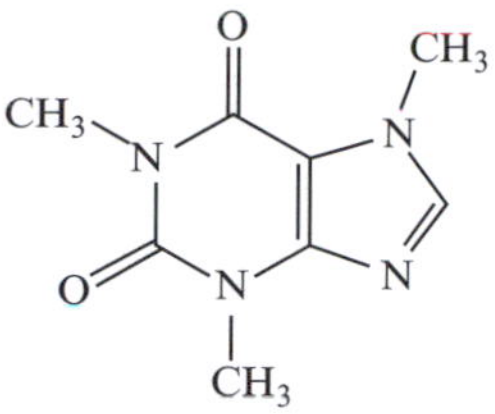

Fig. 12.2. Chemical structure of the methylxanthines.

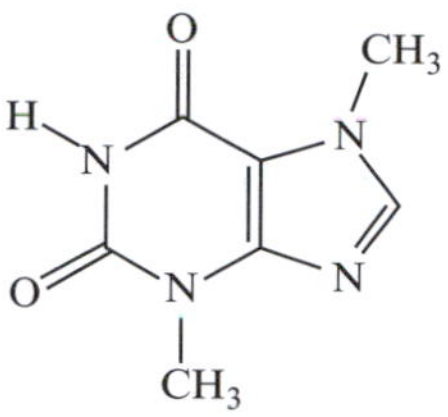

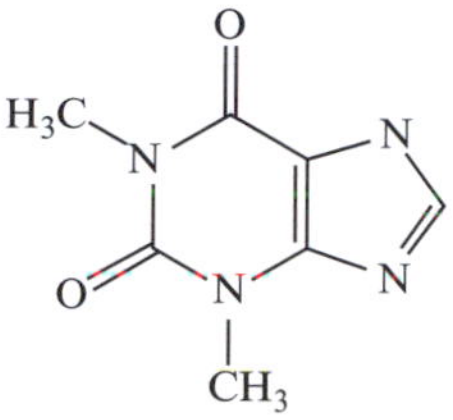

Table 12.3. Relative potency of the methylxanthines on physiological systems.

	Caffeine	Theophylline	Theobromine
CNS stimulation	1	2	3
Respiratory stimulation	1	2	3
Diuresis	3	1	2
Cardiac stimulation	3	1	2
Smooth muscle relaxation	3	1	2
Skeletal muscle relaxation	1	2	3

1 = the most potent effects

nents, such as fiber in the digestive tract (Mandel, 2002).

Caffeine is metabolized by the liver into 1-methyl uric acid and 1-methylxanthene. These metabolites are excreted primarily via the kidneys (Rall, 1985). The 'half-life' of caffeine is the time it takes to eliminate one-half of consumed caffeine from the body. This varies among individuals, and is about three to seven hours in healthy adults. However, a number of factors including reproductive status, age, disease and cigarette smoking can influence metabolism. For example, the half-life of caffeine increases to 6 to 14 h in women who take oral contraceptives, or who are in the last trimester of a pregnancy. The half-life of caffeine is also markedly slower in newborn infants (half-life = 50 h), and in individuals with liver disease (half-life = 60 h) than in healthy adults. In contrast, cigarette smoking significantly decreases the half-life of the drug to approximately three hours (Castellanos and Rapoport, 2002; Mandel, 2002).

Physiological effects of caffeine

Caffeine, theophylline and theobromine have similar physiological effects throughout the body. However, the potency of these drugs varies according to the physiological system under consideration (Table 12.3). For example,

theophylline is a more potent stimulator of the cardiovascular system than caffeine or theobromine, while caffeine leads to more profound stimulation of the nervous system than either of the other two compounds.

Cardiovascular system

The actions of caffeine and the other methylxanthines on the cardiovascular system are complex and sometimes antagonistic. One reason for the difficulty in reaching firm conclusions about the actions of these drugs on cardiovascular functioning is that the drugs' effects depend on an individual's history of consuming methylxanthines, the dose of the drug, and the route of drug administration. Clinical studies indicate that caffeine intake is associated with a rise in blood pressure and increase in heart rate. The effects on blood pressure are most often observed at doses of 250 mg of caffeine or greater. Although the pressor effect of caffeine is seen in men and women, irrespective of race, age or blood pressure, the effect of caffeine on blood pressure is most pronounced in elderly, hypertensive and caffeine-naïve individuals (Green et al, 1996; Myers, 1998; Hartley et al., 2004; James, 2004).

Although caffeine intake can lead to acute increases in blood pressure, epidemiological studies assessing whether caffeine consumption is associated with chronic hypertension have yielded conflicting results. These inconsistent findings reflect the difficulties in accurately determining caffeine intake, the development of tolerance to the drug's pressor actions, and the possibility of confounding factors, such as smoking and body weight, in moderating blood pressure.

Controversy also surrounds the contribution of caffeine intake to high cholesterol levels and the development of cardiac arrhythmias. While concern continues about the contribution of caffeine intake to the development of heart disease, the currently available data suggest that moderate caffeine intake (e.g. less than 400 mg/day) does not have adverse effects on cardiovascular health (Nawrot *et al.*, 2003).

Smooth muscle

The methylxanthines relax a variety of smooth muscles including those found in the bronchi of the lungs. Indeed, as a result of theophylline's ability to dilate the bronchi, the drug is used in the management of asthma. Theophylline and related compounds are prescribed as a prophylactic therapy for asthma, and are used as adjuncts in the treatment of prolonged asthma attacks (Rabe and Schmidt, 2001; Fozard, 2003; Spina, 2003). Additionally, as a result of their ability to stimulate the respiratory system, both theophylline and caffeine have been widely prescribed to prevent episodes of the loss of effective breathing (sleep apnea) in preterm infants (von Poblotzki *et al.*, 2003).

Gastrointestinal system

Caffeine stimulates the secretion of gastric acid and pepsin, the enzyme that begins the breakdown of proteins in the stomach. As result, coffee intake is often considered detrimental to individuals suffering from gastric ulcers. However, as both caffeinated and decaffeinated coffee increase gastric secretions, it appears that caffeine alone is not the culprit, and that there are additional components in coffee, which contribute to the beverage's actions on the gastrointestinal system.

Renal system

The diuretic action of caffeine and other methylxanthines has long been recognized. Acute ingestion of 250–300 mg of caffeine results in the short-term stimulation of urine output and sodium excretion in individuals deprived of caffeine for days or weeks. Regular intake of caffeine, however, is associated with the development of tolerance to the diuretic effects of the drug, so that the actions of the drug on the renal system are reduced in individuals who regularly consume coffee or tea (Maughan and Griffin, 2003).

Caffeine and reproduction

Over the years, concern has been expressed about the potentially harmful effects of caffeine intake during pregnancy. In particular, caffeine intake has been blamed for infertility, miscarriage, low-birth weight and birth defects (Schardt and Schmidt, 1996). Initial concern about caffeine intake during pregnancy was sparked by studies suggesting that caffeine served as a teratogen in laboratory animals. In these studies, providing caffeine to pregnant animals resulted in abnormal organ development in a small percentage of the offspring. The most frequently observed abnormalities were facial and limb defects. However, relatively high doses of caffeine were required to produce these effects, particularly when the drug was incorporated into the animals' food or water. Lower doses of caffeine had negligible effects on fetal development.

Epidemiological studies have assessed the relationship between caffeine consumption during pregnancy and the risk of preterm delivery, low birth weights, and congenital malformations in human populations. Results of this research suggest that heavy caffeine use (greater than 700 mg/day) may be associated with a decreased probability of pregnancy and an increased probability of a woman suffering a miscarriage or having a preterm delivery (Bracken *et al.*, 2003). Additionally, extensive caffeine consumption by a mother may increase the risks of her infant suffering from sleep apnea or sudden infant death syndrome. However, it is important to note that it is extremely difficult to separate caffeine use from other elements in the environment and other behaviors such as smoking or poor nutritional status may confound studies assessing the effects of caffeine on reproduction (Leviton, 1998; Christian and Brent, 2001; Nawrot *et al.*, 2003).

While excessive intakes of caffeine may have unfavorable effects on pregnancy, data indicate that smaller amounts of caffeine (less than 300 mg/day) have few negative effects on pregnancy and infant health. Thus, the American Dietetic Association advises pregnant women to limit caffeine intake to a maximum of 300 mg/day, an amount equivalent to approximately three 8 oz cups of coffee a day (Kaiser and Allen, 2002).

Caffeine and physical performance

Caffeine's physiological effects have made it a boon to athletes. Over the last 10 years, the popularity of caffeine as an ergogenic, or energy producing, aid has risen sharply. Many professional and amateur athletes are committed to using caffeine to improve their physical performance both during training and competition (Wildman and Medeiros, 2000; Graham, 2001; Brouns, 2002). Additionally, caffeine has proven to be an effective strategy to maintain physical performance in military and related situations where sustained operations are a necessity (Lieberman et al., 2002; McLellan et al., 2004).

Caffeine increases heart rate, respiration, blood pressure and blood glucose levels, which together contribute to the positive effects of the drug on physical performance. Additionally, following caffeine intake, energy derived from fat is increased, and energy derived from carbohydrates is decreased, allowing individuals to sustain physical activity for longer periods of time. Another factor that may contribute to caffeine's positive effects on physical activity is that the drug may reduce the perception of the pain resulting from rigorous activity. Caffeine's pain-relieving properties stem, at least in part, from the drug's ability to stimulate the release of beta-endorphin (the body's natural 'pain killer') (Laurent et al., 2000).

The positive effects of caffeine on physical performance are most apparent in, but not limited to, endurance activities. Caffeine, at doses ranging from 2 to 9 mg/kg of body weight, improves performance in a variety of activities (e.g. running, cross-country skiing, cycling) lasting from as little as 60 s to as long as 2 h in both trained and untrained athletes. While caffeine can boost performance of endurance activities, it has minimal effects in enhancing maximal abilities on tasks that require high-power outputs (e.g. lifting and carrying), although caffeine consumption may prolong

the time until fatigue occurs (Graham, 2001; Bell and McLelland, 2003).

Caffeine and sleep

For many, a cup of coffee with dinner can lead to a night with little sleep. Caffeine can delay sleep onset, shorten sleep time, reduce the average depth of sleep, and worsen the subjective quality of sleep. At high enough doses, caffeine can lead to insomnia. However, while for many, sleep disturbances accompany caffeine intake, this is not universally the case. There are those who can consume caffeine-containing beverages late into the evening with minimal adverse affects on their sleep. Generally, those who regularly consume caffeine have fewer problems falling asleep after an evening cup of coffee or tea than those who abstain from caffeine. Moreover, as expected, the effects of caffeine on sleep are dose-dependent with larger quantities of caffeine have more negative effects on sleep than smaller quantities. Finally, as most people know the effect of caffeine intake on their sleep patterns, those with caffeine-related sleep problems tend to limit their evening intake to prevent sleep disturbances. Although caffeine can alter patterns of sleep, there is no strong evidence that caffeine-induced alterations in sleep have a significant effect on subsequent daytime behavior in adults (Smith, 2005).

While caffeine-induced sleep disturbances do not appear to be a major concern for adults, caffeine-induced alterations in sleep may be more problematic in children. The increasing availability of caffeine-containing products marketed to children, make it is possible that caffeine contributes to sleep disturbances and subsequent behavioral issues in children. It could be argued that caffeine intake is part of a cycle where children are using caffeine to offset fatigue brought about by sleep disturbances. Using questionnaires and food diaries, Pollak and Bright (2003) examined the relationship between caffeine consumption in seventh, eighth and ninth graders and sleep disturbances. On average, respondents consumed at least one caffeine-containing item a day, corresponding to about 53 mg of caffeine each day. Soda was the most frequently consumed caffeine-containing item, contributing a little over half of the caffeine consumed. Boys consumed more caffeine than girls. Caffeine intakes were associated with shorter nighttime sleep, more daytime naps, and more interrupted sleep patterns. Since this was a survey study, it is difficult to determine why the respondents were consuming caffeine, and the hypothesis that they are specifically attempting to treat the effects of disrupted sleep cannot be tested. However, this report is an important step in quantifying the actual patterns of caffeine intake in children, and suggests that caffeine consumption may disrupt sleep patterns in children.

Neurophysiological and Behavioral Actions of the Methylxanthines

Although all of the physiological consequences of the methylxanthines are important, it is the action of these drugs on the central nervous system (CNS) and behavior that contributes most significantly to their use. Caffeine, theophylline and theobromine stimulate the activity of the CNS, with caffeine having the most potent effects. Consumption of as little as the amount of caffeine found in one medium cup of coffee (150 mg) stimulates activity in the cortex, the area of the brain involved in higher mental functioning. Higher doses of the drug (500 mg) stimulate activity not only in the cortex, but also in the medulla, a portion of the hindbrain important for the control of respiration, cardiovascular functioning and muscular activity. As described in detail below, when levels of caffeine intake approach 1000 mg, restlessness and insomnia are common, and may be accompanied by sensory disturbances including ringing in the ears and flashes of light.

Personal experience and over 90 years of scientific investigations have confirmed the belief that caffeine has the power to maintain alertness and improve performance on a variety of mental tasks (Hollingwood, 1912; Lieberman, 2003; Smith, 2005). However, there are conflicting reports in the literature as not all studies have found positive effects of caffeine on behavior (Yeomans et al., 2002; Rogers et al., 2003). Before reviewing this research, it is important to consider possible reasons for the conflicting evidence on the actions of caffeine on behavior.

First, most studies investigating the behavioral consequences of caffeine intake have used only a single dose of the drug. Too low a dose of caffeine may not be sufficiently potent to produce a behavioral response, while too high a dose may lead to side effects which adversely affect behavior. In general, data point to an inverted U-shaped dose-response curve for caffeine's effects on behavior. Doses of caffeine ranging from 100 to 600 mg generally increase alertness and concentration while higher doses may lead to restlessness, feelings of anxiety, and deterioration in performance of cognitive tasks. An additional concern when evaluating the effects of varying doses of caffeine on mental performance is the participant's experience with the drug. The same dose of caffeine can have quite different consequences in regular caffeine consumers than in those who refrain from caffeine intake. For example, moderate doses of the drug, which improve cognitive performance in caffeine consumers, may lead to feelings of anxiety and impair performance in those who abstain from caffeine consumption (Lieberman, 2003; Lorrist and Tops, 2003; Smith, 2005).

Other differences in participant populations among studies may also contribute to whether caffeine does or does not improve cognitive performance. Of particular importance is the amount of sleep that individuals have had before being tested for the effects of caffeine on behavior. More positive effects of caffeine on behavioral tasks typically are found in sleep-deprived than in well-rested individuals (Beaumont 2001; Lieberman, 2003). Age, sex and personality characteristics also may play a role in determining responsiveness to caffeine intake. With respect to age, elderly individuals are more sensitive to caffeine's behavioral actions than young and middle-aged adults. With respect to sex, because of their smaller size, women may be more affected by a given dose of caffeine than men (Rees et al., 1999; Johnson-Kozlow et al., 2002; Smith, 2005).

Given the widely-held belief that caffeine has stimulant effects, there is the possibility that expectancy or placebo effects can confound the results of a study. In many experiments, caffeine has been provided in the form of coffee or tea, with decaffeinated coffee or tea used as the control or placebo condition. If these studies fail to find an effect of caffeine on behavior, it cannot be determined if this is because caffeine has no effect, or that a placebo response to the decaffeinated beverage prohibited the drug's action from being observed (Filmore, 1999; Yeomans *et al.*, 2002; Flaten *et al.*, 2003; Smith, 2005). To overcome the possible confounds of expectancy effects when assessing the role of caffeine on behavior, studies have either supplied the drug as a capsule or pill, or used a beverage not normally associated with the drug (e.g. fruit-flavored drink) (Yeomans *et al.*, 2002; Rogers *et al.*, 2003).

There is a continuing debate on whether the effects of caffeine on behavior are primarily an effect of the drug itself, or reflect a reversal of the negative consequences of caffeine withdrawal (Smit and Rogers, 2000; Yeomans *et al.*, 2002; Rogers *et al.*, 2003; Smith, 2005). In regular caffeine users, cessation of caffeine intake is associated with mild withdrawal symptoms including headache, irritability, mental confusion and fatigue. These symptoms typically begin 12 to 24h after the last cup of coffee or tea is consumed (Dews *et al.*, 2002). As in many studies, participants are asked to refrain from using caffeine for at least 12 h before they are tested, some researchers argue that reversal of caffeine withdrawal is a major component of the positive effects of the drug on cognitive behavior. On the other hand, studies demonstrating caffeine-related increases in cognitive performance are observed in non-deprived or drug-naïve individuals raise doubts over whether the effects of caffeine on behavior primarily are due to the reversal of withdrawal symptoms (Smith, 2005).

Although conflicting data exist, the overwhelming majority of research studies support the conclusion that intake of moderate levels of caffeine has beneficial effects on cognitive behavior. In general, caffeine consumption results in an increase in alertness and a decrease in fatigue. However, when the effects of caffeine are examined in more detail it appears that the drug preferentially facilitates performance of tasks requiring sustained attention such as simple reaction time and vigilance tasks.

There is little evidence that caffeine improves intellectual abilities, except perhaps when normal performance has been lowered by fatigue. Sleep-deprived individuals often suffer from impairments in cognitive functioning including a decreased ability to concentrate, and subsequent decrements in tasks requiring sustained attention, logical reasoning and perceptual skills (e.g. driving a car). The best way to reverse the adverse effects of sleep-deprivation is simply to go to sleep. Even a short nap (15–30 min) can alleviate some of the detrimental consequences of sleep deprivation. However, the longer the sleep episode the greater is the restoration in cognitive functioning. If sleep is not an option, consuming a cup of coffee or tea or taking a caffeine pill can help to lessen some of the impairments in cognitive performance associated with sleep deprivation. For example, in a study using Navy SEALS as participants, Lieberman *et al.* (2002) found that caffeine intakes equivalent to that found in approximately 2 cups of coffee were sufficient to reverse the negative effects of extreme psychological stress and 72 h of sleep deprivation on the performance of tasks measuring attention, alertness and reaction time. Caffeine can also reverse the impairments in cognitive performance associated with minor illnesses, such as colds and flu or fatigue related to shifts in diurnal rhythms (e.g. jet lag) (Hindmarch *et al.*, 2000; Beaumont *et al.*, 2001; Leiberman *et al.*, 2002; Leiberman, 2003; Lorist and Tops, 2003; Smith, 2005).

Modes of action of caffeine within the central nervous system

Caffeine exerts its biological actions via several different mechanisms – altered cellular calcium conduction, increased cyclic AMP and antagonism of adenosine receptors. The first two effects are seen at doses greater than ordinarily consumed by most people, and thus are not of major importance in determining the effects of caffeine intake on behavior. The general consensus is that the majority of caffeine's behavioral effects are related to the drug's interactions with adenosine receptors.

Adenosine is formed during the breakdown of adenosine triphosphate (ATP), the primary energy source for most cells in the body. Adenosine is found throughout the nervous system and is considered to be a neuromodulator, which produces its behavioral effects by inhibiting the conduction of messages at synapses that use other neurotransmitters such as dopamine and norepinephrine. Receptors for adenosine are present in the gastrointestinal tract, heart, blood vessels, respiratory system and brain. Stimulation of peripheral adenosine receptors decreases intestinal peristalsis, reduces blood pressure and heart rate and increases bronchial tone. In the brain, adenosine inhibits neuronal activity resulting in feelings of fatigue and behavioral depression. These effects, which are the opposite of many of caffeine's commonly observed actions, have led to the hypothesis that much of caffeine's effects can be attributed to the drug's ability to act as an antagonist at adenosine receptors. In support of this hypothesis, when consumed at levels comparable to those found in 1–3 cups of coffee, caffeine occupies 50% of the adenosine receptors in the brain. By blocking receptors sites, caffeine prevents adenosine from inhibiting neuronal firing, thereby allowing increased stimulation of neuronal activity and behavior (Rall, 1985; Mandel, 2002; Davis *et al.*, 2003; Fisone *et al.*, 2004).

Alterations in adenosine receptors also may play a role in the development of tolerance to and physical dependence on caffeine, which occurs following prolonged use of the drug (see below). Chronic caffeine use is accompanied by an increase in the number of adenosine receptors. As a result, a new balance between endogenous adenosine and the presence of exogenous caffeine occurs leading in a reduction in some of the physiological and behavioral actions of the drug (tolerance). If this balance is altered by severely decreasing or abruptly stopping caffeine use, then the excess adenosine receptors would no longer be blocked by caffeine, and the physiological response to adenosine would be exaggerated resulting in symptoms of caffeine withdrawal.

Caffeine intoxication

While moderate intake of caffeine has relatively benign effects in most individuals, intake of large quantities of the drug can have negative consequences. Extremely high doses of caffeine (10 g) can produce vomiting and convulsions, and in some cases death. Additionally, regular intake of smaller amounts of caffeine, beginning at approximately 1 g/day, can lead to nervousness, irritability, loss of appetite, neuromuscular tremors and vomiting. Repeated high intake of caffeine, over 1 g/day, can lead to a constella-

Table 12.4. Diagnostic criteria for 305.90 caffeine intoxication.

A. Recent consumption of caffeine, usually in excess of 250 mg (e.g. more than 2–3 cups of brewed coffee).
B. Five (or more) of the following signs, developing during, or shortly after, caffeine use:
  1. restlessness
  2. nervousness
  3. excitement
  4. insomnia
  5. flushed face
  6. diuresis
  7. gastrointestinal disturbance
  8. muscle twitching
  9. rambling flow of thought and speech
  10. tachycardia or cardiac arrhythmia
  11. periods of inexhaustibility
  12. psychomotor agitation.
C. The symptoms in Criterion B cause clinically significant distress or impairment in social, occupational or other important areas of functioning.
D. The symptoms are not due to a general medical condition and are not better accounted for by another mental disorder (e.g. an Anxiety Disorder) (American Psychiatric Association, 1994).
An individual must meet the criteria for A, B, C and D to be diagnosed with caffeine intoxication. The removal of caffeine from the diet reverses the symptoms and 'cures' the disorder.

tion of symptoms similar to anxiety neurosis. This constellation of symptoms, listed in Table 12.4 has been termed 'caffeine intoxication' and, classified as an organic mental disorder with known cause (caffeine consumption) in the *Diagnostic and Statistical Manual IV* (American Psychological Association, 1994).

Caffeine and addiction

Caffeine is a drug that produces physiological, psychological and behavioral effects, but does that make it a drug of abuse? There has been considerable debate questioning the abuse potential of caffeine. Many people feel that they are dependent upon caffeine – everyone knows at least one person who cannot seem to face the day without a cup of coffee. However, addiction and dependence are terms that are usually used to describe behaviors relating to drugs such as heroin, nicotine, alcohol and cocaine. In this section we will discuss whether or not caffeine should be considered as an addictive drug.

Before discussing caffeine as a drug, it is important to understand some of the terms used in psychopharmacology, and how a substance is classified as addictive. According to psychopharmacologists and clinicians, for a drug to be considered addictive, it must meet a set of primary criteria and may meet a set of secondary criteria. For example, one hallmark of drug addiction is escalating use of a drug and loss of control over drug-taking behavior. Typically, people who are addicted to a drug need more and more of the drug to achieve the same effect – a phenomenon called tolerance. Moreover, although originally taking the drug may have produced pleasurable – or reinforcing – effects, addicts maintain drug-taking behavior to avoid feeling ill – withdrawal symptoms – when ceasing to take the drug. Thus, drug addition is indicative of a cycle of behaviors that include pursuit of pleasurable effects and avoidance of negative effects – often to the exclusion of other pursuits and to the detriment of the individual.

The first thing to consider about a putative addictive substance is whether or not it produces pleasurable, or reinforcing effects. These pleasurable effects promote drug-taking behavior for the rather obvious reason that people like pleasurable things. Caffeine's reinforcing properties are presumed to be related to the drug's ability to produce physiological arousal, including increased alertness, enhanced mood and increased concentration (Garrett and Griffiths, 1997; Fredholm et al., 1999). Some argue that the reinforcing effects of caffeine are similar in characteristics (but not in magnitude) to psychostimulant drugs such as cocaine or amphetamine (Garrett and Griffiths, 1997). Others argue that although caffeine does produce positive effects (such as mood elevation), the reinforcing effects of caffeine are relatively weak (Daly and Fredholm, 1998). More importantly, unlike typical drugs of abuse, individuals do not normally need to consume increasing amounts of caffeine (drug abuse), but rather use the drug at consistent and moderate levels (drug use).

As mentioned elsewhere in this chapter, it is generally recognized that many of caffeine's effects are mediated by antagonizing adenosine receptors. However, it has been proposed that caffeine also may exert effects on the neurotransmitter, dopamine since (i) caffeine produces similar locomotor and other physiological effects as stimulant drugs that affect dopamine receptors and (ii) low doses of cocaine or amphetamine are reported to be subjectively similar to caffeine. Dopamine is considered to play a key role in the reinforcing properties of almost all drugs. However, it is not clear whether the effects of caffeine on the neurotransmitter are due to the drug's direct effects at the dopamine receptor or via indirect effects on dopamine via inhibition of adenosine (for reviews see: Garrett and Griffiths, 1997; Daly and Fredholm, 1998; Fredholm et al., 1999).

The next issue to consider is the development of tolerance to caffeine. In animals, tolerance to the locomotor-enhancing effects of caffeine is well demonstrated. However, in many animal studies, the doses of caffeine used are significantly greater than those generally consumed by humans (Daly and Fredholm, 1998; Dews et al., 2002). Humans do develop tolerance to some of the physiological effects of caffeine, such as elevated heart rate and blood pressure, but typically do not show tolerance to the mood elevating and sleep-delaying effects of the drug (Daly and Fredholm, 1998; Fredholm et al., 1999). Moreover, the general consensus is that little tolerance develops to the positive effects of caffeine – and this may be why caffeine users do not significantly escalate drug use over time.

The issue of withdrawal may be the most salient consideration in discussing the addictive potential of caffeine. The subjective signs of caffeine withdrawal are in opposition to the effects of taking caffeine and include headache, fatigue, depression, difficulty concentrating, irritability and sleepiness. Symptoms of caffeine withdrawal have been reported to occur in individuals who consume as little as 100 mg/day or the amount found in an 8 oz cup of coffee. As daily caffeine intake increases, withdrawal symptoms typically become more intense. While some do not suffer the adverse consequences of abstaining from caffeine, research suggests that 40% to 70% of individuals who tried to quit caffeine use experience symptoms of caffeine withdrawal.

These symptoms usually begin within 12 to 24 h after terminating caffeine intake. Thus, missing one's morning coffee can have negative consequences in regular caffeine consumers. Peak withdrawal intensity usually is reported 20 to 48 h after abstinence. Fortunately, for those trying to abstain from caffeine, symptoms of withdrawal normally are relatively mild, and subside within a few days. However, in some individuals, withdrawal symptoms can lead to impairments in daily functioning and continue for weeks and sometimes months. Drug withdrawal may lead some to return to regular caffeine use, and contribute to the potentially addictive qualities of the drug (e.g. Evans and Griffiths, 1999; Juliano and Griffiths, 2004).

The question remains, then, is caffeine an addictive drug? Just because a drug has psychoactive properties – can it be a drug of abuse? Do the physiological and psychological effects of caffeine make it likely to be abused, or are the effects more benign? While many researchers are still examining these questions, the evidence thus far suggests that caffeine ingestion does embody some of the criteria for an addictive substance – it produces reinforcing effects, at least in those who already use caffeine. Cessation of caffeine use produces withdrawal symptoms as well. However, many of the classic requirements for drug addiction per se are not met. Although people do seek out the stimulant properties of caffeine, and can experience withdrawal symptoms, they typically do not lose control over their caffeine intake, and generally do not require ever escalating amounts of caffeine to satisfy their caffeine needs. Dews *et al.* (2002) raise an excellent point when discussing caffeine as a drug of abuse, that is, doing so diminishes perceptions of how hazardous drugs such as heroin or cocaine are. Addiction is characterized by many negative physiological, psychological, social, and economic outcomes. To focus on one aspect of addiction – for example, the avoidance of withdrawal – overestimates the abuse liability of a drug.

Conclusion

Although debate on the positive and negative actions of caffeine is likely to continue for some time, a significant reduction in caffeine consumption in the near future is an unlikely event. Caffeine consumption has become a way of life, and for most represents little or no problems. However, too high a dose of caffeine can lead to intoxication, and worsen the symptoms of withdrawal when one abstains from one's daily coffee, tea or soft drink. Thus, as for many foods and beverages, moderation is the key to caffeine intake.

References

American Psychological Association (1994) Diagnostic and Statistical Manual of Mental *Disorders*, 4th edn. American Psychiatric Association, Washington, DC.

Barone J.J. and Roberts H.R. (1996) Caffeine consumption. *Food and Chemical Toxicology* 34, 119–129.

Beaumont, M., Batejat, D., Pierard, C., Coste, O., Doireau, P., Van Beers, P., Chauffard, F., Chassard, D., Enslen, M., Denis, J.B. and Lagarde, D. (2001) Slow release caffeine and prolonged (64-h) continuous wakefulness: effects on vigilance and cognitive performance. *Journal of Sleep Research* 10, 265–276.

Bell, D.G. and McLellan, T.M. (2003) Effect of repeated caffeine ingestion on repeated exhaustive exercise endurance. *Medicine And Science In Sports and Exercise* 35, 1348–1354.

Bernstein, G.A., Carroll, M.E., Thuras, P.D., Cosgrove, K.P. and Roth, M.E. (2002) Caffeine dependence in teenagers. *Drug and Alcohol Dependence* 66, 1–6.

Bracken, M.B., Triche, E.W., Belanger, K., Hellenbrand, K. and Leaderer, B.P. (2003) Association of maternal caffeine consumption with decrements in fetal growth *American Journal of Epidemiology*. 157, 456–466.

Brouns, F. (2002) *Essentials of Sports Nutrition*, 2nd edn. John Wiley & Sons, Chichester, UK, 227.

Cami, J. and Farre, M. (2003) Mechanisms of disease: drug addiction. *New England Journal of Medicine* 349, 975–986.

Castellanos, F.X. and Rapoport, J.L. (2002) Effects of caffeine on development and behavior in infancy and childhood: a review of the published literature. *Food and Chemical Toxicology* 40, 1235–1242.

Christian, M.S. and Brent, R.L. (2001) Teratogen update: evaluation of the reproductive and developmental risks of caffeine. *Teratology* 64, 51–78.

Consumer Reports (2003) Caffeinated kids. *Consumer Reports* 68 (28–29).

Daly, J.W. and Fredholm, B.B. (1998). Caffeine – an atypical drug of dependence. *Drug and Alcohol Dependence* 51, 199–206.

Davis, J.M., Zhao, Z.W., Stock, H.S., Mehl, K.A., Buggy, J. and Hand, G.A. (2003) Central nervous system effects of caffeine and adenosine on fatigue. *American Journal of Physiology. Regulatory, Integrative and Comparative Physiology* 284, R399–R404.

Dews, P.B., O'Brien, C.P. and Bergman, J. (2002) Caffeine: behavioral effects of withdrawal and related issues. *Food and Chemical Toxicology* 40, 1257–1261.

Dicum G. and Luttinger, N. (1999) *The Coffee Book.* The New Press, New York.

Evans, S.M. and Griffiths, R.R. (1999) Caffeine withdrawal: a parametric analysis of caffeine dosing conditions. *The Journal of Pharmacology and Experimental Therapeutics.* 289, 285–294.

Filmore, M.T. (1999) Behavioral effects of caffeine: the role of drug-related expectancies. In: Gupta, B.S. and Gupta, U. (eds) *Caffeine and Behavior: Current Views and Research Trends* CRC Press, Boca Raton, Florida, pp. 207–219.

Fisone, G., Borgkvist, A. and Usiello, A. (2004) Caffeine as a psychomotor stimulant: mechanism of action. *Cellular and Molecular Life Sciences.* 61, 857–872.

Flaten, M.A, Aaslie, O. and Blumenthal, T.D. (2003) Expectations and placebo responses to caffeine-associated stimuli. *Psychopharmacology (Berl)* 169, 198–204.

Forshee, R.A. and Storey, M.L. (2003) Total beverage consumption and beverage choices among children and adolescents. *International Journal of Food Sciences and Nutrition.* 54, 297–307.

Fozard, J.R. (2003) The case for a role for adenosine in asthma: almost convincing? *Current Opinion In Pharmacology* 3, 264–269.

Frary, C.D., Johnson, R.K. and Wang, M.Q. (2005) Food sources and intakes of caffeine in the diets of persons in the United States *Journal of the American Dietetic Association.* 105, 110–113.

Fredholm, B.B., Battig, K., Holmen, J., Nehlig, A. and Zvartau, E.E. (1999) Actions of caffeine in the brain with special reference to factors that contribute to its widespread use. *Pharmacological Reviews* 51, 83–133.

French, S.A., Lin, B.H. and Guthrie, J.F. (2003) National trends in soft drink consumption among children and adolescents age 6 to 17 years: prevalence, amounts and sources, 1977/1978 to 1994/1998. *Journal of the American Dietetic Association* 103, 1326–1331.

Garrett, B.E. and Griffiths, R.R. (1997) The role of dopamine in the behavioral effects of caffeine in animals and humans. *Pharmacology, Biochemistry and Behavior.* 57, 533–541.

Graham, T.E. (2001) Caffeine and exercise – metabolism, endurance and performance. *Sports Medicine* 31, 785–807.

Green, P.J., Kirby, R. and Suls, J. (1996) The effects of caffeine on blood pressure and heart rate: a review. *Annals of Behavioral Medicine* 18, 201–216.

Harland, B.F. (2000) Caffeine and nutrition. *Nutrition* 16, 522–526.

Hartley, T.R, Lovallo, W.R. and Whitsett, T.L. (2004) Cardiovascular effects of caffeine in men and women. *The American Journal of Cardiology* 93, 1022–1026.

Heishman, S.J. and Henningfield, J.E. (1999) Is caffeine a drug of dependence? Criteria and comparisons. In: Gupta, B.S. and Gupta, U. (eds). *Caffeine and Behavior.* CRC Press, Boca Raton, Florida.

Hindmarch, I., Rigney, U., Stanley, N., Quinlan, P., Rycroft, J. and Lane, J. (2000) A naturalistic investigation of the effects of day-long consumption of tea, coffee and water on alertness, sleep onset and sleep quality. *Psychopharmacology (Berl)* 149, 203–216.

Hollingwood, H.L. (1912) The influences of caffeine on mental and motor efficiency. *Archives of Psychology* 22, 1–166.

James, J.E. (1997) *Understanding Caffeine: A Biobehavioral Analysis.* Sage Publications, Thousand Oaks, California.

James, J.E. (2004) Critical review of dietary caffeine and blood pressure: a relationship that should be taken more seriously. *Psychosomatic Medicine* 66, 63–71.

Johnson-Kozlow, M., Kritz-Silverman, Barrett-Connor, and Morton, D. (2002) Coffee consumption and cognitive function among older adults. *American Journal of Epidemiology* 156, 842–850.

Juliano, L.M. and Griffiths, R.R. (2004) A critical review of caffeine withdrawal: empirical validation of symptoms and signs, incidence, severity, and associated features. *Psychopharmacology (Berl)* 176, 1–29.

Kaiser, L.L. and Allen, L. (2002) Position of the American Dietetic Association: nutrition and lifestyle for a healthy pregnancy outcome. *Journal of the American Dietetic Association* 102, 1479–1490.

Lambert, J.D. and Yang, C.S. (2003) Mechanisms of cancer prevention by tea constituents. *The Journal of Nutrition* 133, 3262S–3267S.

Laurent, D., Shneider, K.E., Prusacyck, W.K., Franklin, C., Vogel, S.M., Krssak, M., Petersen, K.F., Goforth, H.W. and Shulman, G.I. (2000) Effects of caffeine on muscle glycogen utilization and the neuroendocrine axis during exercise. *The Journal of Clinical Endocrinology And Metabolism* 85, 2170–2175.

Leviton, A. (1998) Caffeine consumption and the risk of reproductive hazards. *The Journal of Reproductive Medicine* 33, 175–178.

Lieberman, H.R. (2001) Nutrition, brain function and cognitive performance. *Appetite* 40, 245–254.

Lieberman, H.R. (2003) Nutrition, brain function and cognitive performance. *Appetite* 40, 245–254.

Lieberman, H.R., Tharion, W.J., Shukitt-Hale, B., Speckman, K.L. and Tulley, R. (2002) Effects of caffeine, sleep loss, and stress on cognitive performance and mood during U.S. Navy SEAL training. *Psychopharmacology (Berl).* 164, 250–261.

Lorrist, M.M. and Tops, M. (2003) Caffeine, fatigue, and cognition. *Brain and Cognition* 53, 82–94.

Mandel, H.G. (2002) Update on caffeine consumption, disposition, and action. *Food and Chemical Toxicolology* 40, 1231–1234.

Maughan R.J. and Griffin J. (2003) Caffeine ingestion and fluid balance: a review. *Journal of Human Nutrition And Dietetics* 16, 411–420.

McCusker R.R., Goldberger, B.A. and Cone, E.J. (2003) Caffeine content of specialty coffees. *Journal of Analytical Toxicology* 27, 520–522.

McKay, D.L. and Blumberg, J.B. (2002) The role of tea in human health: an update. *Journal of the American College Of Nutrition* 21, 1–13.

McLellan, T.M., Bell, D.G. and Kamimori, G.H. (2004) Caffeine improves physical performance during 24 h of active wakefulness. *Aviatio, Space, and Environmental Medicine* 75, 666–672.

Myers, M.G. (1998) Effects of caffeine on blood pressure. *Archives of Internal Medicine* 148, 1189–1193.

Nawrot, P., Jordan, S., Eastwood, J., Rotstein, J., Hugenholtz, A. and Feeley, M. (2003) Effects of caffeine on human health. *Food Additives and Contaminants.* 20, 1–30.

Pendergrast, M. (1999) *Uncommon Grounds.* Basic Books, New York.

Pollak, C.P. and Bright, D. (2003) Caffeine consumption and weekly sleep patterns in US seventh-, eighth-, and ninth-graders. *Pediatrics* 111, 42–46.

Rabe, K.F. and Schmidt, D.T. (2001) Pharmacological treatment of asthma today *the European Respiratory Journal* (Suppl. 18), pp. 34S–40S.

Rall, T.W. (1985) Central nervous system stimulants. In: Goodman, A.G., Goodman, L.S., Rall, T.W.

and Murad, F. (eds), *Goodman and Gilman's the Pharmacological Basis of Therapeutics*, 7th edn. Macmillan, New York.

Ray, O. and Ksir, C. (2002) *Drugs, Society, and Human Behavior*, 10th edn. McGraw-Hill, New York.

Rees, K., Allen, D. and Lader, M. (1999) The influence of age and caffeine on psychomotor and cognitive function. *Psychopharmacology (Berl)* 145, 181–188.

Rietveld, A. and Wiseman, S. (2003) Antioxidant effects of tea: evidence from human clinical trials. *The Journal of Nutrition* 133, 3285S–3292S.

Rogers, P.J., Martin, J., Smith, C., Heatherley, S.V. and Smit, H.J. (2003) Absence of reinforcing, mood and psychomotor performance effects of caffeine in habitual non-consumers of caffeine. *Psychopharmcology (Berl)* 167, 54–62.

Schardt, D. and Schmidt, S. (1996) Caffeine: the inside scoop. *Nutrition Action Newsletter* 23, 1–7.

Shils, M.E., Olson, J.A., Shike, M. and Ross, A.C. (1999) *Modern Nutrition in Health and Disease*, 9th edn. Williams and Wilkins, Baltimore, Maryland.

Smit, H.J. and Rogers, P.J. (2000) Effects of low doses of caffeine on cognitive performance, mood and thirst in low and higher caffeine consumers. *Psychopharmacology (Berl).* 152, 167–173.

Smith, A. (2005) Caffeine. In: Lieberman, L., Kanarek, R., and Prasad, C. (eds), *Nutritional Neuroscience.* CRC Press, Boca Raton, Florida, pp. 341–361.

Spina, D. (2003) Theophylline and PDE4 inhibitors in asthma. *Current Opinion In Pulmonary Medicine* 9, 57–64.

von Poblotzki, M., Rieger-Fackeldey, E. and Schulze, A. (2003) Effects of theophylline on the pattern of spontaneous breathing in preterm infants less that 1000 g of birth rate. *Early Human Development* 72, 47–55.

Wildman, R.E.C. and Medeiros, D.M. (2000) *Advanced Human Nutrition.* CRC Press, Boca Raton, Florida.

Yeomans, M.R., Ripley, T., Davies, L.H., Rusted, J.M. and Rogers, P.J. (2002) Effects of caffeine on performance and mood depend on the level of caffeine abstinence. *Psychopharmacology(Berl)* 164, 241–249.

13 Alcohol, Brain Functioning and Behavior

R.B. Kanarek

Introduction

Alcohol has long played a significant role in the human diet. Archeological evidence from areas in the Middle East demonstrates that as early as 4000 BC, barley was fermented into beer, and grape-bearing vines were cultivated for the production of wine. In Biblical times, wine was drunk on ceremonial occasions and appreciated for its intoxicating properties by diverse members of the community. The ancient Greeks and Romans further developed viticulture, and wine became an integral part of their diet and culture. In both societies, the demand for wine increased when cults, requiring the drinking of wine as part of their devotions, developed around the Greek god Dionysus (called Bacchus by the Romans). Moreover, as the populations in these areas grew, and as a consequence, the water supply became polluted, illness related to drinking water increased, and wine and beer became the beverages of choice for many.

Although the ancient Greeks and Romans tried their hands at distilling alcohol, large-scale production of distilled beverages, such as brandy, gin, vodka, rum and whiskey, did not become commonplace until the 15th century. Distillation increases the alcohol content of a liquid already containing alcohol by heating the liquid to a point sufficient to boil alcohol, but not water. The resulting vaporized alcohol (steam) is collected and condensed into a liquid with a much higher proportion of alcohol than before. Repeating the process can further increase the alcoholic content of the resulting liquid (Cantrell, 2000; Newman, 2000).

Throughout the ages, the detrimental effects of alcohol on individual behavior and society as a whole have led to prohibitions on alcohol either as a part of a religious doctrine (e.g. Islam) or government policy (e.g. the Prohibition Movement in the USA, 1920 to 1933). However, despite these prohibitions, alcohol consumption remains a fact of life.

In the USA, over 90% of the adult population, at one time or another in their lives, has consumed alcohol, and in 2003, approximately 60% of adult Americans identified themselves as current drinkers. The vast majority of these individuals are considered moderate drinkers defined as the consumption of less than 14 drinks per week for men, and less than 7 drinks per week for women. To better understand this definition, one drink is defined as 12 oz of regular beer (4.5% alcohol), 5 oz of wine (12% alcohol), or 1.5 oz of 80 proof distilled spirits (40% alcohol).

While moderate alcohol intake is the rule for most Americans, approximately 7% of the population are heavy alcohol users (two or more drinks a day for men, and one or more drinks a day for women). While many heavy users consume alcohol on a daily basis, a substantial proportion do not drink each day, but rather engage in binge drinking behavior, defined as five or more drinks on one occasion for men, and four or more drinks on one occasion for women. This pattern of alcohol consumption is associated with a number of health and social problems including violent behavior, child abuse and unplanned and unsafe sex (Alexander and Bowen, 2004; Miller et al., 2004).

Alcohol use is heaviest among young men between the ages of 18 and 25. Fewer women than men in this age group report heavy consumption of alcohol. However, during the last decade, the number of men drinking large amounts of alcohol has remained relatively constant, while the number of young women drinking immoderately has increased substantially. Binge drinking is quite prevalent in men and women in this age group. Surveys of college students conducted indicate that approximately 56% of men and 35% of women engage in heavy episodic drinking at least once during their college career. For those students who binge drink on a regular basis, negative consequences include poor academic and athletic performance, conflicts with friends, driving accidents, unsafe sex and trouble with campus or local police. Additionally, at colleges with high rates of binge drinking, the second-hand effects of this behavior such as interrupted sleep, having to take care of a drunk friend, unwanted sexual advances and vandalism, are more common for non-drinking students than at colleges with low rates of the disorder (Wechsler et al., 2000; Dawson et al., 2004).

Overall, it is estimated that 14 million Americans suffer from alcoholism, and that alcohol-related problems account for 12% of the health budget in this country. Alcohol abuse is the third leading preventable cause of death in this country with approximately 85,000 people dying each year as a direct result of alcohol use (United States Department of Health and Human Services, 2002; Miller et al., 2004).

Interaction of Alcohol and Nutrition

Alcohol is most frequently used and thought of as a drug, and thus its importance to the study of nutrition and behavior may seem curious. However, alcohol has significant nutritional consequences, and can profoundly alter the intake, absorption, digestion and metabolism of a number of essential nutrients, which in turn can affect brain functioning and behavior.

Alcohol provides energy to the body. As a dietary macronutrient, alcohol is metabolized to produce 7 k/cal per gram consumed. In addition, some alcoholic beverages contain significant amounts of carbohydrate (Table 13.1). In those who drink moderately, calories from alcoholic beverages typically account for 3% to 9% of total energy intake (Westerterp, et al., 1999). One question that is often asked is – when individuals drink alcohol do they reduce their intake of other nutrients to compensate for the calories obtained from alcohol? Research aimed at answering this question has led to the conclusion that calories consumed as alcohol do not lead to compensatory reductions in energy intake. Indeed, researchers typically report that food intake is greater after alcohol is imbibed than after consumption of an appropriate control beverage. Thus, it has been suggested that, unlike other macronutrients, alcohol fails to generate feelings of satiety, and actually stimulates caloric intake.

Both metabolic and psychological factors contribute to the stimulatory effects of alcohol on food intake. Metabolically, alcohol suppresses fat and carbohydrate oxidation. This suppression indicates to the body that there is insufficient energy available, which is associated with sensations of hunger. On the psychological side, the ability of alcohol to disinhibit behavior may contribute to the increase in feeding behavior observed after alcohol consumption. Additionally, alcohol consumed with a meal can enhance the pleasurable aspects of feeding behavior (Westerterp-Plantenga and Verwegen, 1999; Yeomans et al., 2003; Caton et al., 2004).

The next logical question that arises from the preceding data is does the short-term stimulatory effect of alcohol on food intake have long-term consequences on body weight. Although contradictory evidence exists, the majority of studies suggest that long-term moderate intake of alcohol is positively correlated with body weight.

Table 13.1. Approximate alcohol, carbohydrate and energy content of selected alcoholic beverages.

Beverage	Quantity ounces	Alcohol grams	Carbohydrates grams	Energy Kcal
Wine				
Red	5	13	3	105
White	5	13	2	100
Dessert, sweet	5	23	18	230
Champagne	5	14	3	100
Beer				
Regular	12	13	13	150
Light	12	11	5	100
Spirits				
Vodka, rum, gin, tequila	1.5	15	0	105
Cognac, brandy	1.0	9	0	64
Mixed Drinks				
Bloody Mary	4.6	14	5	120
Martini	2.0	21	1	145
Gin and tonic	7.0	17	14	170
Frozen Daiquiri	4.7	21	16	190
Screwdriver	7.0	23	16	210
Cosmopolitan	2.5	16	9	145

Source: The alcohol, carbohydrate and caloric content of the beverages represent only approximate values. These values will vary as a function of the proof and brand of alcohol used, the amount of the beverage consumed, and the proportion of the ingredients used to make mixed drinks. Data adapted from www.drinkmixer.com and the United States Department of Agriculture, 2005 Dietary Guidelines for Americans. www.health.gov/dietaryguidelines/dga2005.

The consequences of alcohol use on food intake are more detrimental in heavy drinkers. In chronic alcoholics, calories from alcoholic beverages can account for as much as 50% of total energy intake. As a result, alcoholism is often accompanied by decreases in intake of essential nutrients, nutrient deficiencies and reductions in body weight (Maillot et al., 2001; Lahti-Koski et al., 2002; Wannamethee and Shaper, 2003; Yeomans et al., 2003).

In addition to altering food intake, chronic alcohol consumption compromises nutritional status by interfering with the digestion and absorption of essential nutrients. In heavy drinkers, alcohol inhibits the production of saliva, leading to reductions in the secretion of salivary enzymes, inflammation of the tongue and mouth and increased risk for dental and periodontal disease. As digestion progresses, alcohol slows down peristalsis in the esophagus, and can damage the esophageal sphincter, leading to esophageal reflux and severe heartburn. In the stomach and intestines, alcohol damages the mucosal lining, which consequently impairs the absorption of a number of vitamins, including vitamin B_1 (thiamine), folic acid and vitamin B_{12}.

Chronic use of alcohol hinders the functioning of other digestive organs including the pancreas and liver. Heavy drinking is often associated with inflammation of the pancreas, called pancreatitis. As a result, there is a reduction in the secretion of pancreatic enzymes, which contributes to nutrient malabsorption. Liver damage, which is common in alcoholics, can interfere with the metabolism of a number of essential nutrients including folic acid, pyridoxine, vitamins A, C and D, sodium, potassium and magnesium. Additionally, the enzymes that breakdown fat also metabolize alcohol, so that when alcohol is available, the liver preferentially uses alcohol for energy and stores fat until all of the alcohol is used. Over time, the infiltration of the liver by fat results in the replacement of healthy cells with scar tissue (cirrhosis), which ultimately reduces the amount of blood and oxygen reaching the liver, and impairs the liver's ability to perform its biochemical functions (Todd *et al.*, 1999; Maillot *et al.*, 2001).

Alcohol Consumption, Brain Functioning and Behavior

Acute alcohol intake

Alcohol is rapidly absorbed from the stomach and small intestine into the blood, and is then distributed throughout total body water. The rate of absorption of alcohol into the blood depends on the dose, concentration and type of alcohol consumed. Generally, the more concentrated an alcoholic beverage the more rapid its rate of absorption. Thus, diluting an alcoholic beverage with water will slow down absorption. However, drinking carbonated beverages (e.g. champagne or whiskey with soda) increases the rate of absorption because carbonation facilitates the passage of alcohol across the intestine. Food in the stomach and drugs that decrease gastrointestinal mobility or blood flow delay the absorption of alcohol.

The effects of alcohol on the body are directly proportional to the concentration of alcohol in the blood, or 'blood-alcohol levels'. Blood-alcohol levels are expressed as mg of alcohol per 100 ml of blood. A number of factors including sex, age and the type of beverage consumed influence blood alcohol levels. For example, because women, generally weigh less and have less body water in which alcohol can dissolve than men, when men and women consume identical amounts of alcohol, blood alcohol levels are usually higher in women than in men. With respect to age, the proportion of body water decreases with age, thus, after consumption of similar amounts of alcohol, blood alcohol levels typically are higher in older than in younger individuals.

Alcohol is water soluble, and thus, readily diffuses from the blood across cell membranes into all tissues in the body. Because alcohol readily crosses the blood–brain-barrier, the concentration of alcohol in the brain parallels blood-alcohol levels. Alcohol affects the central nervous system more markedly than any other system in the body. Alcohol acts prima-

rily as a central nervous system depressant. Alcohol suppresses the activity of the brain by altering the properties of neural membranes, cell metabolism, conduction of electrical impulses down the axon and the release of neurotransmitters.

Alcohol first exerts its depressant actions on those parts of the central nervous system involved in the most highly integrative functions. The brain stem reticular activating system, which is important for maintaining alertness, and parts of the cortex are particularly susceptible to the effects of alcohol. Alcohol, initially depresses the activity of inhibitory centers in the brain. Thus, at low doses, a state of disinhibition or mild euphoria is a common consequence of alcohol consumption. At higher doses, alcohol suppresses the activity of the cerebellum, resulting in slurred speech and staggering gait, and of the cortex, leading to impairments in performance of a variety of cognitive tasks (e.g. reaction time tests, memory deficits and intellectual functioning).

At moderate doses, the behavioral responses to alcohol vary widely among individuals. This is because the social setting and an individual's mental state are important determinants of the drug's effects. In one situation, alcohol intake may be associated with euphoria and relaxation, while in another it may lead to withdrawal, hostility and aggression. Setting and state of mind become progressively less important with higher doses of alcohol, since the depressive actions of alcohol predominate leading to difficulties in talking, walking and thinking.

Alcohol decreases alertness, impairs reaction time, leads to disturbances in motor skills and negatively affects the performance of intellectual tasks. Alcohol amnesia or blackouts, after which the drinker cannot remember the events that occurred while he or she was intoxicated, are not uncommon among heavy drinkers, especially those who engage in binge drinking behavior. Consumption of very large quantities of alcohol leads to severe depression of brain activity, producing stupor, anesthesia, coma and ultimately death resulting from inhibition of the respiration centers in the brain stem. The lethal level of alcohol ranges between 0.4% and 0.6% by volume in the blood. However, most individuals pass out before drinking an amount of alcohol capable of causing death (Hanson and Venturelli, 1998; White *et al.*, 2002; Nelson *et al.*, 2004; Zeigler *et al.*, 2005).

Chronic alcohol use

Chronic alcohol abuse is associated with damage to both the peripheral and central nervous system. Alcohol-induced peripheral nerve damage is characterized by numbness in the feet, and muscle discomfort and fatigue, particularly in the lower portions of the legs. With continued drinking, the alcoholic may experience weakness in the toes and ankles, loss of vibratory sensations, impairments in the control of fine movements and ultimately decreased pain sensitivity.

Damage to the central nervous system is one of the most devastating consequences of chronic alcohol intake. This damage is frequently manifest by the appearance of deficits in cognitive behavior. Fifty to seventy percent of detoxified alcoholics display lower performance on tests of learning, memory and perceptual motor skills than their non-alcoholic counterparts (Fadda and Rossetti, 1998; Zeigler *et al.*, 2005).

The first indications of alcohol-induced neurotoxicity, or what is termed Wernicke's encephalopathy, are disturbances in balance and gait, weakness of the eye muscles, difficulties with short-term memory and mental confusion. Continued use of alcohol can lead to Korsakoff's psychosis, a persistent neurological disorder typified by an inability to form new memories (anterograde amnesia), a disordered sense of time, hallucinations, confabulation and dementia.

Autopsies and imaging studies of the brains of chronic alcoholics reveal neuropathological and morphological abnormalities in many parts of the brain. Overall, the brains of alcoholics are reduced in both weight and volume. Individuals with additional medical problems such as cirrhosis or Korsakoff's syndrome display the greatest reduction in brain weight. This reduction in brain weight is due in large part to a decrease in the size of the cerebral cortex, the portion of the brain most involved with processing of cognitive information. While all portions of the cortex are affected by alcohol, the frontal lobes are more seriously affected than other cortical regions. Frontal-lobe damage is believed to account for a number of the behavioral disturbances observed in chronic alcoholics including emotional abnormalities, poor planning and organizational skills, perseverative responding on cognitive tasks, attentional difficulties and problems with spatial memory (Fabba and Rossetti, 1998; Reed *et al.*, 2003; Zeigler *et al.*, 2005).

Other areas of the brain that are particularly vulnerable to the neurotoxic effects of alcohol are the diencephalon, which comprises the thalamus and hypothalamus, the hippocampus and the basal forebrain. Damage to the thalamus resulting from stroke, tumors or trauma, is often associated with memory difficulties similar to those observed in patients with Korsakoff's syndrome. Additionally, brain-imaging studies have found a greater reduction in the size of the thalamus in alcoholics suffering from anterograde amnesia than in alcoholics without amnesic symptoms. The hippocampus and basal forebrain, other brain structures intimately involved in memory, are also frequently damaged in alcoholics. These findings have led to the hypothesis that the memory impairments observed in a large proportion of individuals with chronic alcoholism result in large part from damage to the thalamus, hippocampus and basal forebrain (Fabba and Rossetti, 1998; Reed *et al.*, 2003).

Damage to the cerebellum is also not uncommon in alcoholics. Impairments in functioning of the cerebellum most likely result in the difficulties in walking and coordination often observed in alcoholics (Fabba and Rossetti, 1998).

Nutrition and alcohol-induced neurotoxicity

The ways in which alcohol produces its neurotoxic effects remains unclear. However, there is growing evidence that nutritional deficiencies play a significant role in alcohol-induced brain damage. Particular attention has been paid to thiamine because of the critical role this vitamin plays in brain metabolism. Thiamine serves as a cofactor for a number of enzymes important in maintaining glucose metabolism in nerve cells. In thiamine deficiency, there is a reduction in the production of these enzymes that consequently results in impairment of the energy producing abilities of the cells in the brain.

Thiamine deficiency occurs in approximately 80% of alcoholics. The primary cause of thiamine deficiency is poor diet and lack of nutrient intake. Additionally, however, alcohol (i) damages the lining of the intestine, which decreases intestinal absorption of thiamine, (ii) reduces metabolism of the vitamin and (iii) impairs storage of the vitamin within the liver (Fabba and Rossetti, 1998).

Evidence that thiamine deficiency is an important etiological factor in alcohol-induced neurotoxicity comes from studies demonstrating that thiamine deficiency, resulting from gastrointestinal disease, gastric resection, anorexia nervosa and other disease states, leads to neurological and behavioral outcomes essentially the same as those that occur in Wernicke–Korsakoff's syndrome. Additionally, both research and clinical studies have demonstrated that administration of thiamine can reverse the early symptoms of Wernicke–Korsakoff's syndrome. For example, in patients with Wernicke's encephalopathy, high doses of thiamine can rapidly repair ocular difficulties, gait and balance problems and mental confusion. Unfortunately, thiamine administration is only minimally effective in individuals with Korsakoff's psychosis because damage to the central nervous system is beyond repair (Todd et al., 1999; Day et al., 2004; Pitkin and Savage, 2004).

Although a large percentage of alcoholics suffer from thiamine deficiency, only a small percentage (10%) actually develop Wernicke-Korsakoff's syndrome. One possible explanation is that genetic factors play a part in mediating the effects of thiamine deficiency on brain functioning and behavior. Evidence for this possibility comes from animal studies showing differences among inbred strains in susceptibility to the neurotoxic effects of thiamine deficiency. Further support for this possibility is provided by the observations that (i) the concordance rate for Wernicke–Korsakoff's syndrome is greater in identical than for fraternal twins, and (ii) there are differences among ethnic groups with respect to the number of alcoholics in the population who develop Wernicke–Korsakoff's syndrome (Fabba and Rossetti, 1998).

The preceding information clearly suggests the potential benefits of treating chronic alcoholics with thiamine. However, controversy remains over the exact amount of thiamine that is needed to reverse the symptoms of Wernicke's encephalopathy. Additionally, as most alcoholics suffer from a variety of nutrient deficiencies, it is important to note that thiamine alone may be insufficient to ameliorate the mental problems associated with alcohol abuse. Finally, it must be recognized that if brain damage is extensive, nutritional therapy will not be able to reverse the effects of prolonged alcohol use (Thomson et al., 2002; Stickel et al., 2003; Day et al., 2004).

Fetal Alcohol Syndrome

Although chronic alcoholism can severely damage the brain in adults, it is the brain of the developing organism that is most profoundly affected by alcohol. It has long been suspected that imbibing alcohol during pregnancy can detrimentally affect the developing child. Drinking on the wedding night was forbidden in ancient Greece for fear of the birth of a damaged child, and Aristotle cautioned that women drunkards frequently gave birth to abnormal children. In England, the 'gin epidemic' which occurred between 1720 and 1750 strengthened the suspicion that alcohol could harm fetal development. This epidemic was the direct result of an increase in the availability of new inexpensive food imports in early 18th-century England, and the consequent decrease in the demand for domestic grain. To help English farmers sell their excess grain, Parliament promoted the distilling of grain, and removed taxes on gin, the resulting alcoholic beverage. As alcohol abuse became rampant the number of infants born with developmental and behavioral abnormalities soared. A report by the Royal College of Physicians portrayed the offspring of alcoholic mothers as having a 'starved, shriveled and imperfect look'. In 1751, to protect the health of mothers and infants, Parliament reinstated taxes on gin and other distilled beverages (Abel, 1984).

At the beginning of the 20th century, growing recognition of the possible adverse outcomes of alcohol abuse led to research assessing the association between maternal-alcohol consumption and birth defects. In 1899, Sullivan reported that the infants born to alcoholic mothers had higher mortality and morbidity rates than the infants of non-alcoholic women (Sullivan, 1899). Unfortunately, the scientific community did not actively pursue Sullivan's seminal work, and little was published on the potential adverse affects of maternal alcohol intake during the next 70 years (Abel, 1984).

The modern era of research on the effects of maternal alcohol intake on fetal develop-ment dates from 1968 when Lemoine and colleagues published a paper in France describing a distinct set of physical and behavioral characteristics in children born to alcoholic mothers (Lemoine et al., 1968). Unfortunately, however, because the paper was published in French, it initially received little attention in the USA. Five years later, the publication of two papers provided a more detailed picture of growth failure, dysmorphic facial features and neurological abnormalities in the offspring of alcoholic mothers (Ulleland, 1972; Jones et al., 1973).

In their 1973 publication, Jones and colleagues coined the term fetal alcohol syndrome (FAS) to describe the constellation of abnormalities resulting from maternal alcohol abuse. As shown in Table 13.2, the classic features of FAS include pre- and post-natal growth retardation, a pattern of recognizable facial

Table 13.2. Characteristic features of fetal alcohol syndrome in infants and children.

Documented maternal alcohol exposure.
Growth retardation as evidenced by at least
  one of the following:
  Low-birth weight for gestational age.
  Post-natal growth impairments not due to nutrition.
  Low weight to height ratio.
Dysmorphic facial features including:
  Eyes – wide-set eyes, short palpebral fissures, ptosis, epicanthal folds.
  Ears – posterior radiation.
  Nose – short upturned; hypoplastic philtrum.
  Mouth – thin upper lip, cleft lip or cleft palate.
Abnormalities in CNS development.
Decreased brain size at birth.
Structural brain abnormalities such as:
  Microencephaly.
  Decrease in size of cerebellum.
  Partial absence of the corpus callosum.
Defects in neuronal migration.
Neurological/behavioral problems including:
  Irritability in infancy.
  Disturbances in eating and sleeping.
  Poor hand–eye coordination.
  Impaired fine motor coordination.
  Hearing loss.
  Deficits in attention, executive functioning,
  visual spatial processing.
  Decreased intellectual functioning.
  Deficits in social behavior.

Source: Kelley et al., 2000; Sampson et al., 2000; Burd et al., 2003 b,c; Klug et al., 2003.

abnormalities, and complex alterations in brain structure and functioning, which are associated with impairments in both cognitive and social behavior. In addition, children with FAS may suffer from congenital anomalies including malformations of the cardiovascular, skeletal, renal and auditory systems.

Since 1973, it has been recognized that the classic triad of features of FAS: growth retardation, facial changes and severe cognitive dysfunctions are actually relatively uncommon in the offspring of women who drink heavily during pregnancy. More frequently, children of these women manifest more subtle signs of brain injury and cognitive deficits with or without the physical features of FAS. Thus, in 1996, the Institute of Medicine, added definitions for 'alcohol-related birth defects' (ARBD) and 'alcohol-related neurodevelopmental disorder' (ARND) to the spectrum of alcohol-related birth defects (Sampson et al., 1997, 2000; Adams et al., 2002; Burd et al., 2003c; Klug et al., 2003; Koren et al., 2003).

Behavioral consequences of fetal alcohol syndrome

Of the many devastating consequences of maternal alcohol abuse, impairments in the behavior of the offspring are the most damaging. Early exposure to alcohol is one of the three most common causes of mental retardation in this country (i.e. FAS, Down's syndrome and spina bifida). However, in contrast to the other disorders, mental retardation associated with alcohol intake is completely preventable.

Children with FAS vary widely in their intellectual prowess, but suffer most from mild to moderate mental retardation, with IQ scores ranging from 50 to 70. The severity of the intellectual deficits is directly related to the degree of physical anomalies in children with FAS. Children exposed to alcohol during development, not only suffer from global mental retardation, but also display a variety of more specific cognitive deficits. Children with FAS and ARND exhibit impairments in their organizational skills, ability to learn from previous experiences and to foresee consequences, and speech, language and communication capabilities (Koren et al., 2003).

In addition to deficits in mental abilities, prenatal exposure to alcohol is linked to a multiplicity of behavioral abnormalities. Infants diagnosed with FAS are irritable and jittery, and often display low levels of arousal, abnormal reflexes and a decrease in habituation to repetitive stimuli. Many infants with FAS have a weak sucking reflex, which leads to poor feeding and consequent growth failure during the post-natal period. Sleep disturbances are also common in infants exposed to high doses of alcohol during fetal development.

In older children, hyperactivity and attentional deficits are hallmarks of prenatal exposure to alcohol. Long-term follow-up studies of children with alcohol-related disorders reveal that problems of hyperactivity persist throughout childhood, and may continue into adulthood. In addition, children with FAS and related disorders routinely display impairments in both gross and fine motor behavior (Richardson et al., 2002; Wass et al., 2002).

Recent work indicates that difficulties in social situations frequently plague individuals with FAS and related disorders. In infancy and early childhood, these difficulties can interfere with attachment behavior, and thereby disrupt mother–child interactions (O'Connor et al., 2002). When children with FAS enter school, they display greater than normal levels of aggression and have the social skills of children younger than their chronological age (Coggins et al., 2003).

Unfortunately, the cognitive and social difficulties experienced by young children with FAS do not improve with time, but rather remain a permanent fixture of their lives. During adolescence and adulthood, individuals with FAS frequently encounter problems when engaged in activities requiring sustained attention or abstract reasoning (Table 13.3). Moreover adults with FAS often have problems cooperating with peers, a lack of close friends and display inappropriate behavior in social situations. These deficiencies in social behavior can impair work performance, and increase the possibility that individuals with FAS will need to be dependent on their families and social agencies throughout their lives (Streissguth et al., 1991; Kelly et al., 2000; Burd et al., 2003c; Koren et al., 2003).

Table 13.3. Behavioral characteristics of fetal alcohol syndrome in adolescents and adults.

Problems of attention.
Short-attention span.
Decreased ability to concentrate.
Hyperactivity.
Impulsivity.
Abnormal cognitive functioning.
Memory deficits.
Impairments in abstract reasoning.
Low IQ scores.
Impairments in social skills.
Difficulty responding to social cues.
Lack of reciprocal friendships.
Withdrawn.
Failure to consider the consequences of one's
 actions.
Increased risk of drug dependence.
Bursts of aggressive behavior.

Source: Committee on Substance Abuse and Committee on Children with Disabilities, 2000; Eustace *et al.*, 2003.

Maternal alcohol intake and the developing nervous system

Ethanol readily crosses the placenta and within minutes leads to blood alcohol levels in the fetus equivalent to those of the mother. Alcohol is rapidly distributed throughout fetal tissue including the brain. The question that remains to be answered is how does alcohol damage the developing brain.

Initial research on alcohol-related brain damage in experimental animals demonstrated that prenatal exposure to alcohol decreased the proliferation of new nerve cells, while increasing the death of existing nerve cells (Burd *et al.*, 2003b). These alterations in neuronal development were associated with a reduction in the size of the brain (i.e. microcephaly). Other abnormalities in the brains of animals exposed to alcohol during gestation included incomplete development of the cerebral cortex, aberrations in neuronal migration, particularly in the area of the hippocampus, and abnormalities in neuronal development in the cerebellum and corpus callosum. It has been hypothesized that damage to the hippocampus, an area of the brain involved in

learning and memory, may be directly associated with the cognitive deficits observed in FAS, while damage to the cerebellum contributes to problems in motor behavior.

Studies investigating the effects of prenatal exposure to alcohol on brain development in humans correlate well with the findings of research using experimental animals. Autopsy reports of infants with FAS who died during the neonatal period showed that prenatal exposure to alcohol produces similar changes in brain morphology in humans and experimental animals (Jones and Smith, 1973; Roebuck *et al.*, 1998). More recently, the emergence of techniques that can directly examine the brain in living individuals, such as positron emission tomography (PET) and magnetic resonance imaging (MRI), have confirmed earlier autopsy reports. More specifically, imaging studies demonstrate that maternal alcohol intake is associated with asymmetries in cortical gray matter, with greater decreases in brain surface in the left hemisphere than in the right hemisphere of children with FAS. Moreover, these studies indicate that the corpus callosum, cerebellum, hippocampus and basal ganglia are particularly susceptible to alcohol's teratogenic actions. Imaging studies also have revealed that alcohol-induced aberrations in brain morphology, are not transient, but rather persist into adolescence.

Although at the moment, imaging techniques can only provide information about the consequences of maternal alcohol intake, in the future these techniques could be used as an early screening tool for FAS. Early detection of abnormalities in development could lead to interventions, which could lessen the consequences of alcohol-induced brain damage (Roebuck *et al.*, 1998; Archibald *et al.*, 2001; Mattson *et al.*, 2001; Autti-Ramo, *et al.*, 2002; Sowell *et al.*, 2002 a,b).

An important question that remains to be answered is what does alcohol do in the fetal brain to produce its devastating outcomes. No single mechanism can account for alcohol-induced damage to the developing nervous system. Rather, there are numerous ways in which alcohol can impair the development of the fetal nervous system. For example, alcohol consumption may induce oxidative stress and the production of reactive oxygen species that then damage cellular components such as cell membranes, DNA and protein. Alcohol-induced oxidative stress may also disrupt the function of mitochondria, which generate the energy for the cell, and store and regulate calcium, which is critical for normal neuronal functioning. Recent research suggests that treatment with antioxidants may reduce alcohol-induced neurotoxicity in the developing brain (Kotch *et al.*, 1995; Heaton *et al.*, 2000).

In addition to causing oxidative stress, alcohol may inhibit growth factors that regulate neuronal proliferation and development, alter the number and structure of glial cells, interfere with the activity of neurotransmitters, disrupt the brain's utilization of glucose, and alter gene expression. Moreover, alcohol can impair the fetal nervous system development by indirectly affecting the mother's physiological status. The exact ways in which these mechanisms interact to lead to FAS most likely depend on a variety of factors including the amount of alcohol consumed during pregnancy and the mother's nutritional status (Goodlett and Horn, 2001; United States Department of Health and Human Services, 2002).

Prevalence of fetal alcohol syndrome

As maternal alcohol consumption is the only cause of FAS, it is important to determine how many women consume alcohol while pregnant. Survey data indicate that in the USA approximately 13% of pregnant women report consuming alcohol, while 3% of pregnant women report frequent intake of alcohol (more than 7 drinks per week). Although only a small percent of these women's children will be afflicted with problems associated with maternal alcohol, fetal alcohol exposure remains a major cause of birth defects (Riley *et al.*, 2003).

Across the USA, it is estimated that between 0.7 to 10 children per 1000 births are born each year with problems directly related to maternal alcohol consumption (Eustace *et al.*, 2003). However, as noted previously, not all children whose mothers drink alcohol during pregnancy develop FAS, ARBD or ARND. This leads to the question of why do some, but not all, children born to alcoholic mothers suffer from alcohol-related problems.

One part of the answer is that a number of factors including the mother's race, age, socio-economic status, use of other drugs and nutritional status contribute to whether or not she has a child with FAS or related disorders. For example, maternal use of tobacco, marijuana and other drugs of abuse can facilitate the development of FAS. Additionally, data suggest that both duration of alcohol consumption, and whether or not binge drinking occurs during pregnancy play a role in determining the outcome of maternal alcohol intake (Gladstone *et al.*, 1997; Korkman *et al.*, 2003; Mescke *et al.*, 2003).

It also should be remembered that although children born to mothers who abused alcohol during pregnancy may not display all of the obvious physical consequences of FAS, they may still experience significant behavioral and cognitive problems. Indeed, data suggest that for every child with FAS, three to four additional children suffer from alcohol-related deficits in intellectual, cognitive and psychosocial functioning (Roebuck *et al.*, 1998; May and Gossage, 2001; Sood *et al.*, 2001; Project Choices, 2002; Burd *et al.*, 2003a; Koren *et al.*, 2003; Meschke *et al.*, 2003).

It is difficult to estimate the cost of health care for children with FAS and related disorders. However, we do know that the cost is significant. Data from a recent study in North Dakota found that the average yearly costs of health care for a child with FAS was $2842, which was $2342 greater than health care for a child without the disorder. It is estimated that over 2 million individuals in the USA are affected by FAS, thus the overall health care costs of fetal exposure to alcohol could exceed $4 billion per year (Klug and Burd, 2003).

How much is too much?

One of the most commonly asked questions with regard to FAS is 'How much alcohol is necessary to produce the syndrome?' Unfortunately, the answer to this question is, very simply, 'We don't know'. Research suggests that even low levels of prenatal exposure to alcohol can have adverse consequences on the fetus. The consumption of only one drink a day significantly increases the risk of giving birth to a child with alcohol-related disabilities. Moreover, we know that there is a direct relationship between the quantity of alcohol consumed during pregnancy and the severity of the behavioral and morphological consequences of prenatal exposure to the drug. That is, the more a mother drinks during pregnancy, the greater the possibility that she will have a child with FAS or other morphological and behavioral symptoms associated with alcohol abuse (Sampson *et al.*, 2000; Eustace *et al.*, 2003; Korkman *et al.*, 2003).

One might ask, why it is so difficult to accurately determine the relationship between maternal alcohol consumption and the risk of FAS and related disabilities. Several factors contribute to this difficulty. First, mothers may be hesitant to relate information about alcohol consumption during pregnancy, and thus self-reports of intake may seriously underestimate actual alcohol intake. Second, it is not clear if alcohol intake at one point in pregnancy is more detrimental than intake at other points. There may be a critical period during pregnancy when the fetus is particularly vulnerable to the teratogenic effects of alcohol. Therefore, it is important to know not only how much drinking occurred, but also when drinking occurred during pregnancy. Third, a number of other variables, including nutritional status, multiple drug use, genetic conditions, and stressful life situations may interact with alcohol in the development of FAS. As yet, the precise role of the preceding factors in mediating the effects of maternal alcohol consumption are unknown (Gladstone *et al.*, 1997; Project Choices Research Group, 2002; Meschke *et al.*, 2003).

The question of how much alcohol is safe during pregnancy remains unanswered. Although an occasional drink during pregnancy may have no adverse effects on neonatal development, as noted above, even relatively low levels of maternal alcohol consumption may adversely affect the developing child (Committee on Substance Abuse and Committee on Children with Disabilities, 2000; Sood *et al.*, 2001). Thus, it seems appropriate to err on the side of caution, and to follow the recommendations of government agencies and health organizations, such as the Center for Disease Control and the American Medical Association. To alleviate the possibility of having a child with FAS or other alcohol-related deficits, women should avoid drinking both during pregnancy and if planning to become pregnant (Ebrahim *et al.*, 1999; Committee on Substance Abuse and Committee on Children with Disabilities, 2000; Project Choices Research Group, 2002; Eustace *et al.*, 2003).

Conclusion

Alcohol represents a paradox in today's society. On the one hand, there is evidence that moderate alcohol intake can reduce the risk of heart disease and stroke (Klatsky *et al.*, 2001; Corrao *et al.*, 2004; Gronbaek, 2004; Mann and Folts, 2004). On the other hand, excessive alcohol intake is associated with a myriad of detrimental physiological and behavioral outcomes. While we have not resolved this paradox in this chapter, we hope to have provided sufficient information for you to make informed decisions about the pros and cons of alcohol use.

References

Abel, E.L. (1984) *Fetal Alcohol Syndrome and Fetal Alcohol Effects*. Plenum Press, New York.

Adams, J., Bittner, P., Buttar, H.S., Chambers, C.D., Collins, T.F.X., Daston, G.P., Filkins, K., Flynn, T.J., Graham, J.M., Jones, K.L., Kimmel, C., Lammer, E., Librizzi, R., Mitala, J. and Polifka, J.E. (2002) Statement of the public affairs committee of the Teratology Society on the fetal alcohol syndrome. *Teratology* 66, 344–347.

Alexander, E.N. and Bowen, A.M. (2004) Excessive drinking in college: behavioral outcome, not binge, as a basis for prevention. *Addictive Behaviors* 29, 1199–1205.

Archibald, S.L., Fennema-Notestine, C., Gamst, A., Riley, E.P., Mattson, S.N. and Jernigan, T.L. (2001) Brain dysmorphology in individuals with severe prenatal alcohol exposure. *Development Medicine and Child Neurology* 43, 148–154.

Autti-Ramo, I., Autti, T., Korkman, M., Kettunen, S., Salonen, O. and Valanne, L. (2002) MRI findings in children with school problems who had been exposed prenatally to alcohol. *Developmental Medicine and Child Neurology* 44, 98–106.

Burd, L., Cotsonas-Hassler, T.M., Martsolf, J.T. and Kerbeshian, J. (2003a) Recognition and management of fetal alcohol syndrome. *Neurotoxicology and Teratology* 25, 681–688.

Burd, L., Klug, M.G., Martsolf, J.T. and Kerbeshian, J. (2003b) Fetal alcohol syndrome: neuropsychiatric phenomics. *Neurotoxicology and Teratology* 25, 697–705.

Burd, L., Martsolf, J.T., Klug, M.G. and Kerbeshian, J. (2003c) Diagnosis of FAS: a comparison of the Fetal Alcohol Syndrome Diagnostic Checklist and the Institute of Medicine Criteria for Fetal Alcohol Syndrome. *Neurotoxicology and Teratology* 25, 719–724.

Cantrell, P.A. (2000) Beer and ale. In: Kiple, K. F. and Ornelas, K. C. (eds) *The Cambridge World History of Food.* Cambridge University Press, Cambridge, UK, pp. 619–625.

Corrao, G., Bagnardi, V., Zambon, A. and La Vecchia. C. (2004) A meta-analysis of alcohol consumption and the risk of 15 disease. *Preventive Medicine* 38, 613–619.

Caton, S.J., Ball, M., Ahern, A. and Hetherington, M.M. (2004) Dose-dependent effects of alcohol on appetite and food intake. *Physiology & Behavior* 81, 51–58.

Coggins, T.E., Olswant, L.B., Olson, H.C. and Timler, G.R. (2003) On becoming social competent communicators: the challenge for children with fetal alcohol exposure. *International Review of Research in Mental Retardation* 27, 121–150.

Committee on Substance Abuse and Committee on Children with Disabilities (2000) Fetal alcohol syndrome and alcohol-related neurodevelopmental disorders. *Pediatrics* 106, 358–361.

Dawson, D.A., Grant, B.F., Stinson, F.S. and Chou, P.S. (2004) Another look at heavy episodic drinking and alcohol use disorders among college and non-college youth. *Journal of Studies on Alcohol* 65, 477–488.

Day, E., Bentham, P., Callaghan, R., Kuruvilla, T. and George, S. (2004) Thiamine for Wernicke-Korsakoff syndrome in people at risk for alcohol abuse. Cochrane Database Syst. Rev.

Ebrahim, S.H., Anderson, A.K. and Floyd, R.L. (1999) Alcohol consumption by reproductive-aged women in the USA: an update on assessment, burden and preventions in the 1990s. *Prenatal and Neonatal Medicine* 4, 419–430.

Eustace, L.W., Kang, D.H. and Coombs, D. (2003) Fetal alcohol syndrome: a growing concern for health care professionals. *Journal of Obstetric, Gynecologic, and Neonatal Nursing* 32, 215–221.

Fabba, F. and Rossetti, Z.I. (1998) Chronic ethanol consumption: from neuroadaptation to neurodegeneration. *Progress in Neurobiology* 56, 385–431.

Gladstone, J., Levy, M., Nulman, I. and Koren, G. (1997) Characteristics of pregnant women who engage in binge alcohol consumption. CMAJ 156, 789–794.

Goodlett, C.R. and Horn, K.H. (2001) Mechanisms of alcohol-induced damage to the developing nervous system. *Alcohol Research & Health* 25, 175–184.

Gronbaek, M. (2004) Epidemiologic evidence for the cardioprotective effects associated with consumption of alcoholic beverages. *Pathophysiology* 10, 83–92.

Hanson, G. and Venturelli, P. (1998) *Drugs and Society,* Jones and Barlett Publishers, Boston.

Heaton, M.B., Mitchell, J.J. and Paiva, M. (2000) Amelioration of ethanol-induced neurotoxicity in the neonatal rat central nervous system by antioxidant therapy. *Alcoholism, Clinical and Experimental Research* 24, 512–518.

Jones, K.L. and Smith, D.W (1973) Recognition of the fetal alcohol syndrome in early infancy. *Lancet* 2, 999–1001.

Jones, K.L., Smith, D.W., Ulleland, C.N. and Streissguth, A.P. (1973) Pattern of malformation in offspring of chronic alcoholic mother. *Lancet* 1(7815), 1267–1271, Jun 9.

Kelly, S.J., Day, N. and Streissguth, A.P. (2000) Effects of prenatal alcohol exposure on social behavior in humans and other species. *Neurotoxicology and Teratology* 22, 143–149.

Klatsky, A.L., Armstrong, M.A., Friedman, G.D. and Sidney, S. (2001) Alcohol drinking and risk of hospitalization for ischemic stroke. *The American Journal of Cardiology* 88, 703–770.

Klug, M.G. and Burd, L. (2003) Fetal alcohol syndrome prevention: annual and cumulative cost savings. *Neurotoxicology and Teratology* 25, 763–776.

Klug, M.G., Burd, L., Martsolf, J.T. and Ebertowski, M. (2003) Body mass index in fetal alcohol syndrome. *Neurotoxicology And Teratology* 25, 689–696.

Koren, G., Nulman, I., Chudley, A.E. and Loocke, C. (2003) Fetal alcohol spectrum disorder. *Journal of Canadian Medical Association* 169, 1181–1185.

Korkman, M., Kettunen, S. and Autti-Ramo, I. (2003) Neurocognitive impairment in early adolescence following prenatal alcohol exposure of varying duration. *Child Neuropsychology* 9, 117–128.

Kotch, L.E., Chen, S.-Y. and Sulik, K.K. (1995) Ethanol-induced teratogenesis: free radical damage as a possible mechanism. *Teratology* 52, 128–136.

Lahti-Koski, M., Pietinen, P. Heliovaara, M. and Vartianen, E. (2002) Associations of body mass index and obesity with physical acitivity, alcohol intake, and smoking in 1982–1997, FINRISK studies. *The American Journal of Clinical Nutrition* 75, 809–817.

Lemione, P., Haronsseau, H., Borteryu, J.P. and J.C. Menuet (1968) Les enfants de partents alcooliques. Anomalies observées. À propos de 127 cas. *Quest Medical* 25, 476–482.

Maillot, F., Farad, S. and Lamisse, F. (2001) Alcohol and nutrition. *Pathologie Biologie* 49, 683–688.

Mann, L.B. and Folts, J.D. (2004) Effects of ethanol and other constituents of alcoholic beverages on coronary heart disease: a review. *Pathophysiology* 10, 105–112.

Mattson, S.N., Schoenfeld, A.M. and Riley, E.P. (2001) Teratogenic effects of alcohol on brain and behavior. *Alcohol Research & Health* 25, 185–191.

May, P.A. and Gossage, J.P. (2001) Estimating the prevalence of fetal alcohol syndrome – a summary. *Alcohol Research & Health* 25, 159–167.

Meschke, L.L., Holl, J.A. and Messelt, S. (2003) Assessing the risk of fetal alcohol syndrome: understanding substance use among pregnant women. *Neurotoxicology and Teratology* 25, 667–674.

Miller, J.W., Gfroerer, J.C., Brewer, R.D., Naimi, T.S., Mokdad, A. and Giles, W.H. (2004) Prevalence of adult binge drinking: a comparison of two national surveys. *American Journal of Preventive Medicine* 27, 197–204.

Nelson, E.C., Heath, A.C., Bucholz, K.K., Madden, P.A.F., Fu. Q., Knopik, V., Lynskey, M.T., Whitfield, J.B., Statham, D.J. and Martin, N.G. (2004) Genetic epidemiology of alcohol-induced blackouts *Archives of General Psychiatry* 61, 257–263.

Newman, J.I. (2000) Wine. In: Kiple, K. F. and Ornelas, K. C. (ed.), *The Cambridge World History of Food.* Cambridge University Press, Cambridge, UK, pp. 730–737.

O'Connor, M.J., Kogan, N. and Findlay, R. (2002) Prenatal alcohol exposure and attachment behavior in children. *Alcoholism, Clinical And Experimental Research* 26, 1592–1602.

Pitkin, S.R. and Savage, L.M. (2004) Age-related vulnerability to diencephalic amnesia produced by thiamine deficiency: the role of time of insult. *Behavioral Brain Research* 148, 93–105.

Project Choices Research Group (2002) Alcohol-exposed pregnancy. Characteristics associated with risk. *American Journal of Preventive Medicine* 23, 166–173.

Reed, L.J., Lasserson, D., Marsden, P., Stanhope, N., Stevens, T., Bello, F., Kingsley, D., Colchester, A. and Kopelman, M.D. (2003) FDG-pet findings in the Wernicke-Korsakoff syndrome. *CORTEX* 39, 1027–1045.

Richardson, G.A., Ryan, C., Willford, J., Day, N.L. and Goldschmidt, L. (2002) Prenatal alcohol and marijuana exposure: effects on neuropsychological outcomes at 10 years. *Neurotoxicology and Teratology* 24, 309–320.

Riley, E.P., Mattson, S.N., Li, T.K., Jacobson, S.W., Coles, C.D., Kodituwakku. P.W., Adams, C.M. and, Korkman, M.I. (2003) Neurobehavioral consequences of prenatal alcohol exposure: an international perspective. *Alcoholism, Clinical and Experimental Research* 27, 362–373.

Roebuck, T.M., Mattson, S.N. and Riley, E.P. (1998) A review of the neuroanatomical findings in children with fetal alcohol syndrome or prenatal exposure to alcohol. *Alcoholism, Clinical And Experimental Research* 22, 339–344.

Sampson, P.D., Streissguth, A.P., Bookstein, F.L., Little, R.E., Clarren, S.K., Dehaene, P., Hanson, J.W. and Graham, J.M. (1997) Incidence of fetal alcohol syndrome and prevalence of alcohol-related neurodevelopmental disorder. *Teratology* 56, 317–326.

Sampson, P.D., Streissguth, A.P., Booksteine, F.L. and Barr, H.M. (2000) On categorization in analyzes of alcohol teratogenesis. *Environmental Health Perspectives* 108, 421–428.

Sood, B., Delaney-Black, V., Covington, C., Nordstrom-Klee, B., Ager, J., Templin, T., Janisse, J., Martier, S. and Sokol, R.J. (2001) Prenatal alcohol exposure and childhood behavior at age 6 to 7 years: dose-response effect. *Pediatrics* 108, 1–9.

Sowell, E.R., Thompson, P.M., Mattson, S.N., Tessner, K.D., Jernigan, T.L., Riley, E.P. and Toga, A.W. (2002a) Regional brain shape abnormalities persist into adolescence after heavy prenatal alcohol exposure. *Cerebral Cortex* 12, 856–865.

Sowell, E.R., Thompson, P.M., Peterson, B.S., Mattson, S.N., Welcome, S.E., Henkenius, A.L., Riley, E.P., Jernigan, T.L. and Toga, A.W. (2002b) Mapping cortical gray matter asymmetry patterns in adolescents with heavy prenatal alcohol exposure. *NeuroImage* 17, 1807–1819.

Stickel, F., Hoehn, B., Schuppan, D. and Seitz, H.K. (2003b) Review article: nutritional therapy in alcoholic liver disease. *Alimentary Pharmacology & Therapeutics* 18, 357–373.

Streissguth, A.P. Aase, J.M., Clarren, S.K., Randels, S.P., LaDue, R.A. and Smith, D.F. (1991) Fetal alcohol syndrome in adolescents and adults. *Journal of American Medical Association* 265, 1961–1967.

Sullivan, W.C. (1899) A note on the influence of maternal inebriety on the offspring. *Journal of Mental Sciences* 45, 489–503.

Thomson, A.D., Cook, C.C.H., Touquet, R. and Henry, J.A. (2002) The Royal College of Physicians report on alcohol: guidelines for managing Wernicke's encephalopathy in the accident and emergency department. *Alcohol and Alcoholism* 37: 513–521.

Todd, K.G., Hasell, A.S. and Butterworth, R.F. (1999) Alcohol-thiamine interactions: an update on the pathogenesis of Wernicke's encephalopathy. *Addiction Biology* 4, 261–272.

Ulleland, C.N. (1972) The offspring of alcoholic mothers. *Annals of the New York Academy of Sciences.* 197, 167–169.

United States Department of Health and Human Services (2002) 10th Special Report to U.S. Congress on Alcohol and Health.

Wannamethee, S.G. and Shaper, A.G. (2003) Alcohol, body weight, and weight gain in middle-aged men. *The American Journal of Clinical Nutrition* 77, 1312–1317.

Wass, T.S., Simmons, R.W., Thomas, J.D. and Riley, E.P. (2002) Timing accuracy and variability in children with prenatal exposure to alcohol. *Alcoholism, Clinical and Experimental Research.* 26, 1887–1896.

Wechsler, H., Lee, J.E., Kuo, M. and Lee, H. (2000) College binge drinking in the 1990s: a contin-uing problem. *Journal of American College Health* 48, 199–210.

Westerterp, K.R., Prentice, A.M. and Jequier, E. (1999) Alcohol and body weight. In McDonald, I. (ed.), *Health Issues Related to Alcohol Consumption,* 2nd edn. ILSE Europe, Brussels, pp. 103–123.

Westerterp-Plantenga, M.S. and Verwegen, C.R.T. (1999) The appetizing effect of an aperitif in overweight and normal-weight humans. *The American Journal of Clinical Nutrition* 69, 205–212.

White, A.M., Jamieson-Drake, D.W. and Swartzwelder, H.S. (2002) Prevalence and correlates of alcohol-induced blackouts among college students: results of an email survey. *Journal of American College Health* 51, 117.

Yeomans, M.R., Caton, S. and Hetherington, M.M. (2003) Alcohol and food intake. *Current Opinion in Clinical Nutrition and Metabolic Care* 6, 639–644.

Zeigler, D.W., Wang, C.C., Yoast, R.A., Dickinson, B.D., McCaffree, A., Robinowitz, C.B. and Sterling, M.L. (2005) The neurocognitive effects of alcohol on adolescents and college students. *Preventive Medicine* 40, 23–32.

14 Eating Disorder Syndromes: Anorexia and Bulimia Nervosa

J. Worobey

The last 25 years have witnessed a striking increase in our awareness of eating disorders, most notably the disturbances known as anorexia nervosa and bulimia nervosa. In point of fact, there is a wide variety of problems that may surround eating, ranging from the fear of eating unfamiliar foods (food neophobia), to the eating of non-food substances (pica), to compulsive overeating (binge eating, which will be further addressed in Chapter 15). But due in part to the deaths of Karen Carpenter, a pop singer, and Christy Heinrich, an Olympic gymnast, the public has been made aware that young women, even those who would appear to have achieved fame and fortune, can literally die from the complications of self-imposed starvation. Although her death was due to a car crash, the late Princess Diana reportedly suffered from bulimia. In fact, the prolonged vegetative state that preceded the morbid deathwatch for Terri Schaivo in the United States was supposedly caused by the cardiac arrest brought on from bulimia (http://en.wikipedia.org/wiki/Terry_Schaivo). Indeed, the cover stories appearing in periodicals like *People* magazine on young celebrities like Mary-Kate Olsen would suggest that an eating disorders epidemic is upon us. The research community appears to have embraced this concept, if their journal output is any indication. For example, at the time this book was being written, a literature search on *MEDLINE* using the key words 'eating disor-

ders' revealed 2248 entries for the 20 years from 1975–1994, with 2139 more for the years 1995–2004 – nearly matching the earlier output in half as many years!

In a world where approximately one in every five people experiences chronic hunger, and tens of thousands in underdeveloped countries die each day of starvation, it may seem inconceivable that certain individuals would willingly attempt to starve themselves when sufficient food is available to them. But in a number of westernized cultures an irrational fear of fatness by young women, in particular, has made the disorders of anorexia and bulimia nervosa a topic of great concern to the medical, psychological and nutritional communities. In this chapter, we will define the conditions of anorexia nervosa and bulimia nervosa, examine their prevalence and the existence of related disturbances, describe their physiological and psychological consequences, identify correlates and probable causes of the disorders and discuss treatment strategies for these problems. As fewer than 10% of eating disorders are in males, we will use feminine pronouns throughout most of our discussion, although information on males will be presented where relevant.

Anorexia Nervosa

The eating disorder termed anorexia nervosa can start innocently enough. A teenage girl may initially intend to try and lose a little weight. She cuts out eating sweets and snacks, and is praised by her mother for her will power. As she reaches her desired weight, she may still feel she is overweight and continue to restrict her eating. She avoids all foods she perceives to be calorically dense as well as those that are high in refined carbohydrates. She limits her diet to fruits, vegetables and perhaps cottage cheese. She imposes rules upon herself about when and how much she may eat and follows them rigidly. By the time anyone notices that there is something wrong, she may be consuming no more than 600 cal/day. When a friend confronts her about her excessive weight loss, she complains that she is still too heavy or that a particular region of her body is too fat.

Anorexia nervosa is truly an unusual disorder. Although individuals who suffer from it may show many of the same symptoms that are seen in other forms of starvation, they have one unique characteristic – that their hunger is deliberate and self-imposed. In some ways the disorder presents a paradox, as it is most often seen in young females who are considered well off, yet who are starving in the midst of plenty. The term *anorexia nervosa* even appears to be inappropriate, as it derives from 'an-orex-nervos' (without-mouth-of nervous origin), and suggests the victim has no appetite. But individuals with this disorder do not suffer from a loss of appetite, rather they suffer from an intense fear of gaining weight. Booth (1994) has suggested that *hypophagia* would be a more appropriate term if a Greek-based name is desired, as it means 'deficient eating'. Nevertheless, individuals with anorexia nervosa are frequently preoccupied with eating and other thoughts of food.

History of anorexia nervosa

Historians who study religion have described the pious behavior of several saints as resembling what we now view as anorexic. Saint Catherine of Siena, for example, who lived in the 14th century, led a life of asceticism in order to garner spiritual fulfillment, barely subsisting on a diet that lacked both in quality and quantity. To expiate sin, she abstained from food and drink, except for the communion supper and eventually died of starvation. Robert Bell (1985) coined the term 'holy anorexia' to describe her disorder, though he points out that the cultures in which such women lived valued spiritual health and fasting rather than thinness and self-control.

In the early 1870s physicians in Europe offered the first 'modern' descriptions of anorexia. In an address he delivered at Oxford, Sir William Gull referred to:

> a particular form of disease occurring mostly in young women and characterized by extreme emaciation.... The subjects of this affection are mostly of the female sex and chiefly between the ages of 16 and 23. I have occasionally seen it in males at the same age.... The condition was one of simple starvation.... The want of appetite is due to a morbid mental state.... We might call the state hysterical.... I prefer however the more general term 'nervosa'.   (Gull, 1874)

Gull was in fact the first to use the term 'anorexia nervosa', and his description from well over a century ago still paints a fairly accurate portrait of what the disorder looks like. Thanks to his work, and the reports of anorexia also provided by Dr Charles Lasegue in France, a substantial increase occurred in the medical community's awareness of the disease. With the advent of Freud's influence in the first half of the 20th century, a psychoanalytic perspective dominated clinicians' ideas about the disorder. Specifically, the fear of 'incestuous impregnation' was at the core of the early drive theories of anorexia, and served to explain the patient's decrease in the oral intake of food (Fallon and Bunce, 2000). Although this idea may seem outrageous today, the psychoanalytic approach represented the first serious attempt to understand the etiology of the disorder. When Hilde Bruch, a psychoanalyst, began to study anorectic women in the 1950s, the current wave of interest in anorexia nervosa actually began.

Bruch suggested that the rigid behavior that these anorectic women associated with eating represented a struggle for control. As girls, they had been good children who were quiet, obedient, clean, helpful, dependable, eager to please and excelled at school. When they reached adolescence and were supposed to be self-reliant, they lacked an age-appropriate sense of autonomy and became overcompliant and oversubmissive. Bruch viewed the rigid control of eating and the excessive concern with body size as symptoms of their desperate fight against feeling enslaved, exploited and incompetent. She proposed that their strict limitation of food intake might be one of the only ways the anorectic could feel in control of her life (Bruch, 1973, 1985).

By the 1970s, a dramatic rise in both medical and public interest in anorexia was seen. Researchers began exploring not only etiological factors in the development of anorexia, but also its physiological and psychological correlates. With the high profile death of Karen Carpenter in 1983, public interest was stimulated by an abundance of reports in the popular press. As celebrities came forth with their public confessions of anorexia nervosa in the 1990s (e.g. Victoria Beckham aka Posh Spice), articles in magazines were supplemented with increasing coverage on talk shows, news programs, made for TV movies and documentaries on public television.

Diagnostic criteria

The American Psychiatric Association has recognized 'anorexia nervosa' as a classifiable mental disorder for over 20 years, with its first listing in the 1980 edition of the *Diagnostic and Statistical Manual of Mental Disorders*. Since then, the diagnostic criteria have been reviewed and revised, as research continues to add to our knowledge of its symptoms and prevalence. The current criteria, as defined in the *Diagnostic and Statistical Manual*, 4th edn. (DSM-IV, 1994), appear in Table 14.1.

As shown in the table, there are a number of characteristic symptoms of ongoing anorexia nervosa. Although not explicitly stated in these criteria, a major defining characteristic of the disorder is the active refusal of the patient to eat enough to maintain her normal body weight. As we already mentioned, the refusal to eat is not due to a lack of interest in food. If anything, anorexics are obsessed with food and food consumption, calculating just how many calories they can

Table 14.1. Criteria for anorexia nervosa.

1. Refusal to maintain body weight at or above a minimally normal weight for age and height.
2. Intense fear of gaining weight, even though underweight.
3. Disturbance in the way in which one's body weight or shape is experienced, undue influence of body weight or shape on self-evaluation, or denial of the seriousness of the current low body weight.
4. In postmenarcheal females, the absence of at least three consecutive menstrual cycles.

In the *restricting type*, the individual restricts food without regularly bingeing or purging. In the *bingeing/purging type*, the individual severely restricts food and binges or purges.

Source: adapted from the *DSM-IV – Diagnostic and Statistical Manual of Mental Disorders*, 1994.

and do consume. But their idea of an acceptable amount of calories is ridiculously small. In any case, the result of such a reduced level of food intake is a significant loss of weight, that is, 15% or more. So the first criterion for a diagnosis of anorexia nervosa is the person's weighing 85% or less than what their minimal body weight should be, given their frame and height. For example, a 20-year-old woman of medium build who is 5 feet 4 in tall (1.63 meters) would satisfy this criterion if she dropped to a weight of 105 lb (48 kg) or less.

The second criterion has to do with the irrational fear of gaining weight or becoming fat, even when the individual is losing weight and by all accounts is underweight. The third criterion relates to the second, in that the woman cannot see that she is underweight. She perceives herself as still being overweight, in spite of what the scale reads. Her body image is distorted, both in terms of how she perceives herself and the level of importance she attributes to her physical appearance. What is remarkable about this perceptual problem is that it appears to be confined to the self. In a classic study by Garner et al., (1976) anorexic women adjusted photographs of themselves to create larger images, while they did not adjust the width for pictures of others. In other words, they perceived themselves as heavier than they actually were, although they perceived others of the same proportions to be of normal weight. Many researchers now believe body image issues and disturbances are an important part of the assessment and clinical management of eating disorders (Netemeyer and Williamson, 2001).

Along with loss of weight, fear of fatness and a disturbed body image, a female must stop menstruating in order to be classified as anorexic, or must have her menarche delayed if she is prepubertal. This physiological disturbance has been attributed to primary nervous system dysfunction, but may be better explained by caloric restriction and the lowered fat content of the body (Pomeroy, 1996). Presumably this serves to protect the female from becoming pregnant, which would place even greater demands on her body.

New to the most recent DSM guidelines is the distinction between the restricting type of anorexic and the binge eating/purging type. The restricting type relies on her ability to sustain self-control in not eating. In addition, this type of anorexic will engage in frequent, regular and vigorous exercise as an added means of displacing hunger as well as to work off calories from the minimal amounts of food that she has eaten. As bingeing and purging are a primary characteristic of the bulimic sufferer, these behaviors will be addressed later in this chapter in the section on bulimia nervosa.

Prevalence

As has been already stated, anorexia nervosa occurs most frequently in females, with some 85–95% of the reported cases occurring in adolescent girls. The remaining cases are in prepubertal boys and older women. The prevalence rate has generally been found to be in the 0.5% to 1.0% range for adolescents and at about 1.0% for adults (Lucas et al., 1991; Doyle and Bryant-Waugh, 2000). These rates may not seem high, but they extrapolate to about 10,000 clinical cases in England and around 120,000 in the USA – not an epidemic perhaps, but a matter of serious concern given the severity and potential lethality of the disorder (Gordon, 2000). The mean age of onset is 17 years of age, with peaks at 14 and 18 years (DSM-IV, 1994), ages that would seem to correspond to the girls' transitions to high school and college, respectively. The ratio of female to male anorexics is approximately 10 to 1 (Andersen and Holman, 1997).

For many years, a belief that anorexia nervosa is confined to the upper classes has persisted. Prior to the 1980s clinicians as well as epidemiologists seemed to confirm a concentration of anorexic patients in the upper socioeconomic classes. It may have been the case, however, that only affluent parents could afford to seek treatment for their daughters. More recent research has not shown any associations between the social class of anorexic patients versus members of the general community (Gard and Freeman, 1996), though it may be that the disorder has become more diffused through the population through greater access to education and upward mobility. Religion is another social characteristic that does not appear to bear on the prevalence of eating disorders. There are no clearly established associations between particular religious backgrounds and the development of eating disorders, although some have speculated that anorectics frequently come from backgrounds that are characterized by puritanical attitudes, particularly toward female sexuality (Forthun et al., 2003).

Along with social class, the relative absence of cases among African-American women led to the widespread view that anorexia nervosa was a disease confined to white females. Since the 1980s, however, a number of reports of black people with anorexia nervosa began to appear in the literature. Although there seem to be more black women with eating disorders in the USA than previously thought, evidence suggests that the prevalence remains lower in the African-American than the Caucasian community (Striegel-Moore et al., 2003). Interestingly enough, studies of black and white females suggest that differences in self-esteem and acculturation may be a factor. For example, black teenage girls place less emphasis on weight, appearance and external beauty than their white counterparts (Parker et al., 1995). While black women who scored high on drive for thinness and body dissatisfaction were actually overweight, such distressed attitudes were not correlated with weight in white women. Moreover, black women who most intensely emulated white cultural values evidenced the highest degree of eating disorder symptomatology (Abrams *et al.*, 1993).

How culture may indirectly influence eating attitudes was shown in a study conducted some 20 years ago by Furnham and Alibhai (1983). The researchers compared three groups of women: one of British Caucasians, one of Kenyans and one of Kenyans living in Britain. In accordance with their prediction they found that the Kenyans preferred a larger body shape than the British Caucasians, but surprisingly, the Kenyans who lived in Britain preferred the thinnest body image. With respect to body image, then, the émigrés appeared to overassimilate. The case of South Africa is also interesting. Prior to the 1990s, white South African schoolgirls were indistinguishable from their American and European counterparts in terms of their overvaluation of thinness and vulnerability to eating disorders, with virtually no cases of eating disorders seen in black South Africans (Gordon, 2000). Since the change from apartheid to democratic rule, however, studies of black South African collegiate women reveal scores at least as high on disordered eating measures as their Caucasian classmates (LeGrange *et al.*, 1998). Assimilation may be a partial explanation, but it remains to be seen just what contribution race may make to the likelihood of an eating disorder.

With regard to countries, epidemiological evidence supports an increase of eating disorders in the USA, the UK, Denmark, Japan, the Netherlands and Switzerland. Although such well-designed studies have not been conducted in other countries, the proliferation of published articles and treatment centers suggests that eating disorders have become increasingly prevalent in Czechoslovakia, France, Germany, Hungary, Israel, Italy and Spain. Gordon (2000) has reviewed reports that indicate eating disorders are now observed in relatively affluent societies such as Japan, Hong Kong, Singapore and South Korea, but also, albeit with lower frequency, in less affluent countries such as the Philippines, Mexico, China, Indonesia and India. Despite hunger being a major public health problem for large areas of India, its mid-

dle and professional classes are now quite sizable, and Western influences are pervasive. However, anorexic women in India do not appear to exhibit the body image concerns that characterize westernized cultures (Srinivasin *et al.*, 1998).

Physiological consequences

The medical complications associated with anorexia nervosa are numerous. It affects all major organ systems of the human body, most notably the cardiovascular, dermatological, gastrointestinal, skeletal, endocrine and metabolic systems (Hill and Pomeroy, 2001). Many of the medical complications are similar to those that accompany other forms of starvation, but others do appear to be specific manifestations of anorexia nervosa (see Table 14.2). As might be expected, the severity of the physiological changes that occur in anorexia nervosa varies directly as a function of the degree of reduced food intake and body weight.

Table 14.2. Consequences of excessive weight loss in anorexia nervosa.

Gastrointestinal:
  Delayed gastric emptying.
  Bloating.
  Constipation.
  Abdominal pain.
Hematological:
  Iron deficiency anemia.
  Decrease of white blood cells.
Cardiac:
  Loss of heart muscle.
  Cardiac arrhythmia.
  Increased risk of sudden death.
Osteopathic:
  Decalcification of bone.
  Premature osteoporosis.
Neuropsychiatric:
  Abnormal taste sensations.
  Depression.
  Mild cognitive disorder.
Other:
  Growth of fine hair on trunk.
  Loss of fat stores and muscle mass.
  Reduced thyroid metabolism.
  Difficulty in maintaining body temperature.

Source: adapted from Insel *et al.*, 2004.

Some of the most severe medical complications of anorexia nervosa involve the cardiovascular system. Cardiovascular changes that result from anorexia include low heart rate, low blood pressure, tachycardia, ventricular arrhythmia, congestive heart failure and sudden death due to cardiac failure (Maloney, 1995). In fact, the mortality rate for anorexia nervosa is estimated to be around 18% – a staggering figure for a psychiatric disorder (Hetherington, 2000). Dermatological signs of anorexia include brittle nails, dry, thin and scaly skin, often orange in color due to carotene. While hair loss may occur, undernutrition may result in fine, silky hair (lanugo) on the back, face and extremities (Hill and Pomeroy, 2001).

The entire gastrointestinal system can be affected by anorexia nervosa, with patients frequently complaining of excessive feelings of abdominal bloating and uncomfortable fullness after eating. The severe reduction in food intake results in delayed gastric emptying, which in turn appears to decrease gastric motility (Sharp and Freeman, 1993). Once a pattern of starvation has been established, the delay in gastric emptying likely produces increased feelings of satiety when food is consumed, so that the anorexic feels full while ingesting even less food. The skeletal system may be directly affected through the decreased calcification of bones (osteopenia) due to malnutrition, low calcium intake and estrogen deficiency (Gwirtsman et al., 1989). Because bone accretion peaks in adolescence, the impact on bone density may be greatest if anorexia occurs during these years of development.

Alterations in endocrine functioning are very pronounced in anorexia. One of the first systems to be affected is the hypothalamic-pituitary-gonadotropin axis, which is responsible for promoting gonadal growth and function (Thomas and Rebar, 1990). As mentioned earlier, anorexic women are by definition amenorrheic, which is common in other starvation states and may be attributable to caloric restriction. However, one in six anorexic patients develops amenorrhea before weight is lost and the absence of menses may continue even after their weight is restored. This suggests that for some anorexic women a hypothalamic dysfunction is operating, which may have resulted from dietary changes and psychological stress. Plasma levels of the luteinizing and follicle-stimulating hormones that are produced by the pituitary gland and are critical for normal ovarian function are lower in anorexic patients. Moreover, their secretion in response to gonadotropin-releasing hormones is prepubertal or immature in the anorexic woman. With a return to a higher weight, levels of these hormones will often return to normal, along with the normalization of the uterus. In the male anorectic, serum testosterone levels are decreased (Sharp and Freeman, 1993).

The hypothalamic-pituitary-thyroid axis is also altered, with anorectic individuals tending to exhibit hypothyroidism. Hypothermia, cold intolerance and a decrease in basal metabolic rate are evidence of abnormal thyroid function in these patients (Pirke and Ploog, 1986). Alterations in the hypothalamic-pituitary-adrenal axis are observed in anorexic patients as well, which serves to elevate levels of cortisol, a hormone that regulates fat, carbohydrate and protein metabolism. When anorectic patients resume normal eating, cortisol secretion and metabolism normalize fairly rapidly, suggesting that elevated cortisol secretion is an adaptation to starvation (Hill and Pomeroy, 2001).

The metabolic changes associated with anorexia nervosa are similar to those seen with starvation. After a number of days of semi-starvation, glycogen reserves are first depleted, then protein oxidation increases until ketogenesis kicks in, at which point fat oxidation occurs. This can result in elevated free fatty acids and higher plasma cholesterol. If the individual continues to eat fewer calories than are required for the body's needs, tissue may eventually be consumed in order to supply the energy deficit. Other metabolic problems identified with anorexia include abnormal vasopressin release, which results in increased urine output and a concomitant reduction in intracellular water (Hill and Pomeroy, 2001).

In addition to these physiological consequences, anorexia nervosa can result in electrolyte imbalances, anemia and other mineral deficiencies, kidney stones if chronically dehydrated and edema during the refeeding process.

Taken together, these problems illustrate the severe taxing of the body that self-starvation via anorexia nervosa inflicts on its victim.

Psychological characteristics

If you recall the studies on malnutrition that we discussed in Chapter 5, you will recognize some of the psychological disturbances that are seen in anorexics as similar to the effects of starvation. Irritability, low tolerance for stress and sexual disinterest, but also a preoccupation with food and bizarre eating habits characterize both anorexia nervosa and starvation. Emotions are labile, with the anorexic also avoiding emotional intimacy and social interaction, yet maintaining a dependency on others (Woolsey, 2002). In anorexia, a preoccupation with food may manifest itself by preparing meals for others, collecting recipes, attending cookery classes, or taking courses in nutrition and dietetics (Worobey and Schoenfeld, 1999). Bizarre eating habits may include refusing to eat in the presence of others or taking an extremely long period of time to eat a small amount of food.

Although many of the psychological changes observed in anorexia are similar to those seen in starvation, there are several differences that make the disorder unique. First of all, anorexics tend to display a severe distortion in their body image (Heinberg *et al.*, 1995). They will typically misperceive their body size as larger than they actually are, regardless of what the scale indicates or the assurances of their trusted friends. Second, anorexics frequently misinterpret both internal and external stimuli. For example, internal cues for hunger are redefined as positively reinforcing, with less and less food necessary to feel full, perhaps an outgrowth of the delay in gastric emptying (Robinson, 1989). Anorexics also demonstrate lessened responsiveness to external stimuli such as cold and sexual stimulation (Pomeroy, 1996). Third, unlike starving individuals who become easily fatigued and avoid physical activity, anorexics are often hyperactive and deny feeling fatigued (Hill and Pomeroy, 2001). Indeed, exercise may be used to further assist in weight loss. A fourth distinction between starving individuals and anorexics relates to issues of control (Horowitz, 2004). Anorexics feel helpless in regard to most matters, but they can control their eating, so their self-discipline with respect to not eating is extraordinary. Finally, it may be safely assumed that the fear of fatness that serves to motivate anorexic behavior has no equivalent in a starvation situation.

Bulimia Nervosa

Bulimia nervosa is more prevalent than anorexia nervosa, although it's true incidence is somewhat more difficult to establish because the condition is not as physically obvious. More men suffer from bulimia nervosa than anorexia nervosa, but as with anorexia the disorder occurs primarily in women. While many women with bulimia may also have anorexia, the average bulimic tends to be heavier and older than the typical anorexic patient.

Bulimia nervosa is defined by a binge–purge cycle of food intake. The disorder is more aptly named than anorexia nervosa, as the word bulimia derives from 'buli' (ox). The name thus implies 'ox hunger' or a ravenous appetite, which the bingeing behavior supports. Excessive amounts of calories are indeed ingested, but the individual compensates for the binge by purging through self-induced vomiting or other techniques. The primary distinction between the diagnoses of bulimia and anorexia may in fact be in the eating patterns, as bulimia is characterized by such frequent binges on food, while anorexia includes persistent efforts to restrict food. Some bulimic sufferers may try to diet for a period of days or weeks between binges, but fail in their attempt and binge even more, while others may binge unremittingly (Booth, 1994).

Most bulimic individuals will rarely eat a normal meal. If in a social setting where food is being served, most will consume very little food. However, during a binge episode an astonishing amount of energy may be ingested, from 1000 cal to as much as 50,000 cal by one estimate (Johnson *et al.*, 1981). Foods consumed during a binge tend to be high in fat and carbohydrates, as food is eaten for emotional comfort and not nutritional value. Hence, foods forbidden during dieting, such as ice cream, donuts, cake, cookies, milkshakes and chocolate top the list. Most binge eating is done in the evening and often in secrecy. A variety of conditions can precipitate a binge episode, such as depression, stress, frustration, boredom or just the sight of food. As in our earlier discussion of hunger-satiety mechanisms in Chapter 11, the disinhibition that restrained eaters experience when stressed or depressed may characterize the bulimics who make repeated attempts at dieting to lose weight (Stice and Agras, 1998).

Following a binge, the individual typically feels further anxiety, depression and then guilt. Due to humiliation because of having lost control or recognizing that all those calories will take their toll, the bulimic then seeks to undo overeating. Most will regurgitate the food they eat, and many bulimics will anticipate vomiting in advance of their overeating. For other bulimics, purging is accomplished by using laxatives or diuretics. Unlike the anorexic, the individual with bulimia nervosa is aware of the abnormal behavior and thus attempts to hide it from family and friends.

History of bulimia nervosa

Robert Bell (1985), the historian, noted that Saint Mary Magdalen de' Pazzi, who lived in the 16th century, struggled with food cravings but subsisted on a diet of bread and water. As other nuns reported that she sometimes would gobble food in secret, claiming to be possessed by the devil, Bell speculates that her behavior may be tantamount to the binge–purge pattern of bulimia nervosa. As suggested earlier, however, fasting as a pious act is a different source of motivation than dieting in order to improve appearance.

Clinical reports of bulimic binge eating were published as early as the 1890s, but it was not until the 1940s that detailed reports of compulsive overeating and purging behavior began to appear in the medical literature. Although the majority of reports identified these behaviors in anorexic patients, descriptions of bulimic behavior in non-anorectic samples were also presented. It was not until the 1970s that reports of bulimic behavior among normal weight individuals became more available, with the sur-

prising phenomenon observed in coeds being attributed to the pressures of female socialization. Shortly thereafter, Gerald Russell (1979) first used the term 'bulimia nervosa' in an article that described bulimic symptoms in 30 patients. In addition to providing vivid portraits of these individuals, he suggested diagnostic criteria that included the unmanageable urge to eat, the morbid fear of becoming fat and the avoidance of the effects of fattening foods by inducing vomiting, abusing purgatives or both. Even though the disorder was viewed as less dangerous than anorexia, research on bulimia nervosa exploded over the next decade. In the 1990s, the publicity garnered from admissions of bingeing and purging by celebrities such as Princess Diana, Jane Fonda and Paula Abdul gave thousands of women the courage to come forth and seek understanding and treatment, with the sudden ascendancy of bulimic syndromes described as spectacular (Gordon, 2000).

Diagnostic criteria

The American Psychiatric Association first identified 'bulimia' as a disorder in the 1980 edition of the DSM-III, but basically described it as a syndrome of binge eating (see Chapter 15, this volume). However, it soon became evident that this definition was unsatisfactory as it failed to emphasize the preoccupation with weight and body image that characterized the disorder, as well as the ubiquitous attempts by afflicted individuals compensate for the binge eating. In the revised DSM-IIIR of 1987, the name of the disorder formally became 'bulimia nervosa', and the criteria specified in the current version of the DSM-IV (1994) appear in Table 14.3.

By definition, an individual with bulimia nervosa goes on an eating binge at least twice a week, eating a large amount of food in a short amount of time, and then tries to compensate in an inappropriate manner. The sheer volume of food that is ingested characterizes the binge episode, but the criteria allow for a consideration of context. For example, the American occasion of Thanksgiving Day is a holiday wherein most observers are encouraged to overeat, so eating until feeling bloated

Table 14.3. Criteria for bulimia nervosa.

1. Recurrent episodes of binge eating, characterized by one or both of the following:
   a. eating, in a discrete period of time, an
      amount of food that is definitely larger than
      most people would eat during a similar
      period of time and under similar circum-
      stances
   b. a sense of lack of control over eating during
      the episode.
2. Recurrent inappropriate compensatory behavior in order to prevent weight gain, such as
   self-induced vomiting; misuse of laxatives,
   diuretics, enemas or other medications; fasting; or excessive exercise.
3. The binge eating and inappropriate compensatory behaviors both occur on average at least
   twice a week for 3 months.
4. Body shape and weight unduly influence the
   person's self-evaluation.

In the *purging type*, the individual uses regular
purging behavior. In the *non-purging type*, the
individual uses other inappropriate compensatory
behaviors, such as fasting or excessive exercise,
but does not regularly engage in purging.

Source: adapted from the *DSM-IV – Diagnostic and
Statistical Manual of Mental Disorders*, 1994.

at this event would not qualify for a diagnosis
of bulimia. The fact that guests are pushed by
the cook or host to keep eating also indicates
that control by the individual is publicly
removed, rather than lost.

Regarding the compensatory behaviors,
the key word is inappropriate, as forcing yourself to throw up or taking a laxative when you
are not constipated are anything but a normal
way to conclude a meal. Yet research reveals
that over 75% of bulimic women rely on self-
induced vomiting, while over 60% use laxatives (McGilley and Pryor, 1998). The overlap
indicates that many women use more than one
technique in purging. Johnson *et al.* (1981)
reported that most of their subjects binged at
least once a day, and began to use purging
techniques about a year after they began
bingeing. As with anorexia nervosa, the current DSM-IV criteria specify two types of
bulimics, but in this case it distinguishes
between the purging and non-purging type.
Rather than abuse the body with a chemical
substance to empty the stomach or the bowels,

the non-purging bulimic will employ a more
natural method such as fasting or exercising
excessively.

Much like anorectics, the self-esteem of
bulimic individuals is greatly influenced by
their weight and body shape. But unlike
anorectics, most bulimics maintain a weight
that is within normal limits. Women with
bulimia nervosa typically follow a pattern of
unsuccessful dieting for weight loss that
becomes interspersed with bingeing and
purging behaviors that result in weight fluctuations of 10 lb or more over short periods
of time. Since a normal weight is maintained,
the individual may view purging as a quick
and easy solution to the problem of excess
calories. When we examine the physiological
effects of bingeing and purging, however,
the dire consequences of this cycle will be
evident.

Prevalence

Prospective work suggests that the peak rise for
the onset of binge eating and compensatory
behaviors occurs between 14 and 18 years of
age (Stice *et al.*, 1998). The prevalence rate for
bulimia nervosa is around 1.0% for adolescents and from 1.0% to 3.0% for adults,
although estimates as high as 13% have been
reported (Rosenvinge *et al.*, 1999). As with
anorexia, the ratio of females to males with
bulimia nervosa is highly skewed, with estimates ranging from a low of 4 to 1 up to 19
to 1 (Logue, 1991). These varied estimates may
be due in part to sampling inconsistencies, as
respondents have ranged from high school students to graduate students, and from women
who were interviewed in shopping malls to
those seen at family planning sites. Across
studies, self-report questionnaires were used
which also varied in their items, with the older
studies relying on criteria that were much less
stringent than the current DSM-IV.

Whether the prevalence of bulimia nervosa is increasing, declining or remaining constant cannot be determined at present. A recent
report showed a decline among Harvard
students from 7.2% to 5.1% over 10 years
(Heatherton *et al.*, 1995), and a conservative
estimate for university students in the USA is

around 2% to 3% (Gordon, 2000). Even so, an estimate this low extrapolates to between 1 and 2 million young women.

Since research on bulimia nervosa has been conducted for relatively fewer years than anorexia nervosa, associations between bulimia and social class, country and culture have not been as thoroughly documented. However, it is believed that the sudden exposure of women from traditional backgrounds to a Western cultural experience may heighten their vulnerability to bulimia nervosa. Studies of Pakistani schoolgirls as well as Egyptian university students living in England have shown higher rates for bulimic behavior by these females when compared to their peers who were not forced to assimilate a new culture (Nasser, 1986; Mumford et al., 1991). Girls whose parents tried to exert rigid control and who emphasized traditional cultural values through their language and dress were the most susceptible to eating disorders. Their disordered eating may have reflected the clash between deference to their parents' expectations and the independence they witnessed in their new English environment. Reports of bulimic behavior in Argentina, the most 'European' of the South American nations, also suggest that this disorder is fairly common there (Gordon, 2000).

Physiological consequences

Unlike the anorexic, the bulimic patient may superficially appear to be the picture of health, being of normal weight and shape (Hill and Pomeroy, 2001). But similar to anorexia nervosa, the physical complications of bulimia can affect almost every system of the body (see Table 14.4). They can range from minor problems, such as abrasions on the knuckles from continual use of the hand to induce vomiting, to life threatening difficulties such as electrolyte disturbances resulting from continual purging (Greenfield et al., 1995). Many of the medical complications of bulimia nervosa are side effects of disordered eating practices. The rapid consumption of large amounts of food can lead to acute gastric dilation with resulting discomfort. Inflammation of the pancreas, abdominal distention and

Table 14.4. Consequences of purging in bulimia nervosa.

Gastrointestinal:
  Inflammation of the salivary glands.
  Inflammation of the esophagus.
  Inflammation and enlargement of the pancreas.
  Dysfunctional bowel.
Metabolic:
  Electrolyte abnormalities.
  Low blood magnesium.
Dental:
  Erosion of dental enamel with corresponding decay.
Neuropsychiatric:
  Weakness.
  Fatigue.
  Mild cognitive disorder.
  Seizures.
  Mild neuropathies.

Source: adapted from Insel et al., 2004.

pain and increased heart rate may develop as a consequence of abrupt pancreatic stimulation during frequent binge eating episodes (McClain et al., 1993).

Most bulimic patients vomit regularly after a binge episode in order to remove what they have eaten. However, recurrent vomiting of the stomach's acidic contents can result in erosion of the esophagus, which if torn, can be a life-threatening event in itself. Dental erosion, gum problems and swelling of the salivary glands are also common consequences of continual vomiting, and can serve as a diagnostic indicator of bulimic behavior. Repeated vomiting can also lead to fluid loss, dehydration and electrolyte imbalances. Bulimic patients may experience excessive thirst with decreased urinary output, resulting in edema from excess water being retained. The loss of sodium, potassium and chloride from the body can lead to a variety of cardiac symptoms ranging from irregular heartbeat to congestive heart failure and cardiac death (Hill and Pomeroy, 2001). Mortality rates for bulimia nervosa are estimated at about 3% (Hetherington, 2000).

Despite their frequent vomiting, bulimic women do not appear to develop taste aversions to the food they eat when bingeing. Some believe it is because the vomiting is self-induced rather than imposed externally or caused by illness (Logue, 1991). Others propose that taste receptors on the palate may be damaged from acid in the vomit, so taste sensitivity is decreased (Rodin *et al.*, 1990). For many of these women then, vomiting is something they become quite used to.

Besides vomiting, laxative and diuretic abuse is also a common compensatory behavior. The use of laxatives or diuretics can become addictive, with bulimic patients developing tolerance for their effects and thus resorting to using increasing amounts. Chronic use of laxatives or enemas can result in the loss of normal colon functioning, which may become so severe that colonic resection is necessary. In addition, laxative and diuretic abuse can lead to shifts in fluid balance, electrolyte imbalances, dehydration, malabsorption, abdominal cramping and muscle cramps (Greenfield *et al.*, 1995).

Psychological characteristics

At one level, the psychological profiles of the bulimic and anorexic patients are somewhat similar. Like anorexics, bulimics seem to have a distorted view of their own weight and shape, and desire to weigh much less than they do. Like anorexics, bulimics appear to be obsessed with controlling their food intake. But while anorexics are successful in exercising control around food, bulimics will repeatedly fail in this challenge and end up eating uncontrollably. Their effort at purging what they have just eaten is their shameful recourse for not having had the strength to resist temptation.

Compared to anorexics, bulimics are more likely to display symptoms of depression, show greater lability of mood, and are higher in negative affectivity (Stice and Agras, 1998; Godart *et al.*, 2000). In contrast to anorexics who restrict both their caloric intake and their sexual activity, bulimics tend to engage in more sexual behavior (Zerbe, 1995). And unlike the anorexic patient who tries to resist treatment because of fear of gaining weight, the bulimic patient is usually more embarrassed from having been caught at bingeing and purging than frightened at the prospect of receiving help (Hill and Pomeroy, 2001).

Women with bulimia have been characterized as high achievers, yet tend to be dependent, passive, self-conscious, unassertive and have difficulty communicating their feelings. Moreover, they are extremely vulnerable to rejection and failure and may have problems with impulse control, notably expressed through shoplifting and over consumption of drugs or alcohol (Vogeltanz-Holm *et al.*, 2000).

Partial Syndrome Eating Disturbances

Apart from the individuals who meet the DSM-IV criteria for anorexia or bulimia nervosa, there are untold thousands of males and females who are dissatisfied with their bodies. Weight concerns have been found to exist in 20% of 5-year-old girls (Davison *et al.*, 2000). Studies with 9- to 11- year-olds show that 1 girl out of 3 worries about being fat, with nearly 1 out of 5 boys expressing the same concern (Gustafson-Larson and Terry, 1992). Caucasian teenage girls report greater dissatisfaction with their bodies than their African-American peers, although the latter do endorse a high drive for thinness (Striegel-Moore *et al.*, 2000). Among college students rates of dissatisfaction may be even higher, as some studies indicate as many as 48% of females are bothered by the thought of fat on their bodies, with 20% of males also making this claim (Worobey and Schoenfeld, 1999). In contrast to girls' dissatisfaction that generally reflects a desire to be thinner, however, boys may be unhappy because they desire a more muscular appearance (Smolak *et al.*, 2001).

Regardless of the source of their dissatisfaction, many of these individuals exhibit elements of disordered eating, and may be said to have a subclinical, subthreshold, atypical, partial syndrome, symptomatic, or not otherwise specified eating disorder (Shisslak *et al.*, 1995). For example, some research indicates that bingeing regularly occurs in a substantial number of individuals (Garfinkel *et al.*, 1995), and that fasting and vomiting are used by significant numbers of high school students to supplement their dieting practices (Berg, 1992).

Apart from anorexia and bulimia, the American Psychiatric Association also has a diagnostic category of 'Eating disorders not otherwise specified' for individuals who fall just short of meeting the DSM-IV (1994) criteria. An individual would be typed as sub-threshold anorexic if she met all the criteria for anorexia nervosa except for having regular menses or being at a weight that is not abnormally low. Subthreshold bulimia would be indicated if eating binges are less frequent than twice a week, or vomiting is self-induced after eating a small amount of food, for example. It is estimated that as many as half of all referrals for anorexia or bulimia might receive this diagnosis (Nicholls *et al.*, 2000). In addition, other symptom clusters such as *night-eating syndrome* have been identified and warrant further study (Birketvedt *et al.*, 1999).

Whether or not a diagnosis of anorexia, bulimia or eating disorder not otherwise specified is warranted, it is abundantly clear that disordered eating and inappropriate methods to compensate for overeating are phenomena that are increasingly prevalent in Western societies. Mostly everyone perceives a need to diet at some point in their lives, whether or not it is advisable, and the quality of their everyday life is often compromised due to restrained eating or a lapse in their restraint. We now examine the possible causes that may help to explain why eating, an activity that should be natural and pleasurable, appears to cause difficulties for so many individuals in today's world.

Etiology of Eating Disorders: Possible Risk Factors

It is generally agreed that there is no single cause of eating disorders such as anorexia or bulimia nervosa; rather, such aberrant behavior must be considered the result of several predisposing factors. Not everyone who is predisposed to anorexia will develop the disorder, as many individuals may diet and then resume their previous eating pattern. Likewise, many individuals who binge may never elect to compensate by purging (see Chapter 15), and hence do not become bulimic. A casual, but cutting remark by a parent may trigger one teenage girl's decision to begin starving herself, while another may try to endear her sorority sister's favor by adopting her technique of purging. Therefore, for those who do develop anorexia or bulimia, the precise interaction of predisposing factors at work will vary from person to person, which as one would expect, makes the case history of anyone with an eating disorder unique.

The myriad of risk factors for eating disorders have been conceptualized in a number of models, which despite their varied complexity, may be subsumed under three categories: individual, family and sociocultural (Shisslak and Crago, 2001). As shown in Table 14.5, the list of factors that have been associated with eating disorders is quite extensive. While some are more relevant to anorexia than bulimia and vice versa, they are grouped here in a generalized manner for the sake of brevity. Recognize that researchers who study eating disorders, as well as professionals who work with such patients, differentiate these possible causes to a degree that is beyond the scope of this book. Given the sheer volume of studies that have been conducted and the large number of factors that have been identified, only a few examples of current research will be cited for illustrative purposes.

Individual risk factors encompass biology, personality and behavior. Through scores of correlational studies a wide variety of factors have been associatiated with eating disorders, namely: body dissatisfaction, weight concerns, early maturation, being overweight, low self-esteem, impulsivity, inadequate coping skills, negative affect, dietary restraint, perfectionism and the initiation of dating (Hetherington, 2000; Shisslak and Crago, 2001). For example, research has shown that heterosexual dating is strongly linked to dieting and disordered eating among girls who have recently experienced menarche (Cauffman and Steinberg, 1996). Other work that illustrates current efforts in identifying personal risk factors is exemplified by research on perfectionism, that affirms an association between higher perfectionism and the severity of anorexia (Halmi *et al.*, 2001). In addition, groundbreaking researchers in molecular psychiatry have recently identified an anorexic-related gene, suggesting that identifying the biological causes of eating disorders may be a fruitful area of research in the near future (Vink *et al.*, 2001).

Family risk factors that have been represented in correlational studies attempting to predict eating disorders include: parental overprotection, parental psychopathology, parental

Table 14.5. Risk factors for eating disorders.

Individual risk factors:
Biology
  Early maturation.
  Overweight status.
Personality
  Low self-esteem.
  Impulsiveness.
  Inadequate coping skills.
  Negative affect body dissatisfaction.
  Perfectionism.
Behavior
  Dietary restraint.
  Initiation of dating.
  Weight concerns.
Family risk factors:
Parental
  Obesity.
  Overprotection.
  Loss or absence.
  Psychopathology.
  Neglect.
  Physical or sexual abuse.
Familial
  Conflict.
  Concerns about shape or weight.
  Immediate relative with eating disorder.
Sociocultural risk factors:
Peer
  Weight concerns among peers.
  Teasing by peers.
  Thin ideal by in-group or sorority.
  Thin ideal for sport or team membership.
Societal
  Thin beauty ideal by dominant culture.
  Emphasis on physical appearance for success.
  Gender role conflict.
  Media influences.

obesity, parental loss or absence, parental neglect, physical or sexual abuse, family conflict, family criticism/concerns about shape or weight and having another family member with an eating disorder (Shisslak and Crago, 2001; Worobey, 2002). For example, recent research with high school students has revealed that weight concerns among family members were not a significant predictor of bulimic symptoms, but actual bulimic behaviors by family members served to predict symptoms of bulimia nervosa among the study's participants (Pike, 1995). In another approach, adolescent girls with eating disorders are matched for age and socio-economic status with healthy controls. In such studies, the girls with eating disorders appear to have parents who force them to behave in an exaggerated feminine manner or force them to engage in activities reflecting the parents' ambitions rather than their own (Horesh *et al.*, 1996).

Sociocultural risk factors that have been identified as correlates of eating disorders range from peer to societal influences. Among them are: weight concerns among friends or peers, teasing about weight or shape, a thin beauty ideal for women, an emphasis on appearance for success by women, gender role conflict and media influences (Shisslak and Crago, 2001). A recent study that examined a variety of possible factors relevant to weight concerns, revealed the importance that peers put on weight and eating to be strongest predictor of weight concerns in elementary and middle schoolgirls (Taylor *et al.*, 1998). In another study with middle school girls, the influence of the media in shaping attitudes toward weight was clearly illustrated. The strongest predictor of drive for thinness, weight management and eating disturbances was the extent to which these girls reported that fashion and beauty magazines were an important source of information for them about beauty, diet, fitness and ideal shape (Levine *et al.*, 1994).

Disordered eating, amenorrhea, and osteoporosis are a dangerous combination of problems for which young women who engage in certain competitive sports may be at risk. Collectively, this syndrome is known as the *female athlete triad*, and is seen in sports such as gymnastics and figure skating. Risk factors for athletes include young age, pressure to excel at a chosen sport, focus on achieving or maintaining an ideal body weight or fat percentage, dieting at an early age and participation in competitions that judge performance on aesthetic appeal (Whitney and Rolfes, 2002). Using these guidelines, girls who pursue ballet or cheerleading, and boys who make the wrestling, gymnastics, or crew teams, may also be at risk for disordered eating.

As intuitively reasonable as these risk factors appear to be, however, researchers who study eating disorders have been clear to point out the limitations of these studies. Whether a study is simply a concurrent analysis of variables that are associated with distressed eating attitudes or a retrospective analysis of factors in the histories of eating disordered patients, correlations should not imply causality. To truly qualify as a risk factor then, researchers have proposed that longitudinal (or prospective) studies are necessary to demonstrate a temporal linkage between antecedents and consequences, and ideally, experimental studies of possible risk factors must be conducted to demonstrate causality.

Two recent review articles provide an excellent summary of the current literature on risk factors for eating disorders. Shisslak and Crago (2001) reviewed 26 longitudinal studies that purported to examine any number of risk factors, as long as they provided prospective data. Studies from across the world were reviewed, although the majority of them (77%) were conducted in the USA or England. Based on their analysis, they concluded that eight factors met the criteria of having been supported by two or more longitudinal studies. Four of the factors were specific to eating disorders (i.e. weight concerns, being overweight, body dissatisfaction and dietary restraint) and four additional factors could be considered general (i.e. early maturation, low self-esteem, depression and negative emotionality).

Using a somewhat different approach, Stice (2001) sought to review evidence for only those factors that were supported in at least one prospective or experimental study. His analysis included 41 studies, with 23 that were longitudinal and an additional 18 that were experimental. His list of possible risk factors included adiposity, thin-ideal internalization, body dissatisfaction, dieting, sociocultural pressures to be thin, negative affectivity, perfectionism, timing of puberty, external behaviors, self-esteem, childhood sexual abuse, dysfunctional family systems and awareness of one's internal experience. To attribute causality to a factor, results from longitudinal studies had to be consistent or the hypotheses from experiments had to be supported. Using these criteria his list of causal factors was reduced to four, namely: sociocultural pressures to be thin, body dissatisfaction, thin-ideal internalization and negative affectivity.

The results of these two reviews are fairly consistent. Drawing on their respective conclusions, Table 14.6 displays the risk factors for which some empirical support exists for their potential to cause an eating disorder. The word *potential* is used since any one of these factors is unlikely to induce an eating disorder by itself. Thus any one of them may be a necessity, but by itself, an insufficient cause of disordered eating. For example, certain factors, such as childhood sexual abuse or family dysfunction, do not appear to have support beyond correlational investigations, hence are not viewed as causes. Some factors, such as depression or perfectionism, may interact with other factors to encourage disordered eating, so their causal influence is also questionable (Vohs *et al.*, 1999). Other factors, such as self-esteem, have received empirical support in some prospective studies (Williamson et al., 1995), but have not in others (Keel *et al.*, 1997; Calam and Waller, 1998). The same is true for the timing of puberty (Smolak *et al.*, 1993; Swarr and Richards, 1996). In other instances, some of the factors have the results of correlational as well as prospective research in their favor, but without confirmatory experimental evidence are seen as having only modest support. For example, numerous longitudinal studies show dieting to be a precursor to eating pathology (e.g. Killen *et al.*, 1996; Stice and Agras, 1998). However, a number of exper-

Table 14.6. Risk factors for eating disorders that have demonstrated empirical support.

Correlational Factors
Adiposity.
Depression.
Dieting/dietary restraint.
Dysfunctional parents or family.
Impulsivity/externalizing behavior.
Interoceptive awareness.
Media influences.
Perfectionism.
Self-esteem.
Sexual abuse.
Timing of puberty.
Weight concerns.

Causal Factors
Body dissatisfaction.
Negative affectivity.
Sociocultural pressures to be thin.
Thin-ideal internalization.

iments have shown that long-term dieting results in decreased binge eating and caloric intake (e.g. Wadden *et al.,* 1994; Goodrick *et al.,* 1998).

In sum, although a myriad of risk factors for eating disorders have been identified in hundreds of investigations, adhering to a criterion of prospective and experimental studies serves to reduce the number to a less extensive though no less important listing. Future efforts at determining what factors best predict the onset of an eating disorder will do well to employ multiple methods of data collection, and use developmentally appropriate samples in order to capture the etiologic process as it unfolds. Identifying the interactions between risk factors, examining them over time, and testing pertinent variables in laboratory and ecological experiments are approaches that future research is likely to take. At the same time, new risk factors, mediating factors and protective factors must continue to be investigated, as current models still only explain a small part of the variance in disordered eating (Shisslak and Crago, 2001; Stice, 2001).

Treatment of Eating Disorders

As indicated earlier, both anorexia nervosa and, to a lesser degree, bulimia nervosa can be life threatening. The relatively high mortality rates for these psychiatric disturbances, as well as their other detrimental consequences, make the early detection and treatment of these diseases a critical matter. Because of the complexities of these disorders, a multidimensional treatment approach is usually attempted. The initial step in the medical management of the patient is to correctly diagnose the disorder. A careful medical history including inquiries about dietary habits, weight fluctuations and menstrual irregularities should be taken. This should be followed by a complete physical examination that includes blood tests, thyroid function tests, renal function tests and an electrocardiogram. The physical examination will also allow for the detection of delayed secondary sexual characteristics, lanugo and carotenemia (Hill and Pomeroy, 2001). A psychiatric assessment of the individual and the family should also be undertaken, with questions that examine attitudes toward food and body image disturbance.

For a diagnosis of anorexia nervosa, the first concern is nutritional rehabilitation, which should be planned by the physician in consultation with a registered dietitian. Without correcting the starvation-state and starvation-induced emotional and cognitive states, the patient will not benefit from the accompanying psychological treatment. Caloric increases must be individualized to the patient's medical condition, and must be gradual because rapid caloric replacement during refeeding can be complicated by life-threatening pancreatitis or cardiomyopathy. Normal feeding is preferable to tube feeding or total parenteral nutrition, except for rare emergencies (Mehler and Weiner, 1993). Any therapeutic plan should be individualized, but the patient is typically given 1400 to 1800 kcal per day to start, with a goal of gaining 1 to 2 lb per week (under a kilogram) (Pomeroy, 1996).

Although an eating disorders unit or specialized center is the ideal location for inpatient treatment of anorexia nervosa, there are some conditions when hospitalization may be necessary. Indeed, approximately one-half of patients with anorexia nervosa require hospitalization (Hill and Pomeroy, 2001). Severe or rapid weight loss, that is, weighing less than 75% of the ideal, is a major signal for requiring hospitalization (Hill and Pomeroy, 2001). In addition, life-threatening physical complications such as severe electrolyte imbalances, cardiac arrhythmias and dehydration, risk of suicide or if the patient's social situation interferes with outpatient treatment, are all justifiable reasons for hospitalization (Gore *et al.* 2001). If the patient cannot eat enough on her own to gain half a pound every other day, nasogastric tube feedings with a liquid dietary supplement should begin. It is important, however, that the anorexic patient has a chance to refeed herself before resorting to tube feeding. It is also beneficial to tell the patient that her weight will be carefully monitored so that she does not gain weight 'too fast' (Hill and Pomeroy, 2001).

As the patient adjusts to this feeding regimen, caloric intake is slowly increased by about 300 kcal every other day. A critical feature of effective nutritional management is a therapeutic staff of nurses and a dietitian who can provide the patient with encouragement and support in her efforts to confront her ambivalence and compulsions. The nutritional program may require bed rest until a stable weight gain is evident, informational feedback about weight and calories and gradual assumption of control of eating by the patient. Once the patient begins to gain weight and appears to be motivated, psychological treatment can be instituted (Yager, 1989).

If bulimia nervosa is diagnosed, nutritional counseling may take the form of healthy meal planning in order to normalize eating patterns. Hospitalization is rarely necessary, although inpatient monitoring may be recommended if the patient's medical condition is unstable because of recurrent bingeing and purging or the abuse of laxatives or diuretics that create electrolyte disturbances. The treatment team must lay a solid foundation for nutrition education for the patient, help prevent the sequence of starvation, hunger and overeating, and address her distorted body image and fears of weight gain (Hill and Pomeroy, 2001).

Psychological treatment

Despite the nutritional implications of anorexia and bulimia nervosa in terms of reduced or inconsistent caloric intake and concomitant weight loss, it is clear that these eating disorders are usually psychological in their origin and maintenance. Therefore, it should be no surprise that the primary methods of treatment take a psychological approach. What may be surprising, however, given the relatively recent identification of bulimia nervosa as compared to anorexia nervosa, is that a greater number of well-designed studies of treatment for bulimia exist than for anorexia. This may be due in part to the danger inherent in placing anorexic patients who are at physical risk in a 'no treatment' control group for the purposes of an experiment (Gleaves et al., 2000). Even designs where patients receiving treatment are compared to those who are waiting for treatment may be unethical. For example, in what may be the most methodologically sound study conducted on treatment for anorexia nervosa to date, the researchers reported that three

patients actually died during treatment or while in the 'waiting list' control group (Crisp et al., 1991). As emphasized in Chapter 2, however, experimental approaches are the best way to ensure causality. In this regard, comparative studies, where two or more treatments are compared to each other or a new treatment is compared to a treatment as usual, may be the most ethical approach to advance our understanding of the efficacy of psychotherapy for eating disorders (Gleaves et al., 2000).

No one type of psychotherapy is ideal for anorexia or bulimia nervosa, as even the best therapeutic approaches fall short of helping all patients. Rather, psychotherapeutic strategies must be tailored to the cognitive styles, psychological profiles and developmental levels of the participants. As each patient truly is unique, it is perhaps fitting that a wide variety of therapies for the treatment of eating disorders have been formulated throughout the years. As shown in Table 14.7, no less than ten distinct approaches are currently espoused, though some do appear to be more effective than others (Garner and Needleman, 1996; Miller and Mizes, 2000). The treatments that have received the most empirical research, and are arguably the most effective, are behavior therapy, family therapy, interpersonal therapy and cognitive-behavioral therapy, and will be discussed next.

As applied to bulimia nervosa, the aim of *behavior therapy* (BT) is to alter the environmental antecedents and consequences that are assumed to initiate and maintain the bingeing and purging cycle. Through self-monitoring, the patient assists in identifying the factors that set off her loss of control. Behavioral approaches also include meal planning, psychoeducation and attempts to get the client to reduce dietary restraint (Thackwray et al., 1993). Behavioral treatments sometimes employ a technique called *exposure with response prevention*, wherein patients are exposed to and encouraged to eat foods they view as forbidden, but are then not allowed to purge. Based on the anxiety model of bulimia nervosa, (Williamson, 1990), this approach is somewhat controversial, as its aversiveness to the patient may actually detract from the efficacy of the intervention (Agras et al., 1989).

The outcome studies of BT have shown mixed results, as it has been found to decrease

Table 14.7. Psychotherapeutic approaches for the treatment of eating disorders.

Cognitive-behavioral.
Behavior therapy.
Integrative cognitive.
Interpersonal.
Family.
Supportive expression.
Psychodynamic/psychoanalytic.
Developmental-systems-feminist.
Self-psychology.
Elementary pragmatic.

bingeing, vomiting and depression by some researchers but not others. While it may be not be remarkably effective in isolation, behavioral techniques may be very useful if incorporated into other treatments (see below). For example, behavioral techniques such as exposure, relaxation, modeling and reinforcement are useful in treating anxiety. With respect to anorexics, behavioral techniques such as granting privileges for weight gain have been successfully employed (Gore *et al.*, 2001).

Originally developed for the treatment of anorexia nervosa, *family therapy* (FT) has now been extended to bulimia nervosa. Family therapists argue that the eating disorder may have a distinctive role in precipitating or maintaining certain dysfunctional alliances, conflicts, or interaction patterns within the girl's family. In addition, the eating disorder may serve as a maladaptive solution to the girl's struggle to achieve autonomy, while providing a means by which the parents and child can avoid major conflict (Garner and Needleman, 1996). By observing the family, issues of communication, loyalties, separation and individuation, enmeshment, overprotectiveness and conflict resolution are brought out and dealt with. The emphasis is not on placing blame, but on identifying problematic functions within the family that may be hindering the patient's recovery (Gleaves *et al.*, 2000).

Family therapy has been shown to be especially well-suited for treating families of anorexic girls who are 18 years old or younger and who have had symptoms for a relatively short period of time (Eisler *et al.*, 1997). Therapy that addresses family communication,

conflict and cohesion appears to be beneficial in helping anorexics to gain weight. These findings suggest that FT may be effective with bulimia nervosa as well, although its appropriateness as the sole treatment for bulimia requires further validation (Gore *et al.*, 2001).

The focus of treatment in *interpersonal therapy* (IPT) is on four categories of events that seem to trigger problematic behaviors, that is, grief, role transitions, interpersonal role disputes and interpersonal deficits. For those with bulimia nervosa, role transitions and interpersonal role disputes are most often the focus in therapy (Fairburn, 1993). Treatment involves identifying the interpersonal problems that triggered the development and maintenance of the eating difficulties, devising a therapeutic contract for working on the interpersonal problems and addressing issues related to termination (Wilfley *et al.*, 2000). With respect to eating disorders, what is most remarkable about this treatment method is that it does not directly address eating behavior or attitudes toward eating, weight or body image. As its name implies, the emphasis is solely on improving the patient's interpersonal relationships.

Interpersonal therapy has shown some promise in treating bulimia nervosa in adults, being comparable to BT in reducing dietary restraint, and being more effective than BT in decreasing patients' concerns about their body shape (Fairburn *et al.*, 1991). The applicability of this approach to eating disordered patients who have not yet reached adulthood is feasible, if the focus is directed to the developmental changes that accompany adolescence (Gore *et al.*, 2001).

A fourth approach, cognitive-behavioral therapy (CBT), combines behavioral techniques, such as self-monitoring of food intake and stimulus control, with cognitive strategies designed to combat dysfunctional thoughts about food and weight (Wilson and Pike, 1993). Techniques for coping and preventing relapses are also typically included. It is the most widely studied psychotherapeutic approach for the treatment of bulimia nervosa (Wilson and Fairburn, 1998), but given the greater difficulties in treating anorexia nervosa, there is not as an established database for its efficacy with the latter. As shown in Table 14.8, the approach is highly structured, with 20 sessions spread over a few months for bulimic patients, and 50 sessions over a year for anorexic patients (Pike et al., 1996).

Cognitive-behavioral therapy has been found to decrease bulimic and depressive symptomatology, increase overall adjustment and improve body image adjustment, with these improvements being maintained for at least a year after treatment (Gore et al., 2001). Although the mechanism by which CBT achieves its success is not entirely clear, changing the patient's beliefs and behaviors are thought to be critical. One theory suggests that changing beliefs about the body will lead to changes in eating, while another suggests that changing the eating and purging behavior is what leads to feelings of self-efficacy (Wilson and Fairburn, 1993).

In a landmark study, Fairburn and his colleagues compared the relative efficacy of three of the aforementioned treatment approaches with bulimic patients, namely, behavior therapy, interpersonal therapy and cognitive-behavioral therapy. True to their standard forms, BT focused only on changing eating habits and behaviors, IPT focused on improving interpersonal relationships without addressing eating behavior or attitudes about weight or shape and CBT focused on changing beliefs about weight and shape as well as eating behavior (Fairburn et al., 1991). At the end of the treatment, CBT was found to be superior to the other types with respect to reducing dietary restraint, and equivalent to BT in their greater decrease of vomiting behavior, relative to IPT. Cognitive behavior therapy was also superior to IPT in changing concerns about weight and lowering scores on a measure of disturbed eating habits and attitudes. At the 1-year follow-up, CBT was still superior to BT in decreasing concerns about weight and body shape, as well as in reducing bingeing and purging, but the IPT group was now equivalent to the CBT group (Fairburn et al., 1993). At a 5-year follow-up, the CBT and IPT groups showed a significant and comparable reduction in dietary restraint and shape and weight con-

---

Table 14.8. Phases of cognitive-behavior therapy (CBT).

Phase 1
    a. build a therapeutic alliance
    b. establish the role of the patient as an active collaborator in treatment
    c. assess the core patterns and features of the patient's particular eating disorder
    d. orient the patient to the CBT model of eating disorders
    e. educate the patient about the importance of homework in CBT
    f. establish monitoring procedures for eating and weight
    g. eliminate dieting and normalizing eating throughout the day
    h. develop delay strategies and alternatives to binge eating and purging
    i. learn the skills of imagery, rehearsal and relaxation training
    j. challenge assumptions about the overvaluation of shape and weight
    k. provide psychoeducational information to the patient.

Phase 2
    a. eliminate forbidden foods
    b. identify dysfunctional thoughts
    c. cognitive restructuring
    d. problem solving
    e. continue to challenge assumptions overvaluing weight and shape
    f. broaden the focus of treatment by identifying and challenging the eating disorder self-schema and developing alternative bases for self-evaluation.

Phase 3
    a. review high-risk situations and specific strategies to prevent relapse
    b. promote adaptive coping skills
    c. facilitate recovery from slips.

Source: adapted from Pike et al., 1996.

cerns relative to the pretreatment assessments (Fairburn *et al.*, 1995).

The work of Fairburn and his colleagues clearly substantiates the effectiveness of CBT with bulimic patients, and provides some of the evidence that has led many to consider cognitive-behavioral therapy to be the single best therapy currently available for the treatment of eating disorders (Striegel-Moore and Smolak, 2001). However, their reporting that interpersonal therapy – which did not directly address eating behavior or eating-related attitudes – was just as effective as CBT is an important finding. Given that CBT falls short of helping all patients, a new approach known as *integrative cognitive therapy* has extended the focus of CBT to interpersonal relationships and interpersonal schemas as well as addressing emotional responding and cultural factors (Wonderlich *et al.*, 2001). It is therefore certain that researchers and therapists will continue to evaluate the components of various treatments, while developing and testing other approaches to determine what may be most effective in facilitating the recovery of victims who struggle with eating disorders.

Pharmacological treatment

Although this chapter has emphasized behavioral approaches to the treatment of eating disorders, some mention should be made of the use of medication, as a variety of pharmacological interventions have been employed either in addition to or instead of psychotherapy. Early efforts to treat anorexia nervosa, for example, were based on the idea of treating the delusional beliefs of the anorexic concerning her body weight and image. Hence, drugs that had been developed to treat psychosis, such as L-dopa and lithium, were used with limited success (Mitchell, 1989). More recently, drug treatments have been derived from basic research on the mechanisms of food intake and the regulation of body weight. To date, various appetite stimulants, neuroleptics, opioid antagonists and antidepressants have been tried, but none have been shown to treat the core psychopathology of the disorder (Johnson *et al.*, 1996). Antidepressants are most typically used in an attempt to treat the

accompanying psychopathology such as obsessive-compulsive disorder or depression. Fluoxetine hydrochloride (marketed as *Prozac*™), one of a class of drugs called *selective serotonin reuptake inhibitors*, has shown some recent success in helping recovering anorexics to sustain a normal weight for a year post-hospitalization (Kaye *et al.*, 2001).

Since the symptoms of depression are also common to bulimia, researchers were quick to initiate studies on the effectiveness of antidepressants in ameliorating depression and anxiety in bulimics, as well as in altering their feeding behavior. Several types of antidepressants have been found to be effective in reducing bingeing and purging (Crow and Mitchell, 1996). Serotonin reuptake inhibitors like fluoxetine appear to be the drug of choice for a number of reasons (i) its effectiveness in treating bulimia nervosa is not simply secondary to its effect on depression; (ii) the side effects are less than with tricyclic antidepressants or monoamine-oxidase inhibitors; (iii) improved body satisfaction also seems to result (Goldstein *et al.*, 1999).

The major limitation of pharmacological interventions is that their effectiveness may be short-lived. Patients have been known to relapse after the medication is terminated, though a longer period of treatment may predict longer success (Agras, 1997). However, some studies have shown that even if kept on medication, one-third of bulimics may relapse (Walsh and Devlin, 1995). Antidepressants have been used for children with eating disorders in some cases, though the use of medication may be considered as a last resort if the juvenile has not responded to earlier attempts with psychotherapy or there is also severe depression (Robin *et al.*, 1998).

Conclusion

Our awareness of eating disorders such as anorexia nervosa and bulimia nervosa seems to have grown as rapidly as the incidence of the afflictions themselves. In addition to the number of individuals who may be formally diagnosed, tens of thousands more exhibit some of the signs of an eating disorder. To address this problem, thousands of studies have been conducted over the last 20 years, with clinicians, researchers, parents and spouses desperate for an answer to a problem that seems so hard to be understood. How can one explain the unnatural behaviors of self-starvation or self-abuse via bingeing and purging? As we have discussed throughout this chapter, there may be innumerable factors that act on the developing child or adolescent that influences her relationship with food. Armed with the knowledge of these factors, those that study and treat eating disorders must be joined by those who will try to prevent these disorders.

While the growing number of anorexics, bulimics, and those with subthreshold eating disorders has not yet reached epidemic proportions, in Chapter 15 we will address a serious outcome of eating that does qualify as an epidemic – the increase in overweight persons and obesity in developed nations. Despite their differential outcomes in the extreme cases, that is, emaciation versus morbid obesity, individuals who suffer with either problem have much in common. Both belong to more heterogeneous groups than we first assumed. We will now examine the demographics, personalities, family dynamics and etiology of those who struggle with the reality of overweight.

References

Abrams, K., Allen, L. and Gray, J. (1993) Disordered eating attitudes and behaviors, psychological adjustment and ethnic identity: a comparison of black and white female college students. *International Journal of Eating Disorders* 14, 49–57.

Agras, W.S. (1997) Pharmacotherapy of bulimia nervosa and binge eating disorder: longer-term outcomes. *Psychopharmacology Bulletin* 33(3), 433–436.

Agras, W.S., Schneider, J.A., Arnow, B., Raeburn, S.D. and Telch, C.F. (1989) Cognitive-behavioural and response-prevention treatments for bulimia nervosa. *Journal of Consulting and Clinical Psychology* 57, 215–221.

Andersen, A.E. and Holman, J.E. (1997) Males with eating disorders: challenges for treatment and research. *Psychopharmacology Bulletin* 33(3), 391–397.

Bell, R.M. (1985) *Holy anorexia*. University of Chicago Press, Chicago.

Berg, F. (1992) Harmful weight loss practices are widespread among adolescents. *Healthy Weight Journal/Obesity & Health* 6(4), 69–72.

Birketvedt, G.S., Florholmen, J., Sundsfjord, J., Osterud, B., Dinges, D., Bilker, W. and Stunkard, A. (1999) Behavioral and neuroendocrine characteristics of the night-eating syndrome. *Journal of the American Medical Association* 282, 657–663.

Booth, D.A. (1994) *Psychology of Nutrition*. Taylor & Francis, London.

Bruch, H. (1973) *Eating Disorders: Obesity, Anorexia Nervosa, and the Person Within*. Basic Books, New York.

Bruch, H. (1985) Four decades of eating disorders. In: Garner, D.M. and Garfinkel, P.E. (eds) *Handbook of Psychotherapy for Anorexia Nervosa & Bulimia*. Guilford Press, New York, pp. 7–18.

Calam, R. and Waller, G. (1998) Are eating and psychosocial characteristics in early teenage years useful predictors of eating characteristics in early adulthood? *International Journal of Eating Disorders* 24, 351–362.

Cauffman, E. and Steinberg, L. (1996) Interactive effects of menarcheal status and dating on dieting and disordered eating among adolescent girls. *Developmental Psychology* 32(4), 631–635.

Crisp, A.H., Norton, K., Gowers, S., Halek, C., Bowyer, C., Yeldham, D., Levett, G. and Bhat, A. (1991) A controlled study of the effects of therapies aimed at adolescent and family psychopathology in anorexia nervosa. *British Journal of Psychiatry* 159, 325–333.

Crow, S.J. and Mitchell, J.E. (1996) Pharmacologic treatments for eating disorders. In: Thompson, J.K. (ed.) *Body Image, Eating Disorders, and Obesity: An Integrative Guide for Assessment and Treatment*. American Psychological Association, Washington, DC, pp. 345–360.

Davison, K.K., Markey, C.N. and Birch, L.L. (2000) Etiology of body dissatisfaction and weight concerns in 5-year old girls. *Appetite* 35, 143–151.

Diagnostic and Statistical Manual of Mental Disorders, 4th edn. (1994) American Psychiatric Association, Washington, DC.

Doyle, J. and Bryant-Waugh, R. (2000) Epidemiology. In: Lask, B. and Bryant-Waugh, R. (eds) *Anorexia Nervosa and Related Eating Disorders in Childhood and Adolescence*, 2nd edn. Psychology Press, East Sussex, UK, pp. 41–79.

Eisler, I., Dare, C., Russell, G.F.M., Szmukler, G., LeGrange, D. and Dodge, E. (1997). Family and individual therapy in anorexia nervosa: a 5-year follow-up. *Archives of General Psychiatry* 54, 1025–1030.

Fairburn, C.G. (1993) Interpersonal psychotherapy for bulimia nervosa. In: Klerman, G.L. and Weissman, M.M. (eds) *New Applications of Interpersonal Psychotherapy.* American Psychiatric Press ,Washington, DC, pp. 353–378.

Fairburn, C.G. and Beglin, S.J. (1990) Studies of the epidemiology of bulimia nervosa. *American Journal of Psychiatry* 147, 401–408.

Fairburn, C.G., Jones, R., Peveler, R.C., Carr, S.J., Solomon, R.A., O'Conner, M.E., Burton, J. and Hope, R.A. (1991) Three psychological treatments for bulimia nervosa: a comparative trial. *Archives of General Psychiatry* 48(5), 463–469.

Fairburn, C.G., Jones, R., Peveler, R.C., Hope, R.A. and O'Conner, M. (1993) Psychotherapy and bulimia nervosa: longer-term effects of interpersonal psychotherapy, behavior therapy, and cognitive behavior therapy. *Archives of General Psychiatry* 50, 419–428.

Fairburn, C.G., Norman, P.A., Welch, S.L., O'Conner, M.E., Doll, H.A., and Peveler, R.C. (1995) A prospective study of outcome in bulimia nervosa and the long-term effects of three psychological treatments. *Archives of General Psychiatry* 52, 304–312.

Fallon, A. and Bunce, S. (2000) The psychoanalytic perspective. In: Miller, K.J. and Mizes, J.S. (eds) *ComparativeTtreatments for Eating Disorders.* Springer Publishing Company, New York, pp. 82–127.

Furnham, A., and Alibhai, N. (1983) Cross-cultural differences in the perception of female body shapes. *Psychological Medicine* 13, 829–837.

Forthum, L.F., Pidcock, B.W., and Fischer J.L. (2003) Religiousness and disordered eating: does religiousness modify family risk? *Eating Behaviours,* 4(1), 7–26.

Gard, M.C. and Freeman, C.P. (1996) The dismantling of a myth: a review of eating disorders and socioeconomic status. *International Journal of Eating Disorders* 20(1), 1–12.

Garfinkel, P.E., Lin, E., Goering, P., Spegg, C., Goldbloom, D., Kennedy, S., Kaplan, A. and Woodsie, B. (1995) Bulimia nervosa in a Canadian community sample: prevalence, comorbidity, early experiences and psychosocial functioning. *American Journal of Psychiatry* 152, 1052–1058.

Garner, D.M., Garfinkel, P.E., Stancer, H.C. and Moldofsky, H. (1976) Body image disturbances in anorexia nervosa and obesity. *Psychosomatic Medicine* 38(5), 327–336.

Garner, D.M. and Needleman, L.D. (1996) Stepped-care and decision-tree models for treating eating disorders. In: Thompson, J.K. (ed.) *Body Image, Eating Disorders, and Obesity: An Integrative Guide for Assessment and Treatment.* American Psychological Association, Washington, DC, pp. 225–252.

Gleaves, D.H., Miller, K.J., Williams, T.L. and Summers, S.A. (2000) Eating disorders: an overview. In: Miller, K.J. and Mizes, J.S. (eds.) *Comparative Treatments for Eating Disorders.* Springer Publishing Company, New York.

Godart, N.T., Flament, M.F., Lecrubier, Y. and Jeammer, P. (2000) Anxiety disorders in anorexia nervosa and bulimia nervosa: comorbidity and chronology of appearance. *European Psychology* 15, 38–45.

Goldstein, D.J., Wilson, M.G., Ascroft, R.C. and Al-Banna, M. (1999) Effectiveness of fluoxetine therapy in bulimia nervosa regardless of comorbid depression. *International Journal of Eating Disorders* 25, 19–27.

Goodrick, G.K., Poston, W.S., Kimball, K.T., Reeves, R.S. and Foreyt, J.P. (1998) Nondieting versus dieting treatments for overweight binge-eating women. *Journal of Consulting and Clinical Psychology* 66, 363–368.

Gordon, R.A. (2000) *Eating Disorders: anatomy of a Social Epidemic.* Blackwell Publishers, Malden, Massachusetts.

Gore, S.A., Vander Wal, J.S. and Thelen, M.H. (2001) Treatment of eating disorders in children and adolescents. In: Thompson, J.K. and Smolak, L. (eds) *Body Image, Eating Disorders, and Obesity in Youth: Assessment, Prevention, and Treatment.* American Psychological Association, Washington, DC, pp. 293–311.

Greenfield, D., Mickley, D., Quinlan, D.M. and Roloff, P. (1995) Hypokalemia in outpatients with eating disorders. *American Journal of Psychiatry* 152(1), 60–63.

Gull, W.W. (1874) Anorexia nervosa. *Transactions of the Clinical Society of London* 7, 22–28.

Gustafson-Larson, A. and Terry, R. (1992) Weight-related behaviors and concerns of fourth-grade children. *Journal of the American Dietetic Association* 92, 818–822.

Gwirtsman, H.E., Kaye, W.H., George, D.T., Jimerson, D.C., Ebert, M.H. and Gold, P.W. (1989) Central and peripheral ACT4 and cortisol levels in anorexia nervosa and bulimia. *Archives of General Psychiatry* 46, 61–69.

Halmi, K.A., Sunday, S.R., Strober, M., Kaplan, A., Woodside, Fichter, Treasure, Berrettini and Kaye (2001) Perfectionism in anorexia nervosa: variation by clinical subtype, obsessionality, and pathological eating behavior. *American Journal of Psychiatry* 157(11), 1799–1805.

Heatherton, T.F., Nichols, P., Mahamedi, F. and Keel, P. (1995) Body weight, dieting, and eating disorder symptoms among college students,

1982–1992. *American Journal of Psychiatry* 152, 1623–1629.

Heinberg, L.J., Wood, K.C. and Thompson, J.K. (1995) Body Image. In: Rickett, V.I. (ed.) *Adolescent Nutrition: Assessment and Management.* Chapman and Hall, New York, pp. 136–156.

Herzog, D. and Bradburn, I. (1992) The nature of anorexia nervosa and bulimia nervosa in adolescents. In: Cooper, P.J. and Stein, A. (eds) *Feeding Problems and Eating Disorders in Children and Adolescents.* Harwood Academic, Chur, Switzerland, pp. 126–135.

Hetherington, M.M. (2000) Eating disorders: diagnosis, etiology, and prevention. *Nutrition* 16, 547–551.

Hill, K. and Pomeroy, C. (2001) Assessment of physical status of children and adolescents with eating disorders and obesity. In: Thompson, J.K. and Smolak, L. (eds) *Body Image, Eating Disorders, and Obesity in Youth: Assessment, Prevention, and Treatment.* American Psychological Association, Washington, DC pp. 171–191.

Horesh, N., Apter, A., Ishai, J., Danziger, Y., Miculincer, M., Stein, D., Lepkifker, E. and Minouni, M. (1996) Abnormal psychosocial situations and eating disorders in adolescence. *Journal of the American Academy of Child and Adolescent Psychiatry* 35, 921–927.

Horowitz, L.M. (2004) Interpersonal foundations of psychopathology. American Psychological Association, Washington, DC.

Insel, P., Tumer, R.E. and Ross, D. (2004) *Nutrition.* Jones and Barlett, Sudbury Massachussets, p. 556.

Johnson, C.L., Stuckey, M.K., Lewis, L.D. and Schwartz, D.M. (1981) Bulimia: a descriptive survey of 316 cases. *International Journal of Eating Disorders* 2, 3–15.

Johnson, W.G., Tsoh, J.Y. and Varnado, P.J. (1996) Eating disorders: efficacy of pharmacological and psychological interventions. *Clinical Psychology Review* 16, 457–478.

Kaye, W.H., Nagata, T., Weltzin, T.E., Hsu, G., Sokol, M.S., McConaha, C., Plotnicov, K.H., Weise, J. and Deep, D. (2001) Double-blind placebo-controlled administration of Fluoxetine in restricting- and restricting-purging-type anorexia nervosa. *Biological Psychiatry* 49(7), 644–652.

Keel, P.K., Fulkerson, J.A. and Leon, G.R. (1997) Disordered eating precursors in pre- and early adolescent girls and boys. *Journal of Youth and Adolescence* 26, 203–216.

Killen, J.D., Taylor, C.B., Hayward, C., Haydel, K.F., Wilson, D.M., Hammer, L., Kraemer, H., Blair-Greiner, A. and Strachowski, D. (1996) Weight concerns influence the development of eating disorders. A 4-year prospective study. *Journal of Consulting and Clinical Psychology* 64, 936–940.

Le Grange, D., Telch, C.F. and Tibbs, J. (1998) Eating attitudes and behaviors in 1,435 South African Caucasian and Non-Caucasian college students. *American Journal of Psychiatry* 155, 250–254.

Levine, M.P., Smolak, L. and Hayden, H. (1994) The relation of sociocultural factors to eating attitudes and behaviors among middle school girls. *Journal of Early Adolescence* 14, 471–490.

Logue, A.W. (1991) *The Psychology of Eating and Drinking: An Introduction.* Freeman and Company, New York.

Lucas, A.R., Beard, C.M., O'Fallon, W.M. and Kurland, L.T. (1991) 50-year trends in the incidence of anorexia nervosa in Rochester, Minnesota: a population-based study. *American Journal of Psychiatry* 148, 917–922.

Maloney, M.J. (1995) Eating disorders during adolescence. *Anneles Nestlé* 53, 101.

McClain, C.J., Humphries, L.L., Hill, K.K. and Nickl, N.J. (1993) Gastrointestinal and nutritional aspects of eating disorders. *Journal of the American College of Nutrition* 12(4), 466–474.

McGilley, B.M. and Pryor, T.L. (1998) Assessment and treatment of anorexia nervosa. *American Family Physician* 63, 2743–2752.

Mehler, P.S. and Weiner, K.L. (1993) Anorexia nervosa and total parental nutrition. *International Journal of Eating Disorders* 14, 297–304.

Miller, K.J. and Mizes, J.S. (2000) *Comparative treatments for eating disorders.* Springer Publishing Company, New York.

Mitchell, J.E. (1989) Psychopharmacology of eating disorders. *Annals of the New York Academy of Sciences* 517, 41–48.

Mumford, D.B., Whitehouse, A.M. and Platts, M. (1991) Sociocultural correlates of eating disorders among Asian schoolgirls in Bradford. *British Journal of Psychiatry* 158, 222–228.

Nasser, M. (1986) Comparative study of the prevalence of abnormal eating attitudes among Arab female students of both London and Cairo Universities. *Psychological Medicine* 16, 621–625.

Netemeyer, S.B. and Williamson, D.A. (2001) Assessment of eating disturbance in children and adolescents with eating disorders and obesity. In: Thompson, J.K. and Smolak, L. (eds), *Body Image, Eating Disorders, and Obesity in Youth: Assessment, Prevention, and Treatment.* American Psychological Association, Washington, DC, pp. 215–233.

Nicholls, D., Chater, R. and Lask, B. (2000) Children into DSM don't go: a comparison of classification systems for eating disorders in childhood and early adolescence. *International Journal of Eating Disorders* 28, 317–324.

Parker, S., Nichter, M., Nichter, N., Vuckovic, N., Sims, C. and Ritenbaugh, C. (1995) Body image and weight concerns among African American and White adolescent females: differences that make a difference. *Human Organization* 54, 103–114.

Pike, K.M. (1995) Bulimic symptomatology in high school girls. *Psychology of Women Quarterly* 19, 373–396.

Pike, K.M., Loeb, K. and Vitousek, K. (1996) Cognitive-behavioral therapy for anorexia nervosa and bulimia nervosa. In: Thompson, J.K. (ed.) *Body Image, Eating Disorders, and Obesity: An Integrative Guide for Assessment and Treatment.* American Psychological Association, Washington, DC, pp. 253–302.

Pirke, K.M. and Ploog, D. (1986) Psychobiology of anorexia nervosa. In: Wurtman, R.J. and Wurtman, J.J. (eds) *Nutrition and the Brain,* Vol. 7. Raven Press, New York, pp. 167–198.

Pomeroy, C. (1996) Anorexia nervosa, bulimia nervosa, and binge eating disorder: assessment of physical status. In: Thompson, J.K. (ed.) *Body Image, Eating Disorders, and Obesity.* American Psychological Association, Washington, DC, pp. 177–203.

Robin, A.L., Gilroy, M. and Dennis, A.B. (1998) Treatment of eating disorders in children and adolescents. *Clinical Psychology Review* 18(4), 421–446.

Robinson, P.H. (1989). Gastric function in eating disorders. *Annals of the New York Academy of Sciences* 575, 456.

Rodin, J., Bartoshuk, L., Peterson, C. and Schank, D. (1990) Bulimia and taste: possible interactions. *Journal of Abnormal Psychology* 99(1), 32–39.

Rosenvinge, J.H., Bogen, J.S. and Boerresen, R. (1999) The prevalence of psychological correlates of anorexia nervosa, bulimia nervosa and binge-eating among 15-yr-old students: a controlled epidemiological study. *European Eating Disorders Review* 7, 382–391.

Russell, G.F.M. (1979) Bulimia nervosa: an ominous variant of anorexia nervosa. *Psychological Medicine* 9, 429–448.

Sharp, C.W. and Freeman, C.P.L. (1993) The medical complications of anorexia nervosa. *British Journal of Psychiatry* 162, 452–462.

Shisslak, C.M. and Crago, M. (2001) Risk and protective factors in the development of eating disorders. In: Thompson, J.K. and Smolak, L. (eds) *Body Image, Eating Disorders, and Obesity in Youth: Assessment, Prevention, and Treatment.* American Psychological Association, Washington, DC, pp. 103–125.

Shisslak, C.M., Crago, M. and Estes, L. (1995) The spectrum of eating disturbances. *International Journal of Eating Disorders* 18, 209–219.

Smolak, L., Levine, M.P. and Gralen, S. (1993) The impact of puberty and dating on eating problems among middle school girls. *Journal of Youth and Adolescence* 22, 355–368.

Smolak, L., Levine, M. and Thompson, J.K. (2001) Body image in adolescent boys and girls as assessed with the Sociocultural Attitudes Towards Appearance Scale. *International Journal of Eating Disorders* 29, 216–223.

Srinivasin, T.N., Suresh, T.R. and Vasantha, J. (1998) Emergence of eating disorders in India. Study of eating distress syndrome and development of a screening questionnaire. *International Journal of Social Psychiatry* 44, 189–198.

Stice, E. (2001) Risk factors for eating pathology: recent advances and future directions. In: Striegel-Moore, R.H. and Smolak, L. (eds) *Eating Disorders: Innovative Directions in Research and Practice.* American Psychological Association, Washington, DC.

Stice, E. and Agras, W.S. (1998) Predicting onset and cessation of bulimic behaviors during adolescence: a longitudinal grouping analyses. *Behavior Therapy* 29, 257–276.

Stice, E., Killen, J.D., Hayward, C. and Taylor, C.B. (1998) Age of onset for binge eating and purging during adolescence: a four year survival analysis. *Journal of Abnormal Psychology* 107, 671–675.

Striegel-Moore, R.H. and Smolak, L. (2001) *Eating Disorders: Innovative Directions in Research and Practice.* American Psychological Association, Washington, DC.

Striegel-Moore, R., Schreiber, G.B., Lo, A., Crawford, P., Obarzanek, E. and Rodin, J. (2000) Eating disorder symptoms in a cohort of 11 to 16-year-old Black and White girls: The NHLBI Growth and Health Study. *International Journal of Eating Disorders* 27, 49–66.

Striegel-Moore, R.H., Dohm, F.A., Kraemer, H.C., Taylor, C.B., Daniels, S., Crawford, P.B. and Schreiber, G.B. (2003) Eating disorders in white and black women. *American Journal of Psychiatry* 160(7), 1326–1331.

Swarr, A.E. and Richards, M.H. (1996) Longitudinal effects of adolescent girls' pubertal development, perceptions of pubertal timing, and parental relations on eating problems. *Developmental Psychology* 32, 636–646.

Taylor, C., Sharpe, T., Shisslak, C., Bryson, S., Estes, L., Gray, N., McKnight, K., Crago, M., Kraemer, H. and Killen, J. (1998) Factors associated with weight concerns in adolescent girls. *International Journal of Eating Disorders* 24, 31–42.

Thackwray, D.E., Smith, M., Bodfish, J.W. and Meyers, A.W. (1993) A comparison of behavioral and cognitive-behavioral interventions for bulimia nervosa. *Journal of Consulting and Clinical Psychology* 61, 639–645.

Thomas, M.A. and Rebar, R.W. (1990) The endocrinology of anorexia nervosa. *Current Opinion in Obstetrics and Gynecology* 2, 831–836.

Vink, T., Hinney, A., van Elburg, A.A., van Goozen, S.H.M., Sandkuijl, L.A., Sinke, R.J., Herpertz-Dahlmann, B.M., Hebebrand, J., Remschmidt, H., van Engeland, H. and Adan, R.A.H. (2001) Association between an agouti-related protein gene polymorphism and anorexia nervosa. *Molecular Psychiatry* 6(3), 325–328.

Vogeltanz-Holm, N.D., Wonderlich, S.A., Lewis, B.A., Wilsnack, S.C., Harris, T.R., Wilsnack, R.W. and Kristjanson, A.F. (2000) Longitudinal predictors of binge eating, intense dieting, and weight concerns in a national sample of women. *Behavior Therapy* 31, 221–235.

Vohs, K.D., Bardone, A.M., Joiner, T.E., Abramson, L.Y. and Heatherton, T.F. (1999) Perfectionism, perceived weight status, and self-esteem interact to predict bulimic symptoms: a model of bulimic symptom development. *Journal of Abnormal Psychology* 108, 695–700.

Wadden, T.A., Foster, G.D. and Latizia, K.A. (1994) One-year behavioral treatment of obesity: comparison of moderate and severe caloric restriction and the effects of weight maintenance therapy. *Journal of Consulting and Clinical Psychology* 62, 165–171.

Walsh, B.T. and Devlin, M.J. (1995) Pharmacotherapy of bulimia and binge eating disorders. *Addictive Behaviors* 20, 757–764.

Whitney, E.N. and Rolfes, S.R. (2002) *Understanding Nutrition*, 9th edn. Wadsworth Publishing Company, California.

Wilfley, D.E., Dounchis, J.Z. and Welch, R.R. (2000) Interpersonal psychotherapy. In: Miller, K.J. and Mizes, J.S. (eds) *Comparative Treatments for Eating Disorders*. Springer Publishing Company, New York, pp. 128–159.

Williamson, D.A. (1990) *Assessment of Eating Disorders*. Pergamon Press, New York.

Williamson, D.A., Netermayer, R.G., Jackman, L P., Anderson, D.A., Funsch, C.L. and Rabalais, J.Y. (1995) Structural equation modeling of risk factors for the development of eating disorders symptoms in female athletes. *International Journal of Eating Disorders* 17, 387–393.

Wilson, G.T. and Fairburn, C.G. (1993) *Journal of Consulting and Clinical Psychology* 61, 261–269.

Wilson, G.T. and Fairburn, C.G (1998) Treatments for eating disorders. In: Nathan, P.E. and Gorman, J.M. (eds) *Treatments that Work*. Oxford University Press, New York, pp. 501–530.

Wilson, G.T. and Pike, K.M. (1993) Eating disorders. In: D.H. Barlow (ed.) *Clinical Handbook of Psychological Disorders*, 2nd edn. Guilford Press, New York, pp. 278–317.

Wonderlich, S.A., Mitchell, J.E., Peterson, C.B. and Crow, S. (2001) Integrative cognitive therapy for bulimic behavior. In: Striegel-Moore, R.H. and Smolak, L. (eds) *Eating Disorders: Innovative Directions in Research and Practice*. American Psychological Association, Washington, DC, pp. 173–196.

Woolsey, M.M. (2002) *Eating Disorders: A Clinical Guide to Counseling and Treatment*. American Dietetic Association, Chicago.

Worobey, J. (2002) Interpersonal versus intrafamilial predictors of maladaptive eating attitudes in young women. *Social Behavior and Personality* 30(45), 424–434.

Worobey, J. and Schoenfeld, D. (1999) Eating disordered behavior in dietetics students and students in other majors. *Journal of the American Dietetic Association* 99(9), 1100–1102.

Yager, J. (1989) Psychological treatments for eating disorders. *Psychiatric Annals* 19, 477–482.

Zerbe, K.J. (1995) *The Body Betrayed: A Deeper Understanding of Women, Eating Disorders, and Treatment*. Gürze Books, Carlsbad, California.

15 Behavioral Aspects of Overweight and Obesity

J. Worobey

Despite the fixation that many of us have with appearance, body image and weight loss, the eating disorders we have just discussed affect a relatively small, though significant, proportion of individuals. Quite the opposite, however, in affluent societies such as the USA and UK, where the prevalence of overweight and obesity are much higher. It is ironic then that in a world where starvation still exists in developing countries and food insecurity affects appreciable numbers even in developed nations, the phenomenon of overnutrition would be a significant cause of health problems and psychological distress.

Excessive body weight has been demonstrated to increase the risk of various diseases and disabilities and is associated with a number of adverse social and psychological consequences. Because of the physiological and psychological sequelae of obesity, weight loss has become a preoccupation for many people, and an industry in and of itself. This preoccupation is evident on television, in the supermarket, in bookstores, in the physician's office and in the ever-growing popularity of diet centers and fitness clubs. Although some individuals do manage to lose weight, maintaining that loss for any length of time remains difficult. Yet, the sheer numbers of individuals who are at risk for obesity and its resultant complications demand that something be done to stem the tide of what appears to be an overweight epidemic. Recall the striking increase

in research in eating disorders mentioned in Chapter 14. The increase in research on obesity has been even more dramatic. To illustrate, MEDLINE citations for 'obesity' totaled 1209 in 1994. In 2004, that number more than tripled, to 3973. Perhaps more interesting, PSYCINFO, the literature search engine for the behavioral sciences, listed relatively fewer citations (119) for obesity in 1994, also tripled that amount (to 359) in 2004. It is clear that physicians, psychologists, public health workers and politicians consider obesity to be *the* public health problem of the 21st century.

Defining Obesity and Overweight

The Latin term 'obesus' means to devour, and suggests that overeating was recognized early on as a contributing factor to the condition we call obesity. While the binge eating that was discussed in Chapter 14 as a component of bulimia nervosa may characterize some individuals who are overweight, we now recognize that obesity results from a myriad of causes, not simply overeating, although food intake of course plays a substantive role.

History of obesity

Although obesity as a widespread problem is clearly a modern phenomenon, relics unearthed by archaeologists indicate that overweight women were not only observed during the Stone Age, but in some prehistoric cultures, even revered. Small statuettes of women with pronounced abdominal obesity and pendulous breasts have been found across all of Europe, and may date back some 25,000 years to the Paleolithic era. Numerous figurines excavated in Turkey, purported to be over 7500 years old from the Neolithic and Chalcolithic periods, are said to represent the Mother Goddess and display the exaggerated hips, bellies and breasts that may also characterize fertility (Bray, 2003).

Excessive overweight was not unknown to the Egyptians of 2000 BC, as the mummies of stout Kings and Queens will attest. Although royal mummies represented the higher classes, even then obesity was regarded as objectionable (Darby et al., 1977). The clinical treatment of obesity was first addressed by Hippocrates in the 5th century BC, who suggested hard work before eating if one desired to lose weight, and a limit of one meal per day. Nearly 2000 years ago, Galen declared that running, along with food that provided little nourishment, made his stout patients moderately thin in short order. To these Greco-Roman roots we can add acupuncture by the ancient Chinese, medicinal therapy by the Indians, and diet therapy by the Arabians, as early approaches to the treatment of obesity (Bray, 2004). Based on this evidence, it is abundantly clear that obesity, and the role of diet and exercise in treating obesity, were recognized thousands of years ago.

Determining overweight and obesity

Unlike the eating disorders, obesity is not a psychological disturbance (though it admittedly has psychosocial correlates), but rather is a clinical condition characterized by the excessive accumulation of body fat. Stated simply, the physical measurement of body fat or the approximation of such defines the state of being overweight or obese. There are numerous techniques now available for the direct or indirect measurement of body fat. Direct measures include underwater weighing, total body water analysis, total body potassium analysis, bioelectrical impedance analysis, ultrasound,

computerized tomography, magnetic resonance imaging, dual energy X-ray absorptiometry and neutron inelastic scattering. Although this wide array of techniques indicates that measuring body fat is now a routine matter and can be done with extreme accuracy, none of these approaches are ideal. Space constraints, measurement error, difficulty in interpretation, radiation exposure and the lack of suitability for the severely obese limit many of these procedures. Furthermore, the specialized equipment many of these methods require makes them too expensive and inconvenient for large studies (DiGirolamo et al., 2000).

Because of these drawbacks, indirect measures for assessing body fat are more often used in clinical settings. Because skin is anywhere from 0.5 to 2.0 mm thick, with subcutaneous fat just below the surface, *skinfold thickness* can be determined across multiple sites, such as the mid-triceps, shoulder blade and abdomen (Orphanidou et al., 1994). Special calipers are used to measure the skinfolds, and substantial skill and training is required. Although there is some disagreement about which sites most accurately reflect actual body fat, its utility with the elderly who accumulate fat in additional places, and its tendency to underestimate fat in cases of greater obesity, measuring skinfold thickness is none the less a useful and more economical approach to estimating body fat (Bray, 1989). Waist and hip circumference, with a computed *waist-to-hip ratio*, has also been used to approximate visceral adipose tissue. Waist circumference, in particular, has been shown to correlate strongly with morbid states such as hypertension, Type 2 diabetes and cardiovascular disease (Han et al., 1995).

Since even these indirect approaches to estimating body fat require specialized techniques, the definitions of desirable body weight versus excess body weight or fat can also be based on surrogate measures. Percent of weight in excess of ideal body weight is one approach that has been traditionally used, and derives from life insurance statistics that consider *desirable weight* to be the weight for height and frame for which mortality rates are the lowest. However, this standard is inadequate in a number of ways. For example, the weights only reflect data from individuals who can afford to buy life insurance, and they represent their weight at time of purchase, not time of death. Because of these limitations, an alternate method for estimating obesity that relies on weight and height has been advocated.

The Quetelet Index (1981), or *Body Mass Index* (BMI) as it is more widely known, has been endorsed by the National Institutes of Health of the USA, the National Audit Office of England, and the International Obesity Task Force of the World Health Organization, as providing the most clinically relevant assessment of obesity across varied populations. BMI describes relative weight for height and is calculated by dividing the individual's body weight by the square of his or her height. The formula is:

$$BMI = \frac{\text{weight in kilograms}}{(\text{height in meters})^2} \text{ or } \frac{\text{weight in pounds}}{(\text{height in inches})^2} \times 704.5$$

As shown in Table 15.1, BMI estimates between 18.5 and 25 in adults reflect normal or healthy weight. Overweight status is determined by a BMI of 25 or higher, with obesity reserved for a BMI of 30 or higher. The association between BMI and body fat content will vary across age, sex and ethnic groups because of lean tissue mass and hydration status. However, BMI is significantly correlated with total body fat content, is a more precise measure of total body fat than weight alone, and is a better estimate of health risk than are any actuarial tables from insurance companies (Ford *et al.*, 2001).

Despite the widespread acceptance of BMI as the most practical measure of overweight and obesity in adults, it must be remembered that weight and height are only

a proxy for body composition. For example, a bodybuilder may be classified as overweight by BMI standards, but would not likely be overfat. In addition, BMI is less accurate with individuals who are extremely short or tall, and cannot gauge whether someone who is of normal weight but is extremely sedentary might have excess body fat. With children, growth charts must be used that plot BMI by sex and age (Dietz and Belizzi, 1999). For these reasons clinical assessments are necessary for interpreting BMI in situations where body weight may be affected by increased muscularity or even disease. Nevertheless, for most individuals BMI provides a very good approximation of total body fat.

Prevalence of Overweight and Obesity

Over the last 20 years, the prevalence of obesity has increased at an alarming rate – not just in developed countries, but worldwide. In fact, it has become so common throughout the world that it has begun to displace undernutrition and infectious diseases as the most important contributor to poor health (Kopelman, 2000). In 1980, 8% of women in England were classified as obese, as compared to 6% of men. By 1998, the prevalence for women reached 21% and for men, 17% (Report by the Comptroller and Auditor General, 2001). Data from the National Health and Nutrition Examination Surveys (NHANES) show the percentage of obese adults in the USA increased from 15.5% in the years 1976–1980 to 22.5% in 1988–1994 (Flegal *et al.*, 1998). The results of more recent data are even worse, as the 1999–2000 NHANES estimates the adult obesity rate to be at 31% (National Center for Health Statistics, 2004).

Add to these estimates the individuals who are overweight, and both England and the USA have rates of about one out of every two women and three out of every five men being overweight or obese – truly qualifying as an epidemic. This dramatic increase has led some American experts to predict that if the prevalence continues to rise at the current rate, by the year 2030 *every* adult in the USA

Table 15.1. Body Mass Index (BMI) classifications.

Weight status	BMI (kg/m²)	Obesity class
Underweight	< 18.5	
Normal	18.5–24.9	
Overweight	25.0–29.9	
Obese	30.0–34.9	I
	35.0–39.9	II
Extremely obese	≥ 40	III

Source: adapted from the National Heart, Lung, and Blood Institute Expert Panel on the Identification, Evaluation, and Treatment of Overweight and Obesity in Adults, 1998.

will be overweight (Foreyt and Goodrick, 1995). Data for children suggest that we are assuredly on this path. Estimates for pre-school-age children in the USA indicate a change in overweight and obesity from 22.3% to 27.1% over the 13 years from 1983 to 1995 (Mei *et al.*, 1998). For England the figures are even more striking, as the percentages have grown from 20.1% to 32.8% over the 10 years from 1989 to 1998 (Bundred *et al.*, 2001).

However these two developed nations are not alone, as a study that included 17 European countries, as well as data from Russia, estimated the average prevalence of obesity to be 15% in men and 22% in women (Seidell, 1997). While the prevalence of obesity tends to be lower in less developed nations than in affluent societies, obesity rates also appear to be rising in lower- and middle-income countries (Jain, 2004). Nations that had formerly faced significant problems of malnutrition and famine have attained adequate food supplies, which have been accompanied by changes in diet composition (Popkin, 1998). At the same time their occupational and other types of physical activity have decreased, which as we will soon see, is another contributing factor to excessive weight gain. Although estimates for regions of the world such as Asia, the Middle East and Latin America are uncertain, approximately 7% of the adult world population may be obese (Murray and Lopez, 1996). Since the preva-

lence of overweight (BMI of 25–29.9) is two to three times the prevalence of obesity in most countries, it is plausible that as many as one billion adults are overweight worldwide (Seidell, 1997).

Sociocultural correlates

Many sociocultural variables are associated with the tendency for increased body fat. As shown in Table 15.2, these sociocultural factors may be broken down into social characteristics, social context and socio-economic status. Social characteristics are inherent in the person, and include age, sex and race/ethnicity. Both men and women appear to gain the most weight between 25 and 34 years of age. Thereafter weight may continue to increase, but at a slower rate, and show a decline after the age of 55 (Williamson *et al.*, 1990). As outlined above, men are more likely to be overweight than women, but women are more likely to be obese than men. Interestingly enough, men appear to rate themselves as thin even if they are 5% above their ideal body weight, while women must be at least 10% above their ideal before they will do so (Anderson, 1995). In the USA, black and Latina women have higher rates of overweight than Caucasian women, with the latter seeming to value thinness more than other racial/ethnic groups (James, 1996; Kopelman, 2000).

Table 15.2. Sociocultural correlates of obesity.

Social characteristics:
- Fatness increases over the course of adulthood.
- Fatness declines in the elderly.
- Obesity rates are higher for women than men.

Social contexts:
- Obesity rates are higher in developed countries than developing countries.
- Obesity rates are higher for rural women than urban women.
- Obesity rates are higher for married men than single men.
- Older people living with others have a higher rate of obesity than those who live alone.

Socio-economic status:
- Obesity rates are higher in people with less prestigious jobs.
- Obesity rates are higher in low-income women.
- Obesity rates are higher in less educated women.
- Obesity rates are higher in women who are not employed outside the home.

Source: adapted from Dalton, 1997.

Besides the likelihood of greater body fat among individuals of developed versus developing nations, regional differences in obesity also reflect the possible impact of social context. In the USA, for example, rural women tend to be heavier than women who live in more urban areas, and regionally speaking, southern women are the most likely to be overweight (Sobal et al., 1996). In terms of socioeconomic status, in both England and the USA, the prevalence of obesity increases when moving from the highest to the lowest income categories. Hence, less income, less education and lower occupational prestige are all positively correlated with the likelihood of obesity (Kuczmarski et al., 1994; Joint Health Surveys Unit, 1999). Some experts suggest that obesity may be a causal factor in determining socioeconomic status, as discriminating behaviors toward the obese may reduce their upward social mobility (Enzi, 1994). That is, having a non-preferred body type may negatively influence education, occupation and choice of a marriage partner.

Physiological Consequences

Concerns about the epidemic of overweight and obesity are not simply a matter of physical appearance. Rather, the associated risks for illness and disease are what makes this a significant public health problem (see Table 15.3). Heart disease, for example, which is the leading cause of death in the USA, is associated with a BMI $\geq$ 30, as are hypertension, stroke, diabetes, gallbladder, joint diseases and some forms of cancer. For men, obesity in early adulthood has been linked to cardiovascular disease (Hubert et al., 1983), while for women, weight gain during mid-adulthood has shown a stronger association (VanItallie, 1990). Hypertension is higher in the overweight than in those who are not overweight (Stamler et al., 1978). In combination with high blood cholesterol and high serum triglycerides, which are also linked to being overweight, hypertension contributes to atherosclerosis and coronary heart disease (Blackburn, 1995), though it appears to be a major risk factor for heart disease and stroke in its own right (Rocchini, 2004).

Table 15.3. Consequences of being overweight or obese.

Physical risks
 Hypertension.
 Heart disease.
 Stroke.
 Diabetes.
 Cancer.
 Sleep apnea.
 Osteoarthritis.
 Gout.
 Gallbladder disease.
Psychosocial risks
 Depression about weight and eating.
 Susceptibility to hunger.
 Disinhibition toward eating when stressed.
 Target of prejudice.
 Viewed as less attractive, industrious, intelligent.

Of all the serious diseases, adult onset diabetes (Type 2) appears to have the strongest association with obesity. About 85% of diabetics can be classified as Type 2, and of these, approximately 90% are obese (Albu and Pi-Sunyer, 2004). Obesity compromises glucose tolerance and increases insulin resistance, and diabetes in turn may cause heart disease, kidney disease and vascular problems. Interestingly enough, the location of body fat seems to be a risk factor for disease independent of the amount of fat itself. The 'apple' shape, where fat is collected in the belly, is more characteristic of men who are obese, hence the name android (man-like) (see Fig. 15.1). In contrast, women typically collect fat in their hips and buttocks, giving them a 'pear' shape known as gynoid (woman-like). In general, the 'apple' shape in men is associated with greater health risks than the 'pear' shape pattern more often seen in women since excess fat in the abdominal region appears to raise blood lipid levels, which then interfere with insulin function. Visceral fat (that fat which surrounds the organs of the abdominal cavity) is linked to hyperlidemia, hypertension, heart disease and diabetes (Kissebah, 1996).

Several types of cancer are associated with being overweight and possessing excess abdominal fat. Overweight men are at heightened risk for developing cancer of the prostate, colon and rectum. Overweight women are at

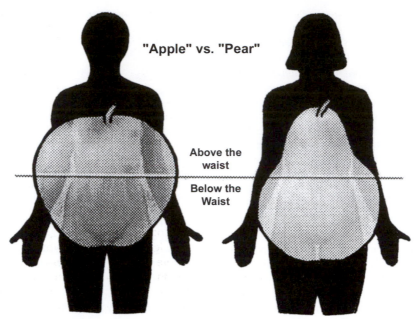

"Apple" vs. "Pear"

Above the
waist

Below the
Waist

Fig. 15.1. The apple and pear shapes that characterize obesity.

greater risk for developing cancer of the colon, gallbladder, uterus, cervix, ovary and breast. In fact, women with an android shape may be at increased risk for breast cancer in particular (Ziegler, 1997). However at present, it is not clear if the increased risk is due to the excess weight or a high fat/high calorie diet. The excess weight that accompanies obesity also appears to increase the risk of osteoarthritis, gout, gallbladder diseases and obstructive sleep apnea (Blackburn, 1995; Ko and Lee, 2004; Wluka *et al.*, 2004).

Psychological Characteristics

As mentioned earlier, obesity is not a psychological disturbance, and rates of general psychopathology do not appear to be any greater in obese groups than in non-obese groups. Moreover, there is little evidence that obese individuals differ from the non-obese on general personality or temperament traits such as extraversion/intraversion, rigidity/flexibility, assertiveness, locus of control and emotionality (Worobey, 2002). On the other hand, obese individuals who seek treatment for their obe-

sity often display higher prevalence rates of psychopathology than does the general population, though this is also true for many individuals who seek treatment for medical or surgical reasons (Goldsmith *et al.*, 1992). All things considered then, there is little evidence for an 'obese personality'. Being distressed enough to seek treatment may be the critical variable, as the obese who seek treatment report more symptoms of personality disorder than comparable obese individuals who do not seek treatment (Fitzgibbon *et al.*, 1993).

Although the obese appear to be as different from each other as are the non-obese on general personality characteristics, for certain psychological characteristics and behavioral patterns they do differ from individuals of lower weight, namely, those factors that are explicitly concerned with weight and eating. Compared to normal weight respondents, overweight individuals are more depressed, self-conscious and pessimistic about their weight and eating, more aware of and susceptible to hunger and more likely to disinhibit when their control over eating is disrupted (Faith *et al.*, 2002). As discussed in Chapter 10, for some individuals disinhibition may result in overeating when limits imposed by dietary restraint are exceeded. Certain subgroups of the obese, such as restrained eaters and binge eaters, may be more prone to emotional eating when stress triggers their disinhibition (Faith *et al.*, 1997).

With respect to body image, obese adults have been found to be less accurate than average weight individuals in judging their body size and see themselves as larger than they actually are. In many individuals who are obese, this may translate into negative body esteem (French *et al.*, 1995). In general, studies of self-esteem in the overweight suggest that obesity is associated with impaired self-esteem in children and adults who may in part motivate their efforts to try and lose weight (Miller and Downey, 1999).

Body image disparagement and poor self-esteem are likely the result of the tremendous disdain that Western societies seem to have for the obese. In American society, for example, overweight and obesity are socially stigmatized, and the perception of others is that the obese individual has little self-control. Unlike a physical deformity or a person's skin color, however, obesity is viewed as intentional, with the obese individual held accountable and responsible for his or her condition (Brown and Bentley-Condit, 1998). In societies where self-worth is tied to physical appearance an individual's body is always on display, and if that body is fat, the individual is discriminated against. Studies have long demonstrated social biases against the obese in renting apartments, gaining college admission or in landing a job (Gortmaker *et al.*, 1993). Negative attitudes toward the obese have even been reported by parents, in providing less financial support for their overweight daughters (Crandall, 1991), and among health professionals, including obesity specialists (Schwartz *et al.*, 2003).

It is patently obvious then that the quality of life for the obese, from both a physiological and psychological level, can be markedly compromised. In a study of the self-perceived impact that obesity had on their lives, Rand and MacGregor (1991) interviewed patients who had lost 100 lb (45 kg) or more through gastric bypass surgery. The patients indicated that they would rather be blind, deaf, dyslexic, diabetic or an amputee than return to their for-

mer morbidly obese status. Such a strong attitude toward their formerly obese state suggests that life was fairly intolerable for these individuals, with the discomfort, prejudice, ridicule and self-loathing they experienced far exceeding any enjoyment they may have derived from eating. As recent research suggests, however, becoming overweight or obese is not simply a matter of excess food intake, but rather a combination of biological and behavioral factors.

Etiology of Obesity

In the preceding sections we addressed the physiological and psychological corrrelates of overweight and obesity. While these factors illustrate what the obese person must contend with, they do not explain the process by which an individual becomes overweight or obese in the first place. The basic formula for the gaining of excess weight is that *over an extended period of time an individual's energy intake is greater than his or her energy expenditure*. A positive energy balance occurs when energy intake exceeds energy expenditure and weight gain is promoted. Conversely, a negative energy balance results in a decrease in fat stores with subsequent weight loss. Body weight is regulated by a series of physiological processes that have the capacity to maintain a stable weight within a narrow range, or set point. In fact, *set point theory* suggests that the body exerts a stronger defense against undernutrition than it does against overnutrition and weight gain (Insel *et al.*, 2004). More will be said about this later. As it is now recognized that obesity has many interrelated causes, we will next examine the current explanations for variation in weight gain that lead to obesity.

Biological influences

Prior to the 20th century, only about 10% of adults were obese, and most likely for genetic reasons (Berdanier, 1996). While the population's gene pool has changed very little if at all over the last century, however, the prevalence of obesity has increased dramatically over the last 30 years. For most individuals then, genes do not cause obesity, although they may influence certain processes that may help lead to it. Nevertheless, there has been indirect evidence for quite some time that heredity plays a part in excess weight gain.

If both parents are obese, for example, it is estimated that the probability that their children will be obese is 80%, whereas if neither parent is obese the chances of an obese child are less than 10% (Bouchard, 1997). Children share the eating environment with their parents as well as their genes, however, so it is imperative to examine the similarity rates of obesity between twins (concordance). Stunkard and his colleagues have done some of the best work in this area using adopted children, showing that the BMI of biological parents corresponds highly to their children they gave up for adoption. In turn, no correspondence was shown between the adoptive parents and the children they adopted. Moreover, in examining twins who were reared together versus apart, these investigators found that the correlation in weight between identical twins reared apart was about twice as high as for fraternal twins who were reared together (Stunkard *et al.*, 1986, 1990).

Recent research suggests that a large number of genes may play a role in the development of obesity. For example, an obesity gene called *ob* has been identified that is expressed in the fat cells and codes for the protein *leptin* (Zhang *et al.*, 1994). Mice with defective *ob* genes do not produce leptin and they become obese. Moreover, they will lose fat if subsequently injected with leptin (Qian *et al.*, 1998). But obese humans generally have high leptin levels, and leptin concentrations usually increase with weight gain. It is therefore speculated that leptin rises with weight gain in order to suppress appetite, but that the obese are resistant to its action in the way that individuals with Type 2 diabetes have high levels of insulin but are resistant to its action (Albu *et al.*, 1997; Ravussin *et al.*, 1997).

Leptin acts as a hormone, primarily in the hypothalamus (Friedman, 1998). The hypothalamus has long been known to act as a control center for integrating messages about energy intake, energy expenditure and energy storage arising from the mouth, gastrointestinal tract and liver. As discussed in Chapter 11, some of these messages influence satiation, while others influence satiety. When leptin is administered to experimental animals that lack this hormone, the animals will attain a normal weight (Das and Roberts, 2001). Leptin may therefore promote a negative energy balance by not only suppressing appetite but also by increasing energy expenditure. Energy expenditure in this case is primarily affected by changes in basal metabolism, which is responsible for up to two-thirds of the energy that the body uses each day in support of metabolic activities such as respiration, circulation, thermoregulation and so forth. The *basal metabolic rate* (BMR), a clinical measure of resting energy expenditure, varies from person to person and is tied to lean body mass. Therefore, conditions which alter lean body mass such as age, weight and physical condition will affect energy requirements and BMR (Schulz and Scheller, 1994).

Genes that code for *uncoupling proteins* may also prove to be important in understanding the development of obesity (Warden *et al.*, 1999). The human body has two types of adipose tissue – the mostly white adipose tissue that stores fat for other cells to use as energy, and brown adipose tissue that releases stored energy as heat. When white adipose tissue is oxidized, the majority of the energy is captured in adenosine triphosphate (ATP) and the remainder is released as heat. In brown adipose tissue, oxidation may be uncoupled from ATP formation producing only heat. This results in the body spending energy instead of storing it. The gene that codes for uncoupling protein-2 is active in brown and white fat, and also influences BMR (Fleury *et al.*, 1997). Animals with high amounts of this protein appear to resist weight gain, while those with minimal amounts gain weight rapidly (Wolf, 1997).

Lastly, the development and metabolism of fat cells themselves may also contribute to overweight and obesity. The amount of fat in a person's body reflects both the number and size of the fat cells that he or she possesses. The *number* of fat cells increases most rapidly during late childhood and early adolescence and more rapidly in obese children than in lean children. As fat cells fill with fat droplets they increase in *size*, and may also divide if they reach their maximum. Obesity can thus develop when a person's fat cells increase in number, size or both. With weight loss, the size of fat cells will reduce, but not their number, and with subsequent weight gain they will readily be refilled (Whitney and Rolfes, 2002).

The enzyme *lipoprotein lipase* (LPL) serves to promote fat storage in fat cells. Obese individuals with high LPL activity store fat especially efficiently, so that even a modest excess in their energy intake has a greater impact than it would on lean people (Kern, 1997). After weight loss, LPL activity increases, and will increase most in those individuals who were fattest prior to their weight loss. In addition, LPL activity is partially regulated by sex-specific hormones. The android and gynoid fat patterns that tend to characterize men and women, respectively, are likely due to abundant LPL activity in the fat cells of the male abdomen, and in the breasts, hips and thighs of the female. The lower body is also less active than the upper body in releasing fat from storage, which explains the greater difficulty in losing weight from the hips and thighs than from around the stomach (Jensen, 1997).

Researchers have determined that after weight loss, or weight gain for that matter, the body adjusts its BMR so as to restore its original weight. Part of this is due to the gene that produces the LPL enzyme appearing to signal the storage of fat in the case where weight is lost, for example. Energy expenditure also mirrors this pattern, increasing after weight gain and decreasing after weight loss, although the greatest contributor to changes in energy expenditure in response to altered energy balance is still volitional activity (Leibel *et al.*, 1995). Interestingly enough, for most people body fat and weight remain fairly constant despite fluctuations in energy intake and expenditure. However, on a population level body weights do tend to edge up over time. As stated earlier, *set point theory* attempts to explain this phenomenon, by assuming that an active regulatory system works to keep the body at a certain fixed weight. That weight may increase is explained by a regulatory system that more vigorously defends against undernutrition than overnutrition. Although many researchers have challenged the validity of set-point theory, because the phenomenon of returning to the earlier weight seems real, the theory remains popular with the overweight public.

Behavioral influences – energy intake

Under the heading of behavioral influences, the two components of the energy balance equation – energy intake and energy expenditure – can readily be considered. Energy intake refers to the food we eat, or caloric intake; energy expenditure is comprised of BMR, diet-induced thermogenesis (the body's generation of heat), and physical activity. Most laypersons would probably venture that the most obvious reason for people becoming obese is that they simply eat too much. Indeed, throughout most of history, gluttony was assumed to be the primary cause of obesity, with the obese thought to suffer from inadequate self-control around food. Given what we know today about the multiple causes of obesity, however, we now realize that energy intake falls short of fully explaining why some people become fat while others seem resistant to weight gain. For instance, diet histories of obese individuals often indicate energy intakes and patterns that are similar to those of normal weight individuals. However, we must acknowledge that diet histories are not the most accurate records of actual intake, as both obese and non-obese people commonly underestimate their dietary intake (Johansson *et al.*, 1998).

Animal models of energy intake may be instructive. For example, genetically obese rats eat much more than their non-obese counterparts during their early post-natal development, and gain weight rapidly. Even when their energy intake is restricted, the obese rats will still gain more weight than will the lean rats (York, 2004). When their adult weight is reached, however, the energy intake of both obese and non-obese rats look similar, even though the obese rats maintain a weight that is double the non-obese rodents. It would thus seem that genetics must work in concert with energy intake in explaining obesity.

Beyond total energy intake, overweight people tend to eat more fat, and it is quite clear that a high fat diet also promotes obesity, especially in those individuals who are genetically predisposed (Heitmann *et al.*, 1997). Dietary fat provides more kilocalories per gram and requires less energy to be metabolized, relative to protein and carbohydrate. This further amplifies energy intake and increases body fat stores (Prentice and Poppitt, 1996). In addition, high fat foods are highly preferred by most individuals, thereby more of such food is likely to be eaten (Blundell and Macdiarmid, 1997). Some argue that relative to protein and carbohydrates, foods higher in fat have little satiating power. This could also encourage overeating, but this hypothesis is still under investigation (Rolls and Bell, 1999). In light of the recent attention being paid to the excess intake of simple sugars and carbohydrates as being the real culprit in weight gain (Taubes, 2001), we may only be at the beginning of understanding how the components of dietary intake combine to influence weight gain.

One thing is certain – individuals in westernized nations are definitely consuming more in the way of total calories. In the USA, for example, it is estimated that the per capita food supply has increased by 300 cal/day, or up 12% over the last 20 years (Putnam *et al.*, 2002). Wherever fast-food restaurants now proliferate, the competition between corporate chains has resulted in promotions that appeal to customers via the upgrading of standard meals – a practice known as 'supersizing' (Collins, 2003). To a meal that is already high in fat, sugar and sodium, the customer is able to further enlarge her soft drink or his order of French fries for a minimal increase in price. In addition, these fast food chains have recently been joined by cafeteria-style restaurants that offer 'all you can eat' buffets with a tremendous variety of foods for one low price. Studies with animals as well as humans demonstrate that food consumption increases when there is greater variety in the meal, and that greater dietary variety is related to increased body fat and weight (Raynor and Epstein, 2001). Even the more traditional, independently run restaurants tend to give generous portion sizes, in hopes of attracting customers by offering a good value for their money. Larger portion sizes have been hypothesized as contributing to the obesity epidemic (Young and Nestle, 2002), with experimental evidence showing that the more food people

are served, the more they overeat (Levitsky and Youn, 2004). Many customers may be too embarrassed to ask the waiter to take half of their meal home for the next day, and instead will overeat, since after all, it was 'prepared especially' for them. Merely consuming foods at restaurants and away from home appears to be an important contributor to the obesity epidemic, at least in the USA (Jeffery and French, 1998; McCrory *et al.*, 1999).

As was mentioned earlier, certain individuals such as restrained eaters and binge eaters are likely to overeat when under stress. The restrained eater often tries to reduce caloric intake by fasting, skipping meals or delaying eating, but will then overeat when some emotional or environmental stressor interferes with the ability to inhibit self-control. This pattern is extremely common in the obese who repeatedly try to lose weight (Arnow *et al.*, 1995). In contrast, the binge eater is not likely to fast or compensate, but will frequently overeat in a compulsive manner. As shown in Table 15.4, the American Psychiatric Association (1994) has established research criteria for this behavioral pattern, signifying that it is under consideration as a possible psychiatric disorder. Unlike the bulimic individual, who binges and purges and may appear to be close to ideal weight, binge eaters are often overweight, and are overrepresented among the enrollees of weight-loss programs (Marcus, 1993).

The causes of overeating in children have also been explored. For example, it has been shown that parents who attempt to control their children's eating during mealtimes may have the unintended effect of increasing the child's tendency to be overweight. That is, parents who use threats or rewards to coerce their children to eat everything on their plate seem to inadvertently interfere with their child's ability to self-regulate energy intake, by forcing them to ignore internal feelings of satiety (Birch *et al.*, 2003). Since most children will eat so-called 'junk foods' if they are available in the house, some have suggested that a laissez-faire attitude toward their children's eating may also be inadvisable (Gable and Lutz, 2000). It is thus apparent that a complex relationship exists between parental control and children's ability to self-regulate their energy

Table 15.4. Research criteria for binge eating disorder.

1. Recurrent episodes of binge eating, characterized by both of the following:
   a. eating in a discrete period of time an amount of food that is definitely larger than most people would eat in a similar period of time under similar circumstances
   b. a sense of lack of control over eating during the episode.

2. The binge eating episodes are associated with three or more of the following:
   a. eating much more rapidly than normal
   b. eating until feeling uncomfortably full
   c. eating large amounts of food when not feeling particularly hungry
   d. eating alone because of being embarrassed by how much one eats
   e. feeling depressed, guilty or disgusted with oneself after overeating.

3. The binge eating is characterized by marked distress.
4. The binge eating occurs at least 2 days a week for 6 months.
5. The binge eating is not associated with the regular use of inappropriate compensatory behaviors.

Source: adapted from the *DSM-IV – Diagnostic and Statistical Manual of Mental Disorders*, 1994.

intake. More research in this area is clearly warranted.

Behavioral influences – energy expenditure

Given the dramatic increase in the prevalence of obesity over the last 20 years, a case can also be made that the increased prevalence of being overweight is due to the lack of physical activity by children and adults. Thanks to modern technology and labor-saving devices, opportunities for physical activity have declined in transportation, at home and at work. We drive automobiles on short errands instead of walking. We use elevators instead of stairs. We buy take-out chicken instead of stuffing a roaster, wash clothing with a machine instead of by hand, cut our grass with a power instead of a push mower, blow snow instead of shoveling it and so on. One hundred years ago, about 30% of the energy used in factory and farm work came from muscle power, while today only 1% does (Whitney and Rolfes, 2002). Even shopping, which used to ensure at least some walking on weekends at the mall, is gradually being replaced by catalog or internet purchasing, which can be done while sitting down in the comfort of one's home. Table 15.5 illustrates the amount of energy expended in certain activities.

If physical inactivity is deemed an important contributor to obesity, television watching probably contributes the most to underactivity (Gortmaker *et al.*, 1990). Television watching increases the likelihood of obesity in a number of ways: (i) watching television is a sedentary experience, where the individual sits, expending little energy beyond what is used for metabolic purposes; (ii) watching television serves to replace time that could be spent in other activities that require movement; (iii) people often eat while watching television, and pay little attention to how much they are ingesting; and (iv) many high fat/high calorie foods are advertised on television, which may influence the subsequent purchases or frequenting of fast-food restaurants by the watcher.

Television advertising may especially influence children. Besides the commercials for fast food on network television, children's programs are routinely sponsored by sugary cereals, candy and soft drinks, which reinforce their image as desirable snacks. Children who watch more television and are less vigorously active have been shown to have higher BMIs (Andersen *et al.*, 1998). Recent analysis in the USA and China using national samples of children in both countries showed that obesity rates were lowest among children who watched one or fewer hours of television per day, and highest among those who watched four or more hours per day (Crespo *et al.*, 2001; Ma *et al.*, 2002).

But as with adults, commercial television is not the only culprit when trying to

Table 15.5. Estimates of energy expenditure for specific activities.

Type of activity	kcal/h/kg	kcal/h/lb	Kcal/lbs at different body weights		
			50kg/110lb	68kg/150lb	91kg/200lb
Aerobics					
Light	3.0	1.36	150	205	273
Medium	5.0	2.27	250	341	455
Heavy	8.0	3.64	400	545	727
Walking					
Strolling <2 mph	2.0	0.91	100	136	182
Brisk pace, level	4.0	1.82	200	273	364
Moderate pace, uphill	6.0	2.73	300	409	545
Running					
Jogging	7.0	3.18	350	477	636
Running 7 mph	11.5	5.23	575	784	1045
Running 10 mph	16.0	7.27	800	1091	1455
Bicycling					
Leisurely <10 mph	4.0	1.82	200	273	364
Moderate 12–14 mph	8.0	3.64	400	545	727
Racing 16–19 mph	12.0	5.45	600	818	1091
Recreation					
Hacky sack	4.0	1.82	200	273	364
Golf	4.5	2.05	225	307	409
Rollerblading	7.0	3.18	350	477	636
Sports					
Ultimate frisbee	3.5	1.59	175	239	318
Downhill skiing	6.0	2.73	300	409	545
Singles tennis	8.0	3.64	400	545	727
Daily activities					
Sleeping	1.2	0.55	60	82	109
Studying/writing	1.8	0.82	90	123	164
Cooking	2.5	1.14	125	170	227
Household upkeep					
House painting	4.0	1.82	200	273	364
Gardening	5.0	2.27	250	341	455
Shoveling snow	6.0	2.73	300	409	545

Source: adapted from Nieman, 1999.

explain the rise in overweight in children. Children now ride buses to school instead of walking, and have fewer classes in physical education than a generation ago. Once they are at home, parents may want to keep their children indoors and encourage them to play quietly, rather than worry about their safety in a neighborhood where danger may be present. A block that has no sidewalks for hopscotch, or a playground that may attract gangs or drug pushers, is unquestionably less desirable than staying indoors. And if confined to the indoors, watching television, videotapes or DVDs, playing video games or 'surfing the net' do not entail much in the way of physical movement (Vandewater *et al.*, 2004).

Physical activity and exercise are the major components of energy output, but recent research has identified another aspect of energy expenditure that may prove to be of some importance in explaining why certain individuals are more resistant to weight gain than others. *Non-exercise activity thermogenesis* (NEAT) refers to the energy we use even when not exercising or attempting to be active, or rather, the energy that is associated with fidgeting, crossing and uncrossing your legs and otherwise maintaining posture. In a study where experimental subjects were overfed, and after accounting for BMR, dietary-induced thermogenesis, and physical activity, those who were higher in NEAT were most resistant to weight gain (Levine et al., 1999). Further studies of this newly identified form of energy expenditure would seem to be warranted (Levine, 2002; Ravussin and Danforth, 1999).

Treatment for Weight Loss

In the USA alone, close to $40 billion per year is spent on efforts to lose weight. However, many individuals who wish to lose weight do not need to do so, many who need to lose weight are not successful, and of the few who do succeed, even fewer meet with permanent success. The last 50 years have seen an evolution in our views of obesity, as we have gone from a belief that failed willpower leads to obesity which must be corrected, to a recognition that obesity results from multiple factors but that physical health is more important than weight loss. As early as the 1940s, the self-help group model first appeared, with commercial programs that sell pre-packaged low-calorie meals emerging in the 1950s and 1960s. In the 1970s, behavioral approaches that focused on changing eating habits were implemented. The value of aerobic exercise was next endorsed, with 'no pain, no gain' a popular mantra. Throughout the 1980s the use of surgical treatments were introduced, and in the 1990s the belief that drugs could serve as a 'magic bullet' was formally tested. Given the scope of the obesity problem, all of these approaches are still employed in one form or another. We will review the major forms of treatment next, beginning with the most radical and moving to what may be the most conservative.

Surgery

The use of surgery as a treatment for weight loss is clearly the most radical form of therapy for the obese. For individuals who are mor-

bidly obese (i.e. 100% or more overweight), this approach has been shown to help those with a severe weight problem to maintain large weight losses for an extended period (Hall et al., 1990). The first extensively used surgical procedure for the treatment of obesity was the *jejunoileal bypass*, wherein the absorptive surface of the small intestine is reduced in length. Patients reported reduced food intake, including less bingeing, snacking and emotional eating, fewer meals and cravings, and smaller portions, along with positive changes in mood, activity level, self-esteem and assertiveness (Stunkard, 1984). Weight loss in excess of 100 lb was typical, but the mortality rate from the procedure ranged from 3–4% and other complications were quite significant (Bray, 1980).

Because of these risks, two types of gastric restriction procedures, that is, *vertical banded gastroplasty* and the *gastric bypass,* were developed. In the former procedure, surgery reduces the stomach's capacity by creating a small pouch. In the latter, a bypass routes food almost directly to the jejunum, bypassing the duodenum and most of the stomach. Complications can still arise, but the mortality rate is a less dangerous 1%. Again, many patients experience increased feelings of self-confidence and improved body image, along with a sense of elation and well-being (Pi-Sunyer, 1999).

Other mechanical approaches to weight loss have fallen in and out of favor. As its name implies, the *intragastric balloon* approach involves a balloon being inserted into the stomach to reduce gastric capacity. Besides complications such as vomiting, ulcers and intestinal obstructions, weight gain typically returns when the balloon is deflated (Morrow and Mona, 1990). With *jaw wiring*, the patient can be expected to lose 4–5 lb (2 kg) per month because of the inability to ingest solid foods and masticate. However, once the wires are removed, patients commonly regain their lost weight. Because both of these approaches by themselves are far less effective than was originally hoped, their use has sharply declined.

One last surgical procedure should also be mentioned. *Liposuction*, which consists of suctioning off subcutaneous fat, has been employed by many to remove targeted fat deposits. This procedure can alter body shape slightly, but has little effect on weight as the body still has billions of fat cells that can store extra fat (Kral, 1988). Popular basically for cosmetic reasons, any improvement in appearance is more than offset by the health risks that include blood clots and nerve damage.

Drugs

Numerous pharmacological approaches to the treatment of obesity have been tried over the years. After all, since many experts view obesity as a chronic disease, it is perhaps inevitable that its treatment would include drugs (Atkinson, 1997). While the early drugs acted to reduce hunger, trigger satiety or stimulate energy expenditure, the newer drugs serve to block the absorption of calories from fat. Since a multitude of factors are now viewed as causing obesity, the current focus is on drugs with distinct mechanisms of action

that can be used in conjunction with proper diet and exercise. In fact, drugs for the treatment of obesity can be classified according to their primary mechanism of action on energy balance. As shown in Table 15.6, anti-obesity drugs may inhibit energy intake, inhibit fat absorption, enhance energy expenditure or stimulate fat mobilization (Campfield and Smith, 2000).

It has been proposed that the ideal anti-obesity drug would meet several criteria:

1. A sustained loss of weight through a reduction in body fat with a sparing of body protein;
2. Maintenance of the weight loss once a desirable body weight has been achieved;
3. Absence of side effects or abuse liability when the drug is chronically administered; and
4. Improved compliance with a weight reduction program of diet and exercise.

Although a number of promising drugs have been developed, tested and marketed over the last 30 years, none of the current pharmacolog-

Table 15.6. Approved and experimental drugs used in the treatment of overweight and obesity.

Drug	Trade name	Mechanism
Over the counter		
Phenylpropanolamine	Acutrim™, Dexatrim™	Suppresses appetite
Prescription		
Phentermine	Fastin™, Phentrol™ etc.	Suppresses appetite
Mazindol	Sanorex™	Suppresses appetite
Diethylproprion	Tenuate™	Suppresses appetite
Clortermine	Voranil™	Suppresses appetite
Sibutramine	Meridia™	Suppresses appetite
Amphetamine	Benzedrine™, Dexedrine™	Suppresses appetite
Benzphetamine	Didrex™	Suppresses appetite
Phenimemetrazine	Anorex™, Adipost™ etc.	Suppresses appetite
Orlistat	Xenical™	Reduces fat absorption
Experimental		
Acarbose	Glucobay™	Reduces carbohydrate absorption
Ephedrine	Metabolife ®	Enhances fat breakdown
Cholecystokinin		Suppresses appetite
Enterostatin		Reduces preference for fat
Leptin		Suppresses appetite, increases energy expenditure
Rimonabant	Acomplia™	Reduces appetite by blocking cannabinoid receptors
Withdrawn		
Fenfluramine	Pondimin™	Suppresses appetite
Dexfenfluramine	Redux™	Suppresses appetite

ical agents satisfy all of these criteria as of yet. For example, as recently as 1996 the Food and Drug Administration (FDA), a regulatory agency of the US government, approved a drug called dexfenfluramine, marketed under the trade name of Redux™. Dexfenfluramine and its sister drug fenfluramine (sold as Pondimin™) work by enhancing levels of serotonin in the brain, which results in the suppression of appetite. Hailed as *the* magic bullet, the demands by the public caused physicians to prescribe these drugs to far more people than were really obese. Within just a few months, close to 5 million people were taking dexfenfluramine or a combination of fenfluramine and phentermine, popularly known as *fen-phen*.

The success story was short-lived, however, as in less than a year the FDA received nearly 150 reports of people who had been taking these drugs to lose weight, but were shortly experiencing pulmonary hypertension and valvular heart disease (Connolly *et al.*, 1997). In the FDA's defense, fenfluramine and phentermine had been separately approved for short-term use by the truly obese (i.e. those with a BMI of 30 or more) or overweight (BMI of 25 or greater) if other risk factors were not present, but not in combination and not for an extended period. Nevertheless, the FDA withdrew fenfluramine and dexfenfluramine from the market on September 15, 1997 (Wadden *et al.*, 1998). Within 3 months of the dexfluramine and fenfluramine recall, the FDA approved another new drug, namely sibutramine, marketed under the name of Meridia™. Sibutamine also enhances serotonin and suppresses appetite, but by a different mechanism. It appears to be safer than fenfluramine, but given it raises blood pressure and increases heart rate, it is obviously not suitable for everyone (Aronne, 1998).

In 1999 another new drug called orlistat, marketed under the trade name of Xenical™, was approved. In contrast to the drugs that enhance serotonin, orlistat works by blocking lipase absorption. In this manner, about one-third of ingested fat will pass through the body and be excreted. Fat that is not absorbed cannot be stored so weight loss results, but this also means that fat-soluble nutrients will be lost, in addition to the unpleasant side effects of diarrhea and flatulence (Drent *et al.*, 1995).

Besides these prescription drugs, a few 'over the counter' medications are also available to consumers. Used as an ingredient in candy or chewing gum, benzocaine numbs the tongue, which reduces taste sensations and thereby discourages eating. Phenylpropanolamine, a type of amphetamine, is a component of pills such as Acutrim™ and Dexatrim™ and purports to work by suppressing appetite. When used with a low-calorie diet it does appear to be somewhat successful in helping individuals to lose weight. However, side effects can include irregular heartbeats, kidney failures, seizures and strokes, as well as behavioral disturbances such as nervousness and sleeplessness (Schteingart, 1995).

What are billed as more natural approaches include products that contain caffeine or fiber, the former to stimulate activity and the latter to provide a feeling of fullness. Caffeine leads to dehydration, which results in only a temporary weight loss since once the pills are stopped normal rehydration should occur. The ever-growing herbal industry has also taken notice, with St John's Wort and ma huang being combined and marketed as 'nature's fen-phen.' But much like the original fen-phen, the ephedrine culled from ma huang has been linked to heart problems as well as seizures. Along with 'dieter's teas' that serve as laxatives – concoctions that contain aloe, buckhorn, cascara, senna and other herbs – these 'natural' products have been implicated in a number of deaths (Kurtzweil, 1997).

The development and marketing of anti-obesity drugs will surely continue in the near future. While some of the current drugs do seem to be of some help in weight loss, all of them have undesirable side effects. And none of them are effective on their own. Diet, exercise, and the modification of eating habits must all be included if substantive weight loss is to be realized (Wadden *et al.*, 2001).

Very-low-calorie diets

For the majority of overweight and obese individuals, dieting represents the primary strategy for losing weight. In the 1980s, obesity treatment centers began to offer what have become known as very-low-calorie diets (VLCDs), an approach deemed suitable for individuals who are moderately obese, that is, from 41% to 100% over their ideal weight. The typical VLCD plan provides no more than 800 kcal, at least 1 g of high-quality protein per kg of body weight, and at least 50 g of carbohydrate, which may not be enough to spare protein. Meals consist of a limited number of foods each day, primarily lean meats, fish and poultry, and often a supplemental powdered formula available by prescription (Apfelbaum et al., 1987). Clients also receive an assortment of vitamin and mineral supplements.

When carefully administered under medical supervision, VLCD diets appear to be relatively safe, although side effects on blood pressure, heart muscle and hormones, as well as headache, cold intolerance and fatigue, have been reported (Atkinson, 1992). While designed to be nutritionally adequate, the body responds to this severe energy restriction as if the person were starving, conserving energy by reducing BMR and slowing fat oxidation. For this reason, a VCLD is only appropriate for short-term use (i.e. 3–4 months), but may help the individual lose some 20 kg (44 lb) over that time interval. Unfortunately, the near starvation it creates primes the body to regain weight at the first opportunity, with two-thirds of the weight loss being regained within a year (Wilson, 1990). Such a rapid loss of weight followed by a steady gain is likely to be detrimental to both physical and psychological health (Whitney and Rolfes, 2002).

Yo-yo dieting

Many individuals who diet will successfully lose weight, but very few are able to maintain their loss for an extended period of time. Nevertheless, they are likely to repeat the strategy of dieting to lose weight, regaining the weight and dieting again, a behavioral pattern known as weight cycling or 'yo-yo dieting'. An oft-cited experiment with rats gave the animals a high-fat diet to induce obesity, followed by restricting their food to reduce them to normal weight, with a repetition of this weight gain-weight loss cycle. In the first cycle it took 45 days for the rats to reach their obese state, and

21 days to lose their excess weight. In the second cycle, however, it only took 14 days for the rats to regain the excess weight, but 46 days to lose it (Brownell et al., 1986).

Such a finding is in line with anecdotal reports by dieters that with every attempt at dieting it takes longer to lose weight and quicker to gain it back. Although some initial studies with humans suggested that weight cycling may affect metabolic functioning and increase health risks, more recent research has not found this to be the case (McCarger et al., 1993; Rebuffe-Scrive et al., 1994). Whether or not weight cycling increases the risk for chronic disease is still a matter of scientific debate, and some would argue that maintaining a stable weight, even if overweight, is less harmful than yo-yo dieting (Jeffery, 1996). However, there are also experts who assert that the potential benefits of weight loss for the obese individual exceed the potential risks of weight cycling (Kirschenbaum and Fitzgibbon, 1995).

Weight Management

As opposed to the extreme forms of dieting that were just described, and the endless number of diet plans that are advertised, adopted and abandoned, a more viable approach to treating obesity is one of striving for a healthy weight, rather than reducing one's weight to conform to a weight-for-height table. In fact, the recent Dietary Guidelines for Americans (2000) listed 'Aim for a healthy weight' as their first piece of advice. Modest weight loss, even if a person remains overweight, can reduce the risk of heart disease and improve control of diabetes. A loss of just 10 to 15 lb (4.5–6.8 kg), for example, can lower an individual's BMI by two units, which will significantly improve his or her health. However, experts recommend a loss of no more than 5% to 10% per year (Whitney and Rolfes, 2002). Not incidentally, 'Find your balance between food and physical activity' is now included in the most recent edition of the Dietary Guidelines (2005). Reducing blood pressure or cholesterol through diet and exercise is therefore a more useful goal than is a mere focus on weight, although the strategies used to do so will result likely in a healthier body weight and composition as well (Abernathy and Black, 1996). Ironically, the unrealistic expectations for weight loss that many people possess may prevent them from appreciating their actual success.

To illustrate, in a recent study of women who were about to enter a weight-loss program, the obese participants (BMIs > 36) were asked to identify the end weights that they would describe as 'disappointing' versus 'ideal'. As would be predicted, all of the weights they indicated were well below their starting weight. After 48 weeks of treatment, the average woman lost 16 kg (~ 35 lb) and reported improvements in the physical, social and psychological domains. However, because they had hoped for a loss of 32% of their body weight but lost an amount closer to 16%, most of the women were dissatisfied with their achievement (Foster et al., 1997). This underscores the role of psychology in weight loss, a factor that along with eating and physical activity must be considered in managing weight or treating obesity. As shown in Fig. 15.2 the multiple factors that contribute to excessive weight gain require a treatment that must also involve multiple components.

Diet composition

A small change in energy intake, such as a reduction of 200–300 kcal/day, is more successful in long-term weight control than is trying to subsist on a daily regimen of 1000–1200 kcal. A realistic energy intake should provide less energy than the person needs to maintain their present body weight, but a daily intake less than 1200 kcal/day could make it difficult to achieve nutritional adequacy (Whitney and Rolfes, 2002). Adequate intake will likelier ensure more successful weight loss than a severely restrictive plan that induces starvation and deprivation, which can lead to bingeing (Polivy, 1996).

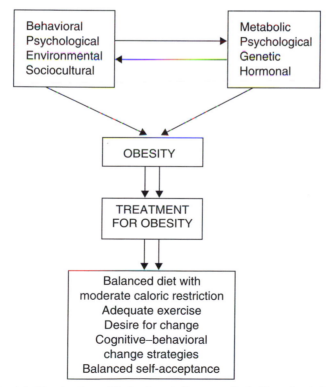

Fig. 15.2. Factors related to obesity and its treatment. Source: adapted from Insel et al., 2004.

Restricting fat intake is an obvious strategy, and studies show that a person who eats a low-fat diet will more readily satisfy their hunger and eat less food (Shah *et al.*, 1994). Such low-fat diets must be high in carbohydrate and adequate in protein, of course, but excessive carbohydrates and out-of-bounds portion sizes should not be used to compensate for the reduction in fat (Insel *et al.*, 2004). Even low-fat foods provide excessive calories if eaten in mass quantities. Complex carbohydrate foods such as fresh fruits, vegetables, legumes and whole grains are low in fat but also rich in vitamins, minerals and fiber. High-fiber foods are also beneficial because they require more effort to chew, in effect slowing down intake while having a strong satiety effect (Burton-Freeman, 2000).

Water, which assists the gastrointestinal tract in adapting to a high-fiber diet, will also help to fill the stomach between meals and dilute the metabolic wastes that the breakdown of fat generates. Drinking water frequently is therefore a useful strategy in maintaining weight. Drinking just any liquid, however, is not as beneficial as plain water. While high in antioxidants, alcoholic beverages are high in calories but low in major nutrients, as are regular soft drinks with their high-sugar content. Moreover, calories as fluids are not well compensated for – individuals do not eat any less when drinking such fluids, resulting in higher energy intake than if fruit, for example, were eaten (Mattes, 1996). And the caffeine in coffee, which serves as a diuretic, gives only the illusion of weight loss.

Physical activity

As has already been discussed, regular physical activity is an essential component of weight management. Aerobic activities such as walking or jogging burn calories directly, while anaerobic activities such as sit ups or lifting weights serve to build muscle mass. In addition, regular exercise can discourage overeating by reducing stress, can produce positive feelings that reinforce a sense of well-being, and will often promote positive social interactions. Overweight individuals who combine diet and exercise may be more likely to lose fat,

retain more muscle and regain less weight than those who only diet. For example, in one study, albeit brief, 20 obese women were randomly assigned to a diet or a diet + exercise plan for 8 weeks. Those in the diet + exercise condition lost 29% more fat mass than those in the diet-only condition (Kempen *et al.*, 1995).

As was earlier illustrated in Table 15.5, physical activity has a direct effect on energy expenditure. While regular exercise of moderate intensity will improve health, in order to lose fat, exercise should be as vigorous as physical shape and time will permit, with intensity offset by the amount of time that is available. For example, a woman who weighs 150 lb (68 kg) would expend approximately 92 calories if she walked for 15 min, versus 103 calories if she ran for 6 min (Wood, 1996). Activity also contributes to energy expenditure indirectly by speeding up basal metabolism. Recall that basal metabolism refers to the energy expended in carrying out bodily functions like breathing, maintaining temperature, etc. Basal metabolism immediately rises after intense and prolonged exercise and will remain elevated for several hours. Over many weeks, however, daily vigorous exercise will build more lean tissue, changing overall body composition. Since lean tissue is more metabolically active, there will be a corresponding rise in BMR, resulting in better weight maintenance (Sjodin *et al.*, 1996).

Physically active individuals are likely to possess good appetites, but exercise itself and eating are incompatible. To support exercise the body must release glucose and fatty acids into the blood as fuels, and simultaneously suppresses its digestive functions. Moreover, by displacing the act of eating, exercise may actually help to curb appetite, especially if anxiety, boredom or depression are typical triggers of overeating for the individual (King *et al.*, 1997).

Behavior change

The National Weight Control Registry, a collaborative venture between a number of universities, is a longitudinal prospective study of individuals 18 years and older who have successfully maintained a 30 lb weight loss for a minimum of 1 year (McGuire *et al.*, 1998). The registry currently includes nearly 3000 individuals, who report having made substantial changes in eating and exercise habits to lose weight and maintain their losses. Although about half of the individuals report having lost weight on their own without any type of formal program or help, their successes underscore the role of behavior change in losing weight and maintaining weight loss. This of course assumes that their self-reports of weight and weight-loss are honest and accurate.

Besides a foundational emphasis on nutrition and exercise, behavioral programs that are designed to facilitate weight management typically include a number of strategies that rely on cognitive-behavioral change. These include *self-monitoring, goal setting, stimulus control, problem solving, cognitive restructuring* and *relapse prevention* (Wing, 2004). For example, in self-monitoring the individuals are taught to write down everything they eat, the caloric content of the foods eaten, as well as the grams of fat. After a few weeks in the weight-loss program, the self-monitoring of physical activity is added. During the initial weeks of a program daily self-monitoring is prescribed, but it may be reduced to periodic self-monitoring when sufficient weight is lost and weight maintenance is desired (Wadden and Letizia, 1992).

In contrast, stimulus control involves managing the near environment so as to avoid cues that encourage inappropriate eating, or to institute new cues that elicit desirable behaviors (Nash, 1997). For the former, the individual may be instructed to place energy-dense foods out of sight (e.g. the cookie jar in a cabinet rather than on a counter), and for the latter, to set up visible reminders to exercise (e.g. keeping sneakers near the doorway). Cognitive restructuring, in turn, refers to eliminating rationalizations for inappropriate eating, as well as countering negative thoughts with positive statements that build self-acceptance (Insel *et al.*, 2004).

Finally, the importance of stress management in managing weight should be mentioned (Christiano and Mizes, 1997). Identifying cues that trigger overeating is a useful way to avoid temptation. Among binge eaters, in particular, chocolate is often eaten under the mistaken belief that it will help to alleviate stress.

However, as may be recalled from Chapter 1, there exists some data on the role of chocolate in the possible altering of mood (Macdiarmid and Hetherington, 1995). Such studies show that instead of facilitating relaxation or reducing depression, the net result of a chocolate binge may be an increase in feelings of guilt! Individuals who are attempting to maintain weight loss and are fond of chocolate, then, may still partake of chocolate on occasions, but should avoid temptation by not keeping it around. Determining coping strategies that do not involve food, such as engaging in exercise or watering houseplants, are best planned in anticipation of the stressful periods that inevitably occur from time to time.

Preventive Approaches to Excess Weight

Given the difficulty of losing weight and maintaining weight loss, it should be obvious that preventing excessive weight gain in the first place is a sensible approach to lifelong health and well-being. Strategies for preventing weight gain are similar to approaches for losing weight, albeit they should begin early and be incorporated into daily living. At an individual level, the following strategies are recommended:

1. Eat regular meals and limit snacking.
2. Drink water instead of high kilocalorie beverages.
3. Regularly select low-fat foods.
4. Limit dietary fat to 30% of daily kilocalorie intake.
5. Become physically active.
6. Limit television-viewing time.

(Bouchard, 1996.)

The dramatic increase in the prevalence of obesity, coupled with the persistent failure of most obesity treatment programs to achieve success, has resulted in prevention research becoming one of the newest areas of inquiry in the obesity area. In a sense, the treatment of obesity in children serves as a means of obesity prevention, if the goal is defined as reducing the risk of obesity in adulthood (Jeffery, 1998). Research suggests that programs utilizing the behavioral strategies previously addressed, which also involve parents in the treatment regimen, may be the most successful approach for working with high-risk children (Epstein *et al.*, 1994). However, the literal epidemic of obesity in adulthood across many developed countries would seem to call out for measures that do more than just target children who have already distinguished themselves as being overweight.

To this end, population-based approaches aimed at reaching children in schools, employees at the work-site, and citizens in the community have all been tried, but admittedly, with less than spectacular results in terms of their effectiveness. For example, in one population-based study, substantial gains in obesity were seen in both the treated and untreated community samples over the 7 years of observation (Jeffery, 1995). Despite such discouraging results, the urgency of the obesity problem demands that innovative strategies be considered and tested.

In a study by Donnelly and his colleagues, a nutrition and physical activity program was implemented with 3rd to 5th graders to attenuate obesity and improve physical and metabolic fitness. The intervention and control schools were matched for ethnicity and socioeconomic status, with participating children across the schools equivalent in BMI and time to run a mile. The nutrition intervention consisted of classroom nutrition education and modified school lunches that were designed to be healthier. The physical activity intervention consisted of non-competitive aerobic activities that were designed to use large muscle groups, for 30–40 min, three times per week. Measures of energy intake and physical activity outside of school were also obtained at the beginning and end of the study. No differences in BMI across schools were found at the study's conclusion. While the intervention lunches were lower in energy, fat and sodium, and higher in fiber, the 24 h diet records revealed sodium intake to be the only nutrient that differentiated the groups at the end of the study. Similarly, while physical activity at school was 6% greater for the intervention compared to the control group, physical activity at home was 16% less for the intervention than for the control children. In both domains, then, it appeared that the chil-

dren in the intervention group compensated at home for their improved behavior displayed at school (Donnelly *et al.*, 1996).

In contrast to directly manipulating nutritional intake and physical activity, Robinson (1999) tested the possibility that merely reducing television and videotape watching and video game use would have a positive impact on children's diet, activity and body composition. As in the Donnelly *et al.* (1996) study, two elementary schools were matched, although target children were restricted to 3rd and 4th graders. The intervention consisted of a classroom-based curriculum that focused on self-help behavioral methods to reduce television viewing. Over the course of the year, there were no changes in physical activity or fitness. However, intervention group children reduced their television, videotape and video game use by about 30%, compared to controls. Eating while watching television declined, and most notably, there were clinically and statistically significant decreases in BMI, skinfold thickness, waist-to-hip ratio and waist circumference, compared to controls. Quite a remarkable result for what would appear to be a rather simplistic intervention. The results of these two studies underscore the complex issues that additionally arise when dealing with children and the need for creativity in formulating solutions to address the obesity epidemic.

While most of the above approaches to reducing obesity derive from the premise that individuals are ultimately responsible for their weight problem, whether it is her genes or his inappropriate eating, an alternate view implicates the environment rather than people. There has been increased discussion in recent years about the 'toxicity' of the environment as it promotes overeating, poor nutrition habits and sedentary behavior (Battle and Brownell, 1998). In theory, there is a range of public health strategies that could be applied to the problem of obesity. While education about health and nutrition will always be the mainstay of public health efforts, policy makers might consider certain limitations on advertising of energy-dense foods or fast-food restaurants, particularly those commercials that are aimed at children, such as high-sugar breakfast cereals. For example, more money is spent on promoting the consumption of foods of questionable nutritional value than is spent on warnings to consumers about their hazards with respect to weight gain (Jeffery, 1998).

Conclusion

In this chapter, as well as throughout this book, we have tried to define the synergistic relationship between nutrition and behavior. The problem of overweight and obesity in our modern world is an appropriate topic on which to close, as it vividly illustrates the complex interactions between diet and development. The disciplines of biology, psychology and economics, among others, along with an appreciation of agricultural and technological advances, are necessary to understand how the current obesity epidemic has occurred. Although weight gain may be explained simply as a matter of energy intake exceeding energy expenditure, the multiple determinants of obesity require a variety of strategies for assisting individuals with weight loss, as well as ensuring that any desired losses are maintained. Prevention is mostly always cheaper than remedial efforts, however, and the policy measures outlined above to regulate dietary intake could be extended even further to promote physical activity. For example, new building codes to make elevators less accessible, new residential areas that include sidewalks to encourage walking, and television programs that are meted out on a fee per show basis. At first glance, such suggestions may appear outrageous, but the serious problem of obesity in the 21st century warrants a radical response.

References

Abernathy, R.P. and Black, D.R. (1996) Healthy body weights: an alternative perspective. *American Journal of Clinical Nutrition* 63, 448S–451S.

Albu, J. and Pi-Sunyer, F.X. (2004) Obesity and diabetes. In: Bray, G.A. and Bouchard C. (eds), *Handbook of Obesity: Etiology and Pathophysiology,* 2nd edn. Marcel Dekker, New York, pp. 899–917.

Albu, J., Allison, D., Boozer, C.N., Heymsfield, S., Kissileff, H., Kretser, A., Krumhar, K., Leibel, R., Nonas, C., Pi-Sunyer, X., VanItallie, T. and

Wedral, E. (1997) Obesity solutions: report of a meeting. *Nutrition Reviews* 55(5), 150–156.

American Psychiatric Association (1994) *Diagnostic and statistical manual of mental disorders,* 4th edn. Washington, DC.

Andersen, R.E., Crespo, C.J., Bartlett, S.J., Cheskin, L.I. and Pratt, M. (1998) Relationship of a physical activity and television watching with body weight and level of fatness among children: results from the Third National Health and Nutrition Examination Survey. *Journal of the American Medical Association* 279, 938–942.

Anderson, A.E. (1995) Eating disorders in males. In: Brownell, K.D. and Fairburn, C.G. (eds), *Eating Disorders and Obesity,* Guilford, New York, pp. 177–182.

Apfelbaum, M., Fricker, J. and Igoin-Apfelbaum, L. (1987) Low- and very low- calorie diets. *American Journal of Clinical Nutrition* 45, 1126–1134.

Arnow, B., Kenardy, J. and Agras, W.S. (1995) The emotional eating scale: the development of a measure to assess coping with negative affect by eating. *International Journal of Eating Disorders* 18, 79–90.

Aronne, L.J. (1998) Modern medical management of obesity: the role of pharmaceutical intervention. *Journal of the American Dietetic Association* 10(2), S23–S26.

Atkinson, R.L. (1992) Low calorie diets and obesity. In: Bills, D.D. and Kung, S.D. (eds), *Biotechnology and nutrition,* Butterworth-Heinemann, Boston, pp. 29–45.

Atkinson, R.L. (1997) Use of drugs in the treatment of obesity. *Annual Review of Nutrition* 17, 383–403.

Battle, E.K. and Brownell, K.D. (1998) Confronting a rising tide of eating disorders and obesity: treatment vs. prevention policy. *Addictive Behaviors* 21(6), 755–765.

Berdanier, C.D. (1996) The candidate gene approach in obesity research. In: Berdanier, C.D. (ed.), *Nutrients and Gene Expression: Clinical Aspects,* CRC Press, Florida, pp. 39–49.

Birch, L.L., Fisher, J.O. and Davison, K.K. (2003) Learning to overeat: maternal use of restrictive feeding practices promotes girls' eating in the absence of hunger. *American Journal of Clinical Nutrition* 78(2), 215–220.

Blackburn, G.L. (1995) Effects of weight loss on weight-related risk factors. In: Brownell, K.D. and Fairburn, C.G. (eds), *Eating Disorders and Obesity,* Guilford, New York, pp. 406–410.

Blundell, J.E. and Macdiarmid, J.I. (1997) Fat as a risk factor for overconsumption: satiation, satiety, and patterns of eating. *Journal of the American Dietetic Association* 97, S63–S69.

Bouchard, C. (1996) Can obesity be prevented? *Nutrition Reviews* 54, S125–S130.

Bouchard, C. (1997) Human variation in body mass: evidence for a role of the genes. *Nutrition Reviews* 55, S21–S30.

Bray, G.A. (1980) Jejunoileal bypass, jaw wiring, and vagotomy for massive obesity. In Stunkard A.J. (ed) *Obesity*. W.B. Saunders, Philadelphia, pp. 369–387.

Bray, G. (1989) Classification and evaluation of the obesities. *Medical Clinics of North America* 73, 161–184.

Bray, G.A. (2004) Historical framework for the development of ideas about obesity In: Bray, G.A. and Bouchard, C. (eds), *Handbook of Obesity: Etiology and Pathophysiology,* 2nd edn. Marcel Dekker, New York, pp. 1–31.

Brown, P.J. and Bentley-Condit, V.K. (1998) Culture, evolution, and obesity. In: Bray, G.A., Bouchard, C. and James, W.P.T. (eds), *Handbook of obesity,* Marcel Dekker, New York, pp. 143–156.

Brownell, K., Greenwood, M.R.C., Stellar, E. and Schrager, E.E. (1986) The effects of repeated cycles of weight loss and regain in rats. *Physiology and Behavior* 38, 459–464.

Bundred, P., Kitchiner, D. and Buchan, I. (2001) Prevalence of overweight and obese children between 1989 and 1998: Population based series of cross-sectional studies. *British Medical Journal* 322, 1–4.

Burton-Freeman, B. (2000) Dietary fiber and energy regulation. *Journal of Nutrition* 130, 272S–275S.

Campfield, L.A., and Smith, F.J. (2000) Pharmacological treatment of obesity: outcomes and new tools. In: Lockwood, D.H. and Heffner, T.G. (eds), *Obesity: Pathology and Therapy,* Springer, Heidelberg, Germany, pp. 177–194.

Christiano, B. and Mizes, S. (1997) Appraisal and coping deficits associated with eating disorders: implications of treatment. *Cognitive Behavior Practica* 4, 263–290.

Collins, K. (2003) How to de-supersize. *Nutrition Notes* (October 13, 2003). American Institute for Cancer Research (www.aicr.org).

Comptroller and Auditor General, (2001) *Tackling Obesity in England.* National Audit Office of England. The Stationery Office, London.

Connolly, H.M., Crary, J.L., McGoon, M.D., Hensrud, D.D., Edwards, B.S., Edwards, W.D. and Schaff, H.V. (1997) Valvular heart disease associated with fenfluramine-phentermine. *New England Journal of Medicine* 337(24), 1783.

Crandall, C.S. (1991) Do parents discriminate against their heavy-weight daughters? *Personality and Social Psychology Bulletin* 31, 724–735.

Crespo, C.J., Smit, E., Troiano, R.P., Bartlett, S.J., Macera, C.A. and Andersen, R.E. (2001) Television watching, energy intake, and obesity in US children: results from the Third National Health and Nutrition Examination Survey, 1988–1994. *Archives of Pediatrics & Adolescent Medicine* 155, 360–365.

Dalton, S. (1997) *Overweight and weight management.* Aspen Publishing, Caithersbing, Maryland, p. 315.

Darby, W.J., Ghalioungui, P. and Gravetti, L. (1977) *Food: The gift of Osiris.* Academic Press, London.

Das, S.K. and Roberts, S.B. (2001) Energy metabolism. In: Bowman, B.A. and Russell, R.M. (eds), *Present knowledge in nutrition,* 8th edn.ILSI Press, Washington, DC.

Dietary Guidelines for Americans (2000) United States Department of Agriculture (USDA) & United States Department of Health and Human Services. *Home and Garden Bulletin* 5(232), 2–39.

Dietary Guidelines for Americans (2005) United States Department of Agriculture (USDA) and United States Department of Health and Human Services. *Home and Garden Bulletin* 6(232).

Dietz, W.H. and Belizzi, M.C. (1999) The use of BMI to assess obesity in children. *American Journal of Clinical Nutrition* 70(Suppl.), 123S–125S.

DiGirolamo, M., Harp, J. and Stevens, J. (2000) Obesity: definition and epidemiology. In: Lockwood, D.H. and Heffner, T.G. (eds), *Obesity: Pathology and Therapy.* Springer, Berlin, pp. 3–28.

Donnelly, J.E., Jacobsen, D.J., Whatley, J.E., Hill, J.O., Swift, L.L., Cherrington, A., Polk, B., Tran, Z.V. and Reed, G. (1996) Nutrition and physical activity program to attenuate obesity and promote physical and metabolic fitness in elementary school children. *Obesity Research* (3), 229–243.

Drent, M.L., Larsson, I., William-Olsson, T., Quaade, F., Czubayko, F., von Bergmann, K., Strobel, W., Sjostrom, L., and van der Veen, E.A. (1995) Orlistat (Ro 18-0647), a lipase inhibitor, in the treatment of human obesity: a multiple dose study. *International Journal of Obesity* 19, 221–226.

Enzi, G. (1994) Socioeconomic consequences of obesity: the effect of obesity on the individual. *Pharmacoeconomics* 5(Suppl.1), 54–57.

Epstein, L.H., Valoski, A., Wing, R.R. and McCurley, J. (1994) Ten-year outcomes of behavioral family-based treatment for childhood obesity. *Health Psychology* 13, 373–383.

Faith, M.S., Allison, D.B. and Geliebter, A. (1997) Emotional eating and obesity: theoretical considerations and practical recommendations. In: Dalton, S. (ed.), *Overweight and Weight*

Management: The Health Professional's Guide to Understanding and Practice. Jones & Bartlett, Boston, pp. 439–465.

Faith, M.S., Matz, P.E. and Jorge, M.A. (2002) Obesity-depression associates in the population. *Journal of Psychosomatic Research* 53(4), 935–942.

Fitzgibbon, M.L., Stolley, M.R. and Kirschenbaum, D.S. (1993) Obese people who seek treatment have different characteristics than those who do not seek treatment. *Health Psychology* 12, 342–345.

Flegal, K.M., Carroll, M.D., Kuczmarski, R.J. and Johnson, C.L. (1998) Overweight and obesity in the United States: prevalence and trends. *International Journal of Obesity* 22, 39–47.

Fleury, C., Neverova, M., Collins, S., Raimbault, S., Champigny, O., Levi-Meyrueis, C., Bouillaud, F., Seldin, M.F., Surwit, R.S., Ricquier, D. and Warden, C.H. (1997) Uncoupling protein-2: a novel gene linked to obesity and hyperinsulinemia. *Nature Genetics* 15(3), 269–272.

Ford, E.S., Moriarty, D.G., Zack, M.M., Mokdad, A.H. and Chapman, D.P. (2001) Self-reported body mass index and health-related quality of life: findings from the Behavioral Risk Factor Surveillance System. *Obesity Research* 9(1), 21–31.

Foreyt, J. and Goodrick, K. (1995) The ultimate triumph of obesity. *The Lancet* 346, 134–135.

Foster, G.D., Wadden, T.A., Vogt, R.A. and Brewer, G. (1997) What is reasonable weight loss? Patients' expectations and evaluations of obesity treatment outcomes. *Journal of Consulting and Clinical Psychology* 65(1), 79–85.

French, S.A., Story, M. and Perry, C.L. (1995) Self-esteem and obesity in children and adolescents: a literature review. *Obesity Research* 3, 479–490.

Friedman, J.M. (1998) Leptin, leptin receptors, and the control of body weight. *Nutrition Reviews* 56(2), S38–S46.

Gable, S. and Lutz, S. (2000) Household, parent, and child contributions to childhood obesity. *Family Relations* 49, 293–300.

Goldsmith, S.J., Anger-Friedfeld, K., Beren, S., Rudolph, D., Boeck, M. and Aronne, L. (1992) Psychiatric illness in patients presenting for obesity treatment. *International Journal of Eating Disorders* 12, 63–71.

Gortmaker, S.L., Dietz, W.H. and Cheung, L.W.Y. (1990) Inactivity, diet, and the fattening of America. *Journal of the American Dietetic Association* 90, 1247–1255.

Gortmaker, S.L., Must, A., Perrin, J.M., Sobol, A.M. and Dietz, W.H. (1993) Social and economic consequences of overweight in adolescence and young adulthood. *New England Journal of Medicine* 329(14), 1008–1012.

Hall, J.C., Watts, J.M., O'Brien, P.E., Dunstan, R.E., Walsh, J.F., Slovotinek, A.H. and Emslie, R.G. (1990) Gastric surgery for morbid obesity. *Annals of Surgery* 211, 419–427.

Han, T.S., van Leer, E.M., Seidell, J.C. and Lean, M.E.J. (1995) Waist circumference action levels in the identification of cardiovascular risk factors: prevalence study in a random sample. *British Medical Journal* 311, 1401–1405.

Heitmann, B.L., Lissner, L., Sorensen, T.I. and Bengtsson, C. (1997) Dietary fat intake and weight gain in women genetically predisposed for obesity. *American Journal of Clinical Nutrition* 61(6), 1213–1217.

Hubert, H.B., Feinlieb, M., McNamara, P.M. and Castelli, W.P. (1983) Obesity as an independent risk factor for cardiovascular disease: a 26-year follow-up of participants in the Framingham heart study. *Circulation* 67, 968–977.

Insel, P., Turner, R.E. and Ross, D. (2004) *Nutrition*, 2nd edn. Jones and Bartlett Publishers, Sudbury, Massachusetts.

Jain, A. (2004) *What works for obesity?* A summary of the research behind obesity interventions. BMJ Publishing Group. www.clinicalevidence.com.

James, W.P. (1996) The epidemiology of obesity. *Ciba Foundation Symposium* 201, 1–11.

Jeffery, R.W. (1995) Community programs for obesity prevention: the Minnesota Hearth Health Program. *Obesity Research* 3(2), 283S–288S.

Jeffery, R.W. (1996) Does weight cycling present a health risk? *American Journal of Clinical Nutrition* 63(3), 452S–455S.

Jeffery, R.W. (1998) Prevention of obesity. In: Bray, G.A., Bouchard, C. and James, W.P.T. (eds), *Handbook of Obesity*, Marcel Dekker Inc., New York, pp. 819–829.

Jeffery, R.W. and French, S.A. (1998) Epidemic obesity in the USA: are fast foods and television viewing contributing? *American Journal of Public Health* 88, 277–280.

Jensen, M.D. (1997) Lipolysis: contribution from regional fat. *Annual Review of Nutrition* 17, 127–139.

Johansson, L., Solvell, K., Bjorneboe, G.E.A. and Drevon, C.A. (1998) Under and overreporting of energy intake related to weight status and lifestyle in a nationwide sample. *American Journal of Clinical Nutrition* 68, 266–274.

Joint Health Surveys Unit (1999) *Health survey for England: The health of minority ethnic groups '99: Findings, methodology and documentation.* (www.archive.official-documents.co.uk/document/doh/survey99/html).

Kempen, K.P.G., Saris, H.M. and Westerterp, K.R. (1995) Energy balance during an 8-wk energy-restricted diet with and without exercise in obese women. *American Journal of Clinical Nutrition* 62, 722–729.

Kern, P.A. (1997) Potential roles of TNF and lipoprotein lipase as candidate genes for obesity. *Journal of Nutrition* 127, 1917S–1922S.

King, N.A., Tremblay, A. and Blundell, J.E. (1997) Effects of exercise on appetite control: implications for energy balance. *Medicine and Science in Sports and Exercise* 29, 1076–1089.

Kirschenbaum, D.S. and Fitzgibbon, M.L. (1995) Controversy about the treatment of obesity: criticisms or challenges? *Behavior Therapy* 26, 43–68.

Kissebah, A.H. (1996) Intra-abdominal fat: is it a major factor in developing diabetes and coronary artery disease? *Diabetes Research Clinical Practices* 30, 25–30.

Ko, C.W. and Lee, S.P. (2004) Obesity and gallbladder disease. In: Bray, G.A. and Bouchard, C. (eds), *Handbook of Obesity: Etiology and Pathophysiology* 2nd edn. Marcel Dekker, New York, pp. 919–934.

Kopelman, P.G. (2000) Obesity as a medical problem. *Nature* 404, 632–634.

Kral, J.G. (1988) Surgical treatment of regional adiposity: lipectomy versus surgically induced weight loss. *Acta Medicus Scandinavia* 723, 225–231.

Kuczmarski, R.J., Flegal, K.M., Campbell, S.M. and Johnson, C.L. (1994) Increasing prevalence of overweight among US adults: The National Health and Nutrition Examination Surveys, 1960–1991. *Journal of the American Medical Association* 272, 205–211.

Kurtzweil, P. (1997) Dieter's brews make tea time a dangerous affair. *FDA Consumer,* 6–11.

Leibel, R.L., Rosenbaum, M. and Hirsch, J. (1995) Changes in energy expenditure resulting from altered body weight. *New England Journal of Medicine* 332, 621–628.

Levine, J.A. (2002) Non-exercise activity thermogensesis (NEAT). *Best Practice and Research Clinical Endocrinology & Metabolism* 16(4), 679–702.

Levine, J.A., Eberhardt, N.L. and Jensen, M.D. (1999) Role of nonexercise activity thermogenesis in resistance in fat gain in humans. *Science* 283, 212–215.

Levitsky, D.A. and Youn, T. (2004) The more food young adults are served, the more they overeat. *Journal of Nutrition* 134(10), 2546–2549.

Ma, G.S., Li, Y.P., Hu, X.Q., Ma, W.J. and Wu, J. (2002) Effect of television viewing on pediatric obesity. *Biomedical and Environmental Sciences* 15(4), 291–297.

Macdiarmid, J.I. and Hetherington, M.M. (1995) Mood modulation by food: an exploration of affect and cravings in 'chocolate addicts.' *British Journal of Clinical Psychology* 34, 129–138.

Marcus, M.D. (1993) Binge eating in obesity. In: Fairburn, C.G. and Wilson, G.T. (eds), *Binge Eating: Nature, Assessment, and Treatment,* Guilford Press, New York, pp. 77–96.

Mattes, R.D. (1996) Dietary compensation by humans for supplemental energy provided as ethanol or carbohydrate in fluids. *Physiology & Behavior* 59(1), 179–187.

McCarger, L., Taunton, J., Birmingham, C.L., Pare, S. and Simmons, D. (1993) Metabolic and anthropometric changes in female weight cyclers and controls over a one year period. *Journal of the American Dietetic Association* 93, 1025–1030.

McCrory, M.A., Fuss, P.J., Hays, N.P., Vinken, A.G., Greenberg, A.S. and Roberts, S.B. (1999) Overeating in America: association between restaurant food consumption and body fatness in healthy adult men and women ages 19 to 80. *Obesity Research* 7(6), 564–571.

McGuire, M.T., Wing, R.R., Klem, M.L., Seagle, H.M. and Hill, J.O. (1998) Long-term maintenance of weight loss: do people who lose weight through various weight loss methods use different behaviors to maintain that weight? *International Journal of Obesity* 22, 572–577.

Mei, Z., Scanlon, K.S., Grummer-Strawn, L.M., Freedman, D.S., Yip, R. and Trowbridge, F.L. (1998) Increasing prevalence of overweight among US low-income preschool children: the Centers for Disease Control and Prevention Pediatric Nutrition Surveillance, 1983 to 1995. *Pediatrics* 101,12.

Miller, C.T. and Downey, K.T. (1999) A meta-analysis of heavy weight and self-esteem. *Personality and Social Psychology Bulletin* 3, 68–84.

Morrow, S.R. and Mona, L.K. (1990) Effect of gastric balloons on nutrient intake and weight loss in obese subjects. *Journal of the American Dietetic Association* 90, 717–718.

Murray, C.J. and Lopez, A.D. (1996) *The Global Burden of Disease.* (WHO World Bank).

Nash, J.D. (1997) *The new maximize your body potential.* Bull Publishing Company, Palo Alto, California.

National Center for Health Statistics (2004) *National Health and Nutrition Examination Survey 1999–2000.* http://www.cdc/nch/nhanes.htm.

Nieman, D.C. (1999) *Exercise testing and prescription.* Mayfield Publishing, Mountain View, California.

Orphanidou, C., McCarger, L., Birmingham, L., Mathieson, J. and Goldner, E. (1994) Accuracy of subcutaneous fat measurement: comparison of skinfold calipers, ultrasound, and computed tomography. *Journal of the American Dietetic Association* 94, 855–858.

Pi-Sunyer, F.X. (1999) Obesity. In: Shils, M.E., Olson, I.A., Shike, M. and Ross, C.A. (eds), *Modern Nutrition in Health and Disease*, 9th edn. Lippincott Williams & Wilkins, Philadelphia, pp. 1395–1418.

Polivy, J. (1996) Psychological consequences of food restriction. *Journal of the American Dietetic Association* 96, 589–592.

Popkin, B. (1998) The obesity epidemic is a worldwide phenomenon: trends in transitional societies. *Nutrition Reviews* 56, 106–115.

Prentice, A.M. and Poppitt, S.D. (1996) Importance of energy density and macronutrients in the regulation of energy intake. *International Journal of Obesity and Related Metabolic Disorders* 20, S18–S23.

Putnam, J., Allshouse, J. and Kantor, L.S. (2002) U.S. per capita food supply trends: more calories, refined carbohydrates, and fats. *Food Review* 25(3), 2–15.

Quetelet, L.A.J. (1981) *Antropometric pour mesure des differentes facultés de l'homme.* C. Muquardt, Brussels, 479.

Qian, H., Azain, M.J., Compton, M.M., Hartzell, D.L., Hausman, G.J. and Baile, C.A. (1998) Brain administration of leptin causes deletion of adipocytes by apoptosis. *Endocrinology* 139(2), 791–794.

Rand, C.S.W. and MacGregor, A.M.C. (1991) Successful weight loss following obesity surgery and the perceived liability of morbid obesity. *International Journal of Obesity* 15, 577–579.

Ravussin, E. and Danforth, E. (1999) Beyond sloth-physical activity and weight gain. *Science* 283, 184–185.

Ravussin, E., Pratley, R.E., Maffei, M., Wang, Friedman, J.M., Bennett, P.H. and Bogardus, C. (1997) Relatively low plasma leptin concentrations precede weight gain in Pima Indians. *Nature Medicine* 3(2), 238–240.

Raynor, H.A. and Epstein, L.H. (2001) Dietary Variety, Energy Regulation, and Obesity. *American Psychological Association Journals: Psychological Bulletin* 127(3), 325–341.

Rebuffe-Scrive, M., Hendler, R., Bracero, N., Cummings, N., McCarthy, S. and Rodin, J. (1994) Biobehavioral effects of weight cycling. *International Journal of Obesity* 18, 651–658.

Robinson, T.N. (1999) Reducing children's television to prevent obesity: a randomized controlled trial. *Journal of the American Medical Association* 282, 1561–1567.

Robinson, T.N., Kiernan, M., Matheson, D.M. and Haydel, F. (2001) Is parental control over children's eating associated with childhood obesity? Results from a population-bases sample of third graders. *Obesity Research* 9, 306–312.

Rocchini, A.P. (2004) Obesity and blood pressure regulation. In: Bray, G.A. and Bouchard, C. (eds), *Handbook of Obesity: Etiology and pathophysiology*, 2nd edn. Marcel Dekker, New York, pp. 873–897.

Rolls, B.J. and Bell, E.A. (1999) Energy intake: effects of fat content and energy density of foods. In: Bray, G.A. and Ryan, D.H. (eds), *Nutrition, Genetics, and Obesity*, Pennington Center Nutrition Series, Vol. 9. Louisiana State University Press, Baton Rouge, Louisiana, pp. 172–191.

Schteingart, D.E. (1995) Phenylpropanolamine in the management of moderate obesity. In: VanItallie, T.B. and Simopoulos, A.P. (eds), *Obesity: New Directions in Assessment and Management*, Charles Press, Philadelphia, pp. 220–226.

Schulz, L.O. and Scheller, D.A. (1994) A compilation of total daily energy expenditures and body weights in healthy adults. *American Journal of Clinical Nutrition* 60, 676–681.

Schwartz, M., Chambliss, H.O., Brownell, K., Blair, S. and Billington, C. (2003) Weight bias among health professionals specializing in obesity. *Obesity Research* 11(9), 1033–1039.

Seidell, J.C. (1997) Time trends in obesity: an epidemiological perspective. *Hormones & Metabolic Research* 29, 155–158.

Shah, M., McGovern, P., French, S. and Baxter, J. (1994) Comparison of a low-fat, ad libitum complex-carbohydrate diet with low-energy diet in moderately obese women. *American Journal of Clinical Nutrition* 59, 980–984.

Sjodin, A.M., Forslund, A.N., Westerterp, H.N., Andersson, A.B., Forslund, J.M., and Hambraeus, L.M. (1996) The influence of physical activity on BMR. *Medicine and Science in Sports and Exercise* 28, 85–91.

Sobal, J., Troiano, R. and Frongillo, E. (1996) Rural-urban differences in obesity. *Rural Sociology* 61, 289–305.

Stamler, R., Stamler, J., Riedlinger, W.F., Alger, G. and Roberts, R. (1978) Weight and blood pressure: Findings in hypertension in screening of 1 million Americans. *Journal of the American Medical Association* 240, 1607–1609.

Stunkard, A.J. (1984) The current status of treatment for obesity in adults. *Research Publications-Association for Research in Nervous and Mental Disorders* 62, 157–173.

Stunkard, A.J., Sorensen, T.I.A., Hanis, C., Teasdale, T.W., Chakraborty, R., Schull, W.J. and

Schulsinger, F. (1986) An adoption study of human obesity. *New England Journal of Medicine* 314, 193–198.

Stunkard, A.J., Harris, J.R., Pedersen, N.L. and McClearn, G.E. (1990) The body-mass index of twins who have been reared apart. *New England Journal of Medicine* 322, 1483–1487.

Taubes, G. (2001) The soft science of dietary fat. *Science* 291(5513), 2536–2544.

Vandewater, E.A., Shim, M. and Caplovitz, A.G. (2004) Linking obesity and activity level with children's television and video game use. *Journal of Adolescence* 27(1), 71–84.

VanItallie, T.B. (1990) The perils of obesity in middle-aged women. *New England Journal of Medicine* 322, 928–929.

Wadden, T.A. and Letizia, K.A. (1992) Predictors of attrition and weight loss in patients treated by moderate and severe caloric restriction. In: Wadden, T.A. and VanItallie, T.B. (eds), *Treatment of the Seriously Obese Patient*, Guilford Press, New York, pp. 383–410.

Wadden, T.A., Berkowitz, R.I., Silvestry, F., Vogt, R.A., St. John-Sutton, M.G., Stunkard, A.J., Foster, G.D. and Aber, J.L. (1998) The fen-phen finale: a study of weight loss and valvular heart disease. *Obesity Research* 6, 278–284.

Wadden, T.A., Berkowitz, R.L., Sarwer, D.B., Prus-Wisniewski, R. and Steinberg, C. (2001) Benefits of lifestyle modification in the pharmacologic treatment of obesity: a randomized trial. *Archives of Internal Medicine* 161(2), 218–227.

Warden, C.H., Kachinskas, D., Gregoire, F., Neverova, M., Easlick, J. and Chomiki, N. (1999) The uncoupling protein family and energy expenditure. In: Bray, G.A. and Ryan, D.H. (eds), *Nutrition, Genetics, and Obesity*, Pennington Center Nutrition Series Vol. 9. Louisiana State University Press, Baton Rouge, Louisiana, pp. 102–121.

Whitney, E.N. and Rolfes, S.R. (2002) *Understanding Nutrition*, 9th edn. Wadsworth Publishing Company, California.

Williamson, D.F., Kahn, H.S., Remington, P.L. and Anda, R.F. (1990) The 10-year incidence of overweight and major weight gain in US adults. *Archives of Internal Medicine* 150, 665–672.

Wilson, M.A. (1990) Treatment of obesity. *American Journal of Medical Science* 299, 62–68.

Wing, R.R. (2004) Behavioral approaches to the treatment of obesity. In: Bray, G.A. and Bouchard, C. (eds), *Handbook of Obesity: Clinical Applications*, 2nd edn. Marcel Dekker New York, pp. 147–167.

Wluka, A., Spector, T.D. and Cicuttini, F.M. (2004) Obesity, arthritis, and gout. In: Bray, G.A., Bouchard, C. (eds), *Handbook of Obesity: Etiology and Pathophysiology*, 2nd edn. Marcel Dekker, New York, pp. 953–966.

Wolf, G. (1997) A new uncoupling protein: a potential component of the human body weight regulation system. *Nutrition Reviews* 55, 178–179.

Wood, P.D. (1996) Clinical applications of diet and physical activity in weight loss. *Nutrition Reviews* 54, S131–S135.

Worobey, J. (2002) Eating attitudes and temperament attributes of normal and overweight college students. *Eating Behaviors* 3, 85–92.

Young, L.R. and Nestle, M. (2002) The contribution of expanding portion sizes to the US obesity epidemic. *American Journal of Public Health* 92, 246–249.

York, D.A. (2004) Rodent models of obesity. In: Bray, G.A. and Bouchard, C. (eds), *Handbook of Obesity: Etiology and Pathophysiology*, 2nd edn. Marcel Dekker, New York, pp. 255–281.

Zhang, Y., Proenca, P., Maffei, M., Barone, M., Leopold, L. and Friedman, J.M. (1994) Positional cloning of the mouse obese gene and its human homologue. *Nature* 372(6505), 425–432.

Ziegler, R.G. (1997) Anthropometry and breast cancer. *Journal of Nutrition* 127(5), 924S–928S.

Appendix
A Primer on Basic Statistics in Nutrition and Behavior Research

J. Worobey

Statistics provide scientists with a method for reporting and evaluating the results of their research. Empirical research is a logical rather than a mathematical process, but as the applied branch of mathematics, statistics provide the means for executing the logical operations that constitute appropriate data analysis (Babbie, 1998). You are undoubtedly aware that full courses in statistics exist; indeed, full courses on specific statistical procedures and analytic strategies are now available at nearly all colleges and universities. In fact, you may have already taken one or more statistics courses. If so, this section should be nothing more than a cursory review of some elementary concepts. But if you have no background in statistics, or you have never read an empirical article in a refereed journal, the summary that follows should provide you with enough background to make sense of the various study results that are presented throughout this book. More important, as you begin to seek out research articles on nutrition and behavior from professional journals, you will have at least a rudimentary acquaintanceship with some of the analytic techniques that the authors may have employed in trying to make sense of their own results.

Descriptive Statistics

Descriptive statistics are used to *describe*, summarize, and determine patterns of association among data from our observations of groups of individuals in an efficient manner. For example, descriptive statistics would allow us to tell how bright the nutrition majors at a university might be as a group, and whether they are at the same level of ability or if they vary widely among themselves. Descriptive statistics could also be used to compare their grades across particular courses. Much of the data gathered using correlational research designs is analyzed with descriptive statistics. The most basic consideration in choosing a descriptive statistic is what type of information we want to obtain. The three questions most commonly asked in psychological research are: (i) what is the central tendency or average of the scores? (ii) how much do the other scores differ from the average score? and (iii) what is the relationship between the variables that represent these different sets of scores (Zimbardo *et al.*, 2000)?

In nutrition–behavior studies, the average score is usually represented by the *mean*, which is calculated by adding together the scores for all subjects on a particular measure, and dividing by the number of subjects. Recognizing that human subjects will differ from each other in their scores on most every behavioral measure (body temperature is a notable exception), it is useful to know how well the mean represents all of the scores in the distribution. The standard deviation is the most common measure of variability, that is, how much each score deviates from the mean.

If the standard deviation is high, it suggests that the scores are widely dispersed, and that the mean may not accurately reflect what the score would be of a typical subject.

Perhaps an illustration from an actual study may help. Worobey (1998) was interested in determining whether 3-month-old infants who are breast-fed would exhibit temperamental differences from infants who are formula fed. As shown in Table A.1, the mean levels of soothability were 4.85 and 5.01 for the breast-fed and formula fed infants, respectively. The standard deviation for the breast-fed group was 0.79 and for the formula-fed 0.72, about a 15% departure from the mean, or average scores. While it indicates some degree of variability, this range is small enough to believe that most of the infants' soothability ratings are in the neighborhood of what the means suggest. But consider the estimates for arm and leg activity – the standard deviations are nearly as high as the means! This suggests that for these variables, the mean may not be a very good reflection of how much motor activity the typical breast- or formula-fed infant displayed.

With respect to the relationship between variables, it should be no surprise that computing correlations would be the statistical technique of choice when using a correlational research approach. The premise behind a correlation is simple enough. If individuals with higher scores on one variable also scored higher on the second variable, this would suggest a positive correlation. Whether or not the correlation truly holds would depend on the individuals who scored lower on one test also scoring lower on the other. Again, a correlation refers to the simultaneous increase, decrease, or change in two variables. If variable 1 increases in its magnitude as variable 2 increases, or if variable 1 decreases in its magnitude as variable 2 decreases, the correlation is positive. If variable 1 increases as variable 2 decreases, or if variable 1 decreases in its magnitude as variable 2 increases, the correlation is negative. Correlational procedures that you are likely to see employed in research studies will often use the Pearson product-moment correlation coefficient (abbreviated as r) or the Spearman rank order correlation coefficient (rho). More sophisticated analytic strategies may use multiple regression or factor analysis, terms we are only mentioning here so that you will recognize them as variants of correlational approaches.

In theory, correlation coefficients like the Pearson r run from −1.00 to 1.00, values that would only be possible if the scores on variables 1 and 2 covaried perfectly. Since people will vary in their level of performance depending on the measure on which they are observed, correlation coefficients will usually be some decimal fraction of the whole number 1. On this continuum, a correlation of 0.00 would indicate absolutely no relationship

Table A.1. Example of means and standard deviations in research temperament ratings and limb activity estimates by feeding method.

	Breast-fed		Formula-fed	
	Mean	Standard Deviation	Mean	Standard Deviation
Temperament Ratings				
Distress	3.50	0.69	3.31	0.74
Soothability	4.85	0.79	5.01	0.72
Fearfulness	2.09	0.61	2.29	0.66
Orienting	4.03	1.13	4.06	1.25
Limb Activity				
Left arm	82.45	79.82	47.16*	41.09
Right arm	57.15	68.29	37.53	44.32
Left leg	10.88	10.36	11.26	12.66
Right leg	47.80	40.88	35.99	39.17

* $p < 0.01$.
Source: adapted from Worobey, 1998.

between the two variables. That is, knowing the value of the first variable would tell you nothing about the value of the second. While correlation coefficients will rarely approach 1.00 (unless the two variables are measuring virtually the same thing), they need to be of a certain magnitude to achieve what is referred to as *statistical significance*. The magnitude of an acceptable coefficient will vary, depending on the number of subjects that comprise the sample. Larger samples can allow for smaller coefficients, and vice versa. It is a general convention among nutritional and behavioral scientists that a 0.05 level of significance is the minimum criterion for accepting the validity of a statistical result. A significance level of 0.05 (indicated by $p < 0.05$) means that the association has only a 5 in 100 chance of not being true, or a 95% chance of reflecting an actual association. A stronger, and likely better, correlation coefficient would achieve a $p < 0.01$ level of significance, meaning that 99 times out of a 100 you would expect this association. A level of $p < 0.0001$ would mean 1 in 10,000, indicating that the results were *anything but chance*.

Espinosa *et al.* (1992) measured food intake, demographic factors, and playground behavior in a sample of moderately undernourished children. Table A.2, derived from their published article, gives us an example of some actual correlation coefficients. As you can see, the coefficients are all between −1.00 and 1.00, in fact, they are between −0.50 and +0.50. Looking at food intake, the coefficients for the line marked kilocalories indicate that

for this sample of boys and girls, energy intake was positively correlated with activity, with a value of 0.38. With a coefficient of −0.21, caloric intake was negatively correlated with anxiety, that is, higher energy intake was associated with lower levels of anxiety. It should not be difficult for you now to determine which if any of the other coefficients are significant, and the direction of the relationships.

Inferential statistics

In contrast to descriptive purposes, inferential statistics would allow us to *infer* how typical our group of nutrition students is of the university population in general. Moreover, inferential statistics would also tell us how much confidence we should have in any inferences that we might make about these students. In essence, inferential statistics give the scientist the ability to generalize from his or her results. In order to develop general theories of nutrition–behavior relationships, it would be neither possible nor desirable to study all human beings under all conditions. Nutritional and behavioral scientists will therefore deduce a specific hypothesis from a theory (or the findings from a correlational study) and design an experiment to test their hypothesis on a sample. *Sampling* refers to the process of drawing a sample from a population, with random sampling the most common approach. To be able to generalize, the sample must be truly representative of the population of interest. For instance, a random sampling of students from

Table A.2. Example of correlation coefficients in research relations between child/family measures and observed playground behaviors.

	Activity	Happy	Anxious	Leadership
Food intake				
Kilocalories	0.38*	0.22*	−0.21*	0.27*
Animal fat-protein	0.21*	0.18	−0.16	−0.02
Physical measures				
Weight for age	0.26*	0.13	−0.05	0.28*
Weight for height	0.23*	0.02	0.06	0.35*
Family measures				
Socio-economic status	0.24*	0.24*	−0.21	−0.03
Parental literacy	0.17	0.08	−0.06	−0.05

* $p < 0.05$.
Source: adapted from Espinosa *et al.*, 1992.

the university would be a much better way to generalize to all students attending the university than assuming that nutrition majors are representative of the typical undergraduate.

While surveys may be conducted with participants who are selected randomly via telephone or letter, experiments must ordinarily rely on volunteers who are apprised of what their involvement will consist of prior to giving their informed consent. Since randomly sampling the population for an experiment is a rather unlikely option, the importance of randomly *assigning* subjects to the experimental versus control groups is all the more important. Random assignment should prevent any pre-existing biases, as the groups should end up as equivalent in terms of subject characteristics such as social class, health, intelligence, and age. As we have already discussed, experiments are usually designed to identify differences between groups after a treatment has been administered, with the researcher hypothesizing that a difference will result.

The purpose of inferential statistics is to test the *null hypothesis*, which states that the population means do not differ and are instead equal, the same as saying that any observed difference would be due to random error. In practical terms, however, the alternate or *research hypothesis* predicts that there *will be* a difference between the groups (Cozby et al., 1989). Put more plainly, the null hypothesis states that the independent variable has no effect, while the research hypothesis states that the independent variable does have an effect.

The null hypothesis thus states that the population means are exactly equal, and is rejected if there is a low probability that the differences between groups as sampled are due to random error. When we speak of statistical significance between groups, we have rejected the null hypothesis and are inferring that the research hypothesis is correct, that is, that the resultant differences between the groups are true and due to the independent variable. As with correlation coefficients, a significance level of $p < 0.05$ is the minimally accepted level, with $ps < 0.01$, 0.001, or 0.0001 indicating increasingly greater confidence in the group differences. Common statistical procedures for testing for differences between groups are the *t*-test (or one-way

analysis of variance), the chi-square test (X^2), or the two-way analysis of variance (*F*-test).

To see such statistical testing in action, let us now look at the results from an actual study on the possible behavioral effects of aspartame, a non-caloric sweetener. Saravis *et al.* (1990) and her colleagues hypothesized that relative to ingesting sucrose, children who ingested aspartame would show reduced mental performance, but heightened alertness and activity. The former would be predicted because of the obvious caloric deficit, and the latter because of the absence of carbohydrates (see Chapter 5, this volume). Using a double-blind crossover design, children who had fasted overnight and ate a standardized breakfast were given a cold drink of strawberry *Kool-Aid*™ sweetened either with sucrose or with aspartame, and then assessed on learning, mood, and behavior. As shown in Table A.3, the mean scores for the aspartame and sucrose groups were similar on most of the measures. Despite numerical values that look slightly different across columns, the analysis of variance did not reveal the mean scores for the learning variables and mood scales to be different from each other, hence, the null hypothesis was not rejected. However, in statistical parlance, a main effect of treatment was shown for the observed gross and minor motor movements, as indicated by the higher *F*-values. Motor behavior, an index of activity, was higher under the aspartame condition. Rejecting the null hypothesis in this case means that the research hypothesis was partially supported.

A Note on Significance

Despite our focus on tests of significance in the last few pages, a note of caution is in order. We have been discussing statistical significance, which is not the same thing as clinical or substantive significance. In nutrition–behavior research, an effect that is due to a particular treatment might be viewed as inconsequential, even though statistically significant. For example, a nutrient added to foods to improve dietary status might also be shown to result in a slight, though statistically significant increase in feelings of nervousness in the test subjects. The researcher and manufacturer may nevertheless

Table A.3. Example of Comparison Tests in Research Effect of consuming aspartame or sucrose on learning, mood and behavior.

	Aspartame	Sugar	F-value
	Mean SE	Mean SE	(df = 1,19)
Learning tasks			
Reaction time in milliseconds	2931 + 203	2775 + 184	0.45
Arithmetic problems correct (%)	78.7 + 2.5	83.0 + 2.0	2.49
Mood scales			
Depression score	5.1 + 1.2	5.7 + 1.5	0.38
State-trait anxiety score	26.6 + 1.1	25.5 + 1.4	0.95
Behaviors observed (5-sec intervals)			
Negative social interaction	0.1 + 0.1	0.2 + 0.1	−0.45
Fine motor activity	14.7 + 2.2	9.8 + 1.8	−3.19**
Gross motor activity	2.2 + 0.6	1.0 + 0.3	−2.42*

* $p < 0.05$ ** $p < 0.01$. SE = Standard Error of the Mean.
Source: adapted from Saravis et al., 1990.

judge this effect to be clinically insignificant when compared to the positive effects the additive has on overall health, and elect to use the ingredient, albeit with a warning label.

Likewise, with a large enough N-size, correlation coefficients of less than 0.10 can achieve statistical significance. This figure is not a misprint – the correlation coefficient itself, not its significance level can be that low. For example, in a recent nutrition paper that included the results of a survey of close to 3000 respondents, an r of −0.08 between two variables achieved significance at the $p < 0.001$ level (Glanz et al., 1998). But the amount of variance that the first variable predicts in the second for a coefficient of that size would be negligible – statistically, about 1% – so you would be hard pressed to predict the value of an individual's second score on a measure by knowing their first. In this case the correlation may have been statistically significant, but it is substantively insignificant.

As a final note, Babbie (1998) makes a striking observation about the nature of statistical significance and their potential to mislead. Suppose a researcher conducts an empirically sound investigation to determine whether eating sun-dried tomatoes reduces feelings of tension. To his dismay, his results show no significant difference between subjects who ate the tomatoes and subjects who drank bottled water. While this may seem a non-result, disseminating his outcome would reduce the chances of another investigator setting up her own experiment to study the same question. But the first investigator's study of sun-dried tomatoes would not likely ever be published, because his results were not significant. Researchers would therefore not know that it was a dead end, and they might continue to run experiments to test the very same question. Getting the same non-results, their studies would not be published either. Scientific time would thus be wasted, when alternate natural remedies might have been pursued and tested.

However, if enough studies were conducted, the laws of probability would predict that one would eventually find a significant difference. If the investigation were conducted by 20 different researchers, for example, we would expect that one of them would achieve significance at the 0.05 level, since that represents the probability of 5 out of 100 (or 1 out of 20). Even with no causal relationship between sun-dried tomatoes and feelings of well-being, the probability is that 1 out of 20 tests will indicate there is. And that would be the study that gets published! This is not to say we should discount published studies as the exceptions, but to simply place the role of statistical significance in its proper context. Statistics are merely tools to help us summarize and make sense of the phenomena we study, and are no substitute for good theory.

References

Babbie, E. (1998) *The Elements of Social Research.* (8th ed.) Wadsworth, California.

Cozby, P.C., Worden, P.E. and Kee, D.W. (1989) *Research Methods in Human Development.* Mayfield, California.

Espinosa, M.P., Sigman, M.D., Neumann, C.G., Bwibo, N.O. and Mcdonald, M.A. (1992) Playground behaviors of school-age children in relation to nutrition, schooling, and family characteristics. *Developmental Psychology* 28(6), 1188–1195.

Glanz, K., Basil, M., Malbach, E., Goldberg, J. and Snyder, D. (1998) Why Americans eat what they do: Taste, nutrition, cost, convenience, and weight control concerns as influences on food consumption. *Journal of the American Dietetic Association* 98(10), 1118–1126.

Saravis, S., Schacher, R., Ziotkin, S., Leiter, L.A. and Anderson, G.H. (1990) Aspartame: effects on learning, behavior, and mood. *Pediatrics* 86(1), 75–83.

Worobey, J. (1998) Feeding method and motor activity in 3-month-old human infants. *Perceptual and Motor Skills* 86, 883–895.

Zimbardo, P.G., Weber, A.L. and Johnson, R.L. (2000) *Psychology.* Allyn & Bacon, Needham Heights, Massachusetts.

Index

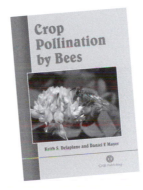
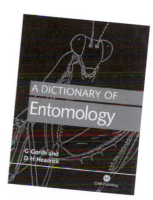